Handbook of Arthurian Romance

Handbook of Arthurian Romance

King Arthur's Court in Medieval European Literature

Edited by
Leah Tether and Johnny McFadyen

In collaboration with
Keith Busby and Ad Putter

DE GRUYTER

ISBN 978-3-11-065580-3
e-ISBN (PDF) 978-3-11-043246-6
e-ISBN (EPUB) 978-3-11-043248-0

Library of Congress Cataloging-in-Publication Data
A CIP catalog record for this book has been applied for at the Library of Congress.

Bibliographic information published by the Deutsche Nationalbibliothek
The Deutsche Nationalbibliothek lists this publication in the Deutsche Nationalbibliografie;
detailed bibliographic data are available on the Internet at http://dnb.dnb.de.

Acknowledgments

The editors would like to express sincere thanks to the many people who have helped this *Handbook* on its way to publication. The collaboration of Keith Busby and Ad Putter was invaluable throughout the process, and particularly so during the scoping phases of this project. Their expertise enabled us to identify an international selection of contributors that is truly demonstrative of the excellence in research across Arthurian Studies today, representing first-rate scholars ranging from early-career to professorial. We thank all of these contributors for their efforts in engaging robustly with the brief and producing a series of studies that strives to bring together approaches new and old, pertinent case studies on texts that step beyond the usual "canon", as well as attentive guidance for the benefit of future Arthurian scholarship. We must also express our gratitude to our meticulous and speedy peer reviewers, who worked at short notice to ensure the quality of this publication. We were also wonderfully supported by the editorial team at De Gruyter, including Jacob Klingner, Maria Zucker and, particularly, Elisabeth Kempf, who was actually responsible for the original conception of the project, as well as for guiding us through the proposal and approvals process, and for helping us to finalize the manuscript. She was responsive, patient and cheerful – the best possible combination for an editor of such a grand project! Thanks must also go to Benjamin Pohl for spotting such a fine cover image. It has been a pleasure to work with this group of people. We have been truly staggered at the breadth and depth of their knowledge, as well as their sheer hard work. We hope this *Handbook* is as much of a pleasure to read as it was to edit.

Table of contents

Section II   Approaching Arthurian Romance: Theories and Key Terms

Section III   **Reading Arthurian Romances: Content, Method and Context**

List of Contributors

Bart Besamusca is Professor of Middle Dutch Textual Culture from an International Perspective in the Utrecht Centre for Medieval Studies at Utrecht University. He has published widely on medieval narrative literature, manuscripts and early printed editions, and manages the research tool Arthurian Fiction in Medieval Europe (www.arthurianfiction.org).

Frank Brandsma is Associate Professor in Comparative Literature (Middle Ages) at Utrecht University and the Utrecht Centre for Medieval Studies. His research focuses on narrative technique and audience in Arthurian romance, especially on the presentation and sharing of emotions. With Carolyne Larrington and Corinne Saunders, he edited *Emotions in Medieval Arthurian Literature* (2015).

Keith Busby is Douglas Kelly Professor of Medieval French Emeritus at the University of Wisconsin-Madison. He has published numerous books and articles on French Arthurian literature. His most recent book is *French in Medieval Ireland, Ireland in Medieval French: The Paradox of Two Worlds* (2017).

Aisling Byrne is Lecturer in Medieval English Literature at the University of Reading. Her publications include *Otherworlds: Fantasy and History in Medieval Literature* (2016) and articles on topics such as Arthurian literature and textual transmission between medieval Britain and Ireland.

Laura Chuhan Campbell is a Teaching Fellow in French at Durham University. Her research focuses primarily on translation and rewriting in medieval literature, particularly French and Italian cultural exchanges, as well as Gender Studies and Ecocriticism. She is the author of the forthcoming *The Medieval Merlin Tradition in France and Italy: Prophecy, Paradox, and* Translatio (2017).

Siân Echard is Professor of English at the University of British Columbia, Vancouver. Her research interests include Anglo Latin literature (especially Geoffrey of Monmouth), Arthurian literature, John Gower, as well as manuscript studies and book history. She has authored and edited several works, most recently including her monograph, *Printing the Middle Ages* (2008).

Andrew B.R. Elliott is Senior Lecturer in Media and Cultural Studies at the University of Lincoln. He has published on historical film, television and video games, from the classical world to the Middle Ages. His most recent book is *Medievalism, Politics and Mass Media: Appropriating the Middle Ages in the Twenty-First Century* (2017).

Stefka G. Eriksen is Head of Research at the Norwegian Institute for Cultural Heritage Research. She publishes on New Philology, authorship and translation theory, orality and literacy, as well as cognitive theory. She is the author of *Writing and Reading in Medieval Manuscript Culture: The Translation and Transmission of the Story of Elye in Old French and Old Norse Literary Contexts* (2014) and editor of *Intellectual Culture in Medieval Scandinavia* (2016).

Christine Ferlampin-Acher is Professor at the Université Rennes 2 and a senior member of the Institut Universitaire de France. Her research mostly focuses on late-medieval French Arthurian texts, such as *Perceforest* and *Artus de Bretagne*. She is the editor of *Artus de Bretagne* (2017).

Helen Fulton is Professor of Medieval Literature at the University of Bristol. She has published widely on medieval English and Welsh literatures including Arthurian literature. She is the editor of *A Companion to Arthurian Literature* (2012).

Paloma Gracia is Professor of Romance Philology at the University of Granada. She has published widely on Arthurian literature and historiography. Her current research focuses on late medieval cyclicity, manuscript compilations and imprints.

Gareth Griffith is a Teaching Fellow and the Director of Part-Time Programmes in English at the University of Bristol. His research focuses primarily on the literature of the Middle English period, with a particular interest in synthesizing literary and manuscript studies to interpret written culture.

Thomas Hinton is Lecturer in French at the University of Exeter. His publications include *The Conte du Graal Cycle: Chrétien de Troyes's* Perceval, *the Continuations, and French Arthurian Romance* (2012), and a special issue of the journal *French Studies* on the medieval library co-edited with Luke Sunderland (2016). He has also published on Arthurian literature, Occitan love lyric and medieval multilingualism, especially Anglo-French.

Marjolein Hogenbirk is Senior Lecturer in Middle Dutch Literature and Book History (codicology and palaeography) at the University of Amsterdam. Her research focuses on Middle Dutch Arthurian literature in its broader European context, relations between Middle Dutch and Old French romances, editions and manuscripts.

Andrew James Johnston is Professor of Medieval and Renaissance English Literature at the Freie Universität Berlin. He has published on Old and Middle English Literature and medievalism. His work includes the monograph *Performing the Middle Ages from* Beowulf *to* Othello (2008) and he has recently co-edited the volumes *The Medieval Motion Picture* (2014) and *The Art of Vision: Ekphrasis in Medieval Literature and Culture* (2015).

Florian Kragl is Professor of Medieval German Literature at the Friedrich-Alexander-University Erlangen-Nürnberg. He has published on Arthurian literature, heroic poetry, Minnesang, the history of poetics and aesthetics and historical narratology. He has (co-)edited several medieval texts, among them two Arthurian romances: the *Crône* by Heinrich von dem Türlin (2012) and the *Lanzelet* by Ulrich von Zatzikhoven (2013) .

Carolyne Larrington is Professor of Medieval European Literature at the University of Oxford and Fellow and Tutor in Medieval English at St John's College. She researches topics in Arthurian literature, Old Icelandic, folklore and medievalism. Her most recent book dealing in part with Arthurian topics is *Brothers and Sisters in Medieval European Literature* (2015).

Charmaine Lee is Professor of Romance Philology at the University of Salerno, Italy. Her main research interest is the romance narrative tradition, the *fabliaux* and Occitan epic and romance.

More recently she has been investigating the French of southern Italy under the Angevin monarchs.

Sofia Lodén is a Postdoctoral Research Fellow at Stockholm University. Her research focuses on the translation of medieval French literature into Old Swedish, as well as depictions of women in courtly literature. Her current project, funded by the Swedish Research Council, is entitled *Maidens and Ladies in Translation. Medieval Francophone Texts and the Beginnings of Swedish Literature.*

Andrew Lynch is Professor in English and Cultural Studies at the University of Western Australia, and Director of the Australian Research Council Centre of Excellence for the History of Emotions, Europe 1100-1800 (CE110001011). He has published widely on medieval and modern Arthurian literature.

Johnny McFadyen holds a PhD in Medieval Latin Arthurian literature from the University of Bristol. His research interests lie in the interpenetration of Latin and vernacular Arthurian literary traditions. He currently works at Oxford University Press.

Matthias Meyer is Professor for Medieval and Early Modern Literature at the University of Vienna and was Dean of the Faculty for Philological and Cultural Studies 2012–2016. He has published on Arthurian Literature, historical narratology and poetry, as well as late Baroque and modern literature.

Patrick Moran is Lecturer of Medieval French Literature at the Université Paul Valéry-Montpellier 3. His research mainly focuses on Arthurian literature, cyclicity and medieval thought. He is the author of *Lectures cycliques: le réseau inter-romanesque dans les cycles du Graal du XIIIe siècle* (2014).

Lowri Morgans holds a PhD in Medieval Welsh Literature from the University of Aberystwyth. Her research focuses on gesture and body language in medieval Welsh poetry and prose, which includes Arthurian literature, as well as the translation of literature from continental languages into Welsh in the Middle Ages.

Giulia Murgia is a Postdoctoral Research Fellow at the University of Cagliari, Italy. Her research interests cover Arthurian literature and Sardinian linguistics. Among her most recent publications is *La* Tavola Ritonda *tra intrattenimento ed enciclopedismo* (2015).

Ad Putter is Professor of Medieval English Literature at the University of Bristol. He has written various books on the *Gawain*-poet and on metre. With Elizabeth Archibald he has edited *The Cambridge Companion to the Arthurian Legend* (2009) and with Myra Stokes the Penguin edition of *The Works of the Gawain Poet* (2014).

Raluca L. Radulescu is Professor of Medieval Literature at Bangor University and Director of the new Centre for Arthurian Studies there. She has written on Arthurian and non-Arthurian romance (more specifically on Thomas Malory), gentry and political culture in late-medieval England and the construction of the past (including Arthurian "history") in Middle English chronicles and genealogies.

Samantha J. Rayner is a Reader at University College London, where she is also Director of the Centre for Publishing. Her research interests are in publishing archives and publishing paratexts, the culture of bookselling, editors and editing, and academic publishing, as well as around the publication histories of medieval and Arthurian texts.

Sif Rikhardsdottir is Associate Professor and former Chair of Comparative Literature at the University of Iceland. She is the author of *Medieval Translations and Cultural Discourse: The Movement of Texts in England, France and Scandinavia* (2012). Her latest projects include a monograph entitled *Emotion in Old Norse Literature: Translations, Voices, Contexts* with Boydell & Brewer.

Robert Rouse is Associate Professor of Medieval English Literature at the University of British Columbia, Vancouver. His research is primarily concerned with medieval romance (both Arthurian and non-Arthurian), having written on issues of historiography, English national identity, saracens and other medieval *others*, the law, the medieval erotic and the medieval geographical imagination.

Michael Stolz is Professor of Medieval German Literature at the University of Bern. He has published numerous books and articles in his field. His research interests cover, among others, intellectual history, the history of reading, editorial philology and Digital Humanities. Most recently he has co-edited (with Gerlinde Huber-Rebenich and Christian Rohr) *Wasser in der mittelalterlichen Kultur. Gebrauch – Wahrnehmung – Symbolik/Water in Medieval Culture: Uses, Perceptions, and Symbolism* (2017).

Alison Stones is Professor Emerita of History of Art and Architecture at the University of Pittsburgh. She researches and writes about illuminated manuscripts.

Jane H.M. Taylor is Professor Emerita of Medieval French at the University of Durham. She has worked extensively on Arthurian literature, most recently on the rewritings of romance in the French Renaissance.

Leah Tether is Senior Lecturer in Digital Humanities at the University of Bristol. She researches the publishing and reading cultures of Arthurian Literature in the medieval and early-modern periods. She is the author of *The Continuations of Chrétien's* Perceval: *Content and Construction, Extension and Ending* (2012) and the forthcoming *Publishing the Grail in Medieval and Renaissance France* (2017).

Richard Trachsler is Professor of Medieval French and Occitan Literature at the University of Zurich. His research interests cover narrative literature in Old French, as well as material and editorial philology.

List of Abbreviations

Ars. = Bibliothèque de l'Arsenal
BBIAS = Bibliographical Bulletin of the International Arthurian Society
BdT = Bibliographie der Trobadors
Bibl. = Bibliothek/Bibliothèque
BL = British Library
BM = Bibliothèque municipale
BMI = Bibliothèque municipal et interuniversitaire
BnF = Bibliothèque nationale de France
BPU = Bibliothèque publique et universitaire
CFMA = Classiques français du moyen âge
CUL = Cambridge University Library
KBR = Koninklijke Bibliotheek van België/Bibliothèque royale de Belgique
MLA = Modern Language Association
NLS = National Library of Scotland
ÖNB = Österreichische Nationalbibliothek
UB = Universitätsbibliothek/Universiteitsbibliotheek
YUL = Yale University Library

NB: All URLs cited in this volume were last accessed on 30 January 2017.

Leah Tether/Johnny McFadyen

Introduction: King Arthur's Court in Medieval European Literature

Arthurian romance is a pan-European phenomenon, with both subtle and overt traces of Arthur and his court interwoven into almost all medieval vernaculars, as well as the Latin tradition. The various stories about King Arthur and his Knights of the Round Table first inscribed in French in the Middle Ages are to be found in many and varied contexts, having been translated, adapted and recast into medieval languages such as Middle High German, Old Norse, Occitan, Latin, Middle English and others. Their manuscript contexts show that medieval consumers of Arthurian literature regarded them not only as literary fictions, but also at times had reason to situate them as chronicles, as education, as history, and more. These many and varied (re-)writings are revealing, in that they offer tangible evidence for a wide, cross-border, cross-cultural and interlingual interest in the key themes associated with Arthuriana, such as chivalric values, questing, kingship and the question of knightly identity. And this interest continued across centuries, albeit subject to some ebb and flow, right up until the present moment, and in an even broader international sense, too, as is demonstrated by recent movie adaptations such as *King Arthur* (2004) or TV series like *Merlin* (2008–2012), as well as literary fictions by authors such as Bernard Cornwall ("The Arthur Books" series 1995–2011) and Kazuo Ishiguro (*The Buried Giant* 2015), and multimedia/gaming programmes, like *King Arthur's Gold* (2011). Even modern literature seeming to have little or nothing to do with Arthur can be shown to draw upon the ever-present appeal of Arthurian motifs, such as the Grail. For example, James Lee Burke's *House of the Rising Sun* (2015), a New York Times Bestseller, re-situates the Grail within the context of early twentieth-century revolutionary Mexico.

There remains, therefore, an undeniably broad and international public interest in Arthurian material, and this inevitably translates into a pointed interest in the subject amongst students of literature, so much so that university literature programmes the world over are rarely to be found without a module or course on Arthurian literature, such is the demand. Indeed, just several weeks prior to assembling this *Handbook*, Bangor University in north-western Wales established a brand new Centre for Arthurian Studies, to include the official *Centre de documentation* [resource centre] for the International Arthurian Society, an active, long-established and international network of scholars, which was officially

Leah Tether (University of Bristol) and **Johnny McFadyen** (Independent Scholar)

DOI 10.1515/9783110432466-001

formed in 1948. Furthermore, in the run-up to the Arthurian Centre's launch, at the launch event of another Bangor centre for excellence (the Stephen Colclough Centre for the History and Culture of the Book), the eminent Bangor-based Malory scholar, P.J.C. Field, delivered a lecture purporting to offer new evidence for the original site of Camelot (suggested by Field to be Slake in Yorkshire), which prompted a media frenzy, with reports of the finding appearing across all forms of international media, from television to radio, and from social media to broadsheet and tabloid.

When Chrétien de Troyes commenced composing his first Arthurian romances in the latter part of the twelfth century, he was writing within the context of a networked European story-telling tradition, the components of which had been largely disseminated through oral means. Indeed, Chrétien's romances show many signs of these varied international, inter-cultural influences. However, the study of Arthurian matter, from its earliest incarnations in the works of twelfth-century historians such as William of Malmesbury, Henry of Huntingdon and William of Newburgh, which sought in part to distinguish history from legend, through to the more sceptical critiques of the sixteenth century and the rise of more recognisably "modern" scholarship in the nineteenth century (Snyder 2006, 3–4), has been largely divided along philological lines. In other words, the language of the Arthurian text in question has become a key means by which we, as scholars, categorize these narratives, such that volumes devoted to the study of this literature frequently divorce text from original context. This can be most clearly seen by series such as *Arthurian Literature in the Middle Ages* – an enormous and significant set of books published by the University of Wales Press, each volume of which provides a collection of essays concerning "The Arthur of..." each language or geographical area (for example, *The Arthur of the French* (Burgess and Pratt 2006), *The Arthur of the North* (Kalinke 2011), and so on). Even collected volumes that do consider Arthurian textuality across different languages such as, for example, *The Cambridge Companion to the Arthurian Legend* (Archibald and Putter 2009) and *A Companion to Arthurian Literature* (Fulton 2009) do not specifically set out connections in approaches and methodology that would allow for the type of true cross-border comparison of Arthurian literature that seems most appropriate for this corpus of interconnected narratives.

None of this is to say, of course, that Arthurian scholarship to date has entirely disconnected texts from sources or intertextual networks, or indeed that linguistically-separate approaches have not been important or useful. This would be a neither fair nor accurate assessment. Existing studies have undeniably enhanced knowledge and established definitively that Arthurian literature represents a phenomenon, or perhaps even a movement, which is largely discrete from other forms of narrative, both medieval and modern, and which thus warrants its own particular approaches and dedicated study. In fact, it is only rarely that there are not at least sideways glances to the cultures and traditions of pre- and co-existing materials, particularly in respect of seminal authors such as Chrétien de Troyes or Geoffrey of Monmouth. Indeed, considerable study has also been devoted to concepts of rewriting and translation from one language to another, as well as from one century to another. But the interrelationships of Arthurian texts are such that tracing developments merely "from one to another" risks oversimplifying the broader connected textual and material tradition, which can claim at least similar, if not equal importance for the study of this inextricably connected and annexed corpus. Of course, no handbook can be truly encyclopaedic, and this one does not claim to be either. As a result, rather than listing every single romance text, exemplary texts are discussed in relation to one particular theme or topic. Similarly, it is not the objective to set out every single theory or concept ever to have been employed in the study of Arthurian romance; instead the focus is on recent trends. The aim of this *Handbook*, in short, is simply to bring together a more meaningful, more complete view of the specifically European context of the Arthurian romances of the Middle Ages, both in terms of textual and material matters, by examining and evaluating current approaches and methodologies that promote, amongst present and future scholars, the more connected study of Arthurian literature across the entirety of its pan-European context.

The challenge that we set for the contributors to our *Handbook of Arthurian Romance* is therefore particularly thorny, since it requires them to step some way outside of their respective home fields. After all, the division of Arthurian study along linguistic lines is not merely to do with matters of methodology, but also (and perhaps more so) to do with language competencies. It would be a tall order indeed to expect all Arthurian scholars to be conversant in all medieval European vernaculars, as well as in Latin. Indeed, there is no one contributor here (or perhaps anywhere) who can claim such a skillset. However, our contributors have been encouraged to start in their home fields and to think about methodologies and approaches that, when broadened out or transferred, might offer insights into both the connections and differences, the (dis-)continuities perhaps, between Arthurian narratives across linguistic and geographical borders. The *Handbook* has, therefore, been divided into three sections, and each of these is dedicated to different aspects of Arthurian romance, seeking to shed light on Arthurian matter from different perspectives. The first two sections offer background information on the literary tradition of Arthurian romance, as well as on recent theoretical perspectives from which romance texts can be approached, while the third is concerned with central topics and motifs of Arthurian romance, discussed in a detailed way on the basis of selected texts. Owing to the diversity of topics, texts, traditions and methods covered by the chapters contained here, we have not provided an overall bibliography, rather a reference list at the end of each chapter, which sets out an indicative and self-contained bibliography ideal for any scholar wishing to read further on the topic(s) or text(s) in question.

Section I, "The Context of Arthurian Romance", gives insight into the various general contexts that frame the text corpus. Its purpose is to highlight central contexts and thus give newcomers to the literature of Arthurian romance an idea of the conditions that shaped the texts. In Chapter 1, Robert Rouse describes the general historical background and explores the concept of chivalry as an aspirational ideology and social code within medieval culture, before moving on to consider briefly its literary construction in Arthurian romance and the many problematic sociological issues to which this gives rise. Samantha J. Rayner then attempts something completely new. Rather than simply exploring the history of scholarship and textual criticism as it relates to Arthurian romance, of which there already exists an excellent example (Lacy 2006), as well as the option to trace more recent scholarship by means of the annual *Bibliography of the International Arthurian Society*, Chapter 2 sees Rayner bring together the previously scattered history of the International Arthurian Society, arguing for precisely how and why the development of Arthurian Studies as a distinctive field has largely to do with the establishment of this Society. In Chapter 3, Aisling Byrne considers the evolution of the critical canon, discussing why certain texts have come to be central or peripheral, arguing that the very concept of a single canon of Arthurian texts is fraught with difficulties, and that there is still much work to be done before a pan-European critical canon, which is both extensive and linguistically diverse, might be established. Patrick Moran's analysis in Chapter 4 provides a meticulous overview of the various text types and formal features associated with Arthurian romance, covering the controversial subject of genre as well as introducing unifying aspects such as the court, rhyme schemes and recurring characters. Moran contends that the French-speaking world imprinted a literary form on Arthurian material that gave other European languages an exemplar to be either emulated or rejected, and that it is the multifaceted vernacular responses to the template set by French-language Arthurian literature that ultimately problematizes notions of genre unity. The history of the Arthur-figure, in respect of its rise in chronicles such as Geoffrey of Monmouth's *Historia regum Britanniae* and its translation to literary texts, forms the subject matter of Chapter 5. Here Meyer draws attention to a perceived distinction between the Arthur of medieval prose and the Arthur-figure as presented within verse romance, but ultimately argues that both serve similar narrative functions within their respective literary traditions. In Chapter 6, Keith Busby offers a study of the manuscript context of Arthurian romance. Busby concentrates on several exceptional books such as, for example, the best-known manuscript containing Chrétien's romances (Paris,

BnF, fr. 794) and an early illuminated manuscript of the *Lancelot-Grail* (Rennes, BM 255), in order to highlight the key characteristics of the dissemination of romance texts in a medieval manuscript context. Busby underlines the fact that Arthurian works were often accompanied by various other non-Arthurian texts, forming a considerable literary corpus that offers insight into the specific requirements and tastes of medieval audiences. This notion of the readership and audience of Arthurian romances provides the focus for Bart Besamusca's analysis in Chapter 7, in which he considers how the reception modes of orality and literacy influenced the composition and dissemination of the texts themselves. He argues that interest in Arthurian literature was, in general, an elite affair, and that in many linguistic areas it was people of royalty and members of the upper echelons of the nobility who served as patrons of medieval authors, thus promoting the production of Arthurian romances and commissioning the manuscripts from which these texts where then later copied.

The second section, "Approaching Arthurian Romance: Theories and Key Terms", gives an overview, critique and evaluation of recent theories in Medieval Studies, offering case studies that showcase how these can be employed in relation to Arthurian romance. Sif Rikhardsdottir, in Chapter 1, addresses questions of temporality, periodization and the discussion of history in the romance tradition, suggesting that Arthurian romance has the potential to offer a generic framework in which its own past can be reconstituted and, as a result, a new future envisioned. This leads into Helen Fulton's discussion in Chapter 2 of the relationships between fictionality and factuality, covering the development of the Arthurian saga from chronicle entries with historical claims to the pure fiction of literary texts that play with different shades of realism. Fulton shows that, whilst questions surrounding Arthur's dubious credentials as a bona fide historical figure were still keenly debated as late as the eighteenth century, Arthurian narrative material itself, as set out in works such as Geoffrey of Monmouth's *Historia regum Britanniae*, and subsequently amplified by later additions from the romance tradition, still to a certain degree enjoyed the status of genuine history until well into the modern period. Jane H.M. Taylor uses Chapter 3 to evaluate the various forms of rewriting that pervade Arthurian literature, with key examples of translation, adaptation and continuation forming the main foci, through which she is able to argue that the act of re-writing (in all its manifold forms) must be understood as an integral component of an evolving dialogue between medieval texts, readers and audiences. The concept of intertextuality is the focus of Chapter 4. Here, Marjolein Hogenbirk explores some of the numerous references to other authors and texts found in Arthurian literature, and analyzes their methods of aestheticization. Through a case study of the Middle Dutch *Roman van Moriaen*, she argues for intertextuality as constituting an intellectual game between author and audience, and that it is therefore a crucial tool for drawing out the possible meaning(s) of a given text. A more traditional, but still relevant, field is discussed in Chapter 5 by Stefka G. Eriksen. Whilst earlier scholars traced the genealogy of texts, more recent trends, which follow Paul Zumthor and Bernard Cerquiglini, regard other manuscript elements (paratexts) as interesting subjects of study; Eriksen here explores the relationship between the primary disciplines for textual criticism in the Middle Ages, classical rhetoric and grammar, and New Philology, in order to foreground the value and potential of the latter as a theoretical framework for "future" philology. Alison Stones' study in Chapter 6 leads on neatly from its predecessor and considers the relationship of text and image in Arthurian romance, as well as the value of its study. Through an examination of the *Lancelot-Grail Cycle*, Stones makes the case for comparative approaches and analyses in the study of text and image, which together enable scholars to identify patterns of similarity or difference in terms of the choice, placement and treatment of images within Arthurian works. This approach, she suggests, promises perhaps the most in terms of telling us about the copying and dissemination of both Arthurian manuscripts and other medieval vernacular literature. Material or Thing Studies are one of the most recent theoretical trends applied in the study of medieval literature; these are addressed in relation to Arthurian romance by Andrew James Johnston in Chapter 7. Johnston argues that the relationship and interaction of (magical) objects, things and persons in texts, which often serve to highlight complex negotiations surrounding questions of materiality in medieval fiction, suggest that in the realm of Arthurian literature it is courtly culture that dictates the parameters within which matter and material must function. The natural world, and ecocriticism in general, is considered in Chapter 8: Christine Ferlampin-Acher here notes that whilst this methodology is mostly applied to contemporary literature, romance texts abound in natural settings like forests, wilderness, oceans and deserts, as well as in various animals, all of which influence and interact with the human protagonists. This, Ferlampin-Acher argues, makes ecocriticism, as a methodological framework, a potentially very important approach to the study of Arthurian literature. Gender roles and conflicts are the focus of Chapter 9. Carolyne Larrington shows that, whilst Arthurian romance is commonly conceived to reinforce medieval gender stereotypes, closer examination serves often to subvert these expectations, which results in a fundamental destabilization of the established conception of Arthurian literature as both socially conservative and heteronormative. Richard Trachsler in Chapter 10 discusses orality and literacy as important key terms in relation to romance texts that develop partly out of a *Minnelied-* and troubadour-tradition, and which – even in their written form – still feature highly active narrator figures. Performativity is also covered in this chapter, showing how literary texts often employ performative strategies to simulate presence, authenticity, corporeality, sensuality and immediacy for the reader. Chapter 11's study of medievalism, put together by Andrew B.R. Elliott, offers a historical overview of later developments of Arthurian subject matter that reaches not only across centuries, but which also introduces new media. Here, Elliott discusses how post-medieval adaptations of Arthurian romance into different media, such as films and series, music, board and computer games, as well as modern literature, have capitalized on the Arthurian legend's inherent flexibility and elasticity, which is an auspicious (though potentially inadvertent) by-product of the various continuations, re-imaginings and contradictions to be found in the medieval romance tradition. Section II closes with Andrew Lynch's evaluation of Post-Colonial Studies in Arthurian literature in Chapter 12. Lynch sets out how this conglomeration of approaches and key terms has played a major role in the study of romance texts, abounding as it does in travels, far-away countries and other cultures, eventually arguing that, even though its value may well now be diminishing in contemporary scholarly debates, the term "post-colonial" can still serve a useful purpose in the study of Arthurian literature, as it encourages modern audiences to consider the wider historical and cultural contexts in which these medieval texts were produced.

Section III, "Reading Arthurian Romance: Content, Method and Context", comprises thirteen text-specific chapters. In each chapter, one romance text is discussed in relation to one particular topic, motif, context or method that prevails in Arthurian literature. Naturally, the European scope of this *Handbook* is reflected in the selection of primary texts, covering with reasonable comprehensiveness the Arthurian tradition in the whole range of European vernaculars, though inevitably some languages do not find representation in this section (such as, for example, Old Scots, Czech and Belarusian, as well as some of the dialects deriving from Old Norse), These are, however, all to be found discussed at various moments in the previous two sections. Chapter 1 sees Florian Kragl discuss Heinrich von dem Türlin's *Diu Crône* and life at the Arthurian Court. Kragl points to Heinrich's own pretensions to create a text that will be regarded as the pinnacle of Arthurian romance, and assesses his achievement through an analysis of the work in both macrostructural terms and with regards to the extravagant level of descriptive detail, which Kragl argues results in a curious hybrid of structural perfection and narrative badinage. The Old Swedish *Herr Ivan*, a translation of Chrétien de Troyes' *Yvain*, is Sofia Lodén's focus in Chapter 2. This story of the knight who loses not only his wife, but also his chivalric honour and reputation, lends itself particularly well to a discussion of chivalric values and negotiations of knightly identity, and Lodén here argues that the Swedish text offers a re-interpretation of the French original designed to present an image of courtly society comprehensible to its Swedish readership, as well as to cater to the tastes of the new Swedish aristocracy. In Chapter 3, Giulia Murgia offers a study of the elements of magic and the supernatural in *La Tavola Ritonda*, a popular Italian Arthurian romance from the fourteenth century that is largely based on the Prose *Tristan*, in which she suggests that the magical elements of the narrative, as presented in the source material, have been marginalized in the Italian text, which seeks instead to recast this supernaturality in either a scientific or Christian miraculous sense. Chrétien de Troyes' *Lancelot, ou le Chevalier de la charette* then forms the textual focus for Chapter 4. Here, Thomas Hinton explores how courtly love, or *fin'amor*, influences knights in their conduct and behaviour, highlighting how multiple aspects of this discourse are shaped by the social setting within the text, and given expression through a delicate balancing act between both private (individual) and public (group) spheres. In Chapter 5, Raluca L. Radulescu tackles the notion of the quest in the Middle English *Sir Percyvell of Galles*, arguing that the Middle English text rejects any spiritual significance present in the original story, and consequently puts forward a very different Arthurian protagonist to the traditional one inaugurated by Chrétien and taken up by his successors. The quest of this protagonist, Radulescu argues, is related to the un-ending circle of family duty, and to the (largely unsuccessful) acquisition of chivalric values, rather than to objects of spiritual import, such as the Grail. The Middle Welsh *Peredur son of Efrawg* is studied by Lowri Morgans in Chapter 6, with a particular focus on the nature of its translation from Chrétien de Troyes' unfinished *Perceval*. Notably, Morgans' comparative analysis of the French and Welsh versions offers valuable insights into the potential discrepancies between audience expectations in both France and Wales during the period of each text's respective composition. Chapter 7 sees Frank Brandsma focus on landscapes and foreign countries as they are depicted in the numerous travels presented in the Middle Dutch *Roman van Walewein*. Brandsma's study shows how, in general, the varied descriptions of topographical details within the *Walewein*, and also in a second contemporaneous Middle Dutch romance (*Moriaen*), are designed more to facilitate the narrative rather than simply to provide realistic description. The Iberian *Post-Vulgate Cycle* is discussed by Paloma Gracia in Chapter 8, with a focus on how cyclicity works in translation in the Portuguese and Spanish versions of this series of texts. Gracia conducts a study which seeks to challenge established perceptions concerning late medieval Arthurian peninsular materials and their perceived relationship to the French *Post-Vulgate Cycle*. Another common motif, the search for the Holy Grail, is studied in Chapter 9 by Michael Stolz on the basis of Wolfram von Eschenbach's *Parzival*. Whilst it is unquestionably an Arthurian romance, the focus of *Parzival* is trained far more on the Grail and Parzival's search for it, than it is on the Arthurian world in which it is situated. Stolz demonstrates how Wolfram's text not only finishes the Grail story as he had it from his French source (Chrétien's unfinished poem), but purposefully adapts, enriches and amplifies the tale in both structural and narrative terms. Chapter 10 turns to the role of women in Arthurian romance. Whilst women are commonly expected to play a rather passive and subordinated role, many romances subvert this expectation and offer a more diverse picture of gender constellations. Here, Laura Chuhan Campbell provides a study of Chrétien de Troyes' *Erec et Enide*, which demonstrates the varied contradictions that emerge from the status of women in Arthurian romance, with a particular focus on the exclusion of female subjectivity within chivalric ideology, as well as the expected role of female characters as passive objects being specifically designed to be bartered away in the system of homosocial relations that underpins the chivalric world. Christian ethics and their interrelationship with the chivalric ideal are studied by Gareth Griffith in Chapter 11. On the basis of the Middle English *Merlin*, which not only features a Christ-like Merlin, but also numerous other Christian elements, Griffith highlights the narrative imperative for Arthurian protagonists to embody not only knightly virtues but also Christian ideals, which leads romance texts to attempt to negotiate the tricky issue of honour and shame that lies at the centre of Arthurian literature's dialogue with medieval Christianity. In Chapter 12, Siân Echard discusses the Latin Arthurian romances *Historia Meriadoci* and *De Ortu Walwanii* guided by Thing Theory. Her examination of the large number of invented objects and pieces of machinery that are the distinguishing feature of these texts demonstrates the ways in which many recognizable romance motifs and structures are defamiliarized within these Latin works, which (depending on the date(s) of composition) could be reflective of the experimental period during which the genre-machinery of romance was being explored and assembled, or alternatively could be designed to send up and deflate the very romance conventions to which later medieval audiences would have been well accustomed. Finally, Charmaine Lee focuses in Chapter 13 on the Occitan romance *Jaufre*, and considers genre boundaries, the interrelationship with other genres and the generic ambiguity inherent in Arthurian romance. Through this analysis, Lee demonstrates the hybridity of this Occitan text, which not only contains references to Chrétien's *oeuvre* and the works of his immediate followers, but also draws upon pre-Galfridian motifs and ideals of courtly ideology, as developed within the troubadour lyric poetry tradition.

Together, the studies found in this *Handbook*, whilst not claiming to be exhaustive, serve to sketch the current scholarly landscape of Arthurian romance studies. By not only discussing exemplary primary texts, but also combining traditional scholarly methodologies with recent theoretical concepts and innovative approaches that guide our interpretations of these texts, a great many similarities and intersections between Arthurian romances composed in different languages begin to emerge. This is particularly evident in Section III, in which the various chapters serve almost as case studies for the efficacy of the concepts, contexts and approaches discussed in Sections I and II. As editors, our objective is of course not to be definitive, but rather to inspire new and existing generations of Arthurian scholars to consider alternative, complementary methods in their studies. The decidedly European perspective of this *Handbook* therefore aims to provide a series of models for future scholarship (and teaching), by means of which the findings of Arthurian Studies, which had hitherto run in parallel across philological divides, might be brought together in a more meaningful and sentenious way, one which is perhaps truer to the original context(s) and transmission of Arthurian romance.

References

Archibald, Elizabeth, and Ad Putter, eds. *The Cambridge Companion to the Arthurian Legend*. Cambridge: Cambridge University Press, 2009.

Burgess, Glyn S., and Karen Pratt, eds. *The Arthur of the French: The Arthurian Legend in Medieval French and Occitan Literature*. Cardiff: University of Wales Press, 2006.

Fulton, Helen, ed. *A Companion to Arthurian Literature*. Oxford: Wiley-Blackwell, 2009.

Lacy, Norris J., ed. *A History of Arthurian Scholarship*. Cambridge: D.S. Brewer, 2006.

Kalinke, Marianne E., ed. *The Arthur of the North: The Arthurian Legend in the Norse and Rus' Realms*. Cardiff: University of Wales Press, 2011.

Snyder, Christopher. "Arthurian Origins." *A History of Arthurian Scholarship*. Ed. Norris J. Lacy. Cambridge: D.S. Brewer, 2006. 1–19.

Section I **The Context of Arthurian Romance**

Robert Rouse
Historical Context: The Middle Ages and the Code of Chivalry

In that last great medieval British retelling of the Arthurian legends, Sir Thomas Malory describes the foundational moment of Arthurian chivalry. Having reclaimed his patrimony by winning the throne of Britain, married Guinevere and established peace within his realm, Arthur calls together his knights and outlines the chivalric tenets and organization of his new Arthurian society:

> Then the King established all the knights, and gave them riches and lands; and charged them never to do outrage nor murder, and always to flee treason, and to give mercy unto him that asketh mercy, upon pain for forfeiture of their worship and lordship of King Arthur for everymore; and always to do ladies, damosels, and gentlewomen and widows succor; strengthen them in their rights, and never to enforce them, upon pain of death. Also, that no man take no battles in a wrongful quarrel for no love, nor for no worldly goods. So unto this were all the knights sworn of the Table Round, both old and young. And every year so were they sworn at the high feast of Pentecost. (*Morte Darthur*, III: 15)[1]

In this moment of communal identity construction, Arthur attempts to suture together two dissonant conceptions of medieval nobility: political and military power and the ideals of chivalric behaviour. In this chapter, I will examine the tensions that manifest between these two concepts within the development of the Arthurian literature of high and late medieval Europe in an attempt show how the changes in real-world aristocratic and gentry culture were reflected in, and negotiated by, the legends of the Arthurian court.

My focus here will be on chivalry, rather than knighthood. Understood here as an ideology, chivalry acts as a social code of behaviour, manifest within both real world practice and within medieval artistic representation. Knighthood is a military role and a class position within medieval society, initially based upon a role as a military professional, but increasingly understood as a measure of social status in the later Middle Ages. Politically, a knight can be defined as a member of the military class of high and late medieval Europe, most often owing military service to a feudal lord as part of the reciprocal system of land tenure and feudal service (Kaeuper and Bohna 2009, 276–277). While there is often an assumed cor-

---

1 All references to the *Morte Darthur* are to Helen Cooper's edition: Malory (1998).

Robert Rouse (University of British Columbia)

DOI 10.1515/9783110432466-002

relation between knighthood and chivalry, both history and literature are at pains to remind us that not all knights are chivalrous, and not all acts of chivalry are performed by knights.

Chivalry, as it manifests in medieval culture, is an aspirational ideology and set of behaviours primarily performed and subscribed to by male members of the medieval military elite. The term itself comes from the Old French *chevalerie*, meaning horse soldiers, but comes to mean something like "the moral and social mores of male members of the ruling elite" as the medieval period progresses. As a sociological phenomenon, chivalry can be seen to develop within medieval culture from the late-eleventh century onwards as a method of moderating the behaviour of a professional warrior class (Kaeuper and Bohna 2009, 274). To explain the problem that chivalry developed to address, one has to understand the paradoxical existence of any body of military-trained and politically-powerful members of and within a society: almost all social groups throughout history have required a body of large, dangerous and military-trained men. The role of these specialized members of a group is, in essence, to protect the society from external threats, and – when required – to enforce normative behaviour and conduct within the group. Over time, the social groups that develop the most effective bodies of trained military figures tend to gain prominence and often come also to dominate neighbouring social groups (Reid 2007; Taylor 2013). However, while the existence of such military-trained members of society offers the group certain advantages, these warriors also present a systemic problem: how does a group regulate the behaviour of large, violent, military-trained men when the latter are not busy fighting other large, violent, military-trained men? Human societies have long struggled with this issue, and have developed a variety of social institutions to manage this aspect of society.

In western Europe during the late-eleventh and twelfth centuries, as political structures began to cohere in the form of more stable kingdoms and feudal structures, chivalry developed as a sociological response to an increasing surplus of under-utilized, trained fighting men (Kaeuper 1999, 11–29). A side effect of the increasingly stable political landscape was a decrease in opportunity for knights to advance themselves through warfare. As patterns of inheritance and land tenure became more predictable, and the opportunities for land acquisition via warfare became less frequent, the problem of landless knights became more acute. As opportunities for legitimate deployment of military prowess and power became more limited, there arose the problem of knightly violence being directed inwards towards the civil population, or in modes of internal competition between knights for land and power. This rise of knightly violence in the form of domestic feuds, succession struggles and outright banditry provides a context for the development of a code of chivalric behaviour that sought to provide systems of self-regulation for the knightly classes (Kaeuper 1999, 11–29).[2]

The proper social role of the knight was a popular topic amongst the political writers of the twelfth century. In his *Policraticus*, John of Salisbury (1990) outlines the divinely-ordained responsibility of the knight to defend the Church and to protect the common folk. This subjugation of the knightly classes to the common good is a central part of the concept of the "three orders" of medieval society, which outlines a mutually supportive, tripartite Christian social structure.[3] This idea was encouraged by both the Church and by the kings, and became a central part of medieval social and political theory. The principle was dramatized by historians and literary writers (such as Geoffrey Chaucer, among the many possible examples) who produced moral histories and fictions in which knights were either rewarded or punished for their adherence to the newly developing chivalric code. Indeed, particularly important in the development of chivalry as a concept was the role of literature. During the twelfth century, a body of literature developed that articulated, promoted and disseminated the tenets and behaviours of chivalry across the noble classes of Europe. Chief amongst this body of literature was the genre of romance, of which the romances of the Arthurian legends, the subject of this *Handbook*, were a popular matter. Arthurian romance operated in part as a cultural vector, a form of entertainment promulgating chivalric ideology through aspirational role models such as Perceval, Erec, Lancelot and, at times, Arthur himself. As we shall see, the figures of Arthurian legend both embody chivalric ideals and act as sites of critique for the chivalric ethos.

Malory's Pentecostal oath moment is worth returning to here. The immediate narrative context for the oath is the aftermath of the adventure of Gawain and the white hart, which ends with Gawain's misfortunate slaying of a noble lady. Overcome with grief and shame, Gawain returns to Camelot to submit himself to Arthur's judgment. Subject, at Guinevere's insistence, to an inquest of the noble ladies of the court, Gawain is forced to swear upon the four Evangelists always to support and defend all gentlewomen in the future, and never to refuse mercy to any chivalric opponent that asks it of him. Gawain here is the embodiment of the undisciplined knight, the warrior whose uncontrolled and unrestrained action leads to conflict, misfortune and the death of innocents. As such he represents the

---

2 Kaeuper (1999, 11–29) provides an extended discussion of the social issues caused by landless knights, which space prevents me from offering here.

3 The "three orders" (those who fight, those who work, those who pray) were originally theorized in *c.* 1023–1025 by Gerard of Florennes, Bishop of Cambrai. See Duby (1980) for an in-depth discussion.

unrestrained potential of the knightly body, the body that needs to be disciplined by the code of chivalry that Arthur institutes through the yearly ritual of the Pentecostal oath. Importantly, the Pentecostal oath links proper chivalric behaviour with the (with)holding of lands and riches by the King. As such, it contains not only tenets of behaviour, but also an explicit account of the consequences of any breach of the code. As we shall see, Arthurian literature would serve as a form of moral history and instruction for its aristocratic audience, offering both positive and negative exempla of chivalric behaviour and the associated consequences.

1 Arthurian chivalry and the individual

The oldest fragments of the Arthurian legend are found in the historical annals and chronicles of Nennius (the *Historia Brittonum*) and Gildas (*De excidio Britanniae*), as well as in the *Annales Cambriae*, and as an intertextual heroic comparison in *Y Gododdin* of Aneirin (see Fulton, *infra*). The Arthur that emerges in the half-light of this early textual landscape is that of the heroic bear, the "*arth*"-figure that emerges as a warlord of the late-fifth or early-sixth century (cf. Meyer, *infra*). It is not until we arrive in the twelfth century that an Arthur appears who will become the lodestone of chivalric culture. In Geoffrey of Monmouth's *Historia regum Britanniae* (composed in the 1130s), we find a vision of the British past in which Arthur's reign is figured as the *fons et origo* [source and origin] of European chivalry, the home of the most chivalric knights of a passed age, as well as the site for the interrogation of chivalric culture for writers over the succeeding centuries. While Geoffrey's *Historia* primarily concerns itself with Arthurian history, we find in his narrative many recognizable elements, which will go on to become the stock material of chivalric narrative. Examples of chivalric practice occur in numerous places, such as the account of the imitation battle that formed part of the Whitsunday festivities (*c.* 1057) in which "Geoffrey briefly illustrates a connection between erotic stimulus and military activity by telling how women spurred the knights on." (Jackson 1994, 9)

The representation of chivalric practice that we find in the *Historia* reminds us that, from the very earliest iterations, chivalry and literature are symbiotic in their relationship. The aristocracy read or listened to the deeds of Arthurian knights as they reflected the aspirational modes of life – the *chivalric habitus* – of their own day-to-day existence and, in like manner, writers such as Geoffrey and the *romanciers* reflected the lifestyles and courtly behaviours of their desired audiences. We can, I suggest, understand the interplay between real-life chivalric practice and its literary representation as that of a dynamic feedback system: practices that became popular in chivalric life soon became part of the literary representation of chivalry, and this representation in turn influenced new audiences of knights both young and old. For example, when Petrus Alfonsi (1977, 115), Henry I's physician, writes in his twelfth-century treatise, *Disciplina Clericalis*, that the seven knightly skills include "riding, swimming, archery, boxing, hawking, chess, and verse-writing," we might rightly wonder whether he is talking of real life or of literary knights. In fact, the question might be considered somewhat beside the point, given the degree of self-fashioning that chivalric knights engaged in. When, for example, one reads the *Histoire de Guillaume le Marechal* (composed *c.* 1220s), the image of William Marshal, 1st Earl of Pembroke, that one receives is at times difficult to disentangle from the literary models to which he – and his biographer – were evidently exposed (Meyer 1891–1901).

One of the difficulties that these literary models presented was the very shape of romance narrative itself. Romance is a genre that almost exclusively concerns itself with the actions of a singular protagonist, often acting as a *Bildungsroman* that tells the story of the rise to power and the maturation of a young aristocratic individual. One social complication with this mode of chivalric literature is that chivalric feats of arms and courtesy are inherently individual activities. As a system that generally rewards competition rather than cooperation, chivalry often has a problematic relationship with real-world politics. Within the Arthurian corpus, we find chivalry most often explored through the tales of the individual knights of Arthur's court, rather than of the legendary King himself. While Arthur institutes, oversees and often stands as judge in the public court of chivalric reputation, his role as king at the centre of the system means that he is often limited in his own chivalric exploits (see Archibald 2012, 139). Scholars have commented on the often non-chivalrous representation of Arthur in many of the romances of individual knights, but this should come as no surprise to us if we remind ourselves that one of the social functions of chivalry as a system was to manage and moderate the actions of the military classes of western medieval society; kings, while they might play at chivalry, were not the target of such an ideological system. As a result, chivalric narratives fit uneasily into the context of broader historical narratives such as Geoffrey's *Historia*, since they are concerned primarily with the ebb and flow of national and regional politics. Therefore, both within the Arthurian canon and without, chivalric literature often concerns itself with the stories of individual knights rather than the geo-politics of medieval history.

2 Chivalry and love

While chivalry began as a social code of conduct that developed to regulate the relation of knightly power with the other orders of medieval society, it soon began to accrete other significations. As chivalry became the *speculum* [mirror] of the aristocratic knightly *habitus* [characteristics], it soon took on desired qualities such as those adumbrated in the writings of Petrus Alfonsi, as we saw above. But in addition to hunting, chess and versification, chivalry also became the locus of that most courtly of aristocratic values, *fin'amor* [courtly love]. Refined love, or courtly love as it is often called, developed in lockstep with the martial aspects of chivalry, and established a code of behaviour to be followed between aristocratic men and women that we are still suffering from to this day. Originating in the romantic poetry and *gai saber* [literally: gay science; the art of composing love poetry] of the eleventh-century Occitan troubadours of Provence and the south, the idea of *fin'amor* spread across Western Europe, becoming an important part of a wider conception of chivalry during the twelfth century (cf. Hinton, *infra*). Nurtured in the courts of powerful female rulers such as Eleanor of Aquitaine and her daughter, Marie de Champagne, *fin'amor* developed into a complex system of intersexual behaviours that were codified by writers such as Andreas Capellanus in his *De Amore* (*c.* 1186–1190). Written at the behest of Marie de Champagne, the work of Capellanus (1972 [1892]) records a sweetly ironic account of the social and sexual mores of Marie's court of the 1170s. While the tone of his work divides opinion – scholars interpret it as ranging from an enthusiastically pedagogical tract to an outright condemnation –, *De Amore* records the principles of *fin'amor* for the reader, raising the same questions of lasting cultural influence as do the romances.

De Amore also provides us with an invaluable context for understanding the important body of Arthurian romances produced during the 1160s and 1170s by another writer patronized by Marie. Chrétien de Troyes served in Marie's court between 1160 and 1172, and between 1170 and 1190 produced some of the earliest and finest of the French Arthurian romances. In addition to the influential narratives of *Perceval* and *Yvain*, Chrétien wrote two of the most enduring love stories of the Arthurian canon: the tales of *Lancelot* (*Le Chevalier de la charrette*) and of *Erec et Enide*. These two poems are largely responsible for introducing the theme of *fin'amor* into the Arthurian legends, such that courtly love has become an integral component not just of the Arthurian world, but of chivalry itself.

Lancelot, ou Le Chevalier de la charrette (*c.* 1177–1181) introduces to the Arthurian corpus the figure of Lancelot, the greatest and most problematic of Arthur's knights. Quite literally an interloper from French culture, Chrétien introduces Lancelot to us as the embodiment of chivalric *fin'amor*. Chrétien's tale begins with the abduction of Guenevere by Meleagant, enabled by the efforts of the ever-bumbling Keu, and follows Lancelot's determined attempts to reclaim the Queen. Lancelot, who is always and inevitably in love with his king's wife, is the model of the courtly lover, following Capellanus' tenets almost to the letter. Disregarding the life of his horse, his honour, his safety and, ultimately, his own freedom, Lancelot pursues the captive queen. Early in the romance, while accompanying a seductive maiden on her travels, Lancelot comes across one of Guenevere's combs on the edge of a well. Trapped in the teeth of the comb is a lock of the queen's golden hair and, upon seeing this, Lancelot falls into a reverie. This has such a profound effect upon him that, as he travels onwards, he is soon attacked by a knight at a ford and accused of unchivalric behaviour as he has been too distracted to hear the knight's challenges. This scene is just one of many moments in the text that illustrate the danger that *fin'amor* poses towards the martial aspects of chivalric performance, and much of the remainder of the romance revolves around the question of how the debilitating effects of romantic love and desire can be balanced with the more traditional demands of chivalry.[4]

Erec et Enide (*c.* 1170) begins in a manner quite unlike most chivalric love stories, with a short account of a courtship replete with chivalric exploits, before moving rapidly to the wedding of the two protagonists. The romance takes as its matter not the deadly pains and love sickness of an unrequited lover such as Lancelot, but the age-old pragmatic question of how one keeps romantic love alive after its consummation. After their marriage, Erec spends his time with his new wife in their garden, relaxing and enjoying the fruits of their love. However, he soon hears the talk of the other young knights, who are saying that he no longer seeks chivalric deeds of adventure. Furious at the loss of his reputation as one of the most chivalrous and *puissant* knights in the land, Erec demands that Enide leave their life of domestic bliss and travel into the forest with him. Erec commands Enide to ride five minutes ahead of him on the trail, and orders her to remain silent, so that he will have many opportunities to save her from the various perils into which she will undoubtedly fall along the way. As we saw in *Le Chevalier de la charrette*, we again find a text that asks the question as to whether love and chivalry are compatible.[5]

Despite the complications that *fin'amor* brought to the wider concept of chivalry, courtly love became an essential component of chivalric culture and literature from the late-twelfth century onwards. For the rest of the medieval period – and beyond – Lancelot continued his tortuous pursuit of his liege's wife

---

4 Hinton (*infra*) provides an in-depth discussion of this matter.
5 See Chuhan Campbell (*infra*), who discusses this in relation to matters of gender.

and queen, and was joined by a legion of lovers, both real and literary, who followed the painful and frustrated model that Chrétien outlined in verse. Next we shall examine another Arthurian text that exploits the complicated ideal of chivalric *fin'amor* as a means of posing yet more questions regarding the role of chivalry.

3 Chivalry critiqued: Sir Gawain and the crisis of "trawthe"

As chivalry develops during the medieval period from a code of martial conduct to an expansive set of social and romantic rules, numerous attempts are made to codify and explain its tenets. During the fourteenth and fifteenth centuries we see the appearance of numerous books and guides to chivalric practice. Such texts, such as the *Livre de chevalerie* of Geoffroi de Charny (*c.* 1352) written for the French Ordre de l'Étoile [Order of the Star], a rival to the English Order of the Garter, outlined particular conceptions or philosophies of chivalry for their individual readerships (Geoffroi de Charny 1996). Designed for a broader, more diverse audience, such guidebooks meant that the fourteenth century also saw an explosion in the number of chivalric romances within the kingdoms of northern Europe. As a result, and in tandem with the expansion of city-based book production and performance, this heralded the beginnings of a widening of the audience for such chivalric romances, so as also to include the gentry and urban mercantile classes (see Radulescu 2013; *infra*).

The resulting increasing complexity of the rules of chivalric knighthood are questioned and critiqued in a range of medieval narratives. One such interrogation of the internal paradoxes of chivalric identity is the alliterative masterpiece *Sir Gawain and the Green Knight*, which particularly pertinently contains the legend "HONI SOYT QUI MAL PENCE" at the end of its sole surviving manuscript (London, BL, Cotton Nero A. X), a close echo of the motto of the above-mentioned Order of the Garter (see Ingledew 2006). The plot of the poem is too well known to rehearse here, but it is worth recalling that the arrival of the Green Knight in Arthur's court begins with an interrogation of identity: "is this Arthur's court?" the Green Knight demands, questioning the very reputation of the body of Arthurian chivalry (*Gawain*-poet 1968, 309–315). This challenge, which provokes a disproportionate response from Arthur himself, reveals the anxiety that lies at the heart of chivalric identity: that public reputation is all, and that this reputation is a fragile construction that relies on the continual performance of chivalric deeds.

The core of the poem concerns the testing of Arthur's champion, Sir Gawain. On the surface, this is made to happen through his Christmas exchange of blows (*gomen*) with the Green Knight, and then more substantially through the games of exchanges with Lord Bertilak the following Christmas. While Gawain successfully travels to the Green Chapel to receive the return blow of the axe, he has a more difficult time with the delicacies of the tests at Castle Hautdesert. On arriving at the castle en route to the Green Chapel, Gawain is welcomed by Bertilak and told to rest for three days before completing his journey. During this time, Bertilak suggests, they will engage in a game of daily exchanges, with Bertilak giving Gawain what he wins from each day he goes out hunting and Gawain proffering up to his host what he receives during his rest days, which coincide. Here is where Gawain's real test begins, with the alluring figure of Lady Bertilak attempting to seduce him while he rests. Over the course of the three days the exchanges occur, with Gawain providing his host with a kiss on the first day, two kisses on the second, and – fatefully – an incomplete exchange of three kisses on the third. Gawain has, of course, held back the last of his day three winnings: he has not offered up the green girdle that Lady Bertilak has promised will protect him (and so, he hopes, will save his life in his encounter with the Green Knight). Here, of course, lies the rub of the test: Gawain keeps the girdle as it may save his life, but he also does so in order to fulfil his promise to the Lady that he will keep a love-token from her. He is caught here between two conflicting chivalric obligations: the first is that he must remain loyal and true to his agreement with his host Bertilak; the second is the obligation of courtesy which, according to the principles of *fin'amor* (intrinsic to the fifth part of his pentangle identity), requires him to keep his dalliance with Lady Bertilak a secret. Caught between the two, Gawain chooses the route that will – he hopes – save his life in what he believes is the real test of truth that awaits him at the Green Chapel. It is only after he arrives at the Chapel, flinches at the first of the blows, again has his identity questioned, and eventually has the tests explained to him, that he realizes the true nature of the tests that he has undergone.

The Green Knight's lenient judgment of Gawain's failure reveals the flawed nature of Gawain's own excessively rigid sense of chivalric identity. Gawain, as the Green Knight recognizes, is caught within the steel teeth of the trap of an overly complicated chivalric identity; he has no real way of manoeuvring between his competing obligations to Bertilak and his Lady wife (Larrington 2012, 261–262). The demands of courtesy (which encompasses *fin'amor*) require him to play the role of courtly lover to the Lady, which places him in an impossible position in relation to his agreement of reciprocal exchange with her husband. The *Gawain*-poet here provides a damning critique of the complexities of chivalric identity, highlighting the paradoxes and contradictions that it entails.

When Sir Gawain is tested in the crucible of Hautdesert we again encounter the conditional question of identity that we first encountered at the beginning of

the poem: whether he is the Gawain of whom reputation speaks. Gawain's identity, as the events of his testing reveal, is one that is defined not just by the twenty-
five principles of chivalric practice represented by his pentangle shield, but also
his extra-/intertextual reputation as the lover-knight of the French literary tradition (cf. Hogenbirk, *infra*). Not merely an elaborate in-joke for the well-read audience member, the repeated references to the reputation of the French Gawain
(Gauvain) lay bare the fact that chivalric bodies are never fully in control of their
complex and often contradictory chivalric identities. Adrift in the open seas of
rumour and gossip, chivalric self-identity is only partly self-defined through personal action and choice, and to a large extent is hostage to fortune and to public
events.

4 Malory and the problem with egalitarianism

To end this overview of chivalry in Arthurian literature, I would like to return to
where I began: to Malory's description of the Pentecostal oath. Malory's articulation of the tenets of the chivalric ethos emphasizes the communal oath of all the
knights of the court, young and old, around the symbolically non-hierarchical
Round Table. Chivalry, in Malory's idealized, secular Arthurian conception, has
no ranks, no system of comparative differentiation. Chivalry is a binary system:
one is either chivalric, or one is not. But this is evidently a fiction. As Malory
repeatedly reminds us throughout the *Morte Darthur*, some knights carry a chivalric renown that is greater than that of others. The chief example of this in Malory
is, of course, Lancelot, as we are reminded by the repeated appellations of his
status as the best knight in this world. While it is true that he has competitors for
this title throughout the *Morte Darthur*, chiefly Sir Tristram and – more briefly –
Sir Gareth of Orkney, his identity as the apogee of secular chivalry is eventually
reaffirmed in the Sir Urry episode. Furthermore, the spiritual hierarchy that is
revealed during the Grail Quest parallels and problematizes this secular hierarchy, thus elevating Galahad, Perceval and the slightly spotted Bors above the
other questing knights, owing to the spiritual associations they become imbued
with as a result of their interactions with the Grail. At every turn the *Morte Darthur*
puts the lie to the fiction of egalitarian chivalry embodied by the Round Table,
laying bare the social, martial and spiritual competitiveness that is at the heart of
the medieval ideology of chivalry.

This problematic fiction complicates not only the egalitarian symbolism and
principles of the Round Table, but also the utility of chivalry as a pragmatic ethical
system. As Cory Rushton (2002, 83) observes, "there is no hierarchy between the

basic tenets which would allow a Round Table knight to make crucial decisions in the field." As we saw clearly in *Sir Gawain and the Green Knight*, the ethical bind that Gawain finds himself in due to the competing chivalric virtues of, on the one hand, honesty in his game of exchanges with Bertilak and, on the other, *courtoisie* towards Bertilak's wife does not allow him to prioritize one over the other. When faced with the Gordian knot that is the green girdle, the code of chivalry that is so central to Gawain's conception of self offers no clear guidance to his actions. Similarly, the oft-encountered conflict between individual chivalric ethics and public political allegiances in the *Morte Darthur* leads ultimately to the discord, confusion and disaster of the final book.

Malory's Arthurian epic narrates not only the death of Arthur, but also what Malory sees as the death of chivalry within the public sphere of English politics. For Malory, writing perhaps in the Tower of London, chivalry has fallen into disrepute as a social institution. As a young knight he grew up in an England still illuminated by the recent glorious reign and renowned deeds of King Henry V. As an adult he lived, fought, raided and, arguably, raped his way through some of the worst years of the civil strife of the mid-fifteenth century. As an older knight he was tried, imprisoned and explicitly not pardoned for his chivalric deeds. As a writer he looked back, not only to the glorious pre-fall age of Arthurian chivalry, but also over the decaying ruins of fifteenth-century chivalric practice: the death of Richard of York at Wakefield; the murder of Edmund of Rutland at Wakefield Bridge; the unprecedented slaughter at Towton; the repeatedly changing direction of noble allegiances; the murder of princes and of kings; the death of an ideal, and of idealism. While chivalry would, of course, be revived under the Tudors – and ironically enough in large part by Caxton's own preface to the very text that lamented its death – in a very real way medieval English chivalry died a death on the battlefields of the Wars of the Roses.

References

Alfonsi, Petrus. *The* Disciplina Clericalis *of Petrus Alfonsi*. Ed. Eberhard Hermes. Trans. P.R. Quarrie. Berkeley: University of California Press, 1977.

Archibald, Elizabeth. "Questioning Arthurian Ideals." *The Cambridge Companion to the Arthurian Legend*. Ed. Elizabeth Archibald and Ad Putter. Cambridge: Cambridge University Press, 2012. 139–153.

Capellanus, Andreas. *Andreae Capellani regii Francorum de amore libri tres*. Ed. E. Trojel. Munich: Fink, 1972 [Copenhagen: Gad, 1892].

Duby, Georges. *The Three Orders: Feudal Society Imagined*. Trans. Arthur Goldhammer. Chicago: University of Chicago Press, 1980.

Gawain-poet, *Sir Gawain and the Green Knight*. Ed. J.R.R. Tolkien, E.V. Gordon. Rev. Norman
    Davis. 2nd edn. Oxford: Oxford University Press, 1968.
Geoffroi de Charny. *The Book of Chivalry of Geoffroi de Charny: Text, Context, and Translation*.
    Ed. and trans. Richard Kaeuper and Elspeth Kennedy. Philadelphia: University of
    Pennsylvania Press, 1996.
Ingledew, Francis. Sir Gawain and the Green Knight *and the Order of the Garter*. Notre Dame,
    IN: University of Notre Dame Press, 2006.
Jackson, W.H. *Chivalry in Twelfth-century Germany: The Works of Hartman von Aue*. Cambridge:
    D.S. Brewer, 1994.
John of Salisbury. *Policraticus*. Ed. Cary J. Nederman. Cambridge: Cambridge University Press,
    1990.
Larrington, Carolyne. "English Chivalry and *Sir Gawain and the Green Knight*." *A Companion
    to Arthurian Literature*. Ed. Helen Fulton. Oxford and Malden, MA: Wiley-Blackwell, 2012.
    252–264.
Kaeuper, Richard W. *Chivalry and Violence in Medieval Europe*. Oxford: Oxford University Press,
    1999.
Kaeuper, Richard W., and Montgomery Bohna. "War and Chivalry." *A Companion to Medieval
    English Literature and Culture, c. 1350–c. 1500*. Ed. Peter Brown. Oxford and Malden, MA:
    Wiley-Blackwell, 2009. 273–291.
Malory, Sir Thomas, *Le Morte Darthur: The Winchester Manuscript*. Ed. Helen Cooper. Oxford:
    Oxford University Press, 1998.
Meyer, Paul, ed. *L'Histoire de Guillaume le Marechal, comte de Striguil et de Pembroke, regent
    d'Angleterre*. 3 vols. Paris: Société de l'histoire de France, 1891–1901.
Radulescu, Raluca L. *Romance and its Contexts in Fifteenth-Century England: Politics, Piety and
    Penitence*. Cambridge: D.S. Brewer, 2013.
Reid, Peter. *Medieval Warfare: Triumph and Domination in the Wars of the Middle Ages*. New
    York: Carroll and Graf, 2007.
Rushton, Cory. "Talk is Cheap: Political Discourse in Malory's *Morte Darthur*." *Disputatio* 5
    (2002): 67–86.
Taylor, Craig. *Chivalry and the Ideals of Knighthood in France during the Hundred Years' War*.
    Cambridge: Cambridge University Press, 2013.

Samantha J. Rayner
The International Arthurian Society and Arthurian Scholarship

> "It is right that present-day Arthurian scholars and those yet to come should understand
> that Societies like ours are not provided by the Welfare State, that the Truro Congress was
> the brain-child of Professor Eugène Vinaver, that without him it would most assuredly not
> have taken place, that, obviously enough, there were three young Oxford men and women
> aiding and abetting him, and that it was he and Professor Jean Frappier who organized the
> Quimper Congress at which our Society was founded." (Thorpe 1973, 187)

The history of academic societies goes back to the seventeenth century and the formation of the Royal Society in London: though the International Arthurian Society (IAS) does not have quite that lineage, it can claim to have created, in less than a century, a distinguished set of achievements, not least of which is the establishment of Arthurian scholarship as a dynamic and evolving academic field. A wider history of Arthurian scholarship has been collected elsewhere (Lacy 2006), so this chapter looks at it through the particular lens of the IAS, a body which has developed all over the world through the efforts of scholars like Vinaver and his successors: a body that, as the quotation above stresses, deserves to be foregrounded as an entity that is built on co-operation and collaboration (as well as confrontation and conflict) from within its membership.

This chapter does not attempt a comprehensive history of the Society, as space makes this impossible, but it will draw out key points in its past, using comments and experiences of members to enhance materials drawn from within the IAS and from outside of it.[1] The aim is to produce a perspective that provides evidence of that claim above: that Arthurian scholarship owes much to the growth of the IAS, and the members who have supported it. There is still a need for a more detailed set of histories from each of the Branches, as communicating with members across the world has already shown a vast, uncaptured sea of information not available elsewhere that would not fit into this chapter. If this piece does its work,

---
1 Without the patient and generous responses from many IAS members over time regarding the Society's histories, this chapter would not have been possible: I would like to thank, in particular, Keith Busby, Bart Besamusca, Frank Brandsma, Cora Dietl, Peter Field, Linda Gowans, Norris Lacy, Philippe Ménard, Raluca Radulescu, Gillian Rogers, Jane Taylor, Toshiyuki Takamiya and Kevin Whetter.

Samantha J. Rayner (University College London)

DOI 10.1515/9783110432466-003

it will inspire others to fill the many gaps left here, and ensure that further histories of this remarkable Society do not get lost.

In 1928, Eugène Vinaver, then a Reader in French at the University of Oxford, formed an Arthurian Society. Two sets of proceedings under the title of *Arthuriana* were published in 1929 and 1930, but then the Society became the Society for the Study of Medieval Languages and Literature in 1932, and the journal was renamed *Medium Aevum*. Vinaver was already known for his work on Arthurian themes at this point (see Vinaver 1929), and his reputation was such that in 1929 Oxford University Press were discussing a new edition of Sir Thomas Malory's *Le Morte Darthur* with him. He was not alone in his conviction that there was a place for an Arthurian Society: a letter published in *History* in 1930, announcing that a conference of Arthurian scholars was to be held in Truro in late August of that year, was signed by Henry Jenner, F.S.A., Signor Giulia Bertoni (Rome), M. Gustave Cohen (Paris), Mr W.F. Gruffydd (Cardiff), Mr. C.B. Lewis (St. Andrews), Mr. R.S. Loomis (New York), M.S. Singer (Bern), Mynheer J. van Dam (Amsterdam) and Mynheer A.G. van Hamel (Utrecht). This international group of names claimed that:

> Arthurian romance, the fountain-head of medieval and modern romantic fiction, in its historical, legendary and literary aspects, has in recent years claimed a good deal of attention from scholars in Great Britain, France, Germany and America. The time seems opportune for a gathering together of those concerned with such studies in order to discuss the many problems arising out of their work. (*History* 1930, 128)

Those interested in taking part were urged to contact Vinaver and Dr. J. Hambley Rowe, a medical practitioner and President of the Royal Cornwall Polytechnic Society. Vinaver (1973, 193) credits Rowe with the idea for the Congress, saying that Rowe wrote to him in Oxford suggesting that an attempt should be made to bring together Arthurian scholars in Cornwall: "the study of the Arthurian legend was to him primarily a means of reviving what he thought was a Cornish tradition." Vinaver (1929) was in favour of the idea, but with the proviso that members of the Congress would be able to express their views freely, "even if this meant denying that Cornwall had any place in the creation of Arthurian romance." As will be seen below, this was to test the hospitality of the Cornish hosts in ways the press picked up on, but also demonstrated the ability of scholarly networks to overcome such local issues without compromising scholarly integrity.

The focus of this Congress was "the problem of Arthurian *origins*" (Vinaver 1969, 115), with papers discussing the source of the Grail Legend (by Professor Roger Loomis, Columbia University, and Dr. C.B. Lewis, St. Andrews University), the importance of French texts in making Arthur famous (by Professor Wilmotte, Brussels University), who the real Arthur was (Henry II, according to Professor

Mary Williams, University College, Swansea), and the discovery of a new manuscript at the Vatican Library (M. Jean Frappier, Marseilles). These papers were part
of an event significant enough to be reported in *The Times*, *The New York Times*,
The Irish Times, *The Observer*, and *The Sun, Baltimore*, among others.[2] This coverage demonstrates the impact – outside of the academy – the Congress had. Local
papers from across Britain reported on the event, and there are letters responding
to the papers and the theories put forward by the academics. In today's terms,
Arthurians were trending across the globe: there was a curiosity around what
the scholars would expose, and a genuine anxiety by some that "many charming
embellishments and details of the old tale are in grave danger" (*The Irish Times*,
26 August 1930: 6) from the learned gathering. "We are not here to discover King
Arthur", said Vinaver, "but to discover the truth about him – which is not necessarily, or always, the same thing." (*The Western Morning News and Mercury*, 26
August 1930: 8)

According to *The New York Times*, about thirty-five delegates attended the
Truro Congress. Henry Jenner, that "white-bearded grand bard of the Cornish
Gorsedd", was appointed President, and the Congress divided its time "between
the little lecture hall in the museum in Truro and charabanc rides which took its
members to Arthurian sites throughout the country." However, this rather genteel
description, complete with information about the Cornish cream the delegates
were given with their tea, sits alongside headlines which made much of Jenner's
sensational assertion that to call Tintagel "King Arthur's Castle" was "an impos-
ture" (*The New York Times*, 21 September 1930: 11). "Tintagel's Legend Faces an
Attack", shouts *The Sun*, in Baltimore (28 September 1930: 8). "New Doubts About
King Arthur Grow From Study of Experts", declares *The New York Times* (21 September 1930: 11). Jenner, a well-known expert on Celtic, Cornish and Arthurian
matters, read a paper that dealt with the textual fault-lines that had created the
association of Arthur and Tintagel: despite this scholarly tour-de-force the report
from *The Times* nonetheless has him wryly admitting at the end that the idea was
"so profitable to hotel and lodging housekeepers that there was very little chance
of getting rid of it." (*The Times*, 29 August 1930: 15) A prescient thought indeed. In

---

2 See e.g., *The Times*, 27 August 1930: 12; *The New York Times*, 21 September 1930: 11; *The Irish
Times*, 26 August 1930: 6; *The Observer*, 31 August 1930: 10; *The Sun, Baltimore*, 28 September
1930: 8; *Yorkshire Post and Leeds Intelligencer*, 25 August 1930: 8; *Western Morning News*, 21 August 1930: 4; *Dundee Courier*, 25 August 1930: 5; the *BBIAS* (1973, 185) reports coverage in at least
thirty-three dailies and weeklies, and gives a full list of these. For ease of use, references to newspaper articles will appear in full in the main text in this chapter, and not in the list of references
at the end.

1975, a report on the Congress of that year in *The Guardian* includes reflections on the first Congress, with people who had been there recalling it "fondly":

> Excursions and sunshine almost every day; a civic reception with a Cornish tea; an Arthurian banquet; and headline-hitting learned papers given al fresco. (*The Guardian*, 15 August 1975: 13)

Along with evocative details like the banquet diners' preference for Ye Chough of Cornwall Pie over Ye Boar of Lancelot with Avalon Sauce, or the perfection of a dessert named Jelly Guinevere, there are marvellings at the spirit of fellowship that was created in this first gathering: these "pioneers" were surprised to find "that people who had fought bitterly in print could, so to speak, lie down peacefully together." (Fox 1973, 187) *The Western Morning News and Mercury* contains a fuller breakdown of the schedule: it was six days of non-stop trips and papers, as the description of Wednesday's plans reveals:

> Excursion to Chapel Point, Gorran, reputed site of Tristram's Leap; Lantyan, St Sampson's, reputed site of King Mark's Palace in the story of Tristram and Iseult; Castle Dore inscribed stone (?Tristram's memorial stone); Castle Dore earthwork (Carhulas, Fort of Gorlois); Cardinham (?King Arthur's memorial stone); Camelford (Slaughter Bridge), the site of traditional (Arthurian?) battle; Tintagel Castle; Kelly Rounds. Egloshayle (Celli Wic) one of King Arthur's homes; Castle-an-Dinas, St Colomb, associated with Arthur by local tradition; and Dameliock, St Dennis (hill fort). (*The Western Morning News and Mercury*, 21 August 1930: 4)

And, just in case that was not enough Arthurian content for one day, "papers will be given en route by Mr Henry Jenner, of Hayle."[3]

In addition to all this scholarly activity, Congress members were invited to the local Gorsedd, at Liskeard, where some Arthurians were initiated as Bards: Dr. Mary Williams took the name "Rhiannon", Professor Loomis "Gwas Geraint", Mrs. Loomis "Merghenid" and Dr. Vinaver "Gwas Gwinear" (*The Western Morning News and Mercury*, 30 August 1930: 10).[4] It was an honour that members took with varying degrees of levity (*BBIAS* 1973, 187–196), but which underlines the closeness of the Congress to local Celtic traditions. The mutual respect shown by locals and academics did much to create a view of the event as part of "those halcyon times. . . [when the] sun never ceased to shine." (Thorpe, 1973, 182) More pertinently to this history of the impact of the IAS, Vinaver (1973, 194) underlined

---

3 A full programme is reproduced in *BBIAS* (1973, 180–181).
4 Also reported in *BBIAS* (1973, 184).

that "something very valuable was achieved during that week spent in Cornwall", and:

> That there were irreconcilable views about the origins of Arthurian literature we knew before we went there. The real value of the meeting lay in the discovery of a vast variety of temperaments behind those views, of people with their individual ways of thinking and feeling which we could not have discovered any other way.

The 1930 Congress concluded with Dr. Hambley Rowe and Dr. Vinaver reporting to a newspaper that the conference had "fully justified itself by the certainty alone that other conferences would follow." Members of the Congress, "did not come to any unanimous conclusion as regards the origin of the Grail legend, but they all felt that the exchange of opinions [had] been of great help, and will no doubt contribute to the advancement of the subject." (Vinaver 1973, 194) Several important decisions had been made: that there would be an International Arthurian Society, with Vinaver as convenor and honorary secretary; that the next Congress would be held in 1932, in Brittany; and that there was a need for a periodical in which Arthurian projects and matters could be published. This last was left to be considered at the next Congress (*BBIAS* 1973, 186).

Despite all these positive results, however, it was not until 1948 that this next Congress took place. Even taking the Second World War into account, this is a considerable gap, and Vinaver admits: "in the years preceding the Second World War I did in fact fail to find enough support among the leading Arthurian scholars for a second Arthurian Congress." (*BBIAS* 1973, 194) Looking in some detail at this first Congress, it is perhaps understandable why this was: the tension in that Cornish location, overcome in many ways by the good nature of hosts and scholars alike, meant that the Congress was described as being "much more of Don Quixote than of Chretien de Troyes" (*BBIAS* 1973, 194)[5] and "a wonderful holiday" (Fox 1973, 188) – and this may have helped create a lack of scholarly drive to participate in the next one. And as R.C. Johnston (1973, 191) said, "enthusiasm, ardour, idealism, naivete – these were somewhat prominent amongst the characteristics of our Society in its earliest days."

In 1954, the President of the Society, Jean Frappier, grappled with defining reasons for the eighteen-year gap between the first and second Congress, and offered a romance-led solution:

---

5 In this citation, Vinaver is quoting Maurice Wilmotte, writing to Vinaver after his return from the Congress.

j'imagine volontiers, aujourd'hui où nous disposons d'une appréciable perspective chronologique, qu'il y eut à cela une cause occulte et profonde en harmonie avec une authentique tradition arthurienne, l'idée d'une préfiguration suivie d'une attente prolongée et traverse d'épreuves, l'obligation d'une période comparable à l'enfance secrète des héros, ou un délai nécessaire au mûrissement de l'espérance bretonne. (Frappier 1954, 89)

[I can readily imagine now, with the benefit of hindsight, that there was a secret and profound reason that is in harmony with Arthurian tradition: the idea of a foreshadowing [or premonition] followed by a prolonged wait, interspersed with trials; the requirement of having a period comparable with the secret childhood of heroes, or a necessary delay in order to ripen Breton hope.]

That there might be some "secret and profound reason that is in harmony with Arthurian tradition" that encompassed trials and a long wait is charming, but it is true that during the years 1930–1948 a curious re-flowering of interest in the Arthurian stories happened, with key scholarship materializing in this gap that changed the shape of areas like Malory studies altogether: Eugène Vinaver's edition of Malory finally appeared in 1947, for example, following years of work (and rework after the discovery of the Winchester manuscript in 1934). Given Vinaver's acknowledged pivotal role in the birth of the Society, this fact, along with the Second World War, can feasibly account for the hiatus in the more formal establishment of the IAS. In a speech that Vinaver gave at the ninth International Congress in Cardiff in 1969, he reflects on the first Congress and its focus on Arthurian origins, drawing a comparison between that and the subsequent flourishing of what he calls "a new kind of medievalism, of a medievalism of *literature as such*." (Vinaver 1970, 116) He talks about the value of human invention, which made things real through art, and that:

the important thing was no longer the fact that the imaginary chivalric life of Arthurian romance had no basis in real life, but the realization that this imaginary life had created its own reality and opened up new vistas of intellectual and aesthetic experience.

These vistas became further enhanced by a widening of media beyond literature, so that by 1987, Norris Lacy, the then President of the Society, hailed the "diversity, both chronological and geographical" represented by the papers at the Congress in Leuven, and the increasing attention to the visual arts, "from medieval manuscripts to modern painting and film." (Lacy 1987, 6) He also makes the point, linking back to Vinaver's reminiscences (1970, 116) about the way people worried about scholarship "destroying our heritage and putting nothing in its place", that Arthurian scholars:

deal with a privileged subject matter. More than virtually any other subject, the Arthurian legend, the *matière de Bretagne* embraces both scholarly and popular publics. There can be few people to whom the name King Arthur does not mean something, and if the popular mind often assumes that Arthur did exist (or does exist?) that belief is the strongest testimony to the power and appeal of the legend.

The Quimper Congress, recorded in the first issue of the *BBIAS* in 1949, had twenty-two delegates and fifteen papers. Of these delegates, only five (Loomis, Vinaver, Lewis, Johnston and Frappier) had been present at the 1930 Congress. Frappier was elected President, with Loomis and Vinaver Presidents of the North American and British Branches, respectively. Frappier was to hold the position of President until 1966, when the term of the presidency came to be limited to three years, and Vinaver took over. The Quimper Congress formally established the International Arthurian Society (IAS) with three main aims: to organize a Congress every three years; to publish an annual *Bibliographical Bulletin*; and to create, in Paris, a *Centre de Documentation arthurienne* [Arthurian Resource Centre]. This first *Bulletin* also records members in Austria, Italy, Belgium and Holland, so right from the beginning, the membership was established as international in scope (*BBIAS* 1959, 5–8). However, the list of members' names in the back of the *Bulletin* only gives the French (thirty-three members) and the Americans (seventy-three members). There is no listing for the British Branch (*BBIAS* 1959, 65–71).

Norris Lacy comments on the "vast and general" nature of some of the papers given at Quimper, including a history of German Arthurian Literature from 1190 to 1500, by J. Riordan, and calls attention to other papers which show an interest in sources, analogues and influences (Lacy 1997, 228). The records of the papers given at the Congresses, which are captured with varying degrees of thoroughness up until 2005, when the Committee decided to stop this practice in order to make the *Bulletin* shorter (*BBIAS* 2005, 386), do show the development of the discipline of Arthurian scholarship over an arc of more than fifty years. It is a shame that the records of more recent Congresses are hard to find, or missing: although the Dutch Branch have a website where reports are held for the 1996, 1999, 2002 and 2005 Congresses,[6] the 2008 Rennes report is now a dead link. The North American Branch website has dead links for its newsletters, which in any case are only listed until 2002.[7] While other sites, like the German and British Branch pages, have more information on them, it is only by going through the Romanian Branch website that a programme for the 2014 Congress, held in Bucharest, can be found.[8] The main link to the Congress webpage results in an error message.

---

6 See <http://www.let.uu.nl/alw/ARTHUR/artcongr.html>.

7 See <http://www.arthuriana.org/arthurias.htm>.

8 See <https://arturieni.wordpress.com/evenements/>.

It is frustrating that the Society's histories are so challenging to access during a time when digital archiving is easier than ever before: hopefully the Society will take steps to preserve its histories more coherently, especially now there is a new *Centre de Documentation arthurienne* at Bangor University.[9]

Despite these challenges, the programme for the Bucharest Congress proves the range of topics now on offer to members: spread over five days, with another day for excursions, the panels range from manuscript studies to Arthurian tourism, magic, power and contemporary remediations of the Arthurian stories.[10] As one new member wrote: "Speakers from all over the world demonstrated that there is still much to write about how the ways in which the mythical or historical figure of Arthur has influenced our imaginations over the centuries." (Linton 2014)

The establishment of a triennial Congress clearly stands at the heart of the Society's success. Bart Besamusca (International President 2003–2005) points out the impact these events have "for establishing and maintaining international contacts and the exchange of ideas", an exchange that makes collaborative research projects on a large scale possible. Besamusca offers proof by way of the Arthurian Fiction Database, and the HERA Dynamics of a Medieval Manuscript Project.[11] Cora Dietl who, at the time of writing, is the current International President, also underlines this aspect: the Congresses "ensure an international networking and co-operation of scholars all over the world", and she highlights the LATE (Littérature Arthurienne Tardive en Europe) Project currently led by Christine Ferlampin-Acher, herself a former International President of the Society (2009–2011) and a contributor to this volume, as just one example of this. She also mentions the Arthurian Fiction Database, the *New Arthurian Encyclopedia*, edited by Norris Lacy, and the series of books known as *ALMA* (Arthurian Literature in the Middle Ages or "The Arthur of..." series), saying these "are all tools for Arthurian Studies that no researcher and no student of Arthurian Studies would like to miss, and that have developed from the international cooperation in the Arthurian Society."[12] Other examples of collaboration include international shared courses and research networks, like Arthurian Emotions, which currently

---

9 See <http://www.internationalarthuriansociety.com/british-branch/news/new-ias-centre-de-documentation>.

10 See <https://arturieni.files.wordpress.com/2015/10/congrc3a8s-sia1.pdf>.

11 See <http://www.arthurianfiction.org> and <http://www.dynamicsofthemedievalmanuscript.eu>. Personal communication from Bart Besumusca, August 2016.

12 Personal communication from Cora Dietl, August 2016.

pull together colleagues from Europe, the USA and Australia. Kathleen Fitzpatrick (2012, 650) explains that:

> societies are above all communities, or clusters of communities, that gather experts in particular fields or subfields in the common project of sharing, discussing, and improving their work. These scholars, in direct, open communication with one another, will be in the best possible position to develop and implement the standards that scholars and their institutions require for the evaluation of new kinds of scholarly projects.

The IAS demonstrates this functionality in the range of professional academic activities it has fostered and supported: apart from those initiatives listed above, *Arthuriana: The Quarterly for the International Arthurian Society-North American Branch* is an ongoing key journal for Arthurian studies, and, also via the North American Branch, The Camelot Project at the University of Rochester provides a wealth of online resources for teaching and research.[13] The Vinaver Trust, set up in 1981, helps scholars to subsidize the publication of books (including the *ALMA* series), and for UK students, the Barron Bequest, set up in memory of W.R.J. Barron, helps support postgraduate studies in Arthurian-related fields.[14] This Bequest is "a lasting memorial to the generosity, in the fullest sense of the word, of a distinguished academic" (Powell 2004): Barron was a long-time Director of the Vinaver Trust, as well as a bibliographer for the *BBIAS*, and his impact on scholars all over the world is still felt.

The Vinaver Trust also demonstrates the felicity of what the writer of Barron's obituary called, "that peculiar mixture of scholarship and speculation, fact and fantasy in medieval Arthurian studies" (Powell 2004); the money in that fund comes not from some scholarly endeavour, but from the proceeds from special edition plates that were made by the Franklin Mint. These plates have become legends of their own within the Society's oral history; Elspeth Kennedy's part in the expanding inventory of endorsed objects, including an Excalibur which she said she kept under her bed, are now part of the unofficial annals of the IAS. Arthurnet, another key resource set up by the American Arthurians, has been invaluable in trying to unpick the truth of this particular tale. This list-serv, which started in 1993, is a portal for Arthurian scholars. Search the archives and you will find plenty of evidence of the generosity of knowledge that circulates within the Society. On the subject of these plates, for example, it is clear from reading a thread on Arthurnet about them that considerable jumbling of memory has

---

13 See <http://d.lib.rochester.edu/camelot-project>.
14 See <http://www.internationalarthuriansociety.com/vinaver> and <http://www.international arthuriansociety.com/british-branch/view/awards>.

clouded the facts, but Judy Shoaf confirms, with reference to the *BBIAS*, that the scheme began in 1990, and that Elspeth Kennedy, then President, supported a deal with the Mint that had, by 1993, already brought in $23,000 to the Society.[15]

Such enterprising moves are rare in academic circles, and not always welcomed by members. Norris Lacy recalls reservations from the membership, and receiving letters "dripping with outrage and invective" from people outside of the Society who claimed it "no longer deserved to be considered a scholarly organization."[16] The IAS certainly attracts interest from outside of its academic boundaries, due to exactly that "peculiar mixture" of elements that appeals to a diverse general audience, too.

Arthurnet is one good example of the informal networking that the IAS has instigated, but it is also, because of its larger appeal to people who are not members, an example of how the Society sometimes has to manage more difficult encounters. In 2014 Judy Shoaf resigned as administrator following the receipt of what she calls a "particularly officious and delusional post."[17] Norris Lacy, in his email to the list (the final one that is archived), notes that despite the attempts to turn discussion threads back towards the great number of Arthurian texts, films and paintings, in recent times there is a very fast "return to the question of various Arthurs, place names, battle sites, and the like." Ironically, as this is where the 1930 Congress started, with debates about the historical Arthur, this is the ground on which Arthurnet foundered. Lacy muses:

> I've often thought that there should really be two Arthurnets: one for those interested in the pseudo-history of Arthur (who he might have been if he were real, what he might have done, and where he might have done it), another for those interested in the myriad literary and other expressions – some of them immortal, others abysmal – of the legend.[18]

Arthurnet may rise again, but for now, like its eponymous hero, it lies waiting for a more propitious time.

On a more positive level, although the Congresses have seen their own share of clashes and high drama over the years, they have also had lasting individual impact, too: time and again scholars point to the generosity shown to them as junior researchers. Frank Brandsma calls the contacts made via the IAS Con-

---

15 See Arthurnet archive, email from Judy Shoaf, "IAS – Franklin Mint Connection," 19 November 2013.
16 Arthurnet archive, email from Norris Lacy, "Franklin Mint – IAS Figurine?" 19 November 2013.
17 Arthurnet archive, email from Judy Shoaf, "Arthurnet," 3 November 2014.
18 Arthurnet archive, email from Norris Lacy, "Re: Arthurnet," 3 November 2014.

gresses "crucial", saying that help from senior people like Elspeth Kennedy, Norris Lacy, Douglas Kelly and Keith Busby were very important to the establishment of his career.[19] Bart Besamusca describes how, in 1987, he made his IAS debut, along with several other Dutch members: "when it was their turn to give a paper [...] Elspeth Kennedy (a scholar whom they did not know personally, but all admired for her Lancelot work), was sitting on the first row at each [...] continuously smiling at them, trying to put them at ease."[20] Current Branch Presidents, Raluca Radulescu (British Branch) and Kevin Whetter (North American Branch) both independently focus on this sense of welcome: Radulescu talks about the "collegiality and positive feedback, the inclusiveness (including the multilingual nature of the research and international membership),"[21] while Whetter emphasizes that "it has definitely been the sense of belonging that has been the greatest benefit – of belonging to an organization that has always fostered and supported my research and one that has introduced me to so many people who are both wonderful scholars and warm and witty individuals."[22]

Similarly, Keith Busby (International President 2012–2014) has many memories of Congress highlights: "the pleasure of putting faces to names of scholars you had been reading,"[23] while Jane H.M. Taylor (International President 2000–2002) emphasizes that the Society is "a receptive and welcoming space [for young scholars] to develop their careers."[24] Cora Dietl, the current International President, stresses the value of the national Branch conferences: "it is these smaller and often more harmonious, if not to say "family-style" conferences that attract young scholars and foster the dialogue between PhD students, active professors, and most honourable retired colleagues."[25] Although online networking is now a part of the IAS portfolio (see below), and members like Whetter worry if, as a result, "traditional society memberships will have the same sort of cache"; he is convinced that "the old-school, or personal, face-to-face element that membership in the branch and society brings is still crucial."[26]

Looking at those original three aims of the Society, there is no mention of creating a network of Arthurian scholars. And yet, when members were asked about the value of the Society, this almost unanimously came out as the most

---

19 Personal communication from Frank Brandsma, August 2016.
20 Personal communication from Bart Besamusca, August 2016.
21 Personal communication from Raluca Radulescu, August 2016.
22 Personal communication from Kevin Whetter, August 2016.
23 Personal communication from Keith Busby, August 2016.
24 Personal communication from Jane Taylor, August 2016.
25 Personal communication from Cora Dietl, August 2016.
26 Personal communication from Kevin Whetter, August 2016.

appreciated benefit. The establishment of national Branches means that there are home contexts for Arthurians in France, Germany, the UK and Ireland, the USA, Japan, Australia and New Zealand, the Netherlands, Romania, Switzerland and Italy, with a Hispanic Branch covering Spain, Portugal and Brazil, and a Nordic Branch covering Iceland, Norway, Sweden and Denmark.[27] Today there are over nine hundred members listed on the IAS website, spread all over the world. Looking at the different Branch webpages gives a snapshot of the breadth of research activity going on, and the variety of different ways in which members engage with each other. For instance, Toshiyuki Takamiya, who kindly sent me a timeline of the history of the Japanese Branch, details a rich scholarly tradition of members including the first Branch President, Teruo Sato, who translated Bédier's *Roman de Tristan et Yseut* and published a study of the Prose *Tristan*. The distinguished outputs from this Branch alone would form plenty of material for a whole chapter: the field of Arthurian study owes much to Japanese skill, which produced, among other key texts, *A Concordance to the Works of Sir Thomas Malory* (Kato 1974). The author, Tomomi Kato of Tokyo University of Electronics published, in 1974, the earliest computer-assisted KWIC (Key Word In Context) concordance of any English work in prose. This innovative and truly ground-breaking achievement was underlined by the eagerness of international scholars to meet Kato at the Congress of 1975, in Exeter: Takamiya describes Kato as being "little known to Malory scholars at home and abroad" before he published the *Concordance*, but he was a star appearance at this Congress.[28]

The 1975 Congress was, in many ways, a key one: not just because it was the first time computer-aided work was a presence, but also because it was the first Congress after one of the core founders, Jean Frappier, died. Although the *BBIAS* records that delegates were "acutely aware" of Frappier's absence (*BBIAS* 1975, 183), it also mentions that four more of the original 1930 Congress attendees were there: Eugène Vinaver, Marjorie Fox, R.C. Johnston and Dominica Legge. In an article in *The Guardian*, Vinaver looks back at the achievements of the IAS since Truro, saying:

> What's happened since then is that we have realized the importance of Arthurian literature as an integral part of our literary heritage. It didn't even occur to me at first, and I said a lot of things that now I bitterly regret. But then I became very interested in thirteenth century prose literature, and it was there I discovered the creative process: the birth of a sense of form. Malory became for me simply the final stage in a process of evolution which produced all the forms of imaginative narrative that we have today. This was completely denied by the

---

27 See <http://www.internationalarthuriansociety.com/branches-and-committees>.
28 Personal communications from Toshiyuki Takamiya and Peter Field, August 2016.

traditional scholars. There was a lot of controversy: we had pretty violent fights, which was what made congresses so exciting. But I think one can say that the young generation have opted in favour of the progressive, rather than the regressive, approach. (*The Guardian*, 15 August 1975)

The controversy was still in evidence: this was the Congress at which Roy F. Leslie read a paper by the deceased William Matthews, which attacked Vinaver's work, and which sparked off a series of responses that have become known as "the Malory debate" (Wheeler, Kindrick and Salda 2000). I have talked about the impact of this elsewhere (Rayner 2015), but this Congress does illustrate the part the IAS played in actively shaping academic debate. Several among the young generation of scholars were deeply impressed by this, their first Congress, with Peter Field and Keith Busby among them: both went on to be International Presidents in the future. This was also the Congress at which German was added to English and French as an operational language of the IAS and when it was agreed at the General Meeting that the Statutes of the Society needed rewriting (*BBIAS* 1975, 201).

The original Statutes are published in the *BBIAS* for 1975, presumably to help with the proposed rewriting task (*BBIAS* 1975, 235–237). There are twelve articles, in French, which cover membership rules, the formation of the Committee and general maintenance of the Society. Article I states that "La Société Internationale Arthurienne est une association qui groupe des professeurs et des chercheurs" [the International Arthurian Society is an association which brings together educators and researchers] but, in contrast to the newer Statutes, it is for the study of "les oeuvres arthuriennes (romans de la Table Ronde) dans la littératures médiévales de tous les pays ainsi que les problèmes qui s'y rattachent." (*BBIAS* 1975, 235) [Arthurian works (books about the Round Table) in the medieval literature of all countries, as well as the problems associated with them.] But by 1975, as a glance at the programme for the Congress reveals, there was research on much more than just the medieval contexts of Arthurian works: a paper on Tennyson, by Dr. J. M. Gray, indicates the start of a sea-change. By the time of the Leuven Congress in 1987, Norris Lacy was able to note the "dramatically" changed spread of topics represented on the programme, including Pre-Raphaelite stained glass, Charles Williams and John Masefield (Lacy 1997, 230–231). New statutes, drawn up by Keith Busby and approved by the IAS in 2014, now include, in the revised Article I, not only a wider membership description ("scholars, teachers, students and other interested parties"), but also a much more inclusive purpose: "to encourage the academic study of the history, literature, material transmission, and other forms of artistic expression, medieval and modern, pertaining to the legend of King Arthur and related subject-matter."[29]

The triennial Congresses, then, have been a constant core aspect of the Society since 1948: but what of the other two initial aims, set out by the founders in that year? The annual *Bibliographical Bulletin* "gives easy access to the scholarly production worldwide, allowing us to get an overview of the state of the art in a certain area within a couple of hours/days."[30] It represents a massive collective endeavour by the bibliographers from each Branch, and has recorded the global output of Arthurian-related scholarship since the Society's formal beginnings in 1948 and the appearance of the first *BBIAS* in 1949. The tireless work of these teams of successive bibliographers has created a resource that scholars such as Peter Field claim has made research faster and generated more advances in the discipline than would otherwise be the case.[31] Cora Dietl also emphasizes the achievement: "there is no other international bibliography dedicated to a central field of research that covers nearly all scholarly publications in that field all over the world, and offers abstracts to all publications – not just to monographs."[32] The *Bulletin* has been more than a bibliography, however; each volume was divided into three sections, the first being the Bibliography, the second, Research and Criticism, and the third, Arthurian News. Until 2011, when the *Bibliography* became an online-only resource (now known as the *Bibliography of the International Arthurian Society* (*BIAS*)), published by De Gruyter, the *Bulletin* held the histories of Arthurian scholarship – and the Society – within its distinctive blue paper covers.

Although the *Bibliography* still exists as *BIAS*, and the Research and Criticism section has morphed into a new journal, the *Journal of the International Arthurian Society* (*JIAS*), the section on Arthurian news has been lost, and although some of this can now be found via the Society's website (<http://www.internationalarthuriansociety.com>), the content here is fragmented and not yet organized into a coherent platform. As discussed earlier, many Branches have their own webpages, which, it is true, are linked to via the main Society website, but some of these are branded with the same design as the main site, and some have taken a different route. Social media has given members other ways to connect and share information, so group pages on Facebook provide more infor-

---

29 "Statutes of the International Arthurian Society"; see <http://www.internationalarthurian society.com/images/uploads/documents/IAS_Statutes_revised.pdf>.
30 Personal communication from Bart Besamusca, August 2016.
31 Personal communication from Peter Field, October 2016.
32 Personal communication from Cora Dietl, August 2016.

mal ways to network. Ironically, this means that it is a challenge to track histories of Branches and the Society as a whole: it would be useful to see an effort to pull key Society event reports together in one central place, and to have other news from the Branch meetings, too, along with obituaries, on the International Society webpages.

More pragmatic functions of the old *BBIAS*, such as supplying a full membership listing has now also been moved to the IAS website, and as the Society adapts to the developing digital tools available to its members, as well as an increasingly time-pressured academic context, it must tackle the issues of whether or not to preserve its histories, and in what format, or they risk becoming lost to future generations. The newly formed *Centre de Documentation arthurienne* at Bangor University might well be the driver for this, although that title is already part of a lost history that underlines the necessity for careful curation of the past. For the third aim of the Society, we will remember, was precisely to create a *Centre de Documentation arthurienne*, in Paris:

> qui comprendrait une bibliothèque, un service de renseignements bibliographiques et, d'une façon générale, s'enfforcerait d'apporter une aide pratique aux chercheurs; il pourrait par exemple faire photographier des manuscrits et des livres rares, dans la mesure où ses moyen financiers le lui permettraient, et commencer ainsi à constituer une collection, dont l'utilité serait considérable, de photographies ou de microfilms. (Frappier 1949, 6)
> [which would include a library, a bibliographic information service and which, in general, would help to provide practical assistance to researchers; it might, for example, arrange for the photographing of manuscripts and rare books to the extent that the financial return would enable the establishment of a collection of photographs and microfilms of considerable utility.]

Frappier emphasized here also that the *Centre* was no less important than the *Bulletin*, and assured members that within a year, it would be up and running. The creation of this physical repository for Arthurian materials has become Avalon-like in its elusiveness from present-day curiosity: tracking through past *Bulletins*, most issues note about a dozen deposits for each year. However, references to the *Centre* disappear after 1999, even though the last printed *BBIAS*, in 2010, still has the *Centre* listed inside the front cover as a main objective of the Society. An attempt to trace the *Centre*'s location (or the location of any of the contents) has so far drawn a blank. While Philippe Ménard reported that the collection was housed at the Sorbonne during the years he was there, from 1975–2002, "sur une étagère d'un placard (fermé à clé) au bout de la Bibliothèque de Littérature française, escalier G, 3e étage" [on a bookshelf in a cupboard (which is locked) at the far end of the Library for French Literature, stairwell G, 3rd floor],[33] the contents seem to have become lost. Ménard himself did not know what had become of the *Centre*, and directed my enquiries towards Dominique Boutet, currently a Professor at the University of Paris-Sorbonne, and another IAS member. He in turn passed me onto Christine Ferlampin-Acher, International President 2009–2011: she confirmed that she also knew nothing about its whereabouts.[34] Keith Busby could not recall why the *Centre* disappeared from the *Bulletin*, and consultations with other members drew blanks, too.[35] It is therefore still a mystery to be solved and, as such, represents a good example of how easily key parts of history can be lost, even in recent times.

There is a hopeful ending to this tale, however: in 2016 an announcement was made to all members of the British Branch of the IAS that Bangor University would be hosting a newly formed *Centre de Documentation*: "the new location is offered not only due to the concentration of Arthurian collections in all languages of the society, and Bangor's continuous standing in Arthurian studies over the past 50 years, but also as an ideal location for the archives of the society."[36] That this new *Centre* has ambitions to curate the Society's history in a more formal way, with a dedicated space, and an already-existing fine collection of Arthurian texts and materials, is very positive: the importance of the Society, "devoted to the study of what is doubtless the western world's largest body of secular literature related to a particular subject or theme" (Lacy 1997, 225), is in its breadth and variety of approaches, methodologies and disciplines. Trying to capture these will, at the very least, enable histories like this one to be more easily accomplished in the future.

The Society's current President, Cora Dietl, says that in its early years the Society "served as a signal of European co-operation and of the search for a common identity in politically very difficult times." She argues that this political value is now largely forgotten, as:

> Arthurian Studies, and Medieval Studies in general, have to fight for recognition, since the Western World tries to be "international" by ignoring its own history, thinking that the knowledge of history might exclude some parts of our societies today.[37]

---

33 Personal email from Philippe Ménard, July 2016.
34 Personal emails from Dominique Boutet and Christine Ferlampin-Acher, July 2016.
35 With thanks to Jane Taylor, Linda Gowans and Peter Field.
36 Email from the British Branch President, Raluca Radulescu, to all British Branch members, April 2016.
37 Personal email from Cora Dietl, August 2016.

Dietl goes on to define what she believes is a main advantage of the Arthurian Society today: "It supports historical (i.e. medieval) studies in the humanities, in their attempt to fight the danger of abolition." Contrast this with the definition of the very first Congress in Truro, where the focus was almost entirely on historical angles, and it is suddenly very clear how much the academic contexts, globally, have shifted in less than one hundred years. Those contexts are shifting again, even as this chapter is written, so it is even more vital that what has been achieved, and the co-operation that this is built upon, is not forgotten: "whatever the future – and there is no indication that the expansion of Arthurian studies or of the IAS will soon end – we owe a great deal to the vision of those who gathered in Truro [...] and of those who, in Quimper, determined that it was time to 'co-ordinate the efforts of Arthurian scholars on an international level.'" (Lacy 1997, 231)

References

Fitzpatrick, Kathleen. "Openness, value, and scholarly societies: The Modern Language Association model." *College & Research Libraries News* 73 (2012): 650–653.

Fox, Marjorie B. "The First Arthurian Congress, Truro, 23–30 August 1930." *BBIAS* (1973): 187.

Frappier, Jean. "Le Congrès de Rennes." *BBIAS* (1954): 87–94.

Frappier, Jean. "La Société Internationale Arthurienne." *BBIAS* (1949): 5–6.

History, New Series, Vol. 15, No. 58 (July 1930): 128.

Johnston, R.C. "The First Arthurian Congress, Truro, 23–30 August 1930." *BBIAS* (1973): 191.

Kato, Tomomi. *A Concordance to the Works of Sir Thomas Malory*. Tokyo: University of Tokyo Press, 1974.

Lacy, Norris J. *A History of Arthurian Scholarship*. Woodbridge: D.S. Brewer, 2006.

Lacy, Norris J. "The International Arthurian Society at 50." *BBIAS* (1997): 228.

Lacy, Norris J. "Excerpts of the President's Address, International Arthurian Congress, Leuven, Belgium, 23 July 1987." *Quondam et Futurus* 7 (1987): 6.

Linton, Phoebe. "Congress Reports: The International Arthurian Society Congress, Bucharest 20–27 July 2014." <http://www.internationalarthuriansociety.com/british-branch/news/ias-2014-congress-reports>.

Powell, Sue. "W.R.J. Barron: Charismatic Arthurian Scholar." *The Independent*, 14 May 2004. <http://www.independent.co.uk/news/obituaries/w-r-j-barron-549929.html>.

Rayner, Samantha J. "The Case of the 'Curious Document': Thomas Malory, William Matthews and Eugène Vinaver." *JIAS* 3 (2015): 120–138.

Thorpe, Lewis. "The First Arthurian Congress, Truro, 23–30 August 1930." *BBIAS* (1973): 187.

Vinaver, Eugène. "The First Arthurian Congress, Truro, 23–30 August 1930." *BBIAS* (1973): 193.

Vinaver, Eugène. "A Speech Made by the President of the International Arthurian Society at a Dinner Offered by the University of Wales on the Occasion of the Ninth International Arthurian Congress in Cardiff, 13 August, 1969." *BBIAS* (1970): 115.

Vinaver, Eugène. *Malory*. Oxford: Clarendon Press, 1929.

Wheeler, Bonnie, Robert L. Kindrick and Michael N. Salda, eds. *The Malory Debate: Essays on the Text of Le Morte Darthur*. Woodbridge: D.S. Brewer, 2000.

Aisling Byrne
The Evolution of the Critical Canon

In *Seven Pillars of Wisdom*, T.E. Lawrence describes the crowded and squalid conditions in which he and his men lived at various points during their itinerant operations. Reading was a welcome escape: "In my saddle-bags was a *Morte d'Arthur*", Lawrence recalled, "It relieved my disgust." (Lawrence 2008 [1926], 495) Lawrence's attachment to Sir Thomas Malory's *Morte Darthur* reflects his romantic streak and his background as a medievalist, but it also testifies to the culturally central status of Malory's work. Malory's *Morte* is a rare instance of a medieval Arthurian text which (in the Anglophone world at least) came close to being a household name, not just a name to conjure with in the academy. Broadly speaking, popular awareness of the medieval Arthurian legend comes in the form of its canon of stories, rather than as a canon of specific texts. The broad outlines of the tales of Lancelot and Guinevere, the quest of the Holy Grail and other key narratives are well known, but only a select few medieval authors or texts have much of a profile beyond the academy. Malory is a case in point, though his prominence may have waned since Lawrence's day.

Awareness of a more extensive and specific range of medieval Arthurian texts is very much the preserve of the academy; however, there are various problems with the idea of a single critical canon of texts, even in this context. On a basic level, what "counts" as an Arthurian text is often open to question (Middleton 2006, 9–10). The texts of the *Tristan* corpus differ considerably in whether, and to what degree, they evoke the Arthurian world as a backdrop for their narrative. Texts like *Perceforest* and *Guiron le Courtois*, focus their narratives on the pre-history of the Arthurian court and on the antecedents of the most celebrated Arthurian knights. It is also fair to say that what we have today might better be described as a range of Arthurian canons, reflecting the core texts around which Arthurian studies in each linguistic tradition have focused their attention. It is a curious fact that, although the spread of the medieval Arthurian legend was a genuinely international phenomenon, modern Arthurian studies can be a very insular discipline (Lacy 2002, 8–9; Besamusca 2007, ix–xi). There are certain key texts, such as Geoffrey of Monmouth's *Historia regum Britanniae* and Chrétien de Troyes' romances, that provide common touchstones for discussions of medieval Arthuriana across various disciplines; however, a scholar working on, say, English Arthurian texts is unlikely to have much knowledge of Italian Arthurian

Aisling Byrne (University of Reading)

DOI 10.1515/9783110432466-004

romance. There is certainly a venerable tradition of source analysis in Arthurian studies, but, by its nature, this sort of work tends to limit its engagement with other languages to Latin, French and, sometimes, Welsh. Despite the fact that we are dealing with a relatively coherent set of stories and with thematic and ideological concerns that recur in texts from across Europe, comparative work on Arthurian texts is still rather limited in quantity.

The key phase of modern canon formation in Arthurian studies was the nineteenth century. In most regions of Europe, including England, France and Germany, where Arthurian material had been particularly popular in the Middle Ages, interest in Arthur waned considerably from the end of the sixteenth through to the end of the eighteenth century, though a steady stream of material was still being produced in this period (Lupack 2009). The revival of widespread interest in the legend in the final decades of the 1700s received impetus from both popular and scholarly movements. Arthurian romance, with its emphasis on the fantastical, seemed to provide a welcome counterbalance to the realism of contemporary neo-classical writing (Matthews 2009, 357). The idealistic chivalric ethos of many of the romances also chimed with the emerging romanticism of the period. Throughout Europe, the rise of linguistic nationalism prompted a new interest in medieval texts in general – the Middle Ages was, after all, the period from which most of the earliest literature in Europe's vernaculars survived. Scholars set to work editing this material with the tools of the emerging discipline of philology (see Eriksen, *infra*).

The linguistic nationalism that fed modern interest in the literatures of medieval Europe also shaped the template of the university that emerged in this period and is still very much with us today. University faculties and departments were structured to reflect modern linguistic realities, however poor a match this might be for the medieval situation. This emphasis, both ideological and institutional, on national vernaculars, has had a longer-term impact on critical canons of Arthurian material, in particular, on the study of Latin literature about Arthur. With the exception of Geoffrey of Monmouth's *Historia regum Britanniae*, Latin literary texts are still relatively marginal to Arthurian studies (Echard 2002, 49). Latin texts obviously do not sit easily within the curricula of the sort of modern language departments where Arthurian literature is now typically studied and classics departments rarely engage with post-classical Latin texts. Even the foundational text of medieval Arthuriana, Geoffrey of Monmouth's *Historia*, has been negatively impacted. Although of all Arthurian texts it has the most claim to being canonical, it has often played a supporting role in both Arthurian scholarship and in university teaching on the subject. Its Latinity presents an obvious issue when it comes to teaching the text on university courses. Geoffrey's presentation of his work as a work of history, not of *romanz* [romance], also places it in something of a no man's land between literary studies and historical studies. Although few would take Geoffrey's truth claims at face value, the fact that the text is written as a history means that it does not respond readily to the tool-kit of literary analysis and cannot easily be read alongside romances, unless as a source. For similar reasons the historiographical tradition of Arthurian writing that Geoffrey inaugurated is considerably more obscure than the romance tradition today.

Although Geoffrey of Monmouth's work lit the fuse that ignited Europe-wide interest in Arthur, some of the most influential accounts of the legend were not produced in Britain, but in France. Modern scholarship on Arthurian romance in medieval France has focused most of its attention on two groups of texts: firstly, the works of Chrétien de Troyes and his early continuators and imitators and, secondly, the prose romances of the thirteenth century, preeminently the *Lancelot-Grail Cycle* and the Prose *Tristan* (Busby and Taylor 2006). The attention devoted to Chrétien, of course, far outstrips that of any other author or body of texts in the French Arthurian tradition. Scholarship on important works like Marie de France's *Lanval* and *Chevrefoil*, Béroul's *Tristan*, the *Post-Vulgate Cycle*, *Perlesvaus* and on writers like Robert de Boron comes in a steady trickle by comparison. French-language Arthuriana is not, of course, limited to works composed in France. Thomas of Britain's *Tristan* and Wace's *Roman de Brut*, both likely to have been written in England, could easily be added to this group and attract attention from both scholars of medieval French and scholars in English studies. The sole surviving Arthurian romance in medieval Occitan, *Jaufre*, receives comparable levels of attention. French material of the fourteenth and fifteenth centuries tends to feature less prominently in the critical canon than material of the twelfth and thirteenth centuries. There are notable exceptions like *Perceforest*, the extensive prose romance probably composed in the second quarter of the fourteenth century; however, this narrative is only marginally Arthurian in its substance. Although the critical canon in French has not changed or enlarged dramatically since the nineteenth century, the terms on which its constituent texts are understood has changed to some extent. It was not until 1909–1913 that the *Lancelot-Grail Cycle* appeared in a single edition – H. Oskar Sommer's seven-volume text and translation. Prior to that point material from the *Lancelot-Grail Cycle* had appeared as separate texts and the tendency to treat the narratives as independent units persisted long after Sommer's work (Busby and Taylor 2006, 96–99).

Chrétien's centrality in French studies is an obvious reflection of his artistry, but it is also a function of his originary status. Although the narrative of Arthur reached a European audience through the Latin account of Geoffrey of Monmouth, it was Chrétien who seems to have refashioned the material for a courtly audience, transforming it from (pseudo-)history into fashionable *romanz*. Chrétien's preeminence may also owe something to other, more anachronistic, factors. These come into focus when the imbalance between the quantity of scholarship produced on the prose romances and scholarship produced on Chrétien's works is considered. The *Lancelot-Grail Cycle* survives in far greater number of manuscript copies than those of Chrétien and his continuators (Middleton 2006, 11–12, 37–38). Although manuscript survival rates are not necessarily a good indicator of a text's popularity with medieval readers, the scale of the disparity is striking. The prose romances are also much more extensive texts than Chrétien's poems. Despite this, scholarly output on Chrétien is vastly greater than that on the prose romances, and this emphasis cannot only be ascribed to his seminal status. Although matters have not been helped by the rather piecemeal and complex editorial history of the prose romances, it seems likely that Chrétien owes some of his modern preeminence to how much more readily his narratives fit the literary expectations of modern readers. As Keith Busby and Jane Taylor (2006, 99) have observed:

> One cannot help wonder whether the relative brevity of Chrétien's romances (6,000–7,000 lines) and the neatness of their beginnings, middles and ends put the apparently prolix prose romances at a critical disadvantage.

For audiences familiar with the narrative arcs of modern novels or short stories, Chrétien's romances can certainly appear more cohesive than the much longer, digressive and episodic prose romances.

These texts also had an impact beyond Francophonia in the Middle Ages. As Karen Pratt (2006, 2) notes, "all the major European literatures originally received their Arthurian rootstock from the Francophone world". Works by Chrétien were translated into other languages, notably German, at an early point. The thirteenth-century French prose romances inspire numerous translations, appearing in part or as a whole in English, Dutch, German, Portuguese, Spanish, Italian, Norse, Greek, Irish and Welsh over the following two centuries. The European impact of these prose texts was not limited to their translation. Many were read beyond France, by courtly audiences who knew French. England, with its close ties to France after the Conquest, is the most obvious example of this, and a great number of French-language Arthurian texts circulated there in the thirteenth and fourteenth centuries. For instance, nearly a third of surviving manuscripts of the *Lancelot-Grail Cycle* are likely to have been in England or Wales at some point in the Middle Ages (Middleton 2003). More surprising, and, perhaps, more indicative of the true impact of these works, is the striking number of French-language manuscripts of prose romances that survive from medieval Italy (Middleton 2006, 56).

Arthurian romance took root in German-speaking lands in the final decades of the twelfth century, shortly after its emergence in France. The major works are based, albeit often very loosely, on French material (Hasty 2009, 175). The German critical canon, like the French one, reflects a long-standing preoccupation with originary texts and with individual, named authors. Like the French canon, texts of the twelfth and thirteenth century are more prominent than texts of later centuries in German studies. The texts afforded indisputably canonical status are by a trio of named authors who flourished in the late-twelfth and early-thirteenth centuries: Wolfram von Eschenbach, Hartmann von Aue and Gottfried von Straßburg. Wolfram's work is by far the most celebrated of the three, though Hartmann literary career begins slightly earlier. Wolfram's *Parzival* and Hartmann's *Iwein* and *Erec* are all modelled on romances by Chrétien (*Perceval*, *Yvain* and *Erec et Enide* respectively). Gottfried's unfinished *Tristan* would appear to be based on another French-language text (though, perhaps, this time a text written in England), Thomas's *Tristan*. Like his source, Gottfried's *Tristan* is only marginally Arthurian; the text mentions Arthur, but none of the usual Arthurian cast of characters takes part in the action. Scholarship devoted to these three authors far outstrips that devoted to other pieces of medieval German Arthuriana, though Heinrich von dem Türlin's *Diu Crône* (see Kragl, *infra*), Der Stricker's *Daniel von dem Blühenden Tal* and the romances attributed to Der Pleier inspire a healthy, though by no means very extensive, range of scholarship.

German Arthurian writing displays a striking freedom in its treatment of its French-language sources. Hartmann's *Erec* (*c.* 1180) adapts Chrétien's *Erec et Enide* and enlarges on many of the key themes of the French. His *Iwein* (*c.* 1200) is considerably closer to Chrétien's *Yvain*. Wolfram's *Parzival* appears to have been composed in the first decade of the thirteenth century and represents a particularly thorough reimagining of his French source material. He approaches Chrétien critically and adds numerous new episodes and an extensive concluding section to the story of Perceval. More manuscripts of *Parzival* have survived than of all the works of Chrétien combined. The total of just under ninety surviving manuscripts and fragments, in addition to various later adaptations and references, must surely reflect a significant medieval popularity for the text (Gibbs and Johnson 2000, 178). As one might expect, given the British setting of much Arthurian narrative, overtly political themes, particularly territorial politics, are not a key focus of German-language Arthurian material. Instead, the emphasis is on the "wonders of Arthur", on personal emotion and on the claims of courtly-chivalric ideals (Hasty 2006).

The modern tradition of popular and scholarly engagement with medieval Arthurian texts emerges particularly early in the German-speaking lands. The rediscovery of medieval Arthurian material begins in the mid-1700s (Classen 2006,

122). Modern translations and paraphrases of Wolfram's *Parzival* and Hartmann's *Iwein* appear at an early point. In 1784 the first edition of one of these texts in the Middle High German original appears: Christoph Heinrich Myller's rendering of Wolfram's *Parzival* (Classen 2006, 122–125). It was in the German-speaking lands, of course, that the new science of philology flourished most notably around this time, providing a key impetus for the transcribing and editing of medieval narrative texts. German Arthuriana benefited from such efforts and a steady stream of editions, translations and studies began to appear. The scholarly methods being pioneered in the German-speaking lands were not limited in their application to German texts; for instance, Wendelin Foerster is often credited with "the introduction of scientific rigour to the edition of Chrétien" through his critical texts of the romances published with extensive introductions and notes in German in the final decades of the nineteenth century (Dembowski 2005, 77; see also Classen 2006, 125).

In Germany, as elsewhere in Europe, romanticism proved fertile ground for the re-emergence of medieval Arthurian texts in the late-eighteenth and early-nineteenth centuries. Key figures in German romanticism urged the merits of the Arthurian texts at an early point. The Schlegel brothers, August Wilhelm and Friedrich, were particularly interested in Arthuriana, and both delivered lectures on the material in the early years of the nineteenth century (Classen 2006, 124). Their central argument, that the chivalric ideals of the Arthurian world offered a model for contemporary society, was a feature of much nineteenth-century engagement with the legend across Europe. Although the Arthurian legend could not be considered a "national" myth, "ethical" approaches, such as those adopted by the Schlegels, were certainly tinged with patriotism, offering the chivalric ideals of the Round Table as a regenerative model for German-speakers under Napoleonic rule (Classen 2006, 123).

Literary rivalry with France may also account for some of the ongoing appeal of Wolfram's *Parzival*, in particular. Since the nineteenth century, *Parzival* has been the central focus for scholarship on Middle High German literature. The appeal of Wolfram's text is not hard to pin down. The artistry of the work is undeniable and it bears favourable comparison with Chrétien's own work. Such comparisons were encouraged by Wolfram himself in his epilogue to *Parizval*. Here he cites a Provençal text by an otherwise unknown poet called "Kyot" as his main source. Kyot's text is, Wolfram insists, more correct and complete than Chrétien's unfinished *Perceval*. The clear implication is that Wolfram's text is similarly superior to *Perceval*:

Ob von Troys meister Cristjân
disem mære hât unreht getân,
daz mac wol zürnen Kyôt,
der uns diu rehten mære enbôt.
[...]
von Provenz in tiuschiu lant
diu rehten mære uns sint gesant,
und dirre âventiur endes zil. (Wolfram von Eschenbach 2003 [1833], 831)
If Master Chrestien of Troyes has done this tale an injustice, Kyot, who sent us the true
tidings, has good reason to wax wroth [...] From Provence into German lands the true tidings
have been sent to us, and this adventure's end limit. (Wolfram von Eschenbach 2004, 264–
265)

Much ink has been spilled on the question of whether or not this, otherwise
unknown, Provençal text by Kyot truly existed or is merely Wolfram's own invention. Regardless of the truth of Wolfram's assertion, this sort of sentiment must
surely have struck a chord with German readers of *Parzival*. For all Chrétien's
poetic talents, it was not much of a leap for modern German-speaking audiences
to imagine Wolfram's text as an advance on Chrétien's work and to embrace
readily a text of evident artistry that claimed to complete and improve on a foundational work of French literature.

When we turn to Britain, the homeland of Arthur, territorial politics inevitably
becomes a more prominent factor in the shaping and reception of the legend. A
good deal of early Arthurian investigation across Europe was concerned with the
potential Celtic origins of the myth. What has been described as "Celtomania"
grew out of a romantic era view of the Celts as an essentially spiritual people, in
tune with nature, and offering a striking contrast to a world undergoing rapid
industrialization (Sims-Williams 1998). Investigating potential connections
between Celtic-language texts and Arthurian romances was a key element in the
study of Arthurian literature right up until the middle of the twentieth century.
This interest in Arthur's "Celticity" raised the profile of Celtic-language literature,
particularly literature in Welsh, in Arthurian studies as a whole. Wales was, of
course, the source of the very earliest references to Arthur, and Geoffrey of Monmouth claimed to be working from earlier Welsh material when he wrote the *Historia*. Three Welsh narratives, in particular, have attained prominence: *Peredur*,
Owain and *Geraint*. These texts first came to widespread attention through Charlotte Guest's translation of medieval Welsh narratives which appeared in 1838
and 1840. Published under the (inaccurate, but influential) title *The Mabinogion*,
Guest's work proved popular with the Victorian reading public and had a marked
impact on the Arthurian works of writers such as Alfred, Lord Tennyson (Matthews 2009, 361). Scholars in Britain, France and Germany also took note. It was

clear from the outset that these three Welsh texts had striking points of correspondence with three texts by Chrétien de Troyes, *Perceval*, *Yvain*, and *Erec et Enide*, and that one set of texts seemed likely to be based, directly or indirectly, on the other (Lloyd-Morgan 2009, 128–129). Questions about the relative primacy of the Welsh and French versions of these stories have never been conclusively resolved, but one result of the long-standing debate was to bring these Welsh texts (albeit usually in translation) to a wider audience beyond Celtic studies. The modern reception of these three texts offers a rare example of Arthurian material in a less widely-spoken vernacular drawing scholarly attention beyond its own field.

While a focus on early and influential works is common to the critical canons of French and German Arthurian texts, the canon of English-language Arthurian material has a rather different profile. Originary texts to compare with Chrétien or Wolfram are notable by their absence from the corpus. Malory's *Morte*, the best known and most influential piece of Middle English Arthuriana, is a particularly late work – it provides the starting point for post-medieval engagements with Arthur, rather than inaugurating a medieval tradition. Another staple of the modern critical canon in English studies, *Sir Gawain and the Green Knight*, appears to have had little to no influence in its own time. Its centrality for modern scholars is largely a function of its poetic merits and, in particular, the extent to which those merits chime with the expectations of modern literary audiences. There may also be a particularly significant disjoint between the modern canon of Arthurian texts in English and what was widely read and influential in England in the Middle Ages. There can be little doubt that a substantial portion of Arthurian literature circulating in England was in French, not in English. As we have seen, a large number of manuscripts of the *Lancelot-Grail Cycle* were circulating in medieval England. Before the late-fourteenth century, the Arthurian texts most familiar to courtly audiences in England may not have differed greatly from the texts that were well known to audiences of a similar background in France.

The cultural prominence of the surviving Middle English Arthurian texts is difficult to evaluate. Like most Middle English romances, they survive in limited manuscript copies of a rather inferior physical appearance. Apart from Chaucer's *Wife of Bath's Tale*, printed as part of the *Canterbury Tales*, Malory's *Morte* is the only Arthurian text printed in English in the early years of that technology. Works which may have had a high profile in the Middle Ages are not necessarily those on which modern scholars focus. In his *Sir Thopas*, Chaucer includes just one Arthurian text in his list of well-known romances:

Men speken of romances of prys,
Of Horn child, and of Ypotys,
Of Beves and sir Gy,
Of sir Lybeux and Pleyndamour (Chaucer 1987, 216)
[Men speak of excellent romances/ Of Horn Child and of Ypotis/ Of Bevis and Sir Guy/ Of Sir
Lybeaus and Plendamour] (my translation)

"Sir Lybeux" is clearly a reference to the eponymous hero of *Libeaus Desconus*, a
Middle English Arthurian text with some similarities to the French *Le Bel Inconnu*.
There are obvious reasons not to take Chaucer's list entirely at face value –
"Ypotys" is not a character from romance, he is the child hero of a pious legend,
and there is no reason to believe a romance of "Pleyndamour" ever existed.
Nonetheless, there are good reasons for taking Chaucer seriously when he states
that the other stories listed were very popular. The prominence of the "Matter of
England" heroes, Sir Guy of Warwick and Sir Bevis of Hampton, in this account
would appear to be reflected in the popular reach of their stories among English-
speaking audiences and in the surviving number of manuscripts, which are at
the higher end for Middle English romances. Chaucer's citation of the romance of
Libeaus Desconus in his romance "canon" is backed up by the fact that no other
Middle English Arthurian text, with the exception of the *Wife of Bath's Tale*, survives in as many copies – six in all. These surviving manuscript copies may not
represent a particularly large total, but when many other Middle English Arthurian texts survive in only one or two copies, it is striking how peripheral *Libeaus
Desconus* remains in modern Arthurian scholarship.

Today, only three texts in Middle English are indisputably canonical: the
late-fourteenth century anonymous poem, *Sir Gawain and the Green Knight*,
Malory's *Morte Darthur* composed in the third quarter of the fifteenth century
and Chaucer's *Wife of Bath's Tale*, probably composed in the 1390s. The scholarship devoted to these three works, and the former two, in particular, is considerably greater than that devoted to other prominent texts like Layamon's *Brut*, the
Stanzaic *Morte Arthur* and the Alliterative *Morte Arthure*. The critical prominence
of the *Wife of Bath's Tale* is very much a function of its status as a Chaucerian
text, rather than an Arthurian one, and the role played by recognizably Arthurian
figures and motifs in the narrative is rather small. The high profiles of Malory's
Morte and *Sir Gawain and the Green Knight* are the result of rather less easily
definable factors.

Malory's *Morte* represents both an end and a beginning. It was probably completed in the late 1460s, and is usually classed as one of the last major achievements of Middle English writing. Most of the tales Malory tells are heavily based
on earlier works in either French or English. On the other hand, the *Morte* gives

us the first known English-language accounts of some of the most well-known Arthurian stories, most notably the quest of the Holy Grail and the story of Lancelot's love for Guinevere (Cooper 2003). Furthermore, its early appearance in print ensured it a post-medieval profile that few non-Chaucerian narratives attained and it became the foundational text for modern, and particularly Victorian, Arthuriana in England. William Caxton's motivations for choosing Malory's work to print in 1485 are difficult to pin down. The comprehensive nature of the text must have been attractive. The fact that Malory's work was in prose, not in verse (the form in which most Middle English romance was written) would also have appealed; firstly, because it underpinned the historicity of the material, on which Caxton was very insistent in his preface to the edition, and, secondly, because prose romance was such a fashionable form at the court of Burgundy where Caxton's tastes seem to have been shaped. That it had long-standing success in print seems evident from the fact that the edition was reprinted five times, at quite regular intervals, and as late as 1634 (Edwards 1996, 241–242). The Malory who has come down to us is very much Caxton's Malory. In his preface to the 1485 edition, Caxton urges the reader to take ethical lessons from the text:

> And I, accordyng to my copye, have doon sette it in enprynte to the entente that noble men may see and lerne the noble actes of chyvalrye, the jentyl and vertuous dedes that somme knyghtes used in tho dayes [...] Doo after the good and leve the evyl, and it shal brynge you to good fame and renommee. (Malory 1971, xv)

T.E. Lawrence's observation that reading the *Morte* "relieved his disgust" when faced with the squalid reality of modern warfare, reflects Caxton's early framing of the *Morte* as a text which brings a nobler, chivalric world to life again, as both an inspiration and an admonition to the present day.

After the 1634 printing of the *Morte* there was a lull in production of the work; the next editions did not begin to appear until 1816 (Edwards 1996, 242, 247). Once again, Malory's work was in the right place at the right time; it tapped into the fascination with the British past that made Walter Scott's novels such a sensation in the same period. Literary figures and artists engaged with the work throughout the nineteenth century. Scott himself was fascinated by the *Morte* and both Keats and Wordsworth owned copies (Edwards 1996, 247–248). Perhaps the most prominent and popular work of poetry to take inspiration from Malory was Tennyson's *Idylls of the King* (1859–1885). In a rather different vein, Mark Twain's *A Connecticut Yankee in King Arthur's Court* (1889) features numerous extracts from Malory's work. The extent to which the *Morte*'s success in Victorian England, in particular, rode on the coat-tails of nationalist and imperialist ideas of the time can be overstated. As David Matthews notes, there was "an underlying acknowledgement that Arthur was in truth a Romano-Celtic figure." (Matthews 2009, 361) Engagement with Malory in nineteenth-century England could be characterized primarily in terms of nostalgia and imitation – readers saw his work as reflecting a socially coherent and ideologically stable society which contrasted with the social fragmentation, urbanization and industrialization of their own day. As among the German romantics, it was the ethical dimension of Arthurian literature that drew Victorian readers to the material. It was felt that "Arthurian chivalry should inform modern behaviour." (Matthews 2009, 359) This emphasis made Malory's work a popular source for children's literature. There were various adaptations of the *Morte* for a younger audience, notably Sidney Lanier's *The Boy's King Arthur* which appeared in 1880 (Edwards 1996, 250). Although recent scholarship has inclined towards a rather darker view of the world Malory describes, the primacy of the *Morte* in the English-language critical canon today is undeniable. Of course, the precise terms on which the text is understood have shifted somewhat over time. The discovery for the first time of a manuscript, rather than print, copy of Malory's *Morte* at Winchester College in 1934 gave fresh impetus to Malorian studies and raised some new questions about the nature of the text. In his edition of the Winchester text, published in 1947, Eugène Vinaver averred that the *Morte* was not envisaged by Malory as a single work, but represented a series independent tales. The title he gave his classic edition of the *Morte* – *The Works of Sir Thomas Malory* – reflected this position.

The rise to prominence of *Sir Gawain and the Green Knight* has marked points of contrast with the reception history of Malory's *Morte*. *Sir Gawain and the Green Knight*'s central status in Middle English studies is a relatively recent phenomenon, particularly when compared to other prominent Arthurian texts I have been discussing, which tend to reemerge in the nineteenth-century. The text was edited as early as 1839 by Frederick Madden alongside other Middle English romances about Gawain, but it was only after the Second World War that it became truly canonical (Dalrymple 2006, 150–151). In the mid-twentieth century, *Sir Gawain and the Green Knight*, previously an admired, but rather specialist, text, became a staple of English university courses. It also began to be adapted and modernized with a degree of regularity for an audience beyond the academy. It is not difficult to see why the text might have found an enthusiastic audience in the post-war era. The *Gawain*-poet's interest in human frailty and his sympathetic exploration of the tensions between lived experience and lofty ideals chimed with a less certain age than that which had embraced texts like the *Morte Darthur*. Literary critical work had for some decades been replacing philological study and source study as the primary focus of medievalists in English departments, and *Sir Gawain and the Green Knight* proved particularly responsive to these new approaches (Dalrymple 2006, 150). Its ironies, lengthy descriptive passages, ornate diction and elaborate structural symmetries responded very readily to the toolkit developed by the New Criticism. Undeniably brilliant, *Gawain* nonetheless offers a prominent example of the discrepancies there can be between modern canonicity and medieval popularity. There is no evidence that *Sir Gawain and the Green Knight* was widely read in medieval England.

The emergence of *Sir Gawain and the Green Knight* as one of the two most prominent Arthurian texts in Middle English studies is a striking example of modern canon reshaping. Reassessing neglected texts has been a point of considerable emphasis in scholarship in the past few decades (Lacy 2002, 5–6). In Middle English studies, this has seen the rehabilitation of a range of romances. Wide-ranging critiques of established canons across literary studies and the rise of New Historicist approaches saw texts previously dismissed as derivative or of poor aesthetic quality undergoing some degree of reevaluation. Helen Cooper's landmark study of romance in medieval England, *The English Romance in Time* (Cooper 2004), is a good reflection of the impact of these developments. Cooper treats neglected texts like *Sir Percyvell of Galles* or *The Carle of Carlisle* alongside established texts like *Sir Gawain and the Green Knight*. However, as Norris J. Lacy notes, the growth in the attention given to other romances is relative, rather than absolute. The number of studies of these works is still utterly dwarfed by the range of scholarly papers and books that appear each year on the two most prominent Middle English texts (Lacy 2002, 5–7). Texts like *Sir Gawain and the Green Knight* are the exceptions; in general, we are still working with the critical canons established in the nineteenth century. No one would dispute the importance of writers like Wolfram and Chrétien, but to focus so much attention on a very small number of texts can be rather limiting and, in the case of French and German Arthuriana, lead to an over-emphasis on the earliest phase of Arthurian production over later medieval texts. In general, the most radical changes in Arthurian studies, at least in the most well-established fields of French, German and English scholarship, have been in methodologies and approaches, not in the texts that are most frequently studied.

Less well-established fields of Arthurian scholarship present a different picture. Languages like Norse, Dutch, Italian, Spanish and Portuguese have their own bodies of medieval Arthuriana, but these have received far less attention than the French, German and English corpora (Lacy 2002, 7–8). There are signs that this is changing and that Arthurian texts in some of these languages are gaining a measure of prominence beyond their own fields. The Arthurian texts of the Scandinavian world, mostly preserved in Icelandic manuscripts, are a good example. Old Norse has a significant body of translated Arthurian texts, but these attracted little attention from scholars of Scandinavian literature before the middle of the twentieth century. Among the surviving works are translations of three works by

Chrétien – *Erec et Enide* (*Erex saga*), *Perceval* (*Parcevals saga*) and *Yvain* (*Ívens saga* and *Herr Ivan* – see Lodén, *infra*) – the same texts that are translated into German at an early point. There is also an adaptation of Geoffrey of Monmouth's *Historia* (*Breta sögur*) and a version of Thomas's *Tristan* (*Tristams saga*). These texts are translated as early as the thirteenth century but, in contrast to some other regional contexts, the translations do not seem to have inspired a local tradition of Arthurian composition. The fact that the surviving medieval Arthurian texts from Scandinavia translate material from Latin and French is at the root of their long-standing neglect. As Sif Rikhardsdottir and Stefka G. Eriksen (2013, 8) observe, scholars in the nineteenth and early-twentieth centuries "favoured the saga form as the 'authentic' voice of the Icelandic people." The eventual decline in the influence of such attitudes did not immediately result in the rehabilitation of the translated Arthurian texts – they were still rather marginal within Old Norse studies, by virtue of their "derivative" status. From the early 1980s, through the work of scholars such as Marianne E. Kalinke, this state of affairs began to change and a wide range of scholarly explorations of these works have appeared in recent years (Rikhardsdottir and Eriksen 2013, 9–10). Scandinavian Arthuriana merited a chapter of its own, alongside contributions on the more well-known German and French Arthurian romances, in the 2009 *A Companion to Arthurian Literature* (Barnes 2009). The addition of *The Arthur of the North* to the long-running "The Arthur of…" series in 2011 also reflects the increased attention these texts are receiving (Kalinke 2011). The fact that a good deal of scholarship on these texts has been published in the English language has also raised their profile beyond Scandinavian studies itself.

I began this discussion by noting that modern study of Arthurian texts tends to take place within, rather than across, a range of national/linguistic canons. With rare exceptions, the texts considered genuinely canonical have not changed, nor have established canons expanded considerably, since the nineteenth century. However, the attention paid on both a popular and a scholarly level to Arthurian texts within each linguistic tradition has varied a good deal. The major texts in French, German and English, for instance, have been intensively mined by scholars and have enjoyed at least some degree of prominence beyond the academy. In many other linguistic traditions, the profile of Arthurian material is rather lower, though there are signs that this is beginning to change. Nonetheless, the problem described by Bart Besamusca remains:

> [t]here is insufficient awareness of the European perspective among Arthurian scholars. The paradox is that a basic element of medieval European culture is studied almost exclusively as if we were dealing with a genre subdivided into national literatures. (Besamusca 2007, xi)

Any attempt to sketch the shape of a genuinely pan-European critical canon bears out this point. Apart from the common touchstones of Geoffrey's *Historia* and Chrétien's romances, there is little common ground among scholars. It is rare that publications appear which address material in three or more languages (Besamusca 2007, x). Ongoing projects, like "The Arthur of..." series by the University of Wales Press and the "*État present*" papers that have appeared in the first issues of the new *Journal of the International Arthurian Society*, provide valuable points of access to specialist fields for interdisciplinary audiences. Interest in multilingual and multidisciplinary perspectives may eventually increase the range of common reference points with which Arthurian scholars work; however, we are still a long way from a situation where an extensive and linguistically-varied pan-European critical canon might emerge.

References

Barnes, Geraldine. "Scandinavian Versions of Arthurian Romance." *A Companion to Arthurian Literature*. Ed. Helen Fulton. Oxford: Wiley-Blackwell, 2009.

Besamusca, Bart. "Introduction: The Pan-European Approach." *Arthurian Literature* 24 (2007): ix–xiv.

Chaucer, Geoffrey. *The Riverside Chaucer*. Ed. Larry D. Benson. 3rd edn. Oxford: Oxford University Press, 1987.

Classen, Albrecht. "German Arthurian Literature." *A History of Arthurian Scholarship*. Ed. Norris J. Lacy. Cambridge: D.S. Brewer, 2006. 122–139.

Cooper, Helen. *The English Romance in Time: Transforming Motifs from Geoffrey of Monmouth to the Death of Shakespeare*. Oxford: Oxford University Press, 2004.

Cooper, Helen. "The Lancelot-Grail Cycle in England: Malory and his Predecessors." *A Companion to the Lancelot-Grail Cycle*. Ed. Carol Dover. Cambridge: D.S. Brewer, 2003. 147–162.

Dalrymple, Roger. "English Arthurian Literature." *A History of Arthurian Scholarship*. Ed. Norris J. Lacy. Cambridge: D.S. Brewer, 2006. 140–157.

Dembowski, Peter F. "Editing Chretien." *A Companion to Chretien de Troyes*. Ed. Norris J. Lacy and Joan Tasker Grimbert. Cambridge: D.S. Brewer, 2005. 76–83.

Echard, Siân. "'Hic est Arthur': Reading Latin and Reading Arthur." *New Directions in Arthurian Studies*. Ed. Alan Lupack. Cambridge: D.S. Brewer, 2002. 49–67.

Edwards, A.S.G. "The Reception of Malory's *Morte Darthur*." *A Companion to Malory*. Ed. Elizabeth Archibald and A.S.G. Edwards. Cambridge: D.S. Brewer, 1996. 241–252.

Gibbs, Marion E., and Sidney M. Johnson. *Medieval German Literature: A Companion*. New York and London: Garland Publishing, 1997.

Hasty, Will. "The Allure of Otherworlds: The Arthurian Romances in Germany." *A Companion to Arthurian Literature*. Ed. Helen Fulton. Oxford: Wiley-Blackwell, 2009. 175–188.

Kalinke, Marianne E., ed. *The Arthur of the North: The Arthurian Legend in the Nordic and Rus' Realms*. Cardiff: University of Wales Press, 2011.

Lacy, Norris J. "Arthurian Research in a New Century." *New Directions in Arthurian Studies*. Ed.
  Alan Lupack. Cambridge: D.S. Brewer, 2002. 1–20.
Lawrence, T.E. *Seven Pillars of Wisdom: A Triumph*. London: Vintage, 2008.
Lloyd-Morgan, Ceridwen. "Migrating Narratives: *Peredur*, *Owain*, and *Geraint*." *A Companion to
  Arthurian Literature*. Ed. Helen Fulton. Oxford: Wiley-Blackwell, 2009. 128–141.
Lupack, Alan. "The Arthurian Legend in the Sixteenth to Eighteenth Centuries." *A Companion to
  Arthurian Literature*. Ed. Helen Fulton. Oxford: Wiley-Blackwell, 2009. 340–354.
Malory, Sir Thomas. *The Works of Thomas Malory*. Ed. Eugène Vinaver. Oxford: Oxford
  University Press, 1971.
Matthews, David. "Scholarship and Popular Culture in the Nineteenth Century." *A Companion
  to Arthurian Literature*. Ed. Helen Fulton. Oxford: Wiley-Blackwell, 2009. 355–367.
Middleton, Roger. "Manuscripts of the Lancelot-Grail Cycle in England and Wales: Some Books
  and their Owners." *A Companion to the Lancelot-Grail Cycle*. Ed. Carol Dover. Woodbridge:
  D.S. Brewer, 2003. 219–235.
Middleton, Roger. "The Manuscripts." *The Arthur of the French*. Ed. Glyn S. Burgess and Karen
  Pratt. Cardiff: University of Wales Press, 2006. 8–92.
Pratt, Karen. "Introduction." *The Arthur of the French*. Ed. Glyn S. Burgess and Karen Pratt.
  Cardiff: University of Wales Press, 2006. 1–7.
Rikhardsdottir, Sif, and Stefka G. Eriksen. "État présent: Arthurian Literature in the North."
  Journal of the International Arthurian Society 1 (2013): 3–28.
Sims-Williams, Patrick. "Celtomania and Celtoscepticism." *Cambrian Medieval Celtic Studies*
  36 (1998): 1–35.
Wolfram von Eschenbach. Parzival, *with* Titurel *and the Love Lyrics*. Trans. Cyril Edwards.
  Cambridge. D.S. Brewer, 2004.
Wolfram von Eschenbach. *Parzival*. Ed. Karl Lachmann. Trans. Peter Knecht. Berlin: De Gruyter,
  2003.

Patrick Moran
Text-Types and Formal Features

To speak of the genre of "Arthurian romance" at a European level may seem self-evident nowadays; yet, if we look at the formal characteristics of this genre and its unique achievements in each language area where it flourished, it is clear that the supposed unity of the genre may be more of a figment of our modern imagination than a medieval reality.[1] Under the "romance" moniker, we group texts that sometimes received very different names in medieval manuscripts, names that were not always consistent from witness to witness. In Old French alone, such diverse generic labels as *roman, conte, livre* or *estoire*, each bearing different connotations and involving incompatible aesthetic hierarchies, make it difficult to group all the texts that tell of Arthur and his Knights of the Round Table into the same category (Baumgartner 1986a; Kelly 1992; Damian-Grint 1997; Gingras 2011, 159–189). The formal diversity of these texts on a European scale can only confirm this reluctance.

Nevertheless, a few major trends, common to the different linguistic backgrounds that produced Arthurian literature, structure the field and can be used to guide the discussion. Among these trends, one of the most powerful is probably the verse-prose divide, which emerges in the Francophone area first and has a strong thematic and structural impact throughout the period (Rychner 1970; Marchello-Nizia 1977). This distinction between Arthurian texts in verse and Arthurian texts in prose manifests itself in almost all other languages involved, and is often dependent on the distinction as first formulated in the Old French area, though in other languages, the verse-prose divide does not always obey the same statistical or thematic distributions. The second major trend that will structure this discussion is the primary role of French-language Arthurian literature. The French-speaking world did not invent the Arthurian legend, but the literary form that it imprinted on the Matter of Britain gave other European languages (with some exceptions) a very powerful template to emulate or, in some cases, to reject.

---

1 More a *classe analogique* than a *classe généalogique*, to quote Jean-Marie Schaeffer's (1989) generic categories.

Patrick Moran (Université Paul Valéry-Montpellier 3)

DOI 10.1515/9783110432466-005

1 Old French between verse and prose

1.1 The octosyllabic form

It seems reasonable, therefore, to trace the major formal trends in Medieval Arthurian literature back to the French tradition. Arthurian romance, when it first appears in Old French in the second half of the twelfth century, is written in octosyllabic couplets. This form is not unique to the Matter of Britain, but is common to the romance genre; the first Arthurian romances – Wace's *Brut*, the verse *Tristans*, the works of Chrétien de Troyes – take part in a formal tradition that took off in the twelfth century but which dates back to some of the oldest *vies de saints*: the *Vie de saint Léger*, written in the late-tenth century, is already octosyllabic, though set in six-line stanzas.[2]

The octosyllabic couplet is a non-musical form, thus opposing the nascent romance genre to the older *chansons de geste*, composed in decasyllabic or dodeca-syllabic *laisses*, which were accompanied by music and were at least partially sung (Zumthor 1972, 122–123). The choice of this form for the young Arthurian genre is in many ways a normative choice: the octosyllabic couplet is perceived as a relatively neutral form, well adapted for narrative. This format allows the emergence of texts of variable length: *romans*, which are usually measured in thousands of lines (most of Chrétien's romances approximate 7,000 lines, while later romances such as *Claris and Laris*, or Jean Froissart's much later *Meliador*, can exceed 30,000 lines), but also *lais*, which generally run to a few hundred lines. The difference in length between the two genres involves thematic differences: the Arthurian *lais*, such as Marie de France's *Lanval*, tend to have subjects that are simpler and more folklore-based than their *roman* counterparts. But the *roman-lai* distinction is fuzzy at best, especially when one considers some of the longer *lais*, like Marie de France's (non-Arthurian) *Eliduc*, which is about 1,200 long, the same length as the verse *roman* of *Le Chevalier à l'épée* or Paien de Maisières' *Mule sans frein* (both late-twelfth or early-thirteenth century). As for the two twelfth-century *Folies Tristan*, which tell brief episodes from the life of Tristan and Iseut, nothing beyond critical habit prevents us from viewing them as *lais*: the Oxford *Folie* has 998 lines and the Bern *Folie* only 584. Thematically nothing distinguishes these texts from Marie de France's *Lai du chèvre-feuille*, which also recounts a ploy devised by Tristan to communicate with Iseut.

---

2 On the origins of French verse and of the octosyllable in particular, see Lote (1949).

1.2 The episodic format and its rivals

The decisive influence of Chrétien de Troyes on Arthurian verse romance can hardly be underestimated. Although Wace's *Roman de Brut* (*c.* 1155), an Anglo-Norman adaptation of Geoffrey of Monmouth's *Historia regum Britanniae*, is technically the first (partly) Arthurian romance in *langue d'oïl*, its formal influence on future generations of texts was limited, beyond its choice of octosyllabic couplets. Chrétien, on the other hand, establishes with his five (surviving) romances (*Erec et Enide, Cligès, Le Chevalier au lion, Le Chevalier de la charrette, Le Conte du Graal*, all written between 1170 and 1190) a model that is widely followed by subsequent romance writers: the model of the individual knightly quest, centred on a single hero and a single episode of his life (Lacy 1987–1988). Arthur serves as a major background character and helps to establish the setting; he is never the lead protagonist. This episodic format lends itself particularly well to courtly topics: from Chrétien onwards, the problems faced by the protagonists are at least partially courtly in nature.[3] This is not to say that all verse romances are courtly or that *courtoisie* cannot be found outside of verse; but it is hardly debatable that the courtly aesthetic finds its fullest and most common manifestation in octosyllabic texts, be they *romans* or *lais*.

While prose romances will tend to move beyond the episodic narrative template, most verse romances of the twelfth and thirteenth centuries submit to it with good grace. Chrétien also introduces some degree of recurrence and stability in his depiction of the Arthurian world: his five romances are set in a relatively stable fictional universe, marked by the return of characters, Gauvain in particular (Busby 1987–1988; Maddox 1996). King Arthur's nephew is never the protagonist of Chrétien's works, but his role as referent or as foil in several of his romances probably justifies, at least in part, the character's popularity with many of Chrétien's epigones, who do not hesitate to make Gauvain the protagonist of their texts (Busby 1980). This popularity is not, however, without its risks; several verse romances centred on Gauvain adopt a humorous or parodic tone. Chrétien himself is famous for his humour and his somewhat ironic take on Gauvain, but his epigones often go further in ridiculing or degrading the character (Adams 1987–1988). This evolution of the Arthurian octosyllabic *roman* towards more parodic practices is also reflected in the *lai*: Robert Biket's *Lai du Cor* (late-twelfth century) or the anonymous *Mantel mautaillé* (late-twelfth or early-thirteenth century) both depict a chastity test imposed on the Arthurian court in an unflattering and satirical light (Koble 2005).

---

3 On Chrétien's works as "problem romances", see Kelly (2006, 144–148).

Though Chrétien gave birth to the tradition of episodic Arthurian romance, centred on a knight and his quest, his own works do not all obey this framework: *Cligès* is a generational tale, straddling two worlds, Britain and Constantinople, and involving two protagonists, Alexandre and his son, Cligès; whereas the unfinished *Conte du Graal* takes the form of a biographical romance of its protagonist, Perceval. After Chrétien, other *romanciers* veer from the episodic template, particularly in the second half of the thirteenth century: *Floriant et Florete*, for instance, is a biographical romance, while *Claris and Laris* or *Les Merveilles de Rigomer* use narrative interlace to weave their multiple protagonists together (Kelly 1969). In the late-fourteenth century, Froissart's *Meliador*, the very last French-language verse romance, also offers a choral narrative. As for Robert de Boron's verse romances (*Joseph d'Arimathie* and *Merlin*, both written at the turn of the twelfth century), they eschew Chrétien's template even more thoroughly: I will return to them shortly.

Another major group of texts in the octosyllabic tradition to avoid the episodic template is constituted by the Continuations to Chrétien's *Conte du Graal* (Bruckner 2009; Hinton 2012; Tether 2012). The unfinished nature of Chrétien's final romance led four successors to complete his tale between the late-twelfth century and the 1230s. These four continuations are diverse in nature and have a complex manuscript tradition. Not all of them aspire to conclude Chrétien's tale: some merely seek to prolong it. *The First Continuation*, in particular, pays little attention to Perceval, in favour of Gauvain's adventures. The Continuations are a particularly interesting series of texts from a formal point of view. Written in verse, they exhibit a number of traits that we associate most commonly with prose: the centrality of the Grail theme, but also the unprecedented scale that the accumulation of continuations gives to the source-romance.[4] As such, it is not unreasonable to consider the late-twelfth-/early-thirteenth-century Continuation trend as a sort of formal interface between the episodic verse romance and the lengthier prose romances that were to come (Moran 2014, 251–288).

Notwithstanding these centrifugal examples, the episodic form constitutes a solid basis in the tradition of octosyllabic Arthurian romance, while allowing a certain degree of tonal flexibility between seriousness and parody. All this will change with the emergence of prose romances in the early-thirteenth century, which profoundly renews French-language narrative practices, and establishes a strong divide between verse and prose romances.

---

[4] The overall Grail tale is further enriched by the potential addition of two short prologues, the *Élucidation* and the *Bliocadran*, which function as miniature retrospective continuations. See Hinton (2012, 105–108).

1.3 The emergence of prose

The origins of Arthurian prose are hard to pinpoint; they tend to merge with the wider question of the origins of Old French prose (Baumgartner 1999). Even the identity of the first Arthurian prose romance is uncertain: while it is commonly held that Robert de Boron's verse *Joseph d'Arimathie* and *Merlin* were put into prose in the early-thirteenth century, the dating of *Perlesvaus* is far more contentious, ranging from the 1190s to the 1250s. To these early examples (or at least assumedly early in the case of *Perlesvaus*), one must also add the Didot-*Perceval*, which completes the story begun in *Joseph* with its own Grail Quest, and of course the Prose *Lancelot*, a first version or first part of which probably dates to the 1210s (Kennedy 1986).

Chrétien's influence is still strong in these early prose tales. *Perlesvaus* functions as a sort of prose continuation to the *Conte du Graal*, while *Joseph* offers a prequel of sorts to the Grail Quest and Didot-*Perceval* functions as a narrative rival to the *Conte du Graal*, influenced in part by the *Second Continuation*. The Prose *Lancelot* centres on the protagonist from *Le Chevalier de la charrette*: the full-length version of the prose romance includes in its centre an expanded version of the "*charrette*" episode, which is largely dependent on Chrétien's text. Thus the prose tradition, at least originally, far from breaking with Chrétien de Troyes' legacy, proposes a reformulation and a rethinking of his narrative propositions.

The first consequence of this reformulation is the eschewing of the episodic template that was favoured by verse romances. The reasons for the introduction of prose in the French Arthurian tradition are unclear, but one element bears mentioning. The earliest appearance of prose (excluding *Perlesvaus*, of uncertain date) is in two texts, *Joseph* and *Merlin*, which are far from courtly: they offer a historical, or rather a pre-historic, perspective on the Matter of Britain and the Grail tradition. At approximately the same time, the field of French language historiographical prose is also beginning to develop: the Latin *Pseudo-Turpin's Chronicle* is translated into French prose c. 1200–1206, at the same time that Geoffroy de Villehardouin and Robert de Clari are writing their memoirs of the Fourth Crusade. At the dawn of the thirteenth century, the emergence of prose seems linked to the emergence of vernacular historiography (Spiegel 1993; Croizy-Naquet 2000). The development of early Arthurian prose represents something of a historical turn in the vernacular tradition: far from verse's courtly and sometimes humorous considerations, prose becomes the domain of a "serious" discourse on Arthur, the Grail and the ultimate fate of the Kingdom of Britain (Baumgartner 1999).

French prose is built around four major fictional topics, which distinguish it from the majority of the verse production. Two of them, Lancelot and the Grail, come from Chrétien and are relatively underused by the octosyllabic tradition.

The other two are independent from Chrétien. The first of these is King Arthur himself, envisioned as the embodiment of a kingdom that emerges, flourishes and perishes: derived from Geoffrey and Wace, this diachronic perspective on the Arthurian kingdom is absent from the verse romances, which take place in a static universe that serves more as a fictional backdrop than as a proper subject-matter (Baumgartner 1986b). The second fictional object that prose reactivates is the Tristan tradition, which virtually vanished from French verse romance after Thomas and Béroul. The Prose *Tristan* (*c.* 1235) brings the characters of Tristan and Iseut back into the fictional spotlight.

1.4 Cycles and *romans-sommes*

The formal divide between verse and prose entails several other differences. As previously noted, prose develops its own thematic preferences, not only by emphasizing specific fictional topics, but also in the way these topics are treated. The historiographical dimension of prose goes often hand in hand with a spiritual, even theological, dimension, especially in Grail romances (Valette 2008). Most of all, prose allows for the development of fictional constructs of far greater dimensions than previously existed. Early proses like *Joseph* or *Merlin* are short because they are based on verse sources; but as soon as the prose tradition begins to produce autonomous texts, their dimensions increase significantly, and the longer prose romances like the Prose *Lancelot* or the Prose *Tristan* far exceed in size the longest verse romances.

In this regard, the formal and thematic aspects of prose combine harmoniously: the historicizing reorientation effected by this form lends itself to lengthy narratives, which aspire to cover a fictional matter in its entirety, be it the whole career of a given knight, the history of the Grail from its appearance in the Holy Land to its final Quest, or the evolution of the Arthurian kingdom, from the days of Uther to the fall of Arthur. In formal terms, this narrative ambition is realized in a variety of ways. In the early period, up to the 1230s, it leads to the formation of narrative cycles, series of independent yet interconnected romances, which, put together, tell a coherent overall narrative (Lot 1918; Frappier 1936; Micha 1987; Besamusca et al. 1994; Sturm-Maddox and Maddox 1996; Moran 2014). The prose *Joseph* and *Merlin* are thus completed by a Didot-*Perceval*, which ties up the threads that were set out in the first two romances. On a much more massive scale, the Prose *Lancelot* serves as basis for a cycle that aims to cover the entire history of the Grail, of Lancelot, and of Arthur's kingdom: structured in five parts

(*Estoire del saint Graal, Estoire de Merlin,*[5] *Lancelot, Queste del saint Graal* and *Mort le roi Artu*), this cycle is enormously successful throughout the rest of the Middle Ages. The fact that medieval scholars often refer to it as the *Vulgate Cycle* highlights how this series of romances sets out to establish an Arthurian canon of sorts.

The cyclical trend in prose romances does not last long: from the 1230s–1240s onwards, more homogenous *romans-sommes* begin to replace cycles (Moran 2014, 543–570). The same period may also have seen the birth of a *Post-Vulgate Cycle*, more centred on the person of Arthur, but traces of its existence are fragmentary and indirect (Bogdanow 1966). *Guiron le Courtois*, a hybrid text with cyclical aspects and a complex manuscript tradition, demonstrates that the cyclic form as manifested in the *Vulgate Cycle* is in decline; *Guiron* also shows a willingness to explore other areas of the Matter of Britain, such as the older generation of knights, before the age of Lancelot (Albert 2010; Morato 2010). Most of all, the Prose *Tristan*, written at the same time, introduces a new template, that of the unified *roman-somme*. Rather than basing itself on the addition of several interconnected romances, the Prose *Tristan*, though similar in size to the *Vulgate Cycle*, presents itself as a unitary work (Baumgartner 1975; De Carné 2010). This formal template remains productive until the late Middle Ages, as shown by later texts like the *Prophecies de Merlin* (c. 1272–1279), *Perceforest* (first half of the fourteenth century) or *Ysaïe le Triste* (late-fourteenth or early-fifteenth century). These last two romances also illustrate the urge to explore other periods and other heroes than those depicted in the central Arthurian canon (i.e. the *Vulgate Cycle*): *Perceforest* effects a unique connection between the worlds of Alexander the Great and of Arthur, by setting its tale in Britain's remote, pre-Arthurian past; *Ysaïe*, on the other hand, takes place after the fall of Arthur, and deals with the adventures of Tristan and Iseut's eponymous son.

Whether in cycles or in *romans-sommes*, French Arthurian prose's most striking narrative technique may be the use of interlace, which involves alternating between different narrative threads such as, for instance, different quests that take place simultaneously (Lot 1918; Vinaver 1970; 1971, 68–99; Baumgartner 1987–1988). The interlace technique is characterized by fixed formulas that punctuate the narrative and weave a complex route among multiple protagonists. Interlace is so popular in the thirteenth century that it can even be found in some of the lengthier late verse romances, such as *Escanor* by Girart d'Amiens (c.

---

5 The *Estoire de Merlin* itself is based on the prose *Merlin*, to which is appended a much longer *Suite*. See Fabry-Tehranchi (2014).

1280). This popularity wanes towards the end of the medieval period, as will be explained later.

2 Arthurian literature in Europe: the anxiety of influence

2.1 Independent areas

It would be inaccurate to say that the Matter of Britain was born in the French-speaking world; however it is reasonable to contend that the forms invented by the Old French tradition represent a starting point of sorts, which serves as inspiration, to varying extents, for most of the other languages. This is not to say that the Arthurian production in other linguistic areas imitates Old French categories wholesale (*roman* vs. *lai*, episodic vs. biographic romance, cyclical vs. unitary prose), but that the choices made in the French-speaking world between the 1150s and the 1250s have a sizable impact beyond the limits of Old French. The verse-prose divide does not always manifest in the same fashion, and texts that would have been in French prose may well be adapted into verse in another language, and vice versa. However, the proportion of adaptations and translations of French texts in all the other Arthurian literatures of Europe means that it is helpful to bear in mind the major trends of *langue d'oïl* romance when examining the "genre" in other languages.

Some linguistic areas, for chronological or hierarchical reasons, eschew French templates to some extent: the two most notable cases are Latin and Welsh. Most Arthurian texts written in Latin in the twelfth century are in prose because they fall within the genre of *historia*, be they a major Arthurian source like Geoffrey's *Historia regum Britanniae*, or more peripheral works like *Arthur and Gorlagon*, *De ortu Walwanii* or *Historia Meriadoci* (on the last two, see Echard, *infra*). These works, despite their differences, all adopt the classical prose form of Latin historiography; the fact that we call the last three "romances" is something of an anachronism. Among the small number of Arthurian texts in Latin, Geoffrey's *Vita Merlini*, composed in dactylic hexameters in a style halfway between epic and burlesque, is the only one to buck this trend. It seems clear in any case that the formal choices made by these Arthurian texts in Latin, all composed between 1136 and the late-twelfth or early-thirteenth century, do not owe much to the vernacular practices that begin to develop in the second half of the twelfth century (Echard 1998; Archibald 2011).

The Welsh production is more difficult to define, since it encompasses texts that were certainly created prior to the *Historia regum Britanniae* and the French vernacular tradition, but also romances that are largely dependent on Chrétien's creations. Among the works that are older than Geoffrey and Chrétien, the verse side includes a number of Welsh Triads devoted to the Arthurian world, as well as the poem *Pa gur yv y porthaur?* These texts are difficult to date with certainty. On the prose side, *Culhwch ac Olwen* is the only "romance" that can be dated with confidence to the pre-Galfridian period (Roberts 1991). Whether in verse or in prose, these early Welsh texts relate to pre-existing genres: in verse, the triadic form encompasses many topics beyond the Arthurian legend; while the prose of *Culhwch ac Olwen* underlines its proximity to the *Mabinogi*, nowadays preserved in the same two manuscripts as the early Arthurian "romance".[6] Afterwards, the three romances of *Geraint*, *Owain* and *Peredur*, as well as later texts such as *Breuddwyd Rhonabwy* or *Y Seint Greal*, all maintain this prose form, even when they are adaptations of verse originals, as is the case for the first three, based on *Erec et Enide*, *Le Chevalier au lion* and *Le Conte du Graal*. This tendency of Arthurian literature to adopt pre-existing forms in the linguistic areas where it emerges, rather than inventing new ones, is widespread, as seen with the octosyllabic couplet in Old French.

2.2 The octosyllabic pattern vs. local traditions

The Old French octosyllable offers a strong template for a number of texts, across a variety of languages. The Occitan romance of *Jaufre* (*c.* 1220–1230), the only surviving Arthurian romance in *langue d'oc*, is written in rhyming octosyllabic couplets. When Henry Lovelich adapts the *Estoire del saint Graal* and the *Estoire de Merlin* from the *Vulgate Cycle* into Middle English (*History of the Holy Grail* and *Merlin*, first half of the fifteenth century), he does it in verse, which may seem surprising; but in both cases he writes in octosyllabic couplets, thus indicating, despite the switch from prose to verse, a keen awareness of the conventions of Old French Arthurian romance (cf. Griffith, *infra*). The Stanzaic *Morte Arthur* (*c.* 1350), though written in eight-line stanzas rather than couplets, is also (mainly) octosyllabic. Instances in which the French octosyllable is more loosely adopted are even more numerous: in Middle High German and Middle English, two Germanic languages that favour accentual verse over syllabic verse, Arthur-

---

6 Aberystwyth, National Library of Wales, Peniarth 4–5, "The White Book of Rhydderch", and Oxford, Bodleian Library, Jesus College 111, "The Red Book of Hergest".

ian texts are frequently composed in four-accent lines set into rhymed couplets, a form which is not so distant, *mutatis mutandis*, from the French octosyllable. In German, it is the form of the overwhelming majority of Arthurian romances; English uses it for instance in *Sir Landevale* (first half of the fourteenth century), *Ywain and Gawain* (first half of the fourteenth century), *Arthur* (late-fourteenth or early-fifteenth century) and *The Carle of Carlisle* (*c.* 1500–1550). This is not to say that these rhymed couplets were specifically designed to adapt the French octosyllabic couplet; German rhymed couplets were in use since at least the ninth century and Otfrid von Weissenburg's *Evangelienbuch* (O'Connell Walshe 1962, 71–85). But the rhythmic proximity to the octosyllabic pattern no doubt contributed to the adoption of this type of verse and stanzaic disposition by Arthurian romance.

The model of the octosyllabic rhymed couplet or of the four-accent couplet, however, is far from hegemonic. Alongside these works, many other verse texts follow traditional forms from their own linguistic tradition: as has already been seen to be the case in French and Welsh, Arthurian fiction frequently adopts pre-established textual patterns. In German, Wolfram von Eschenbach develops a stanzaic form based on long verse quatrains in his *Titurel* (*c.* 1217–1220), followed in this by Albrecht in his continuation, *Jüngerer Titurel* (*c.* 1270); this stanza, the *Titurelstrophe*, is not an *ad hoc* invention, but a repurposing of the *Kudrunstrophe* (developed in the epic poem *Kudrun*, early-thirteenth century), itself a reworking of the *Nibelungenstrophe* (developed in the *Nibelungenlied*, late-twelfth or early-thirteenth century). The *Titurelstrophe* is therefore part of a tradition that encompasses far more than Arthurian romance and can be traced back to German epic poetry (O'Connell Walshe 1962, 71–85). It reappears nevertheless in an Arthurian context in the late-fifteenth century, with Ulrich Fuetrer's *Buch der Abenteuer*, an extensive compilation of German Arthurian material, at over 80,000 lines in length (Bastert 2000). To these Arthurian texts that adopt older or more widespread forms, one can also add all the Middle English romances that participate in the revival of alliterative verse, a form that originally flourished in the Old English period (Turville-Petre 1977). This includes loosely alliterative works like Layamon's *Brut* (early-thirteenth century) and *The Avowynge of King Arthur* (*c.* 1375–1425), or more strictly alliterative poems such as *Joseph of Arimathea* (*c.* 1350), *Sir Gawain and the Green Knight* (late-fourteenth century) the Alliterative *Morte Arthure* (*c.* 1400) or *Golagros and Gawane* (late-fifteenth century, in Scots). Still in the Germanic language family, the Norse *Merlínusspá* (a thirteenth-century adaptation of Geoffrey's *Prophetiae Merlini*) uses the traditional verse form of *fornyrðislag*, which appears both on runic stones and in the *Eddas*.

Conversely, in one notable case, verse offers an opportunity for innovation: the Middle English tail-rhyme stanza, a stanzaic form at least partially derived from the Occitan *rime couee* (Wilson-Costa 2013), but which in English becomes a privileged medium for romance (Purdie 2008). This complex form owes little to the Old French romance heritage, and is a properly insular feature. Several notable Arthurian romances follow this stanzaic scheme: such is the case, for instance, with *Libeaus Desconus* (*c.* 1325–1350), *Sir Launfal* (late-fourteenth century) and *The Weddynge of Sir Gawen and Dame Ragnell* (*c.* 1500), among others.

Much has been said up to this point about verse in a German and English context: this is due to the fact that the Germanic languages, excluding the Scandinavian family, tend to favour verse over prose, be it in Middle High German, Middle Dutch or Middle English (and Scots). Most of the small number of German prose texts are actually *mises en prose* of German verse originals, all dating from the fifteenth century: Middle High German literature went through a *mise en prose* phase similar to the trend that took hold in Middle French at the same time. Eilhart von Oberge's *Tristrant* (late-twelfth century) is put into prose as *Tristan und Isalde*; Wirnt von Grafenberg's *Wigalois* (*c.* 1200–1220) becomes the prose *Wigoleis vom Rade* (1493). The only original German prose romance is the *Prosa Lancelot*, an adaptation of the French Prose *Lancelot*; the first of its three books was probably composed in the mid-thirteenth century, while the next two are from the fifteenth century; the first book was likely translated from a Dutch intermediary (Andersen 2000). This near omnipresence of verse is also true in Dutch, where the only notable prose texts are the *Historie van Merlijn* (*c.* 1534–1544) and the fragmentary Middle Dutch Prose *Lancelot*, a translation of the French romance. Middle English Arthurian prose has a higher profile thanks to Thomas Malory's *Le Morte Darthur* (*c.* 1470, printed 1485), but the only other Arthurian prose that has been preserved is a Prose *Merlin* (*c.* 1450–1460), a translation of the *Estoire de Merlin* from the *Vulgate Cycle*.

In English, there are even a few notable cases of *mise en vers*, where French prose romances are adapted into verse: in addition to Henry Lovelich's two aforementioned romances, *Launcelot of the Laik* (fifteenth century, Scots), is a partial translation of the Prose *Lancelot*. Similarly, the Dutch *Lancelot Compilation* (assembled *c.* 1320) is based primarily on verse adaptations of sections of the *Vulgate Cycle* (Besamusca 1994; 1996; 2000). This assemblage of ten autonomous romances (*Lanceloet, Perchevael, Moriaen, Queeste van den Grale, Wrake van Ragisel, Ridder metter mouwen, Walewein ende Keye, Lanceloet in het met hert witte voet, Torec* and *Arturs doet*) is nearly 90,000 lines in length, and operates in a very similar way to the French prose cycles; had it been produced in a French-speaking region, such an assemblage would certainly have been in prose. In these three Germanic language areas (High German, Dutch and English), prose only seems to become popular at the time of the massive *mise en prose* trend in fifteenth-century France; but the period of original French prose in the thirteenth century seems to have had a very limited formal impact on these three literatures.

2.3 Norse and Romance languages: the triumph of prose

Norse, unlike other Germanic languages, is one of the linguistic areas where prose far outweighs verse. The series of translations and adaptations of French texts initiated by King Hákon Hákonarson (who reigned from 1217 to 1263) imported verse originals into prose, the first of these imports being Brother Robert's *Tristrams saga ok Ísöndar* (*c.* 1226), based on Thomas of Britain's *Tristan*. This is followed by adaptations of *Le Chevalier au lion*, *Erec et Enide*, *Le Conte du Graal*, Marie de France's *Lais* and even the *Mantel mautaillé*. The Icelandic *Saga af Tristram ok Ísodd* (*c.* 1400) is also in prose and follows thematic and narrative patterns typical of the local sagas. In Norse, verse followed prose, contrary to the French order: the earliest Arthurian verse romance is *Hærra Ivan Leons riddare* (or *Herr Ivan*, *c.* 1303–1312; see Lodén, *infra*), an adaptation of the *Chevalier au lion* and one of the three Old Swedish *Eufemiavisor*, translations of French texts commissioned by Queen Eufemia of Rügen and written in the *Knittelvers* form (Lodén 2012). The late Middle Ages also produced Arthurian ballads in Danish, Faroese and Norwegian.

The dominance of prose and the influence of French prose are at their strongest in the other Romance languages. The Iberian peninsula is notable for its prose translations, in the late-fifteenth and early-sixteenth centuries, of various texts from the *Vulgate Cycle* and the *Post-Vulgate* tradition: in Portuguese, *O Libro de Josep Abaramatia* (translation of the *Estoire del saint Graal*) and *A Demanda do Santo Graal* (translation of the *Post-Vulgate* version of the *Queste* and *Mort Artu*); in Spanish, *El Baladro del Sabio Merlin* (translation of the *Post-Vulgate Merlin*) and *La Demanda del Santo Grial* (translated from the *Estoire*) (Hook 2015; cf. Gracia, *infra*). The success of Arthurian prose is even more apparent in Italy, with several adaptations of the Prose *Tristan* (*Tristano Riccardiano*, *Tristano Panciatichiano*...), but also of *Merlin* or *Guiron*. More importantly, the *Tavola Ritonda* (first half of the fourteenth century; see Murgia, *infra*), an original prose romance, offers a totalizing version of the Matter of Britain, from the time of Uther and his *tavola vecchia* to that of Arthur and the *tavola nuova*, with strong Tristanian overtones throughout (Delcorno Branca 1968). On another scale, Arthurian topics also appear in a number of *novelle* and *exempla*, including several sections of *Il Novellino* (*c.* 1280). Italian Arthurian verse is mostly limited to folklore-tinged *cantari* (second half of the fourteenth century) written in *ottava rima*.

2.4 Thematic recurrences and innovations

On a thematic level, certain common characteristics can be observed, regardless of language. The first of these is, of course, the abundance of translations and adaptations of Old French material. In the German, English, Dutch and Norse areas, Chrétien de Troyes is a highly valued source, although specialists have argued that some of the earliest German texts (Ulrich von Zatzikhoven's *Lanzelet*, Wolfram von Eschenbach's *Parzival*) may share a common source with Chrétien or have other independent sources, rather than being actual adaptations of his works (Kolb 1963; Kantola 1982). Adaptations of Chrétien's epigones are more infrequent: two noteworthy exceptions are the Middle English *Libeaus Desconus*, a loose adaptation of Renaut de Beaujeu's *Le Bel Inconnu*, and the Middle Dutch *Wrake van Ragisel*, which adapts Raoul de Houdenc's *Vengeance Raguidel*. Midway between the romance genre and vernacular chronicles, adaptations of the *Historia regum Britanniae* are of course numerous, from Wace's *Roman de Brut* to the Norse *Breta sögur*, Layamon's *Brut* or the Welsh *Brut y Brenhinedd* (Tétrel and Veysseyre 2015).

The single most popular tradition, however, adapted into virtually every Arthurian literature, is the Tristan tradition, even more so than the Grail legend. The three major Tristan romances in Old French, Thomas', Béroul's and the Prose *Tristan*, sow literary seeds throughout Europe. In German, Eilhart von Oberge's *Tristrant* (late-twelfth century) follows Béroul's "common" version of the tale, while Gottfried von Straßburg's *Tristan* (*c.* 1210) adapts Thomas' "courtly" version; Gottfried's romance receives two continuations by Ulrich von Türheim (*c.* 1240) and Heinrich von Freiberg (late-thirteenth century); the anonymous *Tristan als Mönch* is a short tale of disguise and subterfuge, similar to the French *Folies Tristan*. In Czech, the verse *Tristram a Izalda* (*c.* 1400) merges several representatives of the German tradition (Eilhart, Gottfried and Heinrich) to create its own original take on the legend. The Welsh *Ystoria Trystan* intersperses its prose narrative with dialogues in *englynion*, a traditional short poetic form. In Norse, as previously mentioned, the Arthurian tradition begins with a Tristan romance, and the legend resurfaces in Icelandic at the turn of the fourteenth century. In English, *Sir Tristrem* (late-thirteenth century) is based on Thomas of Britain. There is even a Belarusian *Tryščan*. The Prose *Tristan*, meanwhile, was very successful in Italy, where it influenced most Arthurian texts to some extent, from Rustichello da Pisa's French *Arthurian Compilation* (*c.* 1270–1274) to the *Tavola Ritonda* and several direct translations. Last but not least, the Prose *Tristan* also forms the basis for a significant section of Malory's *Morte Darthur*, at the end of the fifteenth century.

Concurrently with these rewritings, translations and adaptations of French texts, a number of original subjects also flourish. In German, this is particularly noticeable among authors of the period that immediately follows the great founders (Wolfram von Eschenbach, Eilhart and Gottfried, Hartmann von Aue, Ulrich von Zatzikhoven): texts like *Diu Crône* by Heinrich von dem Türlin (*c.* 1230; see also Kragl, *infra*) or the romances of Der Pleier (active between 1240 and 1280: *Garel*, *Tandareis und Floribel* and *Meleranz*) all develop topics that owe little to French sources; *Diu Crône* also distinguishes itself through its use of interlace to manage its narrative threads, thus importing a French prose technique into a German verse text (Kratz 1973; Kragl, *infra*). The German tradition as a whole shows a great degree of independence from the French tradition: early romances like *Lanzelet* or *Parzival* offer very singular versions of their subject-matter and are far more parochial than similar texts in other languages. The English Arthurian tradition is more dependent on adaptations of French texts, but it still boasts a number of texts that cannot be fully related to pre-existing sources, the most famous of which is certainly *Sir Gawain and the Green Knight*.

2.5 Abridgments, rewritings and compilations

Another characteristic that many different languages dependent on the Old French tradition have in common is a tendency to simplify and abridge their sources (see also Taylor, *infra*). This tendency is far from systematic, but it can be observed for example in the three Welsh adaptations of Chrétien de Troyes, the Norse sagas, as well as several English romances. Sometimes, the opposite is true: the Middle English *Sir Launfal*, for instance, is an expansion of Marie de France's *Lanval* (1045 lines vs. 646 lines).

When the source is a prose romance, this process of simplification and abridgment frequently leads to a breaking down of the interlace structure: this is a notable feature of the Italian production, for instance. The different narrative threads, rather than being intertwined, are laid out sequentially. This trend becomes widespread in the last centuries of the Middle Ages, including in Middle French: the practice goes hand in hand with the development of Arthurian compilations, a trans-linguistic European phenomenon. In French, the trend begins soon after the heyday of interlaced prose, specifically in Italy, with Rustichello da Pisa's *Compilation* (*c.* 1270–1274), which combines elements from the Prose *Tristan*, the Prose *Lancelot* and *Guiron le Courtois*. The lesser known fourteenth-century Prose *Yvain* is also worth mentioning: rather than a prose version of Chrétien's *Chevalier au lion*, it is a composite object that includes an episode from Chrétien's romance, elements from the *Chevalier aux deux épées*, the *Queste* and the Prose *Tristan*, as well as three episodes that have no known source (Lacy 2004). In the latter part of the fifteenth century, the compilation made by Micheau Gonnot for Jacques d'Armagnac (*c.* 1466–1470), preserved in a single manuscript,[7] is an excellent example of the way compilers overhaul and redesign their source material. Micheau Gonnot recomposes a vast Arthurian narrative from elements taken from the *Vulgate Cycle*, the *Post-Vulgate* tradition, the Prose *Tristan* and *Guiron le Courtois* (Pickford 1959). At the same time, Ulrich Fuetrer undertakes a similar project based on the German Arthurian tradition in his *Buch der Abenteuer*. The fifteenth century, as previously mentioned, is also a period of abundant *mises en proses*, both in French and in German: the *mise en prose* trend and the rise of Arthurian compilations are no doubt related, at a time when scribes are attempting to deliver a definitive and formally homogeneous version of the Matter of Britain.

In this century of compilations, the most historically significant of them all is undoubtedly Thomas Malory's *Morte Darthur*, a vast reconfiguration of Old French prose sources (*Post-Vulgate Merlin*, Prose *Lancelot*, Prose *Tristan*, *Queste* and *Mort Artu*, as well as the English Alliterative *Morte Arthure* and Stanzaic *Morte Arthur*). Similar to Micheau Gonnot, Malory condenses his sources, simplifies the interlace technique and focuses on the essentials (Norris 2008). In his case, these essentials are the life of Arthur: Uther's reign is largely ignored. Malory also reorganizes episodes to give them new meaning; he introduces other episodes that have no known source, such as "The Tale of Sir Gareth of Orkney" or the healing of Sir Urry in "The Book of Sir Launcelot and Queen Guinevere". On a formal level, *Le Morte Darthur* lies somewhere between the cycle and the *roman-somme*. The Winchester manuscript presents the text as a series of eight stand-alone tales (Vinaver 1935), but with a cyclical aspect conferred on them by an overall chronological progression and a recurring cast of characters; William Caxton's 1485 edition, on the other hand, presents Malory's work as a unified, singular romance (Lumiansky 1964; Moorman 1965; Olefsky 1969). The two versions of the compilation re-enact the tension that was already apparent in thirteenth-century French prose, when the *roman-somme* ended up outshining the cyclical form: in Malory's case, print outweighs the manuscript by imposing a unitary version of an assemblage that could have been read in a more discontinuous fashion.

At the end of this exceedingly brief overview, the existence of "Arthurian romance" as a recognizable European genre seems as remote as ever. The differences in formats, in verses and in stanzas, the lack of continuity in the verse-prose distribution, the emergence of singular forms depending on linguistic

---

7 Paris, BnF, fr. 112.

areas – all these factors imperil genre unity. Nevertheless, the centrifugal aspects of the Arthurian tradition cannot entirely hide the underlying characteristics that these texts have in common: the way Arthurian subject-matters take root in traditional poetic forms, typical of their literary environment; the wide dissemination of shared themes, such as the Tristan legend; the widespread retooling of French sources, translated or adapted in a more or less faithful manner; the development of compilations in the fourteenth and fifteenth centuries. There is no doubt that the fundamental characteristic of "Arthurian romance" is its diversity and adaptability – its ability to multiply and differentiate without denying its ties to a shared fictional wellspring.

References

Adams, Alison. "The Shape of Arthurian Verse Romance (to 1300)." *The Legacy of Chrétien de Troyes*. Ed. Norris J. Lacy, Douglas Kelly and Keith Busby. Amsterdam: Rodopi, 1987–1988. 141–166.

Albert, Sophie. *"Ensemble ou par pieces". "Guiron le Courtois", xiiie-xve siècles: la cohérence en question*. Paris: Champion, 2010.

Andersen, Elizabeth A. "The Reception of Prose: The *Prosa-Lancelot*." *The Arthur of the Germans*. Ed. W.H. Jackson and S.A. Ranawake. Cardiff: University of Wales Press, 2000. 155–165.

Archibald, Elizabeth. "Arthurian Latin Romance." *The Arthur of Medieval Latin Literature*. Ed. Siân Echard. Cardiff: University of Wales Press, 2011. 132–145.

Bastert, Bernd. "Late Medieval Summations: *Rappoltsteiner Parzifal* and Ulrich Füetrer's *Buch der Abenteuer*." *The Arthur of the Germans*. Ed. W.H. Jackson and S.A. Ranawake. Cardiff: University of Wales Press, 2000. 166–180.

Baumgartner, Emmanuèle. "Le choix de la prose." *Cahiers de recherches médiévales* 5 (1998): 7–13.

Baumgartner, Emmanuèle. "Le livre et le roman (xiie-xiiie siècles)." *Littérales* 1 (1986a): 7–19.

Baumgartner, Emmanuèle. "Temps linéaire, temps circulaire et écriture romanesque." *Le Temps et la durée dans la littérature au Moyen Âge et à la Renaissance*. Ed. Yves Bellenger. Paris: Nizet, 1986b. 7–21.

Baumgartner, Emmanuèle. *Le "Tristan" en prose: Essai d'interprétation d'un roman médiéval*. Genève: Droz, 1975.

Besamusca, Bart. "The Medieval Dutch Arthurian Material." *The Arthur of the Germans*. Ed. W.H. Jackson and S.A. Ranawake. Cardiff: University of Wales Press, 2000. 187–228.

Besamusca, Bart. "Lancelot and Guinevere in the Middle Dutch *Lancelot* Compilation." *Lancelot and Guinevere: A Casebook*. Ed. Lori J. Walters. New York/London: Garland Reference Library of the Humanities, 1996.

Besamusca, Bart. "Cyclification in Middle Dutch Literature: the Case of the *Lancelot* Compilation." *Cyclification: The Development of Narrative Cycles in the Chansons de Geste and the Arthurian Romances*. Ed. Bart Besamusca et al. Amsterdam: North Holland, 1994. 82–91.

Besamusca, Bart, Gerritsen, Willem P., Hogetoorn, Corry and Lie, Orlanda S.H., eds. *Cyclification: The Development of Narrative Cycles in the Chansons de Geste and the Arthurian Romances*. Amsterdam: North Holland, 1994.

Bogdanow, Fanni. *The Romance of the Grail: A Study of the Structure and Genesis of a Thirteenth-Century Arthurian Prose Romance*. Manchester/New York: Manchester University Press/Barnes & Noble, 1966.

Bruckner, Matilda Tomaryn. *Chrétien continued: a Study of the "Conte du Graal" and its Verse Continuations*. Oxford: Oxford Univeristy Press, 2009.

Busby, Keith. "The Characters and the Setting." *The Legacy of Chrétien de Troyes*. Ed. Norris J. Lacy, Douglas Kelly and Keith Busby. Amsterdam: Rodopi, 1987–1988. 57–90.

Busby, Keith. *Gauvain in Old French Literature*. Amsterdam: Rodopi, 1980.

Croizy-Naquet, Catherine. "Écrire l'histoire. Le choix du vers ou de la prose aux XIIe et XIIIe siècles." *Médiévales* 38 (2000): 71–85.

Damian-Grint, Peter. "*Estoire* as Word and Genre: Meaning and Literary Usage in the Twelfth Century." *Medium Ævum* 66 (1997): 189–206.

De Carné, Damien. *Sur l'organisation du "Tristan en prose"*. Paris: Champion, 2010.

Delcorno Branca, Daniela. *I romanzi italiani di Tristano e "la Tavola ritonda"*. Florence: L.S. Olschki, 1968.

Echard, Siân. *Arthurian Narrative in the Latin Tradition*. Cambridge: Cambridge University Press, 1998.

Fabry-Tehranchi, Irène. *Texte et images des manuscrits du Merlin et de la Suite Vulgate, XIIIe–XVe siècle*. Turnhout: Brepols, 2014.

Frappier, Jean. *Étude sur la "Mort le roi Artu", roman du XIIIe siècle, dernière partie du "Lancelot" en prose*. Geneva/Paris: Droz/Minard, 1936.

Gingras, Francis. *Le Bâtard conquérant : Essor et expansion du genre romanesque au Moyen Âge*. Paris: Champion, 2011.

Hinton, Thomas. *The "Conte du Graal" Cycle: Chrétien de Troyes's "Perceval", the Continuations, and French Arthurian Romance*. Cambridge: D.S. Brewer, 2012.

Hook, David, ed. *The Arthur of the Iberians*. Cardiff: University of Wales Press, 2015.

Kantola, Markku. *Studien zur Reimsprache des Lanzelet Ulrichs von Zatzikhoven: Ein Beitrag zur Vorlagenfrage*. Turku: Turun Yliopisto, 1982.

Kelly, Douglas. "Chrétien de Troyes." *The Arthur of the French*. Ed. Glyn S. Burgess and Karen Pratt. Cardiff: University of Wales Press, 2006. 135–185.

Kelly, Douglas. *The Art of Medieval French Romance*. Madison, WI: University of Wisconsin Press, 1992.

Kelly, Douglas. "Multiple Quests in French Verse Romance: *Merveilles de Rigomer* and *Claris et Laris*." *L'Esprit créateur* 9 (1969): 257–266.

Kennedy, Elspeth. *Lancelot and the Grail: a Study of the Prose "Lancelot"*. Oxford: Clarendon Press, 1986.

Koble, Nathalie. *Les Dessous de la Table Ronde: Le Lai du cor et Le Manteau mal taillé*. Paris: Rue d'Ulm, 2005.

Kolb, Herbert. *Munsalvaesche: Studien zum Kyotproblem*. Munich: Eidos, 1963.

Kratz, Bernd. "Zur Kompositionstechnik Heinrichs von dem Türlin." *Amsterdamer Beiträge zur älteren Germanistik* 5 (1973): 141–153.

Lacy, Norris J. "The Enigma of the Prose *Yvain*." *Arthurian Studies in Honour of P.J.C. Field*. Ed. Bonnie Wheeler. Cambridge: D.S. Brewer, 2004. 65–71.

Lacy, Norris J. "The Typology of Arthurian Romance." *The Legacy of Chrétien de Troyes*. Ed. Norris J. Lacy, Douglas Kelly and Keith Busby. Amsterdam: Rodopi, 1987–1988. 33–56.

Lodén, Sofia. "Le lion d'Yvain revisité. Traduire et adapter Chrétien de Troyes dans les pays nordiques." *Le Moyen Âge par le Moyen Âge, même. Réception, relectures et réécritures des textes médiévaux dans la littérature française des xiv et xv siècles*. Ed. Laurent Brun, Silvère Menegaldo, Anders Bengtsson and Dominique Boutet. Paris: Champion, 2012. 179–194.

Lot, Ferdinand. *Étude sur le "Lancelot" en prose*. Paris: Champion, 1918.

Lote, Georges. *Histoire du vers français*. Paris: Boivin, 1949.

Lumiansky, Robert M., ed. *Malory's Originality*. Baltimore: Johns Hopkins Press, 1964.

Maddox, Donald. "Cyclicity, Transtextual Coherence, and the Romances of Chrétien de Troyes." *Transtextualities: Of Cycles and Cyclicity in Medieval French Literature*. Ed. Sara Sturm-Maddox and Donald Maddox. Binghampton: Medieval and Renaissance Texts and Studies, 1996. 39–52.

Marchello-Nizia, Christiane. "La forme-vers et la forme-prose : leurs langues spécifiques, leurs contraintes propres." *Perspectives médiévales* 3 (1977): 35–42.

Micha, Alexandre. *Essais sur le Lancelot-Graal*. Geneva: Droz, 1987.

Moorman, Charles. *The Book of Kyng Arthur: The Unity of Malory's "Morte Darthur"*. Lexington, KY: University of Kentucky Press, 1965.

Moran, Patrick. *Lectures cycliques: le réseau inter-romanesque dans les cycles du Graal du xiii siècle*. Paris: Champion, 2014.

Morato, Nicola. *Il ciclo di "Guiron le Courtois": strutture e testi nella tradizione manoscritta*. Florence: Edizioni del Galluzzo, 2010.

Norris, Ralph. *Malory's Library: The Sources of the "Morte Darthur"*. Cambridge: D.S. Brewer, 2008.

O'Connell Walshe, Maurice. *Medieval German Literature: A Survey*. Cambridge, MA: Harvard University Press, 1962.

Olefsky, Ellen. "Chronology, Factual Consistency, and the Problem of Unity in Malory." *Journal of English and Germanic Philology* 68 (1969): 57–73.

Pickford, Cedric E. *L'Évolution du roman arthurien en prose vers la fin du Moyen Âge d'après le manuscrit 112 du fonds français de la Biliothèque Nationale*. Paris: Nizet, 1959.

Purdie, Rhiannon. *Anglicising Romance: Tail-Rhyme and Genre in Medieval English Literature*. Cambridge: D.S. Brewer, 2008.

Roberts, Brynley F. "*Culhwch ac Olwen*, The Triads, Saints' Lives." *The Arthur of the Welsh*. Ed. Rachel Bromwich, A.O.H. Jarman and Brynley F. Roberts. Cardiff: University of Wales Press, 1991. 73–95.

Rychner, Jean. *L'Articulation des phrases narratives dans la "Mort Artu": formes et structures de la prose française médiévale*. Geneva: Droz, 1970.

Schaeffer, Jean-Marie. *Qu'est-ce qu'un genre littéraire?* Paris: Le Seuil, 1989.

Spiegel, Gabrielle M. *Romancing the Past: the Rise of Vernacular Prose Historiography in Thirteenth-century France*. Berkeley, CA: University of California Press, 1993.

Sturm-Maddox, Sara, and Maddox, Donald, eds. *Transtextualities: Of Cycles and Cyclicity in Medieval French Literature*. Binghampton/New York: Medieval and Early Renaissance Texts and Studies, 1996.

Tether, Leah. *The Continuations of Chrétien's Perceval: Content and Construction, Extension and Ending*. Cambridge: D.S. Brewer, 2012.

Tétrel, Hélène, and Veysseyre, Géraldine, eds. *L'*Historia regum Britannie *et les "Bruts" en Europe. Tome I, Traductions, adaptations, réappropriations, XIIe-XVIe siècle*. Paris: Classiques Garnier, 2015.

Turville-Petre, Thorlac. *The Alliterative Revival*. Cambridge: D.S. Brewer, 1977.

Valette, Jean-René. *La Pensée du Graal : Fiction littéraire et théologie (XIIe-XIIIe siècles)*. Paris: Champion, 2008.

Vinaver, Eugène. *The Rise of Romance*. Oxford: Clarendon Press, 1971.

Vinaver, Eugène. *À la recherche d'une poétique médiévale*. Paris: Nizet, 1970.

Vinaver, Eugène. *Malory's "Morte Darthur", in the Light of a Recent Discovery*. Manchester: Manchester University Press, 1935.

Wilson-Costa, Karyn. "Of Bards and Troubadours: From *Rime Couée* to the 'Burns Stanza'." *Provence and the British Imagination*. Ed. Claire Davison, Béatrice Laurent, Caroline Patey and Nathalie Vanfasse. Milano: Ledizioni, 2013. 53–62.

Zumthor, Paul. *Essai de poétique médiévale*. Paris: Le Seuil, 1972.

Matthias Meyer
The Arthur-Figure

Thinking about the Arthur-figure in (medieval) European literature, one can start
with the same basic questions as for any (literary) character: when, who, where
and how was Arthur? At first glance, the answers seem simple enough. When?
During the whole Middle Ages and beyond. Who? A (legendary) king. Where? In
the British Isles, but also all over Europe. How was he? Here, it becomes more
complicated (and, of course, the answers to the previous questions also require
more detail). A better question would be: how many Arthur-figures are there and
what are the main differences between them?

One type of answer could be formulated against the backdrop of different
vernaculars. In doing so, one would follow a long established tradition, based on
the nationalistic construction of nineteenth and early-twentieth century national
philology (see Moran, *supra*). This perspective, however, immediately leads to
problems: the most obvious is that Anglo-Norman French was the language of the
Plantagenet court in England. Marie de France (who, in *Lanval* narrates a story
that takes place in the Arthurian world) probably wrote in England; the most
important individual Arthurian author, Chrétien de Troyes, might also have had
a sojourn in the British Isles. But it also obscures similarities between individual
Arthurian texts across linguistic borders, if they are seen only in the tradition
of one language (cf. Byrne, *supra* and Eriksen, *infra*). Furthermore, Arthur came
first into literary prominence in Latin texts – and these could be (and were) read
all over Europe, thus creating a lasting impression on its culture.[1] The Middle
Ages provided many key, seminal motifs in European culture that are still around
today, many very influential: King Arthur and the Round Table, the love potion of
Tristan and Isolde, the quest for the Holy Grail, the invisibility cloak, the immense
hoard (the last two are from the German *Nibelungenlied*), the pact with the devil.
The first three are all, importantly, connected to Arthurian material; their success
is, of course, boosted by the domineering stance of Anglo-American culture in

---

[1] This is not an implicit invective against the formidable series "Arthurian Literature in the
Middle Ages", published as single volumes by language. This series still offers a very important
overview of Arthurian literature. But it also shows the problems with this approach, since, for
instance, the *Historia Brittonum* is dealt with in all of the volumes on the French, English, Welsh
and Latin Arthur.

Matthias Meyer (University of Vienna)

DOI 10.1515/9783110432466-006

today's globalized world (a situation not unlike the influence of the French tradition in the Middle Ages).

1 Is there a historical Arthur?

The questions of the "who" and "when" of Arthur often lead to very awkward terrain in the shape of the question of the historicity of the Arthur-figure (see also Fulton, *infra*). Before I turn briefly to this question, I want to state that any answer that might be given is not important for the literary Arthur-figure that develops from the twelfth century onwards. During much of the twentieth century the historicity of Arthur was not questioned, though different theories were (with quite an astonishing amount of acrimony) set against each other: Arthur was either of Celtic, Roman or Sarmatian heritage. The main reasons given for his historicity were the mentions of him in the *Historia Brittonum* (around 820; some manuscripts attribute the work to a Welsh scribe called Nennius) and the *Annales Cambriae* (surviving in a tenth-century version). Both connect an Arthur with a battle at Mount Badon; the *Annales Cambriae* give 516 as the date for this battle, and Arthur's death together with that of his enemy Medraut (not yet the incestuous son of the later versions) occurs in the battle of Camlann in 537. For a long time, this was seen as proof enough for the historicity of Arthur – although other, older chronicles do not mention Arthur, even if they do mention the battle of Mount Badon. Current research has shown, however, that the *Annales Cambriae* should not be counted as an independent source; furthermore, the brief mention of Arthur in Chapter 56 of the *Historia Brittonum*, while fulfilling an important function within the structure of the work as a whole, shows parallels with earlier chapters on Vortigern and is full of biblical numerical illusions (Higham 2011, 13; Charles-Edwards 1991, 22). The Arthur-figure here has a clearly defined function: Arthur is a Christian military leader, leading the Britons with valour, but he is ultimately unsuccessful against the invading Saxons. In this, he might be – since he is attested nowhere else – a figment of the imagination; he might be real, but since there exists no independent source other than the *Historia Brittonum*, the historicity of Arthur cannot be established or disproved.

There are also Arthurs in poetic sources who are in all likelihood related to the same Arthur we hear about in three brief mentions found in chronicles such as, for example, the Arthur who appears in early Latin Saints' lives. The earliest is probably the *Legenda Sancti Goeznovii* (the text is said to be from 1019, but the date is contested), which shows Arthur as a ruler fighting against the Saxons. Other saints' lives show an Arthur who is a local ruler from the nobility, and who is not necessarily bad in himself, but is usually overcome by a saint. Another Arthur is transmitted in early Welsh poems – of particularly importance are those that clearly predate Geoffrey of Monmouth's history and, of course, the earliest French Arthurian romances. There is no extant evidence of the texts having been transmitted before the dates associated with Geoffrey and the French tradition (a lacuna caused by several factors such as poor storage conditions in Wales and a lack of interest in other linguistic areas where Latin manuscripts from Wales have survived), and so the pre-dating of these texts is based on linguistic and stylistic arguments. While it is very likely that we have several texts that are not influenced by later developments, it seems highly unlikely that we have texts that show us a tradition going back much further than the *Historia Brittonum*. One of the earliest examples is an allusion in the poem *Y Gododdin*, although, again, its very early dating is heavily contested. Here, a hero is praised, "even if he is no Arthur." (Aneirin 1988) Other early poems – transmitted in manuscripts from the fourteenth century – show an Arthur in action, but this time he is not a mere name or a figure to be superseded, but instead appears as an active warrior, accompanied by other fighters – men also of great renown, among them Cai, who is also a great fighter, and not the rather comic seneschal of later romances. But, again, some uncertainties regarding the actual dating of the text remain.

The conclusion here is straightforward: we do not and, barring decisive and conclusive new findings, will never know if a historical Arthur existed and what kind of political role he might have played. What we do know is that stories about an Arthur, a rather shadowy figure, circulated at least from the ninth century onwards, and probably considerably earlier. These stories belong to an oral tradition, using genres and formulas of local oral poetry. This Arthur-figure was an important warrior, fighting battles against the Saxons – a lost cause, as history proves – and he is accompanied by a band of warriors. Some stories suggest that he had a special connection to an Otherworld. Later evidence also leads to the possibility that a wife was attached to this warrior king quite early on. The exact qualities of this Arthur remain undisclosed, but it is safe to say that he was a figure we would put firmly into the tradition of heroic epics, which took root in the period of the barbarian invasions: as with Theoderic the Great, king of the Ostrogoths and ruler of Italy, who was turned into the Germanic literary figure Dietrich von Bern, there might have been a transformation from a historic figure of some kind to the Arthur we find in literature. Since the literary Dietrich is nearly the opposite figure of the historic Theoderic, this parallel also shows that there is no straightforwardly traceable route backwards from the literary Arthur to the historical figure. It is also quite common in the process of turning historical events into heroic epics that a political disaster (the invasion of the British Isles by the Saxons from a Celtic perspective) is sooner or later explained by motifs which have much to do with familial ties and conflict, such as in the case of the role that Guinevere and Mordred fulfil in later versions (see Haug 1971).

2 Geoffrey of Monmouth and his aftermath

In his *Historia regum Britanniae* (*HRB*), Geoffrey of Monmouth recounts that after the death of Uther Pendragon, his son (begotten with help of the magician Merlin) is crowned king:

> Arthur was a young man only fifteen years old; but he was of outstanding courage and generosity, and his inborn goodness gave him such grace that he was loved by almost all the people. Once he had been invested with the royal insignia, he observed the normal custom of giving gifts freely to everyone. (ix.1; 212)[2]

The *HRB* then goes on to tell how Arthur gains the whole of the British Isles, including Ireland, killing many but also – after enough penitential begging – pardoning some:

> He established the whole kingdom in a state of lasting peace and then remained there for the next twelve years.
> Arthur then began to increase his personal entourage by inviting very distinguished men from far-distant kingdoms to join it. In this way he developed such a code of courtliness in his household that he inspired peoples living far away to imitate him. [...] At last the fame of Arthur's generosity and bravery spread to the very ends of the earth [...]. [...] The fact that he was dreaded by all encouraged him to conceive the idea of conquering the whole of Europe. (ix.9, 10; 222)

Here we find much of what will later congeal into a topical set of characteristics: Arthur as a paragon of courtliness, of *largesse* [generosity], the centripetal force of his court. He even marries a lady of Roman descent, Guinevere. However, a striking difference to later traditions is that Geoffrey's Arthur retains his valour: every ruler is afraid that he might come and conquer his territory. This is still a heroic Arthur, turned into some kind of latter day Alexander. While many of his conquests are told more or less summarily (though pointing out such important features as Arthur's willingness to listen to counsel), Arthur's last campaign to counter the letter of the Roman procurator, Lucius, asking him to submit to Roman rule is, however, described in greater detail. It includes details of his most

---

2 All references are to Reeve's edition: Geoffrey of Monmouth (2007).

prominent adventure in the *HRB*, the fight against the Giant of Mont St Michel. Arthur's campaign against Rome is successful, but he returns to England after Mordred has usurped his throne and taken his wife. Whether this has been done against Guinevere's will is uncertain – Geoffrey leaves the point open and prefers not to speak about it (xi.1; 257). In the battle of Camblan, Mordred dies and:

> Arthur himself, our renowned king, was mortally wounded and was carried off to the Isle of Avalon, so that his wounds might be attended to. He handed the crown of Britain over to his cousin Constantine, the son of Cador Duke of Cornwall: this in the year 542 after our Lord's Incarnation. (xi.2; 261)

That an event is related to a concrete year, as here, is an anomaly in the Arthurian section of the *HRB*. As ambiguous as is the complicity of Guinevere in Mordred's adultery is the nature of the end of Arthur: he might be dead, but he could also be alive. His reign, however, is over, and there is no expressed hope for his return at the end of this chapter.

Geoffrey's Arthur is a warrior's king, still related to heroic epics. But his court becomes more important, and the scene that is interrupted by the advent of the letter from Rome is a court feast in all its magnificent splendour, and one which shows every sign of a courtly romance (for example, the inclusion of the sporting knights after the big meal, cheered on by the ladies watching from the city walls, demonstrates analogues with the court feast in the *Yvain*-tradition). Here, Geoffrey, while at the same time applying several *brevitas-topoi*, takes great pains to put the historic Arthur into the framework of contemporary courtly culture, at the same time as constructing a past where his "Britain" leads the world (which, of course, makes a direct connection with the contemporaneous political situation where the English Kings held extensive territories on the Continent).

Much has been written about the political dimension of Geoffrey's "invention" of Arthur. Geoffrey clearly took up oral traditions, whose traces we have seen, and incorporated them into his history. The function of the Arthur-figure here is evident: he is the last "Briton", a kind of autochthon ruler, and his reign is not only successful, but also very nearly leads to an Alexander-like world-encompassing rule. This Arthur fails as a result of family matters: when he leaves for Rome, he has all of Britain and every country he conquered at his service, and he leaves the defence of Britain to his nephew, Mordred, and his wife, Guinevere. In a sense, it is they, not he, who fail. If this is due to the general tendency of the European myth-making process to turn the political into the personal, or if it is a concrete warning about the dangers of family in-fighting to the ruling classes, is a matter open to debate.

Geoffrey's extremely successful *HRB* is the basis for Wace's translation into French, the *Roman de Brut*. Wace's Arthur is essentially the same as Geoffrey's, but one can note several expansions and additions. In the Arthurian section of Wace's text, we find a rising prominence of the theme of (courtly) love. That a king should marry is a question of genealogy, but that he should marry a very beautiful woman, and Guinevere is certainly described as such, is something connected to courtly love. A downside of this, of course, is that Guinevere inevitably becomes part of the "deep wrong" done to the king by Mordred's betrayal. Meanwhile, a motif found for the first time in the *Brut* is the Round Table. The attraction of Arthur's court is so great that many extremely worthy nobles arrive there. To solve the problem of rank, Arthur makes the Round Table. This, in a sense, is more a factoid than a story, but it is one that is developed by later narratives. The English version by Layamon tells a much embellished tale, for instance: after a disaster where squabbles over rank at Arthur's (conventional) table lead to much bloodshed (the fight at the grand hall is a motif from the heroic epics), a Cornish workman offers to make a folding Round Table for Arthur, seating well over 1600 knights.[3]

One of the main differences between Wace and Layamon can be found at the close of their texts: Wace puts as much distance between himself and the open ending of Geoffrey's Arthur as possible. Arthur perished, but it is the belief of the Britons that he might be in Avalon and could return. But Wace's last sentence states that Arthur never came again. Layamon, who further embellishes Arthur's journey to Avalon, tells us that Merlin was a good prophet and that he announced Arthur's return to help Britain. Of both vernacular versions of Geoffrey's *HRB*, Wace's *Brut* is the more romance-like. This is not so much due to the fact that Wace is nearer to Arthurian romances (although this is certainly true regarding the form of the text: octosyllabic rhymes), but because Wace is much less formulaic and has a much more self-reflexive and intrusive author-voice. But the most famous invention of all three is a period of peace in Arthur's realm. This period opens a window of opportunity that is taken up by the later romance poets. That the concept of this period provided a helpful solution to reconciling the miraculous tales that were circulating about Arthur and his men is quite possible; Geoffrey is not interested in them, since he needs a political hero to unify the Britons, and one not connected to Germanic rule – and Wace is too sceptical to include these kinds of tales. But all these tales relate that Arthur's court attracts the other kinds of characters and adventures – as it does in the romances; and as in the romances, this attraction can also prove fatal in the end, as the letter from Rome

---

3 Such hyperbolic numbers are quite usual for heroic epics.

does. But – and this holds true for much of Arthurian literature – this fatal end is hardly Arthur's fault alone. There is, in the end, a didactic streak running through Geoffrey's description of Arthur that lets this section of his text also function as a "Mirror of Princes". But eventually the courtly veneer proves to be rather thin: this Arthur, in essence, is on his way to becoming a courtly hero – but he is still overarchingly a heroic, political figure. Furthermore – and this is an important characteristic – he is a Christian ruler, too.

3 Chrétien de Troyes and the Arthurian verse romance: the mainstream

The above subtitle is misleading, since Chrétien at the same time both establishes and subverts what the European mainstream means for the Arthur-figure in verse. Nevertheless, there is still considerable sense in talking about the mainstream Arthur. There is a simple problem behind this ostensible paradox: Arthur is an ideal figure, but he is also part of a narration, and these are mutually exclusive. This can be seen, for example, in an almost introductory and very simple case that lies in the opening lines of one of the earliest examples of medieval vernacular Arthurian literature: after the prologue containing the famous boast that the name of Chrétien will exist as long as Christianity exists, and the equally famous introduction of the term *bele conjointure* (l. 14)[4] as the aesthetic principle of his literature, Chrétien in *Erec et Enide* switches the plot to speak of King Arthur. It is Easter and Arthur holds court in splendour, but there is no long description, and the king, before he adjourns the court, announces that he wants to reinstate the *coutume* (l. 38) [custom] of the hunt of the white stag. Gauvain is displeased and he argues at length that the end of the *coutume*, whereby the one who is successful at the hunt has to kiss the most beautiful woman, holds potential for conflict at a court where five hundred young ladies of royal blood are present. Arthur agrees but does not change his mind, and it is uncertain from his brief speech as to whether, as a king, he simply cannot renege on his announcement or whether he really wants to go on this hunt. Thus, he creates a problem that in the end has to be solved by an Arthurian knight, and not by Arthur alone. Another motif that is often used to open Arthurian narratives is the rash boon-motif, in which Arthur is usually constrained by his own perfection to grant a wish without knowing its content. Thus, Arthur's hunt, which also explains the absence of other knights, sets the

---

4 References are to Poirion's edition: Chrétien de Troyes (1994).

stage for the entrance of Erec who, by finishing a different *coutume*, a duel for a sparrow-hawk, also wins a wife, Enide. Inserted here is a scene depicting Arthur's return from the stag hunt. Arthur is the winner and he will have to kiss the most beautiful lady. All the men become very aggressive at the prospective slight on their own lady should she not be the chosen one, and the court is on the cusp of mutiny. Arthur is rather helpless, and it is the queen who saves him since it is she who suggests that one should wait for Erec's promised return in three days' time. When Erec returns with Enide, she is immediately taken care of by Guinevere, and the problem of the kiss is solved since Arthur now kisses this beautiful new arrival.

On the level of narrative structure it is clear that this is a prime example of *bele conjointure*: both narratives fit together, one solving the problem of the other. Both narratives also centre around Arthur's court, they take their start- and their end-points from there and, in between, the story returns to the court as well. They also have a common thematic core: female beauty. But they also show that the Arthurian world has to have an "Other", and this "Other" takes many forms: it can be, for example, Erec, who although at Arthur's court takes no part in its sport; it can be Erec's opponent Yder, who does not listen to the queen's command; it is the sparrow-hawk contest taking place at the same time as the hunt. In the end, though, Arthur seems to triumph: Yder will be integrated into the court; Arthur can kiss the most beautiful lady; and Erec, although he briefly returns to his father's country, marries Enide at Arthur's court. That Erec then moves on to his own realm does not mean that he is no longer connected to Arthur: it is the task of every Arthurian knight to make the (narrative) world more Arthurian and for that purpose, he ultimately has to leave the court.

The marriage ceremony is another opportunity for Chrétien to describe the splendour of the court. While at its first mention Chrétien is almost disappointingly brief, he gets into much more detail with each further mention. This court is the epitome of material splendour, and it is also the place where knightly prowess is gleaned. This is also a venue where a high potential for violence is accrued. But Arthur, Gauvain and Guinevere together in their counsel are able to handle the problem – at least long enough to give the narrator time to introduce Enide into his *bele conjointure*. It has to be noted that, despite the very strong courtly ethos, violence is never far away, even in the early Arthurian romances of Chrétien and Hartmann (Hasty 2002). But in the end, paroxysms of violence are avoided by courtly solutions as this brief example shows. It is particularly true of Chrétien that there remains more than a hint of heroic ethos. Erec, his first knightly hero – unlike his identically-named German counterpart – is already a dashing knightly figure. Hartmann's Erec, by contrast, is youthful and inexperienced (Meyer 1999). Both make the mistake of *recreantise* [languor or laziness], but Chrétien's Erec is perfect until then, while Hartmann's protagonist blunders along from the beginning.

In all of this, Arthur functions – more or less – as an unmoved mover. In the qualifier lies the problem of Arthurian narration that comes to the fore in some of the later romances: he functions as a courtly ideal that attracts other characters (see Kragl, *infra*). These others move around the centre of gravity created by Arthur, ultimately leaving Arthur's court but staying in his ethical sphere. This narrative principle, which is Chrétien's invention, has the advantage of being very flexible, since the stable core of Arthurian narration – Arthur's court – allows for a wide variety of narratives, as long as the basic attractiveness of this court is not fundamentally questioned. And the hero's ultimately leaving for his own realm is not only a method of propagating Arthurian values, but also a necessity enabling him to make room for the next hero. The backdrop of this is a court full of named knights without much individual personality, the main (but not the only) exceptions being Gauvain/Gawein/Walewein and Kay/Cai/Keie in their set roles as best knight and seneschal (who are both very early additions that pre-date Geoffrey). Guinevere, in the verse tradition, is mostly a model of female virtue, fitting for Arthur, but with occasional hints of adultery and/or abductions hovering over her. This court, fixed as it is, allows each hero his individual history, as well his faults and problems that come together, eventually, to lead to a final solution.[5] But this introduction makes equally clear that a completely faultless Arthur cannot create narration: if Arthur were absolutely perfect, he would not have proposed the stag hunt. Arthur must commit a few mistakes so that his knight(s) can correct them (Lacy 1996). The other way to create a narrative line is by using the world beyond Arthur's realm: not only can it host monsters and aggressors, but also *coutumes,* regulated customs that can be manipulated to pose a threat, or at least a task, that might disrupt Arthurian society (Köhler 1962; Haug 1971).

What is most important to note is that this construction, artificial and literary as it is, also has a basis in reality in the group that Duby has described as "les jeunes" [the youths]: those young people who do not yet rule (and might never, depending on inheritance customs), and who are in search of a dominion and a wife. These young knights are as far away from their families as is possible in a "cold", unchanging society. Arthur's court is a place removed from the constraints of genealogy and thus also has a utopian potential (or at least a potential for change). Arthur is the figure that integrates into society without being a biological father, but he still functions as a kind of ideal father. And since it is the task of the son to fulfil his father's wishes or to propagate his ideas, this is what

---

5 This central position led Kellermann (1936) to his structural analyses of Arthurian romances, later overly schematized by Kuhn (1948), Fromm (1969) and Haug (1971).

the Arthurian hero does. This is sometimes suggested as the psychological reason for the success of this genre (Wyss 1993).

The subsequent scenes at Arthur's court in *Erec* highlight another function: Arthur confers status, like the status that Erec and Enide lose during their crises, even if ultimately this proves not to be enough because the story has to end with the son becoming independent (with "son" here equating to the young knight for whom Arthur serves as a societal, rather than genealogical, father). This is the narrative sequence incorporated by Chrétien to allow the discussion of ideals: Arthur is the embodiment of an idea(l) and the court or the hero either fall short of it or are attacked because of it. The unfolding narrative reinstates the idea(l) and/or modifies it. The possibilities are almost endless, as long as imagination gives enough variety to the opposing forces, since the possibilities for those on the side of "good" are rather more limited. That this Arthur is a literary invention is made clear from the start: even at the beginning of Hartmann's *Iwein*, it is possible to witness a distancing from the belief of Arthur's countrymen that he might return. Hartmann goes even further and rejects the *laudatio temporis acti-topos*: while in King Arthur's time the court witnessed the deeds of heroes, in Hartmann's world now we can listen to the stories about them, but that is not necessarily a bad thing and can also lead to salvation.

4 The verse romances: minority opinions

There is no successful narrative without a flaw – but there are Arthurian romances that offer more than minor flaws either in Arthur or his court – or both. The first example – which is possibly even earlier than Chrétien – is not a romance, but a lay: Marie de France's *Lanval* takes place mostly at Arthur's court, but Arthur, who is lavish to a fault after a military campaign, forgets one of his best knights, Lanval, who then becomes impoverished. As an outcast, he gains the love – and financial help – of a fairy-like figure, but he cannot mention her existence. Guinevere here plays the role of a sexual predator whose advances are refused, ending in an open accusation against Lanval. Clearly, this Arthurian court on the one hand adheres to courtly values (Arthur's *largesse*), but not all is well. In the end, Lanval leaves the court with his fairy lady, not to be seen again. A lay follows different rules than does a romance, whereby the Otherworld has much more prominence. For *Lanval* to function, Arthur has to be known as the epitome of courtliness (as he is already in Geoffrey) but, moreso than in Chrétien's romances, he is outclassed; here, the Otherworld triumphs.

Yvain and Erec commence their adventure – as do many later heroes – at Arthur's court. But there is a second type of narration – most often connected to the "fair unknown"-motif where the protagonist arrives at Arthur's court not knowing his genealogy/his father. These, again, can be divided into two groups: those where the father has close Arthurian connections, and those where the ties are relatively loose. In both cases, however, the Arthurian episodes have a less evident structural function, since the narrative focus is on the life of the protagonist, especially the problem of finding his genealogical connection. In these romances, the Arthurian realm is not much more than a phase through which the protagonist passes – it is important but not his target, since Arthur's court embodies a society of the best knights, a principle opposed to genealogy. This is especially true if, as in the German *Wigamur*, Arthur's court believes in the worth, valour and value of the protagonist and wants him to marry one of the many ladies he rescues/helps. However, Wigamur himself, not knowing his lineage, sees himself as an incalculable risk for noble lineage, as long as he does not know his origin. Here, clearly, society's conferral of worth upon an individual is superseded by an (older?) genealogical ideal (Ebenbauer 1984; Meyer 2003; cf. for example, the French *Yder*, which also focuses on genealogical thinking and offers a negative portrait of Arthur, even though Gauvain and Guinevere are left more or less uncriticized). The situation is slightly different for romances where the father has some connection (even if it is tenuous) to Arthur's court, such as in those which follow the "Gauvain's son motif" (*Wigalois* and others). Here, the search for the father ends at Arthur's court, but this is not the case for the story-line that follows the life of the protagonist. Both *Wigamur* and *Wigalois*' stories, for example, end in political warfare, and so fit more in the world of the *chansons de geste* or heroic epics. This makes sense, since both are much more connected to the theme of family than other examples of Arthurian romance.

The biographical model might have existed in elaborate examples even before Chrétien, if we believe the source reference of Ulrich von Zatzikhoven in his *Lanzelet*, a Middle High German romance that tells a story about a Lancelot independent of both Chrétien's text and the prose tradition. Lanzelet is a knight who serially loves three women before finding his name at Arthur's court together with acquiring an appropriate wife – only to end up temporarily in another relationship with a fairy-like figure. This Lanzelet embodies sexual morals that are less elaborate than the courtly ones usually connected with Arthur, but does so without casting severe doubt on Guinevere. The courtly mode of Arthurian romance, in this sense, relies heavily on the individual: one protagonist is at its centre, while the court, in respective of its key figures, is individualized. Thus, Arthurian romances that depart from this individual mode seem to point to another ethos: for example, in Der Stricker's *Daniel* we find not only Arthurian story elements, but also direct quotes from the German version of the *Chanson de Roland*, creating a different kind of ethos in this romance. This ethos has to do not only with the protagonist's (in)famous use of cunning, but also, and moreover, with the depiction of Arthur as a warrior king who fights his own battles (even if he is assisted by his knights, which would, of course, also be true of Charlemagne, with whom this draws parallels).

There is another strain in Arthurian romances that goes beyond the standard concept of the courtly Arthur as (more or less unmovable) prime mover. The Arthur of the verse romances is not constrained by the linear passing of time – his existence is timeless. For instance, there is a narrative sequence instigated by Chrétien who apparently places his *Yvain* chronology just after that of the *Charrette* because the absence of the core knights allows for Yvain's adventures in the second part of the romance (and Hartmann has to incorporate a brief version of the abduction episode, unknown to the audience of his *Iwein* to make that clear). Later authors in particular make considerable effort to keep the Arthurian chronology linear (as, for instance, does Der Pleier). But in general, time does not play a major role for Arthur, whose nature and character always remains the same. This is reflected by the constantly favourable weather of Arthurian romance, and by the ubiquitous feasts at Pentecost (and sometimes Easter, leading Wolfram von Eschenbach gently to mock Arthur as *meienbaere* [man of May]). This stasis is broken in some romances, however: *Diu Crône* purports to tell of Arthur's youth (see Kragl, *infra*), and, indeed, starts at Christmas, which is unusual, at least in the German tradition. And it has been argued that the first part of the romance can be read as an account of Arthur's youth where he still has to establish his rule. Another romance that also starts at Christmas and makes much of the motif of Arthur's youth is *Sir Gawain and the Green Knight* (*SGGK*); incidentally, both include the beheading game – in *SGGK* as the central motif, and in *Diu Crône* as one of several themes in the first part of the tale. But the most central motif that destabilizes the literary construction of an Arthurian court is the Grail (see Stolz, *infra*). It has to be noted, however, that Arthurian romance fights back: in Wolfram's *Parzival* the finale at the Grail Castle has many elements of an operetta finale, and has the sense, therefore, that it cannot be taken too seriously. In *Diu Crône*, meanwhile, Gawein finishes the Grail Quest and the Arthurian realm is stable. This, however, is not true for many French romances following Chrétien's enigmatic fragment; here, the Grail world supersedes the Arthurian realm.

5 The prose tradition

After Chrétien's, the most influential Arthurian narratives are probably those that make up the *Lancelot-Grail Cycle*, later embellished to include the prehistory of the Grail and Merlin (*L'Estoire del saint Graal, Merlin, Lancelot, La Queste del saint Graal, La Mort le roi Artu*). The main difference between the prose cycle and the verse romances concerns historicity. While the authors of the verse romances may toy with the idea that Arthur was a historical figure, a belief in Arthur's historical existence is not an essential part of the contract between author and audience. You do not need to believe in Arthur's existence to enjoy Arthurian literature (in fact, it probably helps if you do not). The values that Arthur represents are nevertheless taken seriously – even if Arthur cannot always adhere to them, which makes him even more human. The Arthur of the first chronicles was not a particularly human figure, but rather a politically-motivated Christian and "Briton superman". The Arthur of the prose cycles is human, and not perfect, but often strives for perfection, and, in the end, dies in a tragedy of epic dimensions. Furthermore, he is presented as a (pseudo-)historical figure. While references to sources or literary traditions are *topoi* in the verse romances, in the prose tradition an unbroken chain of transmission is constructed between the events, their first notation and the existing French texts that are already recorded in manuscript, a tradition that spans from the oral to the written tradition.

The Prose *Lancelot*[6] starts with the young life of its protagonist, commencing with the death of his father and his abduction by the Lady of the Lake. Arthur is the second major station on Lancelot's route into the world (the first being the adventures of the Dolorose/Joyeuse Garde). The appearance of Arthur's court is problematic: Arthur forgets to knight Lancelot, Guinevere unwittingly provokes Lancelot's fatal love for her and Arthur, who at the beginning of the text could not save Lancelot's father from King Claudas, is under attack by Galehaut/Galahot, a typical figure from far away (the Outer Isles) who is the son of a giantess. Galahot is attracted by Arthur's worth but is so disappointed by the first battle against Arthur that he gives him a year's reprieve to re-gather his forces. Governed by his dreams and a wise hermit, Arthur improves his situation and establishes his rule during the second attack of Galehot (see also Larrington, *infra*). He integrates Galehot into his court, but only because Lancelot, who is in love with Guinevere, does her bidding. Without Lancelot at this point, Arthur would have been unable to keep his realm, having already nearly lost it twice before. And Arthur's rule is frequently in jeopardy, both from within and without. Initially, Arthur is himself

---

6 I use Lacy (1993–1996).

the main risk: during the war against the Saxons he falls in love (or at least lust) with an enchantress and is seduced by her, and this happens even before the love between Guinevere and Lancelot is consummated. He then falls prey to the machinations of the false Guinevere, and returns to his true wife (who flees with Lancelot to Galehot's realm) only after a papal intervention. It is important to note that, during their exile, Lancelot and Guinevere remain chaste: their love, although adulterous, is a courtly love; it is the love between a queen and the best knight. If Guinevere is no longer queen, their love, or at least their physical love, vanishes (which is also true at the end of the text, after Arthur's death, when Guinevere enters a nunnery and Lancelot becomes a hermit).

In the end, Arthur, who always had the ability eventually to restore order, becomes almost powerless. One of the signs of this is the inadvertent poisoning of a knight by an apple, which was designed as an attack on Gauvain, but the plan goes awry. This almost leads to the burning of the queen, but she is rescued by Lancelot and this sets in motion a train of events that is spurred on by a rivalry between Gauvain and Lancelot. This rivalry ultimately leads to the downfall of the Arthurian realm. It is, as in the chronicles, Mordred who usurps Arthur's throne, but here Guinevere is clearly presented as far more innocent. In between, the Grail appears, but it is a relatively short episode when compared with the episodes that surround it. And the relationship between the Grail world and the Arthurian world is troubled: Lancelot has to engender the Grail hero, Galahad, in a duplicitous, out-of-wedlock sexual encounter. Lancelot, who later ultimately fails in the Grail Quest, sees the Grail frequently before that and it heals his insanity. The Grail leaves the Arthurian world, first for India, but then vanishes from this world. It is a symbol of salvation, but the time for salvation has not yet come. A hopeless world remains, a world of strife, injustice and ruin. Business as usual, in other words.

This conception of Arthur and the Grail proved to be a lasting success. In France, and later in England (Malory), the prose compilation becomes the accepted form of Arthurian literature. It is one of the most complex narrative constructions prior to the advent of the nineteenth-century novel, with its intricately woven strands and its sometimes very realistic, sometimes wonderful depiction of a knightly world that is, of course, fantasy, albeit fantasy presented as history. And thus, this is a world that holds relevance for its readers, since it presents history as utopia, in the guise of a fantastic contemporaneous courtly culture. The fact that, after the downfall of his civilization Arthur returns in a chronicle, a form of literature that regards itself as real(istic), signals a kind of "true" return of the once and future king. This model remains active, especially in British literature, gaining popularity in the nineteenth century first in Europe and subsequently in America, initially in opera and theatre, and then in novel and film.

The Arthur of the prose tradition is thus very different from the comparatively perfect, stable and staid Arthur of the verse tradition – because he also has a history that mirrors that of his realm. But in the end, the function of both Arthurs is the same: they are the anchor figures for a never-ending reservoir of formulaic (if the readers are unlucky) or rather strange (if they are lucky) stories, which, in their co-compilation, both reflect, and reflect on, one another, and open up the possibilities for the first time in European literature to meditate on love, death, human relations, society and more in an all-encompassing literary world.

References

Adams. Alison, ed. and trans. *The Romance of Yder*. Cambridge: Boydell and Brewer, 1983.

Aneirin. *Y Gododdin*. Ed. and trans. A.O.H. Jarman. Llandysul: Gomer, 1988.

Barber, Richard. *King Arthur in Legend and History*. London: Boydell, 1973.

Barron, W.R.J., ed. *The Arthur of the English*. Cardiff: University of Wales Press, 2011.

Burgess, Glyn S., and Keith Busby, trans. *The Lais of Marie de France*. Harmondsworth: Penguin, 1999.

Busch, Nathanael, ed. and trans. *Wigamur*. Berlin: De Gruyter, 2009.

Charles-Edwards, Thomas. "The Arthur of History." *The Arthur of the Welsh*. Ed. Rachel Bromwich, A.O.H. Jarman and Brynley F. Roberts. Cardiff: University of Wales Press, 1991. 15–32.

Chrétien de Troyes. *Oeuvres completes*. Ed. Daniel Poirion, Anne Berthelot, Peter F. Dembowski, Sylvie Lefèvre, Karl D. Uitti and Philippe Walter. Paris: Pleiades, 1994.

Chrétien de Troyes. *Arthurian Romances*. Trans. William W. Kibler and Carleton W. Carroll. New York: Penguin, 1991.

Duby, Georges. "Dans la France du Nord-Ouest aus XIIe siècle: les 'Jeunes' dans la société aristocratique." *Annales* 19 (1964): 835–846.

Ebenbauer, Alfred. "Wigamur und die Familie." *Artusrittertum im späten Mittelalter*. Ed. Friedrich Wolfzettel. Gießen: Schmitz, 1984. 28–46.

Fisher, R.W., trans. *The Narrative Works of Hartmann von Aue*. Göppingen: Kümmerle, 1983.

Fromm, Hans. "Doppelweg." *Werk – Typ – Situation*. Ed. Ingeborg Glier. Stuttgart: Metzler, 1969. 64–79.

Geoffrey of Monmouth. *The History of the Kings of Britain*. Ed. Michael J. Reeve. Trans. Neil Wright. Woodbridge: Boydell, 2007.

Geoffrey of Monmouth. *The History of the Kings of Britain*. Trans. Lewis Thorpe. London: Penguin, 1980.

Green, Thomas. *Conceptions of Arthur*. Stroud: Tempus, 2007.

Hartmann von Aue. *Erec*. Ed. and trans. Volker Mertens. Stuttgart: Reclam, 2008.

Hartmann von Aue. *Gregorius. Armer Heinrich. Iwein*. Ed. and trans. Volker Mertens. Frankfurt a. M.: Deutscher Klassiker Verlag, 2004.

Hasty, Will. *Art of Arms: Studies of Aggression and Dominance in Medieval German Court Poetry*. Heidelberg: Winter, 2002.

Nennius. Historia Brittonum *and* Annales Cambriae: *British History and the Welsh Annals.* Ed. John Morris. London: Phillimore, 1980.

Haug, Walter. *Vernacular Literary Theory in the Middle Ages. The German Tradition, 800–1300 in its European Context.* Cambridge: Cambridge University Press, 2006.

Haug, Walter. "Die historische Dietrichsage. Zum Problem der Literarisierung geschichtlicher Fakten." *Zeitschrift für deutsches Altertum und deutsche Literatur* 100 (1971): 43–62.

Higham, Nick. "The Chroniclers of Early Britain." *The Arthur of Medieval Latin Literature.* Ed. Siân Echard. Cardiff: University of Wales Press, 2011. 9–25.

Jackson, W.H., and S.A. Ranawake, eds. *The Arthur of the Germans.* Cardiff: University of Wales Press, 2000.

Kellermann, Wilhelm. *Aufbaustil und Weltbild Chrestiens von Troyes im Percevalroman*, Halle: Niemeyer, 1936.

Kelly, Douglas. "Chrétien de Troyes." *The Arthur of the French.* Ed. Glyn S. Burgess and Karen Pratt. Cardiff: University of Wales Press, 2006. 135–185.

Kennedy, Elspeth. *Lancelot and the Grail. A Study of the Prose Lancelot.* Oxford: Clarendon, 1986.

Köhler, Erich. "Die Rolle des "Rechtsbrauchs" (costume) in den Romanen des Chrétien de Troyes." *Trobadorlyrik und höfischer Roman. Aufsätze zur französischen und provenzalischen Literatur des Mittelalters.* Ed. Erich Köhler. Berlin: Rütten and Löning, 1962. 205–212.

Kuhn, Hugo. "Erec." *Festschrift Paul Kluckhohn und Herrmann Schneider.* Ed. Wolfgang Mohr. Tübingen: Mohr, 1948. 122–147.

Lacy, Norris J. "King Arthur." *Le Héros dans la réalité, dans la légende et dans la littérature medieval.* Ed. Danielle Buschinger and Wolfgang Spiewok. Greifswald: Reineke, 1996. 67–80.

Lacy, Norris J., ed. *Lancelot-Grail: The Old French Arthurian Vulgate and Post-Vulgate in Translation.* New York: Routledge, 1993–1996.

Layamon. *The Brut.* Ed. W.J.R. Barron and S.C. Weinberg. Harlow: Longman, 1995.

Marie de France. *Lais.* Ed. A. Ewert. London: Bloomsbury, 1995.

Mertens, Volker. *Der deutsche Artusroman.* Stuttgart: Reclam, 2005.

Meyer, Matthias. "Das defizitäre Wunder – Die Feenjugend des Helden." *Das Wunderbare im Artusroman.* Ed. Friedrich Wolfzettel. Tübingen: Niemeyer, 2003. 95–112.

Meyer, Matthias. "Struktur und Person im Artusroman." *Erzählstrukturen der Artusliteratur.* Ed. Friedrich Wolfzettel. Tübingen: Niemeyer, 1999. 145–163.

Putter, Ad, and Myra Stokes, eds. *The Works of the Gawain Poet.* London: Penguin, 2014.

Schmolke-Hasselmann, Beate. *The Evolution of Arthurian Romance: The Verse Tradition from Chrétien to Froissart.* Cambridge: Cambridge University Press, 1998.

Sommer, H. Oskar, ed. *The Vulgate Version of the Arthurian Romances.* Washington: Carnegie Institution, 1908–1916.

Vinaver, Eugene, ed. *The Works of Sir Thomas Malory.* Oxford: Oxford University Press, 1990.

Ulrich von Zatzikhoven. *Lanzelet.* Ed. and trans. Kathleen Meyer. Martlesham: Brewer, 2011.

Ulrich von Zatzikhoven. *Lanzelet.* Ed. and trans. Florian Kragl. Berlin: De Gruyter, 2006.

Wace, Robert. *Roman de Brut.* Ed. I.D.O. Arnold. Paris: Société des Anciens Textes Français, 1938–1940.

Wirnt von Grafenberg. *Wigalois.* Ed. J.M.N. Kapteyn. Trans. Sabine Seelbach and Ulrich Seelbach. Berlin: De Gruyter, 2005.

Wirnt von Grafenberg. *Wigalois: The Knight of the Fortune's Wheel*. Trans. J.W. Thomas. Lincoln, NE: Nebraska University Press, 1977.

Wolfram von Eschenbach. Parzival *with* Titurel *and the Love-Lyrics*. Trans. Cyril Edwards. Oxford: Oxford University Press, 2006.

Wolfram von Eschenbach. *Parzival*. Ed. Karl Lachmann. Trans. Peter Knecht. Berlin: De Gruyter, 2003.

Wyss, Ulrich. "Fiktionalität – heldenepisch und arthurisch." *Fiktionalität im Artusroman*. Ed. Volker Mertens and Friedrich Wolfzettel. Tübingen: Niemeyer, 1993. 242–256.

Keith Busby
The Manuscript Context of Arthurian Romance

Manuscripts of Arthurian romance were produced by the same individuals responsible for other types of books, secular and sacred. The variation in production contexts from the late-twelfth through to the fifteenth centuries, across the many language areas, is considerable, making generalizations difficult. This chapter considers only some circumstances under which manuscripts of Arthurian romance were copied, illustrated and assembled, ranging from what appear to be individualistic and personalized books to those made on a larger, commercial scale. As it is impossible to offer a complete survey here, the focus will be on manuscripts containing romances in Old French, Middle High German, Middle Dutch and Middle English. Particular attention will be paid to some manuscripts which have come to be regarded as important and central to Arthurian studies. The numbers of manuscripts in French and German in particular preclude more than highly selective treatment.

The chronology of manuscript production rarely corresponds to that of romance composition, and there are few extant first generation copies. This is true of medieval vernacular literature in general before the middle of the fourteenth century, when authors' interests in books containing their own works and a more

---

Note: I have given only selected basic bibliographical references in this chapter. Extensive documentation can be found in the *Bibliographical Bulletin of the International Arthurian Society* (to 2011), thereafter *Bibliography of the International Arthurian Society*. Although I give details of printed manuscript facsimiles and URLs to some individual projects, I only provide URLs for digitizations of individual manuscripts in exceptional cases. The majority, often with detailed descriptions, can be accessed via the following websites: <http://gallica.bnf.fr> (French manuscripts held by the Bibliothèque nationale de France, Paris); <http://mandragore.bnf.fr/html/accueil.html> (illuminated manuscripts held by the Bibliothèque nationale de France, Paris); <http://www.handschiftencensus.de> (German manuscripts); <http://www.parzival.unibe.ch/hsverz.html> (manuscripts of *Parzival*); <http://www.bl.uk/manuscripts> (British Library holdings); <http://www.e-codices.unifr.ch> (manuscripts in Swiss libraries). The websites of other major libraries, too numerous to list, include digitized versions of many manuscripts discussed here. See *Medieval Manuscripts on the Web* at <http://faculty.arts.ubc.ca/sechard/512digms.htm>. A good resource on manuscripts containing Old French is <http://jonas.irht.cnrs.fr/>. French Arthurian manuscripts are discussed in the kind of detail not possible here by Middleton (2006). I thank Frank Gentry, Michael Stolz and Raluca Radulescu for reading sections of this chapter.

Keith Busby (University of Wisconsin-Madison)

DOI 10.1515/9783110432466-007

aggressive awareness of authorial identity begin to emerge. That said, in the case of Chrétien de Troyes, it may be possible to argue that not only did he have an acute authorial self-awareness but also that early manuscript transmission points to a recognition of him as an author with an *oeuvre*. Chrétien's catalytic role as the first author of episodic Arthurian romance in verse may have influenced the choice of texts for inclusion in collective manuscripts (*recueils*) and their arrangement within the book, although few reflect directly what literary scholars have perceived as the evolution of the genre. This is why study of the manuscript transmission of Arthurian romance – or anything else – can cast an alternative (or supplementary) light on the nature of medieval texts as they were perceived and received in the Middle Ages. An examination of the manuscript context of Chrétien and early French verse romance will provide a basis for comparison with the traditions of other language areas. I do not consider the Arthurian section of Wace's *Brut*, although the whole text is found alongside romances proper in some of the manuscripts discussed. Prose romance is treated separately.

Accidents of history and vagaries of transmission such as loss of leaves or rebinding over the centuries sometimes obscure the early history of books at the same time as they constitute an object of study. What we see in a manuscript is not always what a medieval user may have seen. Bearing that in mind, it is fair to say that there are essentially two types of manuscripts containing French Arthurian verse romances, namely single item codices and collections. Examples of the first category are relatively rare, most romances being transmitted in *recueils* containing other romances and, most commonly, other types of vernacular narrative. The rare cases of early single-item codices do, however, suggest that individual romances circulated without company before being collected into larger books. The single-item codex is its own context and its physical features may tell us a good deal about its manner of production and reception. Collective manuscripts invite intertextual comparison between their various components which may function through thematic relations and the ordering of texts within the codex. Illumination and rubrication can further suggest how the artisans of the book interpreted what scribes copied and how they attempted to guide or manipulate users.[1]

The earliest complete copies of Chrétien romances are those of *Cligès* in Tours, BM 942 (western France, possibly Anjou, s. 12ex.–s. 13inc.) and *Perceval* in Clermont-Ferrand, BMI 248 (northern France?, s. 13¼). Although the Tours manuscript is both acephalous and acaudal, it has been demonstrated that it contained

---

[1] On reading in manuscript generally, see Busby (2002), which discusses many of the manuscripts considered here.

only *Cligès*; the Clermont-Ferrand *Perceval* also appears to have contained only Chrétien's last, incomplete, romance. Both of these manuscripts are modest, small format books. If the evidence of the so-called "Annonay fragments" (Champagne, s. 13^1/4) is anything to go by, Chrétien's romances may have been gathered into an author collection early, as the fragments include sections from all romances except *Lancelot*. An *oeuvres complètes* would have enabled readers and listeners to form a view of an author and his literary skills. There is no way of knowing precisely how any of these three manuscripts were used, although it is clear that the romances must have been read, in all likelihood aloud, in several sittings. Readers and audiences of Annonay may have listened to the romances in succession, not necessarily in the order of composition established by scholars, and could have been enabled to compare and contrast the individual parts of the Chrétien corpus.[2]

Of the more than forty surviving manuscripts of Chrétien's romances, many are fragments from which little can be deduced, but apart from the above-mentioned, the principal copies fall into four general sub-categories: collections of Arthurian romances; of Arthurian and non-Arthurian romances; of vernacular verse narrative; and of *Perceval* with the Continuations. Within the wider ranging books, there are sections of Arthurian romances, or long sections which link *romans d'antiquité* with British history in a broad universal sweep. The majority of manuscripts were produced in the century between *c.* 1225 and *c.* 1325; there are no fifteenth-century copies. With the exception of London, College of Arms, Arundel XIV, of *Perceval*, and an excerpt from *Erec et Enide* copied in London, BL, Harley 4971 (both England, s. 14^med.), all manuscripts of Chrétien and Arthurian verse romances are continental, with many localizable in northeastern France.

The best known manuscript containing Chrétien's romances is probably Paris, BnF, fr. 794 (Champagne, s. 13^2/4), produced in Provins by a scribe who names himself as "Guiot". This copy has enjoyed prominence because it was used as the manuscript for the series of editions by Mario Roques, Alexandre Micha, and Félix Lecoy, which were long standard texts in scholarly and French university circles. Although Guiot wrote in what may have been close to Chrétien's native Champenois dialect, his text is somewhat anodyne and quirky, suggesting that the most commonly used editions may not contain a text approximating to Chrétien's *ipsissima verba*. Pace Guiot's quirks, BnF, fr. 794 is in many ways a typical *recueil* of its time, containing all of Chrétien's romances, and transmits the Continuations of the *Perceval*, Wace's *Brut*, *Athis et Prophilias*, *Le Roman de Troie*, and *Les Empereurs de Rome* by Calendre.

---

2 The Chrétien manuscripts are listed, described, analyzed and illustrated in Busby et al. (1993).

BnF, fr. 794 is a professional production, but modest in appearance, with only a few painted capitals, the primary decoration limited to the usual red and blue pen-flourished initials (*lettrines*). Chrétien manuscripts are not generally richly illuminated, but there are some exceptions. Princeton, University Library, Garrett 125 (northeastern France, s. 13⁴ᐟ⁴) contains sizeable fragments of *Yvain* and *Lancelot*, *La chevalerie Judas Macchabee*, and the *chanson de geste* of *Garin de Monglane*, with good quality miniatures for the first three texts. It also suggests the apparent codicological compatibility of Arthurian romance with (pseudo-)biblical narrative and epic. That compatibility in turn reflects the tastes of audiences and book-owners. Paris, BnF, fr. 1433 (northeastern France, s. 14¹ᐟ⁴) contains only two Arthurian verse romances, Chrétien's *Yvain*, preceded by the anonymous *Atre périlleux*, both richly illustrated. The distinction between Chrétien and his epigones is perhaps reduced in this kind of manuscript, just as that between *Perceval* and the Continuations recedes to produce copies of what may be perceived as a single long Grail verse romance. The illuminations in such manuscripts as Paris, BnF, fr. 1453 (Paris, s. 14²ᐟ⁴), fr. 12576, fr. 12577, Montpellier, Bibliothèque interuniversitaire, Sect. Méd. H 249 (northern France, s. 13⁴ᐟ⁴), and Mons, BU 331/206 (Tournai, s. 13⁴ᐟ⁴) offer a means of examining the reception of the verse Grail tradition in the thirteenth and fourteenth centuries. BnF, fr. 12576 is copied mainly by the principal scribe of Paris, BnF, nouv. acq. fr. 6614, suggesting organized production in the Arras region, *c.* 1275, while BnF, fr. 12577 is a product of the Parisian *libraire*, Richard de Montbaston, whose books can be dated to *c.* 1330–1340.[3] Chantilly, Musée Condé, 472 (Flanders/Hainaut, s. 13ᵐᵉᵈ) contains Chrétien's *Erec et Enide*, *Yvain* and *Lancelot*, and six epigonal romances (*Les merveilles de Rigomer*, *L'Atre périlleux*, *Fergus*, *Hunbaut*, *Le Bel Inconnu* and *La Vengeance Raguidel*).[4] The position of the long *Merveilles* at the beginning of the manuscript casts it as the fount of adventures, despite its being chronologically the last of the romances in Chantilly 472 to have been composed. Chantilly 472 has much to tell us about the selection of texts it contains, their arrangement and the structure of the book as a whole, as does Paris, BnF, fr. 1450 (northeastern France, s. 13²ᐟ⁴), which begins with the *Roman de Troie* and the *Roman d'Eneas*, continues with Wace's *Brut*, which it interrupts at the *pax arthuriana*, inserting all of Chrétien's romances, reprising and concluding the *Brut*, before ending with *Dolopathos*.[5]

---

3 On manuscript production in Paris generally, see Rouse and Rouse (2000). Richard and Jeanne de Montbaston are covered in the same volume (I, 235–260).
4 The status of the sections of the *Roman de Renart* and the prose *Perlesvaus* in Chantilly 472 are not clear. They may not belong to the original design.
5 On Chantilly 472, see Walters (1994), and on BnF, fr. 1450, Walters (1985).

With a few exceptions, most manuscripts of Arthurian verse romance contain other types of texts. Two exceptions to the usual run of *recueils* are Vienna, ÖNB 2577 containing only Raoul de Houdenc's *Meraugis de Portlesguez* (northeastern France, s. 13ex.–s. 14inc.) (closely related to Dijon, BM 525, with fragments of the same manuscript in Paris, BnF, nouv. acq. fr. 20001), containing seventeen highly accomplished and detailed miniatures, and Cambridge, CUL, Ee. 4. 26 (England, s. 133/4), unillustrated, whose unique text is the anonymous *Yder*. Two other verse romances have survived in single-item codices: *Floriant et Florete* in New York, Public Library, 122 (Île-de-France, s. 13ex.) and *Escanor* by Girart d'Amiens in Paris, BnF, fr. 24374 (Île-de-France, s. 13ex.). *Perceval* with three or four Continuations is sufficient to constitute a single long book, some containing well over 50,000 lines, but this is a unique phenomenon due to the invitation offered by Chrétien's unfinished romance. Generally speaking, Arthurian verse romance in French has a varied codicological context which is by definition lost as soon as the individual texts are forcibly removed to the new setting of a critical edition.[6]

In contrast, manuscripts of Arthurian prose romances provide their own context. The cycle of the *Lancelot-Queste del saint Graal-Mort Artu*, with its two "prequels", the *Estoire del saint Graal* and the *Estoire de Merlin*, is an enterprise of impressive dimensions which sometimes requires division into several volumes.[7] Later prose romances such as the *Tristan* and its derivatives are likewise single-item codices, while the enormous *Perceforest* takes up several volumes. Whereas Chrétien's romances survive in half-a-dozen or so copies and fragments (fifteen for the *Perceval*), and the epigonal romances in smaller numbers, the manuscript corpus of Arthurian prose romance is much larger, responding to wider readership and ownership. Elspeth Kennedy's edition of the non-cyclical *Lancelot* (Kennedy 1980, II, 1–9) lists forty-four manuscripts, while Alexandre Micha's edition of the cyclical version (Micha 1978–1983, I, 10) uses seventeen, although an earlier series of articles describes over a hundred (Micha 1961; 1963; 1964); Jean-Paul Ponceau (Ponceau 1997, I, xxv–xxvii) enumerates forty-two of the *Estoire del saint Graal*, and Micha (Micha 1980, xiv–xix), forty-six of the *Merlin*. There are over fifty surviving copies of the Prose *Tristan* (Baumgartner 1975, 18–20), and over thirty of *Guiron le Courtois* (Lathuillère 1966, 35–96). I mention the Prose *Tristan* here as it integrates the Tristanian world fully into the Arthur-

---

6 I exaggerate here for effect, and do not propose rejecting or abandoning critical editions, but it is incumbent on scholars to look at the varied manuscript environment of whatever text they may be considering.
7 The few Arthurian prose manuscripts containing other texts are mentioned by Middleton (2006, 46–47).

ian; this is not the case with the Old French verse *Tristan* texts, omitted from consideration. Numerous fragments of all of these texts are further testimony to production of prose romances on a commercial, almost industrial, scale. The dissemination of prose romances in Italy (where, although Chrétien is known, manuscripts containing his romances were not produced) is noteworthy, as is the long chronological span of copying, from the second quarter of the thirteenth century through to the early-sixteenth, and in early printed books.

Manuscripts of prose romances run the gamut from modest to luxurious, from plain to lavishly illuminated. Their page dimensions are generally larger than those of verse manuscripts. All tend to use the interlace structure for the location of various types of decoration, from the hierarchy of pen-flourished initials to fully-fledged and detailed miniatures. Interlace formulae such as "Or dist li contes..." [Now the tale says...] provide ready-made narrative pauses and places to embellish the text, attract the reader's attention and manipulate understanding of the romance. Insular copies are rare, although continental French books circulated widely in the British Isles, particularly in higher aristocratic and royal milieus. It is important to note that, from the middle of the thirteenth century onwards, manuscripts of prose romances are copied alongside those containing verse, sometimes in the same "workshops". It is therefore not surprising to find both exhibiting shared characteristics with regard to *mise en texte*, *mise en page* and decoration. As some late verse romances show textual and structural influences from prose romance, so some verse manuscripts show features that first appear in prose. The rise of prose does not bring about the fall of verse, textually or codicologically, although prose romance comes to enjoy a dominant position.

There is little need to consider in detail the kind of modest manuscript of the *Lancelot-Grail* or Prose *Tristan*, whose decoration consists largely of pen-flourished initials. Some may include rubrics (or *tituli*, when not accompanying illuminations) and all reveal careful structuring, in later copies also occasionally seen in a table or tables of contents. These modest copies represent the larger part of the prose romance corpus, but the illuminated copies stand out as examples of what artisans of the book can achieve. In some cases, the more elaborate examples were commissioned and owned by royalty and the highest echelons of the aristocracy. The selection here is an attempt to show the variety of copies of prose romances. At the least it should restore some codicological dimensions to texts either read in unmedieval editions or often referred to in the abstract. The classification of prose manuscripts by their contents is often difficult: not only are many cyclical, containing texts that modern scholarship has isolated, but compilers frequently included texts and sections of texts from different sources.[8]

An early illuminated manuscript of the *Lancelot-Grail* is Rennes, BM 255 (Paris or Champagne, *c.* 1220, lacking *La Queste del saint Graal* and *La Mort le roi Artu*). It is highly unusual as it appears to be contemporary with the composition of the two prequels, the *Estoire del saint Graal* and the *Estoire de Merlin*) and may even impose minor redating of the cycle; its sixty-four historiated initials are placed at the beginning of interlace formulae.[9] One hundred and twenty historiated initials illustrate the *Lancelot-Queste-Mort Artu* trilogy in Paris, BnF, fr. 339 (Paris? s. 13[med.]), and three hundred and forty-four, in Paris, BnF, fr. 344 (Metz or Verdun, s. 13[ex.]). Examples of the richly illuminated manuscripts of the *Lancelot-Grail* cycle are New Haven, Yale University, Beinecke 229 (Thérouanne, s. 13[ex.]); New York, Pierpont Morgan Library, M. 805–807 (northeastern France, 1310–1315); and London, BL, Additional 10292–10294 (St Omer or Tournai, *c.* 1316).[10] These more luxurious manuscripts seem to be clustered in northern regions during the late-thirteenth and early-fourteenth centuries, suggesting the interest of wealthy patrons there. Of the three last-mentioned, only the London copy has rubrics, opening up possibilities for study of relationship between image and a further level of verbal discourse. Careful examination of the text(-rubric)-image nexus enables scholars to understand better the planning and execution of manuscripts, as well as the manner in which the romances were perceived by the makers of the books and their readers. Such study may help tell us what aspects of romance were considered important or indispensable at a particular time and place. Does a manuscript stress the spiritual nature of the Grail, for example? Some Grail romance manuscripts seem reluctant to depict it visually at all. Is the Arthurian *merveilleux* highlighted? Are the illustrations text-specific or generic? It seems clear that from the early decades of the thirteenth century onwards, the rise of prose gives a new impetus to the production and dissemination of Arthurian manuscripts. If prose comes to dominate, verse is not eclipsed.

The popularity of Arthurian prose romance among readers in the fifteenth century is clear from the more than two dozen late copies, ten of which are quite lavishly illustrated. We know more about the patrons and owners of these later

---

8 In addition to Kennedy (1980) and Micha (1978–1983), all manuscripts of the *Lancelot-Grail* are listed, with chronology, provenance and other details, at <http://www.lancelot-project.pitt.edu/lancelot-project.html>.

9 On Rennes, BM 255, see Stones (1977).

10 The full Yale manuscript is online at <http://brbl-dl.library.yale.edu>. See also Stones (1996). Paris, BnF, fr. 95 is very closely related.

books, who are almost all to be found in the highest ranks of the aristocracy or public life: the Duc de Berry (Paris, BnF, fr. 117–120), the Duc de Bourgogne (Paris, Ars. 3479–3480), Prigent de Coëtivy, Admiral of France (manuscript now dispersed), Jacques d'Armagnac (Paris, BnF, fr. 112), Ysembert des Rolin, Chancellor of the Duc de Bourgogne (New York, Pierpont-Morgan Library, M. 38), Jean-Louis de Savoie, Bishop of Geneva (Brussels, KBR 9426 and Paris, BnF, fr. 91). Some of the late copies are well produced, but not illuminated (for example, Cologny, Bibliotheca Bodmeriana, Bodmer 105 [Champagne, *c.* 1480]), while others are extravagant in their decoration. Paris, BnF, fr. 112 has two hundred and fifty-eight illustrations, and Paris, BnF, fr. 113–116 (both Central France, *c.* 1475), has two hundred and five illustrations by the same artist as BnF, fr. 112; both were made for Jacques d'Armagnac.[11]

Manuscripts of the Prose *Tristan* show a similar pattern in terms of chronological production and geographical dissemination (the text was composed a couple of decades after the *Lancelot-Grail*). There are many copies with only pen-flourished initials and some with just *champies* or decorated initials. Others have considerable numbers of well-executed historiated initials and *champies*, such as Paris, BnF, fr. 776 (Arras?, *c.* 1285–1290), or Paris, BnF, fr. 334 (Île-de-France, *c.* 1330). Although these are unexceptional, they are carefully made books, of which an owner would have been proud. The same is true of manuscripts like Paris, BnF, nouv. acq. fr. 6579 (Thérouanne, s. 13$^{3/4}$), decorated with small miniatures (rather than historiated initials) and *champies*. The most lavishly illuminated manuscripts of the *Tristan* are generally later ones: Paris, BnF, fr. 335–336 with *champies*, rubrics, and many pen-wash miniatures (Paris, *c.* 1400); Chantilly, Musée Condé 649 and Dijon, BM 527, two parts of the same manuscript probably made for Charles d'Anjou, Comte du Maine (Val-de-Loire, *c.* 1450–1460); Geneva, BPU 189 and Paris, BnF, fr. 102 (Bourges-Tours, *c.* 1470, illuminated by the same artist). The six-volume copy of *Guiron le Courtois*, Paris, BnF, fr. 358–363 (Bruges, *c.* 1480), was made for Louis de Bruges (de Gruuthuse).

One of the most remarkable features of the manuscript transmission of both the *Lancelot-Grail* cycle and the Prose *Tristan* is the copying and dissemination of both texts in Italy from the late-thirteenth through to the fourteenth century.[12] These range from modest copies with rudimentary marginal illustrations to lavishly illuminated books. Of the cycle, or parts of it, Paris, BnF, fr. 773 (Bologna, *c.* 1290) and fr. 767 (Tuscany, *c.* 1300) have only decorated and pen-flourished

---

11 Paris, BnF, fr. 112 has been studied by Pickford (1960).
12 Italian copies of French Arthurian prose are surveyed by Delcorno Branca (1998); fragments are still being discovered.

initials, while three Genoese manuscripts from *c.* 1290 have the typical northern Italian frameless drawings, quickly executed, and coloured: Paris, BnF, fr. 354; fr. 16998; Udine, Bibl. Arcievescovile 64/177.[13] Often, such drawings are found in margins left purposefully wide, and have the identity of the figures added in red. Examples of comparable copies of the Prose *Tristan* are Paris, BnF, fr. 760; Aberystwyth, National Library of Wales, 446E; and Paris, BnF, fr. 1463 of the compilation of Rustichello da Pisa (all Genoa, *c.* 1290).[14] Of the more richly decorated manuscripts, Paris, BnF, fr. 755 of the Prose *Tristan* (Milan, *c.* 1320–1330) is from the Visconti library, while Paris, BnF, fr. 343, of the Post-Vulgate *Queste* and *Mort Artu* (Milan, *c.* 1380), was made for Bernabò Visconti himself; the former looks like an upmarket version of the Genoese manuscripts just mentioned.[15]

Arthurian literature in French lies at the root of that in other vernaculars. It enjoys chronological priority, an expansive corpus and wide transmission and dispersal. The nature of that transmission and reception is conditioned by the social and cultural contexts of the receiving milieus. Much Arthurian romance in Middle High German, Middle Dutch, Middle Welsh, Middle English, the Nordic languages, Spanish, Catalan and Italian, is directly adapted from French texts, while some is original, but still responds to French romance. Textually, the adaptations reflect the tastes and demands of the new audiences, and this is reflected in the nature of their early manuscript transmission. Later manuscripts have much to tell us about the changing reception of the texts across the decades, centuries, miles and vernacular idioms.

The corpus of Middle High German Arthurian verse romance is smaller than that in French: Ulrich von Zatzikhoven's *Lanzelet*, *Erec* and *Iwein* by Hartmann von Aue,[16] Wolfram von Eschenbach's *Parzival* and *Titurel*, the Rappoltsteiner elaboration of *Parzival* (see Stolz, *infra*), Wirnt von Gravenberg's *Wigalois*, Heinrich von dem Türlin's *Diu Crône* (see Kragl, *infra*) and the anonymous *Wigamur*. Der Stricker's *Daniel von dem blühenden Tal* and Der Pleier's response, *Garel von dem blühenden Tal*, lie somewhat out of the mainstream. Generally speaking, *Wigalois*, *Diu Crône* and *Wigamur* are considered *nachklassich* [post-classical] and the approximate equivalent of the Chrétien epigonal romances. What the

---

13 A full study of the Udine manuscript, with reproductions, is Comelli et al. (1990).

14 BnF, fr. 1463 has been reproduced in facsimile by Cigni and Bertolucci Pizzorusso (1994). It should be noted that Rustichello's compilation was written, as well as copied, in Italy. For texts in Italian, see n. 33 below.

15 Much of BnF, fr. 343 is reproduced in colour by Pastoureau and Gousset (2002).

16 Small fragments have also survived of a *Kliges* attributed to Ulrich von Türheim (author of a continuation of Gottfried's *Tristan* and *Rennewart*, a continuation of Wolfram's *Willehalm*). Fragments of other romances are listed by Schiewer (1988).

corpus lacks in texts, it makes up in numbers of manuscripts: five of *Lanzelet*, four of *Erec*, thirty-three of *Iwein*, eighty-seven of *Parzival*, forty-one of *Wigalois*, three of *Wigamur*, five for Der Stricker and two for Der Pleier. Gottfried von Straßburg's non-Arthurian *Tristan* is preserved in thirty copies; I mention it as it belongs to the same cultural milieus as the Arthurian verse texts listed above. These numbers include fragments.[17]

What distinguishes the tradition of Middle High German manuscripts of the Chrétien adaptations from that of the Old French originals is their number and chronological range. When Chrétien moves into the fifteenth century in French, he does so in prose, in Burgundian adaptations of *Erec et Enide* and *Cligès*. And when French Arthurian literature in manuscript moves into the later fourteenth and fifteenth centuries, it does so in the *Vulgate* and *Post-Vulgate Cycles*, and the Prose *Tristan* and derivatives. With the exception of the *Prosa Lancelot* (ten manuscripts and fragments) and the *Lancelot*, prose and strophic, of Ulrich Fuetrer (three fifteenth-century copies of each), there appears to be limited direct influence of the French prose traditions in German-speaking areas, while persistence of the verse tradition of Hartmann and Wolfram is demonstrated by the multiple copies made as late as the early-sixteenth century and the composition of later romances which respond to them. There is also ample evidence from the copying of vernacular manuscripts that *Parzival* and the other romances come to form part of an extended and varied corpus of what could be termed "canonical" Middle High German literature.[18]

The transmission of Hartmann's and Wolfram's romances shares characteristics with that of Chrétien at the same time as it manifests differences. There are single item manuscripts as well as *Sammelhandschriften* (the equivalent of French *recueils*) containing other Arthurian romances alongside miscellaneous items, secular and spiritual. These latter are susceptible, like French codices, of structural and thematic analysis, although they tend to be generally later in date. There are also a small number of illustrated copies of *Parzival*, mainly late, demonstrating reception of the romance in word and image. It is hard to explain the discrepancy between the transmission of *Erec* and *Iwein*, given the relative similarities between the romances. Although there are two mid-thirteenth-

---

17 Manuscripts of Hartmann and Gottfried are among those discussed by Becker (1977), who also plots the geographical and temporal distribution of manuscripts on maps, as does Schiewer (1988).
18 In his *Buch der Abenteuer*, Ulrich Fuetrer also reworks material from *Parzival*, *Diu Crône* and *Wigalois*, among others. The strophic *Lancelot* is incorporated in three of the five copies of the *Buch*.

century fragments of the former, its principal witness, the so-called "Ambraser Heldenbuch", Vienna, ÖNB 2663 (southern Bavaria, s. 16[inc.]) is post-medieval. This splendid manuscript contains numerous other mainly verse narratives, long and short, including *Iwein*, the *Mantel* and the *Nibelungenlied*.[19] Carefully produced and decorated, it has all the appearance of a personal library; it was assembled for Maximilian I of Habsburg and copied by the chancery scribe, Hans Ried. It demonstrates the accumulation and assimilation of a considerable number of Middle High German verse texts into a canon whose links with the aristocracy proved quite tenacious.

The transmission of *Iwein* is another matter entirely, although the paucity of *Erec* manuscripts may be in part a distortion of historical accident. Of the thirty-three copies of *Iwein*, none are illuminated, although most are carefully produced and decorated.[20] Berlin, Staatsbibliothek, mgf 1062 (Bavaria-Austria, *c.* 1300) is a professionally made copy with simple red and blue alternating capitals, containing other texts of quite different types: Der Stricker's proto-*Schelmenroman*, *Pfaffe Amis*; two Dietrich epics; and the lyrics of Neidhart von Reuental. Florence, Biblioteca Nazionale, BR 226 (Bohemia-Bavaria, *c.* 1300) also transmits Gottfried's *Tristan* and Heinrich von Freiberg's continuation, perhaps more expected codicological company. *Iwein* is found together with *Diu Crône* in Vienna, ÖNB 2779 (Bavaria, s. 14[1/4]), but also with works such as the *Kaiserchronik* and the same Dietrich texts as Berlin, mgf 1062. A late *Sammelhandschrift* is Nela-hozeves (Czech Republic), Lobkowitzsche Bibliothek, Cod. VI Fc 26 (II) (Swabia, 1464–1467), where *Iwein* is accompanied by love treatises and a couplet version of *Wilhalm von Orlens*. Most copies of *Iwein*, however, are single-item codices, ranging in date from the second quarter of the thirteenth century through to the early-sixteenth century. Among the earlier examples are Gießen, UB 97 (southern Germany, s. 13[2/4]) and Heidelberg, UB, Cpg 397 (northern Germany, s. 13[2/4]), the latter written not as verse, but continuously with a punctus at the end of each line, a type of *mise en page* quite common in Middle High German manuscripts, but relatively rare in French. Five copies are from the fifteenth century, including Heidelberg, UB, Cpg 316 (Amberg, 1477) and Rostock, UB, Philol. 81 (Tübingen?, *c.* 1477), both unadorned except for red initials. The last datable copy is Lindau, Stadtbibliothek P II 61 (southwestern Germany, 1521). Single item codices of romances of this length are much less frequent in French, raising questions of the circulation and function of the German manuscripts. None of the manu-

---

19 For the transmission of *Erec*, see Edrich-Porzberg (1994). The "Ambraser Heldenbuch" has been reproduced in facsimile by Unterkircher (1973).
20 On the *Iwein* manuscripts, see Okken (1974).

scripts of *Iwein* are illuminated, but there are visual representations of the text in the celebrated wall-paintings in Schloß Rodenegg (southern Tirol, 1200–1230), Schloß Wilhelmsburg, Schmalkalden (Thuringia, s. 13$^{1/2}$), and Schloß Runkelstein (southern Tirol, *c.* 1390). This iconographic tradition may have been derived from now lost manuscripts.[21]

Parzival is a codicological phenomenon. The manuscripts range in date from the first quarter of the thirteenth century (near coeval with the poem's composition) through to the mid-fifteenth century; an early print dates from 1477. Wolfram's transformation and completion of Chrétien's last romance has consequences for its material transmission. At nearly 25,000 lines, it frequently stands on its own in single-item codices, and rarely invites expansion, although Claus Wisse and Philipp Colin more than double the length of the text with additions comprising the *Nüwe Parzefal* (or "Rappoltsteiner" *Parzival*) composed 1331–1336 in Strasbourg for Ulrich von Rappoltstein and intercalated into Wolfram's romance. The earliest witness to the text is the small set of fragments in Munich, Staatsbibliothek 5249/3c (southwest Germany or Switzerland, s. 13$^{1/4}$). Most of the single-item manuscripts are what could be termed "plain texts" (except for decorated initials of various kinds). Examples are Munich, Staatsbibliothek, Cgm 61 (Bavaria, s. 13$^{2/4}$), written as prose, with red capitals only; Vienna, ÖNB 2708 (Zürich?, s. 13$^{4/4}$), red capitals only; and Vienna, ÖNB 2775 (Rheinland-Franconia, s. 14$^{1/4}$), with majuscules of varying size alternating red and blue. The "Rappoltsteiner" addition is found in Karlsruhe, Landesbibliothek, Donaueschingen 97 (Strasbourg, 1331–1336) and Rome, Biblioteca Casanatense 1049 (Alsace, s. 14$^{2/4}$). The only other manuscript in which *Parzival* can be said to have a "continuation" of sorts is Heidelberg, UB, Cpg 364 (eastern Franconia-Bavaria, s. 14$^{2/4}$), where it is followed by *Lohengrin*, the story of the Swan-Knight, Parzival's son. *Parzival* appears early with other texts. In St Gallen, Stiftsbibl. 857 (southern Tirol?, *c.* 1260), it is assembled with the *Nibelungenlied* and the *Klage*, Der Stricker's *Karl der Große*, Wolfram's *Willehalm* and two short religious poems. This demonstrates the tendency towards codicological assimilation of genres, by means of which Arthurian romance becomes suitable company for Germanic epic and Carolingian narrative. Recognition of Wolfram's position as one of the founders of Arthurian romance in German-language areas is attested by *Parzival*'s appearance with *Wigalois* in Schwerin, Landesbibliothek, no call no. (central Germany, *c.* 1435–1440). More varied is the collection of texts in Hamburg, Staats- und Universitätsbibl., Cod. germ. 6 (Rheinland-Franconia, 1451), where *Parzival* is found with *Wigalois* and versions of the Arthurian horn and mantle tales, but also the *exemplum* of "Der

---

21 The iconography of *Yvain-Iwein* has been studied by Rushing (1995).

König im Bade", items relating to the Middle East, the coronation of Friedrich III, the city of Liège and extracts from the chronicle of Eberhard von Windeck.[22]

Parzival enjoys the richest iconographical tradition of all Middle High German romances. The earliest copy is Munich, Staatsbibliothek, Cgm 19 (eastern Alamannia-Bavaria, s. 13[med.]), with an inserted bifolium,[23] each page of which has a large tripartite miniature, the identity of many figures revealed on scrolls (some not completed); the Grail is depicted discreetly and the *merveilleux* is not emphasized. This manuscript is also to some degree an author manuscript as it contains *Titurel* (Wolfram's fragmentary "side-story" to *Parzival*) and his "Tagelieder" (dawn songs). Munich, Staatsbibl., Cgm 18 (Bavaria, s. 13[4/4]) has an opening miniature and spaces for one hundred and three unexecuted double miniatures; the locations of these can tell us much about the reception of the romance towards the end of the thirteenth century. The next illustrated *Parzival* copy in date is Heidelberg, UB, Cpg 339 (Haguenau [Alsace], 1443–1446), from the workshop of Diebold Lauber, with sixty-four coloured pen-drawings and rubrics stressing the more ceremonial aspects of the narrative (arrival, departure, celebration and so on). Dresden, Landesbibl., Mscr. M 66 is contemporary and from the same workshop, with forty-six drawings, as is Vienna, ÖNB 2914, but with only twenty-five drawings.[24] Bern, Burgerbibl. A A 91 (Switzerland, 1467), contains twenty-eight coloured pen-drawings, and belonged to the Bern "Twingherr", Jörg Friburger; its context is therefore urban (the same could be said, somewhat earlier, of the Rappoltsteiner *Parzival*).[25]

Of the post-classical romances, Wirnt von Gravenberg's *Wigalois* is unusually well attested. An early witness is the set of fragments from the same manuscript in Freiburg im Breisgau, UB 445; New Haven, YUL, Beinecke 481/113; and Vienna, ÖNB 14612 (Bavaria-Austria, *c.* 1220–1230). These may date from no more than a decade after the composition of the romance. Most of the single-item codices containing *Wigalois* are paper copies from the fifteenth century, although Stuttgart, Landesbibliothek HB XIII 5 is a little earlier (Swabia, 1360–1370). *Wigalois* is found with *Iwein* in London, BL, Additional 19554 (?, 1468) and *Parzival* in the Schwerin manuscript noted above; its most varied context is the Hamburg

---

22 A listing of *Parzival* manuscripts is given by Klein (2011) and on the Bern *Parzival* website mentioned in the Note included on p. 97 above.

23 This may have been a more common feature, but untraceable as such bifolia were likely detached from the manuscript.

24 Brussels, KBR 10697 of Gottfried's *Tristan*, with ninety-one illustrations, is also from the Lauber workshop. Other, earlier manuscripts of *Tristan* are also illuminated. See Van D'Elden (2016).

25 The illustrated *Parzival* manuscripts (with wall-paintings and tapestry) are discussed by Schirok (2011).

copy likewise mentioned in connection with *Parzival*. Two copies of *Wigalois* are illustrated: Leiden, UB, Ltk. 537 (Thuringia, 1372), copied by the scribe, Jan von Brunswick for Albrecht II of Braunschweig-Grubenhagen, and the former Donaueschingen manuscript (Alsace, *c.* 1420–1430), now in private hands, attributed to a circle connected with the early Diebold Lauber workshop. The planner of the former seems to know the text well and attempts to provide a reasonable guide to the narrative, while the latter tends to use conventional scenes less closely related to the text. *Wigalois* is also a subject in the wall-paintings at Runkelstein. The single complete manuscript of *Wigamur* is Wolfenbüttel, Herzog August Bibliothek 51.2 Aug. 4° (eastern Swabia, s. 15$^{2/2}$) which contains sixty-seven coloured pen drawings typical of its time and place.[26]

The regions in which Middle Dutch was a major literary language (Flanders, Brabant, Holland) is especially interesting for its Dutch-French bilingualism and, in its southern and eastern parts, for the mixed idioms influenced by Middle High German and Low German. A number of Arthurian manuscripts (of both verse and prose romances in French) were produced close to the Dutch-French border areas, and a larger number are known to have circulated there. The very existence of adaptations from Old French into Middle Dutch confirms this, unless all were made by authors resident in regions of medieval Francophonia. The manuscript transmission of Middle Dutch Arthurian literature is nowhere near as rich as that in Old French or Middle High German, but its principal witness is all the more significant. The corpus of Middle Dutch Arthurian romance is modest: a dozen or so texts in verse and only one prose *Lancelot*, surviving in a total of approximately two dozen manuscripts, many of which are fragmentary.[27]

The Hague, Koninklijke Bibliotheek 129 A 10 was produced in Brabant 1320–1330 and copied by five scribes. It appears to be the second of a two-volume manuscript, the first of which is no longer extant. The organized copying represents only the final stage in the planning of the book, in which original Dutch romances and adaptations of French verse texts are integrated into the French *Lancelot-Grail* trilogy of *Lancelot-Queste del saint Graal-Mort le roi Artu*, the French prose being turned into verse. It is possible that the plan of the manuscript and the changes applied to its constituent parts as a means of ensuring a level of coherence were made by Lodewijk van Velthem, also known to have completed Jacob van Maerlant's *Spieghel Historiael* and *Merlijn-Continuatie*. Opinion

---

26 On this manuscript, see Henderson (1989), Busch (2009, 14–15) and Sullivan (2015, XI–XV).
27 On Middle Dutch Arthurian manuscripts in general, with special attention to KB 129 A 10, see Besamusca and Hogenbirk (forthcoming). The corpus of Middle Dutch romance manuscripts is detailed by Kienhorst (1988), and its dating re-examined by Klein (1995).

on Van Velthem's role in the production of KB 129 A 10 is divided: some believe he may only have corrected the work of the scribes who worked on the manuscript. In any event, the association with Van Velthem links the manuscript to the Brabant-Flanders region and is in some ways paradigmatic of the taste for French literature and the desire to turn it, while adapting to different tastes, into Middle Dutch. The transformation of Old French prose into Middle Dutch verse may suggest that Dutch-language readers considered verse a more appropriate medium for Arthurian romance. There are also fragments from four manuscripts of a Middle Dutch adaptation of Chrétien's *Perceval*, confirming the links of the original with Flanders (Kienhorst 1988, I, 164–168; II, 114–117).

Much of Middle English literature is likewise directly or indirectly dependent on Old French, the dependence no doubt enabled in part by the easy circulation of French manuscripts in the islands. Many of these may have been in insular French (Anglo-Norman), but continental manuscripts were owned and read in Britain and Ireland, and likely formed the basis for adaptations into Middle English or provided models for Middle English originals. The corpus of Middle English Arthurian verse romance is not as extensive as that in French, for although there are about twenty, many are very brief and the total number of lines small in comparison. The manuscript tradition is correspondingly modest.[28]

The rise of romance in Middle English has traditionally been associated with the emergence of a merchant class seeking to emulate the aristocracy, but the unique copy of *Sir Gawain and the Green Knight* is difficult to pin down socially. Linguistically, London, BL, Cotton Nero A. X (s. 14[2/2]) can be localized to Cheshire but attempts to associate it with a patron or owners before the early-seventeenth century are problematic. It is certainly not a luxury object, and its unimposing illustrations were added post-production, but it shows the penetration of Arthurian romance in modest social circles in the North-West Midlands. *Sir Gawain* is preceded in the manuscript by three religious and homiletic poems (also in alliterative verse), *Pearl*, *Cleanness* and *Patience*, suggesting a broad interest on the part of the compiler and patron, and opening the poems up to intertextual readings. Attempts to show that more than one of the poems in Cotton Nero A. X are by the "*Gawain*-poet" or the "*Pearl*-poet" are considered inconclusive.[29]

The so-called "Auchinleck manuscript" (Edinburgh, National Library of Scotland, Advocates' 19. 2. 1 and fragments located elsewhere) was copied in London in the 1330s, possibly for a merchant with aristocratic aspirations, although some

---

28 A good survey of the manuscripts of Middle English romance is Evans (1995).
29 An early black and white facsimile is Gollancz (1923). A colour reproduction has recently been published by The Folio Society (Andrew and Waldron 2016).

have suggested it may be a "woman's book" or may have been commissioned by a family with a history in the crusades. Its sole Arthurian romance is *Of Arthour and of Merlin*, but it also contains other romances, such as *The King of Tars*, *Amis and Amiloun*, *Sir Degare*, *The Seven Sages of Rome*, *Floris and Blancheflour*, two versions of *Guy of Warwick*, *Beues of Hamtoun*, *Lay le Freine*, *Roland and Vernagu*, *Otuel*, *Kyng Alisaunder*, *Sir Tristrem*, *Sir Orfeo* and *Horn Child*. This large book (originally of more than 335 folios) also contains saints' lives and other religious narratives, edifying and allegorical poems, and a metrical chronicle. The contents suggest that Arthurian is only one form of romance, and that by this time, the secular and the sacred were compatible codicological company. Despite its professional production and appearance, Auchinleck looks like a personal book, practically a small library.[30]

Sometime between 1330 and 1340, the Yorkshire landowner, Robert Thornton, compiled and copied Lincoln, Lincoln Cathedral 91. It is usually known as the Lincoln Thornton manuscript, to distinguish it from another book copied by Thornton, London, BL, Additional 31042. The London codex contains two Charlemagne romances, *The Sege of Melayne* and *Otuel and Rowland*, in addition to some edifying items, but the Lincoln book contains the unique text of the Alliterative *Morte Arthure*, *The Awntyrs of Arthure at the Terne Wathelyn* and *Sir Percyvell of Galles*. It contains other romances, religious texts and one gathering with medical items. Thornton seems have copied these manuscripts as a kind of private library, but the decorated initials in Lincoln may have been the work of professional illustrators. In any event, the two books are paradigmatic both of the interest in Middle English Arthurian romance on the part of wealthy individuals far from London and of the medieval refusal to separate the sacred from the secular.[31]

The best known Arthurian text in Middle English is doubtless the *Morte Darthur* of Sir Thomas Malory. Its textual transmission is quite well-known due to the discovery in 1934 of the unique Winchester manuscript, now London, BL, Additional 59678 (southern England, before 1485).[32] The manuscript is known to have been in Caxton's London workshop as it bears traces of his type; since Caxton's edition was published in 1485, this gives us the *terminus ad quem* for the manuscript, which formed some of the basis for Caxton's reworking of most of the

---

30 The manuscript has been digitized at <http://auchinleck.nls.uk/>. A print facsimile is Pearsall and Cunningham (1977). Diverse aspects of the manuscript are examined in Fein (2016).
31 For a facsimile of the Lincoln Thornton, see Brewer and Owen (1978). For studies, see Fein and Johnston (2014).
32 Digital facsimile available at <http://www.maloryproject.com> and print by Ker (1976).

Morte. Additional 59678 is a carefully produced but modest manuscript copied by two scribes, with no illuminations, mainly unflourished red majuscules, with proper names of characters in red in the text; there are also marginal annotations in red. The importance of the 1934 discovery and Eugène Vinaver's 1947 edition lie largely in what they can tell us about the differences between the manuscript and Caxton's text, and the working methods of both Malory and Caxton. Neither manuscript nor printed book is illustrated and any received pictorial views of Malory's "canonical" version in the Anglophone world are usually post-medieval.

Manuscripts of Arthurian literature in other languages – Iberian, Italian, Nordic, and Celtic – have reluctantly been left out of consideration here due to space constraints, and each tradition has its own features, characteristic of place and time.[33] Careful examination of all medieval manuscripts, Arthurian and non-Arthurian, irrespective of language, reveals much about their function in the Middle Ages that is concealed by modern critical editions. The purpose of this chapter has been precisely that: to suggest another, medieval, dimension to Arthurian book culture. Arthurian texts and modern translations have not always been easily and cheaply available, neatly printed on white paper, with helpful scholarly apparatus. For most of the medieval period, they were accessible only to the wealthy, and read, sometimes aloud, in forms which required decoding of *mise en texte*, *mise en page* and *mise en livre*. They were not always alone, but often accompanied by a variety of other texts, comprising a considerable literary corpus linked socially, intertextually and codicologically. The reality of the medieval Arthurian manuscript is of an imperfect, sometimes modest and sometimes luxurious, book, written on animal skin and produced by groups of fallible artisans for individuals with specific requirements and tastes.

---

33 Manuscripts and early prints of Castilian, Catalan, Portuguese and Galician-Portuguese romance (all derived from the French prose traditions) are surveyed by Lucía Megías (2015). On Italian-language manuscripts of texts derived from the French prose *Tristan*, see Heijkant (2014) on the *Tavola Ritonda* and its manuscripts, Delcorno Branca (2014) and on the recent discovery of a Tuscan *Lancelot*, Cadioli (2014). For manuscripts of the Old Norse adaptations of Chrétien, transmitted in late Icelandic copies, see Kalinke (2011) and Bornholdt (2011). The principal Middle Welsh manuscripts, including those containing Arthurian texts, are surveyed in various contributions by Huws (2000). The White Book of Rhydderch (Aberystwyth, National Library of Wales, Peniarth 4–5) is online at <https://www.llgc.org.uk/discover/digital-gallery/manuscripts/the-middle-ages/white-book-of-rhydderch/>, and the Red Book of Hergest (Oxford, Bodleian Library, Jesus College 111), at <http://image.ox.ac.uk/show?collection=jesus&manuscript=ms111>.

References

Andrew, Malcolm, and Ronald Waldron, ed. and trans. *The Pearl Manuscript*. London: The Folio Society, 2016.

Becker, Peter Jörg. *Handschriften und Frühdrucke mittelhochdeutscher Epen*. Wiesbaden: Reichert, 1977.

Besamusca, Bart, and Marjolein Hogenbirk. "Manuscript The Hague, Royal Library, 129 A 10: An Ambivalent and Highly Enigmatic Cycle." (forthcoming).

Bornholdt, Claudia. "The Old Norse-Icelandic Transmission of Chrétien de Troyes's Romances: *Ívens saga*, *Erex saga*, *Parcevals saga* with *Valvens þáttr*." *The Arthur of the North: The Arthurian Legend in the Norse and Rus' Realms*. Ed. Marianne E. Kalinke. Cardiff: University of Wales Press, 2011. 98–122.

Brewer, Derek S., and A.E.B. Owen. *The Thornton Manuscript (Lincoln Cathedral MS. 91)*. London: The Scolar Press, 1977.

Busby, Keith. *Codex and Context: Reading Old French Verse Narrative in Manuscript*. 2 vols. Amsterdam: Rodopi, 2002.

Busby, Keith, Terry Nixon, Alison Stones and Lori J. Walters, eds. *Les manuscrits de Chrétien de Troyes/The Manuscripts of Chrétien de Troyes*, 2 vols. Amsterdam: Rodopi, 1993.

Busch, Nathanael, ed. *Wigamur: Kritische Edition, Übersetzung, Kommentar*. Berlin: De Gruyter, 2009.

Cadioli, Luca. "A New Arthurian Text: The Tuscan Translation of the *Lancelot en prose*." *Journal of the International Arthurian Society* 2 (2014): 63–69.

Cigni, Fabrizio, and Valeria Bertolucci Pizzorusso. *Il romanzo arturiano di Rustichello da Pisa*. Ospadaletto: Pacini Editore, 1994.

Comelli, Antonio, et al., eds. *La grant Queste del Saint Graal (La grande Ricerca del Santo Graal). Versione indeita della fine del XIII secolo del ms. Udine, Biblioteca Arcivescovile, 177*. Udine: Roberto Vattore Editore, 1990.

Delcorno Branca, Daniela. "The Italian Contribution: *La Tavola Ritonda*." *The Arthur of the Italians: The Arthurian Legend in Medieval Italian Literature and Culture*. Ed. Gloria Allaire and F. Regina Psaki. Cardiff: University of Wales Press, 2014. 69–87.

Delcorno Branca, Daniela. *Tristano e Lancilotto in Italia. Studi di letteratura arturiana*. Ravenna: Longo Editore, 1998.

Edrich-Porzberg, Brigitte. *Studien zur Überlieferung und Rezeption von Hartmanns* Erec. Göppingen: Kümmerle, 1994.

Evans, Murray J. *Rereading Middle English Romance. Manuscript Layout, Decoration, and the Rhetoric of Composite Structure*. Montreal and Kingston: McGill-Queen's University Press, 1995.

Fein, Susanna, ed. *The Auchinleck Manuscript: New Perspectives*. Woodbridge: Boydell and Brewer, 2016.

Fein, Susanna, and Michael Johnston, eds. *Robert Thornton and His Books: Essays on the Lincoln and London Thornton Manuscripts*. Woodbridge: Boydell and Brewer, 2014.

Gollancz, Israel. *Pearl, Cleanness, Patience and Sir Gawain, Reproduced in Facsimile from the Unique Ms Cotton Nero Ax in the British Museum*. Oxford: Oxford University Press, 1923.

Heijkant, Marie-José. "From France to Italy: The Tristan Texts." *The Arthur of the Italians: The Arthurian Legend in Medieval Italian Literature and Culture*. Ed. Gloria Allaire and F. Regina Psaki. Cardiff: University of Wales Press, 2014. 41–68.

Henderson, Ingeborg. "Illustrationsprogramm und Text der Wolfenbütteler *Wigamur*-Handschrift." *"In hôhem prîse": A Festschrift in Honor of Ernst S. Dick, Presented on the Occasion of his 60th Birthday, April 7, 1989*. Ed. Winder McConnell. Göppingen: Kümmerle, 1989. 163–181.

Huws, Daniel. *Medieval Welsh Manuscripts*. Cardiff: University of Wales Press, 2000.

Kalinke, Marianne E. "Sources, Translations, Redactions, Manuscript Transmission." *The Arthur of the North: The Arthurian Legend in the Norse and Rus' Realms*. Ed. Marianne E. Kalinke. Cardiff: University of Wales Press, 2011. 22–47.

Kennedy, Elspeth, ed. *Lancelot do Lac: The Non-Cyclic Old French Prose Romance*. 2 vols. Oxford: Oxford University Press, 1980.

Ker, N.R. *The Winchester Malory: A Facsimile*. Oxford: Oxford University Press, 1976.

Kienhorst, Hans. *De handschriften van de middelnederlandse ridderepik. Een codicologische beschrijving*. 2 vols, Deventer: Sub Rosa, 1988.

Klein, Jan Willem. "'Het getal zijner jaren is onnaspeurlijk': een herrijking van de dateringen van de handschriften en fragmenten met Middelnederlandse ridderepiek." *Tijdschrift voor Nederlandse Taal- en Letterkunde* 111 (1995): 1–23.

Klein, Klaus. "Beschreibendes Verzeichnis der Handschriften (Wolfram und Wolfram-Fortsetzer)." *Wolfram von Eschenbach. Ein Handbuch*. Ed. Joachim Heinzle. 2 vols. Berlin/Boston: De Gruyter, 2011. II, 941–1002.

Lucía Megías, José Manuel. "The Surviving Peninsular Arthurian Witnesses: A Description and an Analysis." *The Arthur of the Iberians: The Arthurian Legends in the Spanish and Portuguese Worlds*. Ed. David Hook. Cardiff: University of Wales Press, 2015. 33–57.

Micha, Alexandre, ed. *Lancelot: roman en prose du XIIIe siècle*. 9 vols. Geneva: Droz, 1978–1983.

Micha, Alexandre. "La tradition manuscrite du *Lancelot en prose*." *Romania* 85 (1964): 293–318 and 478–517.

Micha, Alexandre. "Les manuscrits du *Lancelot en prose*." *Romania* 84 (1963): 28–60 and 478–499.

Micha, Alexandre. "Les manuscrits du *Lancelot en prose*." *Romania* 81 (1960): 145–187.

Middleton, Roger. "The Manuscripts." *The Arthur of the French: The Arthurian Legend in Medieval French and Occitan Literature*. Ed. Glyn S. Burgess and Karen Pratt. Cardiff: University of Wales Press, 2006. 8–92.

Okken, Lambertus. *Hartmann von Aue, Iwein: Ausgewählte Abbildungen und Materialien zur Handschriftlichen Überlieferung*. Göppingen: Kümmerle, 1974.

Pastoureau, Michel, and Marie-Thérèse Gousset. *Lancelot du Lac et la quête du Graal*. Arcueil: Éditions Anthèse, 2002.

Pearsall, Derek, and I.C. Cunningham. *The Auchinleck Manuscript: National Library of Scotland, Advocates' MS. 19.2.1*. London: The Scolar Press, 1977.

Pickford, Cedric. *L'évolution du roman arthurien en prose vers la fin du Moyen Age, d'après le manuscrit 112 du fonds français de la Bibliothèque nationale*. Paris: Nizet, 1960.

Rouse, Mary A., and Richard H. Rouse. *Manuscripts and their Makers. Commercial Book Producers in Medieval Paris, 1200–1500*. 2 vols. London: Harvey Miller, 2000.

Rushing, James A. *Images of Adventure: Ywain in the Visual Arts*. Philadelphia, PA: University of Pennsylvania Press, 1995.

Schiewer, Hans-Jochen. "'Ein ris ich dar vmbe abe brach / Von sinem wunder bovme.' Beobachtungen zur Überlieferung des nachklassischen Artusromans im 13. und

14. Jahrhundert." *Deutsche Handschriften 1100–1400. Oxforder Kolloquium 1985*. Ed. Volker Honemann and Nigel F. Palmer. Tübingen: Niemeyer, 1988. 222–278.

Schirok, Bernd. "Die Bilderhandschriften und Bildzeugnisse." *Wolfram von Eschenbach. Ein Handbuch*. Ed. Joachim Heinzle. 2 vols. Berlin/Boston: De Gruyter, 2011. I, 335–365, and II, 1389–1400.

Stones, Alison. "The Illustrations in BN fr 95 and Yale 229, Prolegomena to a Comparative Study." *Word and Image in Arthurian Romance*. Ed. Keith Busby. New York: Garland, 1996. 206–283.

Stones, Alison. "The Earliest Illustrated *Prose Lancelot* Manuscript?" *Reading Medieval Studies* 3 (1977): 3–44.

Sullivan, Joseph, ed. and trans. *Wigamur*. Woodbridge: Boydell and Brewer, 2015.

Unterkircher, Franz. *Ambraser Heldenbuch. Vollständige Faksimile-Ausgabe im Originalformat des Codex Vindobonensis Series Nova 2663 der Österreichischen Nationalbibliothek*. 2 vols. Graz: Akademische Druck- u. Verlagsanstalt, 1973.

Van D'Elden, Stephanie Cain. *Tristan and Isolde: Medieval Illustrations of the Verse Romances*. Turnhout: Brepols, 2016.

Walters, Lori J. "The Formation of a Gauvain Cycle in Chantilly Manuscript 472." *Neophilologus* 78 (1994): 29–43.

Walters, Lori J. "Le rôle du scribe dans l'organisation des manuscrits des romans de Chrétien de Troyes." *Romania* 106 (1985): 303–325.

Reference Works and Websites

Bibliographical Bulletin of the International Arthurian Society, from 2011, *Bibliography of the International Arthurian Society*

The Auchinleck Manuscript, National Library of Scotland: <http://auchinleck.nls.uk>

Digitized Manuscripts, British Library <http://www.bl.uk/manuscripts>

Beinecke Rare Book and Manuscript Library <http://brbl-dl.library.yale.edu>

e-codices: Virtual Manuscript Library of Switzerland <http://www.e-codices.unifr.ch>

Medieval Manuscripts on the Web <http://faculty.arts.ubc.ca/sechard/512digms.htm>

Gallica, Bibliothèque nationale de France <http://gallica.bnf.fr>

Handschriftencensus <http://www.handschriftencensus.de>

Oxford, Bodleian Library, Jesus College 111 online <http://image.ox.ac.uk/show?collection=jesus&manuscript=ms111>

Jonas, Institut de Recherche et d'Histoire des Textes <http://jonas.irht.cnrs.fr>

Lancelot-Graal Project <http://www.lancelot-project.pitt.edu/lancelot-project.html>

The White Book of Rhydderch, National Library of Wales <https://www.llgc.org.uk/discover/digital-gallery/manuscripts/the-middle-ages/white-book-of-rhydderch>

The Malory Project <http://www.maloryproject.com>

Mandragore, Bibliothèque nationale de France <http://mandragore.bnf.fr/html/accueil.html>

Parzifal-Projekt <http://www.parzival.unibe.ch/hsverz.html>

Bart Besamusca
Readership and Audience

Around 1170, Chrétien de Troyes wrote *Erec et Enide*, which "marks a new departure in medieval vernacular narrative" for being the first Arthurian romance (Maddox and Sturm-Maddox 2005, 103). His famous prologue to the text includes the following statement:

> d'Erec, le fil Lac, est li contes,
> que devant rois et devant contes
> depecier et corronpre suelent
> cil qui de conter vivre vuelent. (Chrétien de Troyes 1990, ll. 19–22)
> [This is the tale of Erec, son of Lac, which those who try to live by storytelling customarily mangle and corrupt before kings and counts. (Chrétien de Troyes 1991, 37)]

Chrétien comments here on the dissemination of Erec's story, and he defines the audience of the Arthurian tale in rather specific terms. His remarks will provide the springboard for this chapter's discussion of the subjects of readership and audience.

By referring to professional story-tellers who fail to tell a tale correctly, Chrétien concludes a line of reasoning which he began by stating that a man ought to make use of his "estuide" (ll. 4 and 6) [learning], and that Chrétien's "escïence" (l. 17) [knowledge] enabled him to create a "molt bele conjointure" (l. 14) [very beautiful composition] out of a "conte d'aventure" (l. 13) [tale of adventure]. Since for him literacy is the prerequisite for learning and knowledge, he is indicating how his story came into being. *Erec et Enide* was created at the time of composition, pen in hand. This way of composing a narrative has resulted in a story that will be appreciated as long as Christianity lasts (ll. 24–26), as it is well structured instead of mutilated and corrupted (or: fragmented and incomplete[1]). The implication seems to be that professional story-tellers are deemed to fall short because their tales are orally composed.

The circulation of both oral and written versions of stories is confirmed by Chrétien's contemporaries. In his *Tristan*, Thomas comments on the many variants of the story of Tristan, and motivates his choice for the Tristan version as

---

1 For these translations of "depecier" and "corronpre" by Douglas Kelly, see Burgess and Pratt (2006, 157).

Bart Besamusca (Utrecht University)

DOI 10.1515/9783110432466-008

told by "Breri", whom scholars have identified as the Welsh nobleman Bleddri ap Cadifor (Gallais 2014 [1965]; Boyd 2014). Thomas states that he heard the story told by professional story-tellers many times, and adds: "Asez sai que chescun en dit/ E ço qu'il unt mis en escrit" (Lacy 1998, 102, ll. 2114–2115) [I am well acquainted with the story each has told and with those consigned to writing (Lacy 1998, 103)]. Likewise, Marie de France notes at the beginning of her lay, *Chèvrefeuille*, that the story was often told to her ("Plusor le m'ont conté et dit", Lacy 1998, 188, l. 5) and that she is aware of written versions of the Tristan story ("et je l'ai trové en escrit/ de Tristan et de la roïne", Lacy 1998, 188, ll. 6–7)

The co-existence of oral and written versions of stories may have prompted Chrétien to promote his written composition of the tale of Erec, son of Lac. His point of view was shared by many authors, French and non-French, through-out the Middle Ages. Ample evidence of this feature of the genre of Arthurian romance is provided by the large amount of long verse romances and the enor-mous prose romances that came into being in the various linguistic areas of me-dieval Europe.[2] Their length defies oral composition (but does not exclude aural reception, of course). Other indications of the bookishness of Arthurian romances are the many references to reception situations involving a manuscript. Accord-ing to Denis Piramus in his *La vie de seint Edmund* (c. 1170), for example, the lays of "Dame Mari" (Ravenel 1906, l. 35), Marie de France, were favoured by counts, barons and knights ("cunte, barun et chivaler", l. 42), and in particular by ladies (l. 46): "E si en aiment mult lescrit,/ E lire le funt" (ll. 43–44) [And they loved the writing very much and had it read aloud]. The final lines of the thirteenth-century Welsh *Breuddwyd Rhonabwy* [the Dream of Rhonabwy] stress, albeit ironically perhaps, that the story cannot be recited without the use of a book, due to the number of colours on the horses, arms, trappings, mantles and magic stones (Bromwich et al. 1991, 183). A curious example of recitation from a manuscript is given by Jean Froissart. In his *Chroniques* and *Dit dou Florin*, he relates that in late 1388, when visiting Gaston Fébus, Count of Foix-Béarn, he pleased his host by reading aloud his *Roman de Meliador* over a period of ten weeks, seven folios per night (Burgess and Pratt 2006, 490–491).

The interest of an aristocrat like Gaston Fébus in Arthurian material corrob-orates Chrétien's statement in his prologue to *Erec et Enide* that the story of Erec was told before kings and counts. As will be shown below, his indication of the elite audience of the Arthurian tale remained valid for all parts of Europe for four centuries, from the middle of the twelfth century until the mid-sixteenth century. We will see that in many linguistic areas aristocrats promoted the production of

---

2 For an overview, see the Arthurian Fiction database <http://www.arthurianfiction.org>.

Arthurian romances by acting as patrons of medieval authors and by commissioning manuscripts in which Arthurian texts were copied. The audiences of these romances and books doubtless included the entourages of these patrons and commissioners. We will also see that authors made use of the popularity and the cultural prestige of Arthurian literature to attract aristocratic attention. By dedicating romances to members of the nobility, these writers tried to gain the support of a patron. The popularity and the prestige of the Arthurian genre additionally meant that Arthurian manuscripts, sometimes lavishly illustrated, were present in many aristocratic libraries.

I will start with a discussion of patrons and dedicatees, and continue with a section on commissioners, readers and owners of manuscripts. The order of both sections is loosely chronological. In the conclusion, I will evaluate the persuasiveness of the presented evidence, which is without exception based on explicit references to patrons, dedicatees, commissioners, owners and readers. Conjectural evidence, like the claim that the Red Book of Hergest (Oxford, Bodleian Library, Jesus College 111) was made for the nobleman Hopcyn ap Thomas because it contains praise poems addressed to him and his son (Bromwich et al. 1991, 10–11), has not been taken into account. The data, in first instance, was drawn from the Arthurian Fiction database and the eight volumes of the series "Arthurian Literature in the Middle Ages".[3]

1 Patrons and dedicatees of Arthurian romances

In the essay in which Stephen Jaeger (1996, 46) refreshingly argued that "patrons did not make courtly romance; courtly romance made patrons", he proposed "a guideline for determining the importance of patronage and the role of patron," which is: "[i]f no patron is mentioned, then none exists." (47)[4] Since nothing is known about the patronage of *Erec et Enide*, we should assume, following Jaeger, that Chrétien's romance came into being without a patron in the background. Probably less than a decade after the writing of *Erec et Enide*, somewhere between 1177 and 1181, the French author found an extremely powerful and well-educated

---

3 See <www.arthurianfiction.org>, and Bromwich et al. (1991): *The Arthur of the Welsh*, Barron (1999): *The Arthur of the English*, Jackson and Ranawake (2000): *The Arthur of the Germans*, Burgess and Pratt (2006): *The Arthur of the French*, Kalinke (2011): *The Arthur of the North*, Echard (2011): *The Arthur of Medieval Latin Literature*, Allaire and Psaki (2014): *The Arthur of the Italians* and Hook (2015): *The Arthur of the Iberians*.
4 Bumke (1979) is particularly ground-breaking on patronage.

patron: Marie de Champagne, daughter of Louis VII, King of France, and his first wife, Eleanor of Aquitaine (McCash 2005). Marie, who was born in 1145, married in 1159 and died in 1198, is the exclusive subject of Chrétien's prologue to his *Lancelot*, which he entitles the *Chevalier de la charrette* (Chrétien de Troyes 1984, l. 24). He playfully flatters her, states that he is obeying her wish that he should begin a romance ("vialt que romans a feire anpraigne", l. 2), and acknowledges her role in the genesis of his story – she provided him with the "matiere et san" (l. 26) [matter and meaning], while he did nothing but add "sa painne et s'antancïon" (l. 29) [effort and intention].[5] Scholars have long held the view that Chrétien disliked the romance's subject, that is, the adulterous relationship between Lancelot and Arthur's wife Guinevere, and did not finish the story for that reason – Godefroi de Leigni completed the text, with Chrétien's permission, so he states (l. 7106). More recently, however, it has been suggested that Marie withdrew her support as a consequence of the untimely death of her husband in 1181 (McCash 2005, 22–23).

Perhaps as a result of his fame as a writer of Arthurian romances, Chrétien found a second patron, who was also a member of the high nobility. Philippe d'Alsace, who was Count of Flanders from 1168 to 1191, asked Chrétien to write *Perceval*, which is entitled the "Contes del Graal" in the text's prologue (Chrétien de Troyes 1959, l. 66). In the introductory lines of this unfinished romance, Philippe is excessively praised for his worthiness (he is said to surpasses Alexander the Great) and his generosity (for he gives "sanz ypocrisie et sanz gile" (l. 30) [without hypocrisy or deceit]). Chrétien started to write the greatest story ever told in a royal court (ll. 63–65) "par le comandement le conte" (l. 64) [by the order of the count], who provided the author with his source text: "li quens li bailla le livre" (l. 67) [the count gave him the book]. The count's death in 1191 may well explain the incompleteness of *Perceval*, albeit that around 1230 one of the continuators, Gerbert de Montreuil, claimed that Chrétien died before he was able to finish his work (Burgess and Pratt 2006, 136). It might be that another continuator, Manessier, guessed that a later Flemish ruler would be interested in the patronage of her grandfather. Writing around 1230, Manessier dedicated his romance, which concludes the story of Perceval, to Jeanne, Countess of Flanders between 1205 and 1244. In his epilogue, the author reminds her of Philippe's patronage (Manessier 2004, l. 42653), praises her many virtues and states that inspired by her shining example he was able to finish his text ("Et por ce que tant ai apris/ De ses bonnes meurs a delivre,/ Ai en son non finé mon livre", ll. 42650–42653).

Other twelfth-century French authors were, like Chrétien, engaged in the search for a patron. Wace is an interesting case. In 1155, this Norman cleric

---

5 I follow Douglas Kelly's interpretation of the French terms (Burgess and Pratt 2006, 152).

completed a fifteen-thousand lines long French verse translation of Geoffrey of Monmouth's *Historia regum Britanniae*, presumably under the patronage of King Henry II of England, who granted the author a prebend at the Norman cathedral chapter of Bayeux (Barron 1999, 18; Burgess and Pratt 2006, 96). But Wace does not mention a patron in his *Roman de Brut*. The only piece of evidence we have is provided by the English author Layamon, who translated Wace's chronicle somewhere between 1185 and 1225 (Barron 1999, 22–23). In his prologue, he states that Wace had a copy of his book presented to Henry's wife, Eleanor of Aquitaine (the mother of Marie de Champagne) (Layamon 1995, ll. 22–23). It is conceivable, therefore, that Wace did not mention Henry in his *Roman de Brut* because he wrote the text on his own initiative, and not at the king's request, and was rewarded for it afterwards.

Another intriguing instance of twelfth-century patronage is offered by Gautier d'Arras, who wrote *Ille et Galeron* around 1170. The romance has come down to us in a long and a short version, both probably composed by Gautier (Burgess and Pratt 2006, 398–399). The long version of the text is dedicated to "la bone Beatris,/ Qui est de Rome empereris" (Gautier d'Arras 1956, ll. 5808–5809) [the good Beatrice, who is empress of Rome], the wife of Frederick Barbarossa, Empress Beatrice of Burgundy, who is extensively praised in the prologue. The short version, which is most likely a revision of the long version, adds a second addressee, "le bon cont Tiebaut" (l. 5812), that is Thibaut V, Count of Blois. This addition suggests that Gautier composed the second version of his romance in an attempt to please another aristocrat (Burgess and Pratt 2006, 398).

Royal patronage is strikingly present in thirteenth-century Norway. King Hákon Hákonarson, who reigned between 1217 and 1263, cultivated contacts with outlandish royal courts, in particular that of King Henry III of England, and extensively promoted the translation of French literature in Old Norse (Kalinke 2011, 9–16). The *Tristan* by Thomas of Britain seems to be the first French romance that was introduced in Norway. In 1226, Brother Robert finished the prose text, *Tristrams saga ok Ísöndar*, which was commissioned by the king, according to the prologue: "Var þá liðit frá hingatburði Christi 1226 ár, er þessi saga var á norrænu skrifuð eptir befalningu ok skipan virðuligs herra Hákonar kóngs." [This saga was translated into the Norse tongue at the behest and decree of King Hákon when 1226 years had passed since the birth of Christ.][6] This statement leaves no doubt that King Hákon was a very involved patron.

---

6 Kalinke (1999), I, 28–29 (*Tristrams saga* is edited and translated in this edition by Peter Jorgensen).

Other French romances which came to Norway included three of Chrétien's texts, *Erec et Enide*, *Yvain* and *Perceval*. Only one of them, *Ívens saga*, mentions in its concluding sentence that Hákon ordered the translation (Kalinke 1999, II, 98). This acknowledgement of the king's patronage is repeated in the prologue of *Möttuls saga* (Kalinke 1999, II, 6), which is a translation of the fabliau, *Le Lai du cort mantel*, and in the prologue to the *Strengleikar*, a collection of translated French lays (Kalinke 2011, 11). The author of *Möttuls saga* is the sole translator who comments on Hákon's motivation for requesting the texts. He reveals that the king wanted to provide "gaman" (Kalinke 1999, II, 6) [entertainment] for his courtiers.

Half a century after the death of Hákon Hákonarson, royal patronage in the north of Europe again involved Chrétien's *Yvain*. The author of *Herr Ivan* informs us in the text's epilogue that Queen Eufemia, the wife of Hákon's grandson Hákon Magnússon, ordered him to translate the French romance (Kalinke 1999, III, 298; cf. Lodén, *infra*). *Herr Ivan*, completed in 1303, is a Swedish verse text, which seems to have served a political goal. Scholars assume that the queen requested the translation on the occasion of the betrothal of her daughter, Ingiborg, to the Swedish duke, Erik, brother of the King of Sweden (Kalinke 1999, III, 3).

Like Hartmann von Aue and Wolfram von Eschenbach, the third giant of early German narrative literature, Gottfried von Straßburg, is silent about an alleged patron for his *Tristan*, though the poet may have had planned to mention one, but he did not finish the work. There is irrefutable evidence that people in the high echelons of the German-speaking society were attracted by Gottfried's love story (Rasmussen 2000, 193–194). One of his continuators, Ulrich von Türheim, was probably a ministerial and certainly a productive author – as well as his *Tristan*, he wrote *Rennewart* and a *Cligès* narrative (Jackson and Ranawake 2000, 126). In the prologue to his *Tristan*, which can be dated to around 1240, Ulrich starts by regretting the death of Gottfried, who was "ein kunstricher man" (Ulrich von Türheim 1992, l. 8) [a great artist], as is shown by both the style and the composition of his story (ll. 9–14). Then Ulrich announces his intention to complete the narrative, and states that he acts at the urgent request of the imperial minister Konrad von Winterstetten, who has "mit vlize mich gebeten" (l. 25) [insistently asked me] to do so "im ze liebe" (l. 27) [out of love for him]. Ulrich's extensive praise of his patron's generosity (ll. 33–39) makes us suspect that Ulrich's intentions were not solely artistic.

Half a century later, around 1290, a second *Tristan* continuator was active at the renowned Prague court of Wenceslas II of Bohemia (Jackson and Ranawake 2000, 129). Like Ulrich, this poet, Heinrich von Freiberg, honours Gottfried in the opening lines of his prologue, characterizing his predecessor's work as "meisterlich" (Heinrich von Freiburg 1993, ll. 14 and 18) [masterly]. He then explains that his own writing is inspired by the virtue of a nobleman ("eines herren tugent", l. 55), and reveals his name: Raymond von Lichtenburg (ll. 74–77). The exact role of this powerful aristocrat (Bumke 1991, 486–487) in the genesis of Heinrich's text is, however, not clear due to the poet's phrasing. He writes: "In Behemlant ist er geborn,/ dem ich diz senecliche mer/ mit innecliches herzen ger/ vol tichten und vol bringen sol" (Ulrich von Türheim 1993, ll. 62–65) [he for whom I have to dedicatedly finish the writing of this sorrowful story is born in Bohemia]. This statement may indicate that Raymond was Heinrich's patron, but we cannot rule out the possibility that the poet intended to dedicate his text to the nobleman.

This uncertainty is absent in the case of Girart d'Amiens who, around 1280, wrote one of the last French Arthurian romances in verse, *Escanor*. The genesis of this narrative, which features a remarkably heroic seneschal, Kay (Burgess and Pratt 2006, 442), involved royal patronage, according to Girart's prologue and epilogue. Right at the beginning of *Escanor*, he states that he is obeying a noble, beautiful and wise lady (Girart d'Amiens 1994, ll. 8–9), who is "la pluz vaillant roïne/ Qui onques fust d'Espaigne nee" (ll. 24–25) [the most worthy queen ever born in Spain] and wife of the renowned King of England (ll. 29–33). In the text's epilogue, Girart begs God to protect from dishonour those "Qui ce romant escouteront/ Et qui escrire le feront" (ll. 25913–25914) [who listened to this romance and who had it written], in particular the Queen of England (ll. 25915–25916). This noble lady is Eleanor of Castile, who was married to Edward I, became queen in 1274 and died in 1290 (Burgess and Pratt 2006, 440). In the next section of this chapter, we will see that Edward can be connected to another Arthurian author, Rustichello da Pisa.

Various examples of thirteenth-century authors who dedicate their Arthurian romances to high aristocrats point to the continued appeal of these texts for the upper class of medieval society. The Flemish poet Jacob van Maerlant, for instance, adapted French prose versions of Robert de Boron's *Joseph d'Arimathie* and *Merlin* around 1261 (Jackson and Ranawake 2000, 191–192). In the prologue to his *Graal-Merlijn*, he cleverly relates the high status of the addressee, Albrecht van Voorne, viscount of Zealand, to the contents of the Middle Dutch text: "Desse historie van den grale/ Dichte ick to eren hern alabrechte/ Den heer van vorne wal myt rechte/ want hoge lude myt hoger historie/ Manichfolden zuken er glorie/ Vnde korten dar mede er tijt." (Jacob van Maerlant 1980, ll. 14–19) [I composed this story of the Grail in the honour of Lord Albrecht, the rightful lord of Voorne, because high-placed persons are often in search of honour by means of their important history, and amuse themselves in this way.]

Around the same time, the Occitan poet who composed *Jaufre* tried to attract princely attention by claiming that he heard the story told "en la cort del plus onrat rei / Qe anc fos de neguna lei" (Brunel 1943, ll. 59–60) [at the court of the most honored king who ever followed any faith (Arthur 1992, 4)]. He goes on to flatter this King of Aragon at length (Brunel 1943, ll. 61 and 62–84), who is identified as Jaume I (Hook 2015, 166). Of interest in this context is the case of the German poet Albrecht, who wrote the *Jüngerer Titurel* around 1275. Scholars have argued that Albrecht dedicated his text to Ludwig II of Bavaria, that is Ludwig the Severe (Bumke 1991, 392), in order to gain a new patron after having being abandoned by his original supporters, as the poet laments (Jackson and Ranawake 2000, 76).

An intriguing case of German patronage dates from the fourteenth century. Here we encounter the rare example of an aristocrat who is not supporting a single author, but what looks like an authorial collective (Dietl 2013, 36). The so-called Rappoltsteiner *Parzival*, which came into being between 1331 and 1336, is named after the nobleman who requested the translation of the French *Perceval* Continuations and the *Élucidation*, according to the epilogue (Schorbach 1888, 846.17–23). Ulrich von Rappoltstein, who was a member of a rich and powerful aristocratic family (Jackson and Ranawake 2000, 167–168, 170–172), supported a team of three authors consisting of two goldsmiths from Strasbourg, Phillip Colin (Schorbach 1888, 846.21) and Claus Wisse (854.7), as well as Samson Pine (854.27), their Jewish co-worker who participated in translating the French text (854.26–36).

After the middle of the fourteenth century, the interest of authors in composing Arthurian romances diminished everywhere in Europe, with the notable exception of England (Cooper 2003). There, we finally come across an example of non-noble interest in Arthurian literature. Around 1430, Henry Lovelich made two English verse translations of the French *Estoire del saint Graal* and *Estoire de Merlin* (Cooper 2003, 151). He was a London skinner, who produced the text "at þe instance of harry barton", according to a marginal note in the unique copy of Lovelich's text (Barron 1999, 78). Since Harry (Henry) Barton was, like Lovelich, a member of the Company of Skinners, his request is a clear indication of mercantile interest in Arthurian literature. It should be noted, however, that Barton belonged to the London elite. This is demonstrated by the fact that he served the city twice as Lord Mayor (Ackerman 1952, 476).

The late Middle Ages still witnessed high-placed nobles supporting authors of Arthurian romances. In the last quarter of the fifteenth century, for example, the Munich painter and author Ulrich Fuetrer combined various Grail and Arthurian romances in his huge, strophic *Buch der Abenteuer* (Jackson and Ranawake 2000, 173). In a number of passages the narrator, aptly called Ulrich, praises the aristocrat whose name is revealed by an acrostic right at the beginning of the text: Albrecht IV, Duke of Upper Bavaria. Fuetrer's narrator claims that he would have given up the writing, were it not for his wish to fulfil the duke's request (Bastert 1993, 146–149).

Even royal interest in the patronage of Arthurian literature is documented for this late period. Decades after the invention of printing, Pierre Sala, who worked as an important administrator at the court of France, wrote two Arthurian romances, *Yvain* (around 1522) and *Tristan* (around 1527) (Taylor 2014, 11–37). Although Sala's *Tristan* is in prose, the text starts with a short verse prologue, in which the author addresses his patron. He states that he is writing at the order of a gentleman (Sala 1958, ll. 1–2) who gave him a "vieil Tristan" [old Tristan], quite indecipherably copied in a rather damaged manuscript (ll. 5–8), as his source. At the end of the prologue, he identifies himself as "Vostre Sala, tres humble en vostre chambre" (l. 21) [Your Sala, very modest at your court]. This statement indicates that Sala's patron was none other than François I, King of France (Burgess and Pratt 2006, 546). We will return to Sala, who was both an author and a bibliophile, in the next section.

2 Commissioners, readers and owners of Arthurian manuscripts

Whereas the claim that someone acted as the patron of an Arthurian romance is very often impossible to verify – we will return to this issue at the end of this chapter – and whereas it is unfeasible to find out whether an author successfully dedicated his text to a person (that is, if he or she was rewarded for it, in some way or another), we are on more solid ground in the case of manuscripts. There is very little room for doubt when we read that someone commissioned the production of a codex, had the book in his or her possession or made him- or herself known as the person who added notes to a text. After all, what could be the reason for false statements in these cases? However, it should be noted that the information provided by manuscripts is not unambiguous. It is conceivable, for example, that a commissioner did not order a codex for his own use, but as a gift for someone else. And books that are part of a library may not have been read by the owner of the book collection. In both cases, the crucial aspect related to the books may have been that codices were objects that carried social prestige. It is very likely that commissioners and owners of manuscripts containing Arthurian romances were interested in the texts, but we cannot rule out the possibility that some of these books only served as markers of status. After all, irrespective of its contents, a manuscript expressed both an economic advantage (one could afford a book) and cultural prestige.

In two known instances, an important aristocrat carried an Arthurian manuscript with him across land borders. In these cases, the owners were definitely "addicted" to Arthurian material. The first nobleman was Hugh of Morville, who was one of the hostages of Richard I Lionheart in Germany, according to Ulrich von Zatzikhoven (2006, ll. 9325–9339). The German author states in the epilogue of *Lanzelet*, his idiosyncratic version of the Lancelot story, that Hugh owned "das welsche/ Buch von Lanzelet" (ll. 9340–9341) [the French book of Lanzelet] that the poet used as source text for the production of a faithful translation into German (ll. 9322–9324) at the request of some dear friends (l. 9342). The second nobleman who travelled with an Arthurian book was one of the most powerful men of Europe in his time. In the prologue to his Arthurian compilation, Rustichello da Pisa notes that his text is based on a "livre monseingneur Odoard, li roi d'Engleterre" (Rustichello da Pisa 1994, 233, par. 1.2) [book of Lord Edward, the King of England], and explains what made it possible for the author to be in contact with this royal person. He got the book when Edward "passé houtre la mer en servise nostre Sire Damedeu pour conquister le saint Sepoucre" (par. 1.2) [crossed the sea in the service of Our Lord to conquer the Holy Sepulchre]. Somewhere between 1270 and 1274, when Edward was in the Mediterranean area in order to participate in the unsuccessful crusade under Louis IX of France, Rustichello must have been introduced into Edward's circle (Allaire and Psaki 2014, 23–24). At that time, the future king of England was in the company of his wife Eleanor of Castile, who ordered Girart d'Amiens to write *Escanor* some years later (see above).

Whereas we do not know if Hugh and Edward commissioned the manuscripts they carried with them, there is ample evidence of aristocrats ordering the production of codices. A fine example is the luxurious book that is now in Leiden (UB, Ltk. 537). The single-text codex preserves Wirnt von Grafenberg's *Wigalois*, copied by the Cistercian monk Jan von Brunswick from Amelungsborn ("her jan uon brunswik monek tho amelunges born", f. 117v) in 1372 (Meuwese 2005, 30–31). The monk, who probably painted the forty-seven miniatures as well, made the manuscript at the request of Duke Albrecht II von Braunschweig.

Albrecht evidently had the means to commission a costly codex. The same is true for many other high-placed aristocrats. The manuscript now known as Darmstadt, Hessische Landes- und Hochschulbibliothek 2534, an early-fourteenth-century codex containing parts of the French *Lancelot-Grail* (*Estoire, Merlin, Suite*), for example, was made for the Count of Blois (f. 210), who is thought to be Louis de Châtillon (†1346) (Burgess and Pratt 2006, 58). Another French nobleman, Jacques d'Armagnac, was one of the most famous commissioners of Arthurian manuscripts. This Duke of Nemours, who was decapitated for treason in 1477, was a bibliophile, and possessed multiple copies of various Arthurian romances (Burgess and Pratt 2006, 66–67). He ordered an illustrated copy of the Prose *Tristan*, which was produced by the scribe and priest Micheau Gonnot in 1463 (now Paris, BnF, fr. 99). Some years later, in 1470 and again at the request of the duke, Gonnot completed a unique *Lancelot-Grail* compilation (Paris, BnF, fr. 112; see Pickford 1960). Another bibliophile, connected to the court of France, was introduced above: Pierre Sala. In the 1520s, he commissioned for his own use three illustrated manuscripts in which his own romances, *Tristan* and the *Chevalier au lion*, were copied (Taylor 2013, 153–154).

Examples of royal commissioners include King Pere IV of Aragon. As a result of his lively interest in Arthurian romances, he both bought and ordered books containing these texts (Hook 2015, 169). Archival documentation shows that he commissioned the production of a (French or Catalan prose) *Lancelot* twice, in 1339 and in 1346. Another Iberian monarch, King Enrique IV of Castile, ordered a codex in which the *Libro del cavallero Cifar* was copied. Made in the last third of the fifteenth century, this codex, now Paris, BnF, Esp. 36, contains no less than two hundred and sixty-two miniatures (Hook 2015, 44). The Habsburg Emperor Maximilian I commissioned the so-called Ambraser Heldenbuch (cf. Busby, *supra*). This splendid codex, now in Vienna's Österreichische Nationalbibliothek (ser. nova 2663) contains a large text collection, copied by Hans Ried between 1504 and 1516, including four German Arthurian romances (Hartmann's *Iwein* and *Erec, Der Mantel* and Wolfram's *Titurel*) (Jackson and Ranawake 2000, 237–238).

Albeit scarce, there is also evidence of Arthurian manuscripts which were commissioned by the city elite. A late-thirteenth-century copy of the *Mort le roi Artu* (Chantilly, Musée Condé 649) was made by the scribe Giovanni Gualandi for Brexianus de Salis, who was a top administrator ("capitano del popolo") at Modena around 1281 (Allaire and Psaki 2014, 193). Another example involves the English verse text *Arthur*, which has come down to us in a unique copy that is part of the so-called Red Book of Bath (Warminster, Longleat House 62, 55). This multi-text codex, preserving texts in English, Latin and French, was produced somewhere between 1412 and 1428 for the Magistrate of Bath (Barron 1999, 72).

Assuming that commissioners who ordered codices for their own use and not as gifts for others were often genuinely interested in Arthurian romances, one might expect to find ample evidence of readership in the preserved manuscripts. However, this does not seem the case (albeit that many codices still need to be studied from this perspective). It is quite rare to come across marginal annotations that prove that commissioners or subsequent readers consulted the manuscripts. Of course, this may have been caused, at least in part, by the frequent trimming of codices. A notable exception concerns the English prose *Merlin* in the mid-fifteenth century codex, Cambridge, CUL, Ff. 3. 11. Many users have left their marks on this manuscript, including Elyanor Guldeford, who was a member of a very prominent family, living around 1500. Judging from her many glosses on the narrative, she read the text very carefully (Meale 1986, 97–107). Another attentive reader had Cambridge, CUL, Additional 7071, containing parts of the *Lancelot-*

Grail cycle and the *Suite du Merlin*, on his or her desk. This sixteenth-century, unidentified person added a note to the French text, referring to Caxton's edition of Malory's *Morte Darthur* (Middleton 2003, 234). A final example of readership is a little less straightforward. At the time he was held captive in England, John II of France borrowed two *Lancelot-Grail* manuscripts from the English queen, returning them by the end of 1357 (Burgess and Pratt 2006, 59). It is highly likely that the king wanted these copies for reading purposes.

When we look at acquisitions, next to commissions, it is safe to conclude that Arthurian manuscripts were highly valued throughout the Middle Ages. The impressive documentation, mainly consisting of expenditure statements, wills, inventories of libraries and owners' marks (coats of arms, names), points in particular towards aristocratic families as owners of Arthurian books. For example, Everwin I (†1454), Count of Bentheim, possessed a *Merlin*, three *Lancelot* manuscripts, and a copy of *Perceval*, according to a list written on a folio of a manuscript that is still owned by the counts of Bentheim-Steinfurt (Jacob van Maerlant 1980, 425). French codices, to give another illustrative example, were acquired in large quantities by noble families (Burgess and Pratt 2006, 31–37; 57–84). The successive inventories of the royal library of France, starting in 1373, contain more than thirty copies of Arthurian prose romances (59). Of the nineteen books in the possession of Prigent de Coëtivy (†1450), Admiral of France, five were Arthurian (71). The inventory, which was made after the death of Philip the Good, Duke of Burgundy (†1467), lists more than thirty Arthurian books (62–63).

Non-noble interest in Arthurian literature is attested, finally, by evidence of book ownership. Attracted by the narratives and/or the social prestige attached to manuscripts, middle class representatives, such as merchants, lawyers, doctors, notaries, barbers, tailors and silversmiths, acquired codices containing Arthurian texts. An early example is manuscript Paris, BnF, fr. 12576, which preserves Chrétien's *Perceval* and all four Continuations. A note of rents relating to property in Amiens, written between 1270 and 1290, indicates that this codex was in the possession of a wealthy bourgeois family of that town (Busby et al. 1993, vol. 2, 49–51, 216–224). In addition to many aristocratic families, Italian owners of Arthurian books include notaries, doctors of law, a late fourteenth-century shoemaker, who possessed a book containing the *Tavola Ritonda*, and a late-fifteenth-century soldier, who called himself a trumpeter, and who owned a copy of the same romance (Allaire and Psaki 2014, 190–204). On the Iberian Peninsula, non-noble owners of Arthurian books were members of the bourgeoisie, who were particularly fond of *Tristan* texts (Hook 2015, 324–325). Among them are a pharmacist (1469), a physician (fifteenth century), a painter (1396), a clergyman (1436), the widow of a baker (1464) and many merchants (Hook 2015, 52–54). The dominance of the mercantile class may indicate an economy-driven interest in manuscripts instead of literary curiosity.

3 Conclusion: the persuasiveness of the evidence

Throughout the Middle Ages and in many languages, Arthurian romances were extremely popular (Besamusca and Quinlan 2012). Although we are clearly dealing with a pan-European phenomenon (see also Besamusca and Brandsma 2007), the observations in the two preceding sections suggest that one social class in particular favoured these texts: people of royalty and (high) nobility. However, this conclusion begs a question: how convincing is the evidence presented in this chapter?

It is important to realize that we have applied the inductive method in this enquiry. As a result, there is no conclusive evidence on offer here. Even if we are able to identify hundreds of (documented) aristocratic white swans, we may be unaware of thousands of (undocumented) middle-class black swans. In addition, we could ask if we can trust authors who claim the support of a patron. Their statements are, after all, rather conventional, often impossible to verify, and sometimes entirely false. A famous example of such an untrustworthy claim can be found at the end of the *Queste del saint Graal* (Pauphilet 1949, 280) and the beginning of the *Mort le roi Artu* (Frappier 1964, 1), where it is stated that both romances, composed around 1220–1230, were written by Gautier (Walter) Map (who died, however, in 1209) at the request of King Henry II of England (†1189). Finally, one cannot unconditionally assume that commissioners and owners of manuscripts favoured Arthurian literature, because they may have appreciated the books above all for their economical value and as markers of status.

It is true that these objections cast some doubt on the force of the evidence included in this chapter. However, it is worth noting that the visual arts also support the view that Arthurian literature was an elite affair. Schloß Rodenegg, for example, houses a cycle of wall paintings featuring Iwein, made between 1220 and 1230 (Jackson and Ranawake 2000, 257–259; Allaire and Psaki 2014, 209–210). At Schloß Wilhelmsburg, Schmalkalden, murals painted around the middle of the thirteenth century also tell the Iwein story (Jackson and Ranawake 2000, 259–260). Around 1400, the bankers Niklaus and Franz Vintler commissioned fresco cycles, based on Wirnt von Gravenberg's *Wigalois*, Gottfried's *Tristan* and Der Pleier's *Garel von dem blühenden Tal*, and images of the three greatest knights of the Round Table, Parzival, Gawein and Iwein, at Schloß Runkelstein (Jackson and Ranawake 2000, 261–262; Allaire and Psaki 2014, 210–212). Other Arthurian mural cycles are located in the Ducal Palace at Mantua, in a fortification near Frugarolo, in the Palazzo Ricchieri in Pordenone, in the Castle of Manta and in the French castle, Saint Floret (Allaire and Psaki 2014, 212–219). Since the second half of the fourteenth century, a pictorial series based on *Jaufre* has adorned a room at the royal palace of the Aljafería of Zaragoza (Hook 2015, 167). Philip the Bold (†1404) commissioned a tapestry featuring *Perceval* scenes as a gift for the Duke of York (Burgess and Pratt 2006, 35). These objects and decorated rooms do not argue against middle-class interest in Arthurian literature, of course. But they do confirm that this genre was both a truly pan-European and an elite phenomenon throughout the Middle Ages.

Acknowledgment: I would like to thank my Utrecht colleague and friend Frank Brandsma for his comments on the first draft of this chapter.

References

Ackerman, Robert W. "Herry Lovelich's *Merlin*." *Publications of the Modern Language Association of America* 67 (1952): 473–484.

Allaire, Gloria, and F. Regina Psaki, eds. *The Arthur of the Italians. The Arthurian Legend in Medieval Italian Literature and Culture*. Cardiff: University of Wales Press, 2014.

Arthur, Ross G., trans. *Jaufre: An Occitan Arthurian Romance*. New York: Garland, 1992.

Barron, W.R.J., ed. *The Arthur of the English. The Arthurian Legend in Medieval English Life and Literature*. Cardiff: University of Wales Press, 1999.

Bastert, Bernd. *Der Münchner Hof und Fuetrers* Buch der Abenteuer. *Literarische Kontinuität im Spätmittelalter*. Frankfurt am Main: Peter Lang, 1993.

Besamusca, Bart, and Frank Brandsma, eds. *Arthurian Literature XXIV: The European Dimensions of Arthurian Literature*. Cambridge: D.S. Brewer, 2007.

Besamusca, Bart, and Jessica Quinlan. "The Fringes of Arthurian Fiction." *Arthurian Literature* 29 (2012): 191–242.

Boyd, Matthieu. "Arthurian Vogues: Pierre Gallais's Neglected Evidence." *Journal of the International Arthurian Society* 2 (2014): 80–83.

Bromwich, Rachel, A.O.H. Jarman, and Brynley F. Roberts, eds. *The Arthur of the Welsh. The Arthurian Legend in Medieval Welsh Literature*. Cardiff: University of Wales Press, 1991.

Brunel, Clovis, ed. *Jaufré. Roman arthurien du XIIIe siècle en vers provençaux*. 2 vols. Paris: Société des Anciens Textes Français, 1943.

Bumke, Joachim. *Courtly Culture. Literature and Society in the High Middle Ages*. Trans. Thoman Dunlap. Berkeley, CA: University of California Press, 1991.

Bumke, Joachim. *Mäzene im Mittelalter. Die Gönner und Auftraggeber der höfischen Literatur in Deutschland 1150–1300*. Munich: Beck, 1979.

Burgess, Glyn S, and Karen Pratt, eds. *The Arthur of the French. The Arthurian Legend in Medieval French and Occitan Literature*. Cardiff: University of Wales Press, 2006.

Busby, Keith, Terry Nixon, Alison Stones, and Walters, Lori, eds. *Les manuscrits de Chrétien de Troyes/The Manuscripts of Chrétien de Troyes*. 2 vols. Amsterdam: Rodopi, 1993.

Buschinger, Danielle, and Wolfgang Spiewok, eds. Heinrich von Freiberg, *Tristan und Isolde (Fortsetzung des Tristan-Romans Gottfrieds von Strassburg)*. Greifswald: Reineke-Verlag, 1993.

Chrétien de Troyes. *Arthurian Romances*. Trans. William W. Kibler and Carleton W. Carroll. Harmondsworth: Penguin, 1991.

Chrétien de Troyes. *Les romans de Chrétien de Troyes, édités d'après la copie de Guiot (Bibl. nat. fr. 794) I Erec et Enide*. Ed. Mario Roques. Paris: Champion, 1990.

Chrétien de Troyes. *Lancelot or, The Knight of the Cart (Le Chevalier de la Charrete)*. Ed. and trans. William W. Kibler. New York and London: Garland, 1984.

Chrétien de Troyes. *Le roman de Perceval ou le Conte du Graal*. Ed. William Roach. 2nd edn. Geneva: Droz, 1959.

Cooper, Helen. "The *Lancelot-Grail Cycle* in England: Malory and his Predecessors." *A Companion to the* Lancelot-Grail Cycle. Ed. Carol Dover. Cambridge: Brewer, 2003. 147–162.

Dietl, Cora. "Licht und Erleuchtung im Rappoltsteiner *Parzival*." *Journal of the International Arthurian Society* 1 (2013): 29–49.

Echard, Siân, ed. *The Arthur of Medieval Latin Literature. The Development and Dissemination of the Arthurian Legend in Medieval Latin*. Cardiff: University of Wales Press, 2011.

Frappier, Jean, ed. *La mort le roi Artu. Roman du XIIIe siècle*. Geneva: Droz, 1964.

Gallais, Pierre. "Bleheri, la cour de Poitiers et la diffusion des récits arthuriens sur le continent." *Journal of the International Arthurian Society* 2 (2014): 84–114.

Gautier d'Arras. *Ille et Galeron*. Ed. Frederick A.G. Cowper. Paris: Picard, 1956.

Girart d'Amiens. *Escanor. Roman arthurien en vers de la fin du XIIIe siècle*. Ed. Richard Trachsler. 2 vols. Geneva: Droz, 1994.

Heinrich von Freiburg. *Tristan und Isolde (Fortsetzung des Tristan-Romans Gottfrieds von Strassburg)*. Ed. Wolfgang Spiewok and Danielle Buschinger. Amiens: Centre d'études médiévales, 1992.

Hook, David, ed. *The Arthur of the Iberians. The Arthurian Legend in the Spanish and Portuguese Worlds*. Cardiff: University of Wales Press, 2015.

Jackson, W.H, and S.A. Ranawake, eds. *The Arthur of the Germans. The Arthurian Legend in Medieval German and Dutch Literature*. Cardiff: University of Wales Press, 2000.

Jacob van Maerlant. *Historie van den Grale und Boek van Merline*. Ed. Timothy Sodmann. Köln: Böhlau, 1980.

Jaeger, C. Stephen. "Patrons and the Beginnings of Courtly Romance." *The Medieval Opus. Imitation, Rewriting, and Transmission in the French Tradition*. Ed. Douglas Kelly. Amsterdam/Atlanta: Rodopi, 1996. 45–58.

Kalinke, Marianne E., ed. *The Arthur of the North. The Arthurian Legend in the Norse and Rus' Realms*. Cardiff: University of Wales Press, 2011.

Kalinke, Marianne E., ed. *Norse Romance*, 3 vols. Cambridge: D.S. Brewer, 1999.

Lacy, Norris J., ed. *Early French Tristan Poems, Volume 2*. Cambridge: D.S. Brewer, 1998.

Layamon. *Brut*. Ed. and trans. W.R.J. Barron and S.C. Weinberg. Harlow: Longman, 1995.

Maddox, Donald, and Sara Sturm-Maddox. "*Erec et Enide*: the first Arthurian romance." *A Companion to Chrétien de Troyes*. Ed. Norris J. Lacy and Joan Tasker Grimbert. Cambridge: D.S. Brewer, 2005. 103–119.

Manessier. *La Troisième Continuation du Conte du Graal*. Trans. Marie-Noël le Toury. Ed. William
  Roach. Classiques Champion Moyen Âge, 13. Paris: Champion, 2004.
McCash, June Hall. "Chrétien's Patrons." *A Companion to Chrétien de Troyes*. Ed. Norris J. Lacy
  and Joan Tasker Grimbert. Cambridge: D.S. Brewer, 2005. 15–25.
Meale, Carol M. "The Manuscripts and Early Audience of the Middle English *Prose Merlin*." *The
  Changing Face of Arthurian Romance*. Ed. Alison Adams et al. Cambridge: Boydell Press,
  1986. 92–111.
Meuwese, Martine, ed. *King Arthur in the Netherlands*. Amsterdam: In de Pelikaan, 2005.
Middleton, Roger. "Manuscripts of the *Lancelot-Grail Cycle* in England and Wales: Some Books
  and their Owners." *A Companion to the* Lancelot-Grail Cycle. Ed. Carol Dover. Cambridge:
  D.S. Brewer, 2003. 219–235.
Pauphilet, Albert, ed. *La Queste del saint Graal. Roman du XIIIe siècle*. Paris: Champion, 1949.
Pickford, Cedric Edward. *L'Évolution du roman arthurien en prose vers la fin du Moyen Age
  d'après le manuscrit 112 du fonds français de la Bibliothèque Nationale*. Paris: Nizet, 1960.
Rasmussen, Ann Marie. "Medieval German Romance". *The Cambridge Companion to Medieval
  Romance*. Ed. Roberta L. Krueger. Cambridge: Cambridge University Press, 2000. 183–202.
Ravenel, Florence Leftwich, ed. *La Vie Seint Edmund Le Rei. An Anglo-Norman Poem of the
  Twelfth Century by Denis Piramus*. Philadelphia, PA: John Winston, 1906.
Rustichello da Pisa. *Il romanzo arturino di Rustichello da Pisa*. Ed. and trans. Fabrizio Cigni.
  Pisa: Pacini, 1994.
Sala, Pierre. *Tristan. Roman d'aventures du XVIe siècle*. Ed. L. Muir. Geneva: Droz, 1958.
Schorbach, Karl, ed. *Parzival von Claus Wisse und Philipp Colin (1331–1336). Eine Ergänzung
  der Dichtung Wolframs von Eschenbach*. Strasbourg: Trübner, 1888.
Taylor, Jane H.M. *Rewriting Arthurian Romance in Renaissance France. From Manuscript to
  Printed Book*. Cambridge: D.S. Brewer, 2014.
Taylor, Jane H.M. "Arthur in Manuscript in Renaissance France: The Case of *Ysaïe le Triste*,
  Gotha, MS A 688." *Journal of the International Arthurian Society* 1 (2013): 140–160.
Ulrich von Zatzikhoven. *Lanzelet*. Ed. Florian Kragl. 2 vols. Berlin/New York: De Gruyter, 2006.

Section II **Approaching Arthurian Romance:**
           Theories and Key Terms

Sif Rikhardsdottir
Chronology, Anachronism and *Translatio Imperii*

> "History is played along the margins which join a
> society with its past and with the very act of
> separating itself from that past. It takes place along
> these lines which trace the figure of a current time by
> dividing it from its other, but which the return of the
> past is continually modifying or blurring."
> (De Certeau 1988, 37–38)

Writing about history (the premise of and condition for both chronology and anachronism) in Arthurian literature is particularly difficult as history underlies the very work we do as scholars of medieval literature and so is everywhere, yet the essence of it is hard to define and harder yet to capture. Arthurian literature itself has a past, a present and a future and forms part of the progress of history and so cannot be isolated in a definable past as the subject. It is perpetually in motion, reconfiguring itself and its own past and so as its readers we ourselves must affirm that this engagement is always fleeting and momentary and that the object will have changed the moment we have sought to define it. Moreover, historicity figures as a foundational myth of Arthurian literature, i.e. King Arthur's pastness, the historical reaffirmation of this pastness and the potential future it offers – a future that remains present as we rehearse it.[1] Fundamental to this enactment of past and present historicity is imagination. As Nicholas Watson (2010) has so brilliantly shown, imagination figures as the quintessential mode of mediation of what he so aptly terms "the phantasmal past", through which we seek to encapsulate a mythical past for the present. This imaginary past is perpetually being re-enacted, thereby re-affirming its imaginative relevance and its historical potential. The past as depicted in the stories of King Arthur and his knights – as well as the moment in history of its imaginative re-creation – thus "remains inseparably entangled with the present and will continue to be so." (Watson 2010, 5)

---

1 I draw here on James Simpson's (2002) concept of a constructed past to articulate the fictive past of Arthurian history.

Sif Rikhardsdottir (University of Iceland)

DOI 10.1515/9783110432466-009

This chapter engages with questions of temporality, transmission, chronology and history as they relate to Arthurian romance. Given its broad span, the chapter will by necessity be fairly selective. The aim is to tease out some of the relevant and potentially critically engaging recent theorizations about time and historicity and the nuances of the movement of the *matière de Bretagne*, both temporally and geographically speaking. More figuratively, it seeks to foreground Arthurian romances' recombinative potential as a generic framework for the imaginative reconstitution of its own past and its envisioned future.[2]

1 Temporality, historicity and anachronism

History, historicity and temporality can be said to underlie many of the approaches to Arthurian romance for the past thirty years or so and no single chapter can do its critical history justice.[3] In fact, romance has a particularly fraught relationship with history as a subject and with its own historicity and chronological continuity. The romance's generic history is located in historiographical impulses and the specific staging of the topos of *translatio studii et imperii* as a foundational myth, exhibited in works such as Geoffrey of Monmouth's *Historia regum Britanniae*. While Arthurian romance thus originates in historiography, it simultaneously forges its own history and reconceives the history of its British past as foundational; a Trojan myth recapitalized to be repeated over and over again with a differing perspective, a shifting focus and an ahistorical mutability.

The concept of history is itself notoriously unstable and historicized. The scholarly shift from the poststructuralist critical heritage towards New Historicism in the 1980s and 1990s reveals a historicizing of the field of medieval as well as Arthurian studies that has had a profound impact on how scholars have conceived of the Arthurian legend in history and the temporality of Arthurian chro-

---

2 I utilize Nicholas Watson's (2010) formulation of the "recombinative imagination" here as a mode of articulating the reconstitution of generic components of the disparate romance material through history by which to reconfigure its contemporary significance or future potential.
3 To name just a few examples of the critical works on historicity or temporality in romance: Whitman (2006; 2010; 2013; 2015); Putter (1994); Ingham (2001); Warren (2000); Aurell (2007); Trachsler (2003); Moll (2003); and Walter (1989). For works that focus on historiography or temporality more generally see, for instance, Spiegel (1990; 1993; 1997; 2014); Ashe (2007); Davis (2008); Patterson (1987, 1991); Bloch (1983); Duby (1973); and Lock (1985). The scope here is limited (more or less) to medieval England and the Francophone realm and so works that focus on Scandinavia, the Germanic (including Dutch), Mediterranean, Iberian or Eastern contexts are not included here. For a more expansive overview see, for instance, Whitman (2015).

nology. In fact, Elizabeth Scala and Sylvia Federico (2009, 1) state, citing Fredric Jameson (1999, 4), that "historicism has become the Jamesonian 'cultural dominant' of our field, one whose posture 'allows for the presence and coexistence of a range of very different, yet subordinate, features.'" This dominance of New Historicist tendencies in medieval scholarship has, however, been questioned. Andrew James Johnston and others (2016) have queried the presupposition of historical synchronicity. Bruce Holsinger (2011) has similarly raised questions regarding the implicit presumptions of a definable and accessible historical context, while Carolyn Dinshaw (2007; 2012; 2015) has suggested queer history as an alternative mode of approaching the inherent symbiosis of past and present.[4] What lies at the foundation of "queer historicism" is an acceptance of the unavoidability of anachronism, a recognition of nonlinearity, of temporal crossings and non-historicity, and, ultimately, of the subjectivity of the past as a temporal configuration.

The historicized formulation of temporality as chronological time – and of Arthurian periodization – can in fact be ascribed to the genealogical tendencies of early historiography, evident in medieval chronicles and in Geoffrey's *Historia*. Spiegel (1997, xv) notes that the chroniclers introduced a new model of time that was "transformed by genealogical conceptual paradigms into a continuous, secular stream, in which past and present became an interconnected succession [...] and time itself, because human, was historicized." Geoffrey's *Historia*, although not the first to situate Arthur in the calendarian recording of Britain's fictive past, firmly entrenched the chronological time within which Arthurian temporality could be arranged as an unbroken lineage and out of which the later romance writers would carve out synchronic spaces to flesh out their adventures of the Arthurian heroes.

The historiographic efforts were themselves constituents of the time period, intended to herald and authenticate the ruling elite's legitimacy through genealogy (Spiegel 1993, 2–3). The sequential timeline instituted by the *Historia* became the unquestioned chronology upon which later Arthurian romance staged its accounts. Putter (1994, 1) indeed suggests that Geoffrey's *Historia* was so undisputed "that the Plantagenets frequently claimed Arthur as their forefather, and referred to his alleged conquest of the British Isles to legitimize their ter-

---

4 Holsinger's critique is not directed at New Historicism as such, but rather his essay aims to qualify the practice of historical contextualization and query its presumptions and nuances. See also Camp (2013), Goldberg and Menon (2005) and articles in the special issue on historical contextualization, *New Literary History* 42 (2011), particularly Rita Felski's introduction, "Context Stinks!"

ritorial claims to Scotland and Wales."[5] Stevens (2015, 75–77) suggests similarly that the interest in the Angevin historical framework exhibited in Gottfried von Straßburg's *Tristan* (which incidentally expands the pre-existing background) is directly related to the presumed reading communities and performative setting of the romance, suggesting that the court of the King of Germany and Holy Roman Emperor, Otto IV (*c.* 1175–1218), and the courts of his supporters were likely venues for the performance of the romance and that due to Otto's own dynastic affiliations with the Angevin Empire there might have been a vested interest in the dynastic genealogies.

Geoffrey's *Historia*, which enacts the topos of *translatio imperii* in its configuration of an unbroken genealogical past, itself became subject to the trope as it was translated, adapted or reworked throughout the ages. Its content was co-opted and reframed within new linguistic and ideological contexts, thus reformulating the pseudo-historical material and reshaping the implicit historical perpetuation the *Historia* sought to promulgate. Wace's vernacular translation of Geoffrey's Latin exemplar, *Roman de Brut*, gave the pseudo-historiographic material the shape of romance. Yet, the chronological impulse continued to dominate the reception of the *matière de Bretagne*. Several scholars have, for instance, noted that Chrétien de Troyes' romances were often placed in a chronological sequence in their manuscript contexts, where they were embedded within the historical progression of the *romans antiques* and/or the narrative history of Britain as depicted in Wace's *Brut*.[6]

The Arthurian past was thus fundamentally historicized, becoming part of a chronological passage of time. Yet, it served simultaneously (and anachronistically) to reinforce political and dynastic aspirations of the ruling elites of the high Middle Ages and was later called upon to re-affirm British national ambitions. The periodization of the Arthurian reign provided its recipients with a linear conception of a historical progression, stipulating a pre-Arthurian genealogy, a post-Arthurian period and an Arthurian era that was both historicized *and* mythical. The Arthurian chronology served to mythologize the present-day's own past, providing the current present with an authoritative past, a genealogical lineage and a historicized presence. This self-same periodization of the Arthurian past would later turn on its own creator as the self-conceived Renaissance proclaimed

---

5 The troubled past of Geoffrey's *Historia* as a border text and the associated ethnic and sociopolitical complexities will be discussed further in Fulton (*infra*). See also Warren (2000, particularly 25–59).

6 See, for instance, Huot (1987, 21–28); Putter (1994, 4–5); Walters (1985); Trachsler (2003, 24–25); and Green (2002, 89–91).

its own historicized borders by delineating the Middle Ages as their pre-modern Other.[7]

This impossibility of temporal rigidity is made particularly apparent in Arthurian romance, which fundamentally depends on a conscious blurring of such boundaries and a wilful suspension of temporal borders, inasmuch as its later recipients would have to juggle multiple versions of this fictive Arthur, including his previous textual history. Arthurian romance in some sense can be said to celebrate anachronism as it adopts the legend of the pre-courtly warrior king and refashions him as the ultimate symbol of chivalric glory. It then – in a self-conscious meta-fictive manner – plays on this very temporal convolutedness by heralding its own past as the background against which the story is made to materialize. Anachronism is, obviously, directly interlinked with chronology and the failure to position oneself accurately in a chronological timeline, thus indirectly sustaining and qualifying periodization. Margreta de Grazia (2010, 14) notes that while the term "history" has a long and distinguished past in the English language, there is no equivalent "ancient lineage" for the term "anachrony", which has its first appearance in the seventeenth century. De Grazia (2010, 21) does note that while the concept may be a later invention the notion of anachronistic thinking nevertheless extends further back. Yet, the consciousness of a pre- and postdating temporality intrinsic to anachronism has often been used to define the historical perception of early modern (vs. medieval) thinking.

The notion of anachronism thus firmly and securely places a text and its reader into definable and chronological positions. These positions in turn depend on the sequential boundaries drawn by current presumptions of historical positioning. Yet, the temporal permeance inherent in literary texts is bound to disintegrate those boundaries, throwing the whole linear division into disarray as the past and present inevitably merge to give the text meaning. This meaning draws on the point in time when a literary work is composed (already a fraught notion for medieval literature), its scribal and manuscript history, any intervening periods – which will have loaded the work with referentiality – and ultimately the present position, equally burdened by blurry and indistinct boundaries and only vaguely aware of itself.

The alliterative romance *Sir Gawain and the Green Knight*, for instance, re-articulates Geoffrey's foundational myth of British history only to question its

---

7 For criticism on periodization, both as a critical concept and as a critical practice, see, for instance, Hayot (2011); Watson (2010); Treharne (2006); Davis (2010); Cummings and Simpson (2010); Summit and Wallace (2007) and other essays in the special issue of the *Journal of Medieval and Early Modern Studies* 37 (2007).

temporal validity as the narrative progresses. The poem reframes its own origin by drawing on the historicity of the post-historiographic Arthurian mythology, only to obfuscate this authority through a destabilization of its own historical and mythical origins. The Green Knight poses as a reader of the textual legacy of Arthur, questioning its authenticity when he is confronted with the "sumquat childgered" Arthur in his court and so does the lady when Gawain fails to live up to his fictive (and historicized) repute as a courtly lover (Rikhardsdottir 2014, 9; *Gawain*-poet 2007, l. 86). *Sir Gawain and the Green Knight* thus perfects the art of historical circularity, intrinsic anachronism and meta-fictiveness in the disparity between the perceived reputation and literary legacy of Arthur's court, as an established past within the poem, and the fictive representation of the court in the narrative presence. The play on the multiplicity of temporalities and narrative levels in the poem reveals the plasticity of time and its fictive malleability in the later Arthurian textual tradition.

The penumbra of historicity and its much-dreaded companion, anachronism, has come to the fore in negotiations of intercultural engagements, post-colonial tensions and the East/West divide.[8] As Warren (2000, ix) notes "the ghosts of colonized Britons haunt subsequent formulations of imperial Britain, casting long shadows across European historiography", thus throwing into relief the role of authoritative (Westernized) historiography in shaping the framework of Arthurian romance, both in Britain and in the larger Francophone context. Such socio-political tensions and cultural reckonings underlie the paradigm of *translatio studii et imperii*, which puts such dialectical negotiations of cultural dominion at the forefront.

2 *Translatio studii et imperii*

The concept of *translatio imperii* owes its origin to the historical chronicles and their documentation of the transmission of imperial authority and knowledge from the East to the West. The Latin term *translatio* means "to carry across" and was used originally to indicate the physical movement of objects through space, whether those objects were material entities, such as relics, or more intangible entities, such as knowledge or power:

---

8 For post-colonial approaches to the Middle Ages see for instance Kabir and Williams (2005); Lampert-Weissig (2010); Ingham and Warren (2003); Cohen (2000); and Lynch (*infra*). See also Chakrabarty (2000); Heng (2003); and Huot (2007).

In the later Middle Ages, *translatio* is used in conjunction with the words *imperium, stadium* and *reliquiae; translatio imperii* signifies a transfer of power or dominion (from empire to empire, dynasty to dynasty), *translation studii*, a transfer of learning or knowledge (from one geographic place to another), and *translatio reliquiarum*, a transfer of relics of saints (geographically and between different religions or churches belonging to the same religion). (Stahuljak 2004, 37–38)[9]

The topos of *translatio studii* is articulated as a formulaic and, indeed, a formal means of ordering authoritative transmission and reception in the *romans antiques*, appearing for instance in the prologues of Wace's *Roman de Brut* and Benoît de Sainte-Maure's *Roman de Troie*. It served as an imperial affirmation of dynastic legitimacy, qualifying the genealogical lineage of the Capetians and their claim to the seat of power through the transmission of *imperium* from Rome and their entitlement to authority as the harbinger of knowledge and learning as passed down from ancient Greece (Stahuljak 2004, 145–146; Campbell and Mills 2012, 1).[10] Historiography and the chronicles thus tend to link the *translatio studii et imperii* with geographical expansionism and – in the Middle English chronicles in particular – with the foundation of Britain by Aeneas' descendant, Brutus.

As Helen Cooper (2004, 26–27) notes, the transmission is however not so clear-cut as the topos of *translatio studii* would imply, particularly with respect to the Arthurian material. The Arthurian legend passed from obscure Celtic folkloric materials from the margins of Britain through Geoffrey (who presumably wrote the *Historia* while located in Oxford) and presumably others, to Brittany, and then from Brittany to Chrétien and later back again to their English adapters, and finally across greater Europe, foregrounding the circuitousness of the movement of literary material across both insular and continental Europe. The movement in space, or across terrain, poses as a geographical as well as a geopolitical movement of materials that contain within them codes, a set of references and signifying patterns that will need to be aligned to the pre-existing set of references, whether linguistic, cultural, or literary, but will simultaneously reshape and reformulate those references. *Translatio* as a concept underlies therefore not only this geographic expansionism and the movement of peoples and ideas, but

---

9 For an excellent discussion of the concept of *translatio* and its metaphorical conceptualisations, see Stahuljak (2004) and works cited there. See also Stahuljak (2005), Tymoczko (2014), Campbell and Mills (2012), Goetz (1958) and Copeland (1991). For a study that deals specifically with the concept in Arthurian romance, see Freeman (1979).

10 The genealogy of transmission is nuanced further in Stahuljak's later book, *Bloodless Genealogies* (2005), where the destructive power of the topos and the complexities of (dis)continuation are deliberated.

it also envisions a linguistic shift, the transfer of knowledge inherent in Greek and Latin to the vernacular. It therefore underlies the reformulation of history as a vernacularized romance, a generic shift that morphs the content of Geoffrey's historiography into the generic leviathan of romance, a notoriously generically-unstable and encompassing form that defies its own temporality by the constant reinvention of its own genesis, form and modulations.

The act of "carrying across" implies both a border and a movement in space, a spatial transfer and a conservatory notion in the sense that an object, whether physical (such as a manuscript containing texts being brought from one location to another), or more conceptual (an idea or an ideological concept) that is trans-*located*. The equivocal object is thus simultaneously preserved – as it captures a moment in time of its existence in the act of transference – and mutated – as it is reformulated or re-enacted within its new location. The process of *translatio* is thus not a one-directional mode of transmission as the act itself transmutes both the object it seeks to transfer as well as the system into which the object is being received. The transposition by necessity realigns the very object that is being transposed rather than preserving it intact. There is indeed no intactness. The act of translation presupposes an act of *elucidatio*, or *interpretatio*, both in the moment of conservation and in the moment of its transposition.[11]

Suzanne Conklin Akbari (2005, 106) points out that the historiographic account of Paulus Orosius (*c.* 375–418 AD) frames the account of the movement of imperial power from the kingdom of Babylon through Macedonia and Carthage to Rome through a dichotomy of East and West, with the West framed as a locus of reception rather than as a locus in space. Akbari (108) notes that Orosius' focal point is prescribed by his own geographic positioning and so out of the four cardinal directions, only three of them – the East, the North and the South – are mentioned; the fourth – the West – being his own vantage point, the site from which the others are described. Akbari's astute observation of geographic perspective is relevant here inasmuch as medieval authors' re-enactment of the Arthurian legend prescribe a similar geographic as well as (and more importantly perhaps) temporal vantage point. The site from which the romance figure of King Arthur and his knights is conceived is – like with the Roman historiographer, Orosius – a ground zero, geographically speaking, but significantly also figuratively as it determines the midpoint between the past as material to be harvested and the future where the text will become part of that material presence and thus itself become a part of both its past and its future.

---

11 For a discussion of the vernacularization of the *translatio* topos and its subversive contingencies, see Copeland (1991) and Rikhardsdottir (2012, particularly 24–52).

Romance to some extent in fact exhibits a reversal of the conventional East-West transmissive pattern inherent in the *translatio studii et imperii*. This reversal materializes as a topos within Chrétien de Troyes' romance *Cligès*, where the learning, which, as per the conventional trope, originates in Greece and is passed onwards to Western Europe via Rome, is now to be found in France.

> Par les livres que nos avons
> Lez faiz des anciens savons
> Et dou siecle qui fu jadís.
> Ce nos ont nostre livre apris
> Que Grece ot de chevalerie
> Le premier los et de clergie,
> Puis vint chevalerie a Rome
> Et de la clergie la somme,
> Qui or est en France venue.
> [...]
> Que des Grezois ne des Romains
> Ne dit en mais ne plus ne mains,
> D'eus est la parole remese
> Et esteinte la vive brese. (Chrétien de Troyes 1994, ll. 27–44)
> [Through the books we possess we learn of the deeds of the people of past times and of the world as it used to be. Our books have taught us how Greece ranked first in chivalry and learning; then chivalry passed to Rome along with the fund of transcendent learning that has now come to France. [...] for no longer do people speak at all of the Greeks and Romans – there is no more talk of them, and their glowing embers are dead. (Chrétien de Troyes 2002, 93)]

Not only is France figured as the new site of learning and knowledge, but the trope now includes the code of chivalry in addition to *studii*. More significantly, the court of Arthur has become the locus for this courtly code of chivalry, reversing the previous axis of transmission. The story tells how Cligès' father "Que por pris et por los conquerre/ *Ala de Grece en Engleterre*,/ Qui lors estoit Breteigne dite" (ll. 15–17) [in order to win a reputation and renown, went *from Greece to England*, which at that time was called Britain (Chrétien de Troyes 2002, 93)] only to return later to Greece.[12] The movement of chivalric learning from Arthur's court back to Greece metamorphoses the *translatio studii* inasmuch as it represents both a geographical shift in orientation and, more importantly, a fundamental

---

12 The italics are mine and I have adapted the English translation slightly for syntactical purposes. For a discussion of the topos of *translatio studii* in *Cligès* see, for instance, Freeman (1979) and Nichols (2012, 208), who discusses this reversal as a symptom of an "asynchronious temporality", which he sees as "central to twelfth-century thought" (209).

shift in the *matière* of *translatio studii* by including chivalric behavioural patterns and courtly precepts.

Arthurian romance thus articulates the concept of *translatio studii et imperii* in its re-vocalisation of a Roman past as underlying the reconstitution of a courtly and royal present, while it simultaneously subverts it through a geographic reversal of the point of origin and its transmission. Rather than moving East to West and encompassing cultural authority and knowledge, the cultural transfer is reframed through an act of conscious re-engagement and re-articulation of the Arthurian (British) mythical past as fundamental, both in its ideological message and its inherent value and relevance to its medieval audiences. That modernity has unquestionably assumed this playful re-enactment of cultural transfer and its creative reconstitution to form the material remnants of a cultural heritage of the legacy of Arthur and his knights may itself enact a mode of *translatio imperii* where the myth in transit has become the representative essence of its own obscure and mobile past.

3 Arthurian romance and the inversion of temporality

"Romance, one might say, is situated in and speaks of timeless moments" declares Corinne Saunders (2004, 1) at the beginning of her volume on romance through history. Romance as a matter of fact exhibits simultaneously historiographic temporality and a more subjective temporality that does not abide by the restraints of chronology or the restraints of the linear passing of hours, days and years. This temporality originates in the dialectic between a character's presumed subjectivity and that of the reader, and is contingent upon the magical locus of temporal disavowal that the author and reader engage in to make the events come to life, to give them an urgency that defies their transience, their pastness in a sense. Already at the onset of the Arthurian mythography, in the *Prophetiae Merlini*, the stage is set for this time-defying temporality. Prophecies by definition contest chronology as they reach beyond their historical presence to tell of events yet to come, enacting a profoundly anachronistic gesture of temporal defiance. Merlin's prophecy heralds the coming of Arthur long before his birth, yet the prophecies themselves postdate the very birth that they claim to foretell, signalling a historical consciousness that is simultaneously negated and implemented through the re-enactment of its own historicity.

Like Geoffrey's *Prophecies*, *Sir Gawain and the Green Knight* hovers on the uneasy border between fictiveness and historicity, foregrounding its own pseudo-historical impulse, while simultaneously destabilizing the veneer of historicity and temporality. The entire plot of the story hinges on the impending date at which Gawain will have to present himself before the Green Knight to suffer a blow of his axe. The profound temporal awareness in the poem is made material in the focus on the seasons, their movement and the chronological progress of time.[13] Yet, by its enactment of multiple temporalities, each in turn negated by the other, the chronological passage of time is called into question. As stated before, the legacy of Arthur's court is disputed by his "childgered" presence and Gawain's textual reputation precedes him to Bertilak's castle, where he engages in verbal battles intended to play on those temporal discrepancies. In Chrétien de Troyes' *Yvain ou Le Chevalier au lion*, temporal awareness (or more accurately lack of temporal awareness) instigates the series of events that form the basis of the romance. The often debated forgetfulness of Yvain with respect to the timeframe set for his return to his lady (following fast on the heels of his avid declarations of love for his lady) reveals the narrative functionality of temporality not only as a historicizing factor, but as a subjective positioning where narrative time and its passing is measured in subjective realisations of impending doom or love lost.

Insular romance on the whole is more firmly grounded in historiography when compared with continental romance (Ashe 2010, 3). The non-Arthurian Middle English romance *Havelok*, for instance, indeed seems more firmly placed within an insular historiographical convention that seeks authenticity in the historicized past than *Sir Gawain and the Green Knight*, which, conversely, seems to thematize historicity as a trope only to reject it. In fact, unlike the French romances, Middle English non-Arthurian romances seem distinctly to veer towards a chronicle-like historicity, affirming the *translatio* topos, while their emphasis is nevertheless not on authoritative (textual) lineage, but, more specifically, on paternal hered-ity, its potential rupture or refusal and its eventual reinstatement.

Geoffrey's foundational myth thus endured beyond its pseudo-historiograph-ical intentions and its subsequent perpetuation in romance and was hailed by the Elizabethans as a befitting background to their own national aspirations (Cooper 2004, 24). The post-Chrétien continental romance offered a different direction, one that directly negated the previously established pattern of authoritative transmission and geopolitical orientation of power and knowledge. Following Chrétien's unfinished romance, *Perceval ou Le Conte du Graal*, the Grail material became the foundation for a reformulation of Arthurian historicity as well as its legacy. There is a clear deviation in the Grail material from the previous topos of

---

13 For a discussion of temporality in *Sir Gawain and the Green Knight* see, for instance, Whitman (2013, 84–87) and Bishop (1985).

translatio studii et imperii and historiographic temporality. In the *Lancelot-Grail Cycle* the foundational myth is shifted from Troy to a Biblical past and the creation of the Holy Grail. Its measure of time is thus radically altered as the past serves not as authentication of the present and a foundational lineage for posterity, but as "an eschatological construction with a precise goal to be reached, after which the writer can put down his pen" (Trachsler 2003, 26). Trachsler (31–32) indeed argues that the introduction of the Grail material fundamentally shifts the historiographic orientation of the Arthurian romance towards a spiritual temporality and that this refashioning indeed spells the end of the chivalric romance as known by Chrétien and his audiences.

Ultimately, Arthurian romance, particularly in the fourteenth century, tells a story that has already begun and ended, yet its grand finale lies still in the future. Arthur's relevance (and potential return) to the realm of Britain and to the framework of the courtly romance is a fundamental requirement for the perpetuity of the intrinsic appeal, i.e. the resurgence of a history that has already been laid to pass to make itself relevant again. Arthurian romance thus re-enacts a time-defying gesture of raising the dead, the spectre of a past, like the judge in *St Erkenwald*, summoning the dead for a dialogue so the past can be put to rest, disintegrating into dust as it is re-encapsulated by modernity – or by what amounts to modernity at any given time.

References

Akbari, Suzanne Conklin. "Alexander in the Orient: Bodies and Boundaries in the *Roman de toute chevalerie*." *Postcolonial Approaches to the European Middle Ages: Translating Culture*. Ed. Ananya Jahanara Kabir and Deanne Williams. Cambridge Studies in Medieval Literature. Cambridge: Cambridge University Press, 2005. 105–126.

Ashe, Laura. "Introduction." *The Exploitations of Medieval Romance*. Ed. Laura Ashe, Ivana Djordjević and Judith Weiss. Cambridge: D.S. Brewer, 2010. 1–14.

Ashe, Laura. *Fiction and History in England, 1066–1200*. Cambridge Studies in Medieval Literature 68. Cambridge: Cambridge University Press, 2007.

Aurell, Martin. *La légende du roi Arthur, 550–1250*. Paris: Perrin, 2007.

Bishop, Ian. "Time and Tempo in *Sir Gawain and the Green Knight*." *Neophilologus* 69 (1985): 611–619.

Bloch, Howard R. *Etymologies and Genealogies: A Literary Anthropology of the French Middle Ages*. Chicago: University of Chicago Press, 1983.

Camp, Cynthia Turner. "Spatial Memory, Historiographic Fantasy, and the Touch of the Past in *St. Erkenwald*." *New Literary History* 44 (2013): 471–491.

Campbell, Emma, and Robert Mills. "Introduction: Rethinking Medieval Translation." *Rethinking Medieval Translation: Ethics, Politics, Theory*. Ed. Emma Campbell and Robert Mills. Cambridge: D.S. Brewer, 2012. 1–20.

Chakrabarty, Dipesh. *Provincializing Europe: Postcolonial Thought and Historical Difference*. Princeton Studies in Culture/Power/History. Princeton, NJ: Princeton University Press, 2000.

Chrétien de Troyes. *Cligès*. Ed. and trans. Charles Méla and Olivier Collet. *Chrétien de Troyes: Romans*. Ed. Michel Zink. Classiques modernes. Paris: Librairie Générale Française, 1994. 285–494.

Chrétien de Troyes. "Cligès". *Arthurian Romances*. Trans. D.D.R. Owen. London: Everyman, 2002 [first published 1987, revised introduction in 1993]. 93–184.

Cohen, Jeffrey Jerome, ed. *The Postcolonial Middle Ages*. New York: Palgrave, 2000.

Cooper, Helen. *The English Romance in Time: Transforming Motifs from Geoffrey of Monmouth to the Death of Shakespeare*. Oxford: Oxford University Press, 2004.

Copeland, Rita. *Rhetoric, Hermeneutics, and Translation in the Middle Ages. Academic Traditions and Vernacular Texts*. Cambridge Studies in Medieval Literature 11. Cambridge: Cambridge University Press, 1991.

Cummings, Brian, and James Simpson, eds. *Cultural Reformations: Medieval and Renaissance in Literary History*. Oxford Twenty-First Century Approaches to Literature. Oxford: Oxford University Press, 2010.

Davis, Kathleen. "The Sense of an Epoch: Periodization, Sovereignty, and the Limits of Secularization." *The Legitimacy of the Middle Ages: On the Unwritten History of Theory*. Ed. Andrew Cole and D. Vance Smith. Durham, NC: Duke University Press, 2010. 39–69.

Davis, Kathleen. *Periodization & Sovereignty: How Ideas of Feudalism & Secularization Govern the Politics of Time*. The Middle Ages Series. Philadelphia, PA: University of Pennsylvania Press, 2008.

De Certeau, Michel. *The Writing of History*. Trans. Tom Conley. New York: Columbia University Press, 1988.

De Grazia, Margreta. "Anachronism." *Cultural Reformations: Medieval and Renaissance in Literary History*. Ed. Brian Cummings and James Simpson. Oxford Twenty-First Century Approaches to Literature. Oxford: Oxford University Press, 2010. 13–32.

Dinshaw, Carolyn. "Response Time: Linear, Nonlinear, Queer." *Studies in Gender and Sexuality* 16 (2015): 40–43.

Dinshaw, Carolyn. *How Soon is Now? Medieval Texts, Amateur Readers, and the Queerness of Time*. Durham, NC: Duke University Press, 2012.

Dinshaw, Carolyn. "Temporalities." *Oxford Twenty-First Century Approaches to Literature: Middle English*. Ed. Paul Strohm. Oxford: Oxford University Press, 2007. 107–123.

Duby, Georges. *Hommes et structures du Moyen Age: receuil d'articles*. Le savoir historique 1. Paris: Mouton, 1973.

Felski, Rita. "'Context Stinks!'" *New Literary History* 42 (2011): 573–591.

Freeman, Michelle A. *The Poetics of* Translatio Studii *and Conjointure: Chrétien de Troyes's* Cligés. French Forum Monographs 12. Lexington, KY: French Forum Publishers, 1979.

Gawain-poet. *Sir Gawain and the Green Knight* in *The Poems of the Pearl Manuscript*: Pearl, Cleanness, Patience, Sir Gawain and the Green Knight. Ed. Malcolm Andrew and Ronald Waldron. Rev. 5th edn. Exeter Medieval Texts and Studies. Exeter: University of Exeter Press, 2007. 207–300.

Goetz, Werner. *Translatio imperii*. Tübingen: Mohr, 1958.

Goldberg, Jonathan, and Madhavi Menon. "Queering History." *PMLA* 120 (2005): 1608–1617.

Green, D.H. *The Beginning of Medieval Romance: Fact and Fiction, 1150–1220*. Cambridge: Cambridge University Press, 2002.

Hayot, Eric. "Against Periodization; or, On Institutional Time." *New Literary History* 42.4 (2011): 739–756.

Heng, Geraldine. *Empire of Magic: Medieval Romance and the Politics of Cultural Fantasy*. New York: Columbia University Press, 2003.

Holsinger, Bruce. "'Historical Context' in Historical Context: Surface, Depth, and the Making of the Text." *New Literary History* 42 (2011): 593–614.

Huot, Sylvia. *Postcolonial Fictions in the* Roman de Perceforest: *Cultural Identities and Hybridities*. Cambridge: D.S. Brewer, 2007.

Huot, Sylvia. *From Song to Book: The Poetics of Writing in Old French Lyric and Lyrical Narrative Poetry*. Ithaca, NY: Cornell University Press, 1987.

Ingham, Patricia Clare. *Sovereign Fantasies: Arthurian Romance and the Making of Britain*. The Middle Ages Series. Philadelphia, PA: University of Pennsylvania Press, 2001.

Ingham, Patricia Clare, and Michelle R. Warren, eds. *Postcolonial Moves: Medieval through Modern*. New York: Palgrave Macmillan, 2003.

Jameson, Fredric. *Postmodernism – or the Cultural Logic of Late Capitalism*. Durham, NC: Duke University Press, 1999.

Johnston, Andrew James, Russel West-Pavlov and Elisabeth Kempf, eds. *Love, History and Emotion in Chaucer and Shakespeare:* Troilus and Criseyde *and* Troilus and Cressida. Manchester Medieval Literature and Culture. Manchester: Manchester University Press, 2016.

Kabir, Ananya Jahanara, and Deanne Williams, eds. *Postcolonial Approaches to the European Middle Ages: Translating Culture*. Cambridge: Cambridge University Press, 2005.

Lampert-Weissig, Lisa. *Medieval Literature and Postcolonial Studies*. Postcolonial Literary Studies. Edinburgh: Edinburgh University Press, 2010.

Lock, Richard. *Aspects of Time in Medieval Literature*. Garland Publications in Comparative Literature. New York: Garland, 1985.

Moll, Richard J. *Before Malory: Reading Arthur in Later Medieval England*. Toronto: University of Toronto Press, 2003.

Nichols, Stephen G. "Counter-figural Topics. Theorizing Romance with Eugène Vinaver and Eugene Vance." *MLN* 127 Supplement (2012): 174–216.

Patterson, Lee. *Chaucer and the Subject of History*. Madison, WI: University of Wisconsin Press, 1991.

Patterson, Lee. *Negotiating the Past: The Historical Understanding of Medieval Literature*. Madison, WI: University of Wisconsin Press, 1987.

Putter, Ad. "Finding Time for Romance: Mediaeval Arthurian Literary History." *Medium Ævum* 63 (1994): 1–16.

Rikhardsdottir, Sif. "The Gawain Poet." *Oxford Handbooks Online*. Ed. James Simpson. Oxford: Oxford University Press, 2014.

Rikhardsdottir, Sif. *Medieval Translations and Cultural Discourse: The Movement of Texts in England, France and Scandinavia*. Cambridge: D.S. Brewer, 2012.

Saunders, Corinne. "Introduction." *A Companion to Romance: From Classical to Contemporary*. Ed. Corinne Saunders. Malden: Blackwell Publishing, 2004. 1–9.

Scala, Elizabeth, and Sylvia Federico, eds. *The Post-Historical Middle Ages*. The New Middle Ages. New York: Palgrave Macmillan, 2009.

Simpson, James. *Reform and Cultural Revolution: The Oxford English Literary History*. Vol. 2: 1350–1547. Oxford: Oxford University Press, 2002.

Spiegel, Gabrielle M. "The Future of the Pasts: History, Memory and the Ethical Imperatives of Writing History." *Journal of the Philosophy of History* 8 (2014): 149–179.

Spiegel, Gabrielle M. *The Past as Text: The Theory and Practice of Medieval Historiography.* Parallax, Re-visions of Culture and Society. Baltimore, MD: John Hopkins University Press, 1997.

Spiegel, Gabrielle M. *Romancing the Past: The Rise of Vernacular Prose Historiography in Thirteenth-Century France.* New Historicism: Studies in Cultural Poetics 23. Berkeley, CA: University of California Press, 1993.

Spiegel, Gabrielle M. "History, Historicism, and the Social Logic of the Text in the Middle Ages." *Speculum* 65 (1990): 59–86.

Stahuljak, Zrinka. *Bloodless Genealogies of the French Middle Ages:* Translatio, *Kinship, and Metaphor.* Gainesville, FL: University Press of Florida, 2005.

Stahuljak, Zrinka. "An Epistemology of Tension." *The Translator* 10 (2004): 33–57.

Stevens, Adrian. "Gottfried, Wolfram, and the Angevins: History, Genealogy, and Fiction in the *Tristan* and *Parzival* Romances." *Romance and History: Imagining Time from the Medieval to the Early Modern Period.* Ed. Jon Whitman. Cambridge: Cambridge University Press, 2015. 74–89.

Summit, Jennifer, and David Wallace. "Rethinking Periodization." *Journal of Medieval and Early Modern Studies* 37 (2007): 447–451.

Trachsler, Richard. "A Question of Time: Romance and History." *A Companion to the Lancelot-Grail Cycle.* Ed. Carol Dover. Arthurian Studies LIV. Cambridge: D.S. Brewer, 2003. 23–32.

Treharne, Elaine. "Categorization, Periodization: The Silence of (the) English in the Twelfth Century." *New Medieval Literatures* 8 (2006): 247–273.

Tymoczko, Maria. "Ideology and the Position of the Translator: In What Sense is a Translator 'in Between'?" *Apropos of Ideology: Translation Studies on Ideology – Ideologies in Translation Studies.* Ed. María Calzada Pérez. New York: Routledge, 2014. 181–201.

Walter, Philippe. *La mémoire du temps: Fêtes et calendriers de Chrétien de Troyes à* La Mort Artu. Nouvelle bibliothèque du Moyen Age 13. Paris: Champion, 1989.

Walters, Lori J. "Le rôle du scribe dans l'organisation des manuscrits de Chrétien de Troyes." *Romania* 106 (1985): 303–325.

Warren, Michelle R. *History on the Edge: Excalibur and the Borders of Britain, 1100–1300.* Medieval Cultures 22. Minneapolis, MN: University of Minnesota Press, 2000.

Watson, Nicholas. "The Phantasmal Past: Time, History, and the Recombinative Imagination." *Studies in the Age of Chaucer* 32 (2010): 1–37.

Whitman, Jon, ed. *Romance and History: Imagining Time from the Medieval to the Early Modern Period.* Cambridge: Cambridge University Press, 2015.

Whitman, Jon. "Envisioning the End: History and Consciousness in Medieval English Arthurian Romance." *Arthuriana* 23 (2013): 79–103.

Whitman, Jon. "Posthumous Messages: Memory, Romance, and the *Morte Darthur.*" *The Making of Memory in the Middle Ages.* Ed. Lucie Doležalová. Later Medieval Europe 4. Leiden: Brill, 2010. 241–252.

Whitman, Jon. "Alternative Scriptures: Story, History, and the Canons of Romance." *New Medieval Literatures* 8 (2006): 1–44.

Helen Fulton
Historiography: Fictionality vs. Factuality

The origins of medieval Arthurian romance lie in Latin histories of early Britain in which Arthur is located as a historical figure belonging to a distant Romano-British past at the time of the Anglo-Saxon settlements of the fifth and sixth centuries. Yet these Latin histories were written long after the events of that time, and our only surviving contemporary work, the *De excidio Britanniae* [Concerning the Ruin of Britain] of Gildas, written in the sixth century AD, does not mention Arthur at all. The historical Arthur is therefore pseudo-historical, the product of a generic merging of legend and folklore into what were presented as historical chronicles.

This merging of fiction and non-fiction is characteristic of medieval chronicles in general, and particularly those which were written in Britain (a term which I am using here to signify the island of Britain comprising the medieval kingdoms of Scotland and England and the territory of Wales). In this chapter I will consider some of the ways in which Arthur was presented as a historically real person by medieval historians who routinely used legend and fantasy as part of their historical method. They constructed a discourse of historical naturalism that claimed authority from earlier, often unnamed, sources and elided the boundaries between what we now think of as fiction and history. From the twelfth century onwards in Britain, this elision became hotly contested as historians argued about where to draw the line between historical fact and sheer fantasy, a debate that rumbled on into the Tudor period when the establishment of a definitive and authoritative version of British history was politically necessary to endorse Tudor power and justify their right to rule. In this debate, the figure of Arthur was central. Presented by Geoffrey of Monmouth in the twelfth century as one of a line of historical kings legitimized by prophecy and the supernatural, Arthur's status – was he historical or legendary? – was the subject of competing claims until the eighteenth century.

1 Models of medieval historiography

For much of the twentieth century, medieval history was regarded by modern historians as something not to be taken very seriously, a mixture of fact and fantasy,

Helen Fulton (University of Bristol)

DOI 10.1515/9783110432466-010

hearsay and plain error. Real history, in the modern sense, began with the Tudors, as Peter Burke (1969) argued in his book, *The Renaissance Sense of the Past*. Contrasting medieval history unfavourably with the more rigorous standards of evidence-based reporting adopted by humanist writers of the Renaissance, Burke (1969, 1) suggested the main features of earlier medieval historiography were the juxtaposition of events paratactically, without causative links, a sense of anachronism and a lack of interest in documentary evidence.

For a modern historian, these are serious failures. In the medieval context, however, this approach to writing history simply reveals a different set of priorities and ideologies, an alternative epistemology. Medieval historiography was largely controlled by the church, which viewed history as simply the gradual revelation of God's will. Apparently anachronistic references to Christian worship, for example, when writing about pagan peoples, are not errors so much as examples of external focalization, conscious attempts to link past and present as part of a continuum ordained by God. At a time when the concept of absolute truth was defined entirely in terms of the word of God, medieval writers were free to explore the possibilities of all kinds of relativities of time and meaning.

It is, moreover, not strictly true to suggest that medieval historians had little regard for facts or evidence. Many monastic chronicles were kept as ongoing records of the major events of each year, with the deaths of kings, significant wars and the deeds of aristocratic landowners featuring alongside the more mundane activities of the monastery and its inhabitants. Official documents produced by royal governments were often copied into chronicles as evidence of contemporary events, and although this might be considered as "an attempt [by the government] to create an 'official' national history" (Ruddick 2013, 173), it seems clear that both monastic chroniclers and central governments shared a sense of what history was for.

If the point of medieval history was to record human interaction with God's created world with a view to understanding God's will as it was revealed to human society, the apparent flaws in the medieval historical method can be reinterpreted as logical consequences of the medieval world view, particularly that of the dominant literate class within the church. We can in fact identify two main strands of historiography, the linear and the circular. The first approach, exemplified by Augustine, writing in the fourth century AD, was a universalizing model that brought all local and regional histories into an alignment with the Christian chronology and which led ineluctably and teleologically to the day of judgment (Allen 2003). Drawing partly on classical Latin histories whose path led climactically to either the greatness or the fall of Rome, this linear model formed the basis of what became Tudor history, celebrating the teleological progress of the English nation and its monarchs towards modernity.

But in between classical and Renaissance historiography, medieval writers experimented with a different kind of history, one proposed by Boethius in his *De consolatione philosophiae* [The Consolation of Philosophy] of the sixth century (Boethius 1999). According to Boethius, history is not linear but circular. What goes around comes around. Boethius explained this movement of time as the workings of fortune or fate, which acted as the agent of divine providence to bring individuals to the destiny that God has laid down for them (Marenbon 2003). Just as the operations of Fortuna were conceptualized as a wheel, raising people up only to cast them down again, so the process of history was theorized as a circular movement of recurring events, anticipated by God, prefigured in history and revisited on human society in precise relation to its merit.

This is the model of history that most influenced Geoffrey of Monmouth in his *Historia regum Britanniae* (*c.* 1138) [The History of the Kings of Britain], which provides our earliest most complete biography of Arthur (Geoffrey of Monmouth 2007). Though Geoffrey is working towards the triumph of the Normans as the true rulers of Britain (Ashe 2007; Faletra 2007; Gillingham 2000), he achieves this purpose through a series of "wheels" representing the rise and fall of individuals and peoples. As Troy falls, Rome rises; as each British king dies, another replaces him; the British are for many generations in the ascendant, but then their own moral faults betray them and the Anglo-Saxons conquer them. Arthur himself becomes a legitimate king, rises high in triumph, but is brought down by the treachery that was his destiny.

In both these historical models, fiction and fantasy play their part, just as in the Bible, the ultimate model of both universal and dynastic historiography, supernatural and legendary material supplements and often authorizes the truth-claims of the narrative. The aura of the supernatural that surrounded Arthur from his earliest appearance in Welsh and Latin texts did not, therefore, detract from the claim that he was a historical figure but, if anything, enhanced it.

2 Arthur in early chronicles

The earliest work of history in which Arthur appears as a historical character is the chronicle once attributed to a monk called Nennius, whose authorship is now doubted (Field 1996). The *Historia Brittonum* (Morris 1980) was written in the ninth century, though the earliest surviving manuscript dates from about 1100 (Dumville 1977–1978; Charles-Edwards 2013, 437–452). The chronicle seems to have been written by a Welsh cleric or someone familiar with the political context of the Welsh resistance to the Saxons on the borders of Wales in the early ninth century (Higham 2009). The *Historia Brittonum* was a key source for Geoffrey of Monmouth, who took his account of the prophecy of the two dragons, white and red, fighting for control of Britain, from the *Historia Brittonum* but changed the name of the boy-prophet from Emrys (Latin: Ambrosius) to Merlin, thereby introducing the figure of the Welsh wizard, known in earlier Welsh poetry as Myrddin, to the wider European world (Knight 2009).

Arthur appears in the *Historia Brittonum* as a great battle-leader of the British people, fighting twelve battles across the length and breadth of the island. Carrying a shield bearing the image of the Virgin Mary, Arthur functions as a Christ-like figure with supernatural powers, winning every battle and killing nearly a thousand men single-handedly in one day. Though the precise locations of each of the battles is not known, and many of the place-names may be fictional, the last battle is said to take place at Badon, a place-name mentioned by Gildas as the site of a battle between the British and the Saxons, though Gildas does not mention the name of Arthur. It seems that the author of the *Historia Brittonum* has inserted the figure of Arthur, presumably known to him already from early Welsh legend, into a historical context of warfare, creating from various sources a series of battles which display Arthur's heroic leadership of the British people under threat from the Saxons.

Into this amalgam of history and legend, the chronicle's author has added an element of topographical folklore. Among a list of *mirabilia*, or "marvels", Arthur is associated with a number of place-names, such as Carn Cabal, supposedly named after Arthur's hound, and Llygad Amr, said to be the grave of Arthur's son, Amr, a grave whose length changes each time it is measured (Morris 1980, Ch. 73). Nicholas Higham argues that this folkloric Arthur "seems to precede the warrior Arthur of the *Historia*" (Higham 2009, 34), suggesting an ancient folklore tradition dating back to Roman Britain where the Latin name Artorius [Arthur] was known. What seems clear is that at some stage between Gildas' sixth-century history of Britain and the *Historia Brittonum* of the ninth century, the figure of Arthur as a British leader and hero of various legends emerged into the context of early medieval history (cf. Meyer, *supra*).

This would also explain the appearance of Arthur in two of the annals listed in the *Annales Cambriae* [Annals of Wales], written in the middle of the tenth century (Morris 1980; Charles-Edwards 1991). The first reference, dated to the year 516, describes Arthur at the battle of Badon, "in which Arthur carried the cross of our Lord Jesus Christ for three days and three nights on his shoulders" (Morris 1980, 85), a reference similar to that in the *Historia Brittonum* where Arthur carries an image of the Virgin Mary on his shield at one of the other battles (not at Badon). The second reference, dated as 537, describes Arthur's death at the battle of Camlann, along with Medraut (Medrawd or Mordred), at a time of great plague.

This is possibly the earliest reference we have to Mordred, or at least the earliest datable reference (the name occurs in early Welsh poetry and triads which cannot be dated with great accuracy though the poetry is likely to pre-date Geoffrey of Monmouth). As Rachel Bromwich has pointed out (2014, 455), "The early sources do not claim either that Medrawd was Arthur's nephew or that he was his opponent"; on the contrary, "[t]he early bardic references indicate that Medrawd was looked upon as a paragon of valour and courtesy." The story of Mordred's relationship to Arthur and his treachery which led to the deaths of both of them was almost certainly an invention of Geoffrey's, a dramatic narrative that may well owe its origins to early French romance.

Fragmentary and allusive as it is, the evidence of the *Historia Brittonum* and the *Annales Cambriae* indicates that there was enough interest in Arthur as a supposed battle-leader of the sixth century to include him in accounts of early British history. Whether information about Arthur circulated orally or in written texts, or both, we cannot be certain, but the surviving evidence points clearly to a religious purpose behind the early historical accounts of British downfall and Saxon triumph. As Thomas Charles-Edwards says, the significance of the list of twelve battles in the *Historia Brittonum* lies with "divine providence rather than with human heroism in war" (1991, 28), reminding its readers that the Saxons were divinely ordained to be the rulers of what became England. In the case of Arthur's death, as recorded in the *Annales Cambriae*, "the arrival of plague in the same year implies that the author was presenting Arthur's death as something for which the Lord had punished the Britons." (Higham 2009, 37) In both texts, the biblical model of providential history drives their narratives of Christ-like leaders and the fight for power.

The inexorable rise of the Saxons and the eventual destruction of British sovereignty on the island of Britain emerges as a much more explicit theme in Geoffrey of Monmouth's *Historia regum Britanniae*. By the end of his history, the British are a broken people; following civil war, a great plague, and the exile and death of their last king, Cadwallader, the country is left almost deserted and ripe for occupation by the Saxons. Though Geoffrey has a lower opinion of the Saxons than he does of the British in their prime, his real contempt is for the descendants of the British people, the Welsh:

> As their culture ebbed, they were no longer called Britons, but Welsh, a name which owes its origin to their leader Gualo, or to queen Galaes or to their decline. The Saxons acted more wisely, living in peace and harmony, tilling the fields and rebuilding the cities and towns; thus, with British lordship overthrown, they came to rule all Loegria [England], led by Athelstan, who was the first of them to wear its crown. The Welsh, unworthy successors to the noble Britons, never again recovered mastery over the whole island, but, squabbling

> pettily amongst themselves and sometimes with the Saxons, kept constantly massacring the foreigners or each other. (Geoffrey of Monmouth 2007, 280)

The "noble Britons" so much admired by Geoffrey are represented in his history by the kings of the British who trace their descent from the survivors of Troy. Among these British kings, described in a long chronological line, Arthur is the clear favourite who is given considerably more space than any of the others. When he inherits the crown from his father, Uther Pendragon, Arthur is described by Geoffrey as "a youth of fifteen, of great promise and generosity, whose innate goodness ensured that he was loved by almost everybody." (Geoffrey of Monmouth 2007, 192) On his death in battle against the treacherous Mordred, his nephew, Geoffrey reports: "The illustrious king Arthur too was mortally wounded; he was taken away to the island of Avallon to have his wounds tended and, in the year of Our Lord 542, handed over Britain's crown to his relative Constantinus, son of Cador duke of Cornwall." (Geoffrey of Monmouth 2007, 252)

In between these events, Geoffrey records the main events of Arthur's life, including his marriage to Guinevere, his magnificent coronation at Caerleon, his campaigns against the Gauls and the Romans (in which Arthur carries a shield bearing an image of the Virgin Mary), and finally his usurpation by Mordred. Though Geoffrey does not name his sources, other than saying that his history is actually a translation into Latin of "a very old book in the British tongue" (Geoffrey of Monmouth 2007, 4), it is clear that he was drawing on earlier histories, particularly Gildas' *De excidio Britanniae* (since he refers to Gildas by name) and the *Historia Brittonum*, and on early Welsh material, particularly early poetry and prophecy (Flood 2016). Geoffrey authenticates his history by using techniques familiar from classical historiography: reliance on an earlier written source, reported speeches, dramatic narratives of events, moral evaluations of behaviour and rhetorical devices which emphasize extremes of sin, virtue and divine punishment. Taking a technique from other universalizing Christian histories, Geoffrey suggests that the foundation of Britain by Brutus can be aligned with biblical chronology. Most compellingly, Geoffrey uses the language and form that signify *historia* of the conventional classical type, namely Latin prose.

Geoffrey also authenticates his history by invoking magic and the supernatural as proof that some events are beyond human control and therefore must be ordained. The story of the two dragons fighting underground, Vortigern's consultation with his "magicians", Merlin's prophecies, Uther's supernatural seduction of Ygraine, the extremes of famine and plague, the "angelic voice" that speaks to Cadwallader, are woven into the narrative as part of its providential circularity. It is significant, however, that the supernatural element more or less disappears from Geoffrey's story once Arthur is on the throne. From then until the end of his book, Geoffrey, drawing on earlier histories such as Bede's eighth-century *Historia ecclesiastica gentis Anglorum* [Ecclesiastical History of the English People], becomes increasingly authoritative, apart from highly-coloured accounts of devastation due to plague and war. Geoffrey seems determined that Arthur, almost the last and certainly the greatest of the long line of British kings, should be regarded as a genuinely historical figure from whom the aura of the supernatural has been largely removed. The manner of Arthur's conception, arranged by Merlin the magician, is normalized through Merlin's use of drugs rather than a magic object; Arthur and Merlin never meet or engage with each other in Geoffrey's text; even the reference to Arthur being taken to Avalon "to have his wounds tended" lacks the otherworld atmosphere it acquires in the later romance tradition. In Geoffrey's *Historia*, Arthur represents the high point of British hegemony; because of the workings of providence expressed through plague and famine, and the divine punishment visited on the warring British, the Saxons prevail.

Geoffrey's *Historia*, translated into a large number of vernacular languages and disseminated throughout Europe, was enormously influential for later historians. His account of Arthur's life formed the basis of new histories, expanded with additional information taken from the burgeoning literary traditions, mainly from France, about Arthur, Guinevere, Lancelot and the knights of the Round Table. Two of the earliest and most significant vernacular texts based on Geoffrey's *Historia* are the *Roman de Brut* by the Norman cleric Robert Wace, written in 1155 (Weiss 2002), and the *Brut* written at the end of the twelfth century by an English parish priest, Layamon, "the first chronicler to write in English since the final, tenacious continuators of the *Anglo-Saxon Chronicle*." (Matheson 2009, 60)

Wace's *Roman de Brut* follows the course of Geoffrey's history but adds new details from other sources, drawing especially on French chivalric romance, thus creating a hybrid form of history and romance. Said by Layamon to have been presented to Eleanor of Aquitaine, the wife of Henry II (Weiss 2002, xiii), Wace's narrative poem was intended for oral performance in the setting of the medieval court. It emphasizes the kind of chivalric and affective details typical of French vernacular romance of the time, such as the *Roman de Thebes* and the *Roman d'Eneas*, which are also associated with the court of Henry II in the middle of the twelfth century.

Layamon's *Brut* is an adaptation of Wace into English but expanded to almost double the length including a much longer Arthurian section (Le Saux 1989). Deliberately embracing a native English historiography, Layamon undid the chivalric romance style of Wace and instead emphasized Arthur's status as an old-style British warrior (Tiller 2007; cf. Meyer, *supra*). Unlike Geoffrey's *Historia*, which survives in over two hundred manuscripts, and Wace's *Roman de Brut*, surviving in twenty-four manuscripts up to the fourteenth century, Layamon's

Brut survives in only two manuscripts from the thirteenth century, suggesting a much more limited readership, perhaps due in part to what was perceived as its antiquated heroic English diction and metre (Matheson 1990). Close comparisons between the three texts by Geoffrey, Wace and Layamon suggest different authorial attitudes to Arthur, ranging from admiration of Arthur's martial victories to distrust of his political ambitions and leadership (Donahue 1998; Allen et al. 2013).

The vernacular poetic form of both Wace's *Roman de Brut* and Layamon's *Brut* signalled to medieval readers that these authors were not claiming to be writing history (which was done in Latin prose) but were consciously creating dramatic semi-fictionalized versions of what were assumed to be the historical facts of early British history as set out by Geoffrey of Monmouth. Indeed, Geoffrey's account, mediated through Wace, formed the basis of an Anglo-Norman prose history, the *Brut*, dating from the late-thirteenth century and possibly composed in the north of England (Marvin 2006; Spence 2013). Continuing the history up until the reign of Edward I, the *Brut* shifted the historiographical structure from the rise-and-fall pattern adopted by Geoffrey to a more linear model of the rise of a great people, namely the Normans, the true and legitimate inheritors of the British kingdom. This was later translated into a Middle English version, the Prose *Brut* of the fifteenth century, which circulated widely in England and was regarded as the authoritative history of England. Both the Anglo-Norman and Middle English prose *Bruts* were addressed to the same kind of audiences as the genre of chivalric romance, the nobility and, in the later Middle Ages, the wealthy urban class of merchants and royal administrators.

3 History or legend?

Almost from the date of publication of Geoffrey's *Historia regum Britanniae*, doubts began to be expressed about the factuality of Geoffrey's version of British history, particularly in relation to his story of Brutus as the founder of Britain and in relation to the great claims he made for Arthur. William of Newburgh was a particularly early critic of Geoffrey's historical accuracy. In the preface to his *Historia rerum Anglicarum* [History of English Affairs] of 1190, William denounces the *ridicula figmenta* [ridiculous inventions] that Geoffrey inserted into his account of Arthur, claiming that Geoffrey had drawn these "from the traditional fictions of the Britons, with additions of his own, and endeavoured to dignify them with the name of authentic history." (Howlett 2012, 11) Like other critics, William's scepticism was based on the fact that no mention of Arthur and his period of post-Roman history had been made by earlier historians, particularly Gildas, who was writing at about the same time that Arthur had supposedly been active as a famous military leader. But William's suspicions failed to gain much traction from medieval readers who wanted to believe in the glorious British past of their contemporary Anglo-Norman monarchs, and William's inability to offer any alternative account of early British history allowed others to dismiss or ignore his criticisms of Geoffrey (Matheson 2009).

Gerald of Wales was another twelfth-century historian who criticized Geoffrey's version of events, though Gerald's own historical method was characterized by a reliance on unsupported anecdote, apocryphal stories and an apparent belief in supernatural events which "proved" the power of divine intervention. Gerald, in his *Descriptio Cambriae* [Description of Wales], was scathing about Geoffrey's history, calling it "fabulous" (in the sense that it was based on fables) and "false" in its explanations of place names (Gerald of Wales 1978, *Description of Wales*, Book 1, Ch. 7), though it seems that Gerald was objecting to Geoffrey's historical accuracy rather than doubting the existence of Arthur altogether. In his *Itinerarium Cambriae* [Journey through Wales], he refers to Arthur's great court at Caerleon where he received ambassadors from Rome (Gerald of Wales 1978, *Journey through Wales*, Book I, Ch. V) and, describing the hilltop in south-eastern Wales called Cadair Arthur, "Arthur's Seat", he calls him "the most distinguished king of the Britons." (Book 1, Ch. 2)

Like a number of other commentators, including William of Newburgh, Gerald was dismissive of Geoffrey as a historian but nonetheless accepted the historical existence of Arthur – and of Merlin as well, whose prophecies Gerald cites as evidence of the inevitability of Welsh decline. William of Malmesbury, whose *Gesta regum Anglorum* [Deeds of the English Kings] (1125) was written at least a decade before Geoffrey's *Historia*, was already expressing scepticism about Welsh legends of Arthur's return from the grave, though he does not seem to doubt that Arthur actually existed (Thomson and Winterbottom 1998–1999, 520; cf. Johnston, *infra*). Alfred of Beverley, whose *Annales, sive, Historia de gestis regum Britanniae* [Annals, or, History of the Deeds of the Kings of Britain] were compiled about 1150, based his history mainly on Geoffrey and, although he commented on the lack of corroborating evidence for Arthur's war against the Romans, he did not challenge the view that Arthur was a historical character.

The general acceptance of the historicity of Arthur by clerical writers had a political purpose. The history of Britain, as the prehistory of the English kingdom, was regularly invoked by such writers to support the legitimacy of English monarchs as inheritors of the old British sovereignty over the island of Britain. As R.R. Davies says, "The British past had to be captured and possessed by the English if their claim to the domination of Britain, and with it the revival of Arthur's empire, was to be historically and mythologically legitimized." (Davies 2000, 41) What Arthur symbolized for the English kings, based on Geoffrey's account of his conquests and the later *Brut* retellings, was a unified territory, a single polity mapped on to the island of Britain that was called "England" but managed to include Wales and Scotland as well.

In the first half of the fourteenth century, a monk belonging to the Benedictine abbey of St Werburgh in the northern city of Chester produced a vast universal history spanning the centuries from the Creation to the author's own time, first to the year 1327 and then with additions and revisions up to the author's death in 1362/1363. This was Ranulf Higden, whose Latin *Polychronicon* was the first work of history to offer a serious challenge to the version of British history popularized by Geoffrey of Monmouth. Higden takes his lead from William of Newburgh, revisiting William's scepticism about Arthur and his supposed war against the Romans and echoing William's concern that no other chronicle from any part of Europe mentions such a war or the figure of Arthur as a historical leader of the British. Higden's history was a best-seller: it survives in more than one hundred and twenty manuscripts dating from the fourteenth and fifteenth centuries and it circulated widely among religious and secular audiences, inspiring continuations and subsequent histories of England.

The *Polychronicon* was translated into English by John Trevisa in 1387, becoming in the process a national history for the English people (Taylor 1966; Woolf 2000). But Trevisa's text was not simply a translation; he also added to and commented on Higden's history and, in a significant departure from Higden, took the completely opposite view regarding the historicity of Arthur. While Higden had been sceptical, Trevisa robustly defended Arthur as a genuine figure from history.

In the late fifteenth century, the first printer in London, William Caxton, a shrewd businessman who understood the literary tastes of London readers, published two versions of English history. The first, based on the Middle English Prose *Brut*, appeared in 1480, with a reprint in 1482, under the title *The Chronicles of England*, and contained the section about Arthur that was based ultimately on Geoffrey of Monmouth's account. In the same year, 1482, Caxton published Trevisa's English version of the *Polychronicon* but based his printed edition on a manuscript which did not contain Trevisa's defence of Arthur. What appeared, then, in quick succession, was one history telling Geoffrey's stirring tale of Arthur's Roman wars and another history containing Higden's dismissal of this same event (Matheson 1990; 2009). Though Caxton almost certainly did not intend to present such a contradictory account of English history, this publishing event brought out into the open the struggle to establish the truth about Arthur – was he a historical character or not?

4 Tudor history and Arthurian legend

The sixteenth century saw the rise of what is called humanist historiography, an approach to reconstructing the past that broke with the medieval reliance on unsubstantiated eye-witness accounts and unprovenanced sources, and consciously sought out the evidence of authoritative documents and surviving records of the past, whether written, archaeological or material. One of the earliest examples of this type of history was Robert Fabyan's *New Chronicles of England and France*, a universal history that was published after his death in 1516. Drawing on the earlier printed versions of English history, Fabyan came down somewhere in the middle of the conflicting versions: he accepted that Arthur was a historical figure but he rejected Geoffrey's account of the Roman wars.

The most systematic and persuasive challenge to Geoffrey's history was mounted by the Italian humanist historian, Polydore Vergil (*c.* 1470–1555). Moving to England as a church diplomat in 1502, Polydore had already published a number of works and was invited by Henry VII to write a complete history of England, in Latin, up to the present day. Polydore's *Anglica Historia* was finally published in Basel in 1534, during the reign of Henry VIII, with two updated editions appearing in 1546 and 1555 (Hay 1952; Davies 2015, xxxvi). Inevitably, Polydore turned to Geoffrey of Monmouth's *Historia regum Britanniae* as an important source for his history, but soon experienced similar doubts to those of earlier writers, in particular the insuperable stumbling block that no other historical sources, from classical Latin texts through to medieval Latin and vernacular chronicles from France, substantiated Geoffrey's claims about Brutus and the early British kings, or about Arthur's Roman wars. Polydore quotes in full William of Newburgh's scornful dismissal of Geoffrey's history and, summarizing Geoffrey's account of Brutus, says: "But yet nether Livie, nether Dionisius of Halicarnaseus, who writt diligentlie of the Roman antiquities, nor divers other writers, did ever once make rehersall of this Brutus." (Ellis 1846, I.30)

Writing of the Anglo-Saxon invasions of Britain in Book III, Polydore mainly follows Gildas, who did not mention Arthur at all, but, in deference to the Tudor kings he served, Polydore cautiously accepts the historicity of Arthur as one of the line of British kings, son of Uther Pendragon who followed Vortigern and Vortimer. In 1485, Henry Tudor, a Welshman, had won the throne of England and called his first son Arthur; the prediction made to Cadwallader in Geoffrey's *Historia* that the British (reappearing through the Welsh Tudor family) would one day reoccupy their lost kingdom seemed to have been fulfilled. Polydore referred to this popular prophecy at the time of Henry VII's coronation:

> Thus Henry gained the throne, as had been preordained by God's will and plan, since, as I have recalled earlier, 797 years previously Cadwallader had forecast that his stock would reign once more. Men's minds had already been gripped by the belief that Henry had been brought to the throne by this prophecy, and Henry VI had also predicted it. (Hay 1950, 1)

However, Polydore draws the line at endorsing any of Geoffrey's stories about Arthur's life as a military hero. According to Polydore, it was Uther, not Arthur, who was on the throne at the time of the battle of Badon and he implies, with great scepticism, that much of what has been written about Arthur's exploits, including the Roman wars, belongs to the world of legend rather than history, comparing the Arthurian tales to the stories told about Charlemagne's nephew Roland:

> As concerninge this noble prince, for the marvelus force of his boddie, and the invincible valiaunce of his minde, his posteritee hathe allmoste vaunted and divulged suche gestes, as in our memorie emonge the Italiens ar commonlie noysed of Roland, the nephew of Charles the Great bie his sister. (Ellis 1846, III.121–2)

In this comparison with the Charlemagne legend, Polydore implies that Geoffrey borrowed the theme of uncle and nephew from French romance and that there was no historical basis for Arthur's usurpation by Mordred.

Polydore's rewriting of British history was not welcomed by everyone; in fact, "Vergil's incredulity about Geoffrey of Monmouth's veracity attracted the patriotic, xenophobic, and religious ire of English writers." (Matheson 2009, 67) But he nonetheless reinforced the growing doubts about the historicity of Arthur, and his views were the ones that finally prevailed. While John Leland, a commissioner for Henry VIII, drew on his knowledge of Welsh writing to defend Geoffrey's history against Polydore's aspersions (Davies 2013, xxxviii), the most authoritative Tudor historians of the sixteenth century, Edward Hall (1497–1547), John Stow (1525–1605) and Raphael Holinshed (†1580), followed Polydore's lead in criticizing the Galfridian version of history, with its "fables" of Arthur, and vented their scorn on the figure of Merlin as a false prophet and charlatan. Nevertheless, these historians continued to repeat the basic outline of British history that had been first laid down by Geoffrey of Monmouth.

One of the last supporters of Geoffrey's British history was Sir John Prise (1501/1502–1555), another of Henry VIII's commissioners who undertook the dissolution of the monasteries. A Welsh-speaking Welshman from Brecon, Prise believed that the legitimate claims of the Welsh to the original rulership of Britain were at stake and that a defence of Arthur was a defence of the Welsh as the inheritors of British sovereignty. Prise's Latin treatise, *Historiae Britannicae defensio* [A Defence of the British History], published in 1573 after Prise's death, used humanist techniques to rebut the accusations of Polydore Vergil and others that stories about Arthur were largely figments of Geoffrey's imagination. Defending Geoffrey as the translator of an earlier authoritative work, not the author of a fictitious history, Prise cites numerous works in Latin and Welsh, including early poems attributed to the sixth-century poet, Taliesin, whose British hero, Urien of Rheged, he connects, rather tenuously, with Arthur (Davies 2013, 67–69). Since Urien is associated with Arthur as one of his knights only in Geoffrey's *Historia* (Davies 2013, 282), this is a somewhat circular argument but it is part of a concerted effort by Prise to find evidence for Arthur's existence that pre-dated Geoffrey's work. Prise does not deny that legends about Arthur have been invented since his death: "fables of the kind which tend to be made up about such men of distinction" (Davies 2013, 61); his task is to restore the authentic historical Arthur from the kind of evidence that Geoffrey himself was using, in particular the early histories of the British people told in their own Welsh language. The fact that William of Malmesbury had heard Welsh legends about Arthur a decade before Geoffrey wrote his history was enough proof for Prise that Arthur had been a historical king.

5 The decline of the historical Arthur

Belief in Arthur as a historical king faded away in the wake of the Reformation. With the rise of Protestantism under Elizabeth I and the rejection of medieval practices of prophecy and divination, belief in Galfridian history as a true account of the early history of Britain began to wane. Significantly, the political reasons for supporting such a history were no longer as pressing as they had been; Elizabeth I had no need to shore up her legitimacy by reference to the ancient traditions which had put her Tudor ancestors on the throne. Besides, Arthur himself belonged to a model of history, circular and providential, that was now perceived to be out-dated and almost heretical in its Catholic sense of divine retribution. It is striking that William Shakespeare, brought up on the histories of Hall and Holinshed, did not write any play, historical or otherwise, about King Arthur, as he did about King Lear, another of Geoffrey's British kings, as if Arthur's status was now too uncertain to categorize him as either authentic or legendary.

With the rediscovery of the "Ancient Britons" as a noble people betrayed by the cowardly Saxons, antiquarians expressed admiration for Arthur as a great British king (Piggot 1989). As late as the mid-eighteenth century, David Hume, author of the *History of England* (1754–1762), acknowledged the intrusion of many fables into the life of Arthur but seemed nonetheless to retain a belief in Arthur as a real person, the hero of the Britons and the scourge of the Saxons (Lupack 2009, 342). The strength of Geoffrey's Arthurian narrative, bolstered by additions from romance, therefore retained much of its power as history until the dawn of the modern era.

References

Allen, Michael I. "Universal History, 300–1000." *Historiography in the Middle Ages*. Ed. Deborah Mauskopf Deliyannis. Leiden: Brill, 2003. 17–42.

Allen, Rosamund, Jane Roberts and Carole Weinberg, eds. *Reading Layamon's Brut: Approaches and Explorations*. Amsterdam: Rodopi, 2013.

Ashe, Laura. *Fiction and History in England, 1066–1200*. Cambridge: Cambridge University Press, 2007.

Boethius. *The Consolation of Philosophy*. Trans. Victor Watts. Rev. edn. London: Penguin, 1999.

Bromwich, Rachel. *Trioedd Ynys Prydein, The Triads of the Island of Britain*. 4th edn. Cardiff: University of Wales Press, 2014.

Burke, Peter. *The Renaissance Sense of the Past*. London: Edward Arnold, 1969.

Charles-Edwards, Thomas. "The Arthur of History." *The Arthur of the Welsh: The Arthurian Legend in Medieval Welsh Literature*. Ed. Rachel Bromwich, A.O.H. Jarman and Brynley F. Roberts. Cardiff: University of Wales Press, 1991. 15–32.

Charles-Edwards, Thomas. *Wales and the Britons, 350–1064*. Oxford: Oxford University Press, 2013.

Davies, R.R. *The First English Empire: Power and Identities in the British Isles 1093–1343*. Oxford: Oxford University Press, 2000.

Davies, Ceri, ed. and trans. *John Prise: Historiae Britannicae Defensio, A Defence of the British History*. Oxford: Bodleian Library, 2015.

Donahue, Dennis P. "The Darkly Chronicled King: An Interpretation of the Negative Side of Arthur in Lawman's *Brut* and Geoffrey of Monmouth's *Historia regum Britanniae*." *Arthuriana* 8 (1998): 125–147.

Ellis, Henry, ed. *Polydore Vergil's English History, from an Early Translation, vol. 1*. London: The Camden Society, 1846.

Faletra, Michael. "The Conquest of the Past in the *History of the Kings of Britain*." *Literature Compass* 4 (2007): 121–133.

Flood, Victoria. *Prophecy, Politics and Place in Medieval England: From Geoffrey of Monmouth to Thomas of Erceldoune*. Woodbridge: Boydell and Brewer, 2016.

Geoffrey of Monmouth. *The History of the Kings of Britain*. Ed. Michael D. Reeve. Trans. Neil Wright. Woodbridge: Boydell, 2007.

Gerald of Wales. *The Journey through Wales and The Description of Wales*. Trans. Lewis Thorpe. Harmondsworth: Penguin, 1978.

Gillingham, John. *The English in the Twelfth Century: Imperialism, National Identity, and Political Values*. Woodbridge: Boydell, 2000.

Hay, Denys. *Polydore Vergil, Renaissance Historian and Man of Letters*. Oxford: Clarendon Press, 1952.

Hay, Denys, ed. and trans. *The Anglica Historia of Polydore Vergil, A.D. 1485–1537*. London: Royal Historical Society, 1950.

Higham, N.J. "Early Latin Sources: Fragments of a Pseudo-Historical Arthur." *A Companion to Arthurian Literature*. Ed. Helen Fulton. Oxford: Wiley-Blackwell, 2009. 30–43.

Howlett, Richard, ed. and trans. *Chronicles of the Reigns of Stephen, Henry II, and Richard I, Vol. I: The First Four Books of Historia Rerum Anglicarum of William of Newburgh*. Cambridge: Cambridge University Press, 2012.

Knight, Stephen. *Merlin: Knowledge and Power through the Ages*. Ithaca, NY: Cornell University Press, 2009.

Le Saux, Françoise. *Layamon's Brut: The Poem and its Sources*. Cambridge: D.S. Brewer, 1989.

Lupack, Alan. "The Arthurian Legend in the Sixteenth to Eighteenth Centuries." *A Companion to Arthurian Literature*. Ed. Helen Fulton. Oxford: Wiley-Blackwell, 2009. 340–354.

Marenbon, John. *Boethius*. Oxford: Oxford University Press, 2003.

Marvin, Julia, ed. and trans. *The Oldest Anglo-Norman Prose Brut Chronicle: An Edition and Translation*. Woodbridge: Boydell, 2006.

Matheson, Lister. "King Arthur and the Medieval English Chronicles." *King Arthur through the Ages*. Ed. V.M. Lagorio and M.L. Day. 2 vols. New York and London: Garland, 1990. I, 248–274.

Matheson, Lister M. "The Chronicle Tradition." *A Companion to Arthurian Literature*. Ed. Helen Fulton. Oxford: Wiley-Blackwell, 2009. 58–69.

Morris, John, ed. and trans. *Nennius: British History and the Welsh Annals*. Chichester: Phillimore, 1980.

Piggott, Stuart. *Ancient Britons and the Antiquarian Imagination: Ideas from the Renaissance to the Regency*. London: Thames and Hudson, 1989.

Ruddick, Andrea. *English Identity and Political Culture in the Fourteenth Century*. Cambridge: Cambridge University Press, 2013.

Spence, John. *Reimagining History in Anglo-Norman Prose Chronicles*. York: York Medieval Press, 2013.

Taylor, John. *The Universal Chronicle of Ranulf Higden*. Oxford: Clarendon Press, 1966.

Thomson, R.M., and Michael Winterbottom, ed. and trans. *William of Malmesbury, Gesta Regum Anglorum. The History of the English Kings. Vol. 1*. Oxford: Clarendon Press, 1998–1999.

Tiller, K.J. *Layamon's Brut and the Anglo-Norman Vision of History*. Cardiff: University of Wales Press, 2007.

Wace, Robert. *Wace's Roman de Brut, A History of the British: Text and Translation*. Ed. and trans. Judith Weiss. Exeter: University of Exeter Press, 2002.

Weiss, Judith. "Introduction." *Wace's Roman de Brut, A History of the British: Text and Translation*. Ed. and trans. Judith Weiss. Exeter: University of Exeter Press, 2002. xi–xxix.

Woolf, D.R. *Reading History in Early Modern England*. Cambridge: Cambridge University Press, 2000.

Jane H.M. Taylor
Rewriting: Translation, Continuation and Adaptation

Chrétien de Troyes is unapologetic – self-congratulatory in fact: he has taken his *Erec et Enide* from a *conte d'aventure* [tale of adventure] seemingly doing the rounds of medieval courts (ll. 13–14); his *Chevalier de la charrette (Lancelot)* from not only a *matiere* but a *san* (ll. 26–27) provided by his patroness Marie de Champagne (Kelly 1966, 36–85); his *Cligès* from a manuscript kept in a book-press in Beauvais (ll. 18–30);[1] his *Perceval (Conte du Graal)* from a *livre* [book] given to him by his patron Philippe d'Alsace, Count of Flanders (ll. 61–68). It seems that to claim to do no more than rewrite is laudable: rewriting taps into tradition and established fiction, and allows a poet or *romancier* to demonstrate the ingenuity with which he takes an unformed and commonplace narrative and turns it into meaning and excitement – and, perhaps, to show a flattering intimacy with a duchess or a duke known for their patronage of poets. Rewriting, in other words, is a badge of honour.[2]

Medieval writers, it might be said, are arch-exponents of rewriting,[3] having been so since the very beginning when romance, including Arthurian romance, became a recognized literary genre (Combes 2001, Introduction; Gingras 2015). At the most elementary level, the texts produced by a manuscript culture are in any case necessarily mobile: the mere process of copying produces variation and fluidity, and so also do the subtle scribal changes in wording, word order, sentence construction and dialect, that constitute what Paul Zumthor calls the

---

1 References to Chrétien's works except the *Conte du Graal* are to Poirion's edition: Chrétien de Troyes (1994). For the *Conte du Graal (Perceval)*, I use Busby's edition: Chrétien de Troyes (1995).
2 And one commonly claimed by the writers (transmitters?) of Arthurian romance: witness the elusive Luce del Gast who is said to have *translaté* the prose *Tristan* (Baumgartner 1985, 327–335), as did "Walter Map" the prose *Lancelot*. Note that, as here, I shall take my examples from my own area of expertise, medieval French literature, while cross-referring to other European literatures.
3 Hence a recent proliferation of studies: see Nicholas Arrigo (2015a; 2015b). Monfrin (1963, 61) expresses it well: "Il semble bien que l'on ait rarement eu, avant la fin du Moyen Âge, le souci historique et philologique de laisser ou de retrouver l'oeuvre d'un auteur sous la forme exacte que celui-ci avait voulu lui donner." [It seems that throughout the Middle Ages, few were concerned to restore or to retain the linguistic or historical form that the original author might have chosen].

Jane H.M. Taylor (Durham University)

DOI 10.1515/9783110432466-011

inescapable *mouvance* of the manuscript page.[4] The medieval vernacular literary text, he argues, was not usually thought of as the intellectual property of a particular writer: it was a raw material that could quite legitimately, indeed commendably, be reworked by others.[5] Literary creativity, Douglas Kelly (1996, Introduction) agrees, is thought of in the Middle Ages as far more various than modern conceptions of originality allow: a writer might intervene to explain, to re-tell, to adapt, to re-arrange, to extend: he or she might, on a larger scale, rewrite, translate, continue, adapt – and all of these would be considered not palely imitative, but admirably, delightfully creative.[6]

We have, of course, nothing to tell us what exactly it was – if anything – that Marie or Philippe provided for their tame poet. Was it, for the *Charrette*, the bare outline, a hero risking life and limb, jeopardizing reputation, for the sake of love? Might it have been, for a *Conte du Graal* seemingly heavily imbued with Christian symbolism, a rather more learned disquisition in Latin? In Chrétien's case it seems unlikely that any "source" will surface – but at a date not much earlier, a poet, Wace, living in Normandy and writing in around 1155, "translated" and adapted a pseudo-history, Geoffrey of Monmouth's *Historia regum Britanniae*.[7] The section that Wace devotes to Arthur is freely, cheerfully syncretic: he has for instance, he says with some pride, filtered into Geoffrey's original a motif which was to become canonical, Arthur's "Roünde Table" (*Brut* ll. 9747–9754, quoted Le Saux 2005, 128–130) which has been the subject of *mainte fable* [many a tale] among the British. The Round Table, Wace explains, had been a locus for promoting the chivalry, and equality, which explain Arthur's greatness; we have, here, a refocusing of Geoffrey's version of Britain's "history" according to Wace's own, new, receptor culture, one probably centred in the sophisticated court of Henry II (Le Saux 2005, 82–84; cf. Fulton, *supra*) and looking to celebrate a heroic former

---

4 Zumthor (1973, 65–75) specifically sees connections between anonymity and *mouvance*: an anonymous work, he contends, is considerably more subject to variation than, say, might be a *dit* composed by a Guillaume de Machaut in the fourteenth century.

5 To quote Lewis (1964, 211): "If you had asked Layamon or Chaucer 'Why do you not make up a brand-new story of your own?' I think they might have replied (in effect) 'Surely we are not yet reduced to that?'"

6 Many critics today suggest that the fixity of the modern printed edition is a betrayal of this essential textual mobility: see for instance Dagenais (1994). Modern technologies makes a more holistic, multi-manuscript edition possible: for an example see <https://hridigital.shef.ac.uk/partonopeus/>.

7 I simplify: Wace was combining particular version(s) of the *Historia*, and, it seems, a basket of popular oral tales. For a useful overview of "The Arthur of the Chronicles", see Le Saux and Damian-Grint (2006) and Le Saux (2005, 81–151).

age with analogies to his own.[8] Wace seems, in other words, and like his contemporaries,[9] to have treated the source text as pretext, as a prompt for artful interpretation and reinvention – and invention (Kelly 1978); the process of translation has involved not only the transformation of a linguistic construct, but its reinterpretation (*inventio*) and the eliciting of its "message" (*sententia*). St Jerome's maxim, *non verbum e verbo sed sensum de sensu* [not word for word but sense for sense] is interpreted to encourage and hence to permit the cultural reshaping of an original (Copeland 1985).[10]

That said, medieval readers, and translator-rewriters, were not uncritical:[11] not all rewritings, of predecessors in general and writers of romance in particular, were admired. Chrétien de Troyes, for instance, introduces his Arthurian romance *Erec et Enide* with a scathing denunciation of amateur, incompetent storytellers who distort and pervert ("depecier et corronpre") their source-texts: his version of *Erec*, he says, will on the contrary provide a "molt bele conjointure" (Chrétien de Troyes 1955, ll. 19–22) [literally: very beautiful composition]. Even if the precise meaning of *conjointure* is not altogether clear[12] – for Kelly (1971; 1992, 15–31) it has to do with the artful and satisfying arrangement of parts – and even if we must make allowances for the self-advertisement of a prologue, it is clear that there are aesthetic standards to which rewriters should aspire: old stories – existing stories – are not infinitely malleable. We have no way, I repeat, of accessing whatever *conte d'aventure* lies behind Chrétien's *Erec*, but over and over again, writers of romance who congratulate themselves on their own artful retellings – as does Chrétien himself celebrating the *matiere* and the *san* supplied for the *Charrette* by his patroness, or the *livre* that is, he says, the source of the *Conte du Graal* – also inveigh against the incompetence and bad faith of their rewriting competitors. In what follows here, I want to explore this ambivalence further: what are the

---

8 Typical, of course, of translation practice in the Middle Ages: see Copeland (1991, ch. 6), the papers in Ellis et al. (1989) and Galderisi (2011, esp. Buridant 325–382).
9 Although translation practice did, of course, vary: Hartmann von Aue is considerably "freer" in his adaptation of *Erec* than in his *Iwein*, see Heine (1981).
10 German translations of Chrétien's romances – Hartmann von Aue's *Iwein* and *Erec*, Wolfram von Eschenbach's *Parzival* – are the result of similarly dynamic practices: see Jackson and Ranawake (2000, 38–68), and most recently Perennec (2012). The same is true, seemingly, of Spanish, Italian and Northern material – see Hook (2015, 289–363); for material relating to adaptations of the *Lancelot en prose* and *Tristan*, see Allaire and Psaki (2014, 41–68); of *Tristan* texts, Kalinke (2011, 98–122) – and of course, considerably later, of French originals by a writer like Malory (Batt 1989; Field 1993; Mahoney 2000).
11 Wace himself hesitates to translate *Les Prophecies de Merlin*, since even he could not be sure of their meaning ("jo nel sai interpreter", l. 7540).
12 Note that *conjointure* is a hapax, appearing only in this single context (Kelly 1992, 15).

parameters that govern rewritings – not only the translations but the continua-tions, the adaptations and the *mises en prose* – and what, if any, are the limits on rewriting, what might be involved in the imposition of a new *san*, a new *conjoin-ture*? Interestingly, Chrétien's *Charrette*, left unfinished by the poet for reasons unknown, and completed – continued – by a certain Godefroi de Leigni poses this question in what seems its simplest form. In the colophon of the *Charrette*, Godefroi claims to have continued the romance "par le boen gré Crestiën qui le comança" [with the consent/goodwill of Chrétien who began it] (see Shirt 1975; Brook 1991). Yet again we know nothing of the circumstances in which Chrétien might have recruited a continuator, or of the instructions he might have given – or even indeed if Godefroi was not Chrétien's own invention;[13] moreover, he takes over the romance so seamlessly that had the former not explained his interven-tion, it is doubtful if any reader would have detected a change of authorship (Kelly 1966, 185–186).[14] Godefroi's task is in some ways relatively simple: the story has reached something of an impasse with Lancelot and Guinevere, the lovers, separately imprisoned: Lancelot, the hero, must therefore be freed and arrive just in time for a battle with the villain Meleagant whose death will release Guinevere. Most commentators find Godefroi's continuation poetically less subtle, and there remain some lesser inconsistencies that the continuator has failed to eliminate. But this minor example of continuation (Godefroi is responsible for no more than about 1000 lines of the 7000 or so of the *Charrette*) crystallizes a mechanics of reception and appropriation that must ideally be involved: an aesthetic of expan-sion which demands subservience to the intricacies of the original, understand-ing of its narrative structures, provision of a logical conclusion, cross-textual cohesion – all of which should meet generic and narrative expectations.

The case of Chrétien's *Perceval* (*Conte du Graal*) is far more complex, of course, though an inescapable reference here: like the *Charrette*, Chrétien's original is unfinished, but where Godefroi at least claims to have been licensed by the poet, no fewer than six continuators, and some minor revisers, all seemingly unau-thorized, have relayed each other to prolong this popular instance of Arthurian verse romance.[15] Chrétien would appear – at least according to our present-day

---

13 It is interesting that Genette (1982, 181–202) classes continuation under "forgerie", while Hult (1987) sees Godefroi himself as Chrétien's invention, and hence a fake.

14 Godefroi says simply that he has taken over from the point at which Lancelot was *anmurez*, [imprisoned] by Meleagant. Note that there is some doubt over where Godefroi's contribution begins (Shirt 1975).

15 There exist for the *Conte du Graal* some fourteen manuscripts, ignoring fragments, in which only three are not accompanied by one or more of the Continuations (Busby 1995, ix–lx; Hinton 2012, 245–249; Tether 2012, 9–56).

preferences – to make this the tale of an ignorant young man, Perceval, brought up in isolation deep in the forests, introduced to chivalry and becoming valiant and heroic enough to be able to seek out a mysterious object, the Grail, and to ask the culminating Grail question. We assume the finished version of the tale would have given us explanations for the Grail itself and its perplexing Grail procession (the Bleeding Lance, for instance), for the elusive Grail Castle, and for the enigmatic Fisher King, in which case also we might have understood odd features like the narrative function of what looks like a long digression recounting the much less consequential adventures of Gauvain by which the romance is interrupted. What *conjointure* did Chrétien intend? How did he expect to knit the exploits of his two heroes together? If Chrétien himself died before he was able to complete the romance,[16] then a series of continuators were sufficiently intrigued to take up the challenge of completing it and tying up the loose threads left dangling by the poet himself.[17]

The expressions I have just used, however – "complete", "tying up loose threads" – seem, paradoxically enough, not necessarily to fit the continuators' ambitions; some at least of the latter seem rather to pursue a dynamic of accumulation, that is to prefer to multiply episodes and characters and marvels and to postpone completion (Tether 2012, Ch. 3).[18] The complexities of the *Perceval* Continuations are far too great to be treated in this short chapter, but it is striking that the so-called *First Continuation* or *Continuation-Gauvain* – which exists, incidentally, in three rather different versions, the first of which, the so-called Short Redaction, seems to have been composed shortly before 1200 – seems studiously to have avoided completion, and to have postponed closure while paying occasional lip-service to such an aim. It focuses not on Perceval, whom the modern reader, as we saw, imagines as the obviously destined and paramount hero but

---

16 As claimed by Gerbert de Montreuil in his *Continuation* (l. 6986).

17 The Continuations emerge from a highly complex manuscript tradition and were for many years, and perhaps for that reason, neglected; there has been an upsurge of interest in recent years (see Bruckner 2009, Hinton 2012, Tether 2012, to add to the older but still important Gallais 1988–1989). To discuss the Continuations in any detail is impossible in the short space available here; for an exemplary brief overview of both manuscript history and narrative complexities, see Pickens, Busby and Williams (2006). A reminder however: Chrétien's *Conte du Graal* was composed *c.* 1180; the *First Continuation* in different redactions between 1195 and 1205; the *Second Continuation* between 1205 and 1210; the *Manessier Continuation* between 1225 and 1230; the *Gerbert Continuation* between 1226 and 1230. Two "prequels", the *Élucidation* and the *Bliocadran*, were composed in the early thirteenth century.

18 A rather similar dynamic of continuation-as-accumulation seems to govern, for instance, the Dutch *Walewein* (Haug 1999, Kelly 1999), as well as increasingly to govern late-medieval French Arthurian romances such as *Ysaïe le Triste*, or the *Roman de Perceforest*.

who is ignored here, but rather on Gauvain who, as just one of his pullulating adventures, does twice visit the mysterious Grail Castle, is enlightened on at least some of its mysteries (the Grail is the cup used by Joseph of Arimathea to catch the blood of Christ, the lance is that of Longinus, the Roman soldier who with it pierced the side of Christ's crucified body).[19] The anonymous poet multiplies the heroes (Perceval may be largely ignored, but we have adventures not only, and extensively, for Gauvain, but also for Arthur himself, for Carados, for Bran de Lis, for Guerrehet, among several), and to have revelled in making the marvellous far more multifarious than in Chrétien's sober original. Might this reflect the preferences of a particular court, or a particular socio-cultural environment? At the very least, it must say something about the kinds of episode or the types of problem to which an audience might have responded in the text of Chrétien's original (Bruckner 2009, 15): the discomfort with which, today, we regret Chrétien's diversion to Gauvain is not apparently shared by contemporary audiences, or continuators. Rather than imagining *Perceval* moving forward seamlessly into its continuation, the two being seen as a single fiction,[20] ought we to imagine an audience demanding yet another exciting episode in an "unruly and exuberant narrative"? (Pickens, Busby and Williams 2006, 227)[21]

The remainder of the *Perceval* Continuations, however – the *Second*, the *Manessier* and the *Gerbert Continuations* – do return to Perceval, and do invest increasingly, and successfully, in the expansion followed by the completion of Chrétien's original.[22] Manessier, for instance, the poet of the third of the Continuations, writing somewhere between 1214 and 1227, while accumulating adventures as energetically as his predecessors, seems also to have proceeded as we might expect from a continuation: he brings Chrétien's romance and its two existing Continuations to a satisfying conclusion; he claims to have done so for his patron

---

19 These details are first supplied by the highly inventive and imaginative Robert de Boron, in his own continuation of Chrétien's original, the *Estoire du Graal*, written shortly after 1200 and therefore preceding all of the *Perceval* Continuations (for its manuscript history, and its prose rewriting, see Pickens, Busby and Williams 2006, 247–250). The *Perceval* Continuators therefore are incorporating – accumulating – material provided by Robert rather than creating inventions of their own.

20 Which might well be the case (Bruckner 2009, 14). By far the majority of manuscripts of Chrétien's *Conte du Graal* contain one or more of the Continuations: one might question whether medieval readers, let alone medieval audiences, were actually aware that they were confronting a composite, multi-authored romance.

21 *Perceval* appears to invite continuation: see Jackson and Ranawake (2000, 69–80).

22 Note that Hinton (2012, 29–69) supposes that we are talking not of an original-with-continuations, but of an experiment in the elaboration of a veritable cycle of Grail texts, using interlace and cross-reference as principles of cyclic structure.

Jeanne, Countess of Flanders (Roach 1983, ll. 42643–42644), and presumably is reflecting preferences articulated in the socio-cultural milieu of her court. To do so, he has isolated the key features of those texts, identified their key thematic components, and ensured that they are reprised in ways which might meet narrative expectation. In particular, he seems to have a preference for "reason and reassurance" over "the enigmatic and the bewildering" (Pickens, Busby and Williams 2006, 235). Manessier, initially, reverts to the Gauvain of the *Second Continuation*, but he brings Perceval back, triumphantly, to the Grail Castle. He then manoeuvres matters so that Perceval can heal the Fisher King of his wounds and so that the lineal relationships between the two, adumbrated by Chrétien, can be clarified. After yet more adventures, Manessier has Perceval crowned king of Corbenic, of the Grail Castle therefore, and thus puts a definitive end to the Continuations with Perceval's retreat to a hermitage, and his death and ascent into heaven (taking with him, Grail and Lance).[23]

The *Perceval* Continuations continue to defy all attempts at easy summary; all told – Continuations, prequels – they consist of a total of some 75,000 lines (Pickens, Busby and Williams 2006, 222). What this huge collaborative effort betokens is, of course, a hunger for extensions to a celebrated and inviting original – but they are also evidence of social and cultural practices, and of the relational forces that no doubt drove the literary-fictional life of a particular circle, or court (Combes 2001, 29–105). In the act of continuation, there is a close relationship that links poet and audience, or in medieval terms patron and audience, the tastes that demand completion on the one hand and, on the other, what must have been ambivalent drives towards completion certainly, but paradoxically, also towards that postponement of completion which prolongs readerly pleasure and thus ensures continued patronage. It could be said that continuation, as a strategic and a complex game, acts as a rough barometer of an audience's expectations, and of their sense of the importance, the desirability, of an original; that the interpretative manoeuvres of the Continuators expose a rich and collective history of literary production.

This highly creative, highly collaborative relationship is, on the surface at least, less evident in the case of another variety of rewriting: *mise en prose*, the intralingual prose rewriting of romances, and epics, in the fourteenth, fifteenth

---

23 Gerbert's *Continuation* on the other hand, written somewhere between 1225 and 1230, is conceived as an interpolation, interposed, temporally speaking, between the *Second Continuation* and that of Manessier. Whilst it has been postulated that Gerbert might have intended an end which has since been lost, the text as we have it today does not aim to complete Chrétien's original, and remains resolutely accumulative.

and sixteenth centuries in France (Colombo Timelli and Ferrari 2010) – a genre which has also been much neglected until very recently.[24] The *prosateurs*[25] are unanimous: as the *prosateur* of Chrétien's *Perceval* – once again – says in 1530, the language of the originals has now become "non acoustumé et estrange" [alien and strange], and yet the romances are still in demand: the *prosateur* will devote himself to "translating" it into "prose familiere" [everyday prose].[26] The 1530 *Perceval* is just one of three of Chrétien's romances to have been *mis en prose* in the late Middle Ages and the early Renaissance: two others, *Cligès* and *Erec*, were subjected to the same treatment in the mid-fifteenth century at the Burgundian court, and survive complete in a single manuscript each – and the editorial behaviours of the *prosateurs*, the hierarchies of taste which their procedures suggest, are usefully characteristic. Take, for instance, what might look like a minor detail in the *mise en prose* of Chrétien's *Erec et Enide*:[27] readers of Chrétien's original will remember that when Erec marries Enide and returns to his own country, he dismays his courtiers by neglecting all manly pursuits – hunting, tournaments – and devoting himself to his wife (*Erec*, ll. 2446–2474). All this is perfectly comprehensible, Chrétien implies: Enide is peerlessly beautiful, charming, generous, courtly (*Erec*, ll. 2422–2445). The Burgundian *prosateur*, however, adds or removes one or two details (*Erec en prose*, 170–171) which expand the original: they may look very minor, but they seem to typify the intertextual exchanges between source text and *mise en prose* in which even the most apparently conservative *prosateurs* indulge, and suggest some of the cultural pressures that may govern the remaking and the reshaping of the original. Chrétien extols not only the beauty, but also the virtue of his heroine: no one, he tells us, could ever find reason to disparage her, to reproach her with *folie*, *malvestié*, or *vilenie* [wrongdoing, evil, or transgression]; Erec, on the other hand, seeks nothing but to make love to her ("A sa fame volt dosnoier"; *Erec*, l. 2434). Our *prosateur*, however, adds the following:

---

24 The remarkable collaborative enterprise by Colombo Timelli et al. (2014) provides an invaluable compendium on the *mises en prose*, with full bibliographical details of the primary texts and exhaustive listings of secondary material (to 2014); its dimensions – 929 pp. – show how far interest in the *mises en prose* has grown.

25 I use the French term for which there is no obvious English equivalent.

26 I quote from the prologue to the prose version of *Perceval le Gallois*, published in Paris in 1530 by Jean Longis and others; an edition is in train by Colombo Timelli who has already published the prologue (2014, 682–684). The 1530 *Perceval* is available on Gallica (<http://gallica.bnf.fr>). As well as the Burgundian *Erec* and *Cligès*, to which I refer below, there exists also a *mise en prose* of part of Renaud de Beaujeu's *Le Bel Inconnu* (see Taylor 2014, 119–146).

27 I use Colombo Timelli's edition of the *Erec en prose* (2000).

Chastement se continst Enide avec son mari Erec et, combien que pluseurs aguetemens fussent par envie mis sus elle, il n'y eust oncquez engin d'homme ne de femme tant sceut de mal pencer qui sur elle trouvast une tasche de laidure. (*Erec en prose*, 170)
[Enide behaved most chastely with her husband Erec, and although courtiers set many traps for her, even the most ingenious of men or women was not malicious enough to detect a trace of iniquity.]

This looks innocuous enough – merely a small embroidery on Chrétien's original – but behind it lies a wealth of presupposition which the *prosateur* hopes, apparently, to ward off. There is, in the first place, a very long misogynist tradition surrounding the gallant hero undone by a lascivious woman – the so-called "power of woman *topos*": Samson undone by the womanly wiles of Delilah, Aristotle – in all his wisdom – undone by those of Phyllis (Smith 1995). The adverb *chastement* is surely added precisely to preclude any easy misogynist blame: Enide is not exercising a dangerous sexual influence. When moreover, in the second place, the *prosateur* carefully explains that members of Erec's court set traps ("aguetemens") for Enide, he is – I believe – tapping into another late-medieval commonplace, the corruptions and deceptions of the court (Cooper 1977, 58–74): might an *habitué* of one of the great courts of the fifteenth century, the Burgundian court, be primed to imagine just such nefarious manoeuvrings? I cite what must seem this very inconspicuous example of rewriting because I believe that here as elsewhere (Taylor 1998), we need to be particularly alert to the ways in which a rewriting imposes, surreptitiously but unmistakably, a cultural filter (House 1977, 107) to appeal to a quite specific local constituency, with its own cultural and moral values. And we should also welcome one of the great benefits of looking at rewritings, *mise en prose* included: that they show with particular clarity the adapter's involvement in the creation of meaning, a meaning specific to one particular reading of consciousness and its negotiations with taste and preference.

Throughout this chapter I have, tacitly, distinguished "rewriting", as a category, from translation, from *mise en prose* or from purely scribal interventions: if, for instance, there are indeed different versions of the prose *Lancelot*, cyclic and non-cyclic (Kennedy et al. 2006), or longer and shorter versions of the same romance (Micha 1964–1966, and *pace* Speer 2012), then these have not seemed to me fully to fall into the category of "rewriting". But Arthurian romance is infinitely open to much more wholesale revision and adaptation (see, for instance, Wahlen 2007, 351–360 on the different manifestations of the Morholt). What is now known as the *Post-Vulgate Cycle*, for instance, is a case in point:[28] it occupies a prime position in a sizeable chapter of *The Arthur of the French* entitled "Rewriting Prose Romance" (Bogdanow and Trachsler 2009, 340–392), and deals, at length, with the reframing and reinterpretation of the Grail story as adumbrated by Chrétien, as elaborated by the Continuators whose work we have already explored, and as filled out by those who, like Robert de Boron, saw opportunities for imaginative gap-filling; it seems designed by its writers and compilers to ensure the coherence of what had become a chaotic history of the Grail, and to impose a more consistently moralistic tone (Vinaver 1970, 129–149). I want, however, to turn to a rather less tangled, if also rather later, instance of rewriting, partly for the sake of clarity, partly because it is the work of a writer who makes explicit rewriting's promise of a wholesale, new and textually improved version which mediates a literary past for its readers, a process which, I consider, is particularly advanced in the case of the transition from manuscript to print. Such a promise is, for instance, precisely the programme articulated by the preliminary *Ode* appended to a literary curiosity, Jean Maugin's revision of *Tristan* published in 1554 (Taylor 2014, 183–202). Maugin, an obscure jobbing poet and adaptor who liked to be known as the *petit Angevin*, explains at rather tedious length why old fictions should be renewed, and continues:

> Et pour au vieigl Tristan oster
> Tout le passé, lui fis gouter
> Du fleuve d'obliance,
> Dont Tristan mit tout en obly:
> Ores le voyez ennobly
> De nouvelle eloquence. (Maugin 1554, unpaged)
> [And in order to purge the old Tristan story of all its past, I had it taste the river of forgetfulness, which had had Tristan nearly forgotten: now you may see it exalted with a new eloquence.]

Maugin has, he says significantly, stripped the romance of all its past, all the primitive baggage which had left it forgotten; he has, he claims, restored it to its proper nobility of soul, and equipped it with the *nouvelle eloquence* – Maugin's key phrase – demanded by the reader of 1554.

---

28 As, of course, is the *Perlesvaus*, a reframing and retelling of Chrétien's *Perceval* (Pickens, Busby and Williams 2009, 260–264), and indeed as is also the *Queste del saint Graal* (305–311). For the *Post-Vulgate Cycle*, see Bogdanow (1991–2011), and for a lucid exposition of its extremely tangled codicological history, impossible to deal with here, see Bogdanow and Trachsler (2009, 342–357).

The *Roman de Tristan* had, after all, been published, successfully, several times in the age of print, from the time of Antoine Vérard's handsome *editio princeps* of 1489 (Winn 2009; Taylor 2014, 83–90). A medieval reader would not have found it unfamiliar, either narratively or linguistically: copy-editors, or compositors, had certainly done some modernization: updating of orthography and syntax, addition of occasional picturesque details, but the adjustments are minor, and assume a reader whose tastes will be very similar to those of the thirteenth century. By 1554, however, publication of Arthurian romances had come almost to a halt; Maugin's *nouvelle eloquence* will, he hopes, by adapting *Tristan* to new and more sophisticated taste, bring about a revival.[29] Modern readers may well prefer the spare, laconic style of the original prose *Tristan*; Maugin, however, takes every opportunity to embroider: thus the dawning of love between hero and heroine is translated into the torrents of metaphor and synonymy, threnodies of anguished passion (Maugin 1554, 170–171) – an aesthetic of inflation which does indeed seem to have fuelled the taste for romance in the mid-sixteenth century (Lanham 1976, 216–217) and hence to have driven Maugin's own "re-creation" of the *Tristan* story. His originality consists perfectly licitly – as does that of other rewriters – in the imaginative refashioning and interpretation of inherited materials.

The operations I class here, loosely, under "rewriting" are manifold – something signalled, as we saw, by the wealth of synonyms it attracts: translate, continue, adapt, of course, but also reframe, refashion, revise, reinterpret. It is tempting to think of these different enterprises as acts of poetic piracy, but the rewriters claim, not without reason, to be extending the expressive relevance of their originals. Rewriting, perhaps especially in the Middle Ages, needs to be seen as part of what McGann (1991, 1) calls a "ceaseless process of textual development and mutation": as part of that dialogue between text and reader and audience which, for Arthurian romance, ensures the continuing value of the language of chivalry as a currency for literary esteem.

References

Allaire, Gloria, and F. Regina Psaki, eds. *The Arthur of the Italians. The Arthurian Legend in Medieval Italian Literature and Culture*. Cardiff: University of Wales Press, 2014.

---

29 In which he was to be disappointed: the first book should have been the first part of a four-volume set; although it enjoyed a certain success – there were three further editions – the remaining books never materialized.

Arrigo, Nicholas. "Bibliographie des travaux critiques sur la réécriture française." *Réécritures*. Ed. Dorothea Kullmann and Shaun Lalonde. Toronto: Pontifical Institute of Mediaeval Studies, 2015a. 319–358.

Arrigo, Nicholas. "La réécriture française: quelques éléments pour un état des recherches." *Réécritures*. Ed. Dorothea Kullmann and Shaun Lalonde. Toronto: Pontifical Institute of Mediaeval Studies, 2015b. 301–318.

Barron. W.R.J., ed. *The Arthur of the English: The Arthurian Legend in Medieval English Literature*. Cardiff: University of Wales Press, 2001.

Batt, Catherine. "Malory's Questing Beast and the Implications of the Author as Translator." *The Medieval Translator: The Theory and Practice of Translation in the Middle Ages*. Ed. Roger Ellis, Jocelyn Price, Stephen Medcalf and Peter Meredith. Cambridge: D.S. Brewer, 1989. 143–166.

Baumgartner, Emmanuèle. "Luce del Gat et Hélie de Boron: le chevalier et l'écriture." *Romania* 106 (1985): 326–340.

Besamusca, Bart, and Erik Kooper, eds. *Originality and Tradition in the Middle Dutch* Roman van Walewein. Arthurian Literature 17. Cambridge: D.S. Brewer, 1999.

Bogdanow, Fanni, ed. *La version post-vulgate de la "Queste del saint Graal" et de la "Mort Artu"*. Paris: Société des anciens textes français, 1991–2011.

Bogdanow, Fanni, and Richard Trachsler. "Rewriting Prose Romance: The Post-Vulgate *Roman du Graal* and Related Texts." *The Arthur of the French: The Arthurian Legend in Medieval French and Occitan Literature*. Ed. Glyn S. Burgess and Karen Pratt. Cardiff: University of Wales Press, 2006. 342–392.

Brook, Leslie C. "The Continuator's Monologue: Godefroy de Lagny and Jean de Meun." *French Studies* 45 (1991): 1–16.

Bruckner, Matilda. *Chrétien Continued: A Study of the* Conte du Graal *and its Verse Continuations*. Oxford and New York: Oxford University Press, 2009.

Burgess, Glyn S., and Karen Pratt, eds. *The Arthur of the French: The Arthurian Legend in Medieval French and Occitan Literature*. Cardiff: University of Wales Press, 2006.

Busby, Keith. *Codex and Context: Reading Old French Verse Narrative in Manuscript*. 2 vols. Amsterdam: Rodopi, 2002.

Chrétien de Troyes. *Le Roman de Perceval ou Le Conte du Graal*. Ed. Keith Busby. Tübingen: Max Niemeyer, 1995.

Chrétien de Troyes. *Oeuvres complètes*. Ed. Daniel Poirion. Bibliothèque de la Pléiade. Paris: Gallimard, 1994. *Erec et Enide*, 3–169; *Lancelot ou le Chevalier de la Charrette*, 507–682; *Perceval ou le Conte du Graal*, 685–911.

Colombo Timelli, Maria. "La *Tresplaisante et recreative hystoire du trespreulx et vaillant chevallier Perceval le Galloys* ... (1530), mise en prose tardive du *Cycle du Graal*." *Le Moyen français* 64 (2009): 13–54.

Colombo Timelli, Maria, ed. *L'Histoire d'Erec en prose: roman du XVe siècle*. Geneva: Droz, 2000.

Colombo Timelli, Maria, and Barbara Ferrari, eds. *Mettre en prose aux XIVe–XVIe siècles*. Turnhout: Brepols, 2010.

Colombo Timelli, Maria, Barbara Ferrari, Anne Schoysman and François Suard, eds. *Pour un nouveau répertoire des mises en prose: roman, chanson de geste, autres genres*. Paris: Classiques Garnier, 2014.

Combes, Annie. *Les voies de l'aventure. Réécriture et composition romanesque dans le Lancelot en prose*. Paris: Champion, 2001.

Cooper, Helen. *Pastoral: Mediæval into Renaissance*. Cambridge: D.S. Brewer, 1977.

Copeland, Rita. "The Fortunes of 'non verbum pro verbo': or, Why Jerome is Not a Ciceronian." *The Medieval Translator: The Theory and Practice of Translation in the Middle Ages*. Ed. Roger Ellis, Jocelyn Price, Stephen Medcalf and Peter Meredith. Cambridge: D.S. Brewer, 1989. 15–35.

Copeland, Rita. *Rhetoric, Hermeneutics and Translation in the Middle Ages*. Cambridge: Cambridge University Press, 1991.

Dagenais, John. *The Ethics of Reading in a Manuscript Culture: Glossing the* Libro de buen amor. Princeton, NJ: Princeton University Press, 1994.

Deschepper, Catherine. "'Mise en prose' et 'translation', la traduction intralinguale des romans de Chrétien de Troyes en moyen français." Unpublished doctoral thesis: University of Louvain-la-Neuve, 2003.

Ellis, Roger, Jocelyn Price, Stephen Medcalf and Peter Meredith, eds. *The Medieval Translator: The Theory and Practice of Translation in the Middle Ages*. Cambridge: D.S. Brewer, 1989.

Field, P.J.C. "Sir Thomas Malory's *Le Morte d'Arthur*." *The Arthur of the English: The Arthurian Legend in Medieval English Literature*. Ed. W.R.J. Barron. Cardiff: University of Wales Press, 2001. 225–246.

Field, P.J.C. "Malory and the French Prose *Lancelot*." *Bulletin of the John Rylands University Library of Manchester* 75 (1993): 79–102.

Galderisi, Claudio, ed. *Translations médiévales. Cinq siècles de traduction en français au Moyen Âge (XIe–XVe siècles). Étude et Répertoire*, vol. 1: *De la* translatio studii à l'étude de la translatio. Turnhout: Brepols, 2011.

Gallais, Pierre. *L'imaginaire d'un romancier français de la fin du XIIe siècle: description raisonnée, comparée et commentée de la "Continuation-Gauvain": première suite du "Conte du Graal" de Chrétien de Troyes*. Amsterdam: Rodopi, 1988–1989.

Genette, Gérard. *Palimpsestes: la littérature au second degré*. Paris: Seuil, 1982.

Gingras, Francis. "Les réécritures de *Lancelot du Lac* dans la longue durée: de la tradition manuscrite aux premiers incunables." *Réécritures*. Ed. Dorothea Kullmann and Shaun Lalonde. Toronto: Pontifical Institute of Mediaeval Studies, 2015. 14–27.

Haug, Walter. "The *Roman van Walewein* as a Postclassical Literary Experiment." *Originality and Tradition in the Middle Dutch* Roman van Walewein. Ed. Bart Besamusca and Erik Kooper. Arthurian Literature 17. Cambridge: D.S. Brewer, 1999. 17–28.

Heine, Thomas. "Shifting Perspectives: The Narrative Strategy in Hartmann's *Erec*." *Orbis litterarum* 36 (1981): 95–115.

Hinton, Thomas. *The Conte du Graal Cycle: Chrétien de Troyes' Perceval, the Continuations, and French Arthurian Romance*. Cambridge: D.S. Brewer, 2012.

Hook, David, ed. *The Arthur of the Iberians: The Arthurian Legends in the Spanish and Portuguese Worlds*. Cardiff: University of Wales Press, 2015.

House, Juliane. "A Model for Assessing Translation Quality." *Meta* 22 (1977): 103–109.

Hult, David F. "Author/Narrator/Speaker: the Voice of Authority in Chrétien's *Charrete*." *Discourses of Authority in Medieval and Renaissance Literature*. Ed. Kevin Brownlee and Walter Stevens. Hanover and London: University Press of New England, 1989. 76–96.

Jackson, W.H., and S.A. Ranawake, eds. *The Arthur of the Germans: the Arthurian Legend in Medieval German and Dutch Literature*. Cardiff: University of Wales Press, 2000.

Kalinke, Marianne E., ed. *The Arthur of the North. The Arthurian Legend in the Norse and Rus' Realms*. Cardiff: University of Wales Press, 2011.

Kelly, Douglas. "La conjointure de l'anomalie et du stéréotype: un modèle de l'invention dans les romans arthuriens en vers." *Cahiers de civilisation médiévale* 14 (2007): 25–39.

Kelly, Douglas. "The Pledge Motif in the *Roman van Walewein*: Original Variant and Rewritten Quest." *Originality and Tradition in the Middle Dutch* Roman van Walewein. Ed. Bart Besamusca and Erik Kooper. Arthurian Literature 17. Cambridge: D.S. Brewer, 1999. 29–46.

Kelly, Douglas, ed. *The Medieval Opus: Imitation, Rewriting, and Transmission in the French Tradition. Proceedings of the Symposium Held at the Institute for Research in the Humanities, October 5–7 1995, The University of Wisconsin-Madison.* Amsterdam: Rodopi, 1996.

Kelly, Douglas. *The Art of Medieval French Romance.* Madison, WI: University of Wisconsin Press, 1992.

Kelly, Douglas. "*Translatio studii*: Translation, Adaptation and Allegory in Medieval French Literature." *Philological Quarterly* 57 (1978): 287–310.

Kelly, Douglas. "The Source and Meaning of *Conjointure* in Chrétien's *Erec*." *Viator* 1 (1971): 179–200.

Kelly, Douglas. *Sens and Conjointure in the "Chevalier de la Charrette".* Paris and The Hague: Mouton, 1966.

Kennedy, Elspeth et al. "Lancelot With and Without the Grail: *Lancelot do Lac* and the Vulgate Cycle." *The Arthur of the French: The Arthurian Legend in Medieval French and Occitan Literature.* Ed. Glyn S. Burgess and Karen Pratt. Cardiff: University of Wales Press, 2006. 274–324.

Kullmann, Dorothea, and Shaun Lalonde, eds. *Réécritures.* Toronto: Pontifical Institute of Mediaeval Studies, 2015.

Lanham, Richard A. *The Motives of Eloquence: Literary Rhetoric in the Renaissance.* New Haven, CT and London: Yale University Press, 1976.

Le Saux, Françoise. *A Companion to Wace.* Cambridge: D.S. Brewer, 2005.

Le Saux, Françoise, and Peter Damian-Grint. "The Arthur of the Chronicles." *The Arthur of the French: The Arthurian Legend in Medieval French and Occitan Literature.* Ed. Glyn S. Burgess and Karen Pratt. Cardiff: University of Wales Press, 2006. 93–111.

Lewis, C.S. *The Discarded Image. An Introduction to Medieval and Renaissance Literature.* Cambridge: Cambridge University Press, 1964.

Mahoney, Dhira B. "The Truest and Holiest Tale: Malory's Transformation of the *Queste del Saint Graal*." *The Grail: A Casebook.* Ed. Dhira B. Mahoney. New York: Garland, 2000. 379–396.

Maugin, Jean. *Le Premier livre du nouveau Tristan, prince de Leonnais (...) et d'Yseulte, princeesse d'Yrlande (...) par Jan Maugin, dit l'Angevin.* Paris: Vve M. de La Porte, 1554. Available on Gallica <http://gallica.bnf.fr/>.

McGann, Jerome. *The Textual Condition.* Princeton, NJ: Princeton University Press, 1991.

Micha, Alexandre. "La Tradition manuscrite du *Lancelot en prose*." *Romania* 85 (1964): 293–318, 478–517; 86 (1965): 330–359; 87 (1966): 192–233.

Monfrin, Jacques. "Humanisme et traductions au moyen âge." *Journal des Savants* (Jan–Mar 1963): 161–190.

Perennec, René. "Les adaptations allemandes de romans de Chrétien de Troyes et les jeux de la fiction et de la vérité." *Fictions de vérité dans les réécritures des romans de Chrétien de Troyes. Actes du colloque organisé à Rome du 28 au 30 avril 2010.* Ed. Annie Combes. Paris: Classiques Garnier, 2012. 125–156.

Pickens, Rupert T., Keith Busby and Andrea M. L. Williams. "Perceval and the Grail: the Continuations, Robert de Boron and *Perlesvaus*." *The Arthur of the French: The Arthurian*

Legend in Medieval French and Occitan Literature. Ed. Glyn S. Burgess and Karen Pratt. Cardiff: University of Wales Press, 2006. 215–273.

Roach, W.J., ed. *The Continuations of the Old French Perceval of Chrétien de Troyes*. 6 vols. Philadelphia: University of Pennsylvania Press, 1949–1983.

Shirt, David. "Godefroi de Lagny et la composition de la *Charrete*." *Romania* 96 (1975): 27–52.

Smith, Susan L. *The Power of Women: A Topos in Medieval Art and Literature*. Philadelphia, PA: University of Pennsylvania Press, 1995.

Speer, Mary B. "The Long and the Short of Lancelot's Departure from Logres. Abbreviation as Rewriting in *La Mort le roi Artu*." *Text and Intertext in Medieval Arthurian Literature*. Ed. Norris J. Lacy. New York and London: Routledge, 2012. 219–239.

Taylor, Jane H.M. *Rewriting Arthurian Romance in Renaissance France. From Manuscript to Printed Book*. Cambridge: D.S. Brewer, 2014.

Taylor, Jane H.M. "The Significance of the Insignificant: Reading Reception in the Burgundian *Erec* and *Cligès*." *Fifteenth-Century Studies* 24 (1998): 183–197.

Tether, Leah. *The Continuations of Chrétien's* Perceval: *Content and Construction, Extension and Ending*. Cambridge: D.S. Brewer, 2012.

Vinaver, Eugène. *À la recherche d'une poétique médiévale*. Paris: Nizet, 1970.

Wahlen, Barbara. "Entre tradition et réécriture: le bon Morholt d'Irlande, chevalier de la Table Ronde." *Façonner son personnage au Moyen Âge: Actes du 31e colloque du CUER MA*. Ed. Chantal Connochie-Bourgne. Aix-en-Provence: Publications de l'Université de Provence, 2007. 351–360.

Winn, Mary Beth. "Vérard's Editions of *Tristan*." *Vendanges Tardives: Late French Arthurian Romances*. Ed. Carol J. Chase and Joan Tasker Grimbert. *Arthuriana* 19 (2009): 47–73.

Zumthor, Paul. *Essai de poétique médiévale*. Paris: Seuil, 1973.

Marjolein Hogenbirk
Intertextuality

1 Medieval intertextuality

The term "intertextuality", coined in the late sixties by Julia Kristeva, refers to a literary theory or a reading method for analyzing how individual texts are connected to other texts, a phenomenon which is as old as literature itself.[1] Texts are mosaics of quotations and never entirely new: they are made up of, or connected to, earlier texts and traditions, and they continue them. The earlier texts, the intertexts (or, more accurately, pretexts), resound like other voices in the new text as a result of which the cultural life of the older texts is extended. This way of textual sharing invites a comparison between the textual traditions outside of the actual object of research, and the use of these texts inside it. It asks us to think about how and why an author is choosing a particular text, name or situation in his work and to what effect these older elements are reimagined. Over the years, intertextuality has become a much-used term which has come to be defined in many ways.

Medievalists in particular have developed various critical approaches. Long before the term was coined, they recognized a ubiquitous response to oral or written authorities in medieval literature, since authors "participate in an aesthetic of conventionality which prizes re-writing above "originality" *ex nihilo*." (Bruckner 1987, 222) However, there is no reason to believe that medieval authors just looked at previous texts as models and "classics" to be imitated. They are confronted with a set of choices, which range from taking a mimetic approach to exploring variations on well-known structural schemes, themes and motifs, to making a clean break with conventional patterns. Therefore, we are not dealing with a simple donor-recipient model. Intertextuality is part of the unique identity of medieval works, demanding an analysis of its particular function and use within the boundaries of the single text and its specific historical literary context.

---

1 I have used several studies, papers and commentaries on intertextuality for this chapter. I have benefited especially from the articles in Van Dijk et al. (2013), and from the following invaluable (Arthurian) studies: Bruckner (1987); Wolfzettel (1990); Kelly (1992); Besamusca (1993); Lacy (1996); Thomas (2005); Gordon (2010).

Marjolein Hogenbirk (University of Amsterdam)

DOI 10.1515/9783110432466-012

Literary historians studying medieval texts generally adopt the term inter-textuality in a way that is restricted in relation to the objects of study, focusing mainly on the relationships between written texts. Moreover, they use it more as an analytical instrument for determining the meaning of a literary work, than as a theory. They search for thematic echoes of earlier texts, for quotations and citations and corresponding characters and situations in order to determine the meaning of a literary work within its specific cultural context (Wolfzettel 1990, 6). An axiom of this is that forms of textual sharing are likely to have been inserted deliberately by authors and are meant to be recognized. Consequently, intertextu-ality is considered to be a creative process, an ensemble or a form of play between poets and their readers.

This general approach towards intertextuality and reception raises several problems. The first is obviously the uncertain dating of individual literary works. Most of the time, it is difficult to determine which text refers to which. Seldom do we find the kind of concrete information seen in the thirteenth-century *Hunbaut*, in which the poet denies that he has stolen words from Chrétien (Winters 1984, ll. 186–187). Another difficulty is the problematic authorial status of medieval narratives and the notion of *mouvance*. Texts are fundamentally unstable and move in time and space. Every single text is unique and two manuscript versions of the same text often show considerable differences. As a result, scholars may experience major difficulties in discovering the author's intertextual intentions, assuming, but not knowing for certain, that a specific text in a certain manu-script indeed represents an author's voice. However, the medieval manuscripts in which the texts have survived are the chief witnesses to the reception and use of texts over time, as well as to the culture that created and appreciated them, even if we are generally dealing with later reception phases. So-called miscel-lanies and anthologies, for example, are also manifestations of intertextuality, since they offer numerous possibilities for the study of intertextual patterns both within the individual texts as well as between the texts incorporated in a certain codex.[2]

Another point for consideration when investigating medieval intertextuality concerns the way in which the narratives reached their audiences. The author of a text is usually visible in the narrator's interventions, and these, of course, could be voiced by a performer. All (implied) voices might have engaged the audience to search for correspondences with other episodes and texts (Krueger 1987, 140). However, we actually know very little about reception modes. Were the romances

---

2 See, for instance, an analysis of the famous Arthurian manuscript Chantilly, Musée Condé 472 in Walters (1994). See also Busby et al. (1993) and Busby (2002).

indeed meant to be performed orally, to be read (aloud) in smaller or larger settings or, perhaps most likely, were they received through both means? Another question is to what extent were subtle intertextual references noticed during noisy performances? On the other hand, performances delivered repeatedly, especially through the agency of a knowing jongleur, might have helped to raise audiences' awareness of intertextual allusions, textual correspondences or citations. In any case, in order to recognize subtle or even obvious intertextual borrowing, regardless of the various modes of reception, we must *a priori* presume that there was an audience of *connaisseurs* with a considerable amount of literary baggage, even if there are likely to have been different levels of understanding within and between audiences.[3] The audience for Middle Dutch romances, for example, must have been different from the audience for Chrétien and his direct followers, and may well have been less educated. And yet, we find specific references to French romances, so presumably these audiences, or at least a part of them, could similarly be described as "knowing experts" (Besamusca 1993, 187; Hogenbirk 2011, 130–132).

Apart from the common and more restricted approach to medieval intertextuality, a broader perspective on the phenomenon is possible. First, the notion of "text" may cover not only written texts and the field of literature. Systems, codes and traditions established in other art forms are also crucial to the meaning of literary works, and therefore "text" may also refer to every cultural system operating inside or outside of literary texts. Secondly, all references, intended or otherwise, to the cultural context or to other texts could be considered intertextual in a broader sense. Especially relevant to historical texts is the awareness that we are never able to reconstruct fully the experiences of historical readers and their exact horizon of expectations (I return to this below). We always include our own perspective and run the risk of knowing the author better than the author himself. This is a problematic aspect indeed, but it could also be considered an exciting and promising one. As twenty-first-century readers, we are able to overlook various traditions and may decide for ourselves which texts are engaged in a specific dialogue. Intertextuality, therefore, has no ending, and the potential meaning and interpretation of a text never stops.

---

3 See, for instance, Kelly (1992, 120); Schmolke-Hasselmann (1998, Ch. 8). See also Besamusca (*supra*).

2 The Arthurian perspective

Medieval Arthurian romance could be considered as the intertextual genre *par excellence*, since the intertextual links within the Arthurian tradition are "more elaborate and pervasive than in most other literary forms." (Lacy 1996, vii) Although notions of genre are unstable in the Middle Ages – no single medieval author uses the term *roman arthurien* [Arthurian romance] (see Moran, *supra*) – Arthurian romances form a distinctive group. From the very beginning of their existence in the second half of the twelfth century, the texts share their *matière* in the form of common characters, geography, themes and structures. New works consist of variations on these well-known elements. They function against the backdrop of the tradition as a whole, which makes Arthurian romances excellent objects for intertextual play.

At the same time, medieval authors of Arthurian romances frequently crossed linguistic and generic boundaries, which were obviously diffuse. Especially, but not only, in the later Middle Ages, texts can be characterized by a mixture of various textual models and traditions; the authors' liberty is endless. Romance writers frequently refer to (conventional) elements from other vernacular traditions and genres such as lyric, *chansons de geste*, hagiography, theological and scientific works. They moreover reflect on contemporary social issues and discussions, for instance on juridical practices, gender relations/roles or power structures. Consequently, Arthurian scholars need to unravel a multiple network of cross-references among romances and other texts and contexts, and are plunged into an extremely complex network of textual and cultural relations waiting to be interpreted and understood if, indeed, that were ever possible. The Flemish scholar, J. D. Janssens (1979–1980), therefore compares the study of the Arthurian genre to a quest in "het woud sonder genade" [the forest without mercy], an *autre-monde* location mentioned in the Middle Dutch Arthurian Romance, *De Ridder metter mouwen*.

In order to describe the dynamics of the history of scholarly interest in Arthurian intertextuality, without actually listing one study after another, we may take the four aspects of literary communication as a point of departure: the author, the text itself, the context and the reader/listener. In general terms, a development may be distinguished between an author-centred and production-focused research perspective and a more textual approach, eventually leading to the idea that the meaning of a certain literary work is not innate, but rather dependent upon the interpreting reader or listener and the cultural context resonating within the text. Before the twentieth century, the emphasis in Arthurian scholarship was on the study of the author's intentions and on identifying prior sources or contexts for a given author (see Byrne, *supra*). Borrowing from other works was not considered as a positive characteristic per se, due to a romantic emphasis on originality. However, when scholars became more and more interested in the differences between texts, they concluded that originality and genius could also lie in the way in which authors reworked their material and inscribed it into a certain tradition. The romance genre in particular was seen to map out a set of potentials, which individual romances realize through their own variations, and therefore textual borrowing was advocated as playing a central role in the emergence of the genre. Consequently, authors of medieval narratives were seen more and more as innovators rather than as imitators.

In the 1960s, textual connections were considered an intertextual phenomenon. The focus on creativity and generic conventions resulted in a variety of influence studies of one author on others, or from one language, Latin or vernacular, to another. We also see studies about the influence of oral traditions such as, for instance, the *conte d'aventure* [story of adventure] mentioned by Chrétien, or about the influence of oral literature shown by onomastic evidence, such as in Flanders, where the name "Walawwaynus" (Walewein/Gauvain) was mentioned in a charter as early as 1118.[4] Formalism, structuralism and, later, deconstructionalism directed scholars' focus back to the text itself with its inherent meaning, its *conjointure* and *sen*, resulting in a decline in the study of literary interrelations. From the 1980s onward, scholars focused their attention on the reading and listening audiences, redactors, interpolators and scribes of manuscripts. Intertextuality was considered increasingly as a dialogue, as a two-way circuit between, on the one hand, the intertext and the text reinventing it and, on the other, the readers and listeners receiving the text (Bruckner 1987, 225). It informs us to some extent about the audience's own process of reading and their relationship(s) with contemporary poetic canons, in other words the so-called *Erwartungshorizont* or horizon of expectations. This concept, coined by Jauss, was developed as early as 1967, but for the Arthurian genre fully exploited by Beate Schmolke-Hasselmann in her major study on the Old French verse romances from Chrétien to Froissart (Jauss 1967; Schmolke-Hasselmann 1998). In a shorter article on the initial court episodes of several Old French romances, Schmolke-Hasselmann moreover demonstrates that conventional, intertextual signs direct the audience's attention to meaningful similarities and differences, so that intertextuality is considered as a literary game between author and reader/listener, who is a connoisseur of the genre (Schmolke-Hasselmann 1981). This way of looking at intertextuality implies a restricted perspective: a reference to an intertext is clearly marked in a text by the author and is obviously meant to

---

4 For "Walewein", see Uyttersprot (2004, 175–204).

be recognized and appreciated by the audience. Broader cultural perspectives, which view literature as a product of discursive societal practices, could also be considered as related to intertextuality. Theories by Foucault and Greenblatt (New Historicism) for instance, have been influential in recent decades, resulting in a wide variety of publications about subjects such as power or gender structures, conceptions of honour, and so on.[5]

3 Categorizations of Arthurian intertextuality

Intertextual references may appear in many guises, from exact quotations derived from specific pretexts, to the insertion of well-known characters, to the rewriting of entire episodes with either more or less subtle evocations. Intertextuality may even be created by readers or listeners rather than by authors. In order to understand the intertextual character of a text, we need to distinguish between generic and specific parallels, because of the fact that structural and schematic reproduction of generic models could easily be taken for references to a specific work. In other words: similarities between texts may be the result of direct borrowing, but also of a common tradition or convention. This point was signalled by Matilda Tomaryn Bruckner (1987) in an important study of the relationship between Chrétien de Troyes and his legacy. The study's starting point is the twelfth- and thirteenth-century practice of rewriting and its reception, including not only the reading and listening audience, but also the role of, for instance, interpolators and scribe-editors (225). Bruckner distinguishes three textual Arthurian traditions as each having specific forms of intertextuality. The verse romances represent what she calls (following Bakhtin) a "dialogical" form of intertextuality, continuing the playful game of romance which Chrétien himself began by reinventing and combining aspects from a number of romances. The textual expansion by the use of prose and *entrelacement* (as in, for instance, the Prose *Lancelot* in which the *Charrette* as the central episode is absorbed and retold) can be seen as a second form of intertextuality. Bruckner calls this "centripetal intertextuality". Finally, Bruckner sees the lengthy Continuations of Chrétien's unfinished *Perceval* as examples of "centrifugal intertextuality". This categorization is particularly successful in describing the Old French tradition. Literature

---

5 Amongst many examples, see, for instance, Wolfzettel (1994), and an article on the Middle Dutch *Walewein ende Keye* by Ad Putter (2007), which was inspired by Foucault's economic perspective on "honour". A very good study on the relationship between intertextuality and interdiscursivity (*discours*) is Franssen (2013).

from other vernacular traditions can demonstrate other forms. Later authors of German works, for instance, strove to advance traditions set by those writers conventionally accorded "classic" status in German literary historiography, such as Hartmann von Aue and Wolfram von Eschenbach.[6] Wolfram's *Parzival* has dialogical, centripetal and centrifugal aspects at the same time. For Middle Dutch romance, on the other hand, one could easily state that several texts, especially the original Flemish romances such as the *Roman van Walewein* and the *Roman van Moriaen*, offer a form of dialogical intertextuality, just like the works of their thirteenth-century French colleagues, but in addition, they also sometimes refer to each other.[7]

With Bruckner's categorization, then, we can indeed distinguish several forms and principles of intertextuality within textual traditions, however it is still difficult to distinguish between common participation in the Arthurian genre and the recurrence of schematic models, as well as intertextual references to specific works. The same can also be said of the study by Klaus Ridder (1998, 42–44), in which he mentions specific intertextual categories such as *Gesamtstruktur* and *Strukturzitat* (macro- and microstructural parallels with well-known models from literary tradition), and groupings such as *Episoden-, Motif-* und *Personenzitaten*.

We need instead to look at individual texts, since every text has its own intertextual character and its own way of coming to terms with specific pretexts, the genre or its cultural context. The notion of using less complex definitions of textual borrowing was therefore introduced by Besamusca (1993, 16–17) in a study of the interrelationships of three Middle Dutch Arthurian romances, and I shall summarize this here. Besamusca attempts to define Arthurian intertextuality by taking the convention of rewriting as a vantage point, making a distinction between what he calls "specific intertextuality" and "generic intertextuality". The first refers to the actual rewriting of a specific work, or parts of it, while his notion of generic intertextuality is suggestive of intertextuality within the Arthurian genre and concerns elements that became commonplace and conventional. His examples consist of conventions related to characters, such as Gauvain's problematic relationship with women, typological elements such as the Arthurian romance opening, structures and motifs, which an author can discuss, criticize or approve. A dialogue with the genre as a whole may therefore reveal an author's particular views on conventional elements, and often on a poetic level. Meanwhile, specific intertextuality consists of connections between a text and one or more well-known other texts. Although specific parallels are also always

---

6 See, for instance, the study by Neil Thomas (2005) on the Middle High German *Wigalois*.
7 See, for instance, Besamusca (1993).

mediated by the model of tradition, the particular character of such a parallel offers readers, listeners and researchers sufficient reason to believe that a text reacts to another text. Furthermore, authors almost always mark specific intertextual parallels by inserting signals: a series of remarkable resemblances, verbal similarities, identical names, and so on. In those cases we can usually exclude generic intertextuality.

One might classify another intertextual category, namely, "intergeneric intertextuality" (cf. Besamusca 1993, 194–198).[8] This form of intertextuality refers to the connections of Arthurian works with material drawn from other genres or works. There is an anachronistic aspect connected to this form of textual borrowing, since medieval poets, readers and listeners obviously did not adhere to the modern generic concepts of scholarly discussion, as noted above. However, the term holds considerable promise, since it might allow for the discovery of intertextual references to texts from various generic origins, but also to non-narrative sources available to the author and his audience. One of the most interesting examples can be found in Chrétien's *Chevalier au lion*, where Yvain is ironically compared to Roland and praised for his prowess and his rather unsophisticated way of fighting (Chrétien de Troyes 1971, ll. 3229–3233). Another example is provided by the Middle Dutch *Roman van Walewein*, in which Walewein fights like an epic knight and in which Ysabele shows traits of the Sarasin princesses from certain *chansons de geste* (see Brandsma, *infra*). The two lovers also utter love complaints in style of the troubadour *canso* (Zemel 2010, 1–28; Hogenbirk 2011b). Connoisseurs of Walewein's flawed reputation might have raised their eyebrows here, so a generic play with conventions is also at stake.

Because it is impossible to give a full overview of the intertextual dynamics of a broad and long-lasting tradition as Arthurian romance, I will now elaborate on some general features of Arthurian intertextuality, by using the categories of generic, specific and intergeneric intertextuality in a case study.

---

8 Besamusca does not actually use this specific term. Norris Lacy (1996, viii) does mention "intergeneric intertextuality" and refers to the confusion caused by the ambiguous use of the term "generic intertextuality" as one of the themes of the International Arthurian Society Congress in Bonn in 1993.

Intertextuality —— 191

4 Case study: The Middle Dutch *Moriaen* – contesting convention

Original Middle Dutch Arthurian romances from the thirteenth century have a paradoxical characteristic. They seem to be less sophisticated than most of their sources of inspiration, the French Arthurian romances, and yet they obviously respond to the French tradition. The Flemish *Roman van Moriaen* is a typical example from this tradition, especially with regard to intertextual borrowing.[9] The romance contains an interesting mixture of generic elements derived from different sources, Arthurian and non-Arthurian. Its main source of inspiration seems to be Chrétien's *Conte du Graal*, although there are also specific connections with the Middle Dutch *Roman van Walewein* on which I, however, will not be able to elaborate here.[10]

A small fragment and a complete, reworked version of the narrative have survived. The romance is a story of development and integration, of loyalty and friendship and of a black young knight, Moriaen, who surpasses his famous father, Perchevael. The Grail knight, Perchevael, made his way to the land of Moriane, fathered a son, Moriaen, but abandoned the latter's black mother whilst she was pregnant. Consequently, Moriaen and his mother lost their lands and possessions, an injustice to which fourteen-year old Moriaen wants to see an end by finding his father at Arthur's court and bringing him back to Moriane.[11]

At the beginning of the romance, the young titular hero, Moriaen, is an unknown black knight who is described in a traditional way: tall, black as a raven with teeth as white as chalk. However, he is beautiful in his own way and, above all, he is a Christian. *Moriaen* belongs to the group of Arthurian romances containing elements of the Fair Unknown motif. The author has combined this motif with a youth's search for his father, a biographical theme shared by many other medieval narratives, a group which Friedrich Wolfzettel calls *Enfance* romances (Wolfzettel 1973–1974). Arthurian romances with this theme are, for instance, *Le*

---

9 For my case study I have drawn material from my earlier publications on *Moriaen*: Hogenbirk (2009; 2011a; 2014). In these articles references can be found to other literature about the Middle Dutch romance.

10 For these connections, see Besamusca (1993, 100–110); Brandsma (*infra*) studies this text in some detail.

11 Research has shown that in the original version of the romance, Perchevael must have been Moriaen's father. In the only complete version to have survived, the Grail knight is substituted by Perchevael's brother, Acglovael. Another problem is Moriaen's age. The version in the Lancelot compilation has "xxiiij" years, but this passage is probably corrupt, since the narrator also states that Moriaen is a mere child.

Conte du Graal, *Le Bel Inconnu*, *Fergus* and *Wigalois*. These texts not only draw attention to the quest and development of the young protagonist, but also to the constellation – and more specifically the weaknesses – of the Arthurian court of which the hero finally becomes a member.[12] This is also the case in *Moriaen*. The young black outsider surpasses his well-known father and develops into the ministering angel of a vulnerable Arthurian kingdom by defeating invading Saxons. The similarities with other *Enfance* texts may be seen as a form of generic intertextuality, but there is no reason to believe that the author wanted to refer to this type of text in order to add a specific surplus to *Moriaen*.

Of importance for the romance's meaning, however, are the specific references to Chrétien's *Conte du Graal*. The text offers a specific intertextual response to Chrétien's work and embroiders on the unfinished text. The author must have known the *Conte du Graal* either in Old French or in its surviving Middle Dutch translation.[13] He works towards the closure of Perceval's storyline and explains what becomes of the quests for the Grail and the Bleeding Lance (which appears to be sought by Perceval, and not by Gauvain). Moriaen's quest for his father runs partly parallel with the section of *Le Conte du Graal* in which Perceval, over a period of five years of chivalric deeds during which he attempts to find the Grail, sends sixty prisoners to the court. In the opening scene of the Middle Dutch romance, one of these prisoners, a robber knight, arrives at court and forms the catalyst for the quests of Walewein and Lancelot, who promise Arthur that they will find the Grail knight and bring him back. While they are on their way, they meet Moriaen, who joins them.

Later in the romance, Moriaen's father Perchevael apparently stays with his uncle, the hermit, a familiar figure from the end of Chrétien's unfinished text. Chrétien's hermit episode implicitly suggests that Perceval would return to the Grail Castle to pass the test he had previously failed. The Flemish author introduces a remarkable variation: Moriaen and his friends are told that Perchevael has realized that he would never find the Grail, because he abandoned his mother when he took off to become a knight at Arthur's court, leaving her to die of grief, a part of Perceval's *enfance* that is recounted by Chrétien. In *Moriaen*, Perchevael gives up on his search for the Grail, and has become a hermit, too. His quest for the Grail is a failure, while in Chrétien's text the hermit episode seems to mark a new beginning for Perceval. Moreover, in *Moriaen* Chrétien's hero committed another sin: he abandoned Moriaen's black mother and her unborn child. With

---

12 See Echard (2007), which touches upon the criticism of the Arthurian court and Walewein's role in two other Middle Dutch Fair Unknown stories.
13 For the Middle Dutch *Perchevael* tradition, see Oppenhuis de Jong (2003).

these variations on Chrétien's story of Perceval, the author of the Middle Dutch text makes clear that the Grail knight is not the hero of this romance.

Unlike his father, Moriaen succeeds in his mission. At the outset, he takes care of his mother and makes up for the injustice done to her, thereby also redeeming his father's mistakes. At the end of the romance he brings Perchevael with him to his land, reclaims their property and makes amends for the injustice caused by his father's leave. Perchevael and Moriaen's mother finally marry in Moriane in the presence of their son and his Arthurian friends. With this, Perchevael's chivalric career has reached its end. A new and better hero has surpassed him: Moriaen, who eventually becomes the champion of the Arthurian court, protecting and saving the kingdom of Logres from the invading enemies.

With the character of Moriaen, the author reintroduces a representant of a traditional form of chivalry, different from Chrétien's enigmatic, religiously-inspired chivalric ideals. The Perceval-section in *Le Conte du Graal* shows that the key to transformation, healing and restoration lies in non-violence, nourished by Christian charity. The Flemish poet seems to criticize this new spiritual conception of chivalry. Moriaen's chivalric exploits are not linked to religious values, to sin and absolution, and do not lead to disaster, but rather result in peace. On his way to becoming a true knight, the young hero is inspired by the other protagonist from Chrétien's story, Gauvain (Walewein), who is described without the irony of the French text. Walewein plays a major role as Moriaen's tutor and friend; he teaches the young knight the principles of courtly knighthood. In the structure of his romance, the Flemish author follows Chrétien's pattern of the two interlaced quests of Perceval and Gauvain, but he restores an older hierarchy: Walewein does live up to his reputation here, he is the best knight in court, except perhaps for Moriaen. An interesting variation on common Arthurian schemes and on the *Enfance* texts is that Moriaen, in the end, neither becomes a true member of the Arthurian court nor marries. He takes his leave and continues living with his parents in Moriane. The emphasis of the storyline is entirely on his chivalric development, his out-classing of Perchevael and his friendship with Walewein.

Another source of inspiration for the author of Moriaen seems to come from the *chansons de geste*. In Flanders, the two genres were translated from French at the same time and a mixture of elements is also visible in other Flemish romances from this region. I have argued elsewhere (Hogenbirk 2009) that Moriaen shares characteristics with several Black Saracens from this genre. One of them is Rainouart au Tinel, another youth, who appears in the *Guillaume d'Orange Cycle*. This character is also marked by his blackness (but this time from the fires in the kitchen) and the descriptions of his physical appearance show many similarities to the portrait of the Middle Dutch hero. Rainouart, moreover, integrates into the white court, just like Moriaen. Furthermore, other *chanson de geste* elements can be found in *Moriaen*: formulaic descriptions of fights and an emphasis on male companionship and friendship. Although there are no concrete signs of specific intergeneric intertextuality with texts such as, for instance, *Aliscamps*, or of genre criticism and irony, the mixture of generic elements in Moriaen can be seen as a remarkable characteristic of the romance, and it might tell us something about certain traditional chivalric ideals that the author wanted to emphasize in his text.

I have elaborated here on specific and (intergeneric) intertextuality in *Moriaen*, based on written texts. In addition, a broader perspective may also offer interesting insights into this romance. Medieval culture provides many models of discourse through which the events in *Moriaen* can be interpreted, and modern theories may even prove useful. Postcolonial theories, for example, may shed a light on certain power structures in the romance (see Lynch, *infra*). The author breaks with the contemporary image of black knights in the *chansons de geste*: Moriaen is handsome (although in his own way, according to the narrator), and he quite easily integrates into Arthurian society because he is a Christian, as well as the son of Perchevael. As the narrative proceeds, the narrator pays increasingly less attention to Moriaen's skin colour. By the end of the text, people no longer fear him and he is simply the good knight Moriaen. He seems to become more and more "white" as his integration into the Arthurian world proceeds. This may refer to an underlying cultural discourse on white dominance. From a twenty-first-century perspective we could conclude that the white Arthurian civilization is superior: black Moriaen is rather rough around the edges at the beginning of the romance and, having to adjust to the values of the Arthurian court, must therefore be coached by Walewein in order to integrate into the white world. But of course, there is more research needed into contemporary images, positive and negative, of black cultures in order to identify more concretely a possible underlying socio-historical discussion in *Moriaen*. Wolfram's *Parzival*, with black-and-white-spotted, handsome Feirefiz, the son of Parzival, must also be taken into account in this context, since this romance offers interesting parallels, although the authors did not seem to know each other's work. In sum, an Arthurian romance such as *Moriaen* can be argued as not only referring intertextually to a specific written literary context of pretexts, but as also possibly interacting with contemporary discourse; it is therefore ripe for study from a much broader, cultural perspective.

A final aspect of the intertextual dynamics of *Moriaen* concerns the manuscript context of the romance. The only complete version of the romance has survived in the famous *Lancelot Compilation* of *c.* 1320–1325, a Brabantine manuscript containing ten Arthurian texts.[14] Moriaen can be found in a "Grail context" within this codex: the text is inserted immediately after a drastically reworked version of the *Conte du Graal* and a part of the *First Continuation*, and before the *Queeste van den Grale*. The romance thus literally forms another continuation to Chrétien's text and is also contextualized as a prelude to the completion of the Grail Quest by Galaad in the *Queeste*, in which Perchevael finally dies. In the compilation version of *Moriaen*, Perchevael as father is substituted with Acglovael by the compiler of the manuscript, likely because of the fact that the existence of a son would have been very problematic indeed for the Grail knight, whose achievement is at least partially due to his virginity. Yet, the intertextual links with Chrétien are still clearly visible and are complemented by the manuscript's own intertextual processes. The position amongst Grail texts, all of which are adaptations of Flemish translations of Old French sources, invites a more specific comparison between these compilation versions. Moreover, *Moriaen* and the preceding adaptation of Chrétien's romance have another interesting trait in common with several other texts in the *Compilation*: Walewein is an extremely positive character; he seems, indeed, to be the compiler's favourite. Research into these and other intertextual links, both generic and specific, between the texts in the manuscript promises to offer yet more insights into the reception of *Moriaen* by the compiler and the intended reader(s) of the manuscript. Furthermore, it may shed light on the ideology behind this codex which, in many respects, is still enigmatic.

From this case study, we can conclude that the meaning of an individual Arthurian romance such as *Moriaen* is inevitably shaped by other texts and by discourses, and not only in the author's time, but also in later contexts. Accordingly, research into the way in which authors, scribes or compilers appropriate, adapt and interpret the material they use, whether a restricted scope or a much broader research perspective is used, is a powerful instrument for us to use when attempting to tease out the meaning(s) of either a single text or a text collection. Arthurian texts like *Moriaen* offer their readers endless examples of intertextuality. Indeed, the phenomenon is a crucial element of their literary composition. A lot of work will be necessary to understand fully the bases and effects of textual sharing within the Arthurian genre, especially since each text, vernacular tradition or manuscript contains its own intertextual procedures. Therefore, in order also to identify larger developments in the evolution of the genre, intertextuality is an invaluable analytical tool, even if we do in fact realize that we will not be

---

14 The Hague, Koninklijke Bibliotheek 129 A 10. A study of this codex is to be found in Besa-musca (2003).

able to explore the implications of so vast a notion comprehensively, let alone grasp the ultimate meaning of an individual text. A final key point to remember is that participating in an intellectual game played by medieval authors, readers, scribes and compilers, and thereby searching for the intertextual *surplus* in a text, is one of the most obviously rewarding literary pleasures of the study of Arthurian literature.

Acknowledgment: I thank Leah Tether for correcting my English and for her patience.

References

Besamusca, Bart. *The Book of Lancelot: The Middle Dutch Lancelot Compilation and the Medieval Tradition of Narrative Cycles.* Cambridge: Boydell and Brewer, 2003.

Besamusca, Bart. *Walewein, Moriaen en de Ridder metter mouwen: Intertekstualiteit in drie Middelnederlandse Arturromans.* Middeleeuwse studies en bronnen 39. Hilversum: Verloren, 1993.

Bruckner, Mathilda Tomaryn. "Intertextuality." *The Legacy of Chrétien de Troyes.* Ed. Norris. J. Lacy, Douglas Kelly and Keith Busby. 2 vols. Amsterdam: Rodopi, 1987. I, 57–89.

Busby, Keith. *Codex and Context: Reading Old French Verse Narrative in Manuscript.* 2 vols. Amsterdam and New York: Rodopi, 2002.

Busby, Keith, Terry Nixon, Alison Stones and Lori J. Walters, eds. *Les manuscrits de Chrétien de Troyes/The Manuscripts of Chrétien de Troyes.* 2 vols. Amsterdam and Atlanta, GA: Rodopi, 1993.

Chrétien de Troyes. *Les romans de Chrétien de Troyes, 'Le chevalier au Lion (Yvain)'.* Ed. Mario Roques. CFMA 89. Paris: Champion, 1971.

De Pourq, Maarten, and Carl de Strycker. "Geschiedenis van de moderne intertekstualiteitstheorie: opvattingen, denkers en concepten." *Draden in het donker. Intertekstualiteit in theorie en praktijk.* Ed. Yra Van Dijk, Maarten de Pourck and Carl de Strycker. Nijmegen: Van Tilt, 2013. 15–59.

Echard, Siân. "Seldom does anyone listen to a good exemplum: Courts and Kings in *Torec* and *Die Riddere metter Mouwen*."*Arthuriana* 12 (2007): 79–94.

Franssen, Gaston. "Intertekstualiteit versus interdiscursiviteit." *Draden in het donker. Intertekstualiteit in theorie en praktijk.* Ed. Yra Van Dijk, Maarten de Pourck and Carl de Strycker. Nijmegen: Van Tilt, 2013. 231–248.

Gordon, Sarah. "Intertextuality and Comparative Approaches in Medieval Literature." *Handbook of Medieval Studies: Terms – Methods – Trends, Volume 1.* Ed. Albrecht Classen. Berlin and New York: De Gruyter, 2010. 716–726.

Hogenbirk, Marjolein. "Back to Basics. Reacting to the *Conte du Graal* in the Low Countries." *Wolfram-Studien* (Special issue: Wolframs Parzival-Roman im europäischen Kontext, Tübinger Kolloquium 2012. Ed. K. Ridder et al.) 23 (2014): 51–70.

Hogenbirk, Marjolein. "Dutch Design: The *Romance of Moriaen* as an example of Middle Dutch Arthurian literature." *Zeitschrift für deutsche Philologie* (Special issue: *Dialog mit den*

Nachbarn. Mittelniederländische Literatur zwischen dem 12. und 16. Jahrhundert. Ed. Bernd Bastert et al.) 130 (2011a): 127–140.

Hogenbirk, Marjolein. "The I-word and Genre: Merging Epic and Romance in the *Roman van Walewein.*" *"Li premerains vers": Essays in Honor of Keith Busby.* Ed. Catherine M. Jones and Logan E. Whalen. Amsterdam and New York: Rodopi, 2011b. 157–170.

Hogenbirk, Marjolein. "De carrière van de zwarte ridder Moriaen: Tussen *Conte du Graal* and *Aliscamps.*" *Queeste* 16 (2009): 51–73.

Janssens, Jef D. "De Arturistiek: een 'Wout sonder genade': Beschouwingen over de *Roman van Walewein, Die Wrake van Ragisel,* de *Roman van Ferguut,* de *Lancelotcompilatie* en de *Roman van de ridder metter Mouwen.*" *Spiegel der letteren* 21 (1979): 296–318; 22 (1980): 47–67.

Jauss, Hans Robert. *Literaturgeschichte als Provokation der Literaturwissenschaft,* 1979: <http://latina.phil2.uni-freiburg.de/reiser/einf_jauss.pdf>.

Kelly, Douglas. *The Art of Medieval French Romance.* Madison, WI and London: University of Wisconsin Press, 1992.

Krueger, Roberta, L. "The Author's Voice: Narrators, Audiences and the Problem of Interpretation." *The Legacy of Chrétien de Troyes.* Ed. Norris. J. Lacy, Douglas Kelly and Keith Busby. 2 vols. Amsterdam: Rodopi, 1987. 115–140.

Lacy, Norris J. "Preface," *Text and Intertext in Medieval Arthurian Literature.* Ed. Norris J. Lacy. New York: Garland, 1996 vii–ix.

Maddox, Donald. "Generic intertextuality in Arthurian Literature, the Specular Encounter." *Text and Intertext in Medieval Arthurian Literature.* Ed. Norris J. Lacy. New York: Garland, 1996. 3–24.

Oppenhuis de Jong, Soetje. *De Middelnederlandse Perceval-traditie: Inleiding en editie van de bewaarde fragmenten van een Middelnederlandse vertaling van de* Perceval *of* Conte du Graal *van Chrétien de Troyes, en de* Perchevael *in de* Lancelotcompilatie. Middelnederlandse Lancelotromans 9. Hilversum: Verloren, 2003.

Putter, Ad. "*Walewein ende Keye* and the Strategies of Honour." *Arthuriana* 17 (2007): 55–78.

Ridder, Klaus. *Mittelhochdeutsche Minne- und Aventiureromane. Fiktion. Geschichte und literarische Tradition im späthöfischen Roman: Reinfried von Braunzweig, Wilhelm von Österreich, Friedrich von Schwaben.* Quellen und Forschungen zur Literatur und Kulturgeschichte 12. Berlin and New York: De Gruyter 1998.

Schmolke-Hasselmann, Beate. *The Evolution of Arthurian Romance: The Verse Tradition from Chretien to Froissart.* Trans. Margaret Middleton and Roger Middleton. Cambridge: Cambridge University Press, 1998.

Schmolke-Hasselmann, Beate. "Untersuchungen zur Typik des arthurischen Romananfangs." *Germanisch-Romanische Monatsschrift* 31 (1981): 1–13.

Thomas, Neil. *Wirnt von Gravenberg's* Wigalois. *Intertextuality and Interpretation.* Arthurian Studies 62. Cambridge: D.S. Brewer, 2005.

Uyttersprot, Veerle. *"Entie hoofsche Walewein, sijn gheselle was daer ne ghein": Ironie en het Walewein-beeld in de* Roman van Walewein *en in de Europese middeleeuwse Arturliteratuur.* Brussels: Proefschrift KUB, 2004.

Van Dijk, Yra, Maarten de Pourck and Carl de Strycker, eds. *Draden in het donker: Intertekstualiteit in theorie en praktijk.* Nijmegen: Van Tilt, 2013.

Winters, Margaret, ed. *The Romance of Hunbaut: An Arthurian Poem of the Thirteenth Century.* Davis Medieval Texts and Studies 4. Leiden: Brill, 1984.

Walters, Lori J. "The Formation of a Gauvain Cycle in Chantilly MS 472." *Neophilologus*, 78 (1994): 29–43.

Wolfzettel, Friedrich, ed. *Arthurian Romance and Gender: Selected Proceedings of the XVIIth International Arthurian Congress*. Amsterdam: Rodopi, 1994.

Wolfzettel, Friedrich. "Zum Stand und Problem der Intertextualitätsforschung im Mittelalter (aus romanistischer Sicht)." *Artusroman und Intertextualität: Beiträge der deutschen Sektionstagung der Internationalen Artusgesellschaft vom 16. bis 19. November an der Johan Wolfgang Goethe Universität Frankfurt a. Main*. Giessen: Wilhelm Schmitz, 1990. 1–17.

Wolfzettel, Friedrich. "Zur Stellung und Bedeutung der "Enfances" in der altfranzösischen Epik I, II." *Zeitschrift für französische Sprache und Literatur* 83 (1973): 317–348; 84 (1974): 1–32.

Zemel, Roel. "Walewein en Ysabele in Endi." *Nederlandse letterkunde* 15 (2010): 1–28.

Stefka G. Eriksen
New Philology/Manuscript Studies

The main aim of this chapter is to survey how the advance of New (or material) Philology has influenced the development of Arthurian studies. This will be done, firstly, by giving a short account of the distinction between traditional and New Philology. Even though the term "New Philology" was first introduced in the romance language context, its influence quickly spread to other traditions. Secondly, I will discuss the advance of New Philology most particularly from the perspective of Old Norse Arthurian studies. This will include a summary of the discussion on the value of New Philology as an editorial practice and a short history of editorial practices in Old Norse studies, including Arthurian texts. This is followed by a presentation of the debate on the value of New Philology as theoretical framework, as well as an overview of the research questions addressed to Old Norse Arthurian texts from a new-philological perspective. Finally, I will comment on the relationship between New Philology and classical rhetoric and grammar studies on the one hand, and other modern theories on the other, in order to foreground the value and potential of New Philology as "future" philology.

1 Old Norse Arthurian texts: history, texts and manuscripts

The earliest translations of Arthurian texts into Old Norse were made at the beginning of the thirteenth century, both in Iceland and in Norway. Together with other translations they formed the greater part of what was written down in Old Norse in this initial period of literalization. Because of the relative stability of the Old Norse language, medieval texts, including Arthurian romances, continued to be copied, rewritten and adapted until the beginning of the twentieth century. Judging by the number of preserved manuscripts, Arthurian texts and indigenous romances inspired by them were among the most popular and productive Old Norse genres from the Middle Ages to today. Such a continuous history distinguishes Old Norse literary and manuscript tradition from most other European traditions. Nonetheless the development of Old Norse philology as a field is closely linked to the development of philological theory and practice in general.

Stefka G. Eriksen (Norwegian Institute for Cultural Heritage Research)

DOI 10.1515/9783110432466-013

The oldest Old Norse Arthurian texts include the translation of *Prophetiae Merlini* into *Merlinússpá* and Geoffrey of Monmouth's *Historia regum Britanniae* into *Breta sögur*. Both of these were made in Iceland towards the end of the twelfth or the beginning of the thirteenth century. A few decades later, the Norwegian king Hákon Hákonarson (1204–1263) initiated a major translation programme, starting by commissioning the translation of Thomas of Britain's *Tristan* into *Tristrams saga ok Ísöndar* in 1226. The translation inspired the composition of indigenous rewritings, such as the Icelandic *Saga af Tristram ok Ísodd* in the four-teenth century, and the ballad *Tristrams kvæði*, from the fourteenth to fifteenth centuries. Three of Chrétien de Troyes' romances were translated also: *Yvain ou Le Chevalier au Lion* (*Ívens saga*), *Erec et Enide* (*Erex saga*) and *Perceval ou le Conte du Graal* (*Parcevals saga* and *Valvens þáttr*). Chrétien's *Yvain* was also translated into Swedish (*Hærra Ivan Leons riddare* or *Herr Ivan*; see Lodén, *infra*) in the early fourteenth century, as part of the so-called *Eufemiavisor* – three romances trans-lated for Queen Eufemia, the wife of king Hákon V Magnússon (r. 1299–1319), the grandson of Hákon Hákonarson.[1] In addition we have Arthurian *lais* as part of the collection of short stories called *Strengleikar*, including *Chèvrefeuille* (*Geit-arlauf*) and *Lanval* (*Januals ljóð*). *Le Lai du cort mantel* was translated also, into the thirteenth-century *Möttuls saga*, which in the fifteenth century led to a new independent adaptation, the ballad, *Skikkjurímur*.[2]

The translations of Arthurian romances and *lais* had a considerable influence on indigenous Icelandic literature, and vice versa, in terms of literary motives and narrative structures (Kalinke 2011). In addition, they inspired the blossoming of an independent genre of late- and post-medieval Icelandic romances, ballads and folktales (Driscoll 2011). Even though this survey cannot encompass a full coverage of the scholarship on all these texts, there are recent new-philological studies of the younger material that are important and will be mentioned in this context. Even though a few of the Arthurian texts were allegedly translated in Norway under the commission of King Hákon Hákonarsson, the great majority of the manuscripts that include these texts are Icelandic and none of the pre-served manuscripts are the translator's copy. The one Norwegian manuscript that includes Arthurian texts is Uppsala, Uppsala University Library, De la Gardie 4–7 (hereafter De la Gardie 4–7), produced in the area of Bergen about 1270 (Tveitane 1972). The manuscript includes translations from Old French and Latin and is

---

1 I will mainly focus on the west Norse tradition of Arthurian texts, i.e. mainly those produced in Norway and Iceland. Research on the Swedish and Danish material will be drawn into the discussion where relevant.
2 For a review article on this body of literature, see Rikhardsdottir and Eriksen (2013).

a couple of decades older than the actual translations. In addition to the Norse versions of the texts, it seems that manuscripts of Middle High German romances may have circulated in Norway as well, as is suggested by the fragment of the German romance, *Wigalois* (Bandlien 2012, 109–111).

The Icelandic manuscripts that contain Arthurian texts are all miscellanies of various kinds, from encyclopedic manuscripts such as *Hauksbók* (Reykjavík, Stofnun Árna Magnússonar, AM 371 4to, AM 544 4to and AM 675 4to) to large-format and romance-collection volumes, such as Stockholm, Kungliga Biblioteket, Holm Perg 6 4to (1400–1425; hereafter Holm Perg 6 4to) and Stockholm, Kungliga Biblioteket, Holm Perg 7 fol. (*c.* 1450–1475; hereafter Holm Perg 7 fol.), to smaller every-day collections of romances and fairy tales like the fifteenth-century Reykjavík, Stofnun Árna Magnússonar, AM 489 4to, AM 586 4to, and AM 589 a–f 4to.[3] With regard to the late and post-medieval romances: more than half of them are preserved in forty romances or more, which gives an idea of the popularity of the genre (Driscoll 2011, 194).

Research on Old Norse Arthurian texts has been influenced by the general movement from the national-romantic currents blossoming during the nineteenth and the beginning of the twentieth centuries, towards a greater focus on internationalization and globalization in the humanities during recent decades. As a result of this, attitudes to Old Norse Arthurian texts have changed from being regarded as derivative texts with little, if any, independent literary quality, or impact on the development of Old Norse literature, to being seen as an important literary sub-system which had a dynamic link to indigenous literary production. Further, under the impact of the development of modern translation theory, exemplified by the work of, for example, Gideon Toury, Itamar Even-Zohar and Andrew Chesterman, the research questions to Old Norse Arthurian texts have changed from comparative investigations of the "correctness" or the "faithfulness" of the translation to the source-text, to studies of the function of the translation within their target cultural and literary context(s).[4] The focus on social and cultural contexts of literature may be seen as coinciding with New Historicism and the so-called cultural turn in humanities. These currents were more or less concurrent with the introduction of New Philology at the beginning of the 1990s,

---

3 For a full list of the manuscripts that contain actual Old Norse and Old Swedish translations of Arthurian texts (but excluding the younger post-medieval versions and adaptations), and editions and translations of these texts, see Rikhardsdottir and Eriksen (2013, 24–25).

4 For more detailed surveys of the scholarship on Old Norse translations, see Kalinke (1985); Barnes (2000); Glauser (2005); Rikhardsdottir and Eriksen (2013).

and the relationship between the various theories will be commented on in the conclusion of this chapter.

2 Traditional and New Philology

If one were to generalize, the major distinction between traditional and New Philology is that the former is prescriptive, while the latter is descriptive. According to one of the founding fathers of philology as a discipline, Karl Lachmann (1793–1851), the main aim of the field is to recover, to reconstruct, the oldest and most original form of a text, called the *archetype*, based on the surviving witnesses of that text. The relationship between various witnesses is organized in a *stemma*, which illustrates the common sources of various versions that form separate branches in the family tree. One of Lachmann's followers, Joseph Bédier (1864–1938) reacted to the constructed nature of the *archetype* and proposed a new-philological method: in editorial work, the priority is given to one single manuscript, which contains "the best" witness. Even though the choice of a best witness implies subjective categorization, Bédier's method is at least based on an actual medieval witness, as opposed to a reconstructed one, and as such leads to editions that bring us closer to medieval writership and readership.

Another Romanist, Paul Zumthor (1915–1995), took the discussion a step further by introducing the term *mouvance*, or mobility, and by arguing that mobility is the most essential characteristic of medieval texts. In a similar fashion, Bernard Cerquiglini (1947–) argues that variance is the most essential characteristic of medieval literary tradition, thus foregrounding the individual peculiarities of all versions of a medieval text. The distance between Zumthor and Cerquiglini and New (or material) Philology is actually not all that far. The term was, however, only officially launched in *Speculum* in 1990. There Stephen Nichols,[5] Suzanne Fleischman, R. Howard Bloch, Siegfried Wenzel and Gabrielle M. Spiegel discuss the development of philology and advocate for the primary significance of the medieval manuscript, but also emphasize two other axioms: (1) all aspects of a manuscript, material, graphical, paratextual and textual, and not least the relationship between them, are equally relevant when surveying the artefact; (2) each text and manuscript are produced in, and thus, conditioned by, a specific literary, cultural, social and political context, which should also be taken in consideration when studying that text or manuscript.

---

5 See also Nichols (1994; 1997).

The different concerns and methods of the two philologies are commented upon by John Dagenais, who writes that the physical text does not *represent*, but *is* an authentic/original text and that:

> the awareness of the things we do to physical texts – *correct *error, *recover *lost *meaning of *origins, *fill *in *lacunae, establish the *beginning and *end of texts, and determine if they are *complete – these reveal more than anything else the set of assumptions we bring to the texts we study. (Dagenais 1994, 254; original emphases)

The gradual advancement of these concerns, namely that the material and social aspects of the manuscripts need to be taken into consideration in the study of medieval literature, has led to numerous new-philological studies of Old French Arthurian literature, such as in the work of Keith Busby, Alison Stones, Lori Walters, Tony Hunt, to mention just a few. Because of limitations of space, I will, in the following, mainly focus on Old Norse Arthurian studies and the development in the discipline after the advancement of New Philology, both as an editorial practice and as a theoretical framework.

3 New Philology as editorial practice

Old Norse studies have been the arena of an explicit discussion about the value of New Philology for editorial practices. On the one hand, there are scholars who are of the opinion that New Philology has not caused changes in editorial practices, since "proper" editorial work has always given the required respect and scrutiny to the manuscripts. Kirsten Wolf (1993, 339) eagerly comments on the issue, prompted by the publication of two editions of the Old Norse translation of the *Elucidarium* (called *Elucidarius*): one a synoptically-arranged, diplomatic edition of eight surviving medieval manuscripts and the other a diplomatic edition, both of which "come within the arena" of New Philology. Wolf compares the value and usability of these editions to traditional editions, produced at the Arnamagnaean Institute in Copenhagen and Reykjavík (see below). She claims that the traditional editions aim to present texts and variants which may be used for reconstructing the archetype, but also give a detailed picture of the specific manuscript(s). They also aim to give a coherent narrative that is based on faithful manuscript examination, which is made comprehensible for the reader (Wolf 1993, 340). On the other hand, the main new-philological concern, according to Wolf, is to let the texts speak for themselves. But when each text is given a voice, "we are left not with elucidation, but with a babble of voices clamouring for primacy between two book covers." (Wolf 1993, 343) She characterizes diplomatic editions, which for her are new-philological, as "pseudo-scientific presentation of manuscript letters forms [...] resulting in a curious and indeed controversial breed of text", most of which is "absolutely unreadable." (Wolf 1993, 345) Sverrir Tómasson (2002, 216; see also 2004; 2009) also argues that Old Norse philology has always been "new":

> new philology brings very little as a method to trained editors of Old Norse texts if they have been faithful to the principles of classical philology and if they have taken into account that each text should be put into its correct social and historical place.

Odd Einar Haugen (2010; 2009a; 2009b) nuances the discussion further as he recognizes that some editions from the end of the nineteenth century are work-centred, that is, they cannot really be characterized as new-philological. Most twentieth-century editions, he points out, often represent a single "best" manuscript and variants are included in the critical apparatus: "the spirit of Karl Lachmann reigns in the introduction to Old Norse editions, but that the spirit of his later opponent Joseph Bédier, reigns in the text." (Haugen 2010, 43) Focusing on one *codex optimus*, with synoptic representation of other manuscripts and a presentation of stemma in the introduction is, at least for Haugen, the criteria for characterizing an edition as new-philological. This, he concludes, has been the aim of old philology and therefore "textual philology should, and will, remain old." (Haugen 2009b, 33)

By contrast, scholars such as Matthew Driscoll (2010) argue that Old Norse editorial practices are not yet infused with the main concerns of New Philology. Driscoll points out that even if not all manuscripts of one text can be regarded as equally "good", it is possible that they are equally interesting, albeit to different people and for different reasons. If an edition is to be considered new-philological, it may represent a socially or historically interesting text, even if it is considered "corrupt"; whole manuscripts should be edited, even if a logical coherency and orderly meaning is not obvious; and the manuscript should be regarded as a cultural artefact, and thus represented as closely as possible. Driscoll (2010, 99) claims that editions that focus on the text, and are less, if at all, interested in the materiality of the manuscripts these appear in, are not new-philological. Driscoll also favours the term "artefactual" philology to New (or material) Philology: while "material" only refers to what the manuscripts are made of, "artefactual" philology reflects that it was people who shaped and reshaped the manuscripts, as well as the texts within them. These terms thus advocate giving equal weight to textual and social concerns.

With this general debate as a background, we can now turn to the type of editions that exist of Old Norse Arthurian texts. One of the founding fathers of Old Norse philology, the Norwegian Carl Richard Unger (1817–1897), produced a remarkable number of editions, some of which are still used today. He edited many of the classical Old Norse texts (the kings' sagas, lives of saints, the Norwegian homily book, etc), as well as quite a few translations, including *Strengleikar* (together with R. Keyser). Unger did not have access to all manuscripts that are available now and the premises for his editions are thus easily open to debate.[6] In the twentieth century, Professor Jón Helgason in Copenhagen established the series, "Editiones arnamagnæanæ". The editorial practices of Jón Helgason's school were however never explicitly theorized (Driscoll 2010, 95). Nonetheless, he had a more appreciative attitude towards the value of younger manuscripts compared to his own predecessor, Finnur Jonsson, who dismissed younger manuscripts often without having examined them at all (Driscoll 2010, 97).

A series of the Old Norse Arthurian texts were edited or re-edited in this period. For example, the B series of "Editiones arnamagnæanæ" included new editions of *Erex saga* by Foster W. Blaisdell (1965), as well as of *Möttuls saga* by Marianne Kalinke (1987), and five volumes of *Late medieval romances* by Agnethe Loth (1962–1965). Robert Cook and Mattias Tveitane published a new edition, with an English translation, of *Strengleikar* (1979), while Marianne Kalinke published three volumes of *Norse Romance* (1999).[7] In addition to these textual editions, Old Norse philologists have produced numerous facsimile editions.[8] Most of these editions represent a whole manuscript, irrespective of whether the manuscript contains one text only or several texts. Some, however, contain representations from various manuscripts, such as *Icelandic Illuminated Manuscripts*, edited by Halldor Hermannsson in 1935. Yet, others focus on a saga, such as *Óláfs saga ens Helga*, edited by Jón Helgason in 1942.

A few of these are facsimile editions of manuscripts that include Arthurian texts. The series *Early Icelandic Manuscripts in Facsimile* includes editions by Desmond Slay (1972) of the Icelandic manuscript, Holm Perg 6 4to, made in the early fifteenth century, which includes the translations of Chrétien and *Möttuls saga*; *Fornaldarsagas and late medieval romances*: AM 586 4to and AM 589 a-f 4to (Loth 1977); *The Sagas of Ywain and Tristan and other tales*: AM 489 4to (Blaisdell 1980). The Norwegian manuscript, De la Gardie 4–7, containing *Strengleikar*, is published in the "Corpus codicum Norvegicorum medii aevi" series (Tveitane

---

6 For an overview of all the editions produced by Unger, see Óskarsdóttir (2009, 10). For a more detailed survey of the work of other prominent Old Norse philologists during this period, see Óskarsdóttir (2012, 204).

7 For a list of all editions and modern translations, see Rikhardsdottir and Eriksen (2013, 26–28).

8 *Early Icelandic Manuscripts in Facsimile* (twenty volumes), *Corpus codicum Islandicorum medii aevi* (twenty volumes), *Corpus codicum Norvegicorum medii aevi/ quarto and folio serie* (ten volumes), *Manuscripta Nordica* (three volumes).

1972). The Icelandic manuscript, Holm Perg 7 fol., from the fifteenth century, which includes Icelandic romances derivative of the Arthurian material was recently edited by Christopher Sanders (2000), and includes a digital representation of the facsimiles, in the newly established series "Manuscripta Nordica". The most recent discussion on editorial practices is pursued in connection with electronic editions. Some editors claim that electronic editions generally aim to look exactly like traditional editions (Haugen 2010, 54), while others blame exactly that attitude for the relative lack of success of electronic editions (Driscoll 2010, 102). According to the latter group, the potential of the media remains unused, such as the possibility for interactive text archives, where the reader can choose what and how much to read and, thus, participate in the creation process himself. None of the major projects on electronic Old Norse editions is exclusively centred on Arthurian texts,[9] but some of them such as, for example, *Strengleikar* is edited as part of the MENOTA-project.

4 New Philology as theoretical framework

Foregrounding the artefactual aspects of medieval manuscripts reminds us that philology is much more than a method of producing editions. Sheldon Pollock (2009, 934; 937) defines philology as "the theory of textuality as well as the history of textuality", "the critical self-reflection of language", "the discipline of making sense of texts". He argues that it is exactly because philology has "remained a vague congeries of method" and because of its "lack of disciplinarity" that it is on the verge of extinction (946). Part of the blame lies with philologists themselves:

> We have nearly succumbed from a century or more of self-trivialization – talk about the narcissism of petty differences – and we have failed spectacularly to conceptualize our own disciplinarity. What the theorists say about us "all dressed up and nowhere to go", hits a lot harder than what we say about them: "lots of dates and nothing to wear." (Pollock 2009, 947)

The only exception to the lack of theory in the field is, according to him, romance philology with its concept of New Medievalism and New Philology (947). Critical philology, and especially New Philology, with its hermeneutical nature, sat-

---

9 The MENOTA-project: <http://menota.org/forside.xhtml>; the Scaldic poetry project: <http://www.abdn.ac.uk/skaldic/db.php>; the project on the edition of the Old Norse Legendary Sagas (*Fornaldarsögur Norðurlanda*); see Driscoll (2009).

isfies the main requirements for a theoretical discipline – it is historically self-aware, and methodologically and conceptually global (948). In other words, New Philology is not only a method of editing, but also a way to theorize our starting point when discussing any research question. With its focus on the manuscripts' materiality and sociology, New Philology offers a new approach towards medieval material, a new theoretical framework for understanding and interpreting, a new way of making medieval texts comprehensible for a modern readership. New Philology as a theoretical framework redefines what is legitimate to ask in the scholarly context and how it is legitimate to conduct research. It thus provides new bases for conceptualizing medieval literature and culture.

In Old Norse studies, the introduction of New Philology has imposed the need for new terminology and several scholars have proposed different terms that differentiate various aspects of a text (Driscoll 2010; Wendt 2006). Scholars distinguish, for example, between work or *text-verk* [text-work], as the sum of all possible existent versions: oral, written, drawn or staged; text or text-witness, which is every individual philological witness or manifestation of the work; and artefact or text-carrier, which is any text-bearing object, with all its material and textual aspects. The introduction of New Philology has also resulted in an increased number of case studies of specific manuscripts, as opposed to studies on text-works; groups of manuscripts are also studied together in order to distinguish specific features or characteristics of a certain school or area, or particular time period; the manuscript transmission and reception of a given work is also the topic of several studies.[10]

A number of these studies focus on the manuscripts that include Old Norse Arthurian texts or adaptations. The *Hauksbók* manuscript, for example, which includes *Merlinusspá* and *Breta sögur*, has been studied by a number of scholars. Stephanie Würth (1998) argues that the *Hauksbók* version of *Breta sögur* is a historical narrative in an encyclopedia, while the versions in the now-lost *Ormsbók* and AM 573 4to are more Arthurian in nature.[11] Hélène Tétrel (2010) comments on various versions of the translations of Geoffrey of Monmouth by studying four versions of the Old-Icelandic version of the *Aeneid*. Her main concern is however more traditional than new-philological as she argues for the similarities between these four versions and their link to similar sources. Philip Lavender (2006) pays special attention to *Merlínusspá* from three different perspectives: (1) as an independent poem seen in connection with the native prophecy tradition based on

---

10 For a detailed review of studies on Old Norse manuscripts, irrespective of the type of texts, genres or language that are included in the manuscripts, see Óskarsdóttir (2012, 209–216).
11 See also Gropper (2011).

the two manuscript versions that we have of the poem; (2) in the context of *Breta sögur*; and (3) in connection to indigenous poetry of the eighteenth and nineteenth century based on paper manuscripts from the period. Other scholars do not focus specifically on the Arthurian texts but on the manuscript as a whole: Sverrir Jakobsson (2007) argues that the manuscript represents the contemporary Icelandic worldview of the social class of the manuscript's owner and main scribe, Haukr Erlendsson; Elizabeth Ashmann Rowe (2008) places the manuscript within the contemporary political context; Rudolph Simek (1991) discusses the function of the manuscript and compares it to the encyclopedic collection, *Liber floridus*, compiled by the Flemish monk, Lambert de Saint-Omer.

The readership and reception of Old Norse Arthurian texts have been studied by various scholars. De la Gardie 4–7, including the *Strengleikar* collection, has been studied by Eriksen (2014) in a book-historical investigation. By tracing the relationship between the materiality and textuality of medieval manuscripts, the study illustrates the gradual development of reading habits and book-production industry in Norway and Iceland. Hans Jacob Orning (2012) studies the two Old Norse versions of the Tristan legend in their manuscript contexts and discusses the link between the development of the literary figures and the contemporary political situation. Bjørn Bandlien (2013) discusses the now-lost Icelandic manuscript, *Ormsbók*, which included *Erex saga* and *Ívens saga*, with regard to the process of identity negotiation of its owner Ormur Snorrason. Similar types of questions – about the cultural and political affiliation of the readers – are asked by Roger Andersson (2012) with regard to the three Swedish *Eufemiavisor*.

Even though Old Norse Arthurian manuscripts are not as well illustrated as European Arthurian manuscripts (Busby et al. 1993) or other Norse manuscripts (Driscoll and Óskarsdóttir 2015; Liepe 2009), the focus on the materiality of the manuscripts opens up opportunities for collaborative projects between philologists and art historians. Karoline Kjesrud (2014) studies the representation of a motif from the *Yvain*-material, such as the fight between a dragon and a lion, on the so-called Valþjófsstaðir door. Pia Bengtsson Melin (2012) discusses visualizations of motifs from the stories about Yvain and Tristan, among others, in paintings by Albertus Pictor in Swedish churches and other European monuments, church reliefs and manuscript illuminations. Arthurian motifs such as knights do appear sometimes, even in manuscripts that contain other types of texts, such as Icelandic family sagas (see Liepe 2008).

The Old Norse Tristan material has also been discussed in light of New Philology. The Norse *Tristrams saga* was allegedly translated in the thirteenth century and has been of considerable interest for many medievalists as the only complete medieval version of the lost poem by Thomas. The oldest manuscript of the Norse saga is, however, from the seventeenth century. Comparison with the thirteenth-century poem by Gottfried von Straßburg indicates that the narrative told in the Old Norse version is probably not too different from the original translation, but that the emotional language typical of Thomas and Gottfried is not reproduced in the Norse version. This is also confirmed in a study by Alison Finlay (2004), where she compares the seventeenth-century Norse saga to the thirteenth-century Carlesle fragment of Thomas' poem.

The manuscripts of late and post-medieval transmission of ballads, *rímur* and romances have recently caught the attention of scholars, such as Matthew Driscoll (2011). As already mentioned, manuscripts continued to be produced in Iceland until the beginning of the twentieth century and many of them included genres deriving from the Arthurian romances. This story of transmission and preservation is just barely coming to light, and thus it "stretches our definition of the Middle Ages and medieval literature." (Óskarsdóttir 2012, 216) Old Norse Arthurian material is increasingly studied in comparison with other Arthurian materials from a new-philological perspective. Evelyn Meyer (2011), for example, compares thirteenth-century manuscript copies of the Old French, Middle English, Old Norse and Middle High German stories about Yvain. Due to the nineteenth-century editorial ideal of reconstructing the lost original, many of the endings of the versions were changed. By comparing the story endings in different vernacular manuscript versions of the same literary text, Meyer argues that the versions demonstrate medieval vernacular attitudes to gender and female agency that were erased by the nineteenth-century editors.

5 Conclusion: New Philology as future philology

As already pointed out, New Philology emphasizes the need to contextualize a text not only textually, but also materially and socially. In order to raise our own self-awareness as medievalists, there is also a need to historicize New Philology itself, as a critical and theoretical practice. From a historical perspective, New Philology may be seen as the latest branch of hermeneutics, rhetoric and grammar, as the primary disciplines for textual criticism in the Middle Ages. What we do today, both in terms of new editions and critical research, falls within the tradition of Classical commentary and medieval *translatio*. In other words, the latest edition of a medieval text is just a new version, with commentaries; a *translatio* of the same work which was written, copied and rewritten in the Middle Ages. In her book *Rhetoric, hermeneutics and translation in the Middle Ages*, Rita Copeland (1991, 178) claims that even original rhetorical inventions in the vernacular, such as Chaucer's and Gower's works, "achieve their authority by defining themselves through the very academic discourse they seek to supplant." This duality of academic discourse – always appropriating something old in the creation of something new – is also relevant for our perception of New Philology. New Philology as an academic discourse does not develop autonomously: some aspects of it were well established within the paradigm of traditional philology, especially those relevant for philology as an editorial practice. Other aspects, however, such as those concerned with New Philology as a theoretical perspective, and which demand that the manuscripts are regarded as artefacts produced by and for humans at a certain time and place, are innovative when compared with traditional philological thinking.

When contextualized within contemporary sciences, the establishment of New Philology may be seen as a parallel development to New Historicism and also to the increased interest in the cultural and political context of the artefacts for both art historians and archaeologists. Some claim that, because of its highly theorizing and interdisciplinary nature, New Philology may have severe consequences for the discipline, as theory may take primacy of meaning over text. In addition, it has been argued that New Philology may eventually lead to the death of philology as a separate discipline, because of its interdisciplinary character and its interplay with other disciplines such as history, theology, cultural and mentality studies (De Man 1986).[12] In my view, however, it is exactly a combination of these, its continual creation of textual meaning through new editions, its theorizing nature, and its interdisciplinary potentials, that brings about the novelty of New Philology and guarantees its position as future philology.

References

Andersson, Roger. "Eufemias Publikum." *Eufemia: Oslos Middelalderdronning*. Ed. Bjørn Bandlien. Oslo: Dreyer, 2012. 233–247.
Bandlien, Bjørn. "Arthurian Knights in Fourteenth-Century Iceland: *Erex saga* and *Ívens saga* in the World of Ormur Snorrason." *Arthuriana* 23 (2013): 6–37.
Bandlien, Bjørn. "På sporet av ridderen av det runde hjul." *Eufemia: Oslos Middealalderdronning*. Ed. Bjørn Bandlien. Oslo: Dreyer, 2012. 109–111.
Barnes, Geraldine. "Romance in Iceland." *Old Icelandic Literature and Society*. Ed. Margaret Clunies Ross. Cambridge: Cambridge University Press, 2000. 266–286.
Blaisdell, Foster W., ed. *The Sagas of Ywain and Tristan and other tales: AM 489 4to*. Early Icelandic Manuscripts in Facsimile, 12. Copenhagen: Roskilde and Bagger, 1980.

---

12 For a more detailed discussion, see Pollock (2009, 958).

Blaisdell, Foster W., ed. *Erex saga Artuskappa*. Ed. Editiones Arnamagnæanæ, Series B, vol. 19. Copenhagen: C.A. Reitzels Boghandel, 1965.

Busby, Keith. *Codex and Context. Reading Old French Verse Narrative in Manuscript*. Amsterdam: Rodopi, 2002.

Busby, Keith, Terry Nixon, Alison Stones and Lori J. Walters, eds. *Les manuscrits de Chrétien de Troyes/The Manuscripts of Chrétien de Troyes*. Amsterdam: Rodopi, 1993.

Cook, Robert, and Mattias Tveitane, eds. *Strengleikar: An Old Norse Translation of Twenty-one Old French Lais, ed. from the Manuscript Uppsala De la Gardie 4–7 – AM 666b, 4to*. Oslo: Norsk historisk kjeldeskrift-institutt, 1979.

Copeland, Rita. *Rhetoric, Hermeneutics and Translation in the Middle Ages*. Cambridge: Cambridge University Press, 1991.

Dagenais, John. *The Ethics of Reading in Manuscript Culture: Glossing the Libro de Buen Amor*. Princeton, NJ: Princeton University Press, 1994.

Dagenais, John. "The Bothersome Residue: Towards a Theory of the Physical Text." *Vox Intexta. Orality and Textuality in the Middle Ages*. Ed A.N. Doane and Carol Braun Pasternack. Madison, WI: University of Wisconsin Press, 1991. 246–262.

De Man, Paul. *The Resistance of Theory*. Minneapolis, MN: University of Minnesota Press, 1986.

Driscoll, Matthew J. "Arthurian Ballads, *rímur*, Chapbooks and Folktales." *The Arthur of the North: The Arthurian Legend in the Norse and Rus' Realms*. Ed. Marianne Kalinke. Cardiff: University of Wales Press, 2011. 168–195.

Driscoll, Matthew J. "The Words on the Page: Thoughts on Philology, Old and New." *Creating the Medieval Saga: Versions, Variability and Editoria Interpretations of Old Norse Saga Literature*. Ed. Judy Quinn and Emily Lethbridge. Odense: University Press of Southern Denmark, 2010. 87–104.

Driscoll, Matthew J. "Editing the Fornaldarsögur Norðurlanda." *Á austrvega. Saga and East Scandinavi: Preprint papers of the 14th International Saga Conference Uppsala 9th–15th August 2009, vol. 1*. Ed. Agnete Ney, Henrik Williams, Fredrik Charpentier Ljungqvist. Gävle: Gävle University Press, 2009. 207–212.

Driscoll, Matthew J., and Svanhildur Oskarsdottir. *66 Manuscripts from the Arnamagnæan Collection*. Copenhagen: Museum Tusculanum Press, 2015.

Eriksen, Stefka G. *Writing and Reading in Medieval Manuscript Culture: The Translation and Transmission of the Story of Elye in Old French and Old Norse Literary Contexts*. Turnhout: Brepols, 2014.

Finlay, Alison. "'Intolerable Love': Tristram's Saga and The Carlisle Tristan Fragment." *Medium Aevum* 73 (2004): 205–224.

Glauser, Jürg. "Romance (Translated *riddarasögur*)." *A Companion to Old Norse-Icelandic Literature and Culture*. Ed. Rory McTurk. Oxford: Blackwell, 2005. 372–387.

Gropper, Stefanie. "*Breta sögur* and *Merlínússpá*." *The Arthur of the North: The Arthurian Legend in the Norse and Rus' Realms*. Ed. Marianne E. Kalinke. Cardiff: University of Wales Press, 2011. 48–61.

Haugen, Odd Einar. "Stitching the Text Together: Documentary and Eclectic Editions in Old Norse Philology." *Creating the Medieval Saga: Versions, Variability and Editorial Interpretations of Old Norse Saga Literature*. Ed. Judy Quinn and Emily Lethbridge. Odense: University Press of Southern Denmark, 2010. 39–65.

Haugen, Odd Einar. "An Apology for the Text that Never Was: Reconstructing the King's Mirror." *Medieval texts – Contemporary media: The art and science of editing in the digital age*. Ed. Maria Grazia Saibene and Marina Buzzoni. Como: Ibis, 2009a. 57–79.

Haugen, Odd Einar. "A Quarrel of the Ancients and the Moderns: On the Merits of Old and New Philology in the Editing of Old Norse Texts." *On Editing Old Scandinavian Texts: Problems and Perspectives*. Ed. Fulvio Ferrari and Massimiliano Bampi. Trento: Università degli studi di Trento, 2009b. 9–37.

Haugen, Odd Einar. "Constitutio Textus. Intervensjonisme og konservatisme i utgjevinga av norrøne tekster." *Nordica Bergensia* 7 (1995): 69–99.

Jakobsson, Sverrir. "Hauksbók and the Construction of an Icelandic Worldview." *Saga-Book* 31 (2007): 22–38.

Jakobsson, Sverrir. "Det islandske verdensbillede og dets udvikling fra opblomstring til Renæssance." *Den norröna renässansen: Reykholt, Norden och Europa 1150–1300*. Ed. Karl G. Johansson et al. Rit (Snorrastofa), 4. Reykholt: Snorrastofa, 2005. 63–71.

Jónsson, Erikur, and Finnur Jónsson, eds. *Hauksbók udgiven efter de arnamagnæanske håndskrifter nr. 371, 544 og 675, 4to samt forskellige papirhåndskrifter*. Vol. 1. Copenhagen: Det Kongelige nordiske oldskrift-selskab, 1892–1896.

Kalinke, Marianne E. "Arthurian Echoes in Indigenous Icelandic Sagas." *The Arthur of the North. The Arthurian Legend in the Norse and Rus' Realms*. Ed. Marianne Kalinke. Cardiff: University of Wales Press, 2011. 145–167.

Kalinke, Marianne E. "Norse Romance (*Riddarasögur*)." *Old Norse-Icelandic Literature: Critical Guide*. Ed. Carol J. Clover and John Lindow. Toronto: University of Toronto Press, 2005 [1985]. 316–364.

Kalinke, Marianne E., ed. *Norse Romance*. 3 vols. Cambridge: D.S. Brewer, 1999.

Kalinke, Marianne E., ed. *Mǫttuls saga: with an Edition of* Le Lai du cort mantel *by Philip E. Bennett*. Editiones Arnamagnæanæ, Series B, vol. 30. Copenhagen: C.A. Reitzels Boghandel, 1987.

Keyser, R., and C.R. Unger, eds. *Strengleikar eða Lioðabok: En samling af Romantiske Fortællingen efter Bretoniske Folkesanger (Lais)*. Christiania: Carl C. Werner & Comp.s Bogtrykkeri, 1850.

Kjesrud, Karoline. "A Dragon Fight in Order to Free a Lion." *Riddarasǫgur: The Translation of European Court Culture in Medieval Scandinavia*. Ed. Karl G. Johansson and Else Mundal. Oslo: Novus, 2014. 225–244.

Lavender, Philip. "Merlin and the Vǫlva." *Viking and Medieval Scandinavia* 2 (2006): 111–139.

Liepe, Lena. *Studies in Icelandic Fourteenth Century Book Painting*. Snorrastofa Rit, 6. Reykholt: Snorrastofa, 2009.

Liepe, Lena. "The Knight and the Dragon Slayer: Illumination in a Fourteenth-Century Saga Manuscript." *Ornament and Order: Essays on Viking and Northern Medieval Art for Signe Horn Fuglesang*. Ed. Margrethe C. Stang and Kristin B. Aavitsland. Trondheim: Tapir, 2008. 179–199.

Loth, Agnethe, ed. *Fornaldarsagas and Late Medieval Romances*: AM 586 4to and AM 589 a-f 4to. Early Icelandic Manuscripts in Facsimile, 11. Copenhagen: Roskilde and Bagger, 1977.

Loth, Agnethe, ed. *Late Medieval Romances*, I–V. Editiones Arnamagnæanæ, Series B. Copenhagen: Munksgaard, 1962–1965.

Melin, Pia Bengtsson. "Bilder av Theoderik, Didrik och Dietrich: Från tidigkristen historia till senmedeltida hjältemyt." *Francia et Germania: Studies in Strengleikar and Þiðreks saga af Bern*. Ed. Karl G. Johansson and Rune Flaten. Oslo: Novus, 2012. 167–178.

Meyer, Evelyn. "Manuscript versus Edition: the Multiple Endings of Yvain/ Iwein/ Iven/ Ywayne and their Gender Implications". *Amsterdamer Beiträge zur älteren Germanistik* 68 (2011): 97–141.

Nichols, Stephen G. "Why Material Philology? Some Thoughts." *Philologie als Textwissenschaft: Alte und neue Horizonte.* Ed. H. Tervooren, H. Wentzel. Berlin: Erich Schmidt, 1997. 10–30.
Nichols, Stephen G. "Philology and its Discontents." *The Future of the Middle Ages: Medieval Literature in the 1990s.* Ed. W.D. Paden. Gainesville, FL: University Press of Florida, 1994. 113–141.
Nichols, Stephen G. "Introduction: Philology in a Manuscript Culture." *Speculum* 65 (1990): 1–10.
Orning, Hans Jacob. "Tristram: From Civilizing Hero to Power Politician." *Arthuriana* 22 (2012): 91–108.
Óskarsdóttir, Svanhildur. "Expanding Horizons: Recent Trends in Old Norse-Icelandic Manuscript Studies." *New Medieval Literatures* 14 (2012): 203–223.
Óskarsdóttir, Svanhildur. "To the Letter: Philology as a Core Component of Old Norse Studies." *Scripta Islandica. Årbok* 60 (2009): 7–22.
Pollock, Sheldon. "Future Philology? The Fate of a Soft Science in a Hard World." *Critical Inquiry* 35 (2009): 930–963.
Rikhardsdottir, Sif, and Stefka G. Eriksen. "État present: Arthurian Literature in the North." *Journal of the International Arthurian Society* 1 (2013): 3–28.
Rowe, Elizabeth Ashman. "Literary, Codicological and Political Perspectives on Hauksbók." *Gripla* 19 (2008): 51–76.
Sanders, Christopher, ed. *Tales of Knights: Perg. Fol. Nr 7 in the Royal Library, Stockholm (AM 567 Viß 4to, Nks 1265 IIc Fol.).* Manuscripta Nordica: Early Nordic Manuscripts in Digital Facsimile, 1. Copenhagen: C.A. Reitzel, 2000.
Simek, Rudolf. "Warum sind *Völuspá* und *Merlínusspá* in *Hauksbók* überliefert?" *Deutsch-Nordische Begegnungen: 9. Arbeitstagung der Skandinavisten des deutschen Sprachgebiets 1989 in Svenborg.* Ed. Kurt Braunmüller and Mogen Brønsted. Odense: Odense University Press, 1991. 104–115.
Slay, Desmond, ed. *Romances: Perg. 4:0 nr. 6 in the Royal Library, Stockholm.* Early Icelandic Manuscripts in Facsimile, 10. Copenhagen: Roskilde and Bagger, 1972.
Tétrel, Hélène. "Trojan Origins and the Use of the *Æneid* and Related Sources in the Old Icelandic *Brut.*" *The Journal of English and Germanic Philology* 109 (2010): 490–514.
Tómasson, Sverrir. "The Textual Problems of *Njáls saga*: One Work or Two?" *On Editing Old Scandinavian Texts: Problems and Perspectives.* Ed. Fulvio Ferrari and Massimiliano Bampi. Trento: Università degli studi di Trento, 2009. 39–56.
Tómasson, Sverrir. "The Re-creation of Literature in Manuscripts." *The Manuscripts of Iceland.* Trans. B. Scudder. Ed. V. Ólasson and Gísli Sigurðsson. Reykjavík: Árni Magnússon Institute in Iceland, 2004. 73–80.
Tómasson, Sverrir. "Er nýja textafrœðin ný? Þankar um gamla frœðigrein." *Gripla* 13 (2002): 199–216.
Tveitane, Matthew, ed. *Elis saga, Strengleikar and Other Texts, Uppsala University Library Delagardieska Samlingen Nos. 4–7 Folio and AM 666 b Quarto.* Corpus codicum norvegicorum medii aevi, quarto serie, 4. Oslo: The Society for Publication of Old Norwegian Manuscripts, 1972.
Wendt, Bo-A. "En text är en text är en text? Om en terminologisk tredeling av textbegrepet." *Arkiv för Nordisk Filologi* 121 (2006): 253–274.
Wolf, Kirsten. "Old Norse – New Philology." *Scandinavian Studies* 65 (1993): 338–348.
Würth, Stefanie. *Breta sögur: Der "Antikenroman" in der isländischen Literatur des Mittelalters.* Basel: Helbing and Lichtenhahn, 1998.

Alison Stones
Text and Image

What do images do? Clearly they were important elements in the production of medieval Arthurian manuscripts, as many copies have pictures, and those without narrative images invariably articulate the written page with other kinds of textual markers: painted, pen-flourished, or large initials in a single colour. And small initials may also be coloured. They all contribute, to a greater or lesser degree, to the decorative appearance of the manuscript page and break up the text, serving as markers enabling a reader/viewer to find his/her place again when reading/viewing was interrupted.[1] And of course images, particularly those embellished with gold and colours, add substantially to the cost, and the value, of the book. But images, and other markers, offer a far more complex and interesting network of meanings and functions, which are the focus of this chapter.[2]

Many medieval texts comment specifically on the need for, and the purpose of, illustrations: to help understand aspects of the text and to remember what was written, and even to confirm the truth of what is being said in words. The *Image du monde* of Gossuin de Metz, the *Breviari d'amor* of Matfre Ermengau, and the *Roman de Fauvel* are examples where the purpose of the pictures is to understand the text better, while Richard de Fournival's twin paths of "parole" and "painture" leading to the two doors of seeing and hearing in Memory's Tower is a famous instance of pictures for remembering. And for Henri de Mondeville, author of a surgery treatise dedicated to King Philippe le Bel, his set of anatomical

---

1 Other types of books, especially liturgical books, often have markers in the form of tags made of small strips of parchment attached to the outer margins of pages either by sewing or wound as a knot around a slit cut into the parchment. Among the manuscripts of Chrétien de Troyes, Paris, BnF, fr. 794, the compilation written by Guiot, preserves a tag made of silk thread on f. 361 at the beginning of *Perceval*; the trace of a marker can be seen on ff. 54 (*Cligès*) and 79v (*Yvain*). See Nixon (1993), no. 8, ills. 42, 43, 45. The manuscript is fully reproduced in colour on Gallica <http://gallica.bnf.fr>. Moveable markers also exist. Some rare examples are discussed by Hamburger (2009), kindly drawn to my attention by Hanna Wimmer.
2 I have treated aspects of the function of images in several articles where the examples given below are discussed in more detail. All of them can be consulted on Academia.edu <http://pitt.academia.edu/alisonstones>. Many scholars have investigated aspects of text-picture relationships, priorities and rejections. A useful summary of recent theoretical approaches is to be found in the introductory chapter of Fabry-Tehranchi (2014, 1–24).

Alison Stones (University of Pittsburgh)

DOI 10.1515/9783110432466-014

pictures represented the way to truth.[3] There is nothing quite as explicit in the *Lancelot-Grail* romance, nor, so far as I know, in any other Arthurian text. The presence and usefulness of illustrations must have been taken for granted, as indeed it was in all kinds of books both secular and sacred throughout the thirteenth century and beyond.

1 Lancelot, Morgan and Arthur and the role of pictures

There is, however, one well-known sequence in the text of the *Lancelot* where pictures are the means of unveiling truth. When Lancelot is a captive in Morgan's prison, he looks through the window of his cell and sees in an adjacent room an artist painting on the wall a picture of Aeneas escaping from Troy. It occurs to Lancelot that he could paint pictures of his amorous adventures with Queen Guinevere. The result is so successful that he embraces his picture of the Queen.[4] Morgan plans to show the pictures to King Arthur, so that he will finally realize that the rumours about Lancelot and Guinevere were true. She does so much later in the text, in the *Mort Artu*, and the result is exactly what Morgan had hoped for.[5] This revelation of the betrayal of Arthur by his favourite knight signals the beginning of the downfall of the king.

One might imagine that this sequence would have been an intrinsic part of the iconography of the *Lancelot*, not only for its significance in the story, but at the same time to epitomize the importance of the painted image as a measure of what was considered important in the text in general. On the contrary, only a single illustration of Lancelot's artistic activity has survived, and it does not correspond to what is in the text: Lancelot is shown embracing not his picture of Guinevere on the wall, but a statue of her, on the model of Pygmalion or the *Roman de la Manekine*, where sculpted images take on life-like qualities (London, BL, Additional 10293 (hereafter Add. 10293), f. 325v). And Morgan's revelation to Arthur was also a subject rarely treated pictorially: there are only four instances, two of which simply show Arthur and Morgan in conversation (Paris, BnF, fr. 342, f. 167; New Haven, YUL, Beinecke 229, f. 289), seated together on a bench, with

---

3 A summary is given in Stones (2007).
4 See Stones (1993–1994). Textual references are to Sommer (1909–1916, V 218.8) and Micha (1978–1983, V 51– 52). Sommer hereafter referred to as S and Micha as LM.
5 Equivalent to S VI, 239.14; Frappier (1961, 62.18).

no signs of any painting on the walls. The other two both occur in manuscripts made for Jacques d'Armagnac, one showing Morgan explaining the meaning of the paintings to Arthur (Paris, BnF, fr. 116, f. 688v), the other showing Arthur alone, seeing the pictures and reading the captions placed beneath them (Paris, BnF, fr. 112, vol. III, f. 193v). One can infer that, for Jacques d'Armagnac, the revelation through pictures was indeed a significant episode even if his books do not include an image of the making of those pictures. But why did Add. 10293 not include images of Arthur's discovery of the adultery through Lancelot's paintings? We cannot know. Many of the questions raised by the selection of images are simply unanswerable.

2 Choices and emphases in the illustrations of *Lancelot*

Variations in the number, placing in the text, and treatment of subjects among *Lancelot-Grail* manuscripts indicate that choices were made. No two copies contain exactly the same selections of images and none are identical in pictorial treatment, even when the same artists made them, as the two versions of Arthur seeing Lancelot's pictures show. Another striking example of differences in selection and treatment of images from two manuscripts made in the same workshop is the False Guinevere episode in Add. 10293 and Amsterdam, Biblioteca Philosophica Hermetica MS 1 (hereafter Amst. 1), both made in Flanders in the early years of the fourteenth century.[6] Add. 10293 treats the episode in a lengthy sequence of twenty-four single-column miniatures while Amst. 1 limits its selection to only five images – no doubt a much cheaper option, but one that required a fuller treatment of the subject in just a few miniatures than a more developed sequence of pictures would need. The five miniatures in Amst. 1 depict subjects that are also present among Add. 10293's twenty-four, but they are sometimes placed at different points in the text and they treat the subjects in different ways. Both manuscripts begin the sequence at the same place in the text, with the arrival of the False Guinevere's messenger at Arthur's court.[7] In Add. 10293's version (f. 131) everyone is standing, in two facing groups, one led by King Arthur with his barons behind him, the other by the messenger and her entourage;

---

6 Amst. 1 was sold at Sotheby's on 7.XII.2010, as lot 33. Its present owner has chosen to remain anonymous, so it is convenient still to refer to it as Amst. 1. See also Stones (2012a).
7 Equivalent to S IV 10.14; LM I 18. Cf. Larrington (*infra*).

Arthur and the messenger raise hands in speech gestures. The version in Amst. 1 (ii f. 202) is much more elaborate: the scene takes place in a room framed with pointed arches, turrets and quatrefoil tracery. Queen Guinevere and King Arthur are seated, with barons behind them; Bertholais, standing, presents the False Guinevere's messenger, whose veil has been thrown onto the chequered floor and she opens the box containing the False Guinevere's letter, all details specified in the text but which are absent in Add. 10293's opening miniature.

Add. 10293 continues the story with an image of the reading of the letter before the court, the arrival of the False Guinevere and her companions, and King Arthur seized by King Tholomer's knights. Both manuscripts then have two miniatures each, at the same places in the text, depicting King Arthur imprisoned by the False Guinevere,[8] followed by King Galehot and Queen Guinevere offering the crown to Gauvain because of Arthur's absence.[9] After that, Add. 10293 has nine miniatures depicting debates with King Arthur about his treatment of Queen Guinevere and Lancelot's duel fought as her champion; to these there is no pictorial counterpart in Amst. 1. Both manuscripts include an illustration at S IV 72.9 and LM III 89, but this time the subjects are different. Add. 10293 illustrates the interdiction on Arthur delivered by the Pope using a lighted taper, a motif borrowed from legal illustration such as is found in Gratian's *Decretum*.[10] One can surmise that the legal aspects of the case were of interest to the anonymous patron of Add. 10293 but not to the patron of Amst. 1, where the chosen illustration is the death-bed confession of the False Guinevere. Add. 10293 also includes a death-bed scene but not until three miniatures later, following illustrations of Arthur's own repentance and absolution. The end of the episode is marked in both manuscripts by reconciliation: Lancelot embraced by Arthur in Amst. 1 and Lancelot begged by Guinevere to rejoin the Round Table: in Add. 10293, however, this is the last of five concluding scenes and the corresponding miniature in Amst. 1 occurs at the same place in the text as the fourth scene. There are also differences of format between the two manuscripts, in part because Amst. 1 was copied in two columns and Add. 10293 in three; and Add. 10293 uses *champie* initials for the text opening below the miniatures whereas Amst. 1 has pen-flourished initials. The wording of the rubrics is also different, another aspect of the creation and transmission process that requires further research.

---

8 Equivalent to S IV 50.1; LM I 107.
9 Equivalent to S IV 51.15; LM I 110.
10 A Parisian *Decretum* painted by two artists, the Hospitaler Master and the Méliacin Master, has two miniatures of interdicts being delivered: Arras, BM 46, ff. 82 (Causa XV) and 115v (Causa XXIV).

3 Variations in *Estoire* manuscripts between a model and its copy

In one case one can show a relationship between two manuscripts that suggests the pictures in one were copied from the other, but even then, additions were made and the treatment of the subjects is far from identical. The version of the *Estoire del saint Graal* adapted for Jean-Louis de Savoie, Bishop of Geneva (†1482), by Guillaume de la Pierre and attributed to Jean Colombe or a painter in his entourage: Brussels, BR 9246 (hereafter BR 9246),[11] was most likely based directly on a Parisian copy of the early-fourteenth century illuminated by an artist I have called the Sub-Fauvel Master (Paris, BnF, fr. 105; hereafter fr. 105).[12] Two copies were produced in the Sub-Fauvel workshop, fr. 105 and Paris, BnF, fr. 9123 (the latter a collaboration between the Sub-Fauvel Master and the so-called Maubeuge Master; hereafter fr. 9123). Comparison with BR 9246 shows that it was fr. 105 and not fr. 9123 that served as model for BR 9246, with two possible exceptions. There are eleven miniatures in fr. 9123 that have no corresponding miniatures at the same places in fr. 105 and BR 9246, and twenty-two places where fr. 9123 lacks a miniature to correspond with what is in fr. 105 and BR 9246. Occasionally a miniature in fr. 9123 corresponds to one of the same subjects at a different place in the text in fr. 105 and BR 9246. And there are two cases where a subject included in fr. 9123 but not in fr. 105 takes up part of a miniature in BR 9246 (on ff. 95 and 111), suggesting that perhaps the BR 9246 artist was aware of fr. 9123 and its illustrative programme but had decided not to adopt it as a model for the whole, preferring fr. 105, unless there was another intermediary that is now lost. However, the placing of the miniatures, their subjects and their rubrics are the same in fr. 105 and BR 9246, with two exceptions: BR 9246 introduces two miniatures that are not in the model, and not in fr. 9123 either – and for these there are no rubrics.

---

11 What Jean-Louis de Savoie wanted was a copy whose language was up to date (cf. Busby, *supra*). As Guillaume says on f. 1, "[...]Et pour ce que ils sont escrips en langage ancien et le plus en langue picarde m'a commandé les metre en François[...]" [And because these [words] are written in an old language, and further, the language of Picard, [I] was asked to put them into French]. The intention was for Guillaume to produce a complete *Lancelot-Grail*, but only the *Estoire* in BR 9246 and the *Merlin* and *Suite Vulgate* (Paris, BnF, fr. 91) survive, and the illustrations in the *Merlin* are unfinished, likely because of the death of the patron. See Avril and Reynaud (1993, 360, no. 199); Delamarre (2003); Stones (2015). On the *Merlin* and *Suite Vulgate*, see Fabry-Tehranchi (2012, 36, 45, 91, 115, 340, 355–356, 359, 416, 418, 428, 436, 445, 503, 514, 518; see also figs. 42, 143, 156, 209, 210, 219, 226, 229).

12 The Sub-Fauvel Master is thought to be a lesser painter in the entourage of the major artist known for his work on the *Roman de Fauvel*, Paris, BnF, fr. 146; see Stones (1998).

Given the discrepancy in date between fr. 105 (*c.* 1320–1330) and BR 9246 (1480–1482), it is not surprising that the illustrations are differently treated: Jean Colombe's style in BR 9246 is characterized by a developed interest in architecture, landscape and seascape, in interaction among the protagonists, and in a sophisticated painterly technique, to a far greater degree than the Sub-Fauvel Master of fr. 105, where the miniatures are sketchy and summarily washed in colour. There are differences in format, too: BR 9246's pictures are mostly bigger, often taking up half a page of a two-column text, and sometimes presenting a sequential narrative, expanding what is depicted in fr. 105 and emphasizing the importance of illustration in relation to text. The two additional miniatures depict Titus and Vespasian bidding farewell to Josephé and his followers (f. 13v),[13] and Josephé and his followers before King Elzalach and his men in a room decorated with relief sculptures (or grisaille paintings) of the Life of Christ on the walls (f. 18v). Why these subjects? Both, I suggest, add emphasis to the role of Josephé as hero of the *Estoire* and his evangelizing mission, as would be appropriate for a patron who was also a bishop. The final miniature of the *Estoire* in fr. 9123 depicts the lions that guard the bleeding tomb of King Lancelot (grandfather of the eponymous hero of the Lancelot branch) and lick the blood. Neither fr. 105 nor BR 9246 include a picture at this point in the text, but both give a minor initial and accompany it with a rubric.

4 The role of initials as markers

The role of large initials as substitutes for, or in anticipation of, illustrations, is an area that needs further enquiry. Amst. 1 is a manuscript in which large *champie* initials, mostly accompanied by rubrics, often mark points in the text where in the related manuscripts of Add. 10293 and London, BL, Royal 14 E.III there is a miniature.[14] In this case the use of *champies* must have been in part an economic choice since *champies* would have cost substantially less than full-scale miniatures. The issue is more complicated than that, however, as it raises the question of relative precedence: did the placing of large *champies* or large party-bar initials precede the establishment of pictorial cycles, or vice versa? An examination of the second part of the *Estoire del saint Graal* in some of the earliest unillustrated

---

13 Equivalent to S I 19. 24 + *var* and Ponceau (1997, 34.49, l. 12).
14 London, BL, Royal 14 E.III contains only three of the five branches of the *Lancelot-Grail* romance (*Estoire*, *Queste* and *Mort Artu*) so was not taken into consideration in the comparison of the *Lancelot* episodes discussed above. See Meuwese (1999).

manuscripts in relation to the earliest illustrated copy shows a high correlation in the placing of large pen-flourished initials and narrative illustrations.[15] The earliest illustrated *Estoire* is Rennes, BM 255 (hereafter Rennes 255), *c.* 1220, which has historiated initials at its major textual breaks (Stones 1977; 2010, 47–49). There is also another copy that may be about the same date, with only pen-flourished initials: Nottingham, Nottingham University Library, WLC/Lm7 (hereafter Nottingham Lm7). Both are written above top line.[16] From a generation or so later (*c.* 1250–60), London, BL, Royal 19 C.XII (hereafter Royal 19 C.XII) is written below top line and has only pen-flourished initials. Since Nottingham Lm7 is incomplete, preserving only the second part of the *Estoire*,[17] my comparison also begins from this point.

There are nineteen large pen-flourished initials in Nottingham Lm7 and the same places are also marked by large pen-flourished initials in Royal 19 C.XII. Rennes 255 has sixteen historiated initials at corresponding places but at the beginning of the sequence (no. 1 in Nottingham Lm7 and Royal 19 C.XII) it has only a small *champie* initial, and in two more instances (corresponding to nos. 3 and 4 in Nottingham Lm7 and Royal 19 C.XII) Rennes 255 omits any decoration at all. When we include two copies of the *Estoire* from the same workshop, probably based in Douai, *c.* 1285 (Le Mans, BM 354 and Paris, BnF, fr. 770; hereafter Le Mans 354 and fr. 770 respectively), we find that all nineteen of the large pen-flourished initials of Nottingham Lm7 and Royal 19 C.XII are places also marked in these copies, too, this time with miniatures, historiated initials or large *champie* or party-bar pen-flourished initials. There is a sole exception to this rule: no. 1 which, as also in Rennes 255, has only a small initial (pen-flourished in Le Mans 354 and fr. 770, a small *champie* in Rennes 255). These correlations suggest that Nottingham Lm7 played an important part in the establishment of a system of break-points that stands at the beginning of the illustrative tradition and was drawn upon to a greater or lesser degree in the copies produced subsequently. And the differences between Nottingham Lm7 and Rennes 255 show that there was more than one model in the early stages of the emergence of patterns of textual marking in *Estoire* manuscripts.

---

15 See the comparative tables in Stones (2012b), 81–87.
16 This feature is a dating criterion for English manuscripts. See Ker (1960). A comparable study for French manuscripts is still lacking, but the feature tends to be found in manuscripts of the first half of the thirteenth century and especially the first quarter.
17 At S I 130.6 and Ponceau (1997, 279.445).

5 Conclusion

The examples outlined above have all been examined comparatively. Only through a comparative approach can one detect patterns of similarity or of difference in the choice, placement and treatment of images and thus determine the ways in which a particular copy follows established patterns or breaks new ground. Whilst Arthurian manuscripts are perhaps less marked in this regard than those containing other medieval vernacular literature, such an approach is still important. Sometimes we can suggest reasons for the choices made, particularly, for example, when we know who the patron and/or the makers were. In the absence of detailed payments or other documentary evidence, however, any hypothesis necessarily remains conjectural, though still important as such observations can help to support conclusions drawn on the basis of other available evidence.

References

Avril, François, and Nicole Reynaud. *Les manuscrits à peintures en France 1440–1520*. Paris: Musées nationaux, 1993.
Delamarre, Aurélie. *Copier au XVe siècle du français déjà ancien: l'exemple de l'Estoire del Saint Graal. Commentaire linguistique et édition partielle du ms. B.R. 9246* (unpublished dissertation, École des Chartes, 2003).
Fabry-Tehranchi, Irène. *Texte et images des manuscrits du Merlin et de la Suite Vulgate (XIIIe–XVei siècle)*. Texte, Codex et Contexte XVIII. Turnhout: Brepols, 2014.
Frappier, Jean. *La Mort le roi Artu*. 2nd edn. Geneva: Droz, 1961.
Hamburger, Jeffrey F. "Openings." *Imagination, Books and Community in Medieval Europe: A Conference at the State Library of Victoria (Melbourne, Australia), 29–31 May, 2008*. Ed. Constant Mews. Melbourne: MacMillan Art Publishers, 2009. 50–133.
Ker, Neil Ripley. "From 'above top line' to 'below top line': a change in scribal practice." *Richard Irvine Best Memorial Volume*. Ed. M. Dillon. Celtica 5. Dublin: Dublin Institute for Advanced Studies 1960. 13–16.
Meuwese, Martine. "Three Illustrated Prose *Lancelots* from the same Atelier". *Text and Image: Studies in the French Illustrated Book from the Middle Ages to the Present Day*. Ed. D.J. Adams and Adrian Armstrong. *Bulletin of the John Rylands University Library of Manchester* 81 (1999): 97–125.
Micha, Alexandre. *Lancelot, roman en prose du XIIIe siècle*. 9 vols. Paris and Geneva: Droz, 1978–1983.
Nixon, Terry. "Catalogue of Manuscripts". *Les Manuscrits de Chrétien de Troyes/The Manuscripts of Chrétien de Troyes*. Ed. Keith Busby, Terry Nixon, Alison Stones and Lori Walters. 2 vols. Amsterdam and Athens, GA: Rodopi, 1993. II, 1–85.
Ponceau, Jean-Paul. *L'Estoire del saint Graal*. 2 vols. (CFMA 120, 121). Paris: Champion, 1997.

Sommer, H. Oskar. *The Vulgate Version of the Arthurian Romances*. 7 vols. Washington, DC: Carnegie Institution, 1909–1916.

Stones, Alison. "L'Estoire del saint Graal dans la version adaptée par Guillaume de la Pierre pour Jean-Louis de Savoie, évêque de Genèe: sources et traitement pictural." *Bulletin de la Société nationale des antiquaires de France 2013* (2015), 109–125.

Stones, Alison. "Quelques lecteurs du *Lancelot-Graal* et leurs choix d' images." *Quant l'image relit le texte (Actes du Colloque international 15–16 mars 2011)*. Ed. Maud Pérez-Simon and Sandrine Hériché-Pradeau. Turnhout: Brepols, 2012a. 99–116.

Stones, Alison. "Un schéma d'emplacement pour l'illustration de l'*Estoire del saint Graal* et les débuts de la tradition manuscrite." *Mémoires arthuriennes*. Ed. Danielle Quéruel. Troyes: Médiathèque du Grand Troyes, 2012b. 71–87.

Stones, Alison. "Two French Manuscripts: WLC/LM/6 and WLC/LM/7." *The Wollaton Medieval Manuscripts: Texts, Owners and Readers*. Ed. Ralph Hanna and Thorlac Turville-Petre. Woodbridge: Boydell and Brewer 2010. 41–56.

Stones, Alison. "Why Images? A note on some explanations in French manuscripts c. 1300." *Quand la peinture était dans les livres: mélanges en l'honneur de François Avril*. Ed. Mara Hofmann and Caroline Zöhl. Turnhout: Brepols, 2007. 312–329.

Stones, Alison. "The Artistic Context of *le Roman de Fauvel* and a Note on *Fauvain*." *Fauvel Studies*. Ed. Margaret Bent and Andrew Wathey. Oxford: Clarendon, 1998. 529–567.

Stones, Alison. "Images of Temptation, Seduction and Discovery in the Prose *Lancelot*: a Preliminary Note." *Festschrift Gerhard Schmidt, Wiener Jahrbuch für Kunstgeschichte* 46–47 (1993–1994): 725–735.

Stones, Alison. "The Earliest Illustrated Prose Lancelot manuscript?" *Reading Medieval Studies* 3 (1977): 3–44.

Andrew James Johnston
Material Studies

Over the last two decades, Material Studies have become one of the humanities'
most vibrant fields, and this applies equally to disciplines dealing with modern
issues and to those concerned with pre-modern ones. It seems only natural, then,
to train the gaze of Material Studies on a literary genre so long-lasting and widely
disseminated as Arthurian romance. At the same time, scrutinizing Arthurian
romance through the prism of Material Studies raises certain questions: is there
such a thing as a particularly "medieval" materiality? Does romance as a genre
provide a typical insight into medieval materiality, one markedly different from
other contemporaneous approaches? And if romance does provide a particular
perspective on materiality, can we really speak of a specifically Arthurian materiality? In no case is the answer a clear "yes" or "no". While it is certainly true
that medieval notions of materiality differed considerably from modern ones, it
is impossible to identify a single, or even dominant, medieval take on materiality. Besides, we would first have to define what we actually mean by "materiality". Medieval philosophy, for instance, as Kellie Robertson (2010, 103) points
out, tended to conceive of materiality in terms of Aristotelian hylomorphism, a
perspective that assumes matter and form to be indivisible. Hylomorphism conceives of matter very differently from modern concepts of materiality which tend
to be atomistic and assign a distinctly more passive role to matter. The dominant
strands of medieval philosophy always thought of matter in conjunction with
form because, according to Aristotle, matter simply could not exist without form.
Important as this metaphysical view is, it constitutes merely one of many medieval approaches to materiality: other discourses, such as law, medicine or theology
developed different perspectives – not to mention cultural practices, for example
the cult of relics or the medieval fascination for automata and machines (cf. Lee,
infra). Since romance constitutes an especially fluid genre, we must expect its
negotiations of the material to absorb and refract views on matter from all kinds
of discursive fields.

Even as we realise that the Middle Ages conceived of matter in a variety of
different ways, we must also keep in mind that the boundaries of the material
were drawn in a wide variety of ways. Some issues were approached in a much
more "materialistic" way than we would conceive of them today. For instance, in
some versions of medieval optical theory, sight closely resembled touch (Brown

Andrew James Johnston (Freie Universität Berlin)

DOI 10.1515/9783110432466-015

2007, 47–68). At least as far as its theoretical conceptualization is concerned, medieval vision constituted a decidedly more material experience than its modern equivalent. Besides, medieval views of materiality were prone to stressing the changeability of matter, the ways in which it was subject to corruption, but also to generation and to transformation. Furthermore, it has become increasingly difficult to gauge what exactly a "modern" approach to matter might mean: since scholars and scientists have begun to discuss the Anthropocene as an entirely new era in planetary history, the very concept of a modern materiality is subject to fundamental revision as the boundaries between nature and culture are being redrawn and humanity's very status in the history of the Earth is open to debate (Chakrabarty 2015, 44).

Yet one reason why it makes sense to discuss materiality in Arthurian romance not only despite, but actually because of this diversity of different approaches towards materiality is precisely because the genre is itself remarkably varied in its themes and structures. As Arthurian romance is capable of drawing on many different discourses, it is also capable of imagining matter in a plethora of forms. Our focus ought not, therefore, to be on establishing approaches to materiality characteristic of, or even unique to, Arthurian romance, but rather on Arthurian romance as a literary zone of experimentation where epistemological issues are negotiated in ways not necessarily available to other, extra-literary discourses such as metaphysics, law or theology. Such a stance becomes even more plausible when we consider the profound commitment to fictionality one encounters in Arthurian romances from the works of Chrétien de Troyes onwards (Haug 1997, 118–131; Putter 2009, 44). With its frequently self-conscious emphasis on fiction, Arthurian romance provides a space for probing the many ways in which, during the Middle Ages, matter was understood in relation to human experience.

Taking its cue from these fundamental methodological observations, this discussion will proceed in three steps: rather than attempting a potted history of Material Studies or an overview of the current state of materiality theory,[1] I will focus first on a selection of ideas from Material Studies that seem especially pertinent to Arthurian romance.[2] Second, I will look at a select set of examples that

---

1 This rapidly expanding field has become far too varied to be mastered adequately in so brief a space as this; besides, there is now a burgeoning industry of publications devoted precisely to this kind of information. Here is a brief and by no means exhaustive selection of titles that testifies to the ever-increasing breadth and variety of the field: Barad (2007); Bennett and Joyce (2010); Brown (2003); Cohen (2012; 2015); Dolfijn and van der Tuin (2012); Malafouris (2013); Tilley et al. (2006).

2 It would be just as fruitful to discuss developments in Material Studies that are *not* particularly helpful for medievalists, but for lack of space the issue cannot be addressed here. One interesting

show how important things and matter are to Arthurian romance. In so doing, I shall pay some attention at least to the ways in which questions of "thingness" overlap and segue into matters of the body and of space, neither of which is represented in depth elsewhere within this collection. Finally, I will discuss one particular Arthurian romance chosen for its hyper-canonical status, its sophisticated blending of French and English Arthurian traditions and, above all, its complex negotiations of materiality: the anonymous Middle English alliterative romance *Sir Gawain and the Green Knight*.

1 Medieval materialities: theoretical observations

In her powerful bid for a theory that acknowledges the role of non-human actors in political events, that is her concept of a "vital materiality" that gives expression to the connectedness and interdependence of human and non-human bodies, the political theorist, Jane Bennett, draws, amongst other things, on an Anglo-Norman term from medieval English law: the *deodand*, literally meaning "that which must be given to God". This concept entered English legal discourse around 1200 and was abolished in 1846. The *deodand* referred to an inanimate object accidentally causing harm to, or even killing, a human being. Its epistemic status was ambiguous: while possessing a greater degree of active efficacy than a merely recalcitrant object, it was not endowed with the capacity for deliberate action attributed to human beings (Bennett 2010, 9). The *deodand*'s abolition in 1846 testifies to modernity's desire for absolute distinctions between the human and the non-human, the animate and the inanimate and the subject and the object of (scientific) inquiry. Indeed, it is this desire for rigid epistemic boundaries that Bruno Latour identifies as a crucial characteristic of the "modern constitution" – a system based on radical distinctions that necessarily denounces as "hybrid" anything that straddles its epistemic boundaries. Indeed, as Latour demonstrates, in its drive for epistemic purification, modernity actually produces, at an ever-increasing pace, the very hybrids it so emphatically abhors: objects messily located across the borders of modernity's fundamental epistemic distinctions:

example, for instance, would be the degree to which Material Studies are concerned with "commodities", as signaled by the subtitle of Arjun Appadurai's *The Social Life of Things: Commodities in Cultural Perspective*. Many medievalists would dispute the applicability of the term "commodities" to pre-modern economies. At the same time, medievalists have become interested in the medieval mass market for trinkets and toys, a phenomenon that may help to re-conceptualize the issue of medieval commodities (Ingham 2009).

"the modern Constitution allows the expanded proliferation of the hybrids whose existence, whose very possibility, it denies." (Latour 1993, 34; original emphasis) Frequently, these hybrids are understood as obsolete historical leftovers. With the modern desire for rigid epistemic distinctions comes an equally powerful investment in temporal scenarios of rupture and revolution, in the kind of periodization that gave rise to the notion of the Middle Ages itself: "The moderns have a peculiar propensity for understanding time that passes as if it really were abolishing the past behind it." (Latour 1993, 68) The erasure of the *deodand* from English law is thus doubly significant. It testifies to modernity's rejection of both epistemic and temporal hybrids: a medieval concept anachronistically surviving into modernity and thus being subjected to what Johannes Fabian has called "the denial of coevalness." (Fabian 2002, 31) It is, therefore, no coincidence that a present-day theorist of materiality like Jane Bennett should, for the purpose of overcoming the binary oppositions governing modernity's approach to materiality, find herself invoking medieval concepts.

Some of the most important impulses for the development of Material Studies have come from the history of science where the seemingly objective facts of the hard sciences stand in especially stark contrast to the discursive constructivism increasingly brought to narratives of scientific development. As Lorraine Daston (2008, 16) puts it:

> On the one side there are the brute intransigence of matter, everywhere and always the same, and the positivist historiography of facts that goes with it; on the other side, there are the plasticity of meaning, bound to specific times and places, and the corresponding hermeneutic historiography of culture.

In order to escape from this epistemological binary, a theoretical approach was required that was capable of seeing things as participants in events rather than as mere passive objects: "actants" as Bruno Latour (1993, 138) calls them in his attempt to develop a "symmetrical anthropology" that does away with the classical epistemological hierarchy of subject and object.

In developing notions of materiality that stress the interconnectedness of the material and the supposedly immaterial, of human and non-human as well as animate and inanimate bodies, Martin Heidegger, in particular, proved a powerful source of inspiration, amongst other things through his celebration of the "self-sufficiency" of things, a quality not to be confused with inertness. According to Heidegger (2000 [1950]), the "thingness" of the thing consists in its ability to "gather" other phenomena to it, a characteristic he explained in his discussion of the jug. To Heidegger, a jug is not sufficiently understood if taken for a mere physical entity or simply regarded as an object. Instead, a jug needs to be considered in terms of its manifold relations with the world. A jug contains liquid but also pours it out, it holds wine or water and is thus "entangled" – to use Ian Hodder's term (2012, 88–112) – with the geological and meteorological processes that produce spring water or the equally geological and meteorological, but nevertheless different conditions that coalesce with biological and chemical processes, as well as human agricultural activity, to bring forth wine. And, Heidegger suggests, just as the pouring out can serve very different cultural purposes – including a libation to the Gods – the jug can be seen to dynamically connect the human and the divine spheres, heaven and earth. Material Studies are thus particularly interested in the ways objects and human activities interact, intersect and depend upon each other, how objects are shaped by human actions, desires and requirements and themselves contribute to shaping these desires and requirements, how bodies and things form complex networks and how, within what is seemingly one single thing, a multitude of different relations to other things and bodies exist side by side.

Things also possess a symbolic dimension. One of the central paradoxes in dealing with things is "that things are simultaneously material and meaningful." (Daston 2008, 17) Historians of medieval religious art and literature have been particularly willing to embrace this paradox. In her far-ranging study of Christian materiality, Caroline Walker Bynum draws attention to late medieval spirituality's fascination with that paradox and the very nature of the paradoxical itself, namely that "paradox is the simultaneous assertion (not the reconciliation) of opposites." (Bynum 2011, 34) This recognition of paradox as paradox lies at the heart of many medieval works of art as they play off their self-conscious materiality against their symbolic and spiritual functions. By drawing particular attention to the work of art's materiality a medieval artist would paradoxically enhance instead of diminish its symbolic resonance. As I hope to show towards the end of this contribution, *Sir Gawain and the Green Knight*, despite being, to all intents and purposes, a secular Arthurian romance, shares in this medieval fascination with the paradoxical tensions between the symbolic and the material.

2 Approaches to matter in medieval romance

Arthurian romance engages with matter and materiality in many different ways. At the thematic level, there is the sheer beauty and lavishness of the object world, the riches of the hall and chamber, of palaces and furnishings, of arms and armour as well as fabrics and jewels that time and again capture the imagination of medieval writers. But beauty may prove deceptive even as it expresses the specifically aristocratic aesthetic associated with Arthurian romance. Having grown up in a forest beyond civilization, Chrétien's Perceval naively takes knights for angels, enthralled as he is by their shining armour, which to him assumes an entirely otherworldly quality. His first chivalric adventure consists in his rather callously killing the Red Knight primarily for the sake of his suit of armour. And many of his subsequent adventures are triggered by his inability to place the material in its precise context, to see beyond beautiful surfaces and to understand the symbolic dimension of the things and practices he encounters (cf. Tether 2010).

The Arthurian object-world is laden with symbolic significance. Unsurprisingly, the two most widely-known details from Arthurian legend, details familiar to non-medievalists the world over, are material objects endowed with magical qualities and a powerful political symbolism: the Sword in the Stone and the Round Table. Both have provided titles for modern adaptations of Arthurian romance. At times the Round Table – including the chairs that surround it – assumes the quality of a sentient being when it miraculously displays, in luminous letters, the names of new knights entering the brotherhood. In a similar vein, Malory's *Morte Darthur* cannot end before Sir Bedivere has finally disposed of Arthur's sword Excalibur, after twice lying to his King about having flung it into the lake. When Bedivere does, eventually, obey the royal command, an arm rises out of the water, grasps hold of the sword, brandishes it three times and vanishes below the surface. The sword's disappearance signals the downfall of Camelot, but it is also staged as the object returning to a world of magic that envelops Camelot and intersects with it. The sword connects different epistemologies and different temporalities: a political epistemology, where the sword stands for the royal power that can no longer be exercised by its bearer, and a fairy-tale epistemology that suggests the constant but half-hidden presence of a magical and potentially superior, but also strangely evanescent, Otherworld. Whereas the political sphere appears to be subject to the dictates of a dynastic temporality with its clear-cut periodizations, the Otherworld promises an altogether more fluid and flexible experience of temporality.

Indeed, especially when it comes to dead matter in the literal sense, the Arthurian theme of the *rex quondam rexque futurus* [once and future king] asserts itself, a theme already ridiculed as popular superstition by the twelfth-century historian, William of Malmesbury (Putter 2009, 36). In the Alliterative *Morte Arthure* this theme is inserted at the end of the text as a motto and Malory's *Morte Darthur* declares it to be the inscription on King Arthur's tomb. In the twentieth century, the theme provided the title for T.H. White's Arthurian cycle, *The Once and Future King*. In many versions of the legend Arthur does not in fact die, hovering instead between life and death on an enchanted island, and thus defying the merely physical nature of his bodily existence and the temporality such an existence normally entails.

In Arthurian romance, the sense of a magical indeterminacy of physical objects and their material environments is most powerfully embodied by the Holy Grail, an object taking different shapes in different texts: while in Wolfram von Eschenbach's *Parzival* we encounter the Grail as a large stone, most conventionally it features as the vessel that caught Christ's blood at the Crucifixion. In the latter capacity, the Grail enters into the familiar medieval discourse of the reliquary. Through its identification as something clearly anchored in medieval spiritual practice, the Grail is safely brought into the realm of a spiritual materiality.

For all its concern with magical materialities and otherworldly fluidity, Arthurian romance is perfectly capable of imagining physical space and material boundaries as rigid and constraining in a fashion untainted by the supernatural. The genre investigates how human existence is determined not merely by its ineluctable physicality but also by the degree to which the material is a function of the social. Hence, in Malory's *Morte Darthur* the social nature of space and matter plays a central role in the crucial scene where Lancelot's clandestine relationship with Guinevere is finally and undeniably uncovered. When the lovers are eventually caught in the act by Sir Aggravayne and his associates, Lancelot is trapped in the Queen's bedchamber with merely a sword and his cloak for protection. The onslaught on the Queen's chamber is described as a detailed exercise in domestic siege warfare, with Lancelot opening the door only so much as to provide space for one attacker, Sir Collgrevaunce of Goore, whom Lancelot duly dispatches. He pulls the dead knight's body into the chamber, dons Sir Collgrevaunce's armour with the help of the Queen and her ladies and, after an exchange of rousing words, opens the door and charges at his enemies, all of whom he kills with the exception of Sir Mordred who manages to escape. In this scene, the Queen's chamber becomes a trap in a twofold sense: on the one hand, we witness the conditions of spatial confinement that govern the everyday lives of even the most august personages of the Arthurian court and thus make it well-nigh impossible to carry on a secret affair for any length of time – an issue that provides Chaucer with ammunition for anti-Arthurian satire in the *Squire's Tale*. On the other, the social trap of the Queen's bedchamber becomes a physical trap when it is turned into the scene of a fight. The dual role thus assumed by space and materiality infuses the scene with an almost comical quality, a quality enhanced by the narrative's obvious fascination with the physical details of the event, the mantle tightly wrapped around Sir Lancelot's arm, the bench brought from the hall to serve as a battering ram, the various degrees to which the door is opened at different points in the story and the taking possession of and despoiling of Sir Collgrevaunce's corpse.

Then there is the earlier scene in "Sir Lancelot and Queen Guinevere" where Sir Lancelot pulls out the window's iron grille in order to enter Guinevere's chamber, thus displaying not only obedience to his lady but also his close-to-superhuman strength, a physicality that matches the brutal materiality of the castle's walls where Guinevere had been imprisoned by the evil Mellyagaunt. Lancelot injures his hand and covers the Queen's bed in blood which Mellyagaunt discovers in the morning. He accuses her of having slept with one of the wounded knights sharing her chamber. Mellyagaunt's accusations are based on an understandable misinterpretation of the visual evidence available, and this error makes it possible for Lancelot to defend the Queen's life and honour in single combat without perjuring himself. In an almost fabliau-like fashion, material evidence is misread and the fundamental truthfulness of Mellyagaunt's claims, that is that Guinevere did, indeed, spend the night with one of her knights – albeit not with one of those he actually accuses – is successfully smothered. Here materiality's importance derives from its powerful, yet uneasy involvement in processes of signification.

This ambivalent, if not paradoxical approach to the materiality of the symbolic constitutes an instance of that obsession with the material side of signification that Lee Patterson identified as lying at the heart of medieval chivalric identity (Patterson 1991, 186). It is the kind of problem that the archaically chivalric Othello will face on the Shakespearean stage when he demands "ocular proof" (*Othello* Act 3, Sc. 3, l. 363). And it is a problem that will recur again and again in Arthurian romance when physical tokens of love, affection or respect such as rings or ladies' detachable sleeves are put on display and lead to confusion and even death, as with the Fair Maid of Astolat in Malory's *Morte Darthur*. In her case, the magical subversion of what is deemed physically possible in the material world marks a moment of heightened emotionality as it expresses the tragic inevitability of her fate: as her body comes floating along on a beautifully designed and self-propelled magic ship reminiscent of the one the eponymous protagonist boards in Marie de France's *Guigemar*, readers understand that courtly love may frequently operate in a world beyond human responsibility. Just as nobody steers the Maid's magic boat, nobody, it seems, is to blame for the tragic fate of its passenger.

Much as Arthurian romance probes the boundaries of the material and draws on themes imported from outside the generic confines of romance – such as the discourses of mysticism or of religious relics – the genre also displays forms of materiality centring on the concreteness of bodily experience, including its gross and vile manifestations. The Alliterative *Morte Arthure*, for instance, revels in the gruesome aesthetic and effects that entrails and blood can have on a battlefield, as we witness horses and men falling over each other on a wet and slippery ground drenched in blood and covered with gore. Materiality is here imagined and experienced primarily through excessive representations of the vulnerability of human and animal bodies, representations intensified by an alliterative soundscape imitating the ripping and tearing of flesh and bones. In the Alliterative *Morte Arthure*, garish images of gross materiality are involved also in brutally exposing the homoerotic desire underlying the homosocial ties binding together the almost exclusively male society of the poem's fictional world; this is so, for instance, when Arthur wrestles that half-naked and cannibalistic rapist, the Giant of Mont St Michel, after having cut off the offender's monstrous and highly conspicuous genitals. Monstrosity is thus shown to constitute the Other of the idealized world of Arthurian romance, a monstrosity most clearly expressed in terms of raw and offensive physicality.

Materiality also plays an important role when it comes to the economic base of the chivalric world, a base whose existence the genre overwhelmingly denies. In Chrétien's *Yvain*, the hero rescues three hundred aristocratic women at the Castle Pesme Aventure [most ill adventure], who are held captive by two demi-goblins and forced to weave silk. Here the seemingly serene surface of the fairy-tale world is brutally disturbed by the intrusion of an economic realism that unveils the harsh material conditions that make aristocratic life and aristocratic aestheticism possible in the first place (Perkins 2015, 9). But the scene may allude also to the twelfth-century's burgeoning Flemish textile industry and its specifically urban context threatening the dominance of a chivalric class whose members depend primarily on agriculture for their livelihoods and whose ideological self-image hinges on suppressing the economic as a literary subject (cf. Ferlampin-Acher, *infra*).

Materiality frequently assumes special significance when it comes to either establishing or undermining social boundaries. In Malory's *Morte Darthur* Sir Gareth of Orkney appears incognito at Arthur's court and is given work in the kitchens. The physical space reserved for the servants is invoked not out of a desire for accurately rendering the socio-economic realities of King Arthur's household but rather because Camelot's material underside provides a paradoxical social threshold that elevates those willing to pass it voluntarily. Just as Sir Gareth obediently subjects himself to his humiliation and thereby preserves his incognito, true knights like Sir Lancelot instinctively understand his inborn aristocratic nature and visit him in the kitchens, ignoring the demeaning character of the manual labour Gareth is forced to perform. Whereas Sir Gareth's tale ends happily with the protagonist's marriage to an heiress and his seamless re-integration into the world of Camelot, one of the earliest literary treatments of both Arthurian material and Arthurian *economic* materiality, Marie de France's

Lanval, stages a head-on collision of the Arthurian fairytale world on the one hand, and the harsh social and economic hierarchies governing an aristocratic society celebrating itself in the fictional mirror of Camelot on the other. Lanval faces social and economic death when, for no clear reason, he is overlooked in the Arthurian gift-giving economy. Excluded from the royal fountain of bene-ficence, Lanval must witness his personal economic base collapse and is saved only by events resembling an adolescent wish-fulfilment fantasy *par excellence*: his encounter with a fairy woman who not only becomes his mistress, but also furnishes him with a magic purse. When he has, for the second time, been saved by his fairy mistress, the lay refrains from opting for a romance-like narrative of political and social restoration, but prefers, instead, an abandonment of material reality altogether, as Lanval and his paramour retire to the timeless Otherworld of the Isle of Avalon.

3 Matter in *Sir Gawain and the Green Knight*

One of the most fascinating Arthurian negotiations of the material is offered by the anonymous late-fourteenth-century alliterative romance *Sir Gawain and the Green Knight* (*SGGK*),[3] a text that draws on English and French Arthurian tradi-tions to the point of becoming "a uniquely hybridized version of insular romance." (Larrington, 2012, 252) The poem offers a dazzling panoply of scenes and motifs featuring the material. We witness magnificent displays of costly objects – for instance the detailed descriptions of the Green Knight's attire and the trappings of his horse as well as Gawain's arms, armour and shield – but equally highly evocative descriptions of the winter landscape that reveal what it means to be travelling in the harsh cold wearing a full suit of armour. We encounter a whole array of different architectural settings, the great hall in Camelot, an outside view of Castle Hautdesert's battlements as well as various chambers in the castle with their special emphasis on both comfort and privacy. We experience lavish explo-rations of the sexualized body – the Green Knight's hyper-athletic build and that of Sir Gawain himself, with the elegantly shiny plate armour tightly encasing his muscular thighs, as well as the blatant eroticism of Lady Bertilak's attire with her plunging neckline. And, finally, we become acquainted with an otherworldly space, the Green Chapel, which seems to be designed within a specifically archae-ological frame of reference, inasmuch as it resembles a megalithic burial mound

---

3 All references will be to Tolkien and Gordon (1967).

re-used and re-appropriated by later cultures for different purposes, a motif in medieval literature that reaches back to *Beowulf* (Semple 2013, 224).

The text betrays its fascination both with materiality and with its own textuality from the very beginning: thus, the narrator announces that he will tell his story "with lel letteres loken", "with faithful letters locked together" (*SGGK* l. 34), as though his letters were interlocking metal rings, his language forming a chain and the text assuming the character of chain mail. The romance claims for itself a paradoxical linguistic materiality even as it suggests that the world of chivalry is itself the product of story-telling, of fiction. Indeed, the text's sense of its own literariness is grounded in a keen appreciation of material splendour: "the descriptions of these things adds to the sense of the poem itself as a carefully crafted *objet de luxe*." (Mann 2009, 243)

This theme of a paradoxical materiality resurfaces when, in answer to his prayers, Gawain spies Castle Hautdesert. The building's peculiar aesthetic, its close-to-otherworldly perfection, is expressed in terms once again invoking the paradoxical sense of a specifically textual materiality rather than a physical one:

> So mony pynakle payntet watz poudred ayquere,
> Among þe castel carnelez clambred so þik,
> Þat pared out of papure purely hit semed. (*SGGK* ll. 800–802)
> [So many painted pinnacles were scattered everywhere, clustering so thickly amongst the embrasures of the castle, that it looked just as if cut out of paper. (Barron 1998, 73–75)]

Instead of a real castle we seem to be presented with something approaching a paper model or even a manuscript illumination – *paynted* and *poudred* – an image straight out of the Duc de Berry's *Très Riches Heures*.

The sophistication with which the text deploys and imagines matter can be gleaned especially from passages where the human body is shown to be enveloped by fabric. When Gawain has been freshly attired after his arrival at Castle Hautdesert, the effect of the cascades of cloth draped around him is not an erasure of his body, not a concealment of his physical features, but rather the opposite, as his shapely limbs seem to be enhanced rather than hidden by the effusion of luxuriant textiles. The same is true of the description of the Green Knight, whose tight-fitting clothing emphasizes his physical attractiveness. Yet here we witness something decidedly more compelling: as the half-giant's hyper-fashionable attire is depicted in the most minute detail, we realize the degree to which he constitutes an otherworldly apparition. The surfeit of seemingly realistic physical detail provides for a marked contrast with the intruder's supernatural greenness. It is, therefore, through loving attention to sophisticated worldliness – luxury, fashion, the materiality of textiles and metals, harnesses and hairstyles – that the otherworldly is most powerfully emphasized, a pattern that is repeated when

Gawain strikes off the Green Knight's head. While the intruder's head rolls around the floor in the most realistic fashion – so much so that some of the courtiers actually kick it – and fresh blood spurts from the Green Knight's neck as from a fountain, drenching his tunic, he calmly and politely addresses the company as though nothing out of the ordinary had happened.

Just as the poem's magical, supernatural and otherworldly elements are consistently grounded in their essential materiality, we find the poem's most symbolic aspects depicted in a manner that focuses on the physical: on flesh and blood and on objects and instruments. As far as the actual development of the plot is concerned, the exuberant narratives containing the hunting scenes are virtually superfluous. Yet nowhere else in the poem are we alerted to the sheer materiality of aristocratic life with such extreme care, as it emphatically takes place in a world of physical actors, some animate – hunters and beaters, stags, boars, foxes, hounds and horses – and some not – woods, thickets and rocks as well as swords, daggers, knives, spears and horns. Then there are the transformations that go on within this world, as animals are killed, their entrails mixed with bread and thrown to the dogs while their skins and their meat are skilfully preserved in an almost ritual manner. And all these activities are rendered in expert fashion by celebrating the highly technical nature of hunting through deploying the rich terminology associated with this art: materiality generates language and language engenders materiality. Yet as far as the actual story is concerned, the hunting scenes' principal purpose is entirely symbolic. The physical challenges of the hunts mirror the verbal and erotic challenges experienced in the castle, while the nature of the prey echoes Gawain's ethical performance in the love contest, with the fox standing for his failure to escape from the moral trap into which he has been lured.

Paradoxically, the single object that matters most in the whole romance, the thing around which the whole plot eventually revolves, remains remarkably symbolic and is treated as such. The green baldric, once again described in loving detail with its golden thread and its golden pendants, is never really put to the test. Whether the baldric is truly capable of fulfilling its protective promise remains unclear and, given the fact that Gawain is, in fact, wounded by Lord Bertilak's third stroke, one must assume that it is not. In the end Camelot's courtiers adopt the baldric as their symbol of honour thereby translating an object with a specifically material function into a symbol with a primarily social purpose. Formerly held to be an utterly unique magical thing, a truly singular object, the baldric is now re-constituted as a signifier and as such it can be used by all the courtiers. The baldric ceases to be a thing in the proper sense and transforms instead into a token. This then constitutes the most important – or literally: the most significant – transformation of matter in the whole romance, a poem rich in material transformations. An object marked by the specificity of its original thingness – a richly embroidered and ornamented girdle made of costly fabric, a magical instrument with the properties of a protective charm, the secret gift of a supremely seductive lady of unparalleled beauty and breeding – is re-contextualized through a collective act of signification. The court of Camelot declares it to be a symbol, so it becomes a symbol. Its original function is relegated to the realm of memory, and its original, context-dependent thingness ceases to matter as it is discursively appropriated and its meaning reshaped within a newly established social convention. Clearly, in Camelot matter matters, but the material always matters through discourse. The poem thus ends in a powerful celebration not only of the conventionality of the signifier but also of the general acknowledgment that, in the world of courtly fiction, the material operates primarily within terms dictated by culture.

References

Appadurai, Arjun, ed. *The Social Life of Things: Commodities in Cultural Perspective.* Cambridge: Cambridge University Press, 1986.

Barad, Karen. *Meeting the Universe Halfway: Quantum Physics and the Entanglement of Matter and Meaning.* Durham, NC: Duke University Press, 2007.

Barron, W.R.J., ed. *Sir Gawain and the Green Knight.* Rev. edn. Manchester: Manchester University Press, 1998.

Bennett, Jane. *Vibrant Matter: A Political Ecology of Things.* Durham, NC: Duke University Press, 2010.

Bennett, Tony, and Patrick Joyce, eds. *Material Powers: Cultural Studies, History and the Material Turn.* Milton Park: Routledge, 2010.

Brown, Bill. *A Sense of Things: The Object Matter of American Literature.* Chicago: University of Chicago Press, 2003.

Brown, Peter. *Chaucer and the Making of Optical Space.* Oxford, Bern etc.: Peter Lang, 2007.

Bynum, Carolyn Walker. *Christian Materiality: An Essay on Religion in Late Medieval Europe.* New York: Zone Books, 2011.

Chakrabarty, Dipesh. "The Anthropocene and the Convergence of Histories." *The Anthropocene and the Global Environmental Crisis: Rethinking Modernity in a New Epoch.* Ed. Clive Hamilton, Christophe Bonneuil and François Gemenne. Milton Park: Routledge, 2015. 44–56.

Cohen, Jeffrey Jerome. *Stone: An Ecology of the Inhuman.* Minneapolis, MN: University of Minnesota Press, 2015.

Cohen, Jeffrey Jerome, ed. *Animal, Vegetable, Mineral: Ethics and Objects.* Washington, DC: Oliphaunt Books, 2012.

Cole, Diana, and Samantha Frost. *New Materialisms: Ontology, Agency, and Politics.* Durham, NC: Duke University Press, 2010.

Daston, Lorraine. *Things That Talk.* New York: Zone Books, 2008.

Dolfijn, Rick, and Iris van der Tuin. *New Materialism: Interviews and Cartographies*. Ann Arbor, MI: Open Humanities Press, 2012.

Fabian, Johannes. *Time and the Other: How Anthropology Makes Its Object*. New York: Columbia University Press, 2002.

Haug, Walter. *Vernacular Literary Theory in the Middle Ages: The German Tradition, 800–1300, in its European Context*. Trans. Joanna M. Catling. Cambridge: Cambridge University Press, 1997.

Heidegger, Martin. "Das Ding." *Martin Heidegger Gesamtausgabe. I. Abteilung: Veröffentlichte Schriften 1910–1976. Vol. 7: Vorträge und Aufsätze*. Frankfurt a. M.: Vittorio Klostermann, 2000 [1950]. 165–187.

Hodder, Ian. *Entangled: An Archaeology of the Relations between Humans and Things*. Chichester: Wiley-Blackwell, 2012.

Ingham, Patricia Clare. "Little Nothings: *The Squire's Tale* and the Ambition of Gadgets." *Studies in the Age of Chaucer* 31 (2009): 53–80.

Larrington, Carolyne. "English Chivalry and *Sir Gawain and the Green Knight*." *A Companion to Arthurian Literature*. Ed. Helen Fulton. Chichester: Wiley-Blackwell, 2012. 252–264.

Latour, Bruno. *We Have Never Been Modern*. Trans. Catherine Porter. Cambridge, MA: Harvard University Press, 1993.

Malafouris, Lambros. *How Things Shape the Mind: A Theory of Material Engagement*. Cambridge, MA: The Massachusetts Institute of Technology Press, 2013.

Mann, Jill. "Courtly Aesthetics and Courtly Ethics in *Sir Gawain and the Green Knight*." *Studies in the Age of Chaucer* 31 (2009): 231–265.

Patterson, Lee. *Chaucer and the Subject of History*. Madison, WI: University of Wisconsin Press, 1991.

Perkins, Nicholas. "Introduction." *Medieval Romance and Material Culture*. Ed. Nicholas Perkins. Cambridge: D.S. Brewer, 2015. 1–22.

Putter, Ad. "The Twelfth-century Arthur." *The Cambridge Companion to the Arthurian Legend*. Ed. Elizabeth Archibald and Ad Putter. Cambridge: Cambridge University Press, 2009. 36–52.

Robertson, Kellie. "Medieval Materialism: A Manifesto." *Exemplaria* 22.2 (2010): 99–118.

Semple, Sarah. *Perceptions of the Prehistoric in Anglo-Saxon England: Religion, Ritual, and Rulership in the Landscape*. Oxford: Oxford University Press, 2013.

Shakespeare, William. *Othello*. Ed. E.A. Honigmann. The Arden Shakespeare, 3rd edn. London: Arden, 1999.

Tether, Leah. "Perceval's Puerile Perceptions: The First Scene of the *Conte du Graal* as an Index of Medieval Concepts of Human Development Theory." *Neophilologus* 94 (2010): 225–239.

Tilley, Chris, Webb Keane, Susanne Küchler, Mike Rowlands and Patricia Spyer, eds. *Handbook of Material Culture*. London: Sage, 2006.

Tolkien, J.R.R., and E.V. Gordon, eds. *Sir Gawain and the Green Knight*. Rev. Norman Davis. 2nd edn. Oxford: Clarendon Press, 1967.

Christine Ferlampin-Acher
The Natural World

The theme of nature in the literature of the Middle Ages is a complex subject. It encompasses both what the modern reader understands by the word *nature* (animals, plants, countryside, etc.) alongside a variety of medieval meanings. In the Middle Ages, for example, it was used allegorically in the sense of what is in a person from birth (what is innate) as opposed to *norreture* (what is acquired) as, for instance, in the frequently cited proverb, *nature passe norreture* [nature over nurture]. Restricting the field to just Arthurian literature provides a fitting lens for the study of *nature* in this sense because the former represents such a rich and voluminous corpus, which spans three hundred years from the twelfth to the fifteenth centuries, as well as most of Europe.

Nature as a concept has been studied from the perspective of natural scenery, or countryside, primarily in romantic literature and American nature writing, both which are far removed from the medieval corpus with which I will be concerned here. It is generally thought that medieval writers showed little interest in the landscape except as literary *topoi*, which offer little more than description. The connotation of the word *nature* is anachronistic in the Middle Ages, because it refers etymologically (as well as in Old French) to that which characterizes something or someone from their origins or birth. The word *nature* thus takes on many different values in the Middle Ages – eleven according to Alain de Lille (Solère 2002) – but never the modern meaning of what Zink (2006, 12) calls the "belle nature" [beautiful nature]. *Nature* in this sense is not obviously opposed to *norreture* (what is acquired) and thus raises the question of civilization. This is a theme that receives special treatment in Arthurian literature, particularly in the acts of the members of the Arthurian royal family, who establish courtesy and chivalry as part of a process of civilization.

My particular concern here, however, is more with the way in which nature poses the problem of humankind's relationship with the untamed animal and plant world. The reason for this is that the pertinence of interpretations based on literary ecocriticism remains open to debate. While this school is mainly focused on contemporary literature, some studies on texts from the Middle Ages are starting to emerge. Those that do exist, however, tend to be based on English literature, particularly *Sir Gawain and the Green Knight*, whilst related criticism on medieval French texts is more infrequent. Nevertheless, re-reading Arthurian

Christine Ferlampin-Acher (Université Rennes 2)

DOI 10.1515/9783110432466-016

episodes in light of ecology offers a rich seam to mine. My aim is not to focus on current ecological challenges by showing them as an atemporal constant of human mentality, but rather to use medieval Arthurian texts as a means to demonstrate, on the one hand, that there is a history of ecological thinking and that humankind's relationship with the environment has a cultural, historic, important and constitutive dimension. On the other hand, I wish to show that it is essential to reconstruct the textual significance of representations of nature without anachronism. In literary terms, this approach allows us to look at Arthurian texts from a particularly useful angle. It does not, however, claim to give a complete view of a text, but rather invites us to put into perspective the idea that the Arthurian world is a literary construction, disconnected from the realities of its time and plunged into a bygone era following the death of Arthur; in other words, it is little more than nostalgia. Using traditional approaches that study the representation of nature in texts (studies based on the relationships between *nature* and *culture*), an approach inspired by ecocriticism, alongside a corpus of medieval French Arthurian texts as a test-bed, I aim to set out the potential of such critical approaches to Arthurian material.

1 Scenery and landscapes

While scenery and wild landscapes have been the subject of study in various literary fields since the emergence of Romanticism and nature writing, they have rarely been studied in medieval Arthurian literature. Arthurian texts have mainly been a vehicle for topical representations, where the *locus amoenus*, passed down from antiquity and celebrated by the lyric (Curtius 1956, 317–322), and the *locus terribilis*, more nebulous but just as topical, are pitted against one another (Juan Muela Equerra 2002; Bermejo Larrea 2012; Verelst 1994). On the one hand, there is the welcoming forest, the birds and the *reverdie* [fresh new greenness] in the opening lines of *Le Conte du Graal*.[1] There is also the adventure-filled or love-filled orchard (like that of the *Joie de la Cour* in *Erec et Enide* (Chrétien de Troyes 1989, ll. 5689–5714)), adorned with a spring/fountain and a pine tree, where Tristan and Isolde meet – a scene reproduced on many an ivory casket after

---

1 "Ce fu au tans qu'arbre florissent,/ Fueillent boschaige, pré verdissent,/ et cil oisel an lor latin/ dolcement chantent au matin,/ Et tote riens de joie anflame" (Chrétien de Troyes 1973, ll. 1–5) [It was the time when the trees were blossoming, the woods were becoming covered in leaves, the meadows were turning green, the birds were singing their songs sweetly in the mornings and everything was flushed with happiness] (all translations are my own).

the appearance of the romances by Béroul and by Thomas of Britain. We might also think of the spring/fountain, to which the knights make haste to rest after a battle or to weep over the woman they love, particularly in the Prose *Tristan*.[2] On the other hand, there are places filled with fear, such as dense forests full of dangerous adventures and monsters lying in wait, castles ruled by bad customs, uneasy seas crossed by Tristan and the knights of the Holy Grail and islands with sirens, as in *Le Conte du Papegau* (Charpentier and Victorin 2004, 237), or fairies (like in Avalon). There are also supernatural places, like the Ile d'Aimant (Fer- lampin-Acher 2002, 88–96),[3] mountains (where the monsters hide) and lakes (like the Lac de Lausanne, where the monstrous cat of the *Suite Vulgate* of the *Merlin* lives). There are the fairies, like the Dame du Lac, and ultimately, there are the rivers, which form the gateways to the hereafter. The *loci horribiles* borrow from the infernal imagination, and the *loci amoeni* from Edenic representations. Space is more symbolic than picturesque. The miniatures maintain the vagueness of the evocations, especially in the oldest manuscripts. The pictorial landscape, like the portrait, only undergoes a gradual development prior to the fourteenth century, when literature, including Arthurian literature, begins to accord it some importance, both within the text and in the miniatures.

Although real names are used, the toponymy is often enough to suggest the natural scenery. Take, for example, "Brocéliande" or "Gales" [Wales] in Chrétien de Troyes' *Le Chevalier au lion* or "Escosse" [Scotland], "Wincestre" [Winches- ter] and "Londres" [London] in *La Mort le roi Artu*, which contains a substantial number of mentions of British surroundings, as would be expected. Some names seem to be imaginary, however, and difficult to associate with real places. This is either because the copyist has not recognized the names and misrepresented them or because they have become associated with new meanings. For example, while "Orcanie" refers to the Orkney Islands, the name in this form would have conjured up the disquieting place associated with the classical god, Orcus, in the

---

2 "Cele fontaine estoit aucqes avironnee de granz arbrez qi le lieu fesoient asséz delitable et qi mult l'enbelisoient" (Ménard 1997–2007, § 4; all references to the Prose *Tristan* are to this edi- tion) [This spring/fountain was almost completely surrounded by tall trees, which made it a very pleasant place and much enhanced]; "et trovent adonc la sorse d'une fontaine qi coroit trop clere et trop belle par une arbroie" (§ 18) [and then they fell upon a spring/fountain, which flowed through the trees, quite beautiful and crystal-clear]; "Et la fontaine sordoit en .I. tres biax lieu, environné de trop grant planté d'arbres" (§ 19) [and the spring/fountain gushed out in a very beautiful place, surrounded by many trees].

3 The Arthurian knight travelled mainly by land, through the forests, but when confronted with the spiritual adventures of the Holy Grail, the space of choice for the trial was generally the sea and the islands, particularly in *L'Estoire del saint Graal* (Szkilnik 1991, 22–25).

minds of cultivated medieval readers. But what does "Lamborc" correspond to in *La Mort le roi Artu* and "Landuc" in *Erec et Enide*? While a name based on "reality" would enable medieval readers to create a representation of scenery, not all readers had the same cultural backgrounds, and names that were evocative for one reader might not mean anything to another. The modern reader risks being confused by imagining the Brocéliande in the *Chevalier au lion* (l. 187; l. 697) through the lens of its current touristic reality. In the imaginary toponymy, which characterizes more than it identifies places, the picturesque dimension is much reduced. *Perilleuse forest* [dangerous forest] and *fontaine aventureuse* [adventurous spring/fountain], for example, suggest the function of a place to the reader without describing it. Adventure settings are filled with encyclopaedic-type references, which medieval readers were able to understand and picture in their minds (particularly when they were associated with a *merveille* [marvel]) thanks to knowledge they had acquired from encyclopaedias. Encyclopaedias were relatively accessible as they were written in the vernacular from the thirteenth century onwards. Although this was less the case for Arthurian texts than it was for the material emerging from Rome, as well as for the stories about Alexander the Great, this is possible to see in certain examples such as, for example, that of "Mont Gibel" (Etna) in *Floriant et Florete* (Wolfzettel 2011), and as well as that of the "gouffre de Sathalie" [Gulf of Sathalia], where the *Laide Semblance* lies in *Le livre d'Artus* (Ferlampin-Acher 2002, 304–310).

While the concept of landscape was developing in the pictorial arts and literature during the fourteenth and fifteenth centuries, French Arthurian material was no longer very productive. However, *Perceforest*, which is preserved in fifteenth-century testimonies, sets up a geography that is, on the whole, realistic in response to the ideological challenges of fiction (Ferlampin-Acher 1993; 2010, 168–224). The author presents some descriptions in which nature gives rise to evocations that escape the topical, such as the descriptions of the tide phenomenon in Zealand,[4] the well-kept forest with trees all aligned (Roussineau 2007, Part one, t. I, 139) and the sheep passing peacefully by (Szkilnik 1998). There is no longer any evidence of *topos* in the descriptions of space. It demands interpretation as much by the character, for whom it presents an enigma, as by the reader (Findley 2012). *Perceforest* is a romance situated on the fringes of Arthurian material (it recounts the prehistory of the Arthurian world), and was particularly popular in

---

4 The author mentions the sea, the flat earth, the wetland birds and a hillock, where the shepherds and their flocks would take refuge when the sea level rose (Roussineau 1993, Part three, t. III, 59–60). The wild Zealand was regularly subjected to violent tides and storms and submerged under water.

this Burgundian area, where a new genre of landscape art was emerging (such as, for example, the works of Jan van Eyck). It thus showed a new sensitivity to nature and the landscape in its evocations of a dewdrop or of the malodorous, misty wetlands. Nature in *Perceforest* does not give rise to purely aesthetic descriptions, however. It is often populated with monsters, such as Hollant the giant or savages like the Greeks of Scotland, and interacts with the protagonists in such a way as to make it difficult to extract individual tableaux from the text. Furthermore, the details that produce an effect of reality are often paradoxically linked to marvels. The reader can imagine the stench and mists of Hollant's marshes (Roussineau 1987, 109–112), not from any direct references but because these are the manifestations associated with a monstrous, malodorous, smoke-emitting giant that lives there. This particularly allusive evocation of the marshes is based on both fantastical elements and the diversion of a *topos*. A heron, which is described here in a realistic manner, plays the role of a romantic messenger, thus representing an adaptation of the troubadours' nightingale such that it seamlessly fits into the real fauna of the marshes.

2 What is *nature*?

The meaning of *nature* as constituting a physical world that excludes humans and their creations only dates as far back as the seventeenth century in France. People in the Middle Ages would not have used the term *nature* to refer to the elements discussed above. Words in the *sauvage* [uncultivated] family correspond best in Old and Middle French to our modern idea of nature. In accordance with what its etymology suggests (*sauvage* from the Latin *salvatica* which, in turn, comes from *silva* [forest]), the forest plays an important role in the Arthurian corpus as a place of otherness. It is where we find anything non-human. Animals like stags and lions gather there but also monsters and supernatural figures, like fairies, enchantresses and *Perceforest*'s ladies of the forest. It is also where the classical *genii loci* and the pagan divinities sought refuge after the spread of Christianity. Comparative approaches concerned with beliefs, folklore and mythology help to shed light on this (Ferlampin-Acher 2010; Lecouteux 1995; Walter 1988). Marked by an ontological otherness, fairies,[5] *luitons* [goblins] such as Zéphir in Perceforest, giants and the occasional *beste glatissant* [yelping beast] (Ferlampin-Acher

---

5 The hero in *Artus de Bretagne* meets the fairy Proserpine (Ferlampin-Acher 2017, § 249) beneath an oak tree in the moonlight, in a forest edged by a meadow and a path.

2002, 311–322) rub shoulders in the forest with creatures who are sociologically different, like hideous old women,[6] or *Yvain*'s monstrous Bouvier (Chrétien de Troyes 1982, ll. 276–311),[7] and felons, traitors and thieves of all descriptions, who are sometimes marked by the supernatural, like the sons of *netons* [demons] in *Yvain* (ll. 5263–5331). Confronted with these wild creatures, the heroes antithetically assert themselves as courteous. Many examples of this are presented in the Arthurian corpus. The hero is the civilizing element. King Arthur – even from the earliest texts (such as in Geoffrey of Monmouth's *Historia regum Britanniae*) – is the man who conquers the barbarism of the gigantic Riton, and a refined, courteous civilization grows around him. Also found in this wild place are hermits, like the man who put Perceval back on the right track in *Le Conte du Graal* (he lives in "un desert" [a wasteland]; Chrétien de Troyes 1973, l. 6031), and the Cistercians, as in *La Queste del saint Graal*. The forest, like all nature created by God, offers the character – and the reader – a set of signs to decode. This notion of *integumentum*, or theological nature, also serves as a basis for semiotics, which underpins the interpretation and decoding of the knights' adventures (trials as well as others) in a quest for meaning (Zink 2006, 36–37). Untamed nature provides the framework both for adventure, whether chivalric (fighting giants, monsters, felons, etc.) or spiritual, and for a chivalry that is both terrestrial and celestial.

However, this framework cannot be superimposed onto our own notion of untamed nature, which we imagine as empty of any human mark or presence. On the one hand, it is essential, in order to avoid anachronisms, to base literary approaches on historical knowledge. The relationships between humankind, animals and plants are cultural facts with a historical dimension, which ignorance can lead us to misinterpret.[8] On the other, the untamed nature found in Arthurian romances is not always a deserted place. Emptiness has no meaning for the medieval hero. The forest is peppered with clearings and paths, and it is inhabited. It is where the hero finds the adversaries who are worthy of his heroism and the hermits who guide him. These are not blank spaces in the texts. They are isolated, like the medieval forests, but they are accessible. In reality, the forests were populated areas, where pigs were taken to feed on acorns, where people hunted and

---

6 The castle of the monstrous old woman, horned "aussi comme sauvaige bieste" [like a wild beast] in *Les Merveilles de Rigomer* (Foerster 1915, l. 3510 and l. 3542) lies in the "foriest si parfont" [forest so deep].
7 The Bouvier was found in an "essart" [clearing]. Deforestation was carried out in the Middle Ages. This realistic space, where savagery and civilization meet, represents the character's struggle between human and animal and between natural and supernatural.
8 The portrayal of the stag as an enchantress's pet in *Perceforest* might be considered fantastical, but it was not. Hinds and stags were bred in enclosures in the Middle Ages.

where they moved about from one place to another. It was its ambivalence that was interesting – and not, like today, the dream of untouched authenticity. The romances show an appreciation for intermediate places, like the orchard, which lie somewhere between wild nature and space tamed by humankind. The idea of a land untouched by human hands with no discernible trace of human activity is not relevant in the romances. In French, for example, the word *fontaine* can refer to a natural spring or a man-made fountain. We can see in manuscript miniatures that there is often uncertainty when depicting a scene showing knights at the *fontaine*, with examples oscillating between a natural water course and a man-made construction. Neither does the modern bipartition that opposes nature and the town (such as it is represented in the fabliaux) feature in Arthurian romances. The city is only barely present in the form of the court, and it is often not very city-like, opening onto an orchard. Evocations of the towns and the bourgeoisie are rare, particularly in the twelfth and thirteenth centuries, although Gauvain in *Le Conte du Graal* is attacked by the Escavalon *commune*, which is an opulent city, described by the author as having resident moneychangers and artisans (Chrétien de Troyes 1973, ll. 5692–5716).[9] Later romances, however, give an account of the evolution of the bourgeoisie at the end of the Middle Ages as their readership expanded socially, suggesting that the bourgeoisie became more receptive to evocations of the city, like the descriptions of Argençon in *Artus de Bretagne* (Ferlampin-Acher 2017, § 184).

Our relationship with animals and the supernatural cannot be transposed onto medieval Arthurian texts.[10] The domestic animal is almost entirely absent from the corpus. Husdent is more a hunting dog than a companion, and the horse, while it is often mentioned as a working animal, is given no narrative dimension. The cat that rages by the Lac de Lausanne in the *Suite du Merlin* before becoming a monster is a *petit chaton* [little kitten] pulled from the water and adopted by a fisherman, however it would be a mistake to liken this animal to our modern companions. The fisherman took it in because it would hunt rats and mice, but in transforming it into a monster, the text offers insights into medieval reservations about cats (they often preferred ferrets, and black cats had a rather dark reputation).[11] This monstrous cat did not represent a deviation from a pet cat; it

---

9 However, the town is given a prominent place in classical romances and romances like *Floire et Blancheflor* and *Galeran de Bretagne*.
10 There are many studies (see bibliography in Fabri-Tehranchi and Russakoff 2014, 215–231). However, the Arthurian corpus in its entirety has not been the subject of any specific studies.
11 This episode has an aetiological dimension (it "invents" an origin in the name of the Mont du Chat, which overlooks not the Lac de Lausanne but the Lac du Bourget). This cat is immediately

was a hyperbolic realization of what a cat represented in the Middle Ages. While the domestic animal is rare, however, the beast takes on a totemic quality and becomes a double of the hero, like Yvain's lion or Arthur's "papegau" [parrot] in the *Conte du Papegau*. The animal is often a hostile, evil force like a monster, but it can also be a magical messenger, like white hinds, or providential, like the stag in *La Queste del saint Graal*. Sometimes it is a sign, a presage, as is the case with Sara's foal in *Perceforest* (Ferlampin-Acher 2002, 265). There are many episodes, however, that present the porous nature of the boundaries between humans and animals. Only an era in which people lived in such close proximity with animals (even in close confinement) could be so fascinated by the fragility of what separates humans from animals. This is in spite of the fact that Genesis guarantees the irreducible supremacy of humans over animals.[12] In the Arthurian world, humans metamorphose into animals, as in the episode of Caradoc in the *First Continuation* of the *Conte du Graal* (Roach 1993, ll. 2047–2087).[13] Even Merlin – who is the son of the devil – takes the form of a stag.[14] Metamorphosis into an animal often denotes a sexual issue, such as we find in Caradoc's greyhound bitch, sow and mare, and when Estonné becomes a bear in *Perceforest*. There is also Liriope's greyhound bitch and her lover's magnificent bull, which expiates their amorous impatience at the house of *peneance* [penitence] (Ferlampin-Acher 2002, 268–272).[15] The werewolf is rare in Arthurian literature however (although it serves as a backdrop in *Guillaume de Palerne*). At most, *Perceforest* makes a fleeting allusion to this belief, which was somewhat devalued at the time (Ferlampin-Acher 2011). The porous nature of the boundaries between humans and animals is also found in the representation of hybrids, like the knight-fish in *Perceforest* (see also the part-fish, part-human knight in *Diu Crône*; cf. Kragl, *infra*). These serve not as foils but as models to humans for the creation of tournaments (Ferlampin-Acher

---

fantastical. It is black and can only be unnatural because it likes water (Poirion et al. 2001, ll. 1606–1609).

12 The trend for domestic animals in the modern age shows that humans no longer fear the beast and that they can get close to them emotionally without the fear of any sudden change.

13 An enchanter, in love with Ysaive who married Caradué, successively makes the damsel appear as a greyhound bitch, a sow and a mare, with which the hero mates. This episode, which perhaps transposes the taboo of zoophilia, has often been commented on (Baumgartner 1984).

14 The episode of Grisandole in the Vulgate *Suite du Merlin* (Poirion et al. 2001, ll. 1226–1253) is frequently commented on. In this tale, based on sexual cross-dressing, Merlin takes the form of a savage.

15 While Eliavrés transforms a greyhound bitch into a woman in the story of Caradoc, the reverse is the case in *Perceforest*, where the damsel becomes the greyhound bitch. This animal has an ambiguous symbolism, representing both fidelity and lechery.

2002, 299–304). There are very few occurrences of hybrids in Arthurian material however. The motif of hybridization was most successful at the end of the Middle Ages, after the period during which Arthuriana was at its most popular.

By contrast, the relationship between humans and the plant world receives hardly any attention, even though it usually appears essential to situate texts in relation to associated medieval mentalities and practices (Clément 2008). For example, metamorphoses into plants, which were so popular in the classical texts, are entirely absent from medieval literature, with the exception of Ovidian references. At a stretch, in Arthurian material (and elsewhere) there are some heroines with names that refer to plants, such as Blanchefleur, the damsel Perceval is in love with in *Le Conte du Graal*.[16] Similarly, Arthurian flora shows little variation. *Artus de Bretagne* stands out for the importance placed on the marigold (*solsequia*) and its solar symbolism (Ferlampin-Acher 2016). The rose, lily, oak and pine make frequent appearances, and any mentions that deviate from this norm stand out. The cultural context sheds light on these references, though the modern reader often lacks the right tools to interpret them. *Le Conte du Graal* opposes charm (Chrétien de Troyes 1973, l. 6128) (which rhymes with "desarme" [to disarm], and which the hero ties his horse to when he goes to see the hermit) with oak (l. 6312), which grows in many Arthurian forests and which has a connotation linked to war and warriors (Clément 2008, 107–131). The plant world is thus called upon to evoke spring and the call to love and to create within the framework of the *reverdie* [fresh new greenness] and female beauty. Notwithstanding the presence of harrowmen at Perceval's mother's service *in Le Conte du Graal*, mentions of agricultural practice are rare.

Nature, when set in contrast with humans, does not just define itself in relation to the plant and animal world however. For the modern reader, it also defines itself in relation to the supernatural, which disrupts the natural course of things. Caution must be used when applying this notion, however, since it is specific to the Middle Ages. The soothsayers and demons can disrupt the natural course of things, but as creatures of God, they are part of the world order. Nature in its entirety includes not only the everyday but also the *merveilles* [astonishing happenings]. Therefore, the supernatural is not in opposition to nature, rather it is

---

16 This name has attracted little attention. While it is certainly commonplace (it is shared by the heroine in *Floire et Blancheflor*), is it a coincidence that Perceval, had he asked the right question, would have restored the fertility of the "terre gaste" [wasteland]? Is it by chance that, after having been a great hunter and devouring the little pastries and discovering a food of penitence (which was probably part-plant) from the hermit on his road to redemption, Perceval falls in love with a Blanchefleur?

just an unusual form of it. Furthermore, the supernatural is often represented as hyperbolically natural. The monster – an astonishing *merveille* [marvel] – is a superlative animal, often made up of several animals with a higher concentration of animality indicators than a normal animal, while the fairy is a superlative woman (superlative in beauty, maternal qualities (like the Dame du Lac), treachery (like Morgue), and so on).

The idea of nature is not, therefore, simply part of a binary representation that opposes it to civilization, humans or the supernatural. Rather, it has to do with time and the future, as its etymology suggests, by virtue of its connection with the idea of birth and creation. The word *nature* is most often used to refer to what is innate in human beings. Following in the wake of classical representations of the goddess Natura, it most often appears in allegorical form as the ruler presiding over the future of all living beings, including humans. While nowadays we think about nature in terms of its problematic relationship with humankind and seek some sort of reconciliation, in the Middle Ages nature was within humans as well as all around them. For example, it was an allegorical figure that was able to become a real character, playing an important role in the *Roman de la rose*. In Arthurian romances, which are far removed from this allegorical creation, nature is rather more understated. The exception to this is *Perceforest*, which revived Arthurian material at the end of the Middle Ages. *Perceforest* enters into dialogue with the *Roman de la rose* and even with Alain de Lille's *De planctu naturae*, in which nature is indignant that a virgin can be pregnant (Ferlampin-Acher 2010, 300–340). The *Roman de la rose* uses nature to condemn the seeking of pleasure when it is dissociated from procreation and calls into question the *fin'amor* [courtly love] and thus, indirectly, Arthurian love (even though the romances, more so than the lyrics, ended in marriage). In contrast, *Perceforest* reconciles nature and the Arthurian romance with no hint of prudishness, particularly through the *luiton* [goblin] Zéphir who, as the guardian spirit of the Scottish lineage, is in favour of procreation and allows all Arthurian ancestors and heroes to be conceived.[17]

Aside from this particular case, the nature allegory is also to be found in short ornamental depictions, such as portraits.[18] A number of proverbial utterances also depict *nature*, where the qualities of an individual from birth are

---

17 On *nature* and *culture* in *Perceforest*, see Huot (2007), particularly Part I on the primitive people of Scotland.
18 For example at the Château de la Merveille in *Le Conte du Graal*, Gauvain admires a "pucelle" [virgin], whose cheeks have been coloured rosy red by *nature* (Chrétien de Troyes 1973, l. 7651). This detail is found in many texts.

referred to. This seems to be related to the fact that *nature* in French belongs to the same family as *naître* [to be born] and should therefore be seen as connected to the modern *inné* [innate], which did not enter the French language until the Renaissance as the form *enné*. These qualities are more important than anything education can provide because in the Middle Ages they believed *nature passe norreture* [nature over nurture].[19] This saying is especially frequent in romances that socially disorientate their heroes, as in *Guillaume d'Angleterre, L'Escoufle* and *Guillaume de Palerne*. Although the Arthurian hero can be humiliated by defeat, he is rarely transplanted into another social environment, hence the relative rarity of this proverb in our corpus. There are exceptions to this, however. There is the young Perceval, who was born into a good family but brought up a boor, and who proves to be a highly valued knight by the end of *Le Conte du Graal*. There is also Guillaume le Clerc's *Fergus*, a text which parodies Chrétien's work and presents an ambiguous character, the son of a *vilain* [villain] and a noble lady. He inherits his mother's value – it was assumed that the milk transmitted the maternal qualities to the child. Gauvain's natural sons (Guinglain in Renaut's *Bel Inconnu* and Lionaus, the son of the damsel of Lis in the *First Continuation* of *Le Conte du Graal*) also illustrate this primacy of nature. The fact remains, however, that the Arthurian domain, in its glorification of nobility and only marginal attention to the education of its heroes (I think here of the training that the Dame du Lac organizes for her protégé in the Prose *Lancelot*), is not particularly interested in the relationship between *nature* and *norreture*. Kay, whose mother had breast-fed the future King Arthur but who was himself breastfed by a woman of inferior rank, sees his *nature* corrupted. He is *desnaturé* [unnatural], but while the texts regularly denounce his sharp tongue, they pay hardly any attention to this trait. In other words, the appearances of nature as an allegory and of the term *nature* in the sense of "what comes from birth" are marginal and fairly meaningless in the Arthurian corpus when compared with those found in other medieval texts.

However, the medieval conceptions of nature at the intersection of Christianity and contributions from classical philosophers offer more enlightenment (Solère 2002). Nature in the Middle Ages encompasses the whole of Creation, including humankind; it is an entity that towers above everything. The lines between nature and God can be blurred, but most often, nature is submissive to

---

19 Morawski (1925). A number of proverbs balance *nature* and *norreture*. Most come down in favour of the primacy of *nature*: *Meulz vaut nature que nurreture* (Morawski 1925, n° 1273) [nature over nurture], *Nature ne puet mentir* (n° 1327) [nature cannot lie], *Nature passe norreture* (n° 1328) [nature over nurture], and *Plus trait nature que cent beufs* (n° 1655) [nature means more than one hundred cows].

God as the principal Creator. Hence the frequent references to a nature that forms and shapes and which, as such, can become an authorial representation. When nature gives its beauty to a heroine or pushes a character to act in a certain way, it is the author's disguise. Moreover, romance as a literary genre emerged in the French language during the twelfth-century Renaissance with its Neoplatonism, which revitalized the literary relationship with nature (Ribémont 2002). The hero (like the poet) was therefore in direct contact with the whole of Creation, which he was given in order to acquaint himself with it. Erec's coronation robe, into which was figurally woven all the knowledge in the universe, represents the profound link between the hero and the world (Chrétien de Troyes 1989, ll. 6672–6748; Hart 1981). In the thirteenth century, the resurgence of Aristotelianism prompted a revival of interest in nature and all its manifestations, boosting the distribution of encyclopaedias, including those in the vernacular. Around 1300, in *Artus de Bretagne*, Estienne, knight and scholar, seduces Marguerite by giving an encyclopaedic talk on the world, the planets and meteorology (Ferlampin-Acher 2017, § 217 and § 218). The Arthurian romance was thus able to represent scholarly knowledge on nature, admittedly with the additional challenge of popularizing it, but also and especially with the aim of glorifying the scholar and, through him, the poet, who was the hero knight's rival. With Merlin (and Blaise, see Berthelot 1991) and Estienne in *Artus de Bretagne* (Ferlampin-Acher 1994; 1995), the Arthurian romance writer invents doubles, demonstrating his knowledge of the world and the natural world in particular.

The questions posed by nature, whether considered in terms of its modern meaning or its medieval values, are therefore diverse, and they reveal anthropological problems just as much as poetic ones. Long before the advent of nature writing, Arthurian texts conferred a prominent place to humankind both in the story and in the world, but always under the guardianship of God, a creature among all the others.

3 Ecocritical approaches?

There are still very few studies of Arthurian texts using ecocritical approaches. Contemporary literature has been largely preferred as an object of study for this approach because of current ecological issues. However, even though the contemporary crisis is unprecedented, it presents us with a useful tool for thinking about humankind's place in nature and for shedding light on the archaeology of its representations. Putting the idea of human exceptionalism to the test can be enhanced through medieval representations, which establish a continuum between human beings and animals. This continuum is deeply rooted in the imagination (as is revealed by the metamorphoses and the emergence of totemism) and relayed by Christianity because, even though Christianity establishes a barrier between humankind and the animals in Genesis, it makes them both God's creatures (did we not see this in Francis of Assisi, who is often referred to as the first ecologist?) Moreover, the Middle Ages had its own problems with pollution and climatic disturbances. It may be that the Arthurian texts contain more traces of these than other genres inasmuch as the founding themes are the *terre* [land] rendered *gaste* [wasteland] by human failings and the supernatural storms caused by a human action (for example, at Brocéliande). While the English (Rudd 2014) and even the German (Classen 2015) corpuses have given rise to ecocritical approaches, these have often taken the form of thematic studies, dealing, for example, with trees, the sea, and so on (Rudd 2007), and they have focused only on a few texts (*Sir Gawain and the Green Knight* in particular) or subjects (such as the forest).[20] As far as the French corpus is concerned, there are some studies underway, but these have mainly been carried out in Britain and the United States, by contrast with France where the ecocritical approach has only been employed marginally.

However, there are a number of elements that encourage us to think of medieval literature, and Arthurian literature in particular, as a pertinent field for ecocriticism, provided vigilance is always maintained regarding the meanings of words in the Middle Ages (*nature*, as we have seen, is problematic)[21] and the

---

20 This is the only subject called upon by Aberth (2013) in relation to English Arthurian literature. The forest is in effect an essential space in the medieval tale, Arthurian or otherwise (Saunders 1993). It is also worth noting the collection of essays on medieval Spanish literature, which is organized around a *Nature Untamed, Nature Tamed, Nature Stylized* opposition (Scarborough 2013).

21 Moreover, the word *environnement* is a Middle French creation and more recent than *avironnement* [an *environ*, or that which surrounds]. It had a spatial value and referred to a circuit, a contour, the margins of a page or the act of surrounding and its result. It was only through a semantic borrowing from the English *environment* at the beginning of the twentieth century that it took on the meaning of the set of physical elements and phenomena that surround a living organism. Around 1960, its use extended to the domains of ethology and ecology: "the set of natural and cultural conditions likely to have an effect on an organism." (Rey 2006, 1261) However, we do find evidence of this term in *Artus de Bretagne* (Ferlampin-Acher 2017, § 150, 33) in the Tour Ténébreuse episode, where the initial meaning refers to the mill's grindstones, which surround the Tour with a strong sense of circularity. The episode represents the anxiety surrounding the relatively recent introduction of windmills into Britain, which are characterized by a worrying mechanisation. The hero, the human, is excluded from entering this tower. He has lost his role at the centre of the world, overtaken by the machine, which has also disrupted the rhythm of the

risk of anachronisms. People in the Middle Ages, just as in the Classical world, were always aware of natural disasters and considered them to be destructive disturbances. The majority of medieval encyclopaedias, particularly those that circulated from the thirteenth century onwards, mention cataclysmic events, like earthquakes, storms, and so on. In this period of rediscovering Aristotelianism, they were the objects of scientific knowledge, as they are today, but the explanations given for these disturbances were to do with human fallibility. While causality is typically more scientific today, the idea that human fault should be involved is a notion still present almost a thousand years on. This idea of fault is nowadays often superimposed onto that of responsibility, even if it has to be greatly distorted (Jouanna, Leclant and Zink 2006). The impact of human beings on nature, particularly since the Fall, is thought of as a fault. From the work of Chrétien de Troyes and Robert de Boron onwards, the *graal* [grail] is linked to a *terre gaste* [wasteland], and is replicated by the attack suffered by the *mehaigné* [injured] king and associated with a succession of failings, particularly Perceval's. Perceval does not know how to ask the right questions, and before he learns moderation, particularly from the hermit in relation to food, he devours the little pastries made by the damsel in the tent without restraint. The motif of the Holy Grail, posing the question of food, exhaustion of the land and human sickness, suggests a reflection on abundance and poverty, and one element of this is the opulence of the service of the Holy Grail. Scarcity of food was a worrying prospect for medieval man, and it raised the issue of fault in respect of the bad management of nature and humankind's responsibility.

More than any other body of medieval texts, therefore, Arthurian material poses the pressing problem of uncertain relationships between human beings, the human body, the earth that feeds it and God. Rash acts by knights lead to disasters. While Yvain's Bouvier, for example, knows what to expect from the spring/fountain and guards the herd, careful not to cause any disturbances (Zink 2006, 188 and 193), first Calogrenant and then Yvain disrupt the natural order and trigger a storm. Yvain then has to pass through the madness in the forest for order to be restored. The hermit in *Le Conte du Graal* returns Perceval to both the liturgical and seasonal rhythms. Perceval's excessiveness is particularly strongly denounced in *Fergus*. The romance can of course be interpreted as a simple

---

seasons (Ferlampin-Acher 2013; see also Echard's discussion of machinery, *infra*). In this decentring of nature in medieval thinking, the people perceive themselves to be already thrown aside by early industrialization. *Environnement* refers both to the anthropocentrism of representations (humans want to be at the centre) and to the threat of decentring, where the machine takes the upper hand.

parodic game, but it also seems to set Fergus and Perceval in opposition with each other. Ultimately the true hero, Fergus is the son of a *vilain* [villain], who is close to the "primitive" world and far removed from the world of the court. He is Perceval's double (Ferlampin-Acher 2015), and it is Perceval who goes on to make Fergus a knight, thus marking the transition from one generation to the next. In *Fergus*, the meeting between the eponymous character and the court is preceded by an episode in which Perceval hunts down and violently kills a stag (the text emphasizes the cries of the beast, the blood and the agony, Guillaume le Clerc 1983, ll. 200–232). There are very few texts in which the hunt is presented with such brutality. In Arthurian tales, the hero generally follows the animal, which leads him into an adventure, but he does not actually slaughter it. Perceval is thus discredited, and to a much greater extent than is the uncouth Fergus.

Moreover, the British material, as famously reported by Jean Bodel, is differentiated from the materials of France and Rome by its amusing *merveilles vaines* [pointless marvels]. These *merveilles* are at the intersection of the natural and supernatural. They are astonishing, and they move away from what the character is expecting and invite him (and the reader) to understand. The enchanters (like Merlin) and the fairies regularly disrupt the expected order of things. They embody the Promethean temptation of humans to transform the world, as well as the fear that this arouses. The supernatural thus constitutes a paradigm of the approach to ecological phenomena when they are in a state of crisis. The Arthurian world, after all, is centred around Arthur, whose conception disturbs the natural order of things and who never really dies. Indeed, the great king is condemned to die and his world to be wiped out because both are characterized by a flawed relationship with nature.

The context must also be taken into consideration. The Little Ice Age and the Black Death caused an ecological disaster from the thirteenth century onwards (Bowlus 1980; Aberth 2013), but Arthurian literature gives scant account of these events because it was largely written prior to their onset.[22] Later, however, the numerous storms in *Perceforest* and the frequent dark clouds triggered by Estienne in *Artus de Bretagne* (Ferlampin-Acher 1995; 2008) might be argued as in some way linked to the contemporary meteorological conditions, even if they probably also owe much to the powers of the so-called stormcallers, who are widely documented throughout the Middle Ages.

---

22 It should be noted, however, that the climate prior to 1300 was milder than it is today. This makes the snow exceptional in the *Conte du Graal* and invites us to reconsider the episode of the drops of blood on the snow as a climatic *merveille*.

A parallel must also be drawn between Arthurian literature and the major transformation that Jean Gimpel (1975) considered to be an industrial revolution. In the twelfth and thirteenth centuries, Europe (particularly France, the Burgundian territories and England) experienced the start of industrialization and, with it, an expansion of the cities and towns that prefigured the Industrial Revolution of the nineteenth century. Just as the trial of *Pesme Aventure* in *Yvain* – which sees the hero battling against the supernatural sons of a *netun* [demon] – represents the sad historic status of silk workers in the Middle Ages (Cassagnes-Brouquet 2013), so a number of equally fantastical adventures show, using hyperbolic transposition, that there was already concern over the perverse effects of human activity and pollution (Leguay 1999). *Nigremance* [necromancy], which enabled enchanters to disrupt the order of things, was becoming increasingly demonized at the end of the Middle Ages. In *Artus* and *Perceforest*, for example, it triggers foul-smelling, black clouds. As a result of the *Douloureuse Garde* episode in the Prose *Lancelot*, people were reluctant, frightened even, by the mechanization associated with its machines, arbalests and clocks (Ferlampin-Acher 2012; 2015a; 2015b; Zink 2006, 133). While towns and cities were polluted in real life, none of this was apparent in the fictional cities, but we might link the foul-smelling, black rivers (such as at the Porte Noire and the Tour Ténébreuse in *Artus de Bretagne*) with real-life conditions. In *Perceforest*, the homes of the damsels of the forest draw together representations inspired by contemporary human industry. Similarly, lime kilns were a cause of pollution often condemned in the Middle Ages (Gimpel 1975, 85). In *Perceforest*, the home of Sibille, an enchantress, disappears from view while the nearby lime kilns remain in view. Such a landscape is quite uncommon in Arthurian forests (Roussineau 2007, Part one, t. I, § 216).[23] Likewise, the mining industry (particularly tin) was developing throughout the Middle Ages

---

23 The beginning of the episode mentions Alexandre and Floridas' ride in the forest, which is relevant: "il ne leur souvenoit fors que de regarder la noblesse des arbes et de oÿr le chant des oyseaulx" [they only strongly remembered looking at the nobility of the trees and hearing the song of the birds]. The next element is more surprising, however. They smell "une moult grant fume" [a very big smell], which lures them, and then "ilz troeuvent ung chault four la ou on faisoit chaux" [they found a lime kiln there, where lime was in production]. They question the workers, who tell them about the home of Sibille, which was made invisible by magic. In § 217, a worker explains that he regularly delivers lime to the fairy, who is, like Mélusine, a builder fairy. The juxtaposition in the tale of the smoke from the lime kiln and the invisibility of the castle suggests to the reader a cause and effect relationship, which comes to superimpose itself on the supernatural hypothesis. In Book IV, the lime kiln is used to describe the horrible smoke coming from Hollant the giant, which is so *puante* [foul-smelling] that the birds who breathe it in die: "et sambloit de la fumee qui partoit de lui que ce fust ung chauffour" [Roussineau 1987, Part four 111].

in England (Gimpel 1975, 33–48). Again, this reality is represented through an enchantress in *Perceforest*, since the damsel in the *Chastel d'Estain* is connected with the mines near Cornwall, which had been in use since the time of the Trojans (Roussineau 1987, Part four, §1134). *Artus de Bretagne* invents two supernatural places, the Porte Noire and the Tour Ténébreuse (a kind of fantastical, hyperbolic mill), which offers a view of the disturbance caused by the fairly late introduction of windmills into Britain (Ferlampin-Acher 2013).

At the end of the Middle Ages, the presence of elements in the Arthurian romances open to ecological interpretation seems closely linked to the tendency of romance to become rooted in a place (albeit a fantastical one) that combines indices of reality with the effects of progressive industrialization and political (the Hundred Years' War), spiritual (demonization of the imagination), climatic (the Little Ice Age) and sanitary (the Black Death) crises. Paradoxically, these indices tend to enter into the text in connection with the *merveille* (fairies, monsters, etc.) On the one hand, this suggests that the concerns of everyday life can only be of interest to literature if enhanced by the extraordinary. On the other, it indicates that the supernatural was seen as particularly apt for describing what was perceived, from this era onwards, as heralding in trouble.

It is true that Arthurian texts paint very few landscapes in the modern sense, although such tableaux do appear in the later texts. Nevertheless, we have to keep in mind that this tells us that Arthurian literature, which puts knights to the test in the forest, sets nature and civilization in opposition as modern concerns, and that this literature, which came a long time before the Industrial Revolution, cannot represent ecological issues in the truest sense. The number of studies on the representations of nature and the relationships between humans and animals are growing, however, and a more ecologically-oriented approach may still hold considerable promise, particularly for the later texts. In the end, such approaches may lead to a revision of the idealized image in Arthurian texts of a medieval world that resembled Eden.

References

Aberth, John. *An Environmental History of the Middle Ages: The Crucible of Nature*. London and New York: Routledge, 2013.

Baumgartner, Emmanuèle. "Caradoc ou de la séduction." *Mélanges de langue et de littérature médiévales offerts à Alice Planche*. Ed. Ambroise Queffélec and Maurice Accarie. Paris: Les Belles Lettres, 1984. t. 1, 61–69.

Bermejo Larrea, Esperanza. *Regards sur le locus horribilis. Manifestations littéraires des espaces hostiles*. Zaragoza: Prensas de la Universidad de Zaragoza, 2012.

Béroul. *Tristan et Iseut*. Ed. Daniel Lacroix and Philippe Walter. Paris: Le Livre de Poche, 1989.

Berthelot, Anne. *Figures et fonction de l'écrivain au XIIIe siècle*. Montréal: Institut d'Etudes Médiévales; Paris: Vrin, 1991.

Bogdanow, Fanni, ed. *Queste del Saint Graal*. Paris: Librairie générale française, 2006.

Cassagnes-Brouquet, Sophie. "La Pire des Aventures: le chevalier Yvain et les tisseuses de soie." *Clio. Femmes, Genre, Histoire* 38 (2013): 235–240.

Charpentier, Hélène, and Patricia Victorin, eds. *Conte du Papagaut*. Paris: Champion, 2004.

Chrétien de Troyes. *Erec et Enide*. Ed. Mario Roques. Paris: Champion, 1989.

Chrétien de Troyes. *Le chevalier au lion (Yvain)*. Ed. Mario Roques. Paris: Champion, 1982.

Chrétien de Troyes. *Le Conte du Graal*. Ed. Félix Lecoy. Paris: Champion, 1973.

Classen, Albrecht. *The Forest in Medieval German Literature: Ecocritical Readings from a Historical Perspective*. Lexington: Lexington Books, 2015.

Clément, Myriam. *Contes d'arbres, d'herbes et d'épée: approches du végétal dans le roman arthurien des XIIe et XIIIe siècles*. Unpublished dissertation, Université Rennes 2, 2008.

Curtius, Ernst R. *La littérature européenne et le Moyen Âge latin*. Paris: Presses Universitaires de France, 1956.

Fabry-Tehranchi, Irène, and Anne Russakof, eds. *L'Humain et l'Animal dans la France médiévale (XIIe–XVe s.)*. Amsterdam and New York: Rodopi, 2014.

Ferlampin-Acher, Christine, ed. *Artus de Bretagne*. Paris: Champion, 2017.

Ferlampin-Acher, Christine. "La couronne et le *chapel* de soucis dans *Artus de Bretagne*." *L'œuvre et ses miniatures: Les objets autoréflexifs dans la littérature européenne*. Ed. Luc Fraisse and Eric Wessler. Paris: Garnier, 2016. (page extent not yet known).

Ferlampin-Acher, Christine. "L'arbalète de Passelion dans *Perceforest*: l'objet, entre tension idéologique et jeu." *Engins et machines. L'imaginaire mécanique dans les textes médiévaux*. Ed. Fabienne Pomel. Rennes: Presses Universitaires de Rennes, 2015a. 66–86.

Ferlampin-Acher, Christine. "Dédale et Icare du XIIe au XVe siècle: artifice et arts mécaniques au Moyen Âge." *L'artifice dans les lettres et les arts*. Ed. Timothée Picard and Elisabeth Lavezzi. Rennes: Presses Universitaires de Rennes, 2015b. 273–284.

Ferlampin-Acher, Christine. "Le *locus horribilis* dans *Artus de Bretagne* (XIVe s.): de l'Enfer au moulin, le renouvellement d'un topos." *Le locus terribilis: topique et expérience de l'horrible*. Ed. Juan Muela Equerra. Bern: Peter Lang, 2013. 49–72.

Ferlampin-Acher, Christine. "*Artus de Bretagne* aux XIVe et XVe siècles : du rythme solaire à l'horloge *faee*, le temps des clercs et celui des chevaliers." *Cloches et horloges dans les textes médiévaux*. Ed. Fabienne Pomel. Rennes: Presses Universitaires de Rennes, 2012. 221–240.

Ferlampin-Acher, Christine. "Les métamorphoses du *versipelles* romanesque (*Guillaume de Palerne, Guillaume d'Angleterre, Perceforest*)." *Littérature et folklore dans le récit médiéval*. Ed. Emese Egedi-Kovacz. Budapest: Collège Eötvös Jozsef, 2011. 119–134.

Ferlampin-Acher, Christine. *Perceforest et Zéphir. Propositions autour d'un récit arthurien bourguignon*. Geneva: Droz, 2010.

Ferlampin-Acher, Christine. "Voyager avec le diable Zéphir dans le *Roman de Perceforest* (XVe siècle): la tempête, la *Mesnie Hellequin*, la *translatio imperii* et le souffle de l'inspiration." *Voyager avec le diable: voyages réels, voyages imaginaires et discours démonologiques (15e–17e s.)*. Ed. Thibaut Maus de Rolley and Grégoire Holtz. Paris: Presses Universitaires Paris Sorbonne, 2008. 45–59.

Ferlampin-Acher, Christine. *Fées, bestes* et luitons. *Croyances et merveilles dans les romans français en prose (XIIIᵉ–XIVᵉ siècles)*. Paris: Presses Universitaires de Paris Sorbonne, 2002.

Ferlampin-Acher, Christine. "Grandeur et décadence du clerc Estienne dans *Artus de Bretagne*." *Le clerc au Moyen Age, Senefiance* 37 (1995): 167–195.

Ferlampin-Acher, Christine. "Epreuves, pièges et plaies dans *Artus de Bretagne*: le sourire du clerc et la violence du chevalier." *La violence au Moyen Age, Senefiance* 36 (1994): 201–218.

Ferlampin-Acher, Christine. "La géographie et les progrès de la civilisation dans *Perceforest*." *Provinces, régions, terroirs au Moyen Age, de la réalité à l'imaginaire*. Ed. Bernard Guidot. Nancy: Presses Universitaires de Nancy, 1993. 275–290.

Findley, Brooke Heidenreich. "Interpréter le paysage du *Perceforest*: forêts, jardins, monuments." *Perceforest: un roman arthurien et sa réception*. Ed. Christine Ferlampin-Acher, Rennes: Presses universitaires de Rennes, 2012. 203–211.

Foerster. Wendelin, ed. *Merveilles de Rigomer*. Dresden: Gesellschaft für romanische Literatur; Halle: Niemeyer, 1915.

Gimpel, Jean. *The Medieval Machine: The Industrial Revolution of the Middle Ages*. London: Penguin Books, 1976.

Gimpel, Jean *La révolution industrielle du Moyen Âge*. Paris: Editions du Seuil, 1975.

Guillaume le Clerc. *The Romance of Fergus*. Ed. Wilson Frescoln. Philadelphia, PA: Allen, 1983.

Hart, T. Elwood. "Chrestien, Macrobius, and Chartrean science: the allegorical robe as symbol of textual design in the Old French *Erec*." *Mediaeval Studies* 43 (1981): 250–296.

Hult, David F., ed. *Mort le Roi Artu*. Paris: Librairie générale française, 2009.

Huot, Sylvia. *Postcolonial Fictions in the "Roman de Perceforest": Cultural Identities and Hybridities*. Cambridge: D.S. Brewer, 2007.

Jouanna, Jacques, Jean Leclant and Michel Zink, eds. *L'homme face aux calamités naturelles dans l'Antiquité et au Moyen Âge*. Paris: De Boccard, 2006.

Lecouteux, Claude. *Démons et génies du terroir au Moyen Âge*. Paris: Imago, 1995.

Leguay, Jean-Pierre. *La pollution au Moyen Âge*. Paris: Gisserot, 1999.

Ménard, Philippe, and Christine Ferlampin-Acher (t. V), eds. *Tristan en prose*. Paris: Champion, 1997–2007; t. V, 2007.

Morawski. Joseph, ed. *Proverbes français antérieurs au XVᵉ s*. Paris: Champion, 1925.

Ponceau, Jean-Paul, ed. *Estoire del Saint Graal*. Paris: Champion, 1997.

Poirion, Daniel, and Philippe Walter, et al., eds. *Le livre du Graal. I: Joseph d'Arimathie, Merlin, Les premiers faits du roi Arthur*. Bibliothèque de la Pléiade, 476. Paris: Gallimard, 2001.

Rey, Alain, ed. *Dictionnaire historique de la langue française*. Paris: Le Robert, 2006.

Ribémont, Bernard. *La Renaissance du XIIe siècle et l'encyclopédisme*. Paris: Champion, 2002.

Roach, W., ed. *Première continuation de Perceval*. Paris: Librairie générale française, 1993.

Roussineau, G., ed. *Perceforest*. Geneva: Droz. 1982–2014 (Part one, t. I & II, 2007; Part three, t. III, 1993; Part four, t. I, 1987).

Rudd, Gillian. "Being Green in Late Medieval English Literature." *The Oxford Handbook of Ecocriticism*. Ed. Greg Garrard. Oxford: Oxford University Press, 2014. 27–39.

Rudd, Gillian. *Ecocritical Readings of Late Medieval English Literature*. Manchester: Manchester University Press, 2007.

Saunders, Corinne. *The Forest of Medieval Romance: Avernus, Broceliande, Arden*. Woodbridge: D.S. Brewer, 1993.

Scarborough, Connie, ed. *Inscribing the Environment: Ecocritical Approaches to Medieval Spanish Literature*. Berlin and Boston: De Gruyter, 2013.

Solère, Jean-Luc. "Nature." *Dictionnaire du Moyen Âge*. Ed. Claude Gauvard and Michel Zink. Paris: Presses Universitaires de France, 2002. 967–976.

Szkilnik, Michelle. "Des blancs moutons pasturans les rais du soleil: le paysage dans les marges du *Roman de Perceforest*." *Les Cahiers du S.E.L., Paysage/Paysages (Séminaire Espace Littérature du Département de Lettres Modernes, Université de Nantes)* 2 (1998): 31–54.

Szkilnik, Michelle. *L'archipel du Graal. Étude de l'"Estoire del Saint Graal"*. Geneva: Droz, 1991.

Verelst, Philippe. "Le locus horribilis. Ebauche d'une étude." *La chanson de geste: écriture, intertextualité, translations*. Paris: Université Paris X Nanterre, 1994. 41–57.

Walter, Philippe. *Canicule, essai de mythologie sur Yvain de Chrétien de Troyes*. Paris: SEDES, 1988.

Wolfzettel, Friedrich. "L'Etna dans la littérature médiévale." *Dictionnaire des lieux et pays mythiques*. Ed. Olivier Battistini, Jean-Dominique Poli, Pierre Ronzeaud and Jean-Jacques Vincensini. Paris: Robert Laffont, 2011. 466–467.

Zink, Michel. *Nature et poésie au Moyen Âge*. Paris: Fayard, 2006.

Carolyne Larrington
Gender/Queer Studies

> "for saving I be joined
> To her that is the fairest under heaven,
> I seem as nothing in the mighty world"
> Tennyson, "The Coming of Arthur" (1983, ll. 84–86).

Tennyson takes from Malory, his source for so much in his long poetic sequence, *The Idylls of the King* (published between 1859 and 1885), the romantic idea that love for, and more problematically, the love of, a woman is what inspires the Arthurian male to greatness. Malory's formulation is more nuanced, properly ranking heterosexual love below love for the divine:

> For there was never worshypfull man nor worshypfull woman but they loved one bettir than anothir, and worshyp in armys may never be foyled. But firste reserve the honoure to God, and secundely thy quarell muste com of thy lady. And such love I called vertuouse love."
> (Malory 2013, I: 841)

Yet both authors foreground the masculine as underpinned, defined in some way, by its relation to the feminine. Dorsey Armstrong (2003, 17–18; 28–44) has identified this requirement as *heteronormativity*: the pressure for the visible presence of women within the Arthurian court to defuse the possibility that bonds within the homosocial community of knights might metamorphose into homoeroticism. Men need women therefore, though they are reluctant to grant them agency or subjectivity, preferring to conscript them to the chivalric project and its effortful maintenance. Women too, in Arthurian romance, need men to solve particular problems – usually caused by hypermasculine characters contained within the courtly community only with difficulty.

Recent medieval Arthurian scholarship has flagged up the divergence between popular images of ladies in towers and chivalrous knights and the ways in which the texts interrogate and unpack prevailing gender norms – both medieval and modern. Medieval queer studies, championed in particular by Carolyn Dinshaw, has unsettled the concepts of male and female, of romantic heterosexual love or desire, by seeking out the transgressive, the hybrid – in essence, the queer – across medieval texts (Dinshaw 1994; 1999). This chapter begins by probing versions of Arthurian masculinity, moves on to consider the ways in which the female is imagined and concludes by investigating the queer and non-normative.

Carolyne Larrington (St John's College, Oxford)

DOI 10.1515/9783110432466-017

1 Masculinities

Arthurian masculinities occur in both epic and chivalric formations. In epic, masculinity is relatively clearly defined. Men interact with other men, taking counsel, fighting, dying together in battle. Women are marginal to the project; their function is to participate in strategic alliances, to bear – or fail to bear – children, and to embody a political stability which makes Guenevere an important strategic asset when Mordred seizes the kingdom. More crucial, more emotionally powerful and openly expressed are feelings between men. In the Alliterative *Morte Arthure*, whether as Arthur's righteous anger at the demands of the ambassadors, Gawain's admiring response to his courageous opponent, Priamus, or Arthur's powerful lament over the body of Gawain (Benson 1986, ll. 3949–3969), men feel most strongly about men (Baden-Daintree 2015).

The noble male's primary occupation is to fight; his masculinity is emblematized by his horse and his arms (Lynch 1997, 56–78). Status is defined by standing in the knightly league tables. Lancelot leads always, while Tristan, Gawain, Lamorak, Bors and Gareth are, at different times, highly placed. In individual jousts, and even more in public tournaments, masculinity is measured and assessed: "the tournament is a scene in which chivalric culture acts out the choice – the taking up – of 'masculinity'", writes Louise Fradenburg (1991, 212). To be defeated in combat is shaming, unless one's opponent is manifestly much more highly placed in the rankings. To fail time after time, as Kay does, is to reinforce his different and, to some extent, inadequate performance of masculinity. Kay repeatedly volunteers for adventures, returns discomfited in short order and takes out his frustrations on those less powerful than himself. His position is nevertheless unassailable; his office as Arthur's seneschal is one his foster-brother granted him when Arthur's royal destiny was revealed. Kay's lack of knightly prowess suggests that holding even the highest administrative office is somehow contrary to prevailing masculine norms. No wonder then that Kay sneers at men and women alike.

Lancelot embodies the highest chivalric ideal as a flawed paragon of masculinity. Courageous, determined, unsurpassed in fighting skill and inspired by his passion for Guenevere, Lancelot betrays his lord and king, a betrayal occluded in French and English texts alike. Obsessively faithful to one woman, except when deceived into sexual intimacy by women's machinations, Lancelot is always moving between states of desirability. Enchantresses lust after him: Morgan le Fay captures him more than once in the hope of sexually enjoying him; the strangely necrophiliac, Hallewes, desires him dead if she cannot have him living; the daughter of Pelles succeeds in sleeping with him twice (Malory 2013, I: 193–195; I: 215–216; I: 622–625; I: 632–635; Armstrong 2003, 104–105). Yet Lancelot is icily immune to other women's blandishments. He performs his masculine roles of questing, fighting against and recruiting non-members of the Round Table, jousting in great tournaments and returning to court, with little introspection: "But for to be a weddyd man, I thynke hit nat, for than I muste couche with hir and leve armys and turnamentis, batellys and adventures", he explains defensively to an inquisitive damsel (Malory 2013, I: 206). His relationship with Guenevere is agonizing in French, difficult in English; his bond with Arthur becomes a site of tension only once Agravain and Mordred have given public voice to the allegations against him. Lancelot's excellence excites envy among the ignoble, and admiration among his peers; his sexual relationship piques his conscience only when it appears to bar him from success in the Grail Quest (a crisis differently handled in French and in Malory). In the *Vulgate Cycle*, Lancelot confesses and vows to renounce his love (Bogdanow 2006, 213–226; Matarasso 1969, 89–94); in Malory (2013, I: 696–698); he remains cagey about the extent of his relationship and the confessor moderates the demands he makes on the hero.

Sir Gawain, in contrast, offers a different, perhaps more familiar model of masculinity. In the French tradition (epitomized in such romances as *Le Chevalier à l'épée* [The Knight with the Sword]) he embodies the knight *moyen sensuel*, a doyen of casual sexual encounters and brief marriages (Johnson and Owen 1972; Busby 1980). Maidens are anxious to yield up their virginities to him – a tradition amusingly parodied in *Le Chevalier aux deux épées* [The Knight with Two Swords] where the Damoisele du Castiel du Port is on the verge of surrendering herself to her passionate suitor when she recalls that she has vowed to yield her maidenhead only to Sir Gawain (Rockwell 2006; Larrington 2015b, 132–133). She refuses to believe the highly aroused knight's impassioned claim that he *is* indeed Sir Gawain, and he is compelled to desist. She rides to Arthur's court to discover the truth behind the rumour that Gawain is dead; only then is the Damoisele prepared to believe her lover's claims. Her doubts arise not least because the real Gawain, so she supposes, would never have retreated when she recalled her initial vow. Such play with Gawain's sexual reputation underlies the comedy of the English *Sir Gawain and the Green Knight*. Here the court of Hautdesert rejoices when they learn the identity of their guest, assuming that they will learn "þe teccheles termes of talkyng noble" from him (Andrew and Waldron 2007, l. 917). Morgan le Fay and the Lady also frame their temptation game on the assumption that Gawain is vulnerable to sexual advances. But the women have not recognized that the Gawain who has ridden into their provincial castle is not the French model with his smooth-talking seducer's ways, but rather the more upright English Gawain, with a powerful drive towards the perfection symbolized by the pentangle on his shield, and who understands the difference between *cortaysye* and *luf-talkyng* (Larrington 2006, 60–68; 2009).

Gawain's insistence on chastity (*clannesse*) as bearing equal weight with the other pentangle virtues aligns him here with other knights who chastise their unruly bodies when exposed to sexual temptation. Although Chrétien's version of the Fisher King (in the *Conte du Graal*) gained his unhealable thigh-wound in battle, in Wolfram von Eschenbach's *Parzival* the injury occurred when Anfortas contracted an illicit relationship with a woman, since Grail Knights are sworn to chastity (Wolfram 1998, VII: 478; 2004, 153–154). The mutilation of the knightly body by piercing the thigh – metonymic of castration and horribly incapacitating for the quintessential chivalric requirement of riding horses – punishes sexual desire. In the *Queste*, Perceval is saved from the loss of his own chastity only by a reflex recourse to the sign of the cross before he gets into bed with a lovely lady who proves to be a fiend (Malory 2013, I: 710–713). In response to this near miss, Perceval "therewith [...] rooff hymselff thorow the thiygh." (Malory 2013, I: 712) The elision of the feminine with the diabolical is complete. Sexual relations, whether or not sanctioned by marriage or true love, are repositioned in Grail narratives as devilishly motivated and inimical to salvation: a significant move in romance gender dynamics.

Malory's fledgling court is required in its Pentecostal Oath to swear "never to do outerage nothir mourthir, and allwayes to fle treson, and to gyff mercy unto hym that askith mercy [...] and allwayes to do ladyes, damesels, and jantilwomen and wydowes soccour" (Malory 2013, I: 97). This formulation of chivalry's basic tenets is generated by the failings of the knights who come together at Camelot, collectively engaged in a project to define the boundaries of acceptable courtly masculine behaviour. They have been on a steep learning curve; Pellinor has disregarded the requirement to aid women in distress in his headlong pursuit of adventure. Consequently when the desperate girl who cried in vain to him for help beside the corpse of her dead lover is devoured by wild animals, Merlin reveals her to have been Pellinor's own daughter (Malory 2013, I: 97). If knightliness is not predicated on altruism, on the requirement to help the weak and enforce justice on the overbearing, then its function would be purely to calibrate male competitiveness in military skills. Imagining women also as thinking and feeling subjects is one of the primary challenges the young court has to face. Another early revelation at Arthur's wedding feast is that the same Pellinor had fathered the young Tor on the wife of Ares the cowherd. "Half be force he had my maydynhode", confesses Tor's mother (Malory 2013, I: 80). Pellinor is thus at least partly aligned with Sir Brewse *sans pitié*, an inveterate would-be rapist, and with that traditional and disturbing figure of hypermasculinity, the Giant of Mont St Michel, who first makes his appearance in Geoffrey of Monmouth (Cohen 1999, 66–71; 152–159). The Round Table must reform and re-educate this version of maleness.

Masculinity also strives to efface, to look away from, the damage done to vulnerable male bodies through the violence of knightliness. Wounds are seldom depicted close up in the English tradition. Malory's knights fight like animals – a frequent metaphoric comparison – and much blood is shed: "Than they hurteled togedyrs as too wylde bullys, russhynge and laysshyng with hir shyldis and swerdys, that somtyme they felle bothe on theire nosys" (Malory 2013, I: 203), but no one is really hurt for long. In the Vulgate *Lancelot*, the Lady of Malohaut inspects Lancelot's body after he has distinguished himself in battle against Galehot's forces:

> Et ele esgarde, si vit que il avoit tout le vis enflé et batu et camoissiés des mailles, le col et le nes escorchié et le front enflé et les sorchiex escorchiés et les espaules navrees et detrenchies moult durement et les bras tous pers de cols que il avoit eus et les puins gros et enflés et plains de sanc. (Micha 1978, VIII: 33)
> [She looked and saw that his face was all swollen and battered and bruised by his chainmail, his neck and nose skinned, his forehead swollen and his eyebrows grazed, his shoulders wounded and cut most dreadfully, his arms all black and blue from the blows he had borne, and his hands thick and swollen and full of blood.] (Lacy et al. 1993–1996, II: 125)

The necessity for nursing knights through recovery is acknowledged, but the fear of permanent maiming, of horrible pain, is thoroughly repressed. Even if violence is not usually so graphically described, its effects within a community which has lost its sense of purpose are charted in the figure of Gawain in the *Post-Vulgate Queste* (Bogdanow 1991–2000, II: 462; Lacy et al. 1993–1996, V: 312). Here, inadvertently or in anger, Gawain kills significant numbers of his Round Table fellows. Yet Arthur and the other knights recognize that such casualties are inherent in the chivalric model: when refusing to identify oneself gives conventional grounds for combat, intra-community violence inevitably takes its toll. The final scene in the Round Table's history is epitomized in Robert Bresson's film *Lancelot du Lac* (1974): piles of dead men, former comrades become enemies, bodies on the "colde erthe" in Malory's words (Malory 2013, I: 922). Chivalric masculinity has run its course. The alternative brotherhood in religion adopted by Lancelot and his companions after that final battle now seems the only viable form of community, though Bors, Ector, Blamour and Bleoberis do take up arms once more, to die as Christian martyrs on crusade (Malory 2013, I: 940).

2 Femininities

Arthurian romance develops and nuances its stock female roles over time. The damsel who guides the hero, typified by the close-mouthed maidens of *Le Chev-*

alier de la charrette, evolves into the critical *damoiselle maledisante* figure of Malory's "Tale of Sir Gareth" and "La Cote Male Taille". In contrast to the agents guiding Lancelot towards the land of Gorre and the trial of the sword-bridge who carefully ration information, the *maledisantes* show no inhibitions in criticizing the hero assigned to them, reiterating their socially conservative views that only a noble youth – and certainly not a kitchen-boy – can demonstrate proper knightly masculinity. The young knight must not only prove his prowess but, more challengingly, continue to display courtesy in the face of repeated provocation. The Damoisele Maledisaunt marries La Cote Mal Taille after he has succeeded in his quest; Lyonette, in "The Tale of Sir Gareth" takes on a different role once Gareth has overcome her sister's aggressor, the brutal Red Knight of the Red Laundes. For, rather surprisingly, Lyonette is assimilated to the fairy mistress, but a fairy mistress with a difference (Larrington 2011, 66). Rather than giving free rein to the erotic, as in earlier Arthurian *lai*: Marie de France's *Lanval* and Thomas Chesstre's Middle English version, *Sir Launfal*, Lyonette assumes responsibility for magically policing Lyonesse's sexuality, preventing her sister and Gareth from consummating their love before marriage. Though Lyonesse holds the Castle Perilous in Otherworld territory, "bysyde the Ile of Avylyon", Lyonette does not wish to see her sister compromised (Malory 2013 I: 260–263). She arranges for a supernatural knight to attack and wound Gareth – significantly in the thigh, restricting his sexual performance – and thus safeguards Lyonesse's honour. The fairy erotic is subsumed in contemporary fifteenth-century gentry mores; these acknowledge sexual desire at the same time as enforcing the protection of a girl's value in the marriage market (Cherewatuk 2006, 1–23; Robeson 2005, 114).

Enchantresses, as Lyonette is in a minor way, interestingly figure the female in Arthurian romance. Independent of male control, educated, autonomous, they can operate to support the Arthurian status quo (as does Malory's Lady of the Lake) or to challenge and interrogate it. In the Vulgate *Estoire de Merlin*, Viviane learns all she can from Merlin before she imprisons him in an invisible tower, so that they can be always together. In later versions of the Merlin-tale, Viviane (known under a variety of other names) acts to rid herself of her sexually importunate tutor, locking him away so that she can retain both her magical knowledge and her virginity (Larrington 2006, 105–116). In the *Estoire* however, Viviane loves her teacher and encloses him only in order to remove him from the public world of the court where he is Arthur's key strategic adviser to a private erotic idyll: "quar poi fu de iours ne de nuis que elle ne fust auec luj" [for few days and nights went by when she was not with him], the *Estoire*-narrator assures us (Sommer 1908–1916, II: 452; Lacy et al. 1993–1996, I: 417). Morgan le Fay sets up just such a female paradise through her magical power. She creates the Val des Faux Amants, a valley in which every knight who enters who has been unfaithful to his lady in thought, word or deed becomes entrapped. The enchantment endures for seventeen years, until Lancelot arrives to overthrow it. Nevertheless, although many of the Valley's male inhabitants chafe at their incapacity to pursue their chivalric careers, others are extremely content to remain in the arms of their ladies, enjoying non-aggressive courtly pursuits such as dancing, conversations, music and chess (Larrington 2006, 51–58). What women want and what men want coalesce.

These moves by the enchantresses to extract men from the round of questing and fighting that constitutes knightly masculinity call into question the chivalric enterprise, if always from within the system they seek to problematize. The invitation to remain in feminized space, to abandon the honour-game for private pleasure is tendered in order to question the chivalric code's insistent claim that knights perform their noble deeds for their ladies, that the suffering, isolation and danger that they endure both benefits women and is – crucially – something that women demand. Chivalric women are caught in a classic double-bind: if they love their men and want to be with them, then their female allure distracts men from the pursuits that maintain chivalric identity. As evidenced in *Erec et Enide* (see Chuhan Campbell, *infra*), uxoriousness is damaging to masculinity; as in *Sir Gawain and the Green Knight*, Gawain's confinement to the castle while Bertilak is out hunting puts him in deadly peril in the bedchamber, within "[a] tracery of spaces coded as feminine." (Heng 1991, 501) Women are to blame if men fail in some aspect of knightliness: Gareth grants that psychopathic stalker, the Red Knight of the Red Laundes, mercy explicitly because his murderous siege of Lyonesse's castle is, so the Red Knight claims, at the behest of a lady seeking vengeance for her brother's death. Thus, as R. Howard Bloch (1991) has argued, the idealization of women in courtly rhetoric conceals a misogyny which is quick to surface whenever men fail in performance of their versions of masculinity.

Through magic, enchantresses have the power to exercise agency within the chivalric world. Resisting and unsettling masculine projects is a key part of their textual role; the expression of desire, whether for Merlin, or, in Morgan's case, for a succession of knights, is contingent on their magical authority. Other desiring women in the romance tradition include the mother of Galahad (Sklar 2001) and the Maid of Astolat; they share a name in Malory's account. The first Elayne acts at the behest of her father, deceiving Lancelot into sleeping with her in order to beget Galahad, destined to achieve the Holy Grail. Galahad is already born: Elayne has fulfilled her duty, when, aided by dame Brusen, a version of the cunning old woman of fabliau, Elayne brings Lancelot to her bed simply because she wants him. The consequences are disastrous: a shouting-match between Guenevere and Elayne that risks public scandal. Worse still, Lancelot loses his reason, jumping out of the window and running mad in the forest (Malory 2013, I: 622–625; I: 632–635). Such, it is implied, are the effects of a woman acting on her sexual desire, listening to her body rather than to her father, whose patriarchal project for castigating the Arthurian community sets up the Quest for the Holy Grail.

Elayne of Astolat falls in love with Lancelot without knowing his name or reputation. He treats her with casual instrumentality, wearing her sleeve, accepting her ministrations as nurse, all without considering her perspective on his actions. Bors enquires whether the assiduous girl at the hermitage is "the Fayre Maydyn of Astolat"; Lancelot replies: "Forsothe, she hit ys [...] that by no meanys I can nat put her fro me" (Malory 2013, I: 821), a comment that may be read as appreciative or as long-suffering. When Elayne confronts Lancelot with her desire, with brothers and father as witness, Lancelot is appalled and wrong-footed. The changes that Malory makes to his source texts, the *Mort Artu* and the Stanzaic *Morte*, emphasize Elayne's autonomy. For she loves Lancelot, as her brother Lavayne notes, as strongly and devotedly as does Lavayne himself. But Lavayne is a man and thus can express his love through service; he becomes Lancelot's squire and intimate, even surviving the fall of the Round Table. Elayne cannot be with Lancelot, unless as his nurse or his paramour. Her self-sacrifice in the name of love signals the impending doom of the lovers, the queen and her knight, and of the court. For, if Lancelot had accepted Elayne as wife and retreated with her to his lands in France, the Round Table could have been saved (Larrington 2011, 68–71).

Elayne acts on her own recognizance, her father and brothers astonished bystanders in the drama she creates. Other Arthurian women are permitted less latitude by their male kindred. Sir Persaunt of Inde sends his virgin daughter to Gareth's bed – to test him? To try to snare the prince of Orkney as son-in-law? Gareth passes the test and passes on the girl once he knows she is a virgin (Malory 2013, I: 243–244). Fathers and brothers regard themselves as owning the bodies of their daughters and sisters. So Pelles sanctions his daughter's impregnation by Lancelot; so, in the German romance *Diu Crône* (Felder 2012), the brother of Ginover (Guenevere), Gotegrin, abducts his sister from the court and threatens to murder her when rumours that she had a lover before her marriage to Arthur come to his ears (Samples 1995; 2010). Only the arrival of the supposed lover, Gasozein, in the forest where Ginover and Gotegrin's own retinue are pleading for her life prevents Gotegrin from killing his sister. Gasozein puts Gotegrin to flight, but then attempts to rape the queen. Gawein arrives just in time to rescue the queen from her own rescuer (Larrington 2015a, 150–151).

Arthurian femininities are both multiple and labile, dismantling the popular stereotypes of queen, damsel, enchantress and hag. As romance falls more explicitly under clerical influence, emphasis on chastity and virginity is foregrounded, and the scope for fairy mistresses and enchantresses to exercise sexual autonomy and authority over men is eroded or demonized. Nevertheless, changing mores, in particular moves to re-define marriage as requiring female consent and to involve mutual affection and companionship, inflects the ways in which women are imagined in Malory's chivalric world.

3 Queerness

Carolyn Dinshaw's 1994 article on *Sir Gawain and the Green Knight* has a good claim to inaugurating queer readings of Arthurian texts (see also Zeikowitz 2003 and Pugh 2008). She focuses on the unsettling nexus between the kisses given to Gawain by the Lady and passed on "savory and solemn" (Dinshaw 1994, 205) to her husband, and the implications of Gawain's refusal of sexual intercourse, which is at stake between the heterosexual pair in the mornings and repressed in the interaction between the men in the evenings. Dinshaw (1994, 206) insists that the poem "both produces the possibility of homosexual relations *and* renders them unintelligible." The text's insistent heteronormativity both intimates and suppresses the possibility of erotic attraction between Gawain and his host, in favour of a depiction of Gawain – not as the uninhibitedly sexual seducer of French tradition discussed above – but rather as a young man trying to balance fear of death, adherence to the tenets of the pentangle, the older obligations of guest and host, and sexual desire.

Georges Duby (1983–1984) has highlighted the normative triangulated relationship between the lord, the lady and the other man, whether a young squire, being schooled in courtliness by his lord's wife, or a troubadour poet, expressing his desire for the lady in terms which enhance her lord's status in possessing her. Sarah Kay (1990) has shown how thoroughly the troubadour-patron relationship becomes a dialogue between men, enacted across the body of the woman. She remains silent, ostensibly the object of men's desiring gaze, but in fact that gaze is directed from one man to the other. Similar triangulations exist in Arthurian romance. In the Vulgate *Lancelot*, heterosexual desire is queered by the powerfully reciprocated love of Galehot and Lancelot. Lancelot is destined to share Galehot's grave, not Guenevere's (for she must be returned to her heteronormative status of queen and guarantor of Arthur's rule and masculinity in death). Galehot becomes an intimate of Guenevere's so that both may talk about Lancelot in his absence (Gilbert 2011, 60–102). Marchello-Nizia (1981) notes how Galehot's first challenge to the Arthurian polity is a demand that Arthur should submit to him as his vassal; otherwise he will conquer his kingdom and snatch Guenevere from him. After a truce, Galehot repeats his challenge, but this time, significantly, he has become enamoured of Lancelot; now he threatens to conquer the kingdom and take away the knight in red armour: Lancelot. The interchangeability of queen and knight within Galehot's desiring heart is striking (Marchello-Nizia 1981, 975).

The Lady of Malohaut, who witnesses Guenevere and Lancelot's first kiss also becomes implicated in this queer love triangle (Micha 1982, VIII: 115–116; Lacy et al. 1993–1996, II: 147). She loves Lancelot and has previously tried to seduce him. She uses her knowledge of Lancelot to become the queen's intimate: "'Ha, dame, com est bone compaignie de IIII.'" ["Ah, my lady, four is such good company!"], she exclaims (Micha 1982, VIII: 118; Lacy et al. 1993–1996, II: 147). Once the queen has agreed that the Lady shall become her confidante:

> La nuit ne souffri onques la roine que la dame de Malohaut jeust se avoeques lui non, et chele i jut a moult grant force, car moult doutoit a jesir avoec si haute dame. Et quant eles furent couchies, si commenchierent a parler de ches noveles amors. (Micha 1982, VIII: 121)
> [That night the queen would not allow the lady of Malehaut to sleep anywhere but with her, but she accepted with great reluctance, fearful of sleeping with such a high-placed lady. When they were in bed, they began to speak of this new love. (Lacy et al. 1993–1996, II: 147)]

Although sharing beds with members of the same sex is usual practice in the medieval period, the queen's forcefulness, the Lady's bashfulness, and, on yielding, the mutual pleasure the women take in lying in bed together and speaking of sexual desire strongly mirrors the homoeroticism that quivers between Galehot and Lancelot.

Heteronormativity dictates that the queen should bring the Lady and Galehot together: "'Dame', fait Galahos, 'vous poés fair vostre plaisir de moi, de cuer et de cors'" ["My lady", said Galehaut, "you can do as you wish with me, both body and heart"]. The Lady too agrees, when the queen asks for "vostre cuer et vostre cors" [your heart and your person], to place them "a vostre volenté" [at your will] (Micha 1982, VIII: 123; adapted from Lacy et al. 1993–1996, II: 148). These verbal echoes in the undertakings offered to the queen endow them with the force of a solemn vow; the complex interplay of desire is once again refracted through the bodies of others. The parallel heterosexual love affairs are consummated on the same night in the same castle – if in two separate chambers (Micha 1982, VIII: 444; Lacy et al. 1993–1996, II: 228). Thereafter the queen and the Lady of Malohaut continue to share their sexual secrets, comforting one another when their lovers are absent. Once Galehot dies of a broken heart, believing Lancelot to be dead, the Lady is not long for this world. Outliving her textual usefulness she succumbs to a fatal disease not long after her lover.

As noted above, Lancelot is constantly implicated as the object of different kinds of desire, though he fails absolutely to reciprocate, begrudging even a kiss to the jailer's daughter who offers to release him from captivity in Meleagant's castle (Malory 2013, I: 857). In one episode in Malory, the weary knight falls asleep in a bed in a splendid pavilion. A certain Sir Belleus climbs into bed thereafter:

> He wente that his lemman had layne in that bed, and so he leyde hym adowne by Sir Launcelot and toke hym in his armys and began to kysse hym. And whan Sir Launcelot felte a rough berde kyssyng hym he sterte oute of the bedde lyghtly, and the othir knyght after hym. (Malory 2013, I: 196)

Lancelot comes close to killing his opponent in the battle, though once Belleus has yielded, has explained that he had expected to find his lady in the bed in his own pavilion and now thinks he is likely to die, Lancelot is both apologetic and assiduous in treating his wounds. This is knockabout stuff, as Catherine La Farge argues, comparable with Dinadan's later dressing in women's clothing, a prank so hilarious that the queen falls from her chair, helpless with laughter (La Farge 2011; Armstrong 2003, 93–94; Kelly 1996, 60–61; Batt 2002, 88–89). Yet it speaks also to profound anxieties about male-male intimate contact, to a different kind of bed-sharing from that of Guenevere and the Lady of Malohaut, closer perhaps to the strange night that Galehot spends silently lying alongside the sleeping Lancelot, admiring his physique, and slipping away before morning (Micha 1982, VIII: 78–79; Lacy et al. 1993–1996, II: 136–137; Marchello-Nizia 1981). Dinadan's cross-dressing is part of his disaffected persona, his insistent critique of knightly masculine performance, at the same time as he remains always incorporated within the system. For Arthurian female-male cross-dressing we must wait for the early modern Arthurian epic, Spenser's *The Faerie Queene*, where Britomart, descended from Ariosto's Bradamante, offers a radical challenge to early modern gender assumptions.[1]

4 Conclusion

Judith Butler argues, "gender proves to be performative – that is, constituting the identity it is purported to be [...] In this sense, gender is always a doing, though not a doing by a subject who might be said to pre-exist the deed." (Butler 1999, 25) The heroes of medieval Arthurian romance – in terms of the "storyworld" (Ryan 2007), the Arthurian universe which they inhabit – do pre-exist each individual romance in which their performativity is staged, but knightly masculinity is

---

1 Among Britomart and Bradamante's literary progeny is Brienne of Tarth in George R.R. Martin's "A Song of Ice and Fire" series, and HBO's *Game of Thrones*.

indeed a perpetual work in progress. Hence Lancelot's anguish when he is imprisoned by Morgan le Fay in the Vulgate *Lancelot*; unable to practise chivalry he resorts to drawing his biography on the walls of his prison, rehearsing the constituent elements of his honour (Micha 1980, V: 50–54; Lacy et al. 1993– 1996, III: 219; Larrington 2006, 70–72). Femininity as performance remains oddly elusive: the roles available for chivalric women are multiple and often complex. Their apparent function is to validate knightly endeavours, to provide the heteronormative conditions that enable the pursuit of chivalric masculinity. But for every damsel *maledisante* who insists that it is noble birth, not noble deeds, that makes the knight, there is an enchantress who works to subvert, to interrogate and to thwart the masculine enterprise. Ladies, damsels and sorceresses challenge the dominant gender model, insisting that emotional intimacy, friendship, creativity have their place beside the drive for adventure. In the domestic spaces of romance, the chamber, the pavilion, the garden, women and men experience desires that tug against the definition of "vertuous love" which Malory defines in the quotation at the beginning of this chapter. The polyvalency of desire, of touching, kissing, and above all, talking, can be read through a queer theory lens in ways which fundamentally unsettle the idea of Arthurian romance as heteronormative and socially conservative.

References

Andrew, Malcolm, and Ronald Waldron, eds. *Sir Gawain and the Green Knight. The Poems of the Pearl Manuscript: Pearl, Cleanness, Patience, Sir Gawain and the Green Knight*. 5th edn. Exeter: Exeter University Press, 2007.

Armstrong, Dorsey. *Gender and the Chivalric Community in Malory's* Morte d'Arthur. Gainsville, FL: University Press of Florida, 2003.

Baden-Daintree, Anne. "Kingship and the Intimacy of Grief in the Alliterative *Morte Arthure*." *Emotions in Medieval Arthurian Literature: Body, Mind, Voice*. Ed. Frank Brandsma, Carolyne Larrington and Corinne Saunders. Cambridge: D.S. Brewer, 2015. 87–104.

Batt, Catherine. *Malory's* Morte Darthur: *Remaking Arthurian Tradition*. New York and Basingstoke: Palgrave, 2002.

Benson, Larry, ed. *Morte Arthure. King Arthur's Death*. Exeter: Exeter Medieval Press, 1986.

Bloch, R. Howard. *Medieval Misogyny and the Invention of Western Romantic Love*. Chicago: University of Chicago Press, 1991.

Bogdanow, Fanni, ed. *La Quête du Saint Graal*. Trans. Anne Berrie. Paris: Librairie Général Française, 2006.

Bogdanow, Fanni, ed. *La version Post-Vulgate de la Queste del Saint Graal et de la Mort Artu: Troisième partie du Roman du Graal*. 4 vols. Paris: Picard, 1991–2000.

Robert Bresson, dir. *Lancelot du Lac*. Mara Films, 1974.

Busby, Keith. *Gauvain in Old French Literature*. Amsterdam: Rodopi, 1980.

Butler, Judith. *Gender Trouble: Feminism and the Subversion of Identity*. New York: Routledge Anniversary Edition, 1999.

Cherewatuk, Karen. *Marriage, Adultery and Inheritance in Malory's* Morte Darthur. Cambridge: D.S. Brewer, 2006.

Cohen, Jerome Jeffrey. *Of Giants: Sex, Monsters and the Middle Ages*. Minneapolis, MN and London: University of Minnesota Press, 1999.

Dinshaw, Carolyn. *Getting Medieval: Sexualities and Communities, Pre- and Postmodern*. Durham, NC and London: Duke University Press, 1999.

Dinshaw, Carolyn. "A Kiss is Just a Kiss: Heterosexuality and its Consolations in *Sir Gawain and the Green Knight*." *Diacritics* 24 (1994): 204–226.

Duby, George. *The Knight, the Lady and the Priest*. Trans. Barbara Bray. New York and Harmondsworth: Peregrine, 1983–1984.

Fradenburg, Louise Olga. *City, Marriage, Tournament: Arts of Rule in Late Medieval Scotland*. Madison, WI: University of Wisconsin Press, 1991.

Gilbert, Jane. *Living Death in Medieval French and English Literature*. Cambridge: Cambridge University Press, 2011.

Heinrich von dem Türlin. *Diu Crône*. Ed. Gudrun Felder. Berlin and Boston: De Gruyter, 2012.

Heng, Geraldine. "Feminine Knots and the Other Sir Gawain and the Green Knight." *Publications of the Modern Languages Association* 106 (1991): 500–514.

Johnston, R.C., and D.D.R. Owen, eds. *Two Old French Romances*. Edinburgh: Scottish Academic Press, 1972.

Kay, Sarah. *Subjectivity in Troubadour Poetry*. Cambridge: Cambridge University Press, 1990.

Kelly, Kathleen Coyne. "Malory's Body Chivalric." *Arthuriana* 6 (1996): 52–71.

La Farge, Catherine. "Launcelot in Compromising Positions: Fabliau in Malory's 'Tale of Sir Launcelot du Lake.'" *Blood, Sex and Malory*. Ed. David Clark and Kate McClune. Arthurian Literature 28. Cambridge: D.S. Brewer, 2011. 181–197.

Lacy, Norris J. et al. *Lancelot-Grail: The Old French Arthurian Vulgate and Post-Vulgate in Translation*. 5 vols. New York: Garland, 1993–1996.

Larrington, Carolyne. *Brothers and Sisters in Medieval European Literature*. York Medieval Texts. Woodbridge: Boydell and Brewer, 2015a.

Larrington, Carolyne. "Mourning Gawein: Cognition and Affect in *Diu Crône* and Some French Gauvain-Texts." *Emotions in Medieval Arthurian Literature: Body, Mind, Voice*. Ed. Frank Brandsma, Carolyne Larrington and Corinne Saunders. Cambridge: D.S. Brewer, 2015b. 123–141.

Larrington, Carolyne. "Sibling Relations in Malory's *Morte Darthur*." *Blood, Sex and Malory*. Ed. David Clark and Kate McClune. Arthurian Literature 28. Cambridge: D.S. Brewer, 2011. 57–74.

Larrington, Carolyne. "English Chivalry and *Sir Gawain and the Green Knight*." *Blackwell Companion to Arthurian Literature*. Ed. Helen Fulton. Oxford: Blackwell, 2009. 252–264.

Larrington, Carolyne. *King Arthur's Enchantresses: Morgan and her Sisters in Arthurian Tradition*. London: I.B. Tauris, 2006.

Lynch, Andrew. *Malory's Book of Arms: The Narrative of Combat in* Le Morte Darthur. Woodbridge: D.S. Brewer, 1997.

Malory, Sir Thomas. *Le Morte Darthur*. Ed. P.J.C. Field. 2 vols. Cambridge: D.S. Brewer, 2013.

Matarasso, Pauline, trans. *The Quest of the Holy Grail*. Harmondsworth: Penguin, 1969.

Marchello-Nizia, Christiane. "Amour courtois, société masculine et figures du pouvoir." *Annales. Historie, Sciences Sociales* 36 (1981): 969–982.

Micha, Alexandre, ed. *Lancelot: roman en prose du 13ᵉ siècle*. 9 vols. Paris: Droz, 1978–1983.

Pugh, Tison. *Sexuality and its Queer Discontents in Middle English Literature*. New York and Basingstoke: Palgrave Macmillan, 2008.

Robeson, Lisa. "'Women's Worship': Female Versions of Chivalric Honour." *Re-Viewing Le Morte Darthur*. Ed. Kevin S. Whetter and Raluca Radulescu. Cambridge: D.S. Brewer, 2005. 107–118.

Rockwell, P.V., ed. and trans. *French Romance: III: Le Chevalier as deus espees*. Cambridge: D.S. Brewer, 2006.

Samples, Susann. "An Unlikely Hero: The Rapist-Knight Gasozein in *Diu Crône*." *Arthuriana* 22 (2012): 101–119.

Samples, Susann. "The Rape of Ginover in Heinrich von dem Türlin's *Diu Crône*." *Arthurian Romance and Gender: Selected Proceedings of the XVIIth International Arthurian Congress*. Ed. Friedrich Wolfzettel. Amsterdam: Rodopi, 1995. 196–205.

Sklar, Elizabeth S. "Malory's Other(ed) Elaine." *On Arthurian Women: Essays in Memory of Maureen Fries*. Ed. Bonnie Wheeler and Fiona Tolhurst. Dallas, TX: Scriptorium Press, 2001. 59–70.

Sommer, H. Oskar, ed. *The Vulgate Version of the Arthurian Romances*. 7 vols. Washington, DC: Carnegie Institution, 1908–1916.

Ryan, Marie-Laure. "Toward a Definition of Narrative." *The Cambridge Companion to Narrative*. Ed. David Herman. Cambridge: Cambridge University Press, 2007. 22–36.

Tennyson, Alfred, Lord. "The Coming of Arthur." *Idylls of the King*, Ed. J.M. Gray. Harmondsworth: Penguin, 1983.

Wolfram von Eschenbach. *Parzival*. Trans. Cyril Edwards. Cambridge: D.S. Brewer, 2004.

Wolfram von Eschenbach. *Parzival*. Ed. Karl Lachmann. 6th edn. Berlin: De Gruyter, 1998.

Zeikowitz, Richard. *Homoeroticism and Chivalry: Discourses of Male Same-Sex Desire in the 14ᵗʰ Century*. New York and London: Palgrave Macmillan, 2003.

Richard Trachsler
Orality, Literacy and Performativity of Arthurian Texts

Orality, literacy, performance and performativity are today thriving fields of research. Categories such as orality and literacy are of interest to anthropologists and classicists, historians and philologists who all have been successfully exploring data ranging from Ancient Greece to contemporary cultures in the Middle East. From these general studies emerged a rather polarized picture, with some civilizations being characterized by orality and others already in command of literacy. This "Great Divide", as it is sometimes termed, forces an evolutionary look at the facts and opens a time span of more than a millennium where things, in some ways, are always "in transition", shifting from archaic orality to modern literacy.[1] To the scholar concerned mainly with the western Middle Ages, this binary opposition is of little use: since the medieval period is obviously marked by both orality and literacy, it is an *aural* culture. Slowly but steadily, over recent decades, a new consensus regarding the focus of our studies has emerged: we need to account for the various ways in which the written word was embedded in orality. From the interest in orality stems the relatively new sector of medieval performance studies, since performance gives the text not only a voice, but also a body.[2]

As keywords in medieval studies they may have been coined only quite recently, but terms such as "performers", or, as they were once called, "jongleurs", "minstrels" and "bards", entered the scholarly debate as soon as philology

---

1 The critical bibliography on the subject is enormous: Richter (1994), though concerned mainly with the period prior to vernacular literature, contains a useful introduction to the problem. For the Middle Ages, see Paul Zumthor's *oeuvre* which continues to be very influential in France: Zumthor (1984; 1987). For the German domain, see Green (1994). Coleman (1996) gives an excellent account of prior research and offers a refreshing look at the problem. I also recommend it as a starting point for its personal and determined prose.
2 The epicentre of medieval performance studies is in New York: see the volumes by Birge Vitz et al. (2005), Krueger and Burns (2007) and Duys et al. (2015). The New York team is also involved in several websites, such as the Youtube platform dedicated to "Medieval Tales in Performance": <https://www.youtube.com/channel/UC2wz1uR1Sl93vNMWML2Ieyw>, the showcase "Performing Medieval Narrative Today: A Video Showcase", and, exclusively for Arthurian material, "Arthurian Legend Performed": < http://vimeo.com/ArthurPerform>.

Richard Trachsler (University of Zurich)

DOI 10.1515/9783110432466-018

emerged as a discipline of its own in late nineteenth-century academia. And with them came orality. Scholars were trying to provide a new scientific framework not only to account for the origins, but also for the changes in language, motives and, more generally, texts, plots and stories. It was in that context that the debate on the origins and circulation of the *chanson de geste* and Arthurian literature arose and the first models regarding composition and transmission were elaborated. Since those scholars were rightly concerned mostly with the *Sitz im Leben* [literally: setting in life] of the documents they were reading and explaining, their models relied heavily on emblematic figures such as the troubadour, the cleric, the jongleur and the minstrel. These tutelary figures were responsible for the invention and the transmission of medieval literature and, thus, for what modern critics would later term performance.

To the generation of Gaston Paris, Wendelin Foerster, through to Gustav Gröber, Joseph Bédier and, especially, Edmond Faral in the late-nineteenth to early-twentieth century, jongleurs and bards were key figures for the understanding of medieval literature, since jongleurs, somehow, might have circulated some form of *chanson de geste* before the Oxford version of the *Chanson de Roland*, just as the Celtic bards somehow must have told the stories that Marie de France and Chrétien de Troyes would then have taken up and elaborated. This situation partly explains why the discussion regarding orality has not always separated the two distinct moments of composition and delivery of vernacular literature (Green 1990, 267–280).

On the positive side, one cannot fail to acknowledge that the pioneers of our discipline, by distinguishing different kinds of performers specializing in different kinds of literature, have established a conceptual framework that accounts for differences, on grounds of content, form and milieu, amongst the various types of medieval performances. The jongleur, the cleric, the bard and the troubadour are all tutelary figures of different genres, and they work in distinct environments, such as cities, markets and courts.[3] The genres they performed, by virtue of their formal and thematic differences, probably indicate distinct forms of composition, transmission and circulation of texts. This way of putting the matter, if we think of the distinctions regarding performers and texts not as rigid categories but more as shiftable parameters, definitely helps us to assess medieval performance. The performers can move from one milieu to another, and their repertoire can be adapted, or not, since there is no need to assume that a given audience will only respond to one kind of text. This more open way of looking at medieval

---

3 See the remarkable pioneer study by Faral (1910a) for a general synthesis on the question after three generations of scholarship.

performance also allows us to account for the co-existence of different forms of performance during the Middle Ages and beyond, and also helps to prevent a teleological vision of the evolution of performance in the period, which invariably shifted from oral to written and from more social to individual forms of reading at a uniform pace all across Europe.

The Italian *cantari* offer a case in point. These texts, which to our knowledge are specific to the Italian sphere, are the unique instance in which Arthurian material seems to have continued to be delivered by professional singers in Renaissance Italy and beyond. The *cantari*, short and self-contained episodes usually drawn and adapted from longer accounts, range from four hundred to several thousand lines organized in *ottava rima*, eight-line stanzas, following a pattern used also by Boccaccio in his *Tesiada* and *Ninfale* and later, of course, by Pulci, Boiardo and Ariosto. Clearly, these short stories were sung by *canterini* [singers] whose presence in public places in the South of Italy was still recorded in the nineteenth century, although we do not know how exactly the recitations in the Middle Ages would have taken place, since the texts preserved in the manuscripts certainly seem to allow for improvisation during performance. As far as we can tell from these documents, there was no obvious distinction made between *cantari* of Arthurian content and others based on Carolingian or classical material, which are sometimes contained in the same manuscripts (Bendinelli Predelli 2014, 105–120).[4] Arthurian *cantari* are *cantari* before they are Arthurian.[5]

It may seem arbitrary that the present overview will concentrate on material in French, but, in medieval times, such matter was rather central and an important vector for the dissemination of literature and culture in general on a European scale. Many aspects should thus be adaptable also to other languages and contexts. One should keep in mind though that, although the general political and social organisation in Europe was fairly homogenous throughout the Middle Ages, performing Arthurian literature was unlikely to have been perfectly identical in Britain and other parts of the continent, and might have taken quite different forms, particularly in Scandinavia and in Sicily. The second point that should be kept in mind is that Arthurian literature is not a separate entity in the general panorama of medieval texts. Arthurian literature was probably circulated

---

4 How this oral poetry was fixed in writing is a complex issue; see Degl'Innocenti (2008) and the review of this title by Morato (2011, 194–199). I have not been able to consult Luca Degl'Innocenti's latest book (2016), but it purports to further the argument.

5 Locally- or regionally-specific forms of performance, linked to very specific genres, might survive or arise and it would probably be unwise to make generalizations on a matter we know comparatively little about.

in exactly the same way as other texts presenting the same formal criteria, such as non-Arthurian romance or non-Arthurian *lais*. More significantly, there is no such thing as an "Arthurian performance": Arthurian *lais* would not have been delivered in an identical way to Arthurian verse romance or Arthurian prose, which would again be something entirely different. The key to the understanding of how Arthurian literature was circulated lies not in the *materia*, but in the genre. Before turning to the texts, it might be helpful to start with an overall presentation of the aspects regarding the orality and literacy of Arthurian literature with some contextual facts about its performance and transmission.

1 Enacting

When it comes to the performance of Arthurian literature, the most obvious place to look might be the stage. For the medieval period, there is little to be seen there: in France and all the Latin countries, there is no trace of the existence of any form of Arthurian drama, and in the German tradition the only appearances of Arthur on stage are in the comic context of the late medieval *Fasnachtsspiele* staging a chastity test set at Arthur's court. Only three such plays –all based on the same theme, but using different instruments (the horn, the coat and a crown) – are known, while a fourth play is known only by its title (Kindermann 1966 [1957], 429; Moser 1984; Tailby 2000). Only in Britain is there a "serious" theatrical tradition based on Arthurian texts, but again, this kind of entertainment emerges only in early-modern times (Lupack 1991). Throughout the medieval period, there are, though, the very common forms of the *pas d'armes* [passage of arms] and the tournament, where knights and ladies, but also entire towns, would enact and perform Arthurian characters and episodes.

This kind of entertainment can vary greatly: it might involve only a small group of knights, or an entire court or town. The duration would also range from a more concise event to gatherings across several weeks. All across Europe and beyond, chivalric events, called Round Tables, were organized. Usually the event would involve tournaments and some form of entertainment, loosely inspired by Arthurian or otherwise novelistic material, but the spectacles would become so common and popular that the designation "Round Table" often served as simple synonym for "tournament" (Stanesco 1988, 95). These Round Tables are clearly an international phenomenon that developed wherever there was a knightly culture

in the Western world, including the Baltic coasts and the Holy Land.[6] Philippe
de Novare, a knight who took part in the war in Cyprus and whose testimony
seems reliable, reports that, in 1224 in Beirut, knights had "contrefait les aventures de Bretaigne et de la Table Ronde" (Philippe de Novare 1913, 7) [mimicked
the adventures of Brittany and the Round Table] in celebration of the knighting of
the two sons of a local nobleman. As for Gérard de Montréal, who also travelled
to the East, he records that, in Acre in 1286, tournaments were held where the
participants "contrefirent la Table Reonde [...] et contrefirent Lanselot, et Tristan
et Pilamedes et moult d'autres jeus bias et delitables et plaissans" (Raynaud 1887,
220, § 430; see also Pickford 1960, 248) [mimicked the Round Table [...] as well
as Lancelot, Tristan and Pilamedes and many other similar delightful, pleasant
games]. In most cases, we do not know, unfortunately, in what the *contrefaiture*,
the "imitation", of the Arthurian knights actually consisted. But Lodewijk van
Velthem, a Dutch historiographer of the fourteenth century, in his *Spiegel Historiael*, gives a quite extensive account of a Round Table, organized by Edward I,
King of England.[7]

It is possible that Lodewijk van Velthem, who also adapted French Arthurian romances into Dutch, embellished or invented parts of the event, but it still
remains an instructive piece of evidence, since it must have seemed plausible to
his readers and is not very different from other accounts of similar events that
have come down to us.[8] Lodewijk states that for Edward I's marriage with Eleanor
of Castile, some of his knights were installed as members of the Round Table and
took the names of Arthurian characters, such as Gawain and his brothers, Agravain, Mordred and Gaheriet, followed by Lancelot, Bohort and Lionel, as well as
Kay and Perceval, all impersonated by King Edward's best knights. Sir Kay, in
particular, played a comic part, with quite lengthy dialogue and several practi-

6 The *Artushöfe* established by Hanseatic merchants along the Baltic Sea do not involve people
enacting given Arthurian episodes, but are buildings established and maintained by societies
whose members would think of themselves as a forming a kind of chivalric brotherhood. On
this very interesting phenomenon, see Selzer (1996) and Kugler (2010). There is evidence, too,
for Arthurian activities in the north, as was stated some time ago by Schlauch (1959). See also
Wilhelm (1988).
7 The text of Lodewijk van Velthem's chronicle is conveniently edited and translated in Johnson
and Claassens (2007).
8 Huet (1913) considered that Lodewijk had invented the entire episode, drawing from literary
sources. In his influential contribution, Loomis (1953, 114–117 and 118–119), on the other hand,
was inclined to take the account as fact. For a commentary on the passage, see Barber (2008,
84–99, especially 92–93). The most recent study is by Summerfield (2015), who gives an up-to-
date bibliography.

cal jokes involved, such as cutting saddle-girths. Edward and Eleanor's marriage would have taken place in 1254 at the monastery of Las Huelgas, Burgos. Neither the chronology nor the circumstances of Lodewijk's account match the historic setting. On the whole, though, the description he gives of the actual spectacle nevertheless resembles reasonably well what Sarrasin, an otherwise undocumented author, recalls in his *Roman du Hem*, where the term *roman* in the title merely indicates that the text is an account in romance language. It could more accurately be described as a "'reportage en vers' qui a la valeur d'un document historique" [report in verse, which has the value of a historical document].[9]

The *Roman du Hem* relates a tournament that took place in Hem-Monacu, in the region of Artois, over three consecutive days, from 9–11 October 1278. The event offered jousts alternating with several Arthurian interludes. Together with the *Tournoi de Chauvency*, organized in 1285 and recorded by Jacques Bretel, it contains the most detailed description of such a social event.[10] Unlike the royal marriage recorded by Lodewijk, participants mostly include members of the local noblesse, whose foremost representative was Count Robert II of Artois, the nephew of Saint Louis, King of France, and the Duke of Lorraine, Ferry III. The fact that their tournament would follow a similar scenario to the one recalled in the Dutch chronicle seems to indicate a European aristocratic form of entertainment where real people, not actors, would perform as Arthurian characters. In this case, the anonymous sister of Aubert de Longueval, one of the organizers of the encounter, would play the part of Queen Guinevere, and it was she who also commissioned the text, while Robert II of Artois would be Yvain, the Knight with the Lion. Soredamor would also make an appearance and again Sir Kay would play a comic part; of course there was also the lion, presumably played by an actor wearing a mask and a costume rather than using a real lion, since he was expected to move through the crowd and to pose and growl in accordance with the plot (Freeman Regalado 2005, 114).[11] Of particular interest here is that Arthurian romance not only provides the overall frame and reservoir from which the author drew his inspiration for the interludes, but also that the *Roman du Hem* contains precise textual allusions to Chrétien de Troyes. Not only does Sarrasin mention

---

9 This formula is used by Henry, who produced the impeccable edition of *Le Roman du Hem* (Sarrasin 1939, XII). The text has been much studied in recent years; see Vale (1982); Freeman Regalado (2005; 2007).

10 The *Tournoi de Chauvency* is not based on Arthurian material and shall not be discussed here. For an introductory assessment, see the excellent edition by Delbouille (Bretel 1932). For an extensive overview, see the recent volume by Chazan and Freeman Regalado (2012).

11 One might add the lions were kept even in the *ménageries* of smaller castles and thus could have been used if so wished. See also Lievois and Van den Abeele (2012).

him respectfully by name, and explicitly mentions his *Conte du Graal*, but he also quotes, almost verbatim, several lines from Chrétien's romances (Sarrasin 1939, XII, LVI and n. 1). During a joust on the second day, Sir Kay comically shouts "Or est venu qui aunera" (Sarrasin 1939, l. 1906) ["Here comes the one who will measure all others"], which is the exact line that welcomes Lancelot at the tournament of Noauz in Chrétien's *Chevalier de la charrette* (Freeman Regalado 2005, 106).[12] The public would, we can assume, recognize the quotation and perhaps even verbally participate in the interlude, as the reaction of the damsels in the scene would suggest, since they mock Kay for his self-confidence.

Most of the reports regarding tournaments and Round Tables of this kind are unfortunately not very elaborate, but there is no doubt that Arthurian influences continued to fashion these kinds of spectacles in the later Middle Ages, especially in the form of the *pas d'armes*, a ritualized form of combat, based on literary reminiscences, where knights would joust in pairs, as opposed to Round Tables where the fighting would involve groups and a general *mêlée*. Mathieu d'Escouchy (1863–1864, 251–252) reports that, in 1449 near Saint-Omer, the *Pas d'Armes de la belle Pèlerine* was organized. The challenge was to defend a travelled spot, such as a city gate or bridge, against whoever else put himself forward. The defender would post himself near the designated spot during a period of time publicly announced in advance – on this occasion it would be from the "xve jour de juillet jusques à la feste de l'Assumpcion Nostre-Dame my aoust" (Mathieu d'Escouchy 1863–1864, 252) [fifteenth day of July until the feast of the Assumption of Our Lady in August] – and have two shields hanging outside his tent. One would be Lancelot's, the other Palamède's. Whoever wished to challenge the defender would have to touch one of the two shields: Lancelot's if the opponent wished to fight using a lance, and Palamède's for a fight using swords. The fights would take place on a Wednesday. However, challengers could reserve their turn on any day except Friday, from prime (sunrise) to noon, by contacting a herald and then blowing a horn made available to the challengers. One immediately sees how the preparation and the fight are staged and ritualized by literary tradition. The *Pas d'armes de la belle Pèlerine* pays homage to an episode of the Prose *Tristan*, in which Alexandre l'Orphelin undertakes a similar test for a damsel with precisely that name (Pickford 1951, xvj and n. 70).

Chronicles usually just give summary descriptions of these events, a digest, or a review, but sometimes the original "scenario" has come down to us, too. In these fuller versions of the *pas d'armes*, of which we have several examples, there seems to be little room for improvisation. The rules are very explicitly laid out and

---

12 Henry's note to this line does not include this reference.

every eventuality is discussed. Sometimes, the text even specifies what has to be said in a particular circumstance.[13] It is, of course, difficult to know, based on the evidence of the "script", what the knights in the field actually said, especially since the text contained in the surviving manuscripts breaks down into different redactions, which would suggest that there was room for the adaptation of what otherwise seem like concrete scenarios. All these forms of enacting Arthurian episodes assume a good knowledge of the characters, the plot and the general setting. Obviously, such knowledge could only be gathered by reading the stories or listening to someone telling them.

2 Reading and listening

Jean Froissart, in an often-quoted passage from his chronicles, provides the only explicit account of how an author delivered his work. During the winter months of 1388–1389, Froissart was staying in Orthez at the court of Gaston Fébus, Count of Foix. Gaston, a passionate hunter who would return late from his hunting expeditions and then dine with his court, would order Froissart to join him every night at midnight and read to him from his *Roman de Meliador*, the last Arthurian verse romance ever written in French. *Meliador*, as Froissart points out, had been composed for his former patron, Duke Wenceslas of Bohemia, himself a poet, whose lyrics Froissart has inserted in the romance (a point to which I return later):

> L'accointance de li a moy pour ce temps fu telle que je avoie avecques moy aporté un livre, le quel je avoie fait a la requeste et contemplacion de monseigneur Wincelaus de Boesme, duc de Lucembourc et de Braibant, et sont contenus ou dit livre, qui s'appelle de Melia-der, toutes les chansons, balades, rondeaulx, virelaiz que le gentil duc fist en son temps, lesquelles choses parmi l'ymaginacion que je avoie en dicter et ordonner le livre, le conte de Fois vit moult volentiers; et toutes les nuit aprés son soupper je lui en lisoie, mais en lisant, nul n'osoit parler ne mot dire, car il vouloit que je feusse bien entendu, et aussi il prenoit grant solas au bien entendre. Et quant il cheoit aucune chose ou il vouloit mettre debat ou arguement, trop volentiers en parloit a moy, non pas en son gascon, mais en bon et beau françois. (Froissart 2007, § 13, 188–189)[14]
> [Our acquaintance during that time was such that I brought with me a book that I had made at the request and under the supervision of Wenceslas of Bohemia, Duke of Luxemburg and Brabant. And the book, called *Meliador*, contains all the songs, ballads, rondeaux, virelais

---

13 See the introductory remarks of the *Le Pas du Perron fée*, which is not specifically an Arthurian text (Horn et al. 2013).
14 Froissart gives a similar account of the events in his *Dit dou Florin* (1979, ll. 293–309 and 342–389).

the noble Duke had composed back then. The Count of Foix was happy to see my project regarding the writing and organization of the book. And each night after dinner I used to read to him parts of it, and while I was reading, no one dared to speak or say anything, because the count wished that I should be heard, so great was his pleasure in hearing it. And when there was a point he wished to discuss or debate, he would gladly talk to me in good and nice French, not in his native Gascon.]

This account, stating the privileged position of Froissart at the court of a potential patron who would intervene and discuss the poem that was being recited directly by the author, might be exceptional.[15] What is not exceptional is the practice of noblemen having stories read for their entertainment or instruction. In the second half of the sixteenth century, Charles IX, King of France, would still have people reading to him:

Tantost [le roy] se faisoit lire, ou des vers François, ou les Annales de France, ou Giron le Courtois: quelquefois des anciens Historiens. (Sorbin 1574, f. 30v)[16]
[Sometimes [the king] wished to be read to: it could be verses in French, or the *Annals of France*, or *Guiron le Courtois*; sometimes the works of ancient historians.]

These sessions were private, but not individual. Selected members of the household or of the court would attend and listen. Presumably, the person reading had special skills, but was not necessarily a professional entertainer. In the case of King Charles V, we know he liked his librarian, Gilles Malet, to read for him (Coleman 1996, 22).

Illustrations in manuscripts show precisely this: reading scenes involve the public. There is always a reader with a book in front of an audience that would not only listen, but also watch him. It seems reasonable to suppose that he might have adapted his voice for direct speech and accompanied his lecture with gestures, but we have little evidence to support this. We do not know how such sessions were organized or how long they took. Froissart went to see Gaston de Foix every night during his stay at Orthez. Given that approximately one thousand octosyllables can be recited per hour, depending, of course, upon the amount of

---

15 In fact, the discussion of such sessions is quite similar to what Nykrog (1996) has assumed to be the primary mode of reception of Chrétien's romances.
16 The same can be said of the court of Burgundy a century earlier: "Très renommé et vertueux prince Philippe duc de Bourgogne a dès long-temps accoutumé de journellement faire devant lui lire les anciennes histoires." [The very renowned and virtuous Prince Philip, Duke of Burgundy, has been long accustomed to having ancient [hi]stories read to him daily]. Prologue of the *Histoire abrégée des Empereurs* written by David Aubert for Philippe le Bon en 1457, quoted from Petit (2007, 60).

interaction with the reader, reciting *Meliador* would have taken up several weeks if the session started at midnight and went on for, say, two hours with a few interruptions.[17]

On a larger scale, during feasts and celebrations, professional performers would be invited, sometimes in huge numbers. For the knighting of Prince Edward, in 1302, more than one hundred and nineteen minstrels, most of them musicians, are recorded as having been in attendance.[18] On other occasions, for instance the marriage of Princess Margaret to Jean of Brabant a decade earlier, four hundred and twenty-six minstrels were even paid (Bullock-Davies 1978, 12). It is impossible to know how and what they performed, but some assumptions can be made.[19] It would have been impossible, given both the number of minstrels and the nature of the audience involved, to perform entire romances or even one of the longer *lais*, as the audience would most likely have been disruptive. Extended recitation might have been possible in a more isolated castle or at a village gathering, where there was less competition amongst the minstrels and more stability in the public's attention span. But even then the performer must have been inclined, in order to keep the audience's interest, to modify his performance to suit, and adapt to, the present circumstances. "To do so, he would have needed to deliver short fragments and to modify them appropriately." (Taylor 2002, 66)

That is exactly the reproach an author such as Chrétien de Troyes makes against the professional *conteurs* who tell tales for a living ("cil ki de conter vivre vuelent", *Erec et Enide*, l. 22).[20] They "cut into pieces" and "spoil" (*depecier et corronpre*, l. 21) the author's romance. The storytellers, during their performance, would make use as they pleased of their source material, by cutting it, editing it or rearranging it in order to fit the audience's requests and preferences. Such individually arranged sequences also explain why the *répertoires de jongleurs* that are so frequently inserted into the descriptions of scenes of feasts in romances contain such a great variety of titles, including works we would not associate with minstrels at all, such as the Matter of Rome.[21] When we go through the "titles"

---

17 The numbers are mine, based on personal experience. Rychner stated slightly higher numbers for the *séance épique* [epic session], but, wisely, did not specify how many hours such a *séance* might take (Rychner 1957, 48–49 and 54). Given the amount of artists and scholars actually performing medieval texts, one is surprised that there is not more statistical data available.
18 For a superb study of the documents regarding this well-documented knighting see Bullock-Davies (1978).
19 I here follow Taylor (2002, 65–69) whose suggestions are cautious, yet firm and helpful.
20 All references are to Chrétien de Troyes (1952).
21 For a presentation and discussion of the range of competence of a jongleur, see Faral (1910a). For this paragraph, I refer to Duggan (1989; 1989–1990). It is based essentially on the repertoire

given in such descriptions contained in romances or in the Occitan *ensenhamens* [didactic poems], we are actually mostly confronted with names of famous characters, rather than titles in the modern sense. One minstrel tells the story of Ulysses, another recalls the adventures of Erec and so on. The roll of characters contained in *Flamenca*, for instance, even lists Merlin and Mordred.

During such feasts, where so many jongleurs assembled in one single place, it is unlikely that they were presenting the works *in extenso* and in an orderly fashion. There would be too much noise and agitation and no one could sustain attention for the necessary duration (cf. Hogenbirk, *infra*). It is thus perfectly possible that references to the famous characters actually relate to "excerpts" of longer texts the performers turned into short stories or that, quite simply, they would just recite a part of a long romance (Duggan 1989, 57).[22] Whether these recitations were largely improvised or read from a book remains an open question, one which allows for many answers. There is certainly one type of performance where improvisation is minimal and a second type, which allows for extemporization and composition on the spot, leaving space, between them, for a large variety of possibilities. One is naturally tempted to associate the stable representation, perhaps linked to written text, with a genre like romance and the second, a more improvisational – or rather, composing in performance – mode, with an "oral" genre like the *chanson de geste*. But a careful look at epic texts shows that very often the narrators actually say that they are standing before their audience and reading a text aloud, as opposed to reciting it by memory, so that the book(s) would play an important role during the performance.[23]

3 Manuscript evidence

Given the aural culture of the Middle Ages, we have been assuming here that texts were only read aloud. It is true that silent reading was a reality, though

---

contained in *Flamenca*, one of the longest non-autonomous lists of texts allegedly performed by minstrels. But a similar picture also emerges from the three short satirical pieces going by the title of *Deux Bourdeurs Ribauds* and the Occitan *ensenhamens*. For the text, see Faral (1910b, 83–105) and a discussion in Schulze-Busacker (1984). On the *ensenhamens*, see Pirot (1972) and Monson (1981).

22 "It is generally accepted that medieval poems were not necessarily recited in full and that recorded repertoires often seem to indicate selected episodes rather than complete narratives." (Hunt and Bromiley 2006, 113)

23 See the convincing argument set out by Tyssens (1966).

it remained exceptional until early-modern times.[24] But are there any traces in the manuscripts that would indicate that they were conceived for public recitation? Again, the texts and situations suggest it might be wise to allow for several answers. It is clear that lavishly illustrated manuscripts, with titles, rubrics and tables of contents were made to be looked at, rather than heard. Yet it is not absurd to imagine that the reader can show and share an image with his public in an intimate circle of listeners. Studies of manuscripts, some of which contain Arthurian verse romances, have shown gradual changes in layout and iconographic cycles indicating a shift from aural to visual reception (Busby 1993). On the other hand, the increasing amount of punctuation and improvements in word separation suggest that these manuscripts were intended to be read and, presumably, read aloud, since this kind of information would be particularly precious for somebody performing the text.[25] Especially in the light of the complex syntax of the prose romances and their new stylistic devices, such as emergent direct discourse, there is a sudden shift from indirect into direct speech, which would obviously present a "trap" for any performer. Such grammatical indications, usually in the form of punctuation, would therefore be most welcome by the reader. Yet the evidence presented by the manuscripts is not very conclusive, as some versions simply omit such stumbling blocks altogether, or convert them into either direct or indirect discourse.[26] The manuscripts of the Dutch translation of the *Lancelot* actually do contain some marginal annotations to facilitate the oral delivery of the text, but curiously they do not seem to focus on emergent direct discourse.[27]

There is one kind of evidence, though, that is rarely quoted but which is very helpful in this instance, since it would prove the aural reception of both Arthurian verse and prose romance until a very late stage. One of the formal innovations introduced by authors of the verse romance in the early-thirteenth century is the insertion of lyric pieces into the octosyllabic body of the text.[28] These songs, as far as we can tell, already existed prior to the composition of the romance. They

---

24 The persistence of reading aloud was recognized in early criticism by Balogh (1927). On silent reading, see Saenger (1997), but consult also the comments by Coleman (1996, 21–23).

25 I follow Busby (2005, 61). A similar result is reached for the German tradition, based on a large number of manuscripts, by Palmer (2005, 86): "the use of the *punctus elevatus* in these manuscripts is not in itself an indication that the poems were to be intoned in the manner of liturgical recitative, but it is a strong indicator that the manuscripts offer texts that are to be performed."

26 The term "emergent direct discourse" was coined by Lacy (1994).

27 As shown by Brandsma (2000).

28 For a general presentation of the phenomenon, see Boulton (1993).

circulated as songs and were known as such, in that people knew their words and their melodies. *Escanor* by Girart d'Amiens, for instance, contains four *refrains* all sung by Escanor and his suite on their way to Arthur's court. These *refrains* are also transmitted, in complete versions, in manuscript collections of lyric material. Yet, these *refrains* are woven in to the octosyllabic texture of the narrative, with the last line before the insertion rhyming with the first line of the song, and the same technique is used at the end of the song. The interesting point regarding performance is that these songs, quite clearly, were meant not only to be read, but also to be sung. In the only manuscript of *Escanor* that has come down to us, blanks for musical notation have been left by the copyist. The notes have never been inserted, but the person who prepared the manuscript obviously considered that it would be better to include the melody and thought he had a fair chance of obtaining the tune, and therefore he left some space around the text.[29] The case is not unique at all, as many non-Arthurian manuscripts – including, for instance Girart's *Méliacin* – present the same features. The notation of the melody or blanks clearly prove that the whole romance was read aloud, otherwise it would make little sense to insist on the lyric insert.[30] The interesting point here is that the manuscripts of Arthurian prose romances would respect this tradition. Some manuscripts of the Prose *Tristan* contain the melody of the *lais* or leave blanks for the notation.[31] Even in this case, where the song was no longer an imported, pre-existing piece, but invented *ex novo* for the new romance, the creation would include not only the words, but also the music. In other words, these manuscripts would not simply allow, but rather call for, an aural reception.

4 Internal evidence?

We have not touched, yet, on the internal aspects of the performance and reception of Arthurian literature. Thematic and formal features might also indicate literacy or orality. Rhetoric, style and the general poetics of Arthurian verse and prose romances have been studied in detail, particularly the *persona* of the

---

29 For details, see Girart d'Amiens (1994, 51–54).

30 Jean Froissart's *Meliador*, the only other Arthurian verse text to contain lyric insertions, is an even stronger case in point. Froissart used pieces written by Wenceslas, whose favour he wished to attract by providing a shrine for his *chansons, balades, rondeaulx, virelaiz*, i.e. genres that were clearly still sung and not just recited.

31 For an introductory approach see Fotitch and Steiner (1974). The lyric insertion of the *Guiron-Cycle* have been edited by Claudio Lagomarsini (Guiron le Courtois 2015).

narrator and the authorial voice, which have attracted much critical attention since the early 1970s, when literary studies started to focus almost exclusively on the reflexivity of literature and its tendency to stage its own creation. For verse romances, especially those of Chrétien de Troyes, but also Marie de France's *lais*, phenomena such as *mise en abyme*, *mise en écriture* and interlace of narrative voices of all kinds have been thoroughly investigated.[32] Whereas earlier scholarship concentrated more on showing how Arthurian romance or *lais* articulated a moral or social lesson of an author or a class, recent studies have stressed the conflicting voices within a given text, and *a fortiori*, within the *opera omnia* of an author, or, even, an entire *genre*. In the case of Chrétien de Troyes and Marie de France, critics have insisted on the fact that their texts shift from:

> the fable with a moral to the problem romance. In problem romances, the narrator's point of view looms large, as do the points of view of characters in the plot. They provoke audiences, eliciting reactions form a personal point of view as well. (Kelly 2005, 61)[33]

It is not unlikely that medieval audiences, such as Gaston de Foix listening to Froissart's *Meliador*, would react to what they were hearing, and that the authors, by including scenes like Calogrenant's tale for discussion within the romance, would favour such debates. But we cannot know what was said during or after those performances.

It might be appropriate, though, to point out an additional feature of Arthurian verse production that offers considerable potential for further research, and which might cast some light on the performance and even composition of Arthurian verse romances: recent studies have shown that Arthurian verse romances and medieval French texts in octosyllables in general contain a conspicuous amount of hemistichs or even entire verses that occur several times in the same texts.[34] Not only do such repetitions occur within the same text, but nearly identical lines can also be found in completely unrelated texts. Put another way, we are confronted with formulaic material, as might be expected in an aural context.

As long as studies on oral poetry were concerned mainly with the *chanson de geste*, medievalists did not focus on courtly romance. When scholars conducted the first computer-assisted research on a large corpus of medieval French litera-

---

32 For a recent overview regarding Chrétien de Troyes, see Kelly (2005).

33 On the potential of Arthurian texts to trigger discussion in the audience, see Nykrog (1996). It is interesting to note Spitzer's intuition about Marie's *lais* (Spitzer 1930).

34 Studies on Arthurian material include Trachsler (2009) and Endress (2016). Recently, Cormier (2015) has raised similar questions regarding the *Roman d'Eneas*, one of the most 'learned' texts in the French corpus of romances.

ture in the early 1970s, they succeeded in demonstrating that there exists a high concentration of formulaic material in the *chanson de geste*. Understandably, the octosyllabic production was not at the centre of their focus. Coincidentally, and precisely during those same years, literary scholarship began discovering the narrative devices contained in courtly romance, especially in works by Chrétien de Troyes. Again very understandably, scholars found and investigated exactly what they were looking for: traces of borrowing, quotations and intertextual relations of all kind. In other words, traces of literacy. Arthurian romance, thus, is generally considered to demonstrate that there was a high degree of literacy. If, therefore, Arthurian romance does to some extent contain formulaic material, some of these "quotations" are not "quotations" at all, but rather are simple formulas: standard wording of standard situations and some of the "literacy" of the romance would spill over into the "orality" of the *chanson de geste*.

This potential commonality might be linked to some shared "oral residue" which, to different degrees, informs both epic and romance literature in the Middle Ages and can be traced both in the decasyllables of the *chanson de geste* and the octosyllables of romance.[35] It is still too early to attempt to give finite, or even general answers. But we can at least say that the presence of formulaic material seems to reflect the conditions in which Arthurian verse romances were produced and circulated from the end of the twelfth century onwards. This alone is worth further investigation.

References

Balogh, J. "*Voces Paginarum*. Beiträge zur Geschichte des lauten Lesens und Schreibens." *Philologus* 82 (1927): 84–109 and 202–240.

Barber, Richard. "Why did Edward III hold the Round Table? The Chivalric Background." *Edward III's Round Table at Windsor: The House of the Round Table and the Windsor Festival of 1344*. Woodbridge: The Boydell Press, 2008. 84–99.

Bendinelli Predelli, Maria. "Arthurian Material in Italian *Cantari*." *The Arthur of the Italians: The Arthurian Legend in Medieval Italian Literature and Culture*. Ed. Gloria Allaire and F. Regina Paski. Cardiff: University of Wales Press, 2014. 105–120.

---

35 This point was made, but with an entirely different set of arguments, more than twenty years ago by Birge Vitz (1986; 1987; 1990). "Oral residue" is a term coined by Walter Ong, which means, in essence, a habit of thought and expression from preliterate situations, and a practice that is carried over into a new medium through the inertia or inability to dissociate the new medium from the previous one.

288 —— Richard Trachsler

Birge Vitz, Evelyn. "Chrétien de Troyes: clerc ou ménestrel? Problèmes des traditions orale et littéraire dans les cours de France au XIIe siècle." *Poétique* 81 (1990): 21–42.

Birge Vitz, Evelyn. "Orality, Literacy and the Early Tristan Material: Béroul, Thomas, Marie de France." *Romanic Review* 78 (1987): 299–310.

Birge Vitz, Evelyn. "Rethinking Old French Literature: The Orality of the Octosyllabic Couplet." *Romanic Review* 77 (1986): 308–321.

Birge Vitz, Evelyn, Nancy Freeman Regalado and Marilyn Lawrence, eds. *Performing Medieval Narrative*. Cambridge: D.S. Brewer, 2005.

Boulton, Maureen. *The Song in the Story: Lyric Insertions in French Narrative Fiction, 1200–1400*. Philadelphia, PA: University of Pennsylvania Press, 1993.

Brandsma, Frank. "Emergent Direct Discourse: A Performer's Nightmare ?" *"Por le soie amisté." Essays in Honor of Norris J. Lacy*. Ed. Keith Busby and Catherine M. Jones. Amsterdam and Atlanta, GA: Rodopi, 2000. 15–32.

Bretel, Jacques. *Le Tournoi de Chauvency*. Ed. Maurice Delbouille. Paris: Droz, 1932.

Bullock-Davies, Constance. *Menestrellorum Multitudo. Minstrels at a Royal Feast*. Cardiff: University of Wales Press, 1978.

Busby, Keith. "Mise en texte as Indicator of Oral Performance in Old French Verse Narrative." *Performing Medieval Narrative*. Ed. Evelyn Birge Vitz, Nancy Freeman Regalado and Marilyn Lawrence. Cambridge: D.S. Brewer, 2005. 61–71.

Busby, Keith. "Text, miniature, and rubric in the *Continuations* of Chrétien's *Perceval*." *Les manuscrits de Chrétien de Troyes/ The Manuscripts of Chrétien de Troyes*. Ed. Keith Busby et al. 2 vols. Amsterdam, Rodopi, 1993. II, 365–376.

Chazan, Mireille, and Nancy Freeman Regalado, eds. *Lettres, musique et société en Lorraine médiévale: Autour du "Tournoi de Chauvency" (Ms. Oxford Bodleian Douce 308)*. Geneva: Droz, 2012.

Chrétien de Troyes. *Erec et Enide*. Ed. Mario Roques. Paris: Champion, 1952.

Coleman, Joyce. *Public Reading and the Reading Public in Late Medieval England and France*. Cambridge: Cambridge University Press, 1996.

Cormier, Raymond. "Indications d'oralité dans l'expression poétique du *Roman d'Eneas*." *Romania* 133 (2015): 311–327.

Degl'Innocenti, Luca. *"Al suon di questa cetra." Ricerche sulla poesia orale del Rinascimento*. Florence: Società Editrice Fiorentina, 2016.

Degl'Innocenti, Luca. *I Reali dell'Altissimo. Un ciclo di cantari fra oralità e scrittura*. Florence: Società Editrice Fiorentina, 2008.

Doss-Quinby, Eglal, Roberta L. Krueger and E. Jane Burns, eds. *Cultural Performances in Medieval France. Essays in Honor of Nancy Freeman Regalado*. Cambridge: D.S. Brewer, 2007.

Duggan, Joseph J. "Performance and Transmission, Aural and Ocular Reception in the Twelfth- and Thirteenth-Century Vernacular Literature of France." *Romance Philology* 43 (1989–1990): 49–58.

Duggan, Joseph J. "Oral Performance of Romance in Medieval France." *Continuations: Essays on Medieval French Literature and Language in Honor of John L. Grigsby*. Birmingham, AL: Summa, 1989. 51–61.

Duys, Kathryn A., Elizabeth Emery, Laurie Postlewate, eds. *Telling the Story in the Middle Ages: Essays in Honor of Evelyn Birge Vitz*. Cambridge/Woodbridge and Rochester, NJ: D.S. Brewer, 2015.

Endress, Laura. "Orality and Textual Reworking in *Floriant et Florete*: Another Note on a 'Patchwork Romance'." *Neophilologus* 100 (2016): 1–18.

Faral, Edmond. *Les jongleurs en France au Moyen Age*. Paris: Champion, 1910a.

Faral, Edmond. *Mimes français du XIIIe siècle. Contribution à l'histoire du théâtre comique au Moyen âge, textes, notices et glossaires*. Paris: Champion, 1910b.

Fotitch, Tatiana, and Ruth Steiner, eds. *Les Lais du roman de Tristan en prose d'après le manuscrit de Vienne 2542*. Munich: Fink, 1974.

Freeman Regalado, Nancy. "A contract for an early festival book: Sarrasin's *Le Roman du Hem* (1278)." *Acts and Texts: Performance and Ritual in the Middle Ages and the Renaissance*. Ed. Laurie Postlewate and Wim Hüsken. Amsterdam and New York: Rodopi, 2007. 249–267.

Freeman Regalado, Nancy. "Performing Romance: Arthurian Interludes in Sarrasin's *Roman du Hem* (1278)." *Performing Medieval Narrative*. Ed. Evelyn Birge Vitz, Nancy Freeman Regalado and Marilyn Lawrence. Cambridge: D.S. Brewer, 2005. 103–119

Green, D.H. "Orality and Reading: The State of Research in Medieval Studies." *Speculum* 80 (1990): 267–280.

Girart d'Amiens. *Escanor*. Ed. Richard Trachsler. Geneva: Droz, 1994.

Guiron le Courtois. *Lais, épîtres et épigraphes en vers dans le cycle de Guiron le Courtois*. Ed. Claudio Lagomarsini. Paris: Classiques Garnier, 2015.

Horn, Chloé, Anne Rochebouet and Michelle Szkilnik, eds. *Le Pas du Perron fée. Édition des manuscrits Paris, BnF fr 5739 et Lille BU 104*. Paris: Champion, 2013.

Huet, G. "Les Traditions Arthuriennes chez le Chroniqueur Louis de Velthem." *Le Moyen Age* 26 (1913): 173–197.

Hunt, Tony, and Geoffrey Bromiley. "The Tristan legend in Old French Verse." *The Arthur of the French*. Ed. Glyn S. Burgess and Karen Pratt. Cardiff: University of Wales Press, 2006. 112–134.

Jean Froissart. *Chroniques. Livre III*. Ed. Peter F. Ainsworth. Geneva: Droz, 2007.

Jean Froissart. *Dit dou Florin*. Ed. Anthime Fourrier. Geneva: Droz, 1979.

Johnson, David, and Geert Claassens. "Appendix D." *Edward III's Round Table at Windsor: The House of the Round Table and the Windsor Festival of 1344*. Ed. Julian Munby, Richard Barber and Richard Brown. Woodbridge: The Boydell Press, 2007. 244–268.

Kelly, Douglas. "Narrative Poetic: Rhetoric, Orality and Performance." *A Companion to Chrétien de Troyes*. Ed. Norris J. Lacy and Joan Tasker Grimbert. Cambridge: D.S. Brewer, 2005. 52–63.

Kindermann, Heinz. *Theatergeschichte Europas, Vol. 1: Das Theater der Antike und des Mittelalters*. Salzburg: Müller, 1966 [1957].

Kugler, Hartmut. "Artus in den Artushöfen des Ostseeraums." *Artushof und Artusliteratur: Akten des Kolloquiums der deutsch-österreichischen Sektion der Internationalen Artusgesellschaft in Rauischholzhausen vom 8. bis 11.10.2008*, Ed. Matthias Däumer, Cora Dietl and Friedrich Wolfzettel. Berlin: De Gruyter, 2010. 341–354.

Lacy, Norris. "Emergent Direct Discourse in the Vulgate Cycle." *Arthuriana* 4 (1994): 19–29.

Lievois, Daniel, and Baudouin Van den Abeele. "Une ménagerie princière entre Moyen Age et Renaissance: La Cour des Lions à Gand de 1421 à 1641." *Reinardus* 24 (2012): 77–107.

Loomis, Roger Sherman. "Edward I, Arthurian Enthusiast," *Speculum* 28 (1953): 114–127.

Lupack, Alan. *Arthurian Drama: An Anthology*. New York and London: Garland, 1991.

Mathieu d'Escouchy. *Chronique, vol. 1*. Ed. G. du Fresne de Beaucourt. Paris: Société de l'Histoire de France, 1863–1864.

Monson, Don Alfred. *Les "ensenhamens" occitans: Essai de définition et de délimitation d'un genre*. Paris: Klincksieck, 1981.

Morato, Nicola. "Review: Luca Degl'Innocenti, *I Reali dell'Altissimo. Un ciclo di cantari fra oralità e scrittura*." *Rassegna di Letteratura Europea* 38 (2011): 194–199.

Moser, Dietz-Rüdiger. "Brauchbindung und Funktionsverlust. Zum Nachwirken der *Artus*-Tradition in Fastnachtsbrauch und *Fastnachtsspiel*." *Spätmittelalterliche Artusliteratur: Symposium der Görres-Gesellschaft Bonn*. Ed. Karl-Heinz Göller. Paderborn, Munich, Vienna, Zürich: Schöningh, 1984. 23–39.

Nykrog, Per. *Chrétien de Troyes: Romancier discutable*. Geneva: Droz, 1996.

Palmer, Nigel. "Manuscripts for Reading: The Material Evidence for the Use of Manuscripts Containing Middle High German Narrative Verse." *Orality and Literacy in the Middle Ages: Essays on a Conjunction and its Consequences in Honour of D.H. Green*. Ed. Mark Chinca and Christopher Young. Turnhout: Brepols, 2005. 67–102.

Petit, Aimé. "L'activité littéraire au temps des ducs de Bourgogne: les mises en prose sous le mécénat de Philippe le Bon." *Synergies* 2 (2007): 59–65.

Philippe de Novare. *Mémoires 1218–1243*. Ed. Charles Kohler. Paris: Champion, 1913.

Pickford, Cedric E. *L'Evolution du roman arthurien en prose vers la fin du Moyen Age d'après le manuscrit 112 du fonds français de la Bibliothèque Nationale*. Paris: Nizet, 1960.

Pickford, Cedric E., ed. *Alixandre l'Orphelin: a prose tale of the fifteenth century*. Manchester: Manchester University Press, 1951.

Pirot, François. *Recherches sur les connaissances littéraires des troubadours occitans et catalans des XIIe et XIIIe siècle: Les "sirventes ensenhamens" de Guerau de Cabrera, Guiraut de Calanson et Bertrand de Paris*. Barcelona: Real Academia de Buenas Letras, 1972.

Raynaud, Gaston, ed. *Les Gestes des Chiprois*. Geneva: Fick, 1887.

Richter, Michael. *The Oral Tradition in the Early Middle Ages*. Turnhout: Brepols, 1994.

Rychner, Jean. *La Chanson de Geste: Essai sur l'art épique des jongleurs*. Geneva: Droz, 1957.

Saenger, Paul. *Space between Words: The Origins of Silent Reading*. Stanford, CA: Stanford University Press, 1997.

Sarrasin. *Le Roman du Hem*. Ed. Albert Henry. Paris: Les Belles Lettres, 1939.

Schlauch, Margaret. "King Arthur in the Baltic Towns." *BBIAS* 11 (1959): 75–80.

Schulze-Busacker, Elisabeth. "Gauvain li mauparliers." *Lancelot, Yvain, Gauvain: Colloque Arthurien Belge de Wégimont*. Paris: Nizet, 1984. 113–123.

Selzer, Stephan. *Artushöfe im Ostseeraum. Ritterlich-höfische Kultur in den Städten des Preußenlandes im 14. und 15. Jahrhundert*. Frankfurt a. M.: Lang, 1996.

Sorbin, Arnaud. *Histoire contenant un abrégé de la vie, mœurs, et vertus du roy tres-chrestien et debonnaire Charles IX*. Paris: Guillaume Chaudière, 1574.

Spitzer, Leo. "Marie de France – Dichterin von Problem-Märchen." *Zeitschrift für romanische Philologie* 50 (1930): 29–67.

Stanesco, Michael. *Jeux d'errance du chevalier médiéval. Aspects ludiques de la fonction guerrière dans la littérature du Moyen Age flamboyant*. Leiden: Brill, 1988.

Summerfield, Thea. "The Function of Fiction: King Edward I, King Arthur and Velthem's Continuation." *Journal of the International Arthurian Society* 3 (2015): 32–54.

Tailby, John E. "Arthurian Elements in Drama and *Meisterlieder*." *The Arthur of the Germans: The Arthurian Legend in Medieval German and Dutch Literature*. Ed. W.H. Jackson and Silvia A. Ranawake. Cardiff: University of Wales Press, 2000. 243–247.

Taylor, Andrew. *Textual Situations: Three Medieval Manuscripts and Their Readers*.
    Philadelphia, PA: University of Pennsylvania Press, 2002.
Trachsler, Richard. "Formulas, Orality and Arthurian Romance: A Short Note on a Long Story."
    Romanic Review 100 (2009): 415–429.
Tyssens, Madeleine. "Le jongleur et l'écrit." *Mélanges offerts à René Crozet à l'occasion de
    son soixante-dixième anniversaire par ses amis, ses collègues, ses élèves et les membres
    du C.E.S.C.M., vol. 1.* Ed. Pierre Gallais and Yves-Jean Riou. Poitiers: Société d'études
    médiévales, 1966. 685–695.
Vale, Juliet. "The Late Thirteenth-Century Precedent: Chauvency, Le Hem, and Edward I."
    Edward III and Chivalry: Chivalric Society and its Context 1270–1350. Woodbridge: Boydell,
    1982. 4–24 and Appendices 1–9.
Wilhelm, James, ed. *The Romance of Arthur, III: Works from Russia to Spain, Norway to Italy*.
    New York and London: Garland, 1988.
Zumthor, Paul. *La Lettre et la Voix*. Paris: Editions du Seuil, 1987.
Zumthor, Paul. *La Poésie et la voix dans la civilisation médiévale*. Paris: Presses Universitaires
    de France, 1984.

Andrew B.R. Elliott
Medievalism

Book 21 of Malory's *Le Morte Darthur* contains the by now famous account of the fatal wounding of Arthur and his journey to Avalon. As any Arthurian scholar well knows, despite the meticulously detailed descriptions of other key elements elsewhere in the story, including battles, weaponry, clothing, travels and topology, here Malory coyly omits any explicit narration of the king's death. Instead, we are given only a mere nod towards Arthur's potential return in the claim that "many men say that there is written upon his tomb this verse: *hic iacet Arthurus, Rex Quondam, Rexque Futuris.*" (Malory 1996, bk. 21, chapter VII)

Although the predicted return of Arthur today remains unfulfilled (his periodic "rediscovery" by enthusiastic amateurs notwithstanding), his postmedieval legacy has seen him enjoy more longevity than perhaps any other medieval figure. Certainly, in terms of literature alone, the Arthurian legend has seen more, and more frequent, returns in postmedieval society than at any time during the Middle Ages itself. As Beverly Taylor and Elisabeth Brewer (1983, 15) observe, "Arthur returned to English literature after more than 300 years with an intensity *remarkable for both the quantity and quality* of the works produced" (my emphasis). The landscape of postmedieval Arthuriana is indeed remarkable, and one rarely has to scratch too far below the surface of modern Arthuriana to find the traces of his medieval forebear, either as a direct allusion or else as an oblique reference to names, places, objects or quests.

As a fundamental part of that postmedieval reincarnation, the Arthurian revival of the nineteenth century – as is well documented elsewhere – was characterized by a massive, extensive and furious rewriting of Arthurian legend. In literature, despite the prominence of the much-discussed Victorian novel, the pre-eminent mode for Arthurian legend was the poem, and indeed a remarkable quantity of late-nineteenth-century Arthuriana was written under the long shadow of Alfred, Lord Tennyson's *Idylls of the King* (1859–1885). Though Sir Walter Scott made passing references to Arthur in *The Lady of the Lake* (1810) and more direct ones in *The Bridal of Triermain* (1813), according to David Staines (1975, 267), "the only Arthurian novel of the nineteenth century" was Thomas Love Peacock's historical novel, *The Misfortunes of Elphin* (1829), a well-received novel but one which seemed somewhat out of character for Peacock and an unusual departure for Arthuriana (Burns 1985, 138).

Andrew B.R. Elliott (University of Lincoln)

DOI 10.1515/9783110432466-019

In a modern era of mass media, it is perhaps difficult to appreciate the impact and popularity of Tennyson's "Victorianized" model of Arthurian valour which, according to the poet himself, sold 10,000 copies in the first week of publication (Poulson 1992, 101). It is easier, then, to appreciate the impact of the *Idylls* by considering the effects of the poem on other media, since however much it might be the Arthur of the art-world that is most familiar to modern audiences, the appeal of the legend was by no means exclusively artistic and many of the most familiar Arthurian paintings of the period were directly or indirectly inspired by Tennyson's *Idylls*, and not the other way around. In fact, something of the excitement of the Arthurian revival is communicated by the fact that, in the case of Frederic George Stephens' *Morte d'Arthur* (*c.* 1850–1855), William Holman Hunt's *The Lady of Shalott* (for the 1857 edition of *Idylls*), John Everett Millais' *The Lady of Shalott* (1854), Arthur Hughes' *The Lady of Shalott* (1873), *Sir Galahad* (1870) and *Geraint and Enid* (*c.* 1860), or G.F. Watts' *Sir Galahad* (1862) and *Enid and Geraint* (1879), they were often the *only* Arthurian works in those painters' *oeuvres* (Staines 1982, 158). To the pre-Raphaelites like William Morris, the emergence of a model of chivalry, updated to suit a variety of tastes, was an exciting prospect which offered the long-sought opportunity for integrated symbolism (Prettejohn 2012). Through the simplicity and romantic idealism of Arthurian images, the form could "motivate ideas" about truth, beauty and representational realism, as Ruskin termed it (Udall 1990, 34).

The popularity of Arthurian motifs in paintings established the King as a suitably epic subject, and cemented his importance to Victorian culture as a wise, bold and appropriately English king who fused nobility, bravery and sagacity in a perfect admixture. It also made for fertile ground for future artistic expression in a range of forms, with early experiments in photography, such as Julia Margaret Cameron's *The Passing of King Arthur* (1874), which was also designed to illustrate Tennyson's collection of poems. Passing from fiction into reality, the link between Arthurian chivalry (at least, the variety of chivalry articulated in Tennyson) and Victorian ideals led to a commission for William Dyce to paint an Arthurian fresco (1848–1864) destined to decorate the new Palace of Westminster's Robing Room in London, and in the lesser-known Lords Chamber there hung a Maclise painting, *The Spirit of Chivalry* (1848). The medieval king, then, far from being dead and buried, was very much remade as a guiding influence on the high and mighty of the day. In the USA, it was not the significance of the King but rather the legend as a whole that was mined for its allegorical significance. Edwin Austin Abbey's *Sir Galahad and the Holy Grail* (1895) can still be found in the Boston Public Library in Massachusetts, and a preserved medieval Dutch tapestry of the Nine Worthies hangs proudly on display in the Metropolitan Cloisters in New York.

As the Arthurian revival gave way to the development of new media forms at the end of the nineteenth and twentieth centuries, proliferations of Arthuriana equally began to make their way into a staggering variety of cultural forms. From filmed versions of Wagner's *Parsifal* in the early-twentieth century to television series and comic books at the end of it, from animated children's books to board games, films, video games, and even advertisements, theme parks and a host of incongruous products and brand names, Arthurian legend began to emerge as inherently "multivalent, multinational, and multimedia." (Mancoff 1992, xii; see also Sklar and Hoffman 2002) In Arthur's postmedieval afterlife, however, it is not the rigidity of the legend but precisely its elasticity which is most striking. As Debra N. Mancoff (2013, 278) describes it, the Arthurian revival in England was consequently characterized not by novelty but by "the force of remaking, as much as, if not more than, the spirit of revival." In this mode of remaking rather than revival, it was clear that medieval Arthuriana was not so much an august tradition to be imitated, but rather a starting point for new and fresh re-imaginings.

The elasticity of the legend, in fact, was in part what guaranteed its survival when other legends fell into obscurity. The various continuations and contradictions of the medieval romances offered the medieval legend precisely the kind of "'flexibility' that allows for the idiosyncrasies of individual artists and for each generation to respond to it by virtue of a new idiom furnished for it." (Umland and Umland 1996, 4) As Raymond H. Thompson (1998, 3) describes it, at the same time "as belief in an historical Arthur has dwindled [...] so his appeal to the imagination of creative writers and their audiences has grown." In this sense, then, the flexibility of the Arthurian legend means that modern, medievalist, dreams of Arthur can often reveal as much about our own contemporary anxieties as they do about our medieval ancestors. As Elizabeth Emery and Richard Utz (2014, 4) put it, in clearly psychoanalytical terms, "an individual's interpretation of the Middle Ages always reveals at least as much about that person's present concerns as about whatever the Middle Ages may actually have been."

Though it is scarcely anything new to suggest that the Middle Ages were in themselves a postmedieval invention (see Le Goff and Montrémy 2003, 43; Eco 1987, 66), one of the cornerstones of medievalism and *Mittelalter-Rezeption* is that, as an invention, the period is revealed not as a fixed, unchanging idea, but one which by necessity mutates according to current moods, trends, contexts – or even individuals, as Norman Cantor (1991) has shown with his study of medievalists. Again, Utz and Emery argue that the process of reinvention that inheres in postmedieval interpretations of the period is in fact a key element of medievalism itself, forming part of "the ongoing process of recreating, reinventing, and re-enacting medieval culture in postmedieval times." (Emery and Utz 2014, 2) As a discipline, medievalism (as opposed to medieval studies) is thus characterized not by a genealogical or historical impulse, but by a desire to use the past to explore the present. David Marshall (2007, 2) similarly argues that one of the chief conceptual and methodological differences between medieval studies proper and medievalism is that the latter "interrogates how different individuals or eras, for various reasons, often distortedly, remember the Middle Ages." He continues by stating that Medieval Studies:

> maintains an interest in what the Middle Ages actually were, how they looked and worked in their reality. Medievalism, on the other hand, prompts scholars to ask how the Middle Ages are invoked in their myriad incarnations and for what purpose in relation to the historical context of any given expression of them.

As Louise D'Arcens (2014, 184) observes, piecing these ideas together suggests that the study of medievalism is thus inevitably imbued with a sense of presentism, whose primary object is to unravel "the myriad of modern 'investments' in the medieval past."

It is for this reason, then, that the Middle Ages in their modern iterations can hold such an overwhelming power as a cultural shorthand for a variety of modern concerns. In a medievalist prism, the Middle Ages (and therefore Arthur along with them) nowadays act not only as a distant mirror, as Barbara Tuchman famously suggested, but as *Harry Potter*'s "Mirror of Erised", which shows the viewer only what s/he longs to see in the reflection. In this sense, the postmedieval idea of the Middle Ages can become a repository of "modern investments" in which the past's usefulness to the present is bundled up along with it (see Cantor 1991, 37). It is in this problematic and complex relationship between past and present that modern Arthurian motifs find their expression. The Middle Ages in the modern world come to us as an already fragmentary, heterogeneous and above all constructed body of ideas which are pieced together into modern mosaics. As part of that medieval legacy, Arthur is thus bequeathed to modernity as an already "composite figure", multivalent and "already mythified" (Green 1998, 15) as a "receptive vessel" (Sklar 2002, 9–10) and a "blank slate" (Aberth 2003, 2).

Perhaps the most obvious medium through which the modern Arthur has been transformed is in his postmedieval literary configurations. While *The Misfortunes of Elphin* wears its Arthurian credentials openly, more prominent in the twentieth century were those adaptations that used the Arthurian legend unabashedly as a metaphor to explore modernity, or else as overtly modern updates of the legends, like T.H. White's *The Once and Future King* (1958). Such, for instance, is the imperative in novels like John Steinbeck's *Tortilla Flat* (1935), which uses a free adaptation of the legend to explore friendship and solidarity. Likewise, David Lodge's campus novel, *Small World* (1984), plays with Arthurian legend to lampoon the modern university and its susceptibility to fashionable studies and the various "isms" of influential intellectual traditions.

Nevertheless, even at its most removed from direct adaptation, it is clear that these kinds of novels, as part of the postmedieval Arthurian canon, all depend in one way or another on the medieval versions' familiarity to modern audiences. By their nature such modernizations and metaphorical retellings of the legend frequently increase the distance between modernity and the Middle Ages through deliberate anachronism, modernization or wholesale removal from medieval ancestors, yet at the same time, their status as adaptations rely on an identifiable set of familiar Arthurian tropes and motifs. Onomastic references, even when coded (as in *Small World*'s Persse as Perceval and Fulvia Morgana as Morgana le Fay, or Robert W. Fuller's *The Rowan Tree*'s Adam Blue as Arthur) nevertheless depend on their referents to tell the whole story as metaphor. The modern Arthurian novel thus reflects the fundamentally composite nature of Arthurian legend. Where Tennyson's *Idylls of the King* re-imagines the legend in a late-medieval, Malorian setting, Rosemary Sutcliff's *King Arthur Trilogy* (1979–1981) sets the action in post-Roman Britain, clearly drawing on earlier versions of the legends and, probably, the movements by archaeologist Leslie Alcock to discover the "real" historical basis of Arthur (see Ashe 1987). Nevertheless, both adopt the familiar mock-medieval narrative style of the generic "Middle Ages" familiar from historical novels more generally, and most particularly from Walter Scott.

Indeed, it is precisely because Arthur "means" so many different things at once that literary adaptations have inherited sufficient freedom to be able to rework them in a variety of ways. Meg Cabot transfers Camelot to a modern-day US high school in *Avalon High* (2005), Bryher's *Visa for Avalon* (1965) resurrects Avalon as a modern utopia, while Mark Chadbourn's *The Age of Misrule* trilogy (1999–2001) retells a modern version of the legend. Yet, even in these cases, their reliance on readers' familiarity with the medieval legends makes them updates for new audiences, rather than simply regurgitations of medieval material: it is once again remaking, not revival. When updated to a modern idiom, all of the typical tropes of these rewritings (the relationships between their characters, the reiteration of recognizable Arthurian motifs, the use of specifically Arthurian names) implicitly suggest that the underlying humanity of the characters is universal and timeless. Such an emphasis on an unchanging link between the past and the present even becomes, in Derek Benz and J.S. Lewis' *Grey Griffins* series (2006–), the principal plot point, whereby a group of modern Minnesotan teenagers resist attacks from Morgana le Fay in league, however implausibly, with the Templars. In this mode, even the most egregious modernization unwittingly and paradoxically brings the Middle Ages into conflict with the present by retelling a familiar legend in a fundamentally new way.

It is precisely this freedom from fidelity that brought about a tradition within twentieth-century Arthurian fiction of retelling the tale from traditionally marginalized narrative perspectives, a narratological innovation which, following the logic, actually presumes an extensive familiarity with core elements from the legend in the first place. Probably the most famous of these, Marion Zimmer Bradley's *Mists of Avalon*, retells the Arthurian cycle from a female perspective, offering a view of Camelot from both the outside (as excluded female actors deprived of agency) and the inside (through Bradley's reassertion of the centrality of both femininity and feminine agency). Through its de facto oppositional stand to the legend, Bradley's work offers important narrative and psychological innovations, most notably in the possibility of reconciling contemporary ecological concerns with the medievalism of its Arthurian setting.

Perhaps more importantly for the purposes of modern Arthuriana, the ability to shift the narrative perspective to other characters in the Arthuriad is what opens up the field for later writers such as Nancy McKenzie's *Queen of Camelot* (2002), Garth Nix's short stories in *Under the Lake* (2005) and (to a lesser extent) *Heart's Desire* (2006), or Nancy Springer's *I Am Mordred* (1998) and *I Am Morgana Le Fay* (2001), all of which mine the Arthurian canon to present otherwise overlooked characters' perspectives on familiar tales. In doing so, they often unwittingly follow Bradley's tactic of shifting to female or Othered perspectives in order to challenge the dominant patriarchal narrative voices which dominate both the legends and the voices which have most often retold them.

Despite the undeniable popularity of the Arthurian novel, however, it was the cinema that would ultimately provide some of the most popular and enduring twentieth-century contributions to Arthuriana. In the light of the nineteenth-century explosion of popularity of Arthuriana, and its overflow into other popular media forms, with the emergence of the cinema in the 1890s it was scarcely a surprise that the nascent medium should turn to those same Arthurian subjects for source material. There has been a wealth of scholarship since Kevin J. Harty's pioneering *Cinema Arthuriana* (1991) which has analyzed Arthurian film from a range of different methodological and theoretical viewpoints to explore the ways in which Arthurian subjects have influenced the tradition. For our purposes, it suffices to emphasize the ways in which the popularity of cinema as simultaneously both a high-brow "seventh art" and a vehicle for popular entertainment has been one of the most significant factors helping to introduce Arthur into the popular imagination.

The emergence of the Arthurian film, as Kevin J. Harty (2002) argues, goes hand-in-hand with the very earliest expressions of cinema itself. Given that Arthurian images had already been extensively articulated by the nineteenth-century painters mentioned above, and given the novelty of the medium which was taking its first, faltering steps as a narrative-based and visual medium, it was quite naturally to opera that early Arthurian films would turn, with a filmed version of Wagner's *Parsifal* (Edwin J. Porter) appearing as early as 1904, followed by Mario Caserini's 1912 *Parsifal*. As the cinema began to experiment with longer forms, including two-reelers (a roughly twenty-minute film most frequently used for comic films), Arthurian film would follow suit with its own experiments in longer narrative forms such as *Knights of the Square Table* (1917, Alan Crosland) which re-imagined Camelot as a Boy Scout troop (Harty 1994), or direct adaptations like Emmett J. Flynn's 1921 version of Twain's *A Connecticut Yankee in King Arthur's Court*, and two versions of *Tristan and Yseult* (Albert Capellani, 1911; Maurice Mauriad, 1920).

Nevertheless, as soon as the midpoint of the twentieth century, by which time cinema had established and legitimized itself as a fully-fledged art form, even films that claimed inspiration from Malory, like *Knights of the Round Table* (1953, Richard Thorpe) or *The Black Knight* (1954, Tay Garnett), could incorporate increasing authorial and visual autonomy, and demonstrated a growing willingness to deviate from the Arthurian canon. Thus, following the Second World War, Camelot could once again be found in metaphorical modes in *King Arthur Was a Gentleman* (1942, Marcel Varnel), *Prince Valiant* (1954, Henry Hathaway) or *Camelot* (1967, Joshua Logan), in somewhat loose adaptations like *Siege of the Saxons* (1963, Nathan Juran) or *Sword of Lancelot* (1963, Cornel Wilde), in re-appropriations of national literatures in *Perceval le Gallois* (1978, Éric Rohmer) and *Lancelot du Lac* (1974, Robert Bresson), or else in outright anachronistic versions like Disney's *Unidentified Flying Oddball* (1979, Russ Mayberry) and *Knightriders* (1981, George A. Romero). The removal of Arthur from a fixed setting in a literary tradition offered up a newfound freedom, meaning that artists and filmmakers were able to explore the perennial struggles of Arthur and his court which had become universal. In fact, some of the most effective Arthurian films (effective in the sense of capturing the spirit of the medieval Arthur) include those precisely which, in leaving behind the question of translation fidelity, sought to draw out the perennial themes and to capture the essential spirit of the legend. These include comedies like *Monty Python and the Holy Grail* (1975, Terry Gilliam, Terry Jones), fantasy-dramas like *The Fisher King* (1991, Terry Gilliam) or even films that resurrect the Arthurian framework in order to create an entirely allegorical Arthurian tale – as in *Star Wars* (1977, George Lucas) or *Apocalypse Now* (1979, Francis Ford Coppola).

Ironically, cinema's reign over Arthurian images was really only to be challenged by its closest sibling, with the emergence (in the 1950s) and increasing dominance (in the 1960s and 1970s) of television. Given the decreasing cost-of-entry, coupled with the development of home recording technologies like VCR,

Betamax and, later, DVD, PVR and streaming services, television networks sought
to capitalize on the popularity of cinema not by opposing it, but precisely by imitating it (Stokes 2000). Though initially aimed at more domestic, family audiences, it was not long before television would compete with cinema by securing
libraries and entire back catalogues of studio films to fill up the schedules – particularly with the advent of daytime television with long stretches of less popular
slots to be filled.

Echoing the evolution of Arthurian cinema, once having dominated the
market the new networks found themselves in a strong enough position (com-
mercially and financially) to begin developing their own fare, a move which
saw medieval- and Arthurian-themed series that could substitute breadth for
length (see Elliott 2011 for more on this argument). So it was that the Arthurian
landscape would once again find itself mined for ready-to-use, out-of-copyright
mythical fare with the formulaic *The Adventures of Sir Lancelot* (1956–1957) and
The Adventures of Sir Galahad (1949) giving way to freer adaptations more prone
to mythopoeia, satire and subversion such as *Arthur! The Square Knights of the
Round Table* (1966), Cosgrove Hall's *Alias the Jester* (1985) and, later, Steve Barron's 1998 mini-series *Merlin*, followed by BBC/Shine's own version of *Merlin*
(2008–2012), the Starz series, *Camelot* (2011), and others.

In this respect, while the modern medieval television series might seem to be
a long way away from the medieval legends upon which they are putatively based,
their use of medieval tropes was in many ways inherited directly from the cinema
(and thus indirectly from the literature, opera, art and theatre of the Arthurian
revival). That is not to say that they are slavish imitations of them, however, since
just as with the cinema and other forms, it is precisely their deviations from the
cinematic Arthurian legend that highlight their freedom and ingenuity. This is an
expression once again of the flexibility of the legend. As a relentlessly commercial medium (it is hard to imagine the art-house films of Rohmer being made for
ITV or NBC) in search of novelty and serialized narrative adventures, the small
screen grew to develop a lexicon that afforded a sufficient freedom and flexibility
to play with the Matter of Britain within its own idiom.

In turn, the popularity of visual versions (both televised and cinematic) of
the Arthurian legend led to a greater popular familiarity with the previously high-
cultural Arthurian expressions. Having detached the legend from its position as
an untouchable medieval legacy, pop culture was able, literally, to begin playing
with it through games. With the rise of Arthurian Fantasy in comic books (most
notably *Prince Valiant* in the late 1930s, and *Camelot 3000* in the 1980s), and
the transition from "serious" Malorian films in the 1950s and 1960s to the sword
and sorcery fantasies in the 1970s and 1980s of *Gawain and the Green Knight*
(1973, Stephen Weeks), *Excalibur* (1981, John Boorman) and *Sword of the Valiant*

(1984, Stephen Weeks), the popularity of the fantasy table-top game *Dungeons and Dragons* (1974, 1977, 1981, 1983) made the return of Arthur within yet another medium almost inevitable. The freedoms afforded by films, television, comics and novels offered fertile ground for the fantasy gaming genre precisely because of their conflicting iconography, their variety of motifs and their ability to bring hitherto rarefied cultural capital to the attention of mass audiences. Arthurian elements could be found creeping into *Dungeons and Dragons*, and a number of role-playing games (RPGs) emerged featuring Arthurian references, ranging from *Chivalry and Sorcery* in 1977 (which featured characters and quests from Arthurian myth) to *Age of Arthur* in 2013. However, it was Greg Stafford's 1985 *Pendragon* – a complex RPG based on Malory's *Le Morte Darthur* – that most obviously characterizes the enthusiasm and freedom of the fantasy RPG genre. The game was a hit with players and critics, winning numerous awards for its innovation and gameplay; however, it was also a rare commercial success, shrewdly capitalizing on the massive popularity of Boorman's *Excalibur* four years earlier, and *Pendragon* went on to produce five further editions in a series that stayed in production right up to 2010.

With the astonishingly rapid development of graphic and processor capabilities in the late 1970s and early 1980s, it was not long before the complex RPGs of the table-top would take advantage of a computer's ability to synthesize rules in order to become a kind of mechanized "dungeon master" (the narrator of an RPG and, as such, a non-playing character). Very early video games like *Excalibur* (1983, Atari) and *Sir Lancelot* (1984, ZX Spectrum), which followed simple quests through side-scrolling platforms (2D games which scroll as the player passes through) and text-based adventures, thus grew in complexity, paving the way for more complicated games like *Legion: The Legend of Excalibur* (2002, PlayStation 2) or *Stronghold Legends* (2006, PC) which introduced multi-player options and the ability to play as Arthur or else as his opponents, Count Vlad Dracul or Siegfried of Xanten.

The rapid expansion of the World-Wide Web among domestic users also helped to replicate the social aspects of table-top RPGs. The explosion of popularity of Massively Multiplayer Online Role-Playing Games (MMORPGs), in which huge numbers of players could interact with one another across the Internet meant that the complex open-worlds of Arthurian adventures could finally be experienced in online multi-player modes. In particular, the runaway success of pseudo-medieval games like *World of Warcraft* and *The Elder Scrolls* series offered profitable terrain for the introduction of Arthurian motifs to a new kind of gaming, leading to titles like *Dark Age of Camelot* (2001, Microsoft Windows) which could provide immersive gameplay characterized by individual quests within a broader, virtual world. Once again, the emergence of a new medium was marked by a return to key, familiar themes, such as uniting post-Roman Britain under Arthur (in, for example, 1990's *Spirit of Excalibur* and 2012's *King Arthur II*), completing individual quests (1984's *Sir Lancelot*, or *Avalon* from the same year), defeating evil villains in warfare (1994's *Young Merlin*, 1993's *King Arthur's World*) or, of course, finding the Grail, as in 1992's *Conquests of Camelot*, or Excalibur, as in 1989's *Arthur: The Quest for Excalibur*. The adoption of Arthurian legend into games, following many of the same threads explored in other media, demonstrates that the uses of the past rely on precisely the same delicate mixture of flexibility (to allow freedom of play), adaptation (to ensure a recognizable Arthurian motif) and popular appeal (crossing the boundaries between high and low cultures). As such, despite an eye-watering range and diversity, the postmedieval depiction of Arthur is characterized above all by a paradoxical repetition of core motifs, as well as an astonishing degree of flexibility in the ways in which those motifs are depicted.

In part thanks to its central omissions or open-endedness, and in part thanks to the numerous continuations that replicate, duplicate and embellish the canon, leaving multiple versions of the central tale, the postmedieval Arthurian canon remains sufficiently vast that its power and relevance continues to be assured due to the wide applicability of the legend for a variety of purposes. They may be direct imitations of consciously romanticized legends, but they might equally be attempts to reveal the mythopoeic "truth" of the legend. In the latter mode, they can reflect earnest attempts by both scholars and enthusiastic amateurs who, with alarming regularity, claim to have found the real Arthur of medieval myth, or they might be the more commercially-oriented appropriations of a pseudo-historical Arthur, such as Glastonbury Abbey's discovery of the "tombs" of Arthur and Guinevere, Winchester's "Arthurian Round Table" or the English Heritage's presentation of Tintagel as Camelot. It is, as above, the sheer diversity of forms and the scale of medievalist fantasies of Arthur that most directly encourage new versions to make claims (however plausibly) to be the untold, true version of a pervasive myth.

The postmedieval assertion of the historicity of King Arthur sets up another interesting paradox. Whether claiming to have discovered his origins as a Sarmatian knight (Littleton and Malcor 1994), or to have found the modern locations of "real" battles and sites associated with the legend (Ashe 1987), there is rarely any shortage of claims to have "uncovered" the original Arthur, whether literally or metaphorically (see Kaufman 2015). The paradox emerges, however, precisely through the multiplicity of such varied claims to authenticity: the more vociferously that these Arthurian reinventions lay claim to the truth of their alternate historicity, the more they undermine the credibility of those claims through the endless over-interpretation of the same limited evidence and by implicitly disproving others' claims. The existence of several Arthurs extrapolated from the scant evidence bequeathed to us points, in fact, to no Arthur at all. As Guy Halsall argues, "to pretend to have provided the answers sought by that romantic quest [...] is downright dishonest." (Halsall 2013, 306) It is here that the postmedieval legacy of Arthur thus experiences precisely the same issues as medievalism in general. Medievalism's fervent attempts to re-appropriate medieval legends in the modern era serves both to collapse the temporal distance (through presentism, anachronism or metaphor), as well as to place them into a parallel world. Thus, in part, the key to Arthur's modern survival in literature, films, video games, TV, theatre and opera lies precisely in his refusal to adhere to any kind of historical period, which leaves the myth open to all kinds of revisions, modifications and reworkings.

In the few examples mentioned, it can be seen that in its postmedieval adaptation, the Arthurian tale has found its legacy not in its emphatic assertion of historicity, nor in its insistence on a select few canonical versions, but – in an ironic echo of the medieval Arthurian tradition – in its continuations (see Taylor *supra*). Irrespective of the success or failure of each individual rewriting of the tale, the impulse to rewrite, update, conflate or continue the Arthurian tales is, it scarcely needs to be said, in many respects a similar impulse to the continuations, cycles and rewriting of its medieval ancestors. Where Robert de Boron transports a largely Celtic myth into a conveniently Christian setting, Arthurian works from Edmund Spenser's *The Faerie Queene* (1590–1596) to Fuller's *The Rowan Tree* stand ready to reread the legend as political allegory. Where Chrétien de Troyes pokes fun at the king, modern comedic renditions like *King Arthur's Disasters* (2005–2006) or *Monty Python and the Holy Grail* seek to undermine the seriousness of other adaptations. Where Malory sought to extend the tale and conflate discordant versions into one single edition, so too do, for example, Steinbeck's *The Acts of King Arthur and his Noble Knights* and the Starz series, *Camelot*, aim to integrate a surprising variety of elements of the myth into one single, contiguous tale. Where Geoffrey of Monmouth focuses on one specific character in his *Vita Merlini*, so too can the narrative switch of *Excalibur*, Rohmer's *Perceval le Gallois*, the BBC's *Merlin* or Nancy Springer's *I Am Morgana le Fay* be found as an attempt to explore the psychology of the characters rather than to follow a structural, narratological formulation of heroes, antiheroes and villains. It seems to be the case that, however far they seem to stray from the canon, they often end up reiterating its basic conventions even while making contributions of their own.

Arthur's modern meanings in popular culture thus emerge as a direct result of two overriding impulses. First, his mythification, which was amplified through the various retellings of the legend throughout the medieval period, which could use the trappings of the Matter of Britain as a receptacle for all kinds of contemporary allusions, embellishments or meanings (the Grail, the Round Table, and so on). Each addition to the romantic tradition thus introduced a new mode and precedent for later additions, laying the foundations for a polyvalent, polysemic Arthur divorced from history and fully immersed into the realm of legend. Second, the reintroduction of Arthur in the mid-nineteenth century, and re-articulated over the course of the twentieth and twenty-first centuries, came in tandem with the birth of new media technologies which furnished the traditional Arthurian tales with hitherto unimaginable mass audiences, whose voracious appetite for medievalism further accelerated the recycling of Arthurian motifs. Though the modern fascination with Arthur might have begun with the Gothic revival, it found its most potent carrier in the explosion of mass media technologies like the picture post, pocket-sized novels, cinema, radio, as well as later comic books, television, graphic novels, video games and the Internet.

It is clear that the postmedieval Arthurian cottage industries described by Sklar and Hoffman (2002) whether in books, films, television, games, opera, music or comic books, collectively show no sign of running out of steam anytime soon. Instead, the only limitation is the number of authors ready to produce yet more new versions of the Once and Future King. As I write in summer 2016, advance publicity is already showing teasers for a new King Arthur film to be directed by Guy Ritchie entitled *King Arthur: Legend of the Sword*, in which Arthur is raised "on the streets" to become a plucky Cockney king in what is seemingly a medieval remake of Ritchie's cockney-gangster breakthrough hit, *Lock, Stock and Two Smoking Barrels* (1998). Malory's omission of any account of Arthur's death, then, proved prescient. In the field of medievalism and its presentist impulse, the fewer details we have about the historical King Arthur, the more gaps are left for the postmedieval Arthur industry to fill. Just as Arthur's death could not be contained by the legend, so too is the legend itself one which simply will not, or cannot, be buried.

References

Aberth, John. *A Knight at the Movies*. London and New York: Routledge, 2003.
Ashe, Geoffrey, ed. *The Quest for Arthur's Britain*. Chicago: Chicago Review Press, 1987.
Burns, Bryan. *The Novels of Thomas Love Peacock*. Totowa, NJ: Barnes and Noble, 1985.
Cantor, Norman F. *Inventing the Middle Ages: The Lives, Works, and Ideas of the Great Medievalists of the Twentieth Century*. New York: William Morrow and Company, 1991.
D'Arcens, Louise. "Presentism." *Medievalism: Key Critical Terms*. Ed. Elizabeth Emery and Richard Utz. Cambridge: D.S. Brewer, 2014. 181–188.

Eco, Umberto. "Dreaming of the Middle Ages." *Travels in Hyperreality*. Trans. William Weaver. London: Picador, 1987. 61–72.

Elliott, Andrew B.R. "The Charm of the (Re)making: Problems of Arthurian Television Serialization." *Arthuriana* 21 (2011): 53–67.

Emery, Elizabeth, and Richard Utz, eds. *Medievalism: Key Critical Terms*. Cambridge: D.S. Brewer, 2014.

Green, Thomas. "The Historicity and Historicisation of Arthur." *Arthuriana.co.uk* (1998): <http://www.arthuriana.co.uk/historicity/arthur.htm>.

Halsall, Guy. *Worlds of Arthur: Facts and Fictions of the Dark Ages*. Oxford: Oxford University Press, 2013.

Harty, Kevin J., ed. *Cinema Arthuriana: Twenty Essays*. Jefferson, NC: McFarland, 2002.

Harty, Kevin J. "'The Knights of the Square Table': The Boy Scouts and Thomas Edison Make an Arthurian Film." *Arthuriana* 4 (1994): 313–323.

Harty, Kevin J., ed. *Cinema Arthuriana: Essays on Arthurian Film*. Oxford: Taylor and Francis, 1991.

Kaufman, Amy S. "Touching Arthur." *Arthuriana* 25 (2015): 3–13.

Le Goff, Jacques, and Jean-Maurice de Montrémy. *A La Recherche Du Moyen Age*. Paris: Editions Louis Audibert, 2003.

Littleton, C. Scott, and Linda A. Malcor. *From Scythia to Camelot: A Radical Reassessment of the Legends of King Arthur, The Knights of the Round Table, and the Holy Grail*. New York: Garland, 1994.

Malory, Sir Thomas. *Le Morte Darthur*. Ware, Hertfordshire: Wordsworth Editions, 1996.

Mancoff, Debra N. "To Take Excalibur: King Arthur and the Construction of Victorian Manhood." *King Arthur: A Casebook*. Ed. Edward Donald Kennedy. London and New York: Routledge, 2013. 257–280.

Mancoff, Debra N., ed. *The Arthurian Revival: Essays on Form, Tradition, and Transformation*. Abingdon and New York: Routledge, 1992.

Marshall, David W., ed. *Mass Market Medieval: Essays on the Middle Ages in Popular Culture*. Jefferson, NC: McFarland, 2007.

Poulson, Christine. "The True and the False: Tennyson's *Idylls of the King* and the Visual Arts." *The Arthurian Revival: Essays on Form, Tradition, and Transformation*. Ed. Debra N. Mancoff. Abingdon and New York: Routledge, 1992. 97–114.

Prettejohn, Elizabeth, ed. *The Cambridge Companion to the Pre-Raphaelites*. Cambridge: Cambridge University Press, 2012.

Sklar, Elizabeth S. "Marketing Arthur: The Commodification of Arthurian Legend." *King Arthur in Popular Culture*. Ed. Elizabeth S. Sklar and Donald L. Hoffman. Jefferson, NC: McFarland, 2002. 9–23.

Sklar, Elizabeth S., and Donald L. Hoffman, eds. *King Arthur in Popular Culture*. Jefferson, NC: McFarland, 2002.

Staines, David. *Tennyson's Camelot: The Idylls of the King and Its Medieval Sources*. Waterloo, Ontario: Wilfrid Laurier University Press, 1982.

Staines, David. "King Arthur in Victorian Fiction." *The Worlds of Victorian Fiction*. Ed. Jerome Hamilton Buckley. Cambridge, MA: Harvard University Press, 1975. 267–294.

Stokes, Jane C. *On Screen Rivals: Cinema and Television in the United States and Britain*. London: St. Martin's Press, 2000.

Taylor, Beverly, and Elisabeth Brewer. *The Return of King Arthur: British and American Arthurian Literature since 1900 [i.e. 1800]*. Cambridge: D.S. Brewer, 1983.

Udall, Sharyn R. "Between Dream and Shadow: William Holman Hunt's 'Lady of Shalott'". *Woman's Art Journal* 11 (1990): 34–38.

Umland, Rebecca A., and Samuel J. Umland. *The Use of Arthurian Legend in Hollywood Film: From Connecticut Yankees to Fisher Kings*. Westport: Greenwood Press, 1996.

Andrew Lynch
Post-Colonial Studies

If Arthurian literature has had one major continuing thread over its long life, it is probably the one identified by Stephen Knight (1983, xiv):

> The Arthurian legend, especially in its most sophisticated literary form, is about power in the real world: the texts are potent ideological documents through which both the fears and the hopes of the dominant class are realised.

That feature, "the dynamic political tension inherent in the essential Arthurian story" – especially if "political" is broadly interpreted – is the basis of recent and contemporary interest in the Arthurian tradition as "post-colonial". The long-enduring, diverse and multi-centred linguistic and cultural range of Arthur's legend can be plotted against national, regional and global shifts in power and peoples over many centuries, in a way that shadows the long history of colonialism. On the face of it, the Arthurian tradition seems a prime example of conservative and pro-colonialist attitudes: a white, Western European and Christian affair, male-dominant, aggressively competitive and acquisitive, and centred on the exploits of a small elite group. Yet while this literature has celebrated imperialist ventures in many forms and ages, it has also reflected the problems of empire for both master and subject groups, and made visible within its complex narratives aspects of resistance to colonial control.

Those factors do not in themselves make the tradition "post-colonial" in the strict sense. Knight's study, for instance, notes Arthur's "Norman expansionist vigour" as a colonizer (52), but in an analysis influenced by Marxist historiography he makes no reference to the "post-colonial". "Post-colonialism" is a recent, culturally specific (and contested) interpretative concept, not to be understood simply as part of a recurring historical sequence observed in actuality, and necessarily variable in its formations. As Neil Larsen comments:

> "Imperialism, colonialism, postcolonialism" [...] risks conveying an illusion of conceptual purity or symmetry – a species of category mistake – as a result of which a crucial *historical* perspective is eclipsed. (Larsen 2000, 24)

It has also been pointed out that the term "post-colonial" is not universally accepted, being derived from the discourse of colonizing countries: "nothing

Andrew Lynch (University of Western Australia)

DOI 10.1515/9783110432466-020

similar to [...] 'post-colonialism' came up 'spontaneously' in the national and regional languages of the world outside the Euro-US." (Spivak 2000, xv) The term "colonialism" itself, used to mean "[t]he colonial system or principle", is no older than 1886, according to *OED*. Larsen's survey of the growth of post-colonial studies similarly traces the genealogy of the discourse from "the first great crisis of capitalism in the late nineteenth century (1873–1895)" and specifically excludes ancient and early-modern imperialisms as relevant influences, "except as a source of images and roles in which to play out a modern drama". He does not even mention the medieval period (Larsen 2000, 27). Furthermore, insofar as Arthurian texts are part of the Western literary canon imposed by imperial and colonial rule, they can be considered as part of the problem, whether by excluding non-Western works from proper influence or by endorsing imperialism and colonialism themselves. Alfred, Lord Tennyson's series *Idylls of the King* (1830s–1880s) is a famous example. In it Arthur's mission is to "cleanse the world", bringing "law" and "light", and drawing "all/ The realms together." (Tennyson 1983, 281; Lynch, 2009, 178)

As a result of all these factors, to make the medieval, including the Arthurian, post-colonial required considerable work. There was no explicit connection of the terms until quite recently. Post-colonialism was at first explicitly or implicitly tied to the notion of "modernity", and "question[ed] the very existence of colonialism in the absence of modernity." (Ingham and Warren 2003, 1) Post-colonial studies *per se* can be dated back to Frantz Fanon's *The Wretched of the Earth* (original publication in French in 1961) and Edward Said's *Orientalism* (1978), and to the "Subaltern Studies" group of the 1980s, which Bruce Holsinger suggests had a precursive parallel in the "history from below" method of the *Annales* movement originating around 1930 (Holsinger 2002). Yet it was not until the turn of the twenty-first century that the post-colonial approach became strongly established in medieval studies.

Jeffrey Jerome Cohen's collection *The Post-Colonial Middle Ages* (2000) is considered as one landmark in the field. Questioning and even rejecting the sequential timeline of cause and effect in traditional historiography, Cohen (2000, 2–3) calls for "more complicated narratives of heterogeneity, overlap, sedimentation and multiplicity." His collection does not include a study of Arthurian texts, but the vague origins, long persistence and cultural ubiquity of Arthurian material in Europe and its colonies from the medieval period into the present do seem to sustain his suggestion that we have always been in the "mid-colonial" period: "the time of 'always-already', an intermediacy that no narrative can pin to a single moment of history in its origin or end." (Cohen 2000, 3) If we are to embrace this notion, then it makes little sense to insist on a great divide between the "present" of modernity and the "past" of the medieval pre-modern, and on the radical "alterity" (otherness) of the medieval. Nadia Altschul quotes Dipesh Chakrabarty (2000, 12) to make a similar point:

> humans from any [...] period and region – are always in some sense our contemporaries: that would have to be the condition under which we can even begin to treat them as intelligible to us. Thus the writing of history must implicitly assume a plurality of times existing together, a disjuncture of the present with itself.

Following this logic, Altschul (2008, 596) suggests that "[w]hat postcolonial medievalism proposes instead of alterity is a 'redefinition of the present'."

There was strong opposition to such moves from some quarters. Simon Gaunt (2009, 161) quotes Gabrielle Spiegel's view that theories such as postcolonialism had their power "evacuated [...] by superimposing them on periods and persons for which they were never designed and to which they simply do not apply." (Spiegel 2000, 249–250) Gaunt (2009, 162), with some qualifications, takes the differing view that "there is no need to oppose history and theory; on the contrary, theory – including postcolonial theory – can be used productively in historically informed reflections on medieval culture." It remains true that post-colonial approaches to medieval texts, like Gaunt's, have predominantly justified themselves as historicist. Gaunt makes an excellent further point, that the colonial attitudes of "modernity" did not arise in an imaginative vacuum: "the medieval history of contact between Europe and Asia or Africa is in fact an important element of the longer history of which colonialism and postcolonialism are part." (172) The Arthurian story of conquest and empire remained mainly intra-European in its imagination, unlike, say, the Alexander tradition, but nevertheless it reflected and justified medieval and early-modern ambitions for foreign conquest and then contributed to the "romance" of colonialism.

The association of Arthur with empire, or at least with the claims of right to rule a wide area, goes back to the beginning of the Arthurian tradition. Nicholas Higham (2002) speculates that Arthur, a name relatable to the Welsh *arth* [bear], was a legendary figure of gigantic strength, "used to explain the otherwise inexplicable in the landscape". This figure was then invoked as a historical war leader of "the Britons" by surviving elite British groups in their continuing claims to leadership and military prowess, under the pressure of English encroachment in the sixth to tenth centuries. The Arthur of Welsh heroic poetry and the *Historia Brittonum* was to cast a very long shadow:

> a figure originally developed by a Welsh writer in the ninth century as a symbol of national identity, martial prowess and God-given victory was subsequently taken up by Celto-Norman and Anglo-Norman writers in fulfilment of other agendas, becoming ultimately the

centre of one of the most vigorous "cultural-ideological" myths of the middle ages. (Higham
2002, xxx)

In the process, *King* Arthur succeeded the earlier *dux bellorum* (war leader), and
soon received an imperial mission, most powerfully through Geoffrey of Monmouth's 1130s work, the *Historia regum Britanniae* [History of the Kings of Britain]
(cf. Meyer, *supra*; Fulton, *supra*). In it Arthur conquers all "Britain", the land
whose naming after the Trojan founder, Brutus, vouches for its unitary status,
then assembles a continental empire that reaches from Iceland to Byzantium.
Many subsequent claims were based on Geoffrey. In Wales, Owain Glyn Dŵr's
early-fifteenth-century struggle against the English invoked Arthur as a former
ruler of the entire island (Hawkes 1998, 117–140). In England, Henry VII emphasized his Welshness and bought into the political power of Geoffrey's *Prophetiae
Merlini* by giving the name Arthur to his eldest son. Henry VIII seriously relied
on the existence of Arthur in his claim to have imperial status as King of England
and, in the reign of Elizabeth I, John Dee "argued [...] that Britain possessed a
colonial empire because of imperial conquests, using material from Geoffrey to
give Elizabeth title to much of Europe and even the New World." (Hamilton 1990,
66)

In the early French Arthurian tradition, Chrétien de Troyes celebrated the
long-term transfer of *chevalerie* [chivalry] and *clergie* [learning] from Greece to
Rome to France. The equal presence of "chivalry" – at its basis "body of knights"
or "fighting on horseback" – indicates that this is to be considered an inheritance of military dominance as well as a civilizational and scientific legacy.
The outward forays of knights in Chrétien de Troyes' romances are small-scale
versions of territorial expansion from the Arthurian centre. Erec's conquest of
Yder and Lancelot's actions against Meleagant bring troublesome neighbours
under Arthurian control, either to save or kill. These are "colonizing" actions,
in the sense that they strip a neighbouring locality of power and transfer control
elsewhere, making one location more of a metropolitan "centre", while giving a
formerly co-existing separate entity a new marginal or client status. That these
occurrences simply arise as narrative "adventures" seems designed to clear the
colonizing power of rapacious intent.

"Imperial" and "colonial" Arthur might seem clear enough. But what does
it mean to call a medieval Arthurian text *post*-colonial? Patricia Ingham and
Michelle Warren (2003, 12) draw on influential theory by non-medievalists to
read the *Historia* as post-colonial in the sense of *anti-*, rather than *after-*, colonial: "'Post-colonialism ... begins from the very first moment of cultural contact.
It is the discourse of oppositionality which colonialism brings into being. In this
sense postcolonial writing has a very long history.'" (cf. Ashcroft, Griffiths and

Tiffin 1995, 117) They also cite K. Anthony Appiah's (1991, 336) view that "the post- in postcolonial is the post- of the space clearing gesture." (Ingham and Warren 2003, 7) In her influential study *Sovereign Fantasies*, Ingham (2001, 45) stresses the *Historia*'s "ambivalent political uses" in the post-Conquest period: "This ambivalence [...] links intercultural insular unity to [...] a national fantasy," making reference to Homi Bhabha's emphasis on "both the fantasmatic nature of national narratives and the ways in which such texts always gesture, despite themselves, to the contestations and disunities they earnestly seek to avoid."

For Michelle Warren (2002, 144), writing around the same time, the post-colonial approach highlights the instability of borders: it "mark[s] radical differences along the lines of most intimate contact. By focusing on the limits of difference and resemblance, postcolonial studies situate paradox, ambivalence, and irony in relation to cultural representations." In *History on the Edge*, Warren (2000, 2–3) chooses "to read Arthurian historiography from the regional edges where it was most often written, in an effort to understand its engagements with the dynamics of domination." She emphasizes the (probably Welsh) First Variant of the *Historia*, produced at a time (1136–1155) when Welsh military power was re-asserting itself, as a potentially resistant reading of colonization, boosting the role of the British as Christian monarchs exercising sovereignty over their kingdom, accepting only that a "region" has been lost to them, in distinction from Geoffrey's claim that it was "the whole island". In this way, "[t]he First Variant redactors repossess a portion of the English history appropriated by Geoffrey for the Britons." (67) Even so, Warren argues that in using Geoffrey's story to stake their claim to historical sovereignty, the Welsh narratives inevitably "also record [...] the cultural trauma of colonization." (60)

Ingham's term "sovereign fantasies" had deep resonance in both the contemporary politics and the post-colonial theory of her book's period. Interviewed in 1998, the Ulster writer Seamus Deane (1998, 2) remarked that "[w]here the real and the phantasmal coincide with one another, that's a mark of a colonised society." In Homi Bhabha's (2002, 21) words, "[t]he colonial subject was a kind of split-subject and "knew" it both phenomenologically and historically." When this emphasis on fantasy, unstable reality and split consciousness is applied to a text like the *Historia*, it becomes impossible to find an uncomplicated endorsement within it either for Arthur's imperial regime or for a critique of it. The discourse of post-colonial critique is shot through with intimations of anxiety, ideological fracture and self-defeating literary strategies, even in discussion of texts that might appear propagandist exercises to support territorial expansion. Critics who take a post-colonial approach to medieval texts never consider colonialism as a positive development; their critical practice is a form of political opposition, but equally they are often concerned that their stance is compromised by inevitable involvement in the system and the legacy that they critique. This leads to complex reflections on both critical methodology and historical texts, often in tandem.

Consequently, emphasis on uncertainty of meaning in post-colonial interpretations of texts has often been related to their origin and reception in uncertain historical moments. Higham (2002) associates the growth of early Arthurian historiography with Welsh periods of turmoil and transition. Similarly, Geraldine Heng (2003, 35) cites R.W. Southern's view that "[i]ntensive historical writing follows 'a crisis in national affairs' that alienates a people from its past." She takes Southern's view of the troubling aftermath of the Norman Conquest in England and applies it especially to the new Norman patrons of insular historiography:

> the invasion of foreign lands requires another [kind of cultural work]: especially when that foreign invasion also renders the invaders foreign to themselves and denatured, by their own unrecognizable and self-transformative performance. (35)

Following this trajectory, Heng offers a sophisticated analysis of Arthur's fight with the Giant of Mont St Michel in Geoffrey. In it she reads the monstrous giant as obscurely symbolic of recent Norman violence and atrocity, especially on Crusade, and Arthur as "a cultural saviour plucked from the distant past (an older intact representative of cultural identity) to rescue the contemporary past, and, with giant heroism defeat [...] gigantic horror." (60) In Crusade mode, Arthur triumphs in Geoffrey as a warrior, king and Christian leader; however, in a way that reveals Norman anxieties, he is uncannily like the monstrous giant that he fights.

Heng's reading casts an eerie light on Geoffrey's upbeat account (Faletra 2008, 182–185), troubling but not erasing interpretations of it as pro-imperialist. That Arthur should begin his campaign against Rome with a giant fight recalls the early giant-killing days of Brutus and Corineus in Albion. The defeat of the obscene rapist giant cleanses a famous site in Normandy that has become in Geoffrey's day a great monastic church and place of pilgrimage, and whose ruler is now also King of England. In taking vengeance on a creature who has ravished the niece of his cousin, Hoel of Brittany, Arthur features as a loyal kinsman. In eradicating the giant, he does for the region what its knights have not been able to do for themselves: this first encounter, therefore, brands his armed incursion into Europe as a benefaction. The episode is prefigured by Arthur's dream of a fight between a dragon from the west (himself) and a great bear, variously interpreted as "some giant" and "the Roman emperor". The combined dream-reading seems a method to pass off Arthur's whole invasion as a rightful cleansing of Europe from a despicable regime. Only Mordred's treachery will prevent its fulfilment. Arthur does not get to Rome, but it is hard to see that in Geoffrey's account he should be blamed for trying. Mordred's rebellion is simply one instance of the

Britons' tendency to civil dissension that will eventually bring their rule to a bad end.

To take another instance, Geoffrey's treatment of the Saxons, foolishly invited into Britain by the British king, Vortigern, as allies against the Picts, and then treacherously taking over power, seems designed to minimize a sense that they have any right to belong in Britain or to rule it. That is why historians brought up on Bede's *Historia ecclesiastica gentis Anglorum* [Ecclesiastical History of the English People], like William of Newburgh, later found Geoffrey's work so unpalatable: he writes Bede's England out of the record as much as possible. The British kingdoms are made to last into the seventh century. Saxon rule only comes into being through the weakness and internal conflicts of the British; their pitiful contemporary remnants, Geoffrey says, are the degenerate Welsh. Whilst there is some praise for Athelstan (relocated by Geoffrey in the seventh century), whose reputation lasted long into post-Conquest times, and a vague hope of power granted to the Welsh in an unspecified future, by and large the story arc leaves an obvious space for the Normans as spiritual successors of the noble British like Arthur, and before him, Brutus: they too have earned rule of the land by their own manly military efforts. The Saxons are treated as an aberration. Their notable absence from Geoffrey's *Historia*, except as invading robbers and traitors, figuratively recreates for the recently-arrived Norman rulers the status of the island as *terra nullius* [no man's land], "inhabited only by a few giants", just as when Brutus first arrived in Albion (Faletra 2008, 56).

It has been disputed whether the "colonial" ventures described in Arthurian texts really deserve the name – as it might be applied, for instance, to the crusading states – or if this literature refers merely to "the general expansion of the Frankish 'aristocratic diaspora' [...] seeking to take over a neighboring territory with a shared Latinity, a shared religion, and shared borders (even if maritime)." (Bartlett 1992, 185) There are certainly clear differences from the later establishment of colonies in South America or Australia, for example, and, as Bartlett points out, from other medieval examples, including settlements in the non-Christian Baltic and Middle East (Gaunt 2009, 164; Bartlett 1993, 29–54, 185). All the same, versions of the Arthurian story, as Heng's account of Arthur at Mont St Michel indicates, tend to invest the peoples that Arthur subjugates with outlandish, barbarian and alien qualities. In Wace's *Roman de Brut*, the Irish invaded by Arthur are deeply ignorant and backward: "quite defenceless [*trop nu*]: they had neither hauberks nor shields, they knew nothing of arrows or how to draw a bow [...] nor did they know where to hide." (Weiss 1999, 244) One is reminded of the contempt for the Irish later expressed by Gerald of Wales (2000, 70) in *The Topography of Ireland* (1188):

> this people inhabit a country so remote from the rest of the world, and lying at its furthest
> extremity, forming, as it were, another world, and are thus secluded from civilized nations,
> they learn nothing, and practise nothing but the barbarism in which they are born and bred.

Gerald the Welshman, one might think, comes from a place equally "remote", but as befits a correspondent embedded in the attempted Norman take-over, he speaks of the native population in terms reminiscent of much later colonial ventures in much more distant places.

Similarly, in the later medieval English Alliterative *Morte Arthure*, a text in Geoffrey's tradition, the Romans attacked by Arthur are alienated by their possession of camels, crocodiles, elephants and other "marvellous beasts" (Benson 1994, ll. 2282–2289), and the Roman Emperor is in league with the "Sultan of Syria" (Benson 1994, l. 590). An alienating estrangement of the Roman side as paganized and effete, justifying Arthur's wholesale conquest, also occurs in Thomas Malory's version of these wars (1469), based on the same text. There is remarkably little sense of the Romans as fellow Christians with a shared Latinity or a famously effective structure of government, as they face what Malory calls Arthur's "noble knights of merry England". Forced occupation of others' territory always requires that the indigenous inhabitants of the land, or any opposing claimants to it, be understood as either non-existent or radically unfit to rule. Conversely, as in Warren's account of the Welsh reaction to Geoffrey, it is the colonized who, under pressure, seem more likely to stress their similarities with the colonizers.

The literature of colonialism exists mainly to perform those functions of alienation or self-legitimation, so it might be argued that despite the obvious historical differences between, say, Arthur's supposed conquest of Ireland, Thomas More's justification in *Utopia* of English claims in Ireland and the Americas, and the discourse justifying settler expansion in Australia, in textual terms these are equally "colonial" ventures. The "history" in these texts is evident in the ideological needs embedded in their narratives more than in their relation to reality. Generally speaking, post-colonial readings of literature are wary of treating any Fictions of Empire as more than "culturally constrained and ideologically inflected fabrications", devised for a homeland readership (Parry 2004, 71). It is in the historicized relation between the details of the fabrication and the varied sites of its production and reception that post-colonial attention is concentrated. This kind of analysis finds much to work on in the Arthurian tradition, which reflects differing patterns of emphasis in different places and times. It is notable, for example, that interest in Arthur as a European imperialist, although it continued long in England, had no comparably strong equivalent in vernacular continental Arthurianism, where the history of Arthur's reign is tailored to fit in with the genealogies of local rulers. The French *Lancelot-Grail* cycle, which later fed into works in many other languages, calls Arthur an "emperor" at times, but has limited interest in the basis for that. Even in Malory, where Arthur succeeds in becoming Roman Emperor, there is very little subsequent mention of the fact, partly because the *Morte Darthur* largely follows French sources. Catherine Batt (2002, 29) has suggested that Malory's setting of his Arthuriad in "England" indicates a nationalist streak, but that his treatment of "the French book" as "authorised" still acknowledges the siting of his text in a post-colonial, multi-cultural situation.

It is worth remembering that "Arthurian" itself is not a basic category. To distinguish one medieval or medievalist text from another as Arthurian on the grounds of its reference to particular characters or incidents may well be to over-emphasize a difference that is trivial in relation to other important similarities of genre, form and narrative arc. Chaucer's Arthurian *Wife of Bath's Tale* is far more closely related to his *Franklin's Tale* than, say, to a work like *Of Arthour and of Merlin*. How, and how much, the "Arthurian" quality of a text matters will vary greatly according to other factors, so to draw a continuing Arthurian tradition out of the specific contexts through which it is mediated can be very misleading. What we call the tradition varies greatly according to the selection of texts and genres, and interpretative emphases. There are Welsh saints' lives, for instance, in which Arthur cuts a poor figure. In his late-life *Vita Merlini*, Geoffrey of Monmouth himself provides some resistance to the go-getting imperial Arthur of his *Historia*. Merlin, looking back, speaks approvingly of Arthur's conquests, but he nests the revised story of the Britons in a wealth of other topics, above all in a fascination with the physical universe and natural world – stars, seas, springs, birds and forests. Arthur is favoured most because "applying the moderation of the law, he restored order to his kingdom" (Faletra 2008, 267), in contrast to the *Vita*'s appalled condemnation of the anarchy in King Stephen's reign. Similarly, in Layamon's *Brut*, an early-thirteenth-century English descendant of Geoffrey by way of Wace, while there is a detailed account of Arthur's European campaigns, there is also a deep feeling for what the poet calls "this land" and an inclusive concern for all its inhabitants, high and low; the highlight of Arthur's reign is a twelve-year general peace of unimaginable happiness. The poet's wishes often run counter to the acquisitive and hyperactive nature of the *Historia*'s source material, seeking instead, although doomed to disappointment, to praise a quiet life of content at home as the highest kingly achievement.

Several of the later medieval English Arthurian romances, including *Gawain and Ragnelle* and the *Awntyrs of Arthure* [Adventures of Arthur], seem very local in outlook, centred near Carlisle, and uninterested in foreign affairs, so not obviously of interest as post-colonial. Like *Sir Gawain and the Green Knight,* they focus on truth, courtesy and religion instead of warfare and conquest. Nevertheless, Ingham (2001, 180–181; 187; 190–191) persuasively reads the representation of "land" in these texts, for example in the *Awntyrs of Arthure*, as a "geographic" catalogue that "signifies both the glorious wealth of aristocratic privilege and the unbelievable breadth of a realm", yet is shown as subject to the fear of "sovereign loss" through sin and death. The northern and border lands of these texts, Ingham suggests, show a reluctance to accept central royal power, raising suspicions of an Arthurian "peace" and "unity" that depend on "the injustices of imperial sovereignty" and an "appropriate" violence exercised at (and for) the king's pleasure.

More recently, some scholars have taken a post-nationalist, "cosmopolitan" approach to Arthurian material. So Usha Vishnuvajjala (2014, 117), drawing on work by John Ganim (2005) and others, reads Chrétien de Troyes' *Cligès* as "cosmopolitan in the sense that characters have simultaneous loyalties to different empires and states, where loyalties coexist instead of existing in opposition to world citizenship." This loyalty can exist alongside national identity. A qualifying response might be that in the powerful Arthurian regime celebrated in *Cligès* some shades of difference are tolerated in those, like Alexandre, who can be brought in and advanced to bolster the king's enterprise, but not out of any cosmopolitan spirit. Rank, prowess and courtesy inflect nation, race and ethnicity to a very large extent in Chrétien's work, as in many medieval texts – but there are severe limits: in *Perceval*, written in a Crusading period and dedicated to a more than usually anti-Semitic monarch, he urges that "traitor Jews [...] should be slain like dogs." (Chrétien de Troyes 1985, 70) Tolerance of Otherness in his work can perhaps better be understood as a self-enhancing activity undertaken by the Arthurian centre to draw suitable foreigners into collaboration. Other examples are Feirefiz, the interracial "magpie" knight in Wolfram von Eschenbach's *Parzival* (1197–1210) and Malory's Sir Palomides the Saracen. These are in no way simply "Othered": they are always considered "noble" figures whose full assimilation into the knightly elite is desired, but in each case a corollary of that is that they want to be christened.

It is probably more realistic to look for "middle spaces" of hybridity and overlap in Arthurian texts than for tolerance or cosmopolitanism. David Lawton considers the "Turk" in the English poem *Gawain and the Turk* as typical of several English Arthurian romances, including *Sir Gawain and the Green Knight*, which include "from the start an Other that is not quite other" who then "transform[s] into something more hospitable [...] They are festive and performative others who from the first only pretend to be irreconcilable." (Lawton 2003, 187–188) Lawton further argues that the uncertainly "reformed Turk" of this romance, who operates as both enemy and ally in a complex ethnic and religious border land, troubles the binaries of "Home" and "Away", along with the "determinate identities" of "difference and exoticism" (189–192). The "Turk" might therefore potentially be a mediating figure, offering a "middle term" between "extreme ideological fantasies of identity", in a story that can speak to modern concerns about "East" and "West." More broadly, Lawton's essay is characteristic of an approach which seeks to avoid the conceptual categories that underpin colonizing attitudes. Foremost amongst these categories is "modernity" itself, especially when "[t]he West's sense of its own modernity is [...] grounded by and through colonized bodies suffering pain for belief in that abstraction." (Warren and Ingham 2003, 2)

The decolonizing approach to critique is necessary in Arthurian studies simply because the Arthurian legend has been so closely bound up with the era of nationalism and colonialism. Identifications of Arthur's origins have been controversial matters because they have had strong implications for nationalist and imperialist historiography. Ganim (2005, 46–47) cites the battles between the French scholarly establishment and R.S. Loomis, who insisted on a Celtic background to later Arthurian literature. Post-medieval versions of Arthur have often played upon the notion of a "once and future king" always capable of return as a national leader: Tennyson, for instance, envisaged him as "a modern gentleman of stateliest port", clearly an Englishman. In the Cold War era, as European nations slowly divested themselves of former colonies, the popular figure of Arthur often changed, at least in Anglo-American contexts, to a "Celtic" homeland defender, or "Sarmatian" individualist, without overt imperialist associations, but still a unifying centre for "free" peoples against their enemies, rather like the head of a US-led NATO. Anglo-American cultural and economic agendas are often cryptically attached to such Arthurs, who, like the knights of medieval romance, apparently have no developed political programme and find themselves fighting and killing multiple opponents by accident. The protagonist of Jerry Bruckheimer's film *King Arthur* (2004) is one such: an ethnic and religious outsider, deserted and disillusioned by the Romans, who stays on to ally himself with the indigenous British and fight the Saxons in the cause of "freedom".

There have also been significant anti-colonial versions of Arthurianism, of which the most famous is Mark Twain's *A Connecticut Yankee in King Arthur's Court*. Yet even when colonial attitudes were basically favourable to Arthurian material, they often gave it new employment. Louise D'Arcens (2003, 239) argues that "the seemingly conventional Victorian medievalism" of a nineteenth-century Sydney academic [...] takes on a new significance when expressed in a colonial environment." To Professor John Woolley, it was the anti-materialism in Tennyson's *Idylls* that mattered most in the new country: "Mercantile self-interest is presented [...] as a stumbling block to attaining Woolley's grail of faith, scholarship, and culture." (D'Arcens 2003, 247) That had been a common enough

English response to the *Idylls*, as a "protest [...] against the low and selfish side of a too commercial life," (Knowles 1862, viii) but Woolley was innovative in how he adapted it to Sydney circumstances: Enid plays "cultural muse" to a Gereint coarsened by business; Elayne of Astolat is a fantasist unfit for the harsh realities of colonial life; Guinevere "represent[s] the jaded, directionless colonial subject who succumbs to the 'temptation to indolence or sensuality' that is the colony's greatest pitfall" (D'Arcens 2003, 248–249); Arthur himself is to blame for stifling her industry by failing to allow her a share in his projects. "[T]heir marital failure points to the potential failure of a colonial community in which the administrative reins are held too narrowly." (248–249) D'Arcens shows that with no explicit intention to "write back" to the imperial poet he loved, Woolley still made something very different out of the *Idylls*, giving it a new bent that could only have been imaginable in his particular colonial circumstances.

That obscure and surprising example, which must stand here for many others, indicates that to read an Arthurian text as "post-colonial" means careful attention to historical and cultural situations of utterance and reception, including the reader's own. Ideally, as Gaunt (2009) writes, such an approach will involve comparative studies of different linguistic and literary traditions, including the indigenous traditions that colonial medievalist reference regularly displaces. It will also examine a variety of original text types, in order to avoid the nationalist, canonical, disciplinary and editorial limitations that, as Gaunt puts it, are "bound to occlude important evidence of cultural contact and hybridities." These are counsels of perfection, and very hard to live up to, but their value is reflected in the best insights that have come from scholars working on post-colonial Arthuriana in the last twenty years. While the term post-colonial itself has lost some currency in contemporary debates, explorations of the "layered connections between the disciplines of medieval studies and postcolonial studies" (Lampert-Weissig 2010, xxxix) continue, and their value in making readers think hard about the broader historical and cultural situation of Arthurian literature has been clear. In a Western world increasingly obsessed with border security and fantasies of pure national identity, it remains a highly relevant concern.

References

Altschul, Nadia R. "Postcolonialism and the Study of the Middle Ages." *History Compass* 6 (2008): 588–606.

Appiah, Kwame Anthony. "Is the Post- in Postmodernism the Post- in Postcolonial?" *Critical Inquiry* 17 (1991): 336–357.

Ashcroft, Bill, Gareth Griffiths and Helen Tiffin, eds. *The Post-Colonial Studies Reader*. New York: Routledge, 1995.

Bartlett, Robert. *The Making of Europe: Conquest, Colonization and Cultural Change 950–1350*. London: Penguin, 1993.

Benson, Larry D., ed. *King Arthur's Death: The Middle English Stanzaic* Morte Arthur *and* Alliterative Morte Arthure. Kalamazoo: Medieval Institute Publications, 1994.

Bhabha, Homi, and John Comaroff. "Speaking of Postcoloniality, in the Continuous Present: A Conversation." *Relocating Postcolonialism*. Ed. David Theo Goldberg and Ato Quayson. Oxford: Wiley-Blackwell, 2002. 16–48.

Chakrabarty, Dipesh. *Provincializing Europe: Postcolonial Thought and Historical Difference*. Princeton, NJ: Princeton University Press, 2000.

Chrétien de Troyes. *Perceval, Or, The Story of the Grail*. Trans. Ruth Harwood Cline. Athens, GA: University of Georgia Press, 1985.

Cohen, Jeffrey Jerome, ed. *The Post-Colonial Middle Ages*. New York: St Martin's Press, 2000.

D'Arcens, Louise. "Antipodean Idylls: An Early Australian Translation of Tennyson's Medievalism." *Postcolonial Moves: Medieval through Modern*. Ed. Patricia Clare Ingham and Michelle R. Warren. New York: Palgrave Macmillan, 2003. 237–256.

Deane, Seamus, and Nicholas Patterson. "Different Strokes 1: An Interview with Seamus Deane." *The Boston Phoenix* (June), 1998.

Faletra, Michael, ed. and trans. *Geoffrey of Monmouth: The History of the Kings of Britain*. Peterborough, ON: Broadview, 2008.

Fanon, Frantz. *The Wretched of the Earth*. Trans. Richard Philcox. New York: Grove Press, 2004.

Ganim, John. *Medievalism and Orientalism: Three Essays on Literature, Architecture and Cultural Identity*. New York: Palgrave Macmillan, 2005.

Gaunt, Simon. "Can the Middle Ages Be Postcolonial?" *Comparative Literature* 61 (2009): 160–176.

Gerald of Wales. *The Topography of Ireland*. Trans. Thomas Forester. Rev. Thomas Wright. Cambridge, ON: In Parenthesis, 2000. Available at: <http://www.yorku.ca/inpar/topography_ireland.pdf>.

Hawkes, Terence. "Bryn Glas." *Post-Colonial Shakespeares*. Ed. Ania Looms and Martin Orkin. London: Routledge, 1998. 117–140.

Heng, Geraldine. *Empire of Magic: Medieval Romance and the Politics of Cultural Fantasy*. New York: Columbia University Press, 2003.

Higham, N.J. *King Arthur: Myth-Making and History*. London: Routledge, 2002.

Holsinger, Bruce. "Medieval Studies, Postcolonial Studies, and the Genealogies of Critique." *Speculum* 77 (2002). 1195–1227.

Ingham, Patricia Clare. *Sovereign Fantasies: Arthurian Romance and the Making of Britain*. Philadelphia, PA: University of Pennsylvania Press, 2001.

Ingham, Patricia Clare, and Michelle R. Warren, eds. *Postcolonial Moves: Medieval Through Modern*. New York: Palgrave Macmillan, 2003.

Knight, Stephen. *Arthurian Literature and Society*. London: Macmillan, 1983.

Knowles, J.T. *The Story of King Arthur and his Knights of the Round Table*. London: Griffith and Farrar, 1862.

Lampert-Weissig, Lisa. *Medieval Literature and Postcolonial Studies*. Edinburgh: Edinburgh University Press, 2010.

Larsen, Neil. "Imperialism, Colonialism, Postcolonialism." Ed. Henry Schwarz and Sangeeta Ray. *A Companion to Postcolonial Studies*. Malden, MA: Blackwell, 2000. 23–52.

Lawton, David. "History and Legend: The Exile and the Turk". *Postcolonial Moves: Medieval through Modern*. Ed. Patricia Clare Ingham and Michelle R. Warren. New York: Palgrave Macmillan, 2003. 173–195.

Lynch, Andrew. "Imperial Arthur: Home and Away". *The Cambridge Companion to the Arthurian Legend*. Ed. Elizabeth Archibald and Ad Putter. Cambridge: Cambridge University Press, 2009. 171–187.

Oxford English Dictionary, "colonialism, n. 2".

Parry, Benita. "The Institutionalization of Postcolonial Studies." *The Cambridge Companion to Postcolonial Literary Studies*. Ed. Neil Lazarus. Cambridge: Cambridge University Press, 2004. 66–80.

Said, Edward. *Orientalism*. New York: Pantheon, 1978.

Spiegel, Gabrielle. "Épater les médiévistes." *History and Theory* 39 (2000): 243–250.

Spivak, Gayatri Chakravorty. "Foreword: Upon Reading the *Companion to Postcolonial Studies*". *A Companion to Postcolonial Studies*. Ed. Henry Schwarz and Sangeeta Ray. Malden, MA: Blackwell, 2000. xv–xxii.

Hamilton, A.C., ed. *The Spenser Encyclopedia*. Toronto: University of Toronto Press, 1990.

Vishnuvajjala, Usha. "Loyalty and Horizontal Cosmopolitanism in Chrétien de Troyes' *Cligés*." *Arthuriana* 24 (2014): 111–130.

Warren, Michelle R. *History on the Edge: Excalibur and the Borders of Britain*. Minneapolis, MN: University of Minnesota Press, 2000.

Warren, Michelle R. "Take the World by Prose: Modes of Possession in the Roman d'Alexandre." *The Medieval French Alexander*. Ed. Donald Maddox and Sarah Sturm-Maddox. Albany: SUNY Press, 2002. 143–160.

Weiss, Judith, trans. *Wace's Roman de Brut: A History of the British*. Exeter: University of Exeter Press, 1999.

Section III **Reading Arthurian Romances: Content, Method and Context**

Florian Kragl

Heinrich von dem Türlin's *Diu Crône*: Life at the Arthurian Court

1 The crowning achievement of Arthurian romance

HJe mit hat ein end
Die krone, die mine hend
Nach dem besten gesmidt hant,
Als sie min synn vor yme vant
Vsz einem exemplar.
Vnd wissent das für ware:
Sie enmügent niht wol vff getragen
Zwispel hertzen, valsche zagen,
Wann sie ist jne zü enge.
Sie tragent aber wol die lenge
Die güten vnd die reynen.
Mit so güten steynen
Jst sie vber al beleit,
Das sie wol ir wirdikeit
Zü reht trug vnd zimmt.
Wer sie für sich zú schauwend nymmt,
Wil er sie zú reht schauwen gar,
So mag er wol werden da gewar
Vil maniges fremdes bilde,
Beyde zam vnd wilde,
Des glichen er vor nye gesah,
Ob er sie vor niht machet swah
Von vnkunst ader von nijt.
Mit diser krone gekrönet sijt
Jr frauwen, die nach werde lebent,
Wann vwere grüsze der welt gebent
Freude vnd hohen müt!
Das ist das öberste gút,
Das der welt mag geschehen.
Dirre arbeit wil ich üch jehen,
Wann ich ir dorch üch began,
Wie wenig ich noch daran
Nach dienste han gewonnen.

Florian Kragl (Friedrich-Alexander-Universität Erlangen-Nürnberg)

DOI 10.1515/9783110432466-021

Jr sollent mir nicht enbunnen,
Vwere gnaden grûsze gönnen. (ll. 29966–30000)[1]
[This is the end of the crown that my hands wrought skilfully as I conceived it from a model. Yet you must know that fickle and faithless cowards cannot wear it very well, for it is too tight for them, but those who are noble and good can wear it for a long time. The crown is set all over with such precious stones that it is quite in keeping with their honor. Whoever does not disdain it in advance through ignorance or ill will but examines it carefully may well observe many strange features of all kinds the like of which he has never before seen. May all you ladies who live so as to be highly esteemed be crowned with this diadem! For your warm greetings give the world the greatest good it can have, a joyful and noble spirit. I have you to thank for this work, since I began it for your sake, and though I have not profited from it as I deserve, you should at least not begrudge me a fond greeting and your favor.][2]

These are the last words of one of the longest German Arthurian romances, *Diu Crône* by Heinrich von dem Türlin, who names himself several times (at ll. 8774, 10444, 30011) in his text. The claim Heinrich makes in the lines cited is far from humble. Far from the topical humility of the Arthurian narrator-authors in the twelfth and thirteenth centuries, he presents his work as a richly jewelled crown. It is neither surprising that such a crown needs worthy admirers – a *topos* in German literature around 1200 – nor that this crown is dedicated to ladies, whose grace Heinrich hopes to obtain. What is surprising is the metaphor itself: the "Crown" as a title for this long narrative seems to be extravagant and quite unique, at least in German and French Arthurian literature up to 1230;[3] it is a clear signal that what is told in this *Crône* will surpass everything known before:[4] it is claiming to be, in other words, the pinnacle of Arthurian romance.

The dimensions of Heinrich's text are indeed extraordinary. With its *c*. 30,000 lines, it is even longer than Wolfram von Eschenbach's *Parzival*, and the richness of the plot is considerable. The transmission, by contrast, is not: there is only one complete extant manuscript (now Cod. pal. germ. 374, which is held in the Universitätsbibliothek Heidelberg), which is probably several removes from the text that Heinrich composed in the second or third decade of the thirteenth century, possibly in Carinthia (though both dating and origin have shown themselves very hard to prove). The Heidelberg codex dates from 1479 and is nothing less than

---

1 All references are to Heinrich von dem Türlin (2000 for ll. 1–12281; 2005 for ll. 12282–30042). Other important editions include Heinrich von dem Türlin (2012a; 2012b).
2 All translations are from Heinrich von dem Türlin (1989), with minor amendments.
3 One might think of Bligger's *Umhang*, mentioned by Gottfried von Straßburg in his *Tristan*, which is of course lost.
4 The crown could also symbolize the circular narration that Heinrich uses from time to time; cf. Störmer-Caysa (2003; 2004).

a typical early-modern German adaptation of a Middle High German romance. Surely closer to Heinrich's original is Vienna, ÖNB Cod. 2779, which dates from the first half of the fourteenth century, and which contains just the first two fifths of the text. A few minor fragments complete a picture of rather scant transmission.

The *Crône* seems not to have been a particular hit of the Middle Ages. Heinrich's strange style and his extravagant manner of narration – to which I will return – had little, if any, impact on the literature of the thirteenth century. Rudolf von Ems, one of the most productive writers of the thirteenth century, is the only person to mention Heinrich and his *Crône*, and he does so in his *Alexander* (*c.* 1250), and even then Heinrich is merely listed as one of several courtly authors operating around 1200. This does, though, give us a rough *terminus ante quem*. After Rudolf, however, no further traces of Heinrich are to be found.

When compared with the self-congratulatory epilogue, this tiny example of attention paid to Heinrich does not amount to very much, and we can only speculate about the reasons for the gap between Heinrich's claim and the reception of his text. However, it is clear to see that Heinrich's *Crône* is indeed a unique example within the Arthurian romances of its time (cf. Cormeau 1977; 1984). By contrast with his predecessors, such as Hartmann von Aue, Ulrich von Zatzikhoven, Wolfram von Eschenbach, or even Gottfried von Straßburg, Heinrich does not follow one single designated source. Though he mentions an *exemplar* in the passage from the epilogue cited above, this reference to a single book seems to be merely a symptom of the "pre-existing book" topos. Heinrich does not rely on a single French romance, but rather composes a new story based on a handful of French, as well as some German sources, amongst which we find Chrétien's *Conte du Graal*, some of its Continuations, Wolfram's *Parzival*, alongside shorter texts, including stories preserved in the *Manteau mautaillé*, *La Mule sans frein* and *Sir Gawain and the Green Knight* (cf. Kratz 1973; Zach 1990; Suerbaum 2005). We do not know which exact sources Heinrich had to hand (and from where he got them), but it is highly plausible that it was he who – possibly for the first time in German literary history – compiled an original German romance out of multiple sources. In that sense, his text is certainly unique and special: rather like the eponymous crown.

A second characteristic feature of the *Crône* is the technique that Heinrich uses to combine the motifs and stories he found in his sources. Just like his predecessors (such as Chrétien), he chooses a single protagonist whose adventures are told in a more or less linear fashion (advanced narrative techniques like the *entrelacement* of the French *Vulgate Cycle* remained uncommon in German speaking areas in the early-thirteenth century). Particularly remarkable is the protagonist that Heinrich chooses for his text. At first glance – for around one hundred lines – the *Crône* seems to be a romance about Artus and his youth. At least, this is what Heinrich claims (ll. 161–174). But Heinrich soon leaves this topic behind and brings us to a feast at the Arthurian court, where Artus is no longer in his youth, while his politics, well known from Hartmann, Ulrich and Wolfram, are already well established. We are presented with a passive sovereign (Artus), a lively queen (Ginover), and Gawein is set out as the best knight, while the steward, Kay, is the worst. The feast, which takes up more than 2,000 lines, is, in essence, a test of valour, which is more about the court than the king. After the feast, we return to Artus as the lead protagonist for several thousand lines, but the longer the text continues, the more Artus comes to be superseded by his first knight Gawein, who is present in all previous German Arthurian romances, but never as a lead protagonist (cf. Claassens and Knapp 2010). Here again, we see that Heinrich's text might rightly be considered a crowning achievement in Arthurian literature. The focus is on the core of the Arthurian society (the king, Gawein, the court), and he therefore puts into motion what otherwise is a rather static issue in earlier German Arthurian romance.

It therefore follows that Heinrich's text – whilst not breaking with the conventions of Arthurian literature – constitutes a text full of superlatives. Telling the stories of Artus, his court and Gawein requires nothing less than recounting tales about the best of the best, and about ideals, aspects which are – thanks to the works of authors such as Chrétien and Hartmann – imbued with an aura of timelessness: they are ever present, without a beginning, without downfall, without an evolving storyline in the true sense. Artus' reign brings about no change to this: the rituals and *coutumes* [customs] are as ever they were, and each character has his or her role. However, telling the stories of Artus, his court and Gawein therefore also necessitates the communication of the history of this apparently timeless system, the "historicization" of what is otherwise presented as stable. This, in turn, requires Heinrich to find a way not only to show or discuss – in terms of descriptions or digressions –, but also to narrate the ideal nature of Arthur's kingship. He who wishes to demonstrate what it is to be *and* to become Artus, his court and Gawein (cf. Ebenbauer 1977; Vollmann 2010), and he who wants to avoid irony, will inevitably be confronted with the task of foregrounding ideals and idealism as effects of the narrative progression. This is the third poetic aspect by means of which Heinrich's *Crône* merits its name, since crowns are often regarded as symbols of unquestionable perfection.

Heinrich's *Crône* can thus be seen as a fairly radical attempt to design a new type of Arthurian or even courtly romance. It sets new standards when it comes to the handling of sources; it focuses on the core of Arthurian society; most importantly, it proclaims its driving narrative focus to be a subject that is elsewhere treated as a mere backdrop for Arthurian romance: idealism. The crown as a symbol of coronation, therefore, or as a metonym for the Arthurian *dramatis personae*, or even as a metaphor for perfection, is what this romance is all about.

The first of the three aspects discussed above (Heinrich's choice of sources) belongs to the history of motifs and stories. Its relevance is evidenced most clearly in episodes where two or more storylines converge, often in a playful, and sometimes rather clumsy, manner, such as in passages in which Gawein looks back on deeds he has not yet completed (cf. Störmer-Caysa 2003; 2004). These narratological and motivational lacunae make it almost impossible to break down the plot of the *Crône* into a few sentences. The first section is mostly about Gasozein, a noble knight who claims that he became engaged to Ginover long before Artus even knew her, as well as about Amurfina, who manages to become the wife of Gawein, who for his part errantly and frequently wanders, solving several adventures along the way. In the end, Ginover stays with Artus, Gasozein marries Amurfina's sister, Sgoydamur, and all problems are resolved. But then, Gawein loses his way once again, and a new storyline develops, which is centered around Frau Saelde – that is: Fortuna – and her evil sister, Gyramphiel, who tries to take revenge on Artus and Gawein for an earlier theft. Gawein earns continuous luck for Artus' court (to which I will return), but this luck is quickly lost, before it is won again at the end. Gyramphiel is more or less defeated, while Gawein discovers the Grail and breaks the terrible spell cast on the Grail society, under which they are doomed to exist as pseudo-zombies. But, as mentioned above, these important storylines are easily missed, especially during a first reading of the *Crône*, as Heinrich seems to prefer to foreground details and sub-plots, while being unable (or reluctant) to neatly construct a stable arc of suspense.

Of course, this has an impact on the poetics and the aesthetics of Heinrich's romance. But the impact of the second and third aspects outlined above (the style of narration and the focus on idealism respectively) is even more significant. Narrating the idealism of Artus, his court and Gawein, as well as the idealization of the Arthurian system, is a narratological problem *eo ipso* – and this is a point widely acknowledged by the nascent body of research on the *Crône*. Narration implies movement and progression; idealism, however, is rather more stable and immobile by nature. It is this paradox that epitomizes the poetics of the *Crône*, perhaps more so than anything else. I now turn to an attempt to illustrate this paradox by means of an examination of how "life" invades the Arthurian court. I aim to showcase the poetic techniques that Heinrich uses to manage this paradox, highlighting where he succeeds and when he fails, and why his partial success is crucial for the aesthetics of the *Crône*.

2 Narrative representations of idealism and of its collapse

2.1 Tests of valour

It is one of the classic poetic techniques of Arthurian romance to secure the status of the protagonist through tests of valour. One example of this might be the countless tournaments, which show the primacy of the hero. Typically, tests of valour represent mythical episodes, in which a certain magic object acts as a measuring device for chivalry or virtue, showcasing the excellence or (more frequently) the flaws of the Arthurian court. Such is the case in the *Lanzelet* by Ulrich von Zatzikhoven (*c.* 1195) or in the above-mentioned *Manteau mautaillé*, which was also translated into Middle High German. In both cases, we have a magic coat, whose (variable) length and drapery indicates the degree of perfection or imperfection of the ladies at the Arthurian court. Kay, the seneschal, comments on each participant and ironically exposes several of the shortcomings of the Arthurian court (cf. Baisch 2003; Schonert 2009). One narrative effect of this is comic relief, while another is the clear marking of which knight and which lady are to be the key protagonists of the story.

Heinrich von dem Türlin seems to have been particularly fond of this technique, as he uses it twice in his *Crône*. Both episodes take up so many lines that they are by far the lengthiest tests of valour in all German medieval literature. The first instance is part of the Christmas feast at the Arthurian court at the beginning of the *Crône* (ll. 618–3272). A strange being – part-human, part-fish – comes to court, where he introduces himself as a messenger of the friendly King Priure from the sea and presents a magic cup. Whoever has led a virtuous life can easily drink from this cup. However, he who has not spills the wine over certain parts of his/her body in an amount corresponding to whatever failure he has committed. He who succeeds in this test may keep the cup as a gift. That is the will of King Priure. First, the ladies do their best to win the cup, but they all fail, so the knights take their turn, but they are just as helpless against this magic. Only Artus succeeds. The last to drink from the cup is Kay, who ridiculed the game beforehand and who, of course, spills more than anybody else. The court laughs, but Kay becomes angry and proposes a duel against the part-fish knight, which he loses by some margin. The strange knight bids his farewell, and the feast lasts for three more days. Afterwards, the knights secretly leave for a tournament while Artus and Ginover, along with a few remaining knights, are left alone in boredom.

The second test of valour is again part of a feast, this time at Karidol (ll. 22517–25549); it functions as a kind of turning point. Gawain, who in the meantime was believed to be dead, has returned. The court celebrates after the resolution of a difficult familial issue in Gawein and Artus' family. A messenger girl arrives from Gyramphiel – nobody yet knows that she is Gawein's enemy – bringing a magic glove that Gyramphiel is said to have received from her sister, Saelde. Whoever puts on the glove becomes invisible on his/her right-hand side; but if he or she has committed a failure, the part of his/her body with which s/he failed will stay visible and appear naked. The messenger demonstrates the functionality of the glove before it is the court's turn. Needless to say, this test is even more embarrassing for the participants. Only two pass the test: Artus and Gawein. Once again, it is Kay and his beloved, Galayda, who receive their just desserts more so than anyone else. At the end, the girl bids farewell and the glove stays with the court. Immediately afterwards, a knight on a buck arrives carrying a second glove; this glove allows the left side of the body to disappear. This knight, who claims to be a messenger from Frau Saelde, declares that only with the help of both gloves will Gawein be able to complete his quest for the Grail (which he had been forced to pursue a few episodes earlier). In addition to this, Gawein will need the stone of luck that he obtained from Fimbeus (Gyramphiel's husband) through combat – the fight that caused her hatred for Gawein and for Artus' court. Gawein will also need the ring of luck that Saelde gave to him on his visit to Ordohorht (the palace of Frau Saelde). The messenger offers to demonstrate the interaction of the four symbols of luck: he takes the ring and the stone, puts on the gloves and promptly disappears. The last sixth or so of the text explains how Gawein regains the four items and, eventually, masters the quest for the Grail.

The nature of tests of valour is to praise and to condemn at the same time; this is particularly true in the *Crône*, but also elsewhere. The mediocrity of the court provides space for the excellence of Artus and Gawein. In this sense, the two tests of valour in the *Crône* are conventional. Even though there are two such episodes and both are of extraordinary length, this can be explained away as a symptom of the sheer abundance of narrative material that Heinrich puts into his *Crône*. Indeed, the replication merely points to the difficult narrative structure in which the initial lead protagonist, Artus, is gradually superseded (in narratological terms) by Gawein. This may well be the reason why Artus is the only one to master the magic cup in the first test, while, in the second, Artus and Gawein are shown to have equal courtly strength. This promotion of Gawein seems to be intentional: the narrator complains frequently about Gawein's failure to drink from the magic cup without spilling, but he does not recount the precise events of the scene. By contrast, we hear all of the details for the other knights. If the *Crône* is, in essence, a text with one and a half protagonists, these two tests of valour offer an elegant and apt way to characterize them.

However, two things about the tests of valour are surprising. First, it is strange that the excellence of Artus and Gawein is outshone by the comic elements depicted in the scenes. While few words are wasted for the successful participants, we learn a lot about those who fail. Both the narrator and Kay are playful in what they do (cf. Besamusca 2010), and nearly every failure – especially when it has to do with sexuality – is discussed and explained in a rather bawdy manner. An effect of this is that we glean a kind of intertextual panorama (not only in this scene: cf. Schmid 1994), insofar as some comments recall episodes from other texts like *Erec*, *Iwein* and *Parzival*. Kay becomes the hero-in-disguise of these passages, exposing the Arthurian court as a mere shadow of what it is supposed to be: it represents courtly degeneration instead of courtly perfection. That Kay even mocks Artus and Gawein, despite their passing the test(s), shows clearly that these scenes are not really about testing, but rather about an ironical interpretation of what happens. Hence, the *amplificatio* of the test of valour in the *Crône* does not underline Arthurian perfection, but rather undermines it.

Second, the narrative implementation of the tests appears to be purposefully awkward. The first test is presented as a typical introduction to the story: an opportunity for adventure arrives at the court (in form of the part-fish knight with his magic cup) and the king is confirmed as the best of the best. One might expect that a narrative complication would arise from such a configuration – even just a plea from King Priure or similar – but no such thing occurs. The whole of the Christmas scene is free from any such narrative consequences, as if the test was in vain, rather like an overture that does not lead into the operatic melodies that follow. The second test, on the other hand, is closely woven into the narrative progression. In fact, the ruse of the knight with the buck motivates almost everything that follows. But it is curious that a test of valour in which Artus and Gawein succeed should lead to disaster and destruction, even raising the possibility that Gawein will lose his life as a result of Artus and his court having lost their hard-won luck. Worse still, the ruse of the knight with the buck only succeeds because of the pride of the Arthurian court, the members of which never refuse to take on such tests, regardless of the consequences. Virtue, in other words, gets lost in its exemplification.

2.2 The objects of Frau Saelde

If the tests of valour are meant to exemplify the excellence of Artus and Gawein, then the objects of Frau Saelde are meant to symbolize, and secure, the everlasting luck of the whole Arthurian court. Both arise from a similar narrative cue: it is well known in German literature, following Hartmann's *Erec*, that Arthur and his court are blessed with luck. However, he who establishes as protagonists Artus, his best knight Gawein, and the Arthurian court, as does Heinrich von dem Türlin, must exceed the superlatives used for Artus in earlier texts. He will have to make sure that the everlasting luck is not simply woven into the mechanics of the narrative, but also takes on further meaning. Once again, Heinrich uses a traditional narrative technique to manage this: allegory. Whilst it is difficult to narrate everlasting and unclouded luck satisfactorily, it is rather easier to symbolize such luck by using allegorical tools. This is exactly what happens in the *Crône*, and it happens no fewer than four times. The tools in question have already been named. They are the ring, the stone and the two gloves.

First, the ring: Gawein obtains it more or less exactly after the first half of the text (ll. 14927–15945). After having managed to escape the first attack of Gyramphiel on his life and having seen the first *Wunderkette* (to which I will return) whilst wandering, as he often does in the *Crône*, he comes to the palace of Saelde in Ordohorht. There he finds Saelde – who, as mentioned above, is the medieval Fortuna (cf. Cormeau 1995) – sitting on her wheel, and by her side is her child, called Heil. Mankind hangs on the Saelde-wheel, with the lucky ones on the right and the unlucky ones on the left, until the moment Gawein enters the palace. In his presence, the ever-winding wheel stops, and all unfortunate ones are allowed to move to the right side. Frau Saelde assures everlasting luck for Artus and his court by giving Gawein a ring that protects this luck. Gawein is to give it to Artus. By entering the allegorical district of Saelde – that is to say: by making the narration an allegorical one – the *Crône* shows what would otherwise be impossible to see: the way in which Gawein overcomes the unreliability of luck. At the same time, the (newly-achieved) luck of the Arthurian court is captured in an allegorical object (the ring), which Gawein transports out of the allegorical district into the literal Arthurian world.

Second, the stone: the stone's story begins long before the story told in the *Crône*, and we can know about this only by way of some flashbacks that the narrator or his characters allow us to see (ll. 4867–4888, 9039–9040, 14937–15004, 23211–23436, 24359–24363). As outlined above, the story of this stone and its theft is the impulse for nearly everything that happens in Heinrich's romance; the centre of motivational gravity, in other words, lies far beyond the actual storyline. If we order the various flashbacks into a linear story, it would run as follows: Gyramphiel had her sister, Saelde, fabricate a splendid belt for her husband, Fimbeus. Laid into the belt buckle is a stone which guarantees luck for the wearer of the belt. Gyramphiel's idea is to protect her husband whilst he embarks on adventures. At the Arthurian court, however, this belt, which also makes the people appreciate its wearer, is seen and desired by Ginover. Fimbeus offers her the belt as a token of love, but the queen refuses. However, she borrows the belt for a little while and enjoys being adored whilst wearing it. Her greed increases, and eventually she sends Gawein after Fimbeus to win the belt for her, a deed he achieves by means of a stroke of luck: the magic stone falls out of its frame, which seems momentarily to stun luck, and Gawein takes it (and the belt?)[5] with him. He gives the belt to Ginover, who later on gives it as a present to her apparent lover, Gasozein. But Gawein keeps the stone. It will help him to slay a dragon after which Gyramphiel sends him just prior to his arrival at Saelde's palace. He will not lose this stone (just like the ring) – at least, that is, not until the knight with the buck tricks him. This stone, too, is an allegorical symbol of luck, gained from Frau Saelde, and whoever owns the stone is the master of Saelde. Thirdly, the gloves: compared with ring and stone, the gloves play only a minor part, helping the knight with the buck (and his companion girl) to steal the ring and the stone. Their symbolic state, however, stays obscure.

The superficial effect of those four lucky items is relatively easy to grasp: they safeguard and showcase the stable and continuous luck of Artus, his court and Gawein in a way that a simple narrative explanation never could, since what actually goes on to happen strongly contradicts what would be expected of everlasting luck. However, the importance of luck in the *Crône* is to be found in the fact that it is precisely those lucky items that are meant to stabilize luck which, in fact, make it flexible. This is mainly achieved through two narrative operations: the first could be understood as an unlucky interaction between the four lucky items. It may seem – superficially – to strengthen Gawein's and his fellows' luck that he owns both ring and stone (the gloves, as mentioned, seem to be less important). Upon closer inspection, however, one might justly wonder what this duplication of luck does to the ring and the stone. Gawein winning the ring at Frau Saelde's palace is the allegorical climax of the whole text. But what if this success is simply due to the fact that Gawein has the stone that places luck (personified by Saelde) under his spell? This seems rather pleonastic. Indeed, if Gawein already has the luck in form of the stone, then what use is the ring he obtains? Or, what would happen if the ring and stone had different owners (possibly fighting each other), or what if – though this is never the case – Gawein lost one object and kept the other? And what about luck herself (Saelde) if she does not grant the luck of the Arthurian court voluntarily, but rather is forced into it by virtue of the fact that Gawein has the stone? Is such luck of any worth? Or is all of this nothing more than an ingenious allegorical representation of the Arthurian paradox whereby Artus and his men are continuously lucky *and* constantly earn luck.

---

5 Some details are obscured by these flashbacks; this, however, does not detract from my argument.

While this is paradoxical, even aporetic (though also ingenious and a clever poetic trick), Heinrich's second narrative manoeuvre does considerable damage to the Arthurian system, as well as to Arthurian luck. The problem lies in the fact that luck, which is epitomized by an allegorical symbol, can leave the allegorical sphere and become an object of the "real" world. Allegorical objects in a non-allegorical setting are constantly in danger of being lost, stolen or damaged. This is exactly what happens in the *Crône*, and on several occasions. In allegorical terms, we might wonder how Gawein could ever win his fight against Fimbeus, who is wearing the belt with the lucky stone. Or we might wonder how the Arthurian court could lose luck on between two and four occasions. It is, however, unsurprising that a magic object should be partially damaged (the belt) or that magic objects can be stolen. If the allegorical symbol becomes a magic object, then it is transferrable, but not only from the allegorical to the literal dimension, also between owners. The more luck imbued in an allegorical object, the more stable it seems to be. However the more such objects are transferred into a non-allegorical narrative dimension, the more flexible they become. The absolute narrative assurance of Arthurian luck, in other words, is in its radical destabilization (cf. Kaminski 2005).

3 Enhancement and subversion

It would be easy to add further examples, but in a deeper sense most of the narrative phenomena are alike: Heinrich von dem Türlin works hard to make the Arthurian court an ideal one. He does this by adapting and amplifying common narrative structures and motifs. In doing so, however, he exaggerates poetic techniques, so that he does not only tell the best of all possible Arthurian romances, with the best of all possible kings and the best of all possible knights, but implicitly also allows space for their exact opposites. The tests of valour superficially expose the perfection of the protagonists, but in the way that Heinrich tells them, it is the losers that gain the narrative attention. The allegorization of Arthurian luck simultaneously embeds it deep into the narrative texture, but the more Heinrich exploits this semi-allegorical technique, the more he undermines what the allegory should establish.

To a certain extent, the reasons for these paradoxes are systematic. Excessive praise of some selected characters inevitably outclasses others while, if luck is embedded in a tangible object, it is subject to bargaining and robbery. However, what is noteworthy about Heinrich's conception is that he does not invest any poetic energy in sugar-coating these contradictions. On the contrary, all of the narrative details in the *Crône* seem to revel in inherent subversion. All of the paradoxes and aporias addressed above seem thoroughly intentional, precisely as if the *Crône* was simply about foregrounding them.

This poetic principle is not limited to the issue of Arthurian idealism. It encompasses nearly all aspects of the text. At this point, it is important to discuss the three so-called *Wunderketten* (cf. Wyss 1980) of the *Crône*. These wonders – just like the bridges in Chrétien's *Chevalier de la charrette* – function primarily as accessories of liminal situations. The first *Wunderkette* moves Gawein into the allegorical district around Saelde, while the second leads him back into Arthurian "normality". The third, meanwhile, transports him to the Grail Castle; return transport is not necessary, as Gawein releases the pseudo-zombies around the Grail from their miserable existence – a marvellous parody on *Perceval/Parzival* – and thereby destroys the Otherworld that the *Wunderkette* had led him into. However, the depictions of these three *Wunderketten* are of such length, and so fascinating, that the reader or listener easily misses their macrostructural function. Gawein, and with him the reader or listener, is magnetized by the surreal tableaux, but he never takes his time to reflect on them, simply riding on to the next example of phantasmagoric scenery (cf. Däumer 2010). The fact that the *Wunderketten* are pathways into Otherworlds gets completely lost. The *limes*, in the end, is more attractive than the realm it encloses.

I suggest that this is where the key to the cases mentioned above lies. The *Wunderketten* are undoubtedly the most aesthetic passages of the text. But is not vice – in an aesthetic sense – more thrilling than virtue, and is not a lack of luck a more compelling narrative topic than everlasting luck? Heinrich puts to the test several ambitious, and occasionally rather elegant, methods of narrating perfection (cf. Knapp 1977). But in their installation, the means often extend beyond their purpose, thus giving Heinrich's *Crône* the narrative flexibility it needs. I am tempted to consider this strategy deliberate. The verve injected by Heinrich speaks against mere coincidence. One of the consequences of this multiple (narrato-) logical collapse is an unbridled lust for narration, which unhinges itself from the idealistic restrictions that Heinrich establishes and then, somewhat ironically, avoids. It is no wonder that it is Kay who becomes – at least in the scenes at the Arthurian court – a third protagonist (besides Gawein and Artus), and that the *Crône* does not come to an end before Kay is rescued and has returned to the court. The final return of a hero is reserved here for the anti-hero of Arthurian literature. The stylistic driver of these poetic paradoxes is Heinrich's usage of the Middle High German language. It imitates the oscillation between idealism and its narrative decomposition by alternating between stark digressions and quick-moving episodes that lead the reader or listener through the narrated world in the style of a fast-cut movie.

It is no surprise at all that this enigmatic mixture of idealistic gravity and impish deconstruction has become a primary subject for study recently. For a long time the *Crône* was considered to be difficult: too confused, too bawdy, too shrill. But, at least since the 1970s, it is exactly this element of the text that has given it a prominent position in Arthurian studies and made it a kind of academic cult romance (cf. Cormeau 1977; Jillings 1980; Mentzel-Reuters 1988; Meyer 1994; Bleumer 1997; Keller 1997; Gutwald 2000; Stein 2000; Shockey 2002; Thomas 2002; Vollmann 2008).

We should not forget, however, that this energetic narrative structure represents but one facet of the piece. Heinrich intended to forge an Arthurian crown, and it would be too simplistic to regard the *Crône* merely as a matter of parody. It is not only the tectonic architecture of the text that drives towards this purpose. Heinrich also emphasizes it clearly in his epilogue (in the passage cited at the beginning of this article). In the end, both sides of the coin are misleading insofar as Heinrich reaches his intended purpose in macrostructural terms, while at the same time deconstructing it through the sheer level of narrative detail. Hence, a better description for the poetic tension of this extraordinary hybrid of perfection and persiflage may be found in the final lines that Heinrich writes immediately prior to his epilogue:

> Die auentùre ich hie la.
> Ob ich halt hette zü sagen,
> Das wolt ich darvmb vertagen,
> Das alle auentùre
> Von Gaweins tùre
> Sagent. Wie vil sin sij,
> Was töhte denn swaches bly
> So wol gesmidter krone,
> Die edel gestein vil schone
> Jn golde gezieret hat,
> Als es kunst vnd witze rat
> An dem adel bekennen kan?
> Wùrt vermischet ettwa dar an
> Ein blúme ader ein bild,
> Das es tumben lùten wild
> Jst zü bedrahten vnd zů sehen –
> Das villicht mag geschehen,
> Ob es zü tieff ergraben was –,
> Vnd wil fùr swaches glasz
> Jr edele gesteine kiesen:
> Was mag sie daran verliesen,
> Ader der meister, der sie hat gesmiedt?

Da wùrt niht wan jhener mit
Bedrogen, den sie kostet. (ll. 29910–29933)
[And thus the story ends. Even if I had more to say, I would keep it to myself, since all adventures tell of Gawein's excellence. No matter how many there are, it is not fitting to add base lead to such a well-crafted crown, which has embellished beautiful gems by setting them in gold, as art and skill make possible with precious stones. Should a flower or a figure be mixed in here and there, so that simple, uncouth people may regard it as wild – which might easily happen if the engraving is too deep – and should they think the jewels nothing but cheap glass, what has the crown, or the master who made it, lost as a result? No one else is deceived but he who looks at it (or: he who pays for it).]

References

Baisch, Martin. *"Welt ir: er vervellet / Wellent ir: er ist genesen!* Zur Figur Keies in Heinrichs von dem Türlin *Diu Crône." Aventiuren des Geschlechts. Modelle von Männlichkeit in der Literatur des 13. Jahrhunderts.* Ed. Martin Baisch et al. Aventiuren 1. Göttingen: V&R University Press, 2003. 155–180.
Besamusca, Bart. "Characters and Narrators as Interpreters of Fidelity Tests in Medieval Arthurian Fiction." *Neophilologus* 94 (2010): 289–299.
Bleumer, Hartmut. *Die* Crone *Heinrichs von dem Türlin. Form-Erfahrung und Konzeption eines späten Artusromans.* MTU 112. Tübingen: Niemeyer, 1997.
Boor, Helmut de. "Fortuna in mittelhochdeutscher Dichtung, insbesondere in der *Crône* des Heinrich von dem Türlin." *Verbum et signum. Beiträge zur mediävistischen Bedeutungsforschung. Studien zur Semantik und Sinntradition im Mittelalter. Fs. für Friedrich Ohly, Vol. 2.* Ed. Hans Fromm, Wolfgang Harms and Uwe Ruberg. Munich: Fink, 1975. 311–328.
Claassens, Geert, and Fritz Peter Knapp. "Gauvainromane." *Höfischer Roman in Vers und Prosa.* Ed. René Pérennec and Elisabeth Schmid. GLMF 5. Berlin and New York: De Gruyter, 2010. 249–310.
Cormeau, Christoph. "Fortuna und andere Mächte im Artusroman." *Fortuna.* Ed. Walter Haug and Burghart Wachinger. Fortuna Vitrea 15. Tübingen: Niemeyer, 1995. 23–33.
Cormeau, Christoph."Zur Gattungsentwicklung des Artusromans nach Wolframs *Parzival." Spätmittelalterliche Artusliteratur. Ein Symposion der neusprachlichen Philologien auf der Generalversammlung der Görres-Gesellschaft Bonn, 25.–29.9.1982.* Ed. Karl Heinz Göller. Beiträge zur englischen und amerikanischen Literatur 3. Paderborn and Vienna: Schöningh, 1984. 119–131.
Cormeau, Christoph. Wigalois *und Diu Crône. Zwei Kapitel zur Gattungsgeschichte des nachklassischen Aventiureromans.* MTU 57. Munich: Artemis, 1977.
Däumer, Matthias. "'Hje kam von sinen augen/ Das wunderlich taugen': Überlegungen zur Sinnesregie in den Wunderketten- und Gralspassagen der *Krone* Heinrichs von dem Türlin." *Artushof und Artusliteratur.* Ed. Matthias Bäumer, Cora Dietl and Friedrich Wolfzettel. Schriften der Internationalen Artusgesellschaft 7. Berlin and New York: De Gruyter, 2010. 215–235.

Ebenbauer, Alfred. "Fortuna und Artushof. Bemerkungen zum 'Sinn' der *Krone* Heinrichs von dem Türlin." *Österreichische Literatur zur Zeit der Babenberger.* Ed. Alfred Ebenbauer, Fritz Peter Knapp and Ingrid Strasser. Wiener Arbeiten zur germanischen Altertumskunde und Philologie 10. Vienna: Halosar, 1977. 25–49.

Felder, Gudrun. *Kommentar zur* Crône *Heinrichs von dem Türlin.* Berlin and New York: De Gruyter, 2006.

Gutwald, Thomas. *Schwank und Artushof. Komik unter den Bedingungen höfischer Interaktion in der* Crône *des Heinrich von dem Türlin.* Mikrokosmos 55. Frankfurt a. M. et al.: Lang, 2000.

Heinrich von dem Türlin. *Die Krone: Unter Mitarbeit von Alfred Ebenbauer †.* Trans. Florian Kragl. Berlin, Boston: De Gruyter, 2012a.

Heinrich von dem Türlin. *Diu Crône. Kritische mittelhochdeutsche Leseausgabe mit Erläuterungen.* Ed. Gudrun Felder. Berlin, Boston: De Gruyter, 2012b.

Heinrich von dem Türlin. *Die Krone (Verse 1–12281). Nach der Handschrift 2779 der Österreichischen Nationalbibliothek nach Vorarbeiten von Alfred Ebenbauer, Klaus Zatloukal und Host P. Pütz.* Ed. Fritz Peter Knapp und Manuela Niesner. ATB 112. Tübingen: Niemeyer, 2000.

Heinrich von dem Türlin. *Die Krone (Verse 12282–30042). Nach der Handschrift Cod. Pal. germ. 374 der Universitätsbibliothek Heidelberg nach Vorarbeiten von Fritz Peter Knapp und Klaus Zatloukal.* Ed. Alfred Ebenbauer and Florian Kragl. ATB 118. Tübingen: Niemeyer, 2005.

Heinrich von dem Türlin. *The Crown: A Tale of Sir Gawein and King Arthur's Court.* Trans. J.W. Thomas. Lincoln, NE and London: University of Nebraska Press, 1989.

Jillings, Lewis. Diu Crône *of Heinrich von dem Türlein: The Attempted Emancipation of Secular Narrative.* GAG 258. Göppingen: Kümmerle, 1980.

Kaminski, Nicola. *"Wâ ez sich êrste ane vienc, Daz ist ein teil unkunt". Abgründiges Erzählen in der* Krone *Heinrichs von dem Türlin.* Heidelberg: Winter, 2005.

Keller, Johannes. Diu Crône *Heinrichs von dem Türlin: Wunderketten, Gral und Tod.* Deutsche Literatur von den Anfängen bis 1700 25. Bern et al.: Lang, 1997.

Knapp, Fritz Peter. "Virtus und Fortuna in der *Krône.* Zur Herkunft der ethischen Grundthese Heinrichs von dem Türlin." *Zeitschrift für deutsches Altertum und deutsche Literatur* 106 (1977): 253–265.

Kratz, Bernd. "Zur Kompositionstechnik Heinrichs von dem Türlin." *Amsterdamer Beiträge zur älteren Germanistik* 5 (1973): 141–153.

Mentzel-Reuters, Arno. *Vröude. Artusbild, Fortuna- und Gralkonzeption in der* Crône *des Heinrich von dem Türlin als Verteidigung des höfischen Lebensideals.* Europäische Hochschulschriften. Reihe I: Deutsche Sprache und Literatur 1134. Frankfurt a. M. et al.: Lang, 1988.

Meyer, Matthias. *Die Verfügbarkeit der Fiktion. Interpretationen und poetologische Untersuchungen zum Artusroman und zur aventiurehaften Dietrichepik des 13. Jahrhunderts.* GRM-Beiheft 12. Heidelberg: Winter, 1994.

Schmid, Elisabeth. "Text über Texte. Zur *Crône* des Heinrich von dem Türlîn." *Germanisch-Romanische Monatsschrift, neue Folge* 44 (1994): 266–287.

Schonert, Christiane. *Figurenspiele. Identität und Rollen Keies in Heinrichs von dem Türlin* Crône. Philologische Studien und Quellen 217. Berlin: Schmidt, 2009.

Shockey, Gary. *Homo viator, Katabasis and Landscapes: A Comparison of Wolfram von Eschenbach's* Parzival *and Heinrich von dem Türlin's* Diu Crône. GAG 674. Göppingen: Kümmerle, 2002.

Stein, Peter. *Integration – Variation – Destruktion. Die* Crone *Heinrichs von dem Türlin innerhalb der Gattungsgeschichte des deutschen Artusromans.* Deutsche Literatur von den Anfängen bis 1700 32. Bern et al.: Lang, 2000.

Störmer-Caysa, Uta. "Zeitkreise in der *Crône* Heinrichs von dem Türlin." *Kulturen des Manuskriptzeitalters. Ergebnisse der Amerikanisch-Deutschen Arbeitstagung an der Universität Göttingen vom 17. bis 20. Oktober 2002.* Ed. Arthur Groos and Hans-Jochen Schiewer. TRAST 1. Göttingen: V&R University Press, 2004. 321–340.

Störmer-Caysa, Uta. "Der Gürtel des Fimbeus und die Chronologie. Versuch über die lineare Zeit in der *Crône* Heinrichs von dem Türlin." *Literatur – Geschichte – Literaturgeschichte. Beiträge zur mediävistischen Literaturwissenschaft. Festschrift für Volker Honemann zum 60. Geburtstag.* Ed. Nine Miedema and Rudolf Suntrup. Frankfurt a. M. et al.: Lang, 2003. 209–224.

Suerbaum, Almut. "*Entrelacement*? Narrative Technique in Heinrich von dem Türlîn's *Diu Crône.*" *Oxford German Studies* 34 (2005): 5–18.

Thomas, Neil. Diu Crône *and the Medieval Arthurian Cycle.* Arthurian Studies 50. Cambridge: D.S. Brewer, 2002.

Vollmann, Justin. "Krise des Individuums – Krise der Gesellschaft. Artusroman und Artushof in der *Krone* Heinrichs von dem Türlin." *Artushof und Artusliteratur.* Ed. Matthias Bäumer, Cora Dietl and Friedrich Wolfzettel. Schriften der Internationalen Artusgesellschaft 7. Berlin and New York: De Gruyter, 2010. 237–251.

Vollmann, Justin. *Das Ideal des irrenden Lesers. Ein Wegweiser durch die* Krone *Heinrichs von dem Türlin.* Bibliotheca Germanica 53. Tübingen and Basel: Francke, 2008.

Wyss, Ulrich. "Die Wunderketten in der *Crône.*" *Die mittelalterliche Literatur in Kärnten. Vorträge des Symposions in St. Georgen/Längsee vom 8. bis 13.9.1980.* Ed. Peter Krämer. Wiener Arbeiten zur germanischen Altertumskunde und Philologie 16. Vienna: Halosar, 1980. 269–291.

Zach, Christine. *Die Erzählmotive der* Crône *Heinrichs von dem Türlin und ihre altfranzösischen Quellen. Ein kommentiertes Register.* Passauer Schriften zur Sprache und Literatur 5. Passau: Rothe, 1990.

Sofia Lodén

Herr Ivan: Chivalric Values and Negotiations of Identity

Le Chevalier au lion has sometimes been described as the romance that marks the peak of Chrétien de Troyes' literary career: according to Jean Frappier (1969, 11–12), it contains all the elements of a courtly romance. Concrete examples of its success are the many translations into other languages. At the beginning of the fourteenth century, Queen Eufemia of Norway (1270–1312, r. 1300–1312) commissioned a translation of *Le Chevalier au lion* into Swedish.[1] This translation, *Herr Ivan*, was written in verse and was followed by two other translations: *Hertig Fredrik av Normandie*, which is said to be a translation from a German text with a French origin (none of these texts are preserved, however) and *Flores och Blanzeflor*, a translation from the Old Norse version of the French *Le Conte de Floire et Blanchefleur*. These three Swedish texts are commonly known as the *Eufemiavisor* [Songs of Eufemia].[2] The main source of the Swedish translation was Chrétien's romance, at the same time as the Old Norse prose translation, *Ívens saga*, from the thirteenth century, functioned as a secondary source.[3]

This essay aims to explore how Yvain's chivalric identity was manipulated in the Swedish translation *Herr Ivan*. I will look closer at the episodes in the French and Swedish texts that depict how Yvain loses his chivalric identity and goes mad: first, when he realizes that he has broken his word to Laudine and is rejected by her, and then when he, accompanied by his lion, is reminded of his misery at the spring where his adventures had started. I will show that the Swedish translator

---

1 Eufemia was of German origin and it is possible that she was influenced by the richly developed German tradition of Arthurian romance.

2 The *Eufemiavisor* have interested several scholars lately. See for example Ferm et al. (2015).

3 The question of the sources of *Herr Ivan* is examined thoroughly in my doctoral dissertation (Lodén 2012). *Ívens saga* was written at the same time as a group of other Old Norse translations of romances. Five translations refer to King Hákon Hákonarson (King of Norway 1217–1263) as their commissioner: *Tristrams saga* (*Tristan et Yseut*), *Ívens saga* (*Le Chevalier au lion*), Möttuls saga (*Le Mantel mautaillé*), *Elíss saga* (*Élie de Saint-Gilles*) and *Strengleikar* (Marie de France's *Lais*). On this subject, see Eriksen (2014, 106–107). Also other translations, like *Erex saga* (*Erec et Enide*), *Parcevals saga* (*Le Conte du Graal*) and *Karlamagnús saga* (a compilation of different *chansons de geste*), belong to the same translation context, even though they do not mention King Hákon.

Sofia Lodén (Stockholm University)

DOI 10.1515/9783110432466-022

shifts the focus from love to honour (cf. Hinton, *infra*), as well as briefly discuss the reasons behind this shift. Even though the Old Norse *Ívens saga* helped the Swedish translator in his work with certain passages – especially the prologue, but also other parts of the text – it is improbable that it influenced this rewriting of chivalric values significantly.[4] I will, therefore, only make limited references to this text.[5]

The question of marriage is at the centre of Chrétien's romances. But whereas *Erec et Enide* seems to resolve how chivalric adventure can be reconciled with love for a lady, *Le Chevalier au lion* does not present any real solution to this. The sinister beginning of the love story between Yvain and Laudine sets the tone: Yvain falls in love with Laudine just after having killed her husband and needs the help of the lady's maiden, Lunete, in order to convince Laudine about his love. Once they are a couple, he fails to keep his promise to her and stays away for longer than a year. It is only through the cunning intervention of Lunete, once again, that the two of them finally marry.

In *Le Chevalier au lion* and other romances, the question of marriage is intimately linked with that of identity, which is another central theme in Arthurian literature and one which has fascinated scholars for a long time.[6] To conceal and reveal identity is a common theme (Lacy 2005, 374) and anonymity is a frequent topic (Gordon 2008). In Chrétien de Troyes' *oeuvre*, for example, a central question is how to reconcile the subjective and objective identity: "He [i.e. Chrétien] often focuses, in fact, on the irony generated by the discrepancy between what a character thinks he is and what others think he is." (Lacy 2005, 366) Perceval offers an excellent example of this. For Yvain, his identity is partly defined by the lion that accompanies him: from the moment the knight rescues it from the serpent, Yvain is identified as the knight of the lion. But whereas the animal functions as a marker of something constant in his identity as it is seen by others, his relationship and marriage to Laudine stretches the bounds of who he really is.

---

4 The prologue is analyzed in Lodén (2012, 56–62).

5 It should be noted that the manuscript situation of the Old Norse text is particularly complicated, since the saga is not only preserved in later copies, but these copies are also Icelandic and not Norwegian, as would have been their lost original. This makes the comparisons with *Herr Ivan*, written before these preserved copies, tricky.

6 For a wider discussion of identity in medieval romance, see Gordon (2008), Hardman (2002), Lacy (2005) and Maddox (2000).

1 A specular encounter at the court

In a study on medieval French literature, Donald Maddox has drawn attention to what he calls "specular encounters" – encounters in which the protagonist is confronted with a character that reflects a negative side of him: "featured individuals are placed before a mirror that reflects unsettling circumstances and aspects of selfhood." (Maddox 2000, 201) According to Maddox, this type of encounter is the centrepiece of both Marie de France's *Lais* and Chrétien's romances. In *Le Chevalier au lion*, the encounter in question takes place when Yvain has failed to return to Laudine within a year and Laudine sends a female messenger to King Arthur's court, where Yvain is to be found:

> Yvain must contend with public humiliation by proxy, and after this devastating specular encounter he takes refuge in wilderness, where he regresses in distinct phases, from abjection and self-hatred to loss of memory and predatory subsistence on raw meat. (Maddox 2000, 86)

There are some major differences between the messenger's speech in *Le Chevalier au lion* and *Herr Ivan*, when it comes to both its content and its role in the bigger narrative. To begin with, nothing in Chrétien's romance is said about the messenger in order to introduce her; we only learn: "il [Yvain] vit venir / une damoisele a droiture" (ll. 2704–2705) [[he] saw a damsel coming straight towards them].[7] *Herr Ivan* adds the following about the maiden: "hon var baþe høvisk ok bald" (l. 2125) [she was both courtly and splendid].[8] The statement tones down any negative expectation.[9] In the French text, Yvain is condemned even before the maiden has started her real speech:

> Si dist que sa dame salue
> Le roy et monseigneur Gavin
> Et tous les autres fors Yvain,
> Le desloial, le jangleour,
> Le menchongnier, le guileour,
> Qui l'a gabee et descheüe. (ll. 2716–2721)

---

7 The quotations from *Le Chevalier au lion* follow Hult's edition (Chrétien de Troyes 1994). All translations of the French romance come from Kibler's version (Chrétien de Troyes 1991).
8 The quotations and translations of *Herr Ivan* follow Williams and Palmgren (1999).
9 In *Ívens saga*, she is said to be fair: "ein fríð mær" (66) [a fair maiden], which may have influenced the Swedish translator. The quotations and translations of *Ívens saga* follow Kalinke (1999).

[She said that her lady sent greetings to the king and my lord Gawain and all the others except Yvain, that liar, that deceiver, that unfaithful cheat, for he had beguiled and deceived her.]

There is no such passage in *Herr Ivan*, where it is only said that the maiden spoke in a strange way: "sva underlika hon til orþa fik" (l. 2128) [she began to speak quite strangely].[10] Thus, although she is a courteous character according to the translator, her behaviour is immediately distanced from courtliness. Then, in Chrétien's text, the maiden's speech is introduced by a passage dedicated to the nature of love and the way in which Yvain has stolen Laudine's heart. In *Herr Ivan*, there is no such passage, but the knight is compared to a thief more generally: "han ær værre æn nokor þiuf" (l. 2140) [he is worse than any thief].[11] The same goes for the passage that follows in the French text, which describes the suffering that Yvain has caused his lady. The Swedish text omits all references to Laudine's pain and only establishes: "hon varþer þik aldrigh af hiærtæ hus" (l. 2149) [she will never be devoted to you in her heart].[12]

As shown by Maddox, the maiden's speech marks a turning point in the narrative: from now on, Yvain's identity as a knight will be tested continuously. In the French romance, her speech is followed by a passage about Yvain's suffering:

Et ses anuis tous jours li croist
Et quanquë il voit li encroist
Et quanquë il ot li ennuie:
Mis se voudroit estre a la fuie
Tous seus en si sauvage terre
Quë on ne le seüst ou querre,
N'omme ne femme n'i eüst,
Ne nuls de lui riens ne seüst
Nient plus que s'il fust en abisme.
Ne het tant riens com li meïsmes,
Ne ne set a qui se confort
De lui meïsmes qu'il a mort.
Mix ameroit vis erragier
Quë il ne s'en peüst vengier
De lui qui joie s'est tolue. (ll. 2781–2795)
[And his anguish grew constantly, for everything he saw added to his grief and everything he heard troubled him; he wanted to flee entirely alone to a land so wild that no one could

---

10 This verse has no equivalent in *Ívens saga*.
11 Also the maiden in *Ívens saga* refers to the knight as a thief: "þú ert undirhyggjumaðr, svikall ok þjófr" (66) [you are a deceitful man, a traitor and thief].
12 *Ívens saga* does not make the same type of omissions, but follows Chrétien more closely.

follow or find him, and where no man or woman alive could hear any more news of him than if he had gone to perdition. He hated nothing so much as himself and did not know whom to turn to for comfort now that he was the cause of his own death. But he would rather lose his mind than fail to take revenge upon himself, who had ruined his own happiness.]

The Swedish translator rewrites important parts of Chrétien's account:

Hærra Ivan sara i hans hærta sveþ;
þæn riddare hiolt sik svo ømkelik;
han vare þa hælder døþer æn qvik
ok sva langt þæþan komin bort
þæt ænin finge til hans sport,
hvarte vin æller frænde,
at ængin man honum kænde.
Han haver nu mist al þæn æra
þær han i væruldinne hafþe bæra
ok þær til baþe vit ok sinne;
slikt fanger man for stolta qvinnæ;
þera hoghmoþ ær alt ofbald,
þær þe giva þolik þiænista giald. (ll. 2168–2180)
[Sir Ivan's heart ached grievously; the knight behaved quite pitifully. He would rather have been dead than alive and so far away from there that nobody would know his whereabouts, neither friend nor kinsman, and that nobody knew him. Now he has lost all the honour he had borne on earth and furthermore both his wits and mind. That is what happens because of haughty women; their arrogance is much too great, when they give such reward for service.]

Even though the knight suffers in both texts, his grief is not given the same explanation. While the French Yvain wants to hide from everyone because of his great pain, the Swedish Ivan prefers to leave the court because of the shame that he feels after having been rejected by his lady. According to Chrétien, Yvain has lost his *joie*, whereas the Swedish translator chooses to refer to the loss of Ivan's *æra* [honour]. The self-hatred that is depicted in the French passage has also been toned down; nothing is said about the knight's wish to take revenge upon himself. On the contrary, the translator turns Ivan into a victim of female arrogance, something that has no equivalent in the French romance.[13]

---

13 Even though *Ívens saga* abbreviates, it does not make these modifications: the saga does not refer to honour or female arrogance. Just as in Chrétien's text, the knight is said to hate himself: "Hataði hann þá ekki jafnmjök sem sjálfan sik" (68) [He now hated no one as much as himself].

2 Naked in the woods

After having listened to the maiden's speech, Yvain flees the civilized world of the court and loses his identity as a courteous knight: he runs into the wild forest, where he becomes unhinged, tears off his clothes and lives naked like a savage, before finally being found and rescued by a group of courtly women. The Swedish translation follows the overarching lines of this episode, at the same time as it makes significant modifications. In the French text, Chrétien briefly tells us that Yvain lives on raw meat from animals that he has hunted:

> Les bestes par le bois aguete
> Et lors ochist, et si menjue
> La venoison trestoute crue. (ll. 2824–2826)
> [He stalked wild animals in the forest and killed them and ate their raw flesh.]

In *Herr Ivan*, the text reads as follows:

> ok skøt þær diur til sinna føþa
> – han fik þem þo eigh utan møþo –
> ok at þem ra ræt sum en høk –
> han hafþe hvarte yrter ælla løk.
> Iak haver eigh annat sannare hørt,
> hans ætan var fyr alt annorlund giørt.
> Han lifþe þær længe for utan brøþ
> ok þolde þa baþe hunger ok nøþ. (ll. 2207–2214)
> [shooting animals for his food – yet he did not get them without effort – and ate them raw just like a hawk; he had neither herbs nor onions. I have never heard anything more true; in former days his food was prepared quite differently. He lived there long without bread, enduring both hunger and distress.]

On the one hand, the translator emphasizes the effort behind the hunting; on the other hand, he adds a reference to the knight's previous life at court, where food was properly cooked with spices and where bread was a natural part of the meal, thus underlining the change of lifestyle and identity.[14] This type of reminder of the knight's past returns later in the text: "Man haver þæt stundom fyrra set,/ hans ætande tiþ var bæter ret." (ll. 2235–2236) [On occasion one formerly saw that his meals were better prepared.]

---

14 *Ívens saga* does not make these additions, but follows Chrétien: "skaut sér dýr, ok át hrátt kjöt þeira" (68) [[he] shot animals and ate their meat raw].

When the Lady of Noiroson and her maidens find the knight asleep in the forest, the maiden who first takes a look at him does not recognize him immediately because of his nakedness:

> Ja l'avoit ele tant veü
> Que tost l'eüst reconneü
> Së il fust de si riche atour
> Com ele l'ot veü maint jour. (ll. 2897–2900)
> [yet she had seen him so often that she would have recognized him immediately had he been as richly attired as he had been so frequently in the past.]

As pointed out by Norris Lacy (2005, 368), clothing thus becomes intimately linked to chivalric identity:

> Although Chrétien might reasonably have related this non-recognition to the change in his [Yvain's] physical state, the poet chooses instead to emphasize the absence of his customary attire. Thus, his undoubtedly long and unruly hair and beard and his generally unkempt appearance are less an obstacle than the absence of his customary clothing. Just as clothes make the man, nakedness makes him unrecognizable. Clothing is not only an index of social or economic status, but also an essential key to his very name and identity.

In the Swedish text, however, the knight's nakedness does not seem enough to make him unrecognizable, but the following comment is added about his change of colour: "hans huþ var svart, þæt sæghir iak þik,/ þy var han eigh kænnelik." (ll. 2275–2276) [His skin was dark, I tell you; hence he was not recognizable].[15] It is finally through a scar on his face, "une plaie qu'il ot el vis" (l. 2904) [a scar he had on his face], that the knight is recognized. In *Herr Ivan*, it is added where the scar came from: "et ar þæt han hafþe fangit i striþ" (l. 2284) [a scar of a wound that he had received in a battle].[16] Once again, the narrator chooses to stress the protagonist's knightly origin.

The maiden is then astonished to find Yvain in such a sorry state and rides back to her lady, saying:

> Dame, jë ay Yvain trouvé,
> Le chevalier mix esprouvé
> Del mondë, et mix entichié;
> Mais je ne sai par quel pechié

---

15 *Ívens saga* presents a third version of the passage: "Var hann þá ólíkr því sem fyrr var hann" (68) [He was at this point very unlike what he had been before].

16 *Ívens saga* once again follows Chrétien: "sárs er hann hafði í andliti" (68) [a scar that he had on his face].

Est au franc homme meschieü.
Espoir aucun duel a eü
Qui le fait ainsi demener,
C'on puet bien de duel forsener;
Et savoir et veoir puet l'en
Que il n'est mie bien en son sen,
Que ja voir ne li avenist
Que si vilment se contenist
Së il n'eüst le sens perdu. (ll. 2921–2933)
[My lady, I have found Yvain, the most accomplished knight in the world, and the most vir-
tuous; but I do not know what misfortune has befallen the noble man. Perhaps some grief
has caused him to behave in this manner; one can certainly go mad with grief. And one can
clearly see that he is not in his right mind, for truly nothing could have made him behave so
shamefully if he had not lost his mind.]

The passage is modified as follows in *Herr Ivan*:

Min kæra frugha, iak sæghir sva,
han var en fromare æn andre tva;
þæt magho fruor ok iomfruor kæra
at han sva ømkelika ligger hæræ,
þæn bæzta riddara man æn fan,
konung Yrians son hærra Ivan.
Iak kan mik eigh þær a forstanda
hvat honum ær nu komit til handa,
utan þæt se for stolta qvinna
at han haver mist baþe vit ok sinne. (ll. 2301–2310)
[My dear lady, I can say he was more capable than two together; ladies and maidens must
regret that he is lying here so pitifully, the best knight ever found, King Yrian's son, Sir Ivan.
I cannot understand what has happened to him, unless for the sake of a noble lady he has
lost both his senses and mind.]

According to the maiden in Chrétien's text, the reason why Yvain has lost his
mind and acts *vilment* [shamefully] must be a great sorrow. In the Swedish text,
the knight's folly is directly linked to a lady.[17] The difference might seem subtle,

---

17 This is not the case in *Ívens saga*: "Frú min,' kvað hún, 'ek hefi fundit herra Íven, þann bezta
riddara er vápn hefir borit. En ek veit eigi fyrir hverja misverka er svá þungliga fallit duganda
manni. Þat grunar mik, at hann hafi ofmikinn harm ok hafi týnt viti sínu, þvíat eigi mundi hann
ella halda sik svá ef hann væri í fullu viti sínu. [...]" (68) ["My lady," she said, "I have found Sir
Íven, the best knight who has ever borne weapons. But I don't know for what misdeed such a
serious misfortune has befallen such a valiant man. I suspect that he suffers excessive sorrow
and has lost his senses, for else he would not comport himself in such a manner if he had full
use of his reason"].

but does indeed reflect an ideological discrepancy between the two texts. While the French Yvain suffers out of love, the Swedish Ivan needs his lady in order to increase his knightly honour.

3 Regained identity

In order to help Yvain, the Lady of Noiroson gives one of her maidens a magic ointment that should be put on him – an ointment that she had once received from Morgan le Fay, King Arthur's sister whose magical powers are well known in Arthurian literature. The lady also procures new clothes for the knight: "Robe vaire, cote et mantel,/ Li fait porter, de soie en graine" (ll. 2974–2975) [She sent along a bright-coloured gown, a coat, and a mantle of red-dyed silk]. In *Herr Ivan*, nothing is said about the colour or material of the clothes, whereas their value and suitability for a knight are stressed: "Hon lot hænne rik klæþe fa/ þær en riddara matte mæþ ærom i ga" (ll. 2351–2352) [She let her have costly clothes, which a knight could wear with honor].[18]

When the knight wakes up in the forest, the maiden has already treated him with the ointment without him having noticed. He puts on the clothes that she has secretly put next to him and then finds the maiden, who brings him back to the lady's castle where their female care helps him to regain fully his identity as a knight:

> Et Monseigneur Yvain aaisent
> De tout che püent et sevent,
> Si le baignent et son chief levent
> Et le font rere et rouongnier,
> Car on li peüst apongnier
> Le barbe a plain poing seur le faiche.
> Ne veut chose c'on ne li faiche:
> S'il veut armes, on li atourne;
> S'il veut chevax, on li sejourne,
> Grant et isnel, fort et hardi. (ll. 3132–3141)
> [and [they] proceeded to look to my lord Yvain's comfort in every way they could: they bathed him, washed his hair, and had him shaved and trimmed, for one could have grabbed a whole fistful of beard on his face. Whatever he wished they did for him: if he wanted armour, it was laid out for him; if he wanted a horse, a large and handsome, strong and hardy one awaited him.]

---

18 *Ívens saga* only says: "Hún fekk henni nýja gangveru af skarlati ok hin smæstu línklæði" (70) [She gave her new clothes of scarlet and the finest linen].

Even though the Swedish translation of the passage gives fewer details, it follows the general lines of the French romance:

> iomfruan monde til hærra Ivans ga;
> hon giorþe sum I maghin høra
> hon lot honum lut ok karbaþ gøra
> ok skipaþe honum ræt alla maka
> ok skar hans har ok lot han raka.
> Þa han krafþe et ælla tu,
> þa bøþ hon honum væl siæx ælla siu. (ll. 2486–2492)[19]
> [The maiden went to Sir Ivan; she did as you will hear: soap and a hot bath she prepared for him and arranged all sorts of comfort for him and cut his hair and had him shaved. When he asked for one or two things, she offered him at least six or seven.]

4 Yvain's second bout of madness

Later in the narrative, when Yvain has rescued the lion from the dragon, he arrives by mere chance at the spring where his adventures once began. He is reminded of the loss of his lady and becomes miserable once again:

> La par poi ne se forsena
> Mesire Yvains autre feïe,
> Quant le fontaine ot aprochie
> Et le perron et le chapele.
> Mil fois las et dolent se claime,
> Et chiet pasmés, tant fu dolans (ll. 3488–3493)
> [Alas, my lord Yvain nearly lost his mind again as he neared the spring, the stone, and the chapel. A thousand times he moaned and sighed, and was so grief-stricken he fell in a faint.]

This time, the Swedish translator also mentions the knight's misery, by referring to his lost joy:

> Þa hærra Ivan kældona sa,
> þa mælte han ok saghþe sva:
> "Alla mina glæþi haver iak hær mist,
> hvat skal mik længer lifsins frist?
> Þæn æræ iak hær forþum fik,
> mæþ sorgh hon braþelik mik forgik."

---

19 *Ívens saga* abbreviates the passage: "ok kendi stólpann ok þegar fell á hann svá mikil æði, at hann fell náliga í óvit" (74) [and he recognized the pillar and at once such great madness overcame him that he nearly lost consciousness].

Af anger fik han sva mykin qvala,
han fiol i ovit ok la i dvala (ll. 2815–2822)
[When Sir Ivan saw the spring, he spoke and said: "All my joy I have lost here; what is the use of living on? The honor I had in times past has passed sadly and rapidly from me." He was so troubled by his misery that he fainted and lay unconscious.]

Nevertheless, the joy in question does not seem to refer to the love for the lady but rather the honour that she once represented and that is now gone.

When Yvain faints, his sword slips and pierces his neck, which starts to bleed. Seeing this, the lion believes his master to be dead and tries to kill itself out of sadness. Yvain wakes up just in time and the lion's suicidal efforts cease. However, the knight's misery remains just as severe:

[...] Que fait qu'il ne se tue,
Cis las qui joie s'est tolue?
Que fais je, las, qui ne m'ochi?
Comment puis je demourer chi
Et veoir les choses ma dame?
En mon cors pour quoi arreste ame?
Que fait ame en si dolens cors? (ll. 3527–3533)
["Why does the wretch who's destroyed his own happiness not kill himself?" he asked. "Why do I, wretch that I am, not kill myself? How can I stay here and behold my lady's possessions? Why does my soul remain in my body? What good is a soul in such a sad body?"]

Once again, the Swedish translation clearly links the lost joy to a question of honour:

Hvat dugher mik længer for døþin fly!
Iak vil mik dræpa ok gøra sva
mæþan ængin man hær ser up a,
þy at al min glæþi ær nu ænd
ok sarlika mik til sorghina vænd,
æ siþan iak miste þæn høghelik æræ
þær iak hafþe mæþ min hiærtæ kære. (ll. 2862–2868)
[What is the use of fleeing from death! I want to kill myself and do it while no one here is watching, because all my joy has now ended and has sadly turned into sorrow, since I have lost the great honor I had with my heart's beloved.]

It should be noted that the Old Norse translation this time also refers to the loss of honour, which may have influenced the Swedish translator.[20]

The difference between the French and Swedish texts culminates in the last part of the knight's lamentation. *Le Chevalier au lion* says:

> Dont n'ai je chest leon veü
> Qui pour moi a si grant duel fait
> Qu'il se veut m'espee entresait
> Par mi le pis el cors bouter?
> Et je doi le mort refuser
> Qui ai joië a duel changie?
> De moi s'est la joie estrangie.
> Joie? La quels? N'en dirai plus,
> Que che ne porroit dire nus,
> S'ai demandee grant oiseuse.
> De joie fu la plus joieuse
> Chele qui m'iert asseüree,
> Mais mout m'ot petite duree.
> Et qui che pert par son meffait,
> N'est drois que boine aventure ait. (ll. 3544–3558)

[Have I not observed this lion so disconsolate just now on my behalf that it was determined to run my sword through its breast? And so should I, whose joy has changed to grief, fear death? Happiness and all comfort have abandoned me. I'll say no more, because no one could speak of this; I've posed a foolish question. Of all joys, the greatest was the one assured to me; yet it lasted such a little while! And the man who loses such joy by his own mistake has no right to good fortune.]

Whereas Chrétien discusses the nature of joy at length, as well as the consequences when joy is lost, *Herr Ivan* presents a completely different perspective:

> Þæt ær nu min mæsta kæra
> þæn harm þær leonit for mik bæra,
> iak vilde hælder vara døþ
> æn se a hænne þolika nøþ.
> Opinbara iak þæt ter,
> ok vil iak þær til sighia mer,

---

20 *Ívens saga* says: "Til hvers skal ek lifa? Vesall maðr var ek, svá ógeyminn. Hvat skal ek útan drepa mik sjálfr? Ek hefi týnt huggan minni ok fagnaði, ok um snúit af sjálfs míns glæp virðing minni, ok vent tign minni í týning" (74) [For what reason should I live? I was a wretch of a man, so heedless. What am I to do but kill myself? I have lost my consolation and joy, and through my own fault brought down my honor and turned my reputation into loss]. Even though the saga mentions the knight's lost honour, the other quoted passages show that it does not present the same rewriting of chivalric values as *Herr Ivan*.

iak vilde mik siælver fordærvæ,
skulde eigh diævulen siælinæ ærvæ. (ll. 2873–2880)
[My greatest concern is now the sorrow the lion feels for me; I would sooner be dead than see it suffer so. I show it openly and furthermore I want to say, I would kill myself, were not the Devil to inherit my soul.]

In this way, the lady, and the joy that she represented, are not only excluded from the translation, but also replaced by the lion: according to the translator, it is the sight of the lion's suffering that causes the knight's greatest misery.[21] One may, of course, wonder whether this interpretation is a misunderstanding on the part of the translator.[22] However, when analyzed in its textual context, it rather appears to be a conscious rewriting of the love theme. When Chrétien speaks of the joy Yvain had together with the lady, the translator consequently underlines the honour that their marriage would procure. The last verses of the quoted passage therefore reflect the moralizing focus of *Herr Ivan*, according to which suicide should be condemned.

The differences between *Le Chevalier au lion* and *Herr Ivan* must be understood in light of their different literary and historical contexts. The French romance has its roots in a long literary tradition, while the Swedish translation marks the beginnings of a new literary tradition. While we cannot exclude the possibility that similar translations had existed earlier, the *Eufemiavisor* remain the oldest surviving Swedish literary texts; the runic inscriptions and law texts that precede them are not narrative literary texts to the same extent.[23] When Chrétien writes about Yvain's lost joy and suffering, the allusions to the troubadour tradition and the theme of *fin'amor* are obvious. The Swedish translator, on the other hand, does not seem familiar with these references, or at least not interested in them, since he chooses a different interpretation of the knight's suffering: the loss of honour.

As several scholars have shown, *Herr Ivan* has a clearly didactic outlook. Joseph Sullivan (2009, 65) describes it as follows:

---

21 In *Ívens saga*, the knight does not refer to the lion in his speech: "ok vent [...] yndi mitt í angrsemi, líf mitt í leiðindi, hjarta mitt í hugsótt, unnustu mina í <ó>vin, frelsi mitt í friðleysi; eða hví dvel ek at drepa mik?" (74) [and [I have] turned [...] my delight into suffering, my life into loathing, my heart into anxiety, my beloved into my enemy, my freedom into outlawry; why do I delay in killing myself?]
22 The transformation of the role played by the lion is discussed in Lodén (2012, 248–261).
23 See Ferm (2015).

Indeed, its representation of appropriate socio-political conduct within a feudal-courtly milieu likely has much to do with an authorial agenda to educate his Swedish audience, in much the way a manual of conduct might, on how to live successfully in a feudalized world.

The translator's negotiation of the knight's identity is undoubtedly linked to this didactic focus: the poetically sophisticated suffering of the French Yvain is given a concrete interpretation which is centred on the question of marriage and the honour represented by marriage. Nevertheless, the gap between the two texts should not be exaggerated. As I have shown elsewhere, *Herr Ivan* does not misinterpret the French romance but rather interprets it for the sake of intrinsic coherence (Lodén 2012, 278–280). Whereas Chrétien often remains ambiguous, the Swedish translator clarifies sophisticated literary themes such as the role of the courtly adventure, female characters and love, and links them to courtliness and honour. His intent may therefore have been to present an edifying and easily comprehensible picture of the courtly knight to the Swedish readership, to whom King Arthur and his knights must have appeared peripheral. This characterization certainly seems to fit with that requested by Queen Eufemia – a political character that would set an example of courtly behaviour to the public at the Swedish court. But Ivan was just as much a literary character: the relatively new Swedish aristocracy, in essence, needed its own literature, with all of the fitting and appropriate aesthetic ideals and values.

References

Chrétien de Troyes. *Le Chevalier au lion ou Le roman d'Yvain*. Ed. David F. Hult. Paris: Librairie Générale Française, 1994.

Chrétien de Troyes. *Arthurian Romances*. Trans. William W. Kibler. Harmondsworth: Penguin, 1991.

Eriksen, Stefka G. *Writing and Reading in Medieval Manuscript Culture: The Translation and Transmission of the Story of Elye in Old French and Old Norse Literary Contexts*. Turnhout: Brepols, 2014.

Ferm, Olle. "The Emergence of Courtly Literature in Sweden. A Critical Discussion of Swedish Research." *The Eufemiavisor and Courtly Culture: Time, Texts and Cultural Transfer: Papers from a Symposium in Stockholm 11–13 October 2012*. Ed. Olle Ferm, Ingela Hedström, Sofia Lodén, Jonatan Pettersson and Mia Åkestam. Stockholm: Kungl. Vitterhets historie och antikvitets akademien, 2015. 109–120.

Ferm, Olle, Ingela Hedström, Sofia Lodén, Jonatan Pettersson and Mia Åkestam, eds. *The Eufemiavisor and Courtly Culture: Time, Texts and Cultural Transfer: Papers from a Symposium in Stockholm 11–13 October 2012*. Stockholm: Kungl. Vitterhets historie och antikvitets akademien, 2015.

Frappier, Jean. *Étude sur Yvain ou le Chevalier au lion de Chrétien de Troyes*. Paris: Société d'édition d'enseignement supérieur, 1969.

Gordon, Sarah E. "The Man with No Name: Identity in French Arthurian Verse Romance." *Arthuriana* 18 (2008): 69–81.

Hardman, Philippa, ed. *The Matter of Identity in Medieval Romance*. Rochester, NY: D.S. Brewer 2002.

Kalinke, Marianne E., ed. and trans. *Ívens saga*. Cambridge: D.S. Brewer, 1999.

Lacy, Norris J. "On Armor and Identity: Chrétien and Beyond." *"De sens rassis": Essays in Honor of Rupert T. Pickens*. Ed. Keith Busby, Bernard Guidot and Logan E. Whalen. Amsterdam: Rodopi, 2005. 365–374.

Lodén, Sofia. *Le chevalier courtois à la rencontre de la Suède médiévale: du Chevalier au lion à Herr Ivan*. Unpublished dissertation, Stockholm University, 2012.

Maddox, Donald. *Fictions of Identity in Medieval France*. Cambridge: Cambridge University Press, 2000.

Sullivan, Joseph M. "Laudine: The Old Swedish *Herr Ivan* Adapts a Character from Chrétien's *Yvain*." *Yearbook of the Society for Medieval German Studies* 1 (2009): 50–75.

Williams, Henrik, and Karin Palmgren, eds. and trans. *Hærra Ivan*. Cambridge: D.S. Brewer, 1999.

Giulia Murgia
La Tavola Ritonda: Magic and the Supernatural

"Qual è quello cavaliere che si diletti d'esser tenuto e d'avere in sè prodezze, sia pro' nella sua opera e avere ardito il cuore, e sia forte di membra, savio e ingegnoso nello combattere; e non affalsi sue prodezze con incantate armadure" (§ LXXXVII) [1] [Best is the knight that has and uses his own prowess, both in his works and in his courageous heart, and who is strong of limb and wise and clever in battle, and who does not falsify his strengths with enchanted arms]. These are the words pronounced by Tristan when Sir Lasancis attempts to bequeath him his enchanted armour in the *Tavola Ritonda* [Round Table]. The message is clear: the perfect knight errant cannot give in to exploiting magical shortcuts; his value is measured only through the demonstration of his courage, strength and nobility of heart, all of which he proves at court and in combat.

If Tristan limits himself to underlining the incompatibility between chivalry and magic,[2] thereby implicitly recognizing its existence, elsewhere in the *Tavola Ritonda*, the condemnation of the use of the magical arts is even more definitive, even to the point of undermining its ontological status.[3] Following the trial of the enchanted horn, which demonstrated the faithlessness of many of the ladies of Cornwall, King Mark wants to condemn these women to burn at the stake. Sir Dinasso, however, opposes him precisely because he does not want to give credence to the spells of Logres. He affirms: "non vogliamo dare fede nè credere agli incantamenti di Longres, che sono tutti fallaci e falsamente ordinati" (§ XLIII) [we want not to have faith or belief in the enchantments of Logres, as they are all deceiving and falsely made].

Similar considerations show that one of the principal questions the *Tavola Ritonda* attempts to answer is how to define the supernatural. The very breadth of its sources and its adoption of a detached and autonomous attitude limit the

---

1 All references are to Polidori's edition of *La Tavola Ritonda* (1991 [1864–1866]), unless otherwise noted.
2 For more on the notion of the "magical" in the medieval period, see Chandès (1992); CUER-MA (1999); Kieckhefer (2000 [1989]); Sweeney (2000); Bartlett (2008).
3 On the theme of the "magical" in the *Tavola Ritonda*, see Delcorno Branca (1968, 75–79); Heijkant (1997, 33–36).

Giulia Murgia (University of Cagliari)

DOI 10.1515/9783110432466-023

Tavola Ritonda to reconciling conflicting arguments: on the one hand, magic, being an essential legacy of Arthurian and Grail lore, as well as that of the *cantari*;[4] on the other hand, the fact of speaking to the new audience of medieval communes in Italy, which imposed a certain sceptical detachment from the *merveilleux* [marvellous]. *La Tavola Ritonda* (in the so-called "Polidori" version, after its first editor) is, in fact, the conventional title given to a work of Tuscan origin, composed by an anonymous author during the first half of the fourteenth century, who translates, abridges and re-elaborates the Prose *Tristan*, the imposing thirteenth-century French romance; but in this text it is easy to recognize the author's knowledge of other Arthurian sources, such as the Prose *Lancelot*, the *Mort le roi Artu*, the *Queste del saint Graal* and *Guiron le Courtois*, interpolated freely and autonomously, as well as the revival of some episodes originating from the metrical versions of the Tristan legend (the poems of Thomas of Britain and Béroul, as well as the *Folies Tristan*) and from the *cantari fiabeschi* (*cantari* with fairy-tale roots), which were amply diffused throughout Italy at the time (Delcorno Branca 2014; Heijkant 2014). Besides the Tuscan version, there were various other redactions of the *Tavola Ritonda*, including the so-called Po Valley Redaction attested by Florence, Biblioteca Nazionale, Palatino 556 (1446) – hereafter Palatino 556. Palatino 556 is a unique witness to the Tristan tradition in Italy due to its two hundred and eighty-nine ink drawings, and it is related to the Tuscan redaction by its descent from a common antigraph.[5]

In the *Tavola Ritonda* the Tristan myth becomes a sort of canvas for a new kind of depiction of social ritualism, painted with both seriousness and playfulness. Indeed, the *Tavola Ritonda* is a knowing mirror of a society which loves to "play at knights", both because it likes to and needs to. In it, the courtly, rather frivolous *galateo*, or rules for polite behaviour, of a now-extinct society is represented, though it is still able to nourish the Italian imagination, now as bourgeois as it is aristocratic. If, to our modern eyes, the stories it contains seem like an innocuous literary diversion designed exclusively for entertainment, in the

---

4 "*Cantari* are short narrative poems, from 400 to several thousands lines, that emerged as a genre in late medieval Italy. Although some *cantari* represent religious or classical episodes, most have epic or romance subjects. In the hands of semi-learned authors, the genre furnished a matrix in which the Matter of France and the Matter of Britain became conflated. *Cantari* are characterised by eight-line stanzas (*ottava rima*) [...]. The genre was destined for oral presentation, being 'sung' in public by a *canterino*." (Bendinelli Predelli 2014, 105) For a bibliography on the *cantari*, see Picone-Bendinelli Predelli (1984); Picone-Rubini (2007).
5 Citations from the Po Valley redaction will refer to Cardini (2009). There is also an Umbrian redaction attested by Florence, Biblioteca Nazionale, Palatino 564 (for more on which, see Guida 1979), which, however, is not an object of the present analysis.

Italy of medieval city states, the title of knight allowed access to a series of civil offices much more prosaically, such that the rites of the world of chivalry became a *de facto* model for the identification of a new emerging class in search of status symbols and objects, including cultural ones, a system which would vindicate the knight's social ascent (Cardini 1983; 1997; 2006).

The "truth" of our romance's message would descend only with difficulty from the practical adaptability of the chivalric model that it proposes on real life, but this truth should rather be sought in the drive to rationalization and moralization in the retold Tristan legend. Thus, the objective of the present work will be to examine the treatment of magic in the Tuscan and Po Valley redactions (in Palatino 556) of the *Tavola Ritonda*, considering how it is recast and to what extent it is marginalized (though never completely eliminated), and, finally, how it is refunctionalized in a "scientific" sense, as well as in the sense of the Christian miraculous.

The chief driver of the marvellous in the *Tavola Ritonda* is the prophet Merlin.[6] Although here (as similarly occurred in the Prose *Tristan*) the Breton enchanter is given only limited space, it is still he who directs, through the prophecies that he leaves carved on rocks scattered throughout the romance (§ CXXVI), the narrative comings and goings of the text, anticipating the destiny of the Round Table and of the knights errant.[7] Merlin is the ultimate possessor of the supernatural; he is the original repository of the magical knowledge that he then transmits to the numerous fairies of the *Tavola Ritonda*: not only the Lady of the Lake and Morgan, figures well-known in the transalpine tradition as well, but also other feminine figures such as the Savia Donzella [Wise Lady], Medeas, Elergia, Escorducarla, and the Gaia Pulzella [Cheerful Damsel], known only in the Italian tradition. In Italian romance, magic and the supernatural are, in fact, principally pertinent to the female sphere: the fairies (Harf-Lancner 1989), students of Merlin, distinguish themselves through their wisdom and their capacity for the arts of magic; they are characterized by their strong seductive qualities and they conduct transgressive lives; they open the doors for the other characters to the Otherworld (Rider 2000), leading them into a dimension that is not geographically distant or unreachable (indeed, it is in perilously close contact with the ordinary world), but which is still located beyond time and memory.

The first fairy who comes onto the stage in the *Tavola Ritonda* is the Lady of the Lake, who appears in the section dedicated to the boyhood of Lancelot. This

---

6 The vastness of the bibliography on Merlin prohibits a brief overview. However, the fundamental works of Zumthor (1943 [1973]) and Trachsler (2000) are particularly pertinent.

7 The Po Valley Redaction will be referred to as Pal. 556.

section is modelled on Chrétien de Troyes' *Perceval* and is even sung in octaves in the *cantari* of Carduino (Delcorno Branca 1999, 39–64).[8] Lancelot, raised by the Lady of the Lake in an environment sheltered from any contact with the outside world, makes his first acquaintance with chivalry, which becomes the object of his astonished, ecstatic contemplation (§ VI). Pal. 556 opens with this episode. In fact, one of the tendencies that seems to differentiate Pal. 556 from the Tuscan redaction is the concession of a larger space to this knight, the friend and enemy of Tristan (Delcorno Branca 2009, 14). Beyond the invocation of the Virgin (which reflects the spirit of Marian devotion widely diffused in Italy at the time) and the exhortation of the public to listen attentively and in silence ("per cortesia intendite, bona zente" [pray listen well, good people]), the compromise of Pal. 556's *incipit* with the world of the *cantari* is rendered even more evident by the fact that in the first folios there is an attempt – quickly abandoned, possibly because of the burden of work that it would have required – to versify the text. It is particularly the Po Valley redaction, by contrast with the Tuscan one, which underlines the magical abilities of the Lady of the Lake by means of the insistent repetition of the syntagma "per arte" [by her arts/by means of magic]. This occurs when she decides to raise Lancelot ("tolselo per arte e fecilo nutrire" (Pal. 556, 135) [she took him by her arts and caused him to be nourished]) and is able to prophesy his future glories: "vedea, per arte, ch'ela sapea fare", (Pal. 556, 135) [she saw, by her arts, because she knew how to do it]. The sense of the recovery of this episode in the *Tavola Ritonda* in both the Tuscan and Po Valley versions, does not, however, valourize magical implications; instead, the intent is perhaps to accompany the reader into the text with the same naiveté and the same childish joy that the first sighting of the three knights gives to Lancelot, a sight which is "troppo bella cosa a vederli" (§ VI) [a thing too beautiful to behold].

The Lady of the Lake only reappears much later in the romance, when she will intervene in order to liberate King Arthur (§ LIX-LX),[9] who is imprisoned in the "palagio maraviglioso del Grande Disio" [marvellous palace of Great Desire], a marvellous feat of architecture so named because it constitutes a place of perdition in which one can give into the expression of his or her impulses. It is inhabited by Elergia, the daughter of another fairy who is the lady of the island

---

8 The training and education of a young knight represents one of the principal themes of Arthurian fairytale *cantari* (Delcorno Branca 1999, 13). This episode is present also in the Prose *Tristan*, but at a later narrative moment, and with Perceval as the protagonist (Löseth 1891, § 308).

9 Later, it will be the Lady of the Lake herself who "imprisons", by means of a stratagem, first Tristan and Lancelot, and then Iseut and Guinevere in an enchanted castle (§§ CV-CVI-CVII). I return to this below.

of Vallone, Escorducarla (§ LXXXVII). Escorducarla, in her time, had caused the castle to be built expressly for the purpose of imprisoning Merlin; this attempt having failed, the fortress is now Elergia's, who follows her mother's example and proceeds to entrap knights there. Elergia, in the Tuscan *Tavola Ritonda*, is clearly a Morganian fairy, expert "delle sette arti della gramanzia, e anche della opera d'incantamento" (§ LIX) [in the seven arts of magic, and also in the work of enchantment]. This figure, like that of her mother, is reminiscent of the story narrated in the *Suite du Merlin*, in which it was Vivian – there identified with the Lady of the Lake, adoptive mother of Lancelot – who leads Merlin to a similar palace and who, later, takes responsibility for his death in the famous episode of his entombment. This episode is further rewritten in the *Prophecies de Merlin*, where the Lady of the Lake is cast as the *Bianca Serpente* [White Serpent] who will trick the prophet in order to defend her chastity (Murgia 2015b). In Elergia, the medieval mythology of the fairy is re-envisioned: along with the other fairies in our text, she is characterized by the same negative qualities that the *Tavola Ritonda* suggests for the Lady of the Lake, who, by contrast, is depicted in a completely positive light as a maternal figure.

For example, Elergia gives Arthur a magical object, a ring that causes him to lose his memory:

> io la richiesi d'amore, ed ella mi donò un anello; e sì com'io l'ebbi in dito, così fui io tanto duramente innamorato di lei, ch'io non mi ricordava della reina Ginevra nè degli miei cavalieri; e presi della donzella tutto il mio volere. (§ LX)
> [I asked her for love, and she gave me a ring; and when I had it on my finger, then did I become so enamored of her, that I did not remember Queen Guinevere or my knights; and all my volition was taken by the lady.]

Because the power of a fairy can be combatted only with magical weapons, it will be another fairy, the Lady of the Lake, who makes possible the restoration of Arthur and who allows the decisive intervention of Tristan by sending a damsel who will remove the ring from Arthur's finger and free him from the spell. Upon his liberation, Arthur executes Elergia by cutting off her head: the summary execution of a woman is framed as part of the general task of extirpating wicked *coutumes* [customs] from the realm.

As is usual in the *Tavola Ritonda*, however, the border between natural and supernatural is blurred and unstable. Although Elergia retains her origins within the fairy realm, the wonders of the marvellous architecture *del Grande Disio* are re-read and explained in a scientific-naturalistic tone. The castle upon which Tristan stumbles in the Prose *Tristan* is scarcely described (Löseth 1891, § 74a), while in the *Tavola Ritonda* it is transfigured according to the body of knowledge contained within lapidaries: thus the extraordinary luminosity of the castle is ascribed to the use of a stone called "carboncello" [carbuncle stone], a mineral which in the medieval period was considered to be endowed with intense luminescence. Meanwhile the magic of the semi-transparency of the door, which renders the inside invisible to those on the outside, is retraced to the physical properties of jasper, a type of quartz (Murgia 2015a, 302–321).

The death of Elergia will not remain unpunished (§ LXXXVII; Pal. 556, 222–226). Her mother, Escorducarla, is represented as a woman weighed down by the worst of tragedies: not only does the king of Camelot decapitate her daughter, Elergia, but a knight in the service of Arthur kills her four sons. Thus, Escorducarla conceives a plan of terrible revenge: the destruction of the knights errant and the Round Table. She decides to entrust this work to her elderly brother, Sir Lasancis, to whom she gives enchanted armour and a magic lance which will allow him to defeat his enemies (Delcorno Branca 1998, 201–223). After Lasancis has imprisoned many knights, thanks to these enchanted instruments, it will be Tristan's turn to face Lasancis. Warned by a hermit about the magical weapons, Tristan will devise a stratagem that allows him to triumph, free the prisoners and melt the enchanted arms and armour in a furnace. The story concludes with the quotation with which we opened this article: a harsh attack on the marvellous by Tristan, who underlines how knights should not use enchantments and spells. The opposition between natural and supernatural, or rather between the human and the superhuman, is evident in the attitude of Tristan, who faces Lasancis like a new David before Goliath:[10] "Ma vostra forza niente vi varrae sanza la virtude dello ingegno" (§ LXXXVII) [But your strength will avail you naught without the virtue of cleverness].

The episode of Escorducarla's revenge and the knight with the enchanted arms has no correspondence with the Arthurian tradition preceding the *Tavola Ritonda*, but it should certainly be considered along with the ten octaves of a surviving fragment of the *Cantare di Lasancis*, made *c.* 1372 (Delcorno Branca 1999, 110–112).[11] Moreover, this narrative canvas is also similar to that of two other *cantari*, the *Falso Scudo* and the *Astore e Morgana* (Delcorno Branca 1999, 204). By comparing the numerous magical-fabulous elements present in these *cantari* we can perceive, in the rewriting of the *Tavola Ritonda*, "una traduzione in termini razionali [...] dell'originaria vicenda magico-miracolistica" (Delcorno

---

10 The comparison of Tristan to David has already been made in Tristan's combat with Morolt; see Denomy (1956); Bertolucci Pizzorusso (1998).

11 The account contained in the *Tavola Ritonda* and the object of reworking in the *cantare* do not seem to derive one from the other, but rather from a preceding adaptation of this sequence built around the Tristan legend in Italy (Delcorno Branca 1999, 181).

Branca 1999, 204) [a translation in rational terms [...] of the original magical-miraculous tale].[12]

Furthermore, Arthur is not the only knight of the *Tavola Ritonda* seduced by a fairy. Often duplicating narrative structures (Mula 2014), as is typical of the prose romance, the *Tavola Ritonda* cheerfully creates games of reflection across its various sections. The account of the imprisonment of Arthur (§§ LIX-LX), in fact, is little more than a duplication of the episode of the imprisonment of Sir Meliadus (§ XII-XIII; Pal. 556, 147–150), who – as already narrated in the Prose *Tristan* (Löseth 1891, § 20) – falls victim to the seduction of an enchantress. As he awaits the birth of his first son (Tristan, in fact) by his wife, Eliabella, Meliadus participates in a stag hunt, a traditional prelude to the entrance into the Other-world and to the encounter with the fairy, who, in the *Tavola Ritonda*, is called the Savia Donzella [Wise Lady], a name which emphasizes her deep familiarity with magic. The Savia Donzella conducts Meliadus to a castle, evocatively named the "Torre dello Incantamento" [Tower of Enchantment], which she has had built in a remote and inaccessible location, "con piantature spinose per tal modo e sì bene, che lo sentiero non si vedeva nè non se ne sapeva altri accorgere" (§ XII) [with spiny plants placed so well, that the path could not be seen by anyone else]. The Savia Donzella locks Meliadus in a room that – as with Arthur and the magic ring of Elergia – causes complete amnesia. In this case, too, the breaking of the enchantment and the subsequent liberation of Meliadus is only possible thanks to the intervention of another enchanter, Merlin, who sends two knights to kill the Savia Donzella.

The castle of the Savia Donzella is the place where, later in the romance, Tristan and Iseut will spend a period of serenity after their flight from King Mark (§ XLV). It is only in the Italian tradition, in the castle, which is now free of the fairy's presence, that Tristan dreams of a stag which "gli facea due fedite; e dell'una non parea ch'egli si curasse, tanto era lo dolore de l'altra" (§ XLV) [gave him two wounds; and of one wound it seemed he could not be cured, so great was the pain of the other]. Beyond the interpretation of the symbology of the dream,[13] the presence of the fairy seems to reverberate even after her death, as though her spirit has continued to infest the castle, even influencing the dreams of the hero

---

12 The episode will later be retold by Matteo Maria Boiardo and by Ludovico Ariosto (Delcorno Branca 1999, 222).

13 Heijkant (1989, 60) gives this interpretation: "la prima ferita corrisponde a quella causata dal giovinetto, la seconda, più grave a quella causata dal re Marco, il quale rapisce Isotta" [the first wound corresponds to that caused by the youth, the second, graver wound to that caused by King Mark, who kidnaps Iseut].

in order to prophesize his tragic fate through the presence of the animal guide, in the form of a stag, who had already taken Tristan's father, Meliadus, to the Torre dell'Incantamento.

Other than the stag, the laconic mention of which is here only a vague remembrance of its symbolic significance according to medieval folklore, there are other magical animals that appear in the *Tavola Ritonda*. We will remember the opening section, in which a serpent keeps Lady Rima prisoner (§ CXXV). The skirmish is described very briefly in the Tuscan version, but the Po Valley version describes a more articulated narration of the fight between Tristan and the serpent (Pal. 556, 319). Pal. 556, in fact, demonstrates a greater inclination towards magical-marvellous elements than does the Tuscan version; the same interest for the episode of the serpent is clearly shared, too, by the illustrator of the codex, who accompanies the narration with a drawing of a winged dragon.[14] The narrative elements belonging to Pal. 556 – the dramatization of the battle, the odour of the swelling corpse of the serpent, and the unguent with which the freed maiden cures Tristan's poisoned wounds – repeat and valourize the theme of the hero as a vanquisher of monsters, aiming to transform Tristan into a new Hercules or another St George (Delcorno Branca 2009, 13).[15]

An allusion to the tradition of the *cantari*, and in particular to the fight between the serpent and Gawain in the *Cantare di Ponzela Gaia* (Barbiellini Amedei 2000), deserves comment. In this *cantare*, the story begins with Gawain departing to hunt in the forest, only to come upon a monstrous serpent, who challenges him to fight and transforms into Ponzela Gaia, the fairy who will become his lover. Although the story narrated in the *Tavola Ritonda* could not be identical to that of the *cantare* because Tristan is not free to form a love bond with the maiden he saves, it should nevertheless be observed that Lady Rima (or Gierina, as she is called in Pal. 556) comes out into the open only after the death of the serpent, as though the woman were coming out of the serpent, and it represents a kind of metamorphosis. Moreover, the "unguento molto prezioso" [very precious unguent] with which the maiden in Pal. 556 cures the wounds of Tristan can perhaps be compared to that "pretiosa medicina" [precious medicine] with which the fairy Morgan heals Astore in the *cantare* of the same name (Delcorno Branca 1999, 85–94).

There are other fairies, too, who belong exclusively to the *Tavola Ritonda*, some of them only appearing in the Tuscan version. The episode of the Castello

---

14 Images of Pal. 556 are available at: <http://www.bncf.firenze.sbn.it/Bib_digitale/Manoscritti/Pal_556/main.htm>.
15 For more on this, see Cigni (2002).

Crudele [Cruel Castle], in which Tristan is imprisoned, presents some typically fabulous elements in the Prose *Tristan* (Löseth 1891, § 187), and these are then reused in the *Tavola Ritonda* (§ LXXVIII): the bridge is built "per sì fatto incantamento e per tale maestria, che quando voi siete di làe, potete bene passare di qua; ma essendo di qua, non potete mai vedere il ponte, se la donna non vi ci mena per mano" [by such enchantment and such mastery, that when you are there, you can well pass by it to here; but when you are here, you will never see the bridge, if the woman does not lead you by the hand], while the magic ring given to him by Iseut reveals to Tristan the presence of the bridge even when it is invisible to all others.

The Tuscan *Tavola Ritonda* does revise the brief allusion of the Prose *Tristan* to the mistress of the Castello Crudele: the lady commences a habit of imprisoning various knights, year after year, because of her lustful nature, because "voleva ogn'anno a suo diletto tramutare uno cavaliere" (§ LXXIX) [every year she wanted to bend a knight to her pleasure]. The lady of this castle, significantly, is called Medeas. Her fairy nature is rendered evident by the fact that she lives in an enchanted castle that leads to the Otherworld; her own name, which relates her to the Medea of the classical world, refers to the various re-readings of Medea in the medieval period, which impelled her image towards an ever more perturbing representation; she is more than just a "donna sapiente, donna divina, ma strega, fattucchiera terrificante." (Caraffi 2003, 40) [wise woman, divine woman, but a witch, a terrifying sorceress.] In the Italian text Medea has four sisters, all with classical names (Lavina, Agnena, Bresenda, Pulizena), and they are descendants of Calistra, queen of the kingdom of Femminoro: they are all women who refuse matrimony and interact with men for the sole reason of satisfying their lust. Thus, by inserting the Castello Crudele against a background that the medieval period considered to be endowed with its own historicity, like that represented by the kingdom of Femminoro, as well as alluding to the misogyny that was typical in Italian literature, the Tuscan compiler is consolidating his own extensive knowledge in order to strengthen and rationalize customs, like that of the Castello Crudele, which would otherwise have left a fourteenth-century Italian reader rather incredulous and unsatisfied (Murgia 2015a, 169–185).

All of the fairy figures (wise and lecherous, vengeful and unfortunate) that we have rapidly reviewed (Elergia, Escorducarla, the Savia Donzella, Medeas) are little more than an insistent multiplication of the model of Morgan (Harf-Lancner 1984). In the *Tavola Ritonda*, Morgan is the daughter of Uther Pendragon, sister of Arthur, and, as is typical in the Italian tradition, also the sister of the Lady of the Lake and mother of the Gaia Pulzella. In the text, Morgan carries out a prophetic and anticipatory function: it is she who preannounces the fatal destiny of love and death that awaits Tristan. She does this by sending certain magical objects:

the enchanted horn, the shield split in half, the green shield and the poisoned lance.

Already present in the Prose *Tristan* (which, in its turn, is borrowed from the Prose *Lancelot*), the episode of the *écu fendu* [the split shield] undergoes a significant process of transformation in the *Tavola Ritonda* (§ XXVIII-XXIX; Löseth 1891, § 37). The shield features two lovers about to kiss, but they are forever rent apart by a deep fissure that splits the shield in half. With respect to the French text, the *Tavola Ritonda* alters the sender and the lovers who are represented. In the Prose *Tristan* it was the Lady of the Lake who conceives of the shield, with the benevolent goal of supporting the love of Guinevere and Lancelot, but in the Italian text it is Morgan who sends the shield, which now represents Tristan and Iseut. The final aim of this shift is the competitive comparison between the amorous paradigms proposed by the two couples; the fairy is thus principally called upon to embody an enunciative instance: she, "la quale sa quello che è stato e quello che dee essere, e vuole dare a intendere ch'ella il sa" (§ XXIX) [who knew that which had been and that which would be, and wanted to make known that which she knew], definitively confirms the superiority of Tristan over Lancelot. The metaphor figured on the metamorphic shield of the *Tavola Ritonda* is also bearer of a moralizing re-reading: the mending of the *écu fendu*, here too, as in the *Lancelot* and later in the Prose *Tristan*, represents the physical consummation of love, but in the Italian text it cannot impose any moral condemnation because their love is a direct consequence of that *beveraggio amoroso* [love potion] that the two drink unknowingly.

Among the various magic objects conceived by Morgan there is also the enchanted horn, which the fairy sends to Arthur to demonstrate the guilt of Guinevere (§ XLIII). This magic object can distinguish faithful women from adulterers: the latter cannot drink from the horn without spilling its contents. In the hands of Amorotto, the knight planning revenge against Tristan, the horn reaches not the court of Camelot, but the court of King Mark in Cornwall. This proof of chastity (Besamusca 2010), whose thematic nucleus descends directly from the late thirteenth-century work, the *Lai du cor* (Lecco 2004), attributed to a certain Robert Biket and characterized by a clear misogynist slant, is also present in the Prose *Tristan* (Löseth 1891, §§ 47–48), albeit with some nuances. In the *Tavola Ritonda,* only thirteen of the six hundred and thirty-eight Cornish women put to the test are able to demonstrate their conjugal faithfulness, and because Iseut is among the adulterers, King Mark wants to condemn them all to burn at the stake. It is the argument of Sir Dinasso against the magic of Logres, cited above, that convinces Mark to desist.

In other instances, Morgan emphasizes Tristan's indissoluble love for Iseut. For example, when she decides to renounce any attempts to seduce Tristan or to give him her daughter, the Gaia Pulzella, in marriage,[16] because she knows that the heart of the hero can belong only to the queen of Cornwall, she predicts his death. And so she entrusts to Tristan a green shield (§ LXXX; Löseth 1891, §§ 190–191), which is not a magic shield, but a symbolic one, the double of the *écu fendu* because of its function as an informant: "Ma sappiate che la fata ingannava Tristano, però che quello scudo ella lo avea fatto fare in disinore altrui; chè significava che Lancelotto s'avea messo sotto i piedi e fatto disinore allo re Artù e alla reina Ginevra" (§ LXXX) [But know that the fairy was deceiving Tristan, because she had had that shield made in order to give dishonour to another; it meant that Lancelot had trampled on and dishonoured King Arthur and Queen Guinevere]. When Onesun the Bald (father of the Gaia Pulzella and husband of Morgan) sees that Tristan bears his wife's fairy shield, he fights to get it back and is killed by Tristan. On his tomb Morgan writes the prophecy that predicts Tristan's death: "sarete morto con quello ferro medesmo collo quale voi avete morto lui" (§ LXXX) [you will die by that same blade with which you killed him].

This prophecy is connected to the masterly web of references, absent in the Prose *Tristan,* which anticipate the hero's tragic end, when he will be fatally wounded by his uncle, Mark, with the lance sent to him by Morgan (the same with which Tristan had killed Onesun). Morgan charges a lady to bring the lance to King Mark for this purpose, and along the road the lady encounters Tristan, who asks what her mission is (§ CXXIV). The maiden gives a response that Tristan does not understand, but which is explicit for the reader: she brings that lance as a gift to King Mark so that the king might use it when he goes hunting, "sappiendo ch'egli con essa trarrà a fine la fiera la quale fa tremare tutte l'altre fiere: e quella fine si ricorderà mentre che 'l mondo durerà" (§ CXXIV) [knowing that with this he will lay low the beast which makes other beasts tremble: and that end will be remembered so long as the world endures]. The compiler takes care to clarify the sense of the maiden's words, adding that Morgan has not enchanted the lance, but she has poisoned it to ensure that, as soon as Tristan is wounded, he cannot be cured even by Iseut's considerable healing powers (§ CXXIV).[17] This image will

---

16 La Gaia Ponzela is one of the most celebrated heroines of the *cantari* and belongs exclusively to the Italian tradition (Barbiellini Amidei 2000). Unique to the *Tavola Ritonda* is the episode which casts her as the protagonist beside a knight called Burletta della Diserta (§ LXXXI), who stains his honour with an attempt at rape; see Heijkant (2002).

17 Morgan makes her last appearance when she goes to her brother Arthur, once he has been mortally wounded in the final battle with Mordred, and she takes him to an island to die: "E tale conveniente, si crede che la fata Morgana venisse per arte in quella navicella, e portòllo via in una isoletta di mare; e quivi morì di sue ferite, e la fata il sopellì in quella isoletta" (§ CXLIV) [And in such good time, that it is believed that Morgan came by her arts in that boat, and brought him

figure in Tristan's prophetic dream the night before King Mark kills him (§ CXXVI). He dreams that a naked maiden brings him before a woman called Legista, who shows him a great church and tells him: "Qui ti riposa" (§ CXXVI) [Here shall you rest]. Again, the Tuscan compiler glosses the sense of Tristan's nocturnal vision: the naked maiden embodies the love which guides Tristan towards death, while Lady Legista is the fairy Morgan, who, having sent the poisoned lance, occasions the physical death of the hero.

It is not only Morgan who abets the competitive game of comparisons between Tristan and Lancelot (Richard 2007). The intent to compare them emerges in other sequences characterized by a fabulous atmosphere, one which is unique to the *Tavola Ritonda*. In a world where magic is primarily in the domain of the fairies, rarely do we come upon a male figure with magical-demonic qualities. However, the *Tavola Ritonda* inserts an original section centred around the "Cavaliere Fellone" [Fell Knight] (§§ CXIII–CXIV), constructed through a process of contamination that re-elaborates material of the Grail Quest and is particularly indebted to the *Queste*. The Cavaliere Fellone possesses the attributes characteristic of the knight from hell: he is of gigantic stature, he rides a black horse and he has the strength of five knights. He takes Lancelot prisoner and Tristan liberates him. This time it is not cunning that allows Tristan to win, but his ability to call upon Christian miracles. Only through the strength of his prayers and the promise to not sin again with Iseut is Tristan able to weaken his adversary, pronouncing the phrase: "Cristo crocifisso, aiutami" (§ CXIV) [Crucified Christ, help me].

Pal. 556 strengthens the magical dimension of this episode (Heijkant 1999), as is evident from the insistent repetition of the word *incantamento* [enchantment] and the fact that the Cavaliere Fellone, in the Po Valley text, is called also the "chavalero Incantatore" (Pal. 556, 288) [Knight Enchanter]. The Po Valley version, moreover, adds or amplifies certain elements taken directly from the fable, inserting, for example, a magic hat, "lo più belo capelo che mai fose veduto et era atermegiato di pene di pavone" (Pall 556, 295) [the most beautiful hat that had ever been seen, and it was ornamented with peacock feathers]. That the Cavaliere Fellone represents the diabolical is, in the Po Valley text, even clearer: in the fortress of the Cavaliere Fellone, the devil, called "lo Inemico" [the Enemy], appears in the guise of various people linked to Tristan, not only his beloved Iseut, but also her handmaiden, the faithful Bragina, and the hound given to him by the daughter of King Fieramonte. The episode thus becomes a representation of Tristan's internal conflict with his ghosts and his sins.

---

away to a little island in the sea; and there he died of his wounds, and the fairy buried him on that island].

Another episode aimed at confronting Tristan and Lancelot is a new addition to the narrative which has no counterpart within the French tradition. It is found in the *Tavola Ritonda* in the chapters CV–CVI–CVII.[18] Here the protagonist is the Lady of the Lake, who decides to "imprison" the two perfect couples, Lancelot and Guinevere and Tristan and Iseut, so that they might all enjoy an idyll together within a "padiglione, lo quale era fatto per arte in tale maniera, che pareva ad altrui uno bello palagio" (§ CV) [pavilion, which had been made by her arts in such a way that it seemed to others a beautiful palace]. The Lady of the Lake hides the disappearance of Tristan and Lancelot from King Arthur and his court by faking their deaths and placing false cadavers along the road to the castle. These are so realistic that no one realizes a thing, not even Iseut as she clutches the false corpse of Tristan to her breast.[19] Another magical element in this sequence is the use of a dust that "per arte, di subito misse una sì oscura e folta nebbia e tanto grande, che lo re Artù e gli altri cavalieri, per la grande oscuritade, l'uno non vedea l'altro. E a quel punto sì sparì il palagio e le due corpora" § (CVII) [by art, immediately gave out such a dark and thick fog, and so wide, that King Arthur and the other knights, because of the great darkness, could not see one another. And at that point the palace and the two corpses disappeared]. After two weeks of amorous idyll, it is time for the lovers to return to reality: the story that the four will recount upon their return to court to justify their long absence places all the blame on the Lady of the Lake, who, they say, had given them a certain *beveraggio* [sleeping draught]. This episode, too, closes with the condemnation of magic and enchantments, as Arthur threatens to burn the Lady of the Lake at the stake – the punishment he had already proposed, as the text reminds us, for his sister, the fairy Morgan (§ CVII).

It is significant that in this episode there is the allusion to the *beveraggio amoroso* [love potion] administered to Tristan and Iseut on the ship while the latter is being brought to the shores of Ireland as the betrothed of King Mark. This is the fulcrum upon which the Tristan legend turns. The love potion that induces the passion between Tristan and Iseut has always been the object of careful attention by critics,[20] especially the question of whether the potion is magical or merely symbolic. In fact, recognizing the love potion as a magical object has seemed to some a form of rigid determinism that would then result in the re-casting of the much-celebrated perfection of the link between the two faithful lovers. For

---

18 It is also present in Pal. 556, 254–258.

19 The simulation of the dead body is a theme retraceable to the thirteenth-century poem, *Tristan als Mönch* (Classen 1994).

20 On the nature and the capacities of the philter in *Tristan*, see Frappier (1963).

some, the philter is only a symbol, a tangible representation of the feeling that had really manifested itself before the drinking of the potion and of the dynamic of falling in love (Vinaver 1927; Ferrante 1973, 40; Doggett 2009, 112). The *Tavola Ritonda* falls within this school of thought, opting to confer a rational form to the symbol (Murgia 2015a, 325–350): it thus transforms the love potion into a medical compound (§ XXXIV; Pal. 556, 188), following the interpretation already partly proposed in the Prose *Tristan* (Löseth 1891, § 39). Brandina and Governale, because of their imprudent treatment of such a dangerous *beveraggio*, are the *toxicatores* [poisoners] of the events, while the philter is presented as no less than *venenum* [poison].

In the Prose *Tristan* the shift toward the scientific interpretation occurs mostly through a network of allusions to medical knowledge already common among its readers, and particularly through a precise correspondence between the effects of the love poison and the excess of black bile. In the Tuscan *Tavola Ritonda*, by contrast, the anonymous Tuscan compiler rationalizes the philter by multiplying its prodigious physical capabilities: for the first time the love potion is capable of acting even in the domain of the natural. This is evident when the fall of the philter provokes the release of a silvery foam and its vapour induces a physical change, welding the planks in the deck of the ship together just as it will unite forever the hearts of Tristan and Iseut; its properties also imply the involvement of others present, since Governale and Brandina inhale the fumes, while the little dog, Idonia, licks the deck where the drops fell. Nothing and no one who comes into contact with the philter – neither inert material, nor the protagonists, nor even animals – can resist the power of the *beveraggio amoroso*. The re-reading of the properties of the love potion in this physical-naturalist key thus fulfils the double objective of absolving Tristan and Iseut from any moral responsibility as well as subtracting pieces of the tale from the domain of the irrational, thus mitigating, once again, the impact of the magical and the supernatural in the *Tavola Ritonda*.

References

Allaire, Gloria, and Psaki, F. Regina, eds. *The Arthur of the Italians: The Arthurian Legend in Medieval Italian Literature and Culture*. Cardiff: University of Wales Press, 2014.
Barbiellini Amidei, Beatrice, ed. *Ponzela Gaia: Galvano e la donna serpente*. Milan: Luni, 2000.
Bartlett, Robert. *The Natural and the Supernatural in the Middle Ages*. Cambridge and New York: Cambridge University Press, 2008.

Bendinelli Predelli, Maria. "Arthurian Material in Italian Cantari." *The Arthur of the Italians: The Arthurian Legend in Medieval Italian Literature and Culture*. Ed. Gloria Allaire, and F. Regina Psaki. Cardiff: University of Wales Press, 2014. 104–120.

Bertolucci Pizzorusso, Valeria. "L'arpa d'Isotta. Variazioni testuali e figurative." *Miscellanea Mediaevalia. Mélanges offerts à Philippe Ménard*. Ed. Jean-Claude Faucon, Philippe Ménard, Alain Labbé and Danielle Quéruel. I. Paris: Champion, 1998. 101–119.

Besamusca, Bart. "Characters and Narrators as Interpreters of Fidelity Tests in Medieval Arthurian Fiction." *Neophilologus* 94 (2010): 289–299.

Biket, Robert. *Il corno magico*. Ed. Margherita Lecco. Alessandria: Edizioni dell'Orso, 2004.

Caraffi, Patrizia. *Figure femminili del sapere. XII–XV secolo*. Rome: Carocci, 2003.

Cardini, Franco. "L'autunno del medioevo fiorentino. Un "umanesimo cavalleresco"?". *Mito e storia nella tradizione cavalleresca*, Atti del XLII convegno storico internazionale (Todi, 9–12 ottobre 2005). Spoleto: CISMA, 2006. 513–528.

Cardini, Franco. *L'acciar de' cavalieri. Studi sulla cavalleria nel mondo toscano e italico (secc. XII–XV)*. Florence: Le Lettere, 1997.

Cardini, Franco. "Concetto di cavalleria e mentalità cavalleresca nei romanzi e nei cantari fiorentini." *I ceti dirigenti nella Toscana tardo comunale*, Atti del III convegno (Firenze, 5–7 dicembre 1980). Monteoriolo: Papafava, 1983. 157–192.

Cardini, Roberto, ed. *Tavola Ritonda. Manoscritto Palatino 556 della Biblioteca Nazionale Centrale di Firenze*. Rome: Istituto della Enciclopedia Italiana, 2009.

Cigni, Fabrizio. "Da un'avventura tristaniana al mito di Eracle: la sconfitta del Moroldo." *Rinascite di Ercole*, Atti del Convegno Verona, maggio 2002. Ed. Anna Maria Babbi. Verona: Fiorini, 2002. 183–198.

Cigni, Fabrizio. "Un nuovo testimone del cantare *Ultime imprese e morte di Tristano*." *Studi Mediolatini e Volgari* 43 (1997): 131–191.

Chandès, Gérard, ed. *Le Merveilleux et la magie dans la littérature, Actes du colloque de Caen, 31 août–2 septembre 1989*. Amsterdam: Rodopi, 1992.

Classen, Albert, ed. *Tristan als Mönch*. Greifswald: Reineke, 1994.

CUER-MA. *Magie et illusion au Moyen Âge. Sénéfiance* 42 (1999), <http://books.openedition.org/pup/3355>.

Delcorno Branca, Daniela. "The Italian Contribution: *La Tavola Ritonda*." *The Arthur of the Italians: The Arthurian Legend in Medieval Italian Literature and Culture*. Ed. Gloria Allaire and F. Regina Psaki. Cardiff: University of Wales Press, 2014. 69–87.

Delcorno Branca, Daniela. "Le carte piene di sogni. Introduzione alla *Tavola Ritonda* padana." *Tavola Ritonda. Manoscritto Palatino 556 della Biblioteca Nazionale Centrale di Firenze*. Ed. Roberto Cardini. Roma: Istituto della Enciclopedia Italiana, 2009. 3–18.

Delcorno Branca, Daniela, ed. *Cantari fiabeschi arturiani*. Milan-Trento: Luni editrice, 1999.

Delcorno Branca, Daniela. *Tristano e Lancillotto in Italia. Studi di letteratura arturiana*. Ravenna: Longo Editore, 1998.

Delcorno Branca, Daniela. "Per la storia del *Roman de Tristan* in Italia." *Cultura neolatina* 40 (1980): 211–231.

Delcorno Branca, Daniela. "I cantari di Tristano." *Lettere Italiane* 23 (1971): 289–305.

Delcorno Branca, Daniela. *I romanzi italiani di Tristano e la* Tavola Ritonda. Florence: Olschki, 1968.

Denomy, Alexander J. "Tristan and the Morolt: David and Goliath." *Mediaeval Studies* 18 (1956): 224–232.

Doggett, Laine E. *Love Cures. Healing and Love Magic in Old French Romance*. Philadelphia, PA: Pennsylvania State University Press, 2009.

Donà, Carlo. "Cantari e fiabe: a proposito del problema delle fonti." *Rivista di Studi testuali* 6–7 (2004–2005): 105–137.

Ferrante, Joan M. *The Conflict of Love and Honor: The Medieval Tristan Legend in France, Germany and Italy*. Paris: Mouton, 1973.

Frappier, Jean. "Structure et sens du *Tristan*, version commune, version courtoise." *Cahiers de Civilisation Médiévale* 6 (1963): 255–281, 441–454.

Gardner, Edmund G. *The Arthurian Legend in Italian Literature*. London and New York: Dent/ Dutton, 1930; New York: Octagon Books, 1971.

Guida, Salvatore. "Per il testo della *Tavola Ritonda*. Una redazione umbra." *Siculorum Gymnasium* 32 (1979): 637–667.

Harf-Lancner, Laurence. *Les fées au Moyen Age. Morgan et Mélusine. La naissance des fées*. Paris: Champion, 1984.

Heijkant, Marie-José. "From France to Italy: The Tristan Texts." *The Arthur of the Italians: The Arthurian Legend in Medieval Italian Literature and Culture*. Ed. Gloria Allaire and F. Regina Psaki. Cardiff: University of Wales Press, 2014. 41–68.

Heijkant, Marie-José. "La mésaventure érotique de Burletta della Diserta et le motif de la pucelle esforciée dans la *Tavola Ritonda*." *Zeitschrift für romanische Philologie* 118 (2002): 182–194.

Heijkant, Marie-José. "Tristan im Kampf mit dem Treulosen Ritter. Abenteuer, Gralssuche und Liebe in dem italienischen *Tristano Palatino*." *Tristan und Isolt im Spätmittelalter, Vorträge eines interdisziplinären Symposiums vom 3 bis 8 Juni 1996 an der Justus-Liebig-Universität Gießen*. Ed. Xenja von Ertzdorff. Amsterdam: Rodopi, 1999. 453–472.

Heijkant, Marie-José. *La tradizione del* Tristan *in prosa in Italia e proposte di studio sul* Tristano Riccardiano. Nijmegen: Sneldruck Enschede, 1989.

Hoffman, Donald L. "*Radix Amoris*: The *Tavola Ritonda* and Its Response to Dante's Paolo and Francesca." *Tristan and Isolde. A Casebook*. Ed. Joan Tasker Grimbert. New York and London: Routledge, 2002. 207–222.

Kieckhefer, Richard. *Magic in the Middle Ages*. Cambridge: Cambridge University Press, 1989 [2000].

Löseth, Eilert. *Le Roman en prose de Tristan, le roman de Palamède et la compilation de Rusticien de Pise. Analyse critique d'après les manuscrits de Paris*. Paris: Bouillon, 1891.

Mula, Stefano. "Narrative Structure in Medieval Italian Arthurian Romance." *The Arthur of the Italians: The Arthurian Legend in Medieval Italian Literature and Culture*. Ed. Gloria Allaire and F. Regina Psaki. Cardiff: University of Wales Press, 2014. 91–104.

Murgia, Giulia. *La* Tavola Ritonda *tra intrattenimento ed enciclopedismo*. Rome: Sapienza Università Editrice, 2015a.

Murgia, Giulia. "L'allegoria della Bianca Serpente nelle *Prophecies de Merlin*: una lettura dell'enserrement di Merlino alla luce di Genesi (1–3)." *In altre parole. Forme dell'allegoria nei testi medievali*. Ed. Patrizia Serra. Milan: FrancoAngeli, 2015b. 153–176.

Picone, Michelangelo, and Bendinelli Predelli, Maria, eds. *I cantari. Struttura e tradizione, Atti del Convegno internazionale di Montréal, 19–20 marzo 1981*. Florence: Olschki, 1984.

Picone, Michelangelo, and Luisa Rubini, eds. *Il cantare italiano fra folklore e letteratura, Atti del Convegno internazionale di Zurigo, Landesmuseum, 23–25 giugno 2005*. Florence: Olschki, 2007.

Polidori, Filippo-Luigi, ed. *La Tavola Ritonda o l'Istoria di Tristano*. 2 vols. Bologna: Romagnoli, 1864–1866; Milan-Trento: Luni Editrice, 1997.

Richard, Adeline. *Amour et passe amour. Lancelot-Guenièvre, Tristan-Yseut dans le* Lancelot en prose *et le* Tristan en prose. *Étude comparative*. Aix-en-Provence: Publications de l'Université de Provence, 2007.

Rider, Jeff. "The Other Worlds of Romance." *The Cambridge Companion to Medieval Romance*. Ed. Roberta L. Krueger. Cambridge: Cambridge University Press, 2000. 115–131.

Sweeney, Michelle. *Magic in Medieval Romance: from Chrétien de Troyes to Geoffrey Chaucer*. Dublin: Four Courts Press, 2000.

Trachsler, Richard. *Merlin l'enchanteur. Étude sur le Merlin de Robert de Boron*. Paris: SEDES, 2000.

Villoresi, Marco. *La fabbrica dei cavalieri. Cantari, poemi, romanzi in prosa fra Medioevo e Rinascimento*. Rome: Salerno, 2005.

Vinaver, Eugène. "The Love Potion in the Primitive Tristan Romance." *Medieval Studies in Memory of Gertrude Schoepperle Loomis*. Paris and New York: Champion/Columbia University Press, 1927. 75–86.

Zumthor, Paul. *Merlin le prophète. Un thème de la littérature polémique, de l'historiographie et des romans*. Lausanne: Payot, 1943; Geneva: Slatkine, 1973.

Thomas Hinton
Chrétien de Troyes' *Lancelot, ou le Chevalier de la charrette*: Courtly Love

"Courtly love" (*fin'amor*) has long been a term medievalists cannot live with, yet cannot live without. It famously first appeared – in the French form *amour courtois* – towards the end of the nineteenth century in a two-part article by Gaston Paris (1881/1883), in the context of a discussion of the love between Lancelot and Guenevere in Chrétien de Troyes' *Le Chevalier de la charrette*. As argued by Hult (1996), Paris' coinage answered a set of disciplinary, ideological and personal concerns specific to a late-nineteenth-century (French, male) scholar of medieval literature; the formulation is relatively rare in medieval texts themselves.[1] The scholar's fear of anachronism is reflected in the widespread tendency to couch the term in scare quotes, keeping it at one remove – certain critics have even gone so far as to repudiate the concept altogether as an unhelpful modern invention.[2] However, Boase (1977) has demonstrated the longevity of scholarly discussion of a distinctive and influential treatment of love originating in certain medieval vernacular texts, stretching back to Italian humanists in the sixteenth century.[3] Then as now, the primary material from which evidence was gleaned was chivalric romance, especially that written in French, and the Occitan lyric poetry of the troubadours. The *Charrette* itself was invoked as early as 1647 in Jean Chapelain's dialogue, *De la lecture des vieux romans*, where one character argues that the text is "une représentation naïve, et une histoire certaine et exacte des moeurs qui régnaient dans les Cours d'alors" (1870, 13) [a naïve representation, and a true and exact account of the mores that reigned in the courts of that time]; above all, Lancelot's love is singled out for its sincerity and intensity: "Lancelot ne joue point l'amoureux, il l'est véritablement" (31) [Lancelot does not act the part of lover, he truly is one]. The relationship between Arthur's champion and his

---

1 For examples of medieval usage, and an argument in favour of the expression's medieval authenticity, see Ferrante (1980).
2 Most famously (and polemically) Robertson (1968), as stated baldly in his title ("Courtly Love as an Impediment to the Understanding of Medieval Texts") and conclusion: "The study of courtly love, if it belongs anywhere, should be conducted only as the subject is an aspect of nineteenth and twentieth century cultural history." (17)
3 We could take this even further back if we included medieval practitioner-theorists like Dante in our purview.

Thomas Hinton (University of Exeter)

DOI 10.1515/9783110432466-024

queen has thus long been at the centre of discussion of courtly love – henceforth I happily throw off the scare quotes – and continues to act as a touchstone for treatments of the subject.

Following in the vein of the most compelling recent scholarship, I start from the position that courtly love is best conceived not as an idealized behavioural code (a view which still holds currency in the popular domain)[4] but as a discursive field of exploration and debate.[5] The first half of this chapter will consider how the *Charrette* exemplifies the tendency to idealize and simultaneously problematize a certain conception of love in medieval courtly literature. I want to give full weight to the "courtly" element in courtly love, and demonstrate how multiple aspects of the discourse are shaped by the social setting within which texts like the *Charrette* were written, and which they mirror in their own depictions of love in court society. Accordingly, the second half of the chapter will focus on how the expression of inner emotion finds its place – and value – in the public world of the court; I argue that love offers medieval authors a compelling lens through which to examine the competing demands of private and public imperatives.

1 Courtly love, contradiction and interpretation

Le Chevalier de la charrette is usually dated to the late 1170s. Its appearance was part of a minor explosion of compositional activity in the second half of the twelfth century which introduced a host of new vernacular textual forms: Arthurian romance and the *roman antique* established themselves alongside the earliest French lyric poetry. These poets, or *trouvères*, wrote love songs modelled on the troubadour *canso* which at the same time was coalescing into what is held to be its canonical form in Occitania (cf. Lee, *infra*). Chrétien de Troyes sits at the heart of these developments. Alongside his five Arthurian romances, he was himself among the earliest-known *trouvères*, with at least two securely attributed surviving songs.[6] One of these has been read as engaged in a dialogue with the trou-

---

4 The scholars most responsible for popularizing the view of courtly love as a set of rules are probably C.S. Lewis (2013 [1936]) and Denis de Rougemont (1939).

5 Alongside scholars mentioned herein, see Schnell (1989) and Corbellari (2009), who both insist on the discursive and multifaceted nature of *amour courtois*.

6 His name is also associated with two non-Arthurian narratives, *Guillaume d'Angleterre* and *Philomena*. See Kay (1997) for a thought-provoking discussion of how the name "Chrétien de Troyes" can be seen to function as a textual tag, irrespective of questions of authenticity or integrity of the corpus.

badour, Bernart de Ventadorn, about the quality of Tristan's love for Yseut (Ron-caglia 1958). Courtly love is thus the connecting thread that brings Occitan and French lyric into contact with the *Tristan* legend and the earliest known Arthur-ian romances;[7] these cultural interactions are the crucible for the emergence of a "literature of public entertainment" in Europe, and therefore shaped what we think of as the "literary" today (see Kay 2001).[8]

Gaston Paris' 1883 account of courtly love stressed four features that have remained central to most definitions of the concept: (i) the lover's position is one of inferiority, with the lady frequently depicted as haughty or capricious in her treatment of the suitor;[9] (ii) love is ennobling and an incitement to improvement and acts of valour; (iii) love is furtive and transgressive, which usually means adulterous. Paris' fourth contention, already noted above, is that courtly love consisted of a set of behavioural rules to be applied to the best of one's abilities, yet even in the short summary given here we can see how the first three charac-teristics generate tensions which would make it difficult, if not impossible, for the first three criteria to be obtained simultaneously as a coherent code. The lover's willing abasement would appear difficult to reconcile with the contention that his love improves his status. Moreover, if true love is secret and furtive, how is it to generate the social capital of recognized value that would confirm its power to improve the loving subject?

Where scholars working in the wake of Paris saw the *Charrette* as an exem-plification of a medieval code of love, recent work has found in the same text a material demonstration of the contrasting thesis that courtly love is inherently paradoxical, a site of debate rather than a revered doctrine.[10] Several scholars

---

7 For readings that highlight the value of thinking about Chrétien's romances through the lens of troubadour love lyric, see the following: Bogdanow (1981); Bruckner (2005, 145–146); Grimbert (2005); Stahuljak et al. (2011).

8 Compare with Lewis (2013 [1936], 2–5): "Every one has heard of courtly love, and every one knows that it appears quite suddenly at the end of the eleventh century in Languedoc [...] the most momentous and the most revolutionary elements in it have made the background of Euro-pean literature for eight hundred years. [...] Compared with this revolution the Renaissance is a mere ripple on the surface of literature."

9 The lady's superiority has long been unmasked as a rhetorical pose which imprisons her with-in "social rules and regulatory systems that privilege heterosexual men as the desiring, speak-ing, and most visible subjects of amorous exchange" (Burns 2001, 25); see Burns (1985); Gravdal (1991); Krueger (1993); Gaunt (1995).

10 Paris himself notes that even the *Charrette* is not a perfect fit: having held up Guenevere as the model of female perfection (1883, 517), he is forced to concede that certain of the traits he is describing must be sought in other Arthurian romances (518). See Hult (1996, 215); and also Burns (2001, 24 n. 3).

have argued that the double-facing language of love in courtly texts, moving freely between sacred and erotic registers, reflects "the particular social configuration of twelfth-century courts, where clerics and lay people of both sexes gathered, and where cultural tastes and exchanges could flourish." (Gaunt 2006, 42) Courtly love fictions are part of a negotiation between "the lay and clerical interests of the various courtiers and their masters." (Kay 2000, 92; see also Kay 1996)[11] Attention has also been paid to the relationship – and frequent disjunction – "between inner intensity and outward decorum" (Kay 2000, 85); love becomes a prism through which to test the implications of the fact that "the life of the court divides human beings into outer mask and inner man." (Jaeger 1985, 239)

A similar shift of emphasis has occurred in *Charrette* criticism, from trying to pin down its philosophy of love to appreciating slipperiness and ambivalence as the core of its poetic project; the key text here was Bruckner (1986). The *Charrette* thus remains an invaluable aid to thinking through the implications and contradictions of courtly love in the Middle Ages. The romance's title, *Le Chevalier de la charrette*, refers to a key event early in the narrative: chasing after the evil Meleagant who has abducted Arthur's queen, the as-yet-anonymous Lancelot meets a dwarf pulling a cart – which, our narrator explains in a historical aside, was used in Arthur's time as a mobile pillory for criminals. The dwarf invites the knight to climb in if he wishes to learn where the queen has gone, and after the briefest of hesitations Lancelot follows his instruction. The degree of his commitment to finding Guenevere is highlighted by Gauvain, also present, who declines to follow his example: "Car trop vilain change feroit/ Se charrete a cheval chanjoit" (ll. 391–392) [for it would be too shameful an exchange to trade a horse for a cart].[12] The paradox of being "the knight of the cart" is thus laid bare. Lancelot's willingness to abase himself for his lady leads, in this instance, to an apparent abdication of his chivalric status, and the dishonour of stepping into the cart marks a series of subsequent meetings with other members of court society, for whom this action is as damning as it is baffling. Our hero's adherence to a supposed ideal of absolute commitment in love service leads to humiliation in the eyes of his peers, a stain on his identity that proves hard to shake off. For characters, narrator and audience alike, he remains "the knight of the cart" until the moment, halfway through the narrative, when Guenevere reveals to all that this knight is "Lanceloz del Lac." (l. 3660)

---

11 For a wider analysis of the negotiation between sacred and secular discourses, see also Bolduc (2006).

12 All references to *Le Chevalier de la charrette* are from Zink's edition (Chrétien de Troyes, 1994a); all translations into English are my own.

The *Charrette* thus offers a useful vantage point from which to think about courtly love, but it is important to stress that no single text alone can represent the essence of the phenomenon. If courtly love is best thought of as "a large grid crisscrossed with conflicting opinions" (Jaeger 1999, 120), the adulterous passion of Lancelot and Guenevere is no more or less archetypal than the many Arthurian heroes who settle down into marriage with their beloved, whether this be the conclusion of their adventures (e.g. *Fergus*, *Jaufre*) or a starting point for further crisis and questioning (e.g. *Erec*, *Yvain*). Kay (2000) and Jaeger (1999, Ch. 14) offer concordant models of a spectrum of representations ranging from idealization of a desire that flaunts social rules (represented notably by the *Tristan* tradition) to domestication of sexuality by "patriarchal interest" (Kay 2000, 90), as it is redirected through the institutions of marriage or religion. One might say that whereas the latter pole subjects private passion to the laws of public order, the former subjects public behaviour to the whim of private passion.

Seeing each individual text as a negotiation between these two poles allows a way out of a conundrum that has weighed heavily on *Charrette* scholarship: how to square the adulterous treason of that romance with the depiction in Chrétien's earlier Arthurian narratives (*Erec*, *Cligès*, *Yvain*) of marriage as the natural conclusion of falling in love (Kelly 1966; Noble 1982). Taking the Jaeger/Kay line, we can see each individual romance as an experiment in testing possible answers to the balance of private and public imperatives. And what applies across the body of an author's work applies equally within the individual text, which may explore multiple conflicting standpoints without necessarily resolving their contradictions.

Here again, the *Charrette* offers much encouragement for studying the contradictions of courtly love, for it insistently asks its audience simultaneously to interpret the unfolding narrative and to query the value or grounding of that interpretation. Is Lancelot love's fool or love's champion? Is he traitor or hero? Wherever we look, we are either faced with a choice to make, or asked to witness a choice being made. The early part of the text, up to the encounter with the cart (ll. 30–320), is programmatic in this respect. Meleagant, having entered Arthur's court and announced that many of the king's knights and countrymen are being held captive in his father's land of Gorre, offers to fight any of Arthur's knights who dares to escort Guenevere to an agreed meeting-point in the forest: if he loses, the prisoners will be released, but if he wins, the queen becomes his. Arthur's seneschal, Keu, tricks the king into awarding him the mission (through the device of the Rash Boon). Following him into the forest at the suggestion of Gauvain, the assembled courtiers are horrified to see Keu's horse returning without its rider, the saddle bloody and broken (ll. 257–267). No explanation is necessary, for characters or audience, before these visual clues – all are able to read the signs of

Keu's defeat and Guenevere's abduction correctly. At this point Gauvain, who is at the head of the group, meets a knight riding on an exhausted horse, who asks for one of the two mounts that Gauvain's squires are leading. Gauvain accepts, inviting the knight to choose the horse he prefers, and the knight leaps onto the one closest to him; explicitly, we are told that he "N'ala pas querant le meillor/ Ne le plus bel ne le graignor" (ll. 291–292) [did not look for the better, nor the more handsome, nor the larger]. Gauvain next stumbles upon more visual markers of battle: the horse he has given lies dead, the ground is covered with hoofprints and broken weapons. "Bien resanbla que grant estor/ De plusors chevaliers i ot,/ Se li pesa molt et desplot/ Ce que il n'i avoit esté" (ll. 310–313) [It looked very much as if there had been a pitched battle involving several knights, and it grieved and displeased him greatly that he had not been there]. Again, there is little doubt about what the visual clues mean, but this time certain mysteries remain: if there were several knights present, who were the knight's adversaries? Was Meleagant involved – does he have an accomplice? Like Gauvain, we arrive late to the scene and have to piece together an interpretation from what we see, and in relation to what we already know. A little further on still, Gauvain catches up with the knight, who is on foot, and who has himself reached the cart of infamy. The stage is set for an internal debate between Amor and Reison [Love and Reason] before the knight decides to take up the dwarf's challenge to get into the cart. This momentary hesitation is resolved when Love "commands" him to jump in, and so he does, "caring nothing for the shame [involved]." (ll. 375–377)[13]

By this point, less than four hundred lines into the text, we and the characters have repeatedly been forced to interpret narrative action along two different axes: to understand what is happening and to judge the better of two courses of action.[14] Along the first axis, beyond the battlegrounds we (through Gauvain) are called to witness; we may also be trying to work out who this anonymous knight is. A clue is offered, as the queen's last speaking part before she is escorted away by Keu is addressed to an absent "ami" [friend]: "Ha! amis, se le seüssiez,/ Ja, ce croi, ne me lessissiez/ Sanz chalonge mener un pas!" (ll. 209–211) ["Oh my love! If you knew about this, I do not believe you would ever let someone take me even one step without challenge!"][15] The care she takes to speak out of earshot points to

13 "Amors le vialt et il i saut,/ Qu de la honte ne li chaut/ Puis qu'Amors le comande et vialt."
14 See Krueger (1983) for analysis of how the "inscribed audiences" of the *Charrette* and *Yvain* relate to these texts' real and implied audiences.
15 It should be noted that only manuscript *A* (Chantilly, Musée Condé, 472) carries the reading "amis"; *C* (Paris, BnF, fr. 794) has "Ha rois!", which should probably be disregarded given that Arthur explicitly *is* aware of (and has reluctantly endorsed) Keu's gamble with the queen's safety. Although the other manuscripts also omit the word "ami" here, their upholding of "se [vos] le

an illicit relationship, which one might surmise contemporary audiences would already have known involved Lancelot.[16] Even for those in the audience able to identify the knight, further mysteries subsist: how does Lancelot happen to arrive just after the abduction, and how does he seem to know what has befallen her? Where has he come from?

Alongside this flurry of puzzling and unglossed information which forces us to consider and filter evidence, we repeatedly witness Lancelot placed in situations where he must choose between alternatives, a state of affairs that engages his judgment and simultaneously requires the audience to assess for itself the soundness of his decisions. The relatively insignificant choice of horses offered by Gauvain in the passage discussed above soon emerges as merely the first instance of this *leitmotif*: immediately after, Lancelot finds himself confronted with the dilemma of the cart; in a subsequent episode, a simulated rape prompts another internal monologue about the merits of intervention; later still, he and Gauvain must choose between two routes of unequal peril to get into Gorre. The proliferation of characters who subsequently pass judgment – for good or ill – over Lancelot's behaviour further prompts us to consider whether we wish to endorse either the praise for his valour or the excoriation of his shame in getting in the cart, or both. One of the important psychological mechanisms underlying this is the question "what would *you* do?", inviting reflection on the negotiations between public reputation and private commitment which – as noted above – are central to survival and success in the world of the court.

2 Courtly love as love-at-court: public and private language

It is believed that Chrétien de Troyes wrote the *Charrette* at the same time as he was working on another Arthurian romance, *Yvain*. That text opens with a lively court scene, where knights, ladies and damsels mingle:

Li un recontoient nouveles,
Li autres parloient d'Amours,

---

seüssiez", with the addressee not specified, points again to an absent figure sufficiently close to Guenevere that she would expect him to defy the king's arrangement with his seneschal.

16 Certainly, when Guenevere reveals Lancelot's name at l. 3660, the other characters' reactions suggest that audiences were expected to recognize the name and to know something of the character already.

Des angousses et des dolours
Et des grant biens qu'en ont souvant
Li desiple de son couvant,
Qui lors estoit riches et boens;
Mais or y a molt poi des siens,
Qui a bien pres l'ont tuit laissie,
S'en est Amours mout abaissie;
Car chil qui soloient amer
Se faisoient courtois clamer
Et preu et largue et honnorable;
Or est Amours tournee a fable
Pour chou que chil qui riens n'en sentent
Dient qu'il ayment, mes il mentent;
Et chil fable et menchonge en font
Qui s'en vantent et droit n'i ont. (*Yvain*, ll. 12–28)[17]
[Some were sharing news; others were speaking about Love, about the anguish and pain and great benefits that are often conferred upon disciples of her Order, which in those days was rich and powerful; but now she has few loyal followers, for almost everyone has abandoned her, and Love is dishonoured as a result. For in the olden days those who loved had themselves called "courtly", and worthy, generous and honourable; now Love is turned to fable, because those who feel nothing say they are in love, and they are lying; and by boasting about it when they have no right to do so, they make love into a fable and a lie.]

This lengthy exposition of the Golden Age *topos* confirms some of the observations made in the preceding section. Love, here, is both an inner feeling (expressed, with a typical admixture of sacred and profane, as submission to a quasi-monastic Rule) and a public performance; those who espouse the latter without the former are condemned as hypocrites. Indeed, the author goes further by linking the question of sincerity and sociability to matters of class:

Mais pour parler de chix qui furent
Laissons chix qui en vie durent,
Qu'encor vaut mix, che m'est a vis,
Un courtois mors c'uns vilains vis. (*Yvain*, ll. 29–32)
[But let us leave those who are still alive in order to speak of those who lived before; for it seems to me that a dead courtly man is still worth more than a live commoner [*vilain*].][18]

The narrator's striking antithesis contrasts the true and therefore courtly lovers of old with the false lovers of his day, whose hypocrisy aligns them with the

---

17 All references are to Zink's edition (Chrétien de Troyes, 1994b).
18 On the parodic use and potential instability of the *courtois/vilain* opposition, see Gravdal (1989), especially Ch. 1 on *Fergus* as parody of Chrétien de Troyes.

non-noble *vilain*. The conviction of proverbial formulae such as this depend on a shared understanding of its terms of reference: to be *courtois* is to be recognized as such by the community. But it is precisely the community's failure to police the adequacy of seemingly true feelings that has brought Love's stock so low. Similarly, the reflexive logic in "*se faisoient* courtois clamer" highlights the negotiation necessary between the putative *courtois* and his third-party arbiter, and places strong emphasis on the social context of the term. Presumably, then, those modern courtiers that Chrétien's narrator castigates here also "have themselves called 'courtly'" through their skill in public performance, but the lack of genuine emotion underlying their words and gestures debars them in his eyes from meriting that epithet.

The problem with this position is that, if *courtois* is a label bestowed in recognition of public performance, the defining criterion must be entirely external: one's ability to perform in the appropriate manner. The *Yvain* narrator's supplementary condition depends on a claim to be able to tell the true from the false which is unverifiable, partly because it rests on an ineffable criterion (inner sincerity) and partly because the narrator's own vocabulary of value is indistinguishable from that of the conventional frame he is purporting to challenge. Unilateral redefinition of terms agreed through social interaction runs the risk of making the new frame of reference unintelligible to the community.

The narrator's final comment, that a dead courtly man is worth more than a live *vilain*, reconfirms the primacy of public language and reputation, since it evokes the courtly lover's capacity to act as a memorandum, a lasting model for the behaviour that should be expected of all lovers. But of course the problem of hypocrisy raised earlier in the prologue, of false love successfully passed off as the real thing, casts doubt on the ability of such a model to function. The *Yvain* prologue thus threatens to undermine the Rule of courtly love at the same time as it celebrates (and mourns) it – and in doing so, it offers an excellent example of how the discourse on love in these texts revolves around debate, contradiction and paradox (cf. Lodén, *supra*).

Perhaps because of the productive contradictions it generates, the spectre of hypocrisy and feigned love is never far from the surface of courtly literature; insistence on inner authenticity itself becomes part of the public performance. In love lyric, the term *lauzengier* is invoked obsessively by the lyric subject to designate rivals who threaten his relationship through malicious slander and feigned sincerity; several scholars have recognized that these figures are critical to the textual logic of lyric (Köhler 1964; Gaunt 1995, Ch. 3; Kay 1996).[19] The same vocabulary appears in the prologue to the *Charrette*, again in the context of hypocritical speech. Chrétien begins by praising his patroness, Marie de Champagne, in a dazzling display of having your cake and eating it:

> Puis que ma dame de Champaigne
> Vialt que romans a feire anpraigne,
> Je l'anprendrai molt volentiers
> Come cil qui est suens antiers
> De quanqu'il puet el monde feire
> Sanz rien de *losange* avant treire.
> Mes tex s'an poïst antremetre
> Qui i volsist *losenge* metre,
> Si deist, et jel tesmoignasse,
> Que ce est la dame qui passé
> Totes celes qui sont vivanz (ll. 1–11, emphasis mine)
> [Since my lady of Champagne wants me to begin a romance, I will begin most willingly, as one who is entirely hers in everything he may accomplish in this world, without including the slightest *flattery*. But someone else might take on the task who would want to use *flattery*; he would say, and I could bear witness, that she is the lady who surpasses all others who are alive [...]]

He ostentatiously refuses to flatter (*losange*) Marie, drawing a distinction between himself and the hypocrite: "Par foi, je ne sui mie cil/ Qui vuelle *losangier* sa dame" (ll. 14–15, emphasis mine) [In faith, I am not one who wishes to flatter his lady]. But this is done in such a transparently disingenuous fashion that the distinction is undermined – indeed, he even declares his readiness to bear witness to the truth of the flatterer's discourse. The difference between truth and the flatterer's lies collapses as the two are revealed to be identical in form. If the *Yvain* narrator appears to seek a personal idiom that will bring to public attention the deficiencies in conventional love-language, the *Charrette* narrator affects to use the disavowal of public praise to convey a more sincere version of the same. Ultimately, both find that public language is not up to the task of sorting truth from falsehood.

Other scenes in the *Charrette* serve to remind us that the realm of public speech is not only slippery, it is also frequently dangerous for the expression of private sentiment. Guenevere's apostrophe to the absent Lancelot as she is being led away by Keu is intended as a private monologue, but the intimacy of court life turns it into a potentially dangerous indiscretion: "Molt le cuida avoir dit bas,/

---

19 See also Paterson (1993), who draws on contemporary depictions of the court environment to contextualize the *lauzengier* theme in Occitan lyric.

Mes li cuens Guinables l'oï,/ Qui au monter fu pres de li" (ll. 212–214) [She thought she had said it very quietly, but Count Guinable heard it, for he was close to her as she was mounting her horse]. Nothing develops from this incident, but it acts as a hint of the danger of the public domain, as well as a reminder of the adulterous treason involved in Lancelot and Guenevere's love, which Chrétien generally avoids addressing directly.[20]

Stephen Jaeger (1999, 139) reminds us that "courts are dangerous places, where the urge to ruin reputations is always alive and at work and even the appearance of wrongdoing can serve it." Surviving evidence (including from literary texts) suggests that adultery could be sanctioned by humiliating execution.[21] The precise relationship between real court behaviour and its literary analogues is probably impossible to determine, but the staging of Guenevere's indiscretion should remind us that she and Lancelot were playing for very high stakes.

Lancelot reaches Gorre by crossing the Sword Bridge and incurring stigmata-like wounds on his hands and feet, marks of his private devotion to Guenevere which function for those around him as public signs of his exceptional courage as a knight; for once, public and private discourses are in harmony. Yet the conjunction is short-lived. Lancelot soon bests Meleagant in an interrupted duel, thereby freeing all of Gorre's prisoners including the queen. In the public arena, he is the liberator whose arrival was foretold in an inscription on a mysterious tomb encountered on his journey (ll. 1900–1909). But when King Bademagu, the well-intentioned father of Meleagant and ruler of Gorre, brings him to the queen, she snubs him in front of everyone. Guenevere's actions cause sufficient discomfort among the court that Bademagu deems it necessary to take Lancelot to one side to express his confusion and embarrassment (ll. 3981–3999). The king's discretion here serves to underscore the imprudence of Guenevere in showing her emotions and flouting social convention that demanded she offer a warm welcome to her liberator. "She is wrong," opines Bademagu, "since you have risked fatal adventure for her." (ll. 3997–3999)[22]

---

20 On the displacement of commentary on the adultery onto other parts of the narrative, see Bruckner (1989, 60–108); Prior (2006).

21 Benton (1968, 24–27) mentions several examples, including (26) the case of Philip of Flanders (later to be named as patron of Chrétien's *Conte du Graal*) who caught his wife Isabelle of Vermandois with one of his knights and had the lover drowned in a latrine in 1175, around the time that Chrétien was writing the *Charrette*; we might also think of Francesca and Paolo in Dante's *Inferno* V, murdered by her husband for an affair that began while reading the (prose) tale of Lancelot and Guenevere.

22 "– Certes, fet li rois, ele a tort,/ Que vos vos estes jusqu'a mort/ Por li en avanture mis."

When the lovers are later reconciled, Guenevere reveals that her hostility was motivated by learning that he had hesitated before stepping into the cart (ll. 4484–4489). She thus reverses the public meaning of this incident, as it has been signalled to us repeatedly by the succession of characters mocking Lancelot's "honte" [shame]. Where in public discourse the cart signifies disgrace and Lancelot's hesitation a concern for his honour, Guenevere's reaction implies that – within her private discourse of love – the hesitation is the true shame, and the most honourable conduct would have been to embrace the public indignity without a backward glance. Deployed before the public gaze of the court, Guenevere's redefinition of terms leads to confusion and embarrassment; it is only when the lovers can find a moment to speak without being overheard that she is able to make herself understood to Lancelot. Yet the scope for this kind of private communication is always limited. Although the lovers are finally able to engineer a night together, their joy can only be short-lived: public life makes its demands which are as imperious as those of Love. Thus, we are told, Lancelot is in tears at the moment of departure: "Del rasanbler n'est pas pris termes,/ Ce poise lui, mes ne puet estre" (ll. 4705–4705) [No arrangements are made for the next meeting; this upsets him, but it cannot be otherwise]. Moreover, in entering Guenevere's chamber, Lancelot cuts himself and bleeds onto her sheets, a mishap which nearly gives the lovers away.[23] Isolation from the discourse of the court is both temporary and fraught.

The final significant incident before Lancelot's concluding defeat of Meleagant is a tournament organized at Noauz, where Lancelot fights incognito. Thinking she recognizes him, but cautious about indiscretions, Guenevere sends a damsel to tell him to fight "au noauz" [for the worst], punning on the name of the tournament's location; by his willingness to obey, she recognizes him as her lover. The cart scenario plays out a second time: the public reaction to Lancelot's inept knightly performance is to mock, while Guenevere evaluates it according to a reversed hierarchy where social shame translates to private worth. If the prologue suggested that a private language of authenticity was impossible, the Noauz tournament and the cart episode create a space where private love communication can be clearly distinguished from the conventions of public language, as long as the lover's behaviour is sufficiently excessive to render it identifiable. Yet

---

23 As Méla (1989, 296) notes, the meaning of blood fluctuates in this part of the romance to underscore the duality of Lancelot's character; on the Sword Bridge, Lancelot's wounds are proof of his election as best knight in the world (l. 3172); in Guenevere's chamber the blood is evidence of his treasonous adultery, though the explosive truth remains locked away within the realm of private discourse.

it is an ephemeral success, not only for the practical reasons adduced above but also because this private language is itself parasitic on public language. Its reversal of the poles of shame and honour, using the performance of what is publicly "shameful" as the marker of absolute devotion, depends on the stability of those conventional meanings, a stability to which the private discourse must eventually give way. Once Guenevere is certain of Lancelot's identity, she sends word again that he is to do his best, which proves to be better than anyone else at the tournament. There is no durable way to be best knight in the world and remain within the behavioural sphere of private meaning.

At Noauz, and again when Lancelot arrives at Arthur's court to face Meleagant for the final time, we see Guenevere much more guarded with her language and behaviour: she laughs silently at the damsels swooning over Lancelot's prowess in the tournament; she holds back from welcoming him to court until she can meet him in "Un boen leu et un plus privé" (l. 6851) [a better and more private place]. She has "learned to avoid the kind of problematic exposure that occurred with her cold reception; she has accepted the necessity to wait for the appropriate moment to show her private feelings." (Bruckner 2005, 149) Guenevere's actions now suggest that the correct public "performance" of authentic emotion is *not* to perform it. But then how is one to know that it exists at all?

3 Conclusion: measuring up

The *Charrette* takes up and tests a number of hypotheses regarding the relationship between private sensitivity and public behaviour in court life. In vernacular literature of the twelfth century, love is the privileged domain through which to work through this problem, and it might be argued that it is peculiarly suited to doing so, and that this helps to explain the extraordinary success of courtly literature. Its particular conceptual contours at any time are historically contingent and publicly agreed; but the public concept will always tend be measured against the pre-linguistic emotional states to which individual subjects may claim to have privileged access.[24] The theme of adultery allows the *Charrette* to explore positions that are perhaps more invested in privacy than those of certain other romances whose interest lies in the bonds and demands of marriage; but its

---

24 This observation might allow us to reconcile the sociohistorical bent in much courtly love criticism (including this chapter) with Peter Dronke's claim that what he calls the "courtly experience" is "at least as old as Egypt of the second millennium B.C. and might indeed occur at any time or place." (Dronke 1965, ix)

emphasis on the pitfalls and conflicts involved in maintaining a space of inner feeling in the face of court life is, I would suggest, a common factor across courtly literature.

Lancelot arrives incognito at the tournament of Noauz, but is immediately recognized by a herald. Having been sworn to secrecy on pain of death, the herald contents himself with a single cry, which he utters whenever Lancelot takes the field: "Or est venuz qui l'aunera!" (ll. 5563, 5571, 5617, 5963) [Now here is the one who will take the measure!] For him, Lancelot and the reader, the meaning of this enigmatic utterance is clear, and gestures once more to the potential for a private language to signify meaningfully, if ephemerally, below the surface of public discourse. But the herald's cry goes further still. It does not only confer value on Lancelot; it sets him up as a new public standard, in terms of which other knights are to be measured. "Auner" is a verb derived from the textiles industry, referring to the act of measuring cloth, an activity regulated by law; the same word may also mean "to gather together" or "come together".[25] The herald's unusual turn of phrase thus sits at the intersection of social cooperation and social control. It lays bare the role of the community in defining what counts as valour, but suggests that an exceptional individual can challenge and even redefine the collectively agreed hierarchy. The herald's cry offers a glimpse of potential for Lancelot's valour – which in turn is fuelled by his love for Guenevere – to transform the public discourse on personal worth. It is the delicate balance between the private and the social, the individual and the group, the absolute and the contingent, that the *Charrette*'s treatment of courtly love serves to examine.[26]

References

Benton, John F. "Clio and Venus: An Historical View of Medieval Love." *The Meaning of Courtly Love: Papers of the First Annual Conference of the Center for Medieval and Early Renaissance Studies*. Ed. F. X. Newman. Albany, NY: State University of New York Press, 1968. 19–42.

Boase, Roger. *The Origin and Meaning of Courtly Love: A Critical Study of European Scholarship*. Manchester: Manchester University Press, 1977.

---

25 Godefroy (1965 [1880]), I, 499–500.

26 Arthurian prose romance further develops the idea of heroic exceptionality which redefines the social order, through the figure of Lancelot's son, Galahad: here the passion that motivates the hero is love for the divine, and the Grail Quest is explicitly framed as a re-evaluation of the worth of each of Arthur's knights.

Bolduc, Michelle. *The Medieval Poetics of Contraries*. Gainesville, FL: University Press of Florida, 2006.

Bruckner, Matilda Tomaryn. *"Le Chevalier de la Charrette*: That Obscure Object of Desire, Lancelot." *A Companion to Chrétien de Troyes*. Ed. Norris J. Lacy and Joan Tasker Grimbert. Cambridge: D.S. Brewer, 2005. 137–155.

Bruckner, Matilda Tomaryn. *Shaping Romance: Interpretation, Truth, and Closure in Twelfth-Century French Fictions*. Philadelphia, PA: University of Pennsylvania Press, 1989.

Bruckner, Matilda Tomaryn. "An Interpreter's Dilemma: Why Are There So Many Interpretations of Chrétien's *Chevalier de la Charrette?*" *Romance Philology* 40 (1986): 159–180.

Burns, E. Jane. "Courtly Love: Who Needs It? Recent Feminist Work in the Medieval French Tradition." *Signs* 27 (2001) 23–57.

Burns, E. Jane. "The Man behind the Lady in Troubadour Lyric." *Romance Notes* 25 (1985): 254–270.

Chapelain, Jean. *De la lecture des vieux romans*. Ed. A. Feillet. Paris: Aubry, 1870.

Chrétien de Troyes. "Lancelot. Lancelot ou le Chevalier de la Charrette." *Chrétien de Troyes: Romans*. Ed. Michel Zink. Paris: Livre de Poche, 1994a.

Chrétien de Troyes. "Yvain. Yvain ou Le Chevalier au Lion." *Chrétien de Troyes: Romans*. Ed. Michel Zink. Paris: Livre de Poche, 1994b.

Corbellari, Alain. "Retour sur l'amour courtois." *Cahiers de recherches médiévales et humanistes* 17 (2009): 375–385.

De Rougemont, Denis. *L'Amour et l'occident*. Paris: Plon, 1939.

Dronke, Peter. *Medieval Latin and the Rise of European Love-Lyric*. Oxford: Clarendon Press, 1965.

Ferrante, Joan M. *"Cortes'amor* in Medieval Texts." *Speculum* 55 (1980): 686–695.

Gaunt, Simon. *Love and Death in Medieval French and Occitan Courtly Literature: Martyrs to Love*. Oxford: Oxford University Press, 2006.

Gaunt, Simon. *Gender and Genre in Medieval French Literature*. Cambridge: Cambridge University Press, 1995.

Godefroy, Frédéric. *Dictionnaire de l'ancienne langue française et de tous ses dialectes du IXe au XVe siècle*. Vol. 1. Vaduz: Kraus, 1965 [1880].

Gravdal, Kathryn. *Ravishing Maidens: Writing Rape in Medieval French Literature and Law*. Philadelphia, PA: University of Pennsylvania Press, 1991.

Gravdal, Kathryn. *Vilain and Courtois: Transgressive Parody in French Literature of the Twelfth and Thirteenth Centuries*. Lincoln, NE & London: University of Nebraska Press, 1989.

Grimbert, Joan Tasker. *"Cligés* and the Chansons: A Slave to Love." *A Companion to Chrétien de Troyes*. Ed. Norris J. Lacy and Joan Tasker Grimbert. Cambridge: D.S. Brewer, 2005. 120–136.

Harvey, Ruth. "Courtly Culture in Medieval Occitania." *The Troubadours: An Introduction*. Ed. Simon Gaunt and Sarah Kay. Cambridge: Cambridge University Press, 1999. 8–27.

Hult, David F. "Gaston Paris and the Invention of Courtly Love." *Medievalism and the Modernist Temper*. Ed. R. Howard Bloch and Stephen G. Nichols. Baltimore, MD and London: Johns Hopkins University Press, 1996. 193–224.

Jaeger, C. Stephen. *Ennobling Love: In Search of a Lost Sensibility*. Philadelphia, PA: University of Pennsylvania Press, 1999.

Jaeger, C. Stephen. *The Origins of Courtliness: Civilizing Trends and the Formation of Courtly Ideals, 939–1210*. Philadelphia, PA: University of Pennsylvania Press, 1985.

Kay, Sarah. "Courts, Clerks, and Courtly Love." *The Cambridge Companion to Medieval Romance*. Ed. Roberta L. Krueger. Cambridge: Cambridge University Press, 2000. 81–96.

Kay, Sarah. *Courtly Contradictions: The Emergence of the Literary Object in the Twelfth Century*. Stanford, CA: Stanford University Press, 2001.

Kay, Sarah. "Who Was Chrétien de Troyes?" *Arthurian Literature* 15 (1997): 1–36.

Kay, Sarah. "The Contradictions of Courtly Love and the Origins of Courtly Poetry: The Evidence of the *Lauzengiers*." *Journal of Medieval and Early Modern Studies* 26 (1996): 209–253.

Kelly, Douglas. *Sens and conjointure in the* Chevalier de la charrette. The Hague: Mouton, 1966.

Köhler, Erich. "Observations historiques et sociologiques sur la poésie des troubadours." *Cahiers de Civilisation médiévale* 7 (1964): 27–47.

Krueger, Roberta L. *Women Readers and the Ideology of Gender in Old French Verse Romance*. Cambridge: Cambridge University Press, 1993.

Krueger, Roberta L. "Reading the *Yvain/Charrete*: Chrétien's Inscribed Audiences at Noauz and Pesme Aventure." *Forum for Modern Languages Studies* 19 (1983): 172–187.

Lewis, C.S. *The Allegory of Love: A Study in Medieval Tradition*. Cambridge: Cambridge University Press, 2013 [1936].

Méla, Charles. *La Reine et le Graal: La conjointure dans les romans du Graal, de Chrétien de Troyes au Livre de Lancelot*. Paris: Seuil, 1989.

Noble, Peter S. *Love and Marriage in Chrétien de Troyes*. Cardiff: University of Wales Press, 1982.

Paris, Gaston. "Études sur les Romans de la Table Ronde." *Romania* 10 (1881): 456–496 / 12 (1883): 459–534.

Paterson, Linda. *The World of the Trobuadours: Medieval Occitan Society, c.1100–c.1300*. Cambridge: Cambridge University Press, 1993.

Prior, Sandra Pierson. "The Love That Dares Not Speak Its Name: Displacing and Silencing the Shame of Adultery in *Le Chevalier de la Charrete*." *The Romanic Review* 97 (2006): 127–153.

Robertson, D.W., Jr. "The Concept of Courtly Love as an Impediment to the Understanding of Medieval Texts." *The Meaning of Courtly Love: Papers of the First Annual Conference of the Center for Medieval and Early Renaissance Studies*. Ed. F.X. Newman. Albany, NY: State University of New York Press, 1968. 1–18.

Roncaglia, Aurelio. "*Carestia*." *Cultura neolatina* 18 (1958): 121–138.

Schnell, Rüdiger. "L'Amour courtois en tant que discours courtois sur l'amour." *Romania* 110 (1989): 72–126 and 331–363.

Stahuljak, Zrinka, Virginie Greene, Sarah Kay, Sharon Kinoshita and Peggy McCracken, eds. *Thinking Through Chrétien de Troyes*. Cambridge: D.S. Brewer, 2011.

Raluca L. Radulescu
Sir Percyvell of Galles: A Quest for Values

By the time *Sir Percyvell of Galles* (henceforth *Percyvell*) made its entrance on the medieval English Arthurian romance scene in the later Middle Ages, the story of his exploits had been enjoyed by audiences in a number of languages and geographical spaces, from Chrétien de Troyes' unfinished *Conte du Graal* and Wolfram von Eschenbach's *Parzifal* to the Welsh *Peredur son of Efrawg*. The Middle English *Percyvell* survives in only one manuscript, in 2,288 tail-rhyme lines, in the mid-fifteenth-century Lincoln anthology (Lincoln, Lincoln Cathedral 91; hereafter Lincoln Thornton), copied and owned by a member of the Yorkshire gentry, Robert Thornton (see also Busby, *supra*). Here Percyvell is Arthur's nephew, a detail unique to this version, acknowledged by Thornton in his explicit to the romance: "Here endys þe Romance of Sir Percevell of Gales Cosyn [sic] to kyng Arthour." (Brewer and Owen 1978; Fein and Johnston 2014)[1]

Although the Middle English version only survives in this copy, there is evidence that medieval English audiences would have likely encountered the hero and his exploits in other contemporary late Middle English texts, as attested by his inclusion in a list of romance heroes in the *Laud Troy Book* and, more famously, by Geoffrey Chaucer's own parody of popular romance in his unfinished "Tale of Sir Thopas" from his *Canterbury Tales*.[2] The anonymous author of the Middle English *Percyvell* was also likely familiar with both Chrétien's unfinished *Conte du Graal*, the *First Continuation* and the *Perlesvaus*, from which he skilfully combined elements, as David Fowler (1975) and Keith Busby (1987; 1978) have demonstrated.[3] Although modern critics have been quick to dismiss the Middle English version on the grounds of its aesthetic inferiority by comparison with the more complex earlier French and German versions, *Percyvell* does, however, present a series of striking features which point to a rather different outlook on this Arthurian character from the traditional one inaugurated by Chrétien.

Conversely, however, *Percyvell*'s modern defenders have explored the assimilation of the story into the broader popular romance tradition in England (see

---

1 The explicit to *Percyvell* is found at f. 176ra. References to *Percyvell* are to Mills (1992).
2 The romance heroes' list is to be found in the anonymous *Laud Troy Book* (*c.* 1400). See Wülfung (1902–1903, ll. 39–40).
3 In-depth comparisons with the sources are available in these studies.

Raluca L. Radulescu (Bangor University)

DOI 10.1515/9783110432466-025

the seminal articles by Putter 2004; 2009), while the use of comedy as a device in attracting audience sympathy for the protagonist has also been praised for its contribution to a more rewarding, if simplified, narrative (Eckhardt 1974).[4] Mary Braswell (2011) succinctly summarizes the absence from this version, of any "lance, procession to the chapel, maimed king, or wasteland" – in short, of all the elements that would recommend the text as a relative of the Grail narrative established since Chrétien's twelfth-century classic story. Without a Grail Quest to accomplish, and therefore neither questions to ask, nor healing to perform (and fail), the spiritual import of Percyvell's adventures is absent, as is the evident commentary on his unpreparedness for the Quest, and his resulting inability to cope with its (mysterious) demands, which are foregrounded in Chrétien's *Conte*. Since the intrinsic quest structure cannot, therefore, turn on the quest for the Grail, a different kind of pivot is required. Indeed, it quickly becomes evident that the author of this adaptation of the *Perceval* story made significant and dramatic choices in developing the quest motif found in his source. Layers of spiritual significance are removed from the original story, and other aspects are enhanced: family values, including the agency of the son in restoring the mother to sanity; the comedy of "chivalric manners"; and a strong element of free will. Indeed, Percyvell's trajectory seems to be more actively shaped by his own decisions than those of his French, German and Welsh counterparts. Where *Percyvell* falls short of the sophistication encountered in the French and German versions, greater clarity of purpose and direct progression in the narrative more than compensate. Ad Putter (2004, 176) also finds *Percyvell* "a shorter and more straightforward story with a very satisfying shape and conclusion." He draws attention to the value and specifics of the anonymous author's method of simplifying the narrative, in other words the direct and uncomplicated ("unscrambled") story line when compared with Chrétien's original:

> The main effect of the *Percyvell*-poet's alternative prehistory and re-ordering of events is to make the past immediately accessible to us and to the hero, since the line that connects the past with the present is direct and unbroken.

Putter finds these simplifications both interesting and telling, especially in the reduction both of retrospect and of convoluted plots that propel the protagonist on his quest.

---

4 Eckhardt's article contains a number of close textual comparisons of Chrétien's and Wolfram's texts, as well as extensive references to earlier comparative studies of the French, English and German versions.

Another factor that might play a role in our understanding of this adaptation of the quest and its associations is the manuscript context in which the story survives. In the Lincoln Thornton, *Percyvell* keeps company, in Booklet 2, with numerous other popular Middle English romances of the "family" type (*Octavian*; *Sir Isumbras*; *Erl of Tolous*; *Sir Eglamour of Artois*), which may explain, in part at least, the more evident focus on bloodlines and the hero's return to his mother before her death. In fact, the plotline may have been reshaped precisely to suggest that Percyvell's quest, in this romance, points to the un-ending circle of family duty rather than the spiritual duties of his literary Grail predecessors. Responding to specific concerns in each cultural space, therefore, but retaining a core set of recognizable motifs, including that of the orphan who finds his way back to his destined role and reveals the noble ancestry of his line, the Middle English version of the story evolves in unexpected ways, guiding the audience to a different quest outcome than its forerunners.

There are at least two ways in which this romance text and its altered quest motif can profitably be explored in the context of current debates: the first is the author's apparently deliberate attempt to break away from tradition, ignoring all the *topoi* encountered in Grail stories that would otherwise have rendered this version an obvious heir, or at least familial relation, of the distinguished *Perceval* of the French tradition; the second is the text's position in the transmission of Middle English Arthurian romance (both in a specific manuscript context and against broader cultural exchanges across linguistic and geographical borders).

To start with, *Percyvell of Galles* defies the Grail tradition known from the *Conte du Graal* by offering an original "back-story" to the central character. Young Percyvell is here related by blood to none other than Arthur himself, whose sister, Acheflour, is Percyvell's mother. Percyvell's father has been killed in combat with the Black Knight in front of Percyvell (who was still very young); it is understood that the father's pride in his prowess led to his downfall. By implication, the "yyng" ("childe") Percyvell's first encounter with Arthur's knights, Gawain, Ywain and Kay, is accompanied by several other unifying features centred around kinship, as bloodlines are given more precedence here than in Chrétien's version, leading to what Putter (2004, 237) calls "unity of action". Moreover, Percyvell's strong sense of duty to his mother, manifested in the author's manner of orchestrating the son's return to look for his mother on his own initiative (unlike any of his other namesakes in Welsh, French or German) and while she is still alive, is a key to understanding the shape of his quest. In fact, one may go as far as to suggest that the Middle English Percyvell's adventures, motivated as they are by his desire to become a knight of Arthur's court, and to recover the honour and reputation of his family, appear to be designed (ultimately) to remind him of his first duty to his mother, to whom he is linked by the typical recognition token usually destined to return a chivalric knight to his beloved: the ring she gave him on his departure. This ring is a family object and not a spiritual one and, furthermore, it is this item that also elicits a response from the mother's wild self and paves the way to her recovery and reinstatement as a courtly lady (also bringing her full circle, as it were). Metaphorically, therefore, the shape of Percyvell's quest is circular, replicating the shape of the ring his mother gives him, wanting him to return to her rather than participate in the chivalric world of adventure that she had removed him from in his infancy.

Another aspect that characterizes this enhanced focus on the importance of returning to family is the mother's hasty advice prior to Percyvell's departure:

> "Sone, thou has takyn thi rede
> To do thiselfe to the dede!
> In everilke a strange stede,
> Doo als I bydde the.
> Tomorne es forthirmaste Yole day   [first day of Christmas]
> And thou says thou will away
> To make the knyghte if thou may,
> Als thou tolde mee:
> *Lytill thou can of nu[r]toure*;
> *Luke thou be of mesure*   [take care; be restrained]
> Bothe in haulle and in boure,
> And fonde to be fre."   [strive; act nobly]   (ll. 389–400; my emphasis)

Percyvell's mother gives him little practical advice here, first warning him that he is unprepared for the courtly life ("little thou can of nurtoure"), and then emphasizing restraint ("be of mesure") and a very few basic rules of etiquette:

> Than seide the lady so brighte,
> "There thou meteste with a knyghte,   [Whenever]
> Do thi hode off, I highte,   [Take; charge (you)]
> And haylse hym in hy."   [greet; at once]   (ll. 401–404)

No mention is made, for example, of the equivalent moment in the other versions where the mother advises her son to take food and drink, rings and the love of a lady, whether or not she consents – which traditionally casts doubt over the mother's motivations, and justifies Perceval's/Parzifal's/Peredur's subsequent need to be educated by his uncles, who are absent in *Percyvell*. On the other hand, more space is dedicated to Percyvell's good (and good-natured) instincts, which pertain less to chivalry as advised by his mother than to magnanimity and fairness. Eckhardt (1974, 207) is right to point out that, in this context, "the mental habit so stressed by Chrétien of the boy's failing to listen, of his rudely neglecting to care about the feelings of others, is much less in evidence here." Indeed, the protagonist's words to his mother are ever-caring, both at the beginning and at the end of the story: "Swete modir" (ll. 197, 241, 405; cf. "My modir [...] dere," l. 2223) and he cannot be accused of harsh or selfish arrogance in his address to others either, as he might be in the *Conte*. In fact, his gesture of halving the food he finds on his first adventure signals an endearing character feature:

The corne he partis in two,	[divides]
(Gaffe his mere the tone of thoo)	[one (half)]
And to the borde gan he goo,	
Certayne that tyde.	[then]
He fande a lofe of brede fyne	
And a pychere with wyne,	
A mese of the kechyne,	[dish (of food) from]
A knyfe ther beside;	
The mete ther that he fande,	
He dalte it even with his hande,	[divided; exactly]
Lefte the halfe lyggande	
A felawe to byde.	
The tother halfe ete he –	
How my3te he more of mesure be?	(ll. 449–462)

Here, unlike the protagonist of the French, German and Welsh versions, Percyvell displays the pragmatism of one unaccustomed to anything other than simple living. Whether or not this should be seen as "foolishness" and "simplicity", with the poet adding an element of "harmless humour", as Eckhardt (1974, 211) suggests, is open to interpretation. Eckhardt continues by justifying this critical interpretation in the light of Percyvell's thought of sharing food "both for himself and his mare", framed as it is by the (poet's) rhetorical question "How might he be more 'measured'?", as an indication of Percyvell's own literal application of his mother's word "mesure". Should the Middle English gobble their lunch in the way that Chrétien's carefree Perceval and Wolfram's Parzival do? The answer might be found not within the tale itself, but rather in the context in which medieval English audiences would have understood it – that of popular romance. In the other "family" romances copied into this booklet in the Lincoln Thornton manuscript, we see the same middle-class values and the educational core of manuals of nurture (the actual word used by Percyvell's mother); in other words, a "proper" way of doing things can be taken literally. That Percyvell *has to* behave this way, because this is the only way he has learned whilst at home, is a dimension that would not be lost on the Middle English audience of the text within this particular manuscript context. The protagonists of *Sir Isumbras* and *Octavian* are evidently not of the same status as the Perceval of Chrétien's *Conte*, but for now

Percyvell joins their ranks, reassuringly perhaps for the Lincoln Thornton's audience, through his behaviour, outside of the courtly context in which manners are expected of noble born protagonists.

Within this context, several other aspects of Percyvell's trajectory, or the shape of his quest, take on different interpretations. For example, with Gawain's help, Percyvell of the Middle English popular romance learns and then forgets that taking a vanquished knight's armour can be done by the expert untying of the laces rather than by burning the corpse, in a development that is as comical as it is profoundly unsettling. This is undoubtedly an intentional feature developed by the anonymous author, the tragi-comedy, which would have been immediately apparent to the original audience:

> Now es Percyvell lyghte   [eager]
> To unspoyle the Rede Knyghte –   [disarm]
> Bot he ne couthe never fynd righte
> The lacynge of his wede.   [fastenings; armour]
> He was armede so wele
> In gude iryn and in stele,
> He couthe not gett of a dele,   [scrap (of it)]
> For nonkyns nede!   [Not to save his life]
> He sayd, "My moder bad me
> When my dart solde broken be,
> Owte of the iren bren the tree: [wood]
> Now es me fyre gnede."   [lacking]
> Now he getis hym flynt,
> His fyre iren he hent,
> And then withowtten any stynt,   [delay]
> He kyndilt a glede.   [fire]
> [...]
> A grete fyre made he than
> The Rede Knyghte in to bren –   [burn]
> For he ne couthe nott ken   [did not know how]
> His gere off to take.
> Be than was sir Gawayne dyght,
> Folowede after the fyghte
> Betwene hym and the Rede Knyghte,
> For the childes sake.
> [...]
> Than sir Gawayne doun lyghte,
> Unlacede the Rede Knyghte;
> The childe in his armour dight,   [arrayed]
> At his awnn will.   [just as he wished] (ll. 741–756; 761–768; 785–788)

In relation to this passage Eckhart (1974, 206) contends that:

> the English poet ignores, or softens, the crueler aspects of his hero's personality, so that the growing awareness of serious fault so important in Chrétien is absent, and there results a brighter, if rougher, comedy, without undertones of moral darkness.

One might wonder if rough comedy is the only aspect of the "adventure" that an audience would perceive, especially in the context of middle-class values being explored at length in the popular romance tradition. It is both puzzling and disturbing that Percyvell has no consideration for the vanquished knight's bodily integrity; after all, he believes his opponent still alive, and nonetheless tries to burn him. If our modern assumptions lead us to value comedy over the moral meaning of the story, we might believe that the middle-class audience of this text is unable or unwilling to engage with moral considerations; this does not mean the audience would not additionally enjoy the story for fun. This judgment takes the side of an older argument about the presumed unsophisticated audiences of popular romances; at the same time it also reads *Percyvell* in isolation from the literary context in which it has survived, that is in terms of both the popular romance tradition in general and the particular manuscript context into which it was copied.

A brief look at the other romances (Arthurian and non-Arthurian) in the Lincoln Thornton helps to elucidate the context for the reading of this version of the *Perceval* story by fifteenth-century gentry audiences. Each of the protagonists of the popular romances copied into the manuscript in the vicinity of *Percyvell* undergoes trials that involve physical as well as moral growth. Isumbras loses his status, only to regain it at the end of a penitential journey during which he also learns the value of honouring his family. Interestingly, in *Isumbras*, the ring functions as a typical recognition token in a highly emotional scene when the eponymous hero and his estranged wife are reunited by chance. In the only other Arthurian romances copied by Thornton in the same booklet as *Percyvell*, specifically the Alliterative *Morte Arthure* and the *Awntyrs of Arthure*, the latter copied just before *Percyvell*, heavy emphasis is placed on moral responsibility for past actions, and chivalric conduct comes under scrutiny more than once, in both overt and subtle ways. Without suggesting that one text copied into an anthology as varied as the Lincoln Thornton's necessarily fits in with the specific concerns of another, or that one text is modified to suit another, we should consider the context in which the text survives as an indication of the depth and sophistication with which middle-class readers of *Percyvell* were familiar, and likely enjoyed.

In more ways than one Percyvell's actions – for example, his attempt to burn the knight so as to get his armour – are glossed over in this text. The effect of this omission possibly hints at a deeper concern with how chivalric or unchivalric exploits are measured only against noble rules of conduct, rather than on a humane level. Bearing in mind the lessons of the *Awntyrs of Arthure*, the text that precedes *Percyvell* in this manuscript, the reader might ponder on the unfair advantage that Gawain has in the *Awntyrs* over Galeron, because Gawain is Arthur's nephew, and thus the audience is predisposed to favour his exploits even when he is unfair to others. On the same level of interpretation, both Percyvell's rash decision to burn the Red Knight in order to get the armour, and Gawain's assistance with "doing things properly" merely highlight the sense of entitlement these knights possess in "despoiling" and humiliating others (to use the term Gawain employs in *Awntyrs*). While the earlier French and German versions of the story contain this scene, with little variation, the deeper spiritual implications of the Grail and the associated trials Perceval/Parzifal faces during his quest make this initial blunder a distant memory. In the English *Percyvell* the audience is simply not allowed to forget because there is far more emphasis on both *what* Percyvell does and *how* he does it, from a pragmatic point of view, when he encounters an opponent. The English protagonist displays boundless energy and a greed for full-on combat, forgetting, in all likelihood, that to be a knight means to grow into one, hence necessitating a lot more than just the display of physical strength.

This interpretation becomes even more relevant as this Percyvell does not learn from his experience, and finds himself thinking again of burning another enemy, without any thought for Gawain's previous advice and assistance in the earlier episode:

> Fayne wolde he hafe hym slayne,
> This uncely sowdane,   [accursed]
> Bot gate couthe he get nane –   [way (into the armour)]
> So ill was he kende.   [taught]
> Than thynkes the childe
> Of olde werkes full wylde: [past deeds]
> "Hade I a fire now in this filde,
> Righte here he solde be brende!"   (ll. 1673–1679)

Although on this occasion his enemy, the sultan Gollerotham, is not dead, but very much alive and well, it takes Gawain's advice to remind Percyvell that a better tactic might be to fight with the sultan on foot and thus win the fight, which Percyvell does. The episode also includes a somewhat recognizable, though completely changed, scene, in which Percyvell is stunned and in a reverie. On this occasion, however, he is thinking not of his beloved (as in the equivalent scenes in the French and Welsh versions), but about the terminology for his means of transport (since Gawain has revealed, rather amusingly, that not all horses are mares):

> Than his swerde drawes he,
> Strykes at Percevell the fre:
> The childe hadd no powsté   [skill]
> His laykes to lett.   [attack; parry]
> The stede was his awnn will;   [master]
> Saw the swerde come hym till,
> Leppe up over an hill –
> Five stryde mett!
> Als he sprent forby,
> The sowdan keste up a cry:
> The childe wan nowt of study   [came; perplexed state]
> That he was inn sett.
> [...]
> He [Percyvell] says, "Now hase thou taughte me
> How that I sall wirke with the!"
> Then his swerde drawes he
> And strake to hym thro.
> He hit hym even one the nekk bane
> Thurgh ventale and pesane: [neck and chest armour]
> The hede of the sowdane
> He strykes the body fra.
> [...]
> Many mirthes then he made [...]
> That he had slane the sowdane
> And wele won that wymann
> *With maystry and myghte.*   (ll. 1700–1711; 1716–1723; 1728; 1733–1735; my emphasis)

Once again, while the French and German Percevals are criticized more for their lack of depth in coping with the demands of the Grail Quest, the Middle English Percyvell is unable to remember the practical advice that would enable him to fulfil part of his own quest and display proper chivalric behaviour. It is ironic, therefore, that he is recognized by Gawain for this action rather than as a result of his chivalric exploits per se: "with maystry" would indicate skill, but Percyvell is not a master; rather he has employed the style he sees the sultan using ("now hast thou taughte me").

That *Percyvell* and its quest structure might be better interpreted from a middle-class perspective is also supported by the anonymous author's treatment of Lady Lufamour. The latter displays instant pragmatism, a feature that works well in the context of Thornton's "gentry romances", as Michael Johnston (2014) has called a selection of texts copied into the Lincoln Thornton manuscript (albeit not this one). When Chrétien's Laudine from *Yvain* (*Le Chevalier au lion*) – who may be seen as a distant analogue of Lufamour, the defenceless lady who needs a champion – finds herself without a protector, she takes a while to warm to the prospect of a new suitor, in spite of Yvain's good looks and superior prowess to her (now dead) husband. By contrast, Lufamour immediately judges Percyvell's physical strength to be sufficient enough to recommend him as her champion:

> Faste the lady hym behelde;
> Scho thought hym worthi to welde,
> And he myghte wyn hir in felde
> With maystry and myghte. (ll. 1309–1312)

Her decision is quickly acted upon, and our "country bumpkin" is invited to sit at the high table and is served while seated in nothing less than a golden chair:

> The childe was sett on the dese   [dais]
> And served with reches   [splendidly]
> (I tell yow withowtten lese)   [truly]
> That gaynely was get;   [quickly]
> In a chayere of golde
> Bifore the fayrest to beholde   (ll. 1317–1322)

At this point Lufamour makes her promise that "Who that may his bon [*slayer*] be,/ Sall hafe this kyngdome and me/ To welde at his will." (ll. 1338–1339) Thus Lufamour does not need (as, for example, does Chrétien's Laudine) to hear of her suitor's lineage. Lufamour only finds out about Percyvell's lineage from Arthur some two hundred lines further on in the romance, when she is surprised by Percyvell's unpolished behaviour, both in the court and on the battlefield:

> At the first bygynnyng
> Scho frayned Arthour the kyng   [questioned]
> Of childe Percevell the yyng –
> What life he had in bene.
> Grete wondir had Lufamour
> He was so styffe in stour
> And couthe so littill of nurtour,   [courtesy]
> Als scho had there sene.   (ll. 1560–1567)

The values put forward by this text, therefore, also revolve around pragmatism of choice; Lady Lufamour chooses Percyvell despite his evident unpreparedness for a courtly life. The anonymous author thus highlights her unromantic appreciation of his sheer determination and physical strength at the expense of any sophistication and courtly manners. By the end of the romance there are no signs that Percyvell has learned any more in the way of either chivalric behaviour in combat or in courtly society, yet this does not disqualify him from becoming the king of Lufamour's lands. For this reason it is perhaps obvious that the author's attitude toward his romance material might be, as Eckhardt (1974, 207) suggests, that of "happy gusto, with many a belly-laugh, several times a snort of amusement, but no complicated, sophisticated, quiet jokes, no literary parody," as well as something else. The tone and structure are uncomplicated indeed – deliberately so. Yet the way in which Lufamour readily accepts Percyvell as her champion and, later, her husband before she learns of his noble lineage reminds us of Sir Thomas Malory's later creation of another Fair Unknown, the unlikely kitchen knave, Beaumains, who turns out to be Sir Gareth, truly one of Arthur's nephews. However, while both Gareth's courtly manners and his chivalric prowess are without reproach throughout his story, Percyvell cannot boast the same nobility of action by the end of his adventures – just the nobility of his birth. In true fifteenth-century fashion, one might say, the middle-class dreams and aspirations of this text's readers might well be vindicated in Percyvell's unchanged "country bumpkin" behaviour: one can have the lovely rich heiress, be revealed to be related to no less than King Arthur, and still not be required to change one's ways.

Moving on to the last scenes of the romance, where Percyvell's quest comes full circle, his thoughts turn to his mother, who has not, as in Chrétien's version, fallen into a deadly faint at her son's departure. Percyvell needs no one to remind him of his duty to the mother, and he leaves his new wife as easily as he did his mother. However, it is interesting to note that his thoughts turn to her as he recalls that he left her "manles" – without a protector, at the end of a year he has enjoyed in his new position as king in Lufamour's lands, as that lady's protector:

> Til it byfelle appon a day,
> Als he in his bedd lay,
> Till hymselfe gun he say
> (Syghande full sare):   [sighing]
> "The laste Yole day that was
> Wilde ways I chese;
> My modir all manles   [without male protector]
> Leved I thare."   (ll. 1780–1791)

His pragmatic thoughts match the tone of the romance and mark the return to middle-class considerations. When he puts on the clothes he used to wear, for the sake of his mother, so as to bring her back to sanity, he clearly acknowledges both the long way he has come, and the value of those family bonds he was taught by his mother:

His armour he leved therein;
Toke one hym a gayt skynne
And to the wodde gan he wyn,   [made his way]
Among the holtis hare.
A sevenyght long hase he soghte;
His modir ne fyndis he noghte,
Of mete ne drynke he ne roghte,   [took no heed]
So full he was of care.   (ll. 2196–2223)

This passage reminds the reader not only of Percyvell's old ways but also of another hero of Middle English romance, the protagonist of *Sir Orfeo*, whose self-imposed exile is the key to his finding his lost wife. Percyvell's return to the woods does not detract from his achievements (a lovely lady and a kingly crown), but it does restore a sense of a natural state – unambiguously advocating that love for the mother is the pillar of his development. Only after his healing of the mother does Percyvell return to his wife and position, and eventually, and rather cursorily, leaves for the Holy Land, where his achievements are more of the worldly, rather than spiritual, kind:

Sythen he went into the Holy Londe,
Wanne many cites full stronge,
And there was he slayne, I undirstonde,
Thus gatis endis hee.   [In this way]
Now Jhesu Criste Hevens Kyng,
Als he es lorde of all thyng,
Grante us all his blyssyng:
Amen for charité!   (ll. 2280–2287)

Does this mean that the moral and spiritual components in *Percyvell* actually pertain to his unending love of the mother, rather than, as is the case for the French and German Percevals, to the love of God? The ring brings Percyvell and his mother together, but it is the mother's love and his love for her that acts as a circle that has to be completed.[5] However, a new turn in the story gives precedence to the year-long absence, during which Percyvell has accomplished so much, but which started on Christmas Day ("tomorne es forthirmaste Yole day [...]" l. 393), unlike the timing of Chrétien's setting, which was spring (Putter 2004, 183). The circularity of the movement in the story predicts that Percyvell's impetuousness is matched by the series of events that unfold, each leading him closer to a solu-

---

5 Putter and Eckhardt make similar points. See Putter (2004); Eckhardt (1974); see also Baron (1972).

tion for his mother's madness – the recovery of the ring from the maiden from whom he took it a year before, ready now for the moment he is reunited with his mother. Whether or not we agree with the anonymous author's choices in reshaping Percyvell's quest into a circular, and rather more worldly, trajectory, we have to admit the resulting structure is, indeed, satisfying and does not leave the reader wanting more complexity.

Finally, without fanfare, the anonymous author of *Percyvell* gestures toward "bookish" romances. When Arthur sees Percyvell for the first time, he cries out, recalling the story of Percyvell's father; he further announces that "The bokes says that he mon/ Venge his fader bane." (ll. 567–568) The circular movement of the story in this Middle English version is thus helped by the hint to predestination – a different kind from the complicated and spiritually edifying story of the French *Perceval*, but one that is valid in its own right nonetheless. This study has shown that the alteration of the quest motif from one that is concerned with seeking a spiritual object to one that is about reconnecting with certain worldly (family) values is unquestionably dramatic, but in some ways also familiar. The perennial question remains, therefore, as to whether *Percyvell* should be considered sufficiently related to its Grail counterparts to warrant further investigation of its sources, or be treated simply as a free interpretation of the original story, rejecting the spiritual messages and complicated esoteric associations of both the Grail and the educational trajectory of a naïve protagonist.

References

Baron, F. Xavier. "Mother and Son in *Sir Perceval of Galles*." *Papers in English Language and Literature* 8 (1972): 3–14.

Braswell, Mary Flowers. "The Search for the Holy Grail: Arthurian Lacunae in the England of Edward III." *Studies in Philology* 108 (2011): 469–487.

Brewer, D.S., and A. E.B. Owen, eds. *The Thornton Manuscript (Lincoln Cathedral Ms. 91)*. London: Scolar Press, 1978.

Busby, Keith. "Chrétien de Troyes English'd." *Neophilologus* 71 (1987): 696–713.

Busby, Keith. "*Sir Perceval of Galles, Le Conte du Graal* and *La Continuation-Gauvain*." *Études Anglaises* 31 (1978): 198–202.

Eckhardt, C.D. "Arthurian Comedy: The Simpleton-Hero in *Sir Perceval of Gales*." *Chaucer Review* 8 (1974): 205–220.

Fein, Susanna, and Michael Johnston, eds. *Robert Thornton and His Books: Essays on the Lincoln and London Thornton Manuscripts*. Woodbridge: Boydell and Brewer/York Medieval Press, 2014.

Fowler, David C. "*Le Conte du Graal* and *Sir Perceval of Galles*." *Comparative Literature Studies* 12 (1975): 5–20.

Johnston, Michael. *Romance and the Gentry*. Oxford: Oxford University Press, 2014.

Mills, Maldwyn, ed. *Ywain and Gawain, Sir Percyvell of Gales, The Anturs of Arther*. London: J.M. Dent, 1992.

Putter, Ad. "Arthurian Romance in English Popular Tradition: *Sir Percyvell of Gales*, *Sir Cleges*, and *Sir Launfal*." *A Companion to Arthurian Literature*. Ed. Helen Fulton. Oxford and Malden, MA: Wiley-Blackwell, 2009. 235–251.

Putter, Ad. "Story Line and Story Shape in *Sir Percyvell of Gales* and Chrétien de Troyes's *Conte du Graal*." *Pulp Fictions of Medieval England*. Ed. Nicola McDonald. Manchester: Manchester University Press, 2004. 171–196.

Wülfung, J. Ernst, ed. *Laud Troy Book (c. 1400)*. London: Kegan Paul, Trench, Trübner and Co, 1902–1903.

Lowri Morgans
Peredur son of Efrawg: The Question of Translation and/or Adaptation

The Welsh texts of *Peredur, Owain* and *Geraint* have been subject to much debate by critics, in particular in terms of their narrative structure, style, motifs and themes. A particular subject of interest has been the question of translation and/or adaptation of the text *Peredur son of Efrawg* and its relationship with the French text, *Perceval* (the *Conte du Graal*).[1] There is an obvious connection between the tales of *Peredur, Owain* and *Geraint* and their French counterparts, *Perceval, Yvain* and *Erec* by Chrétien de Troyes, and it is one which has fuelled much scholarly debate about the precise ways in which they interconnect. In the case of *Peredur*, this question arguably poses the most difficulty as the manuscript tradition of the story is complex, and the authorship and date of the tale remain uncertain.

Eleven medieval Welsh tales form the corpus commonly known as the *Mabinogion*. These are tales of myth and legend from medieval Wales which reflect its culture and Celtic traditions. Although the stories are referred to collectively as the *Mabinogion*, they do not share the same "date, authorship, sources, background and content." (Davies 1988, 133) It is suggested that they were written down between the eleventh and fourteenth centuries, during a period where there were "foreign influences on native prose and poetry." (Davies 1988, 134) Some of the stories are about the adventures of the native heroes and others, such as *Peredur*, tell the story of King Arthur and his knights. The *Mabinogion* tales were labelled for convenience by Lady Charlotte Guest during the nineteenth century, and she separated the native Welsh prose tales and grouped them as follows: the *Four Branches of the Mabinogi, Culhwch ac Olwen*, the two dreams, *Cyfranc Lludd a Llefelys. Peredur, Owain* and *Geraint* were referred to collectively as the "three romances" which, given their form, is little more than a useful label, and used only because of their correspondence with the works of Chrétien de Troyes (Davies 2007, xi).

The collection of the *Mabinogion* tales which includes *Peredur* is found in the "White Book of Rhydderch" (Aberystwyth, National Library of Wales, Peniarth

---

1 For detailed analysis on the arguments surrounding the source of the Welsh romances, examples include: Jones (1956–1957, 208–227); Foster (1959, 192–205); Roberts (1976, 203–243); Goetinck (1975); Lloyd-Morgan (1986, 78–91).

Lowri Morgans (Independent Scholar)

DOI 10.1515/9783110432466-026

4–5, dated *c.* 1350) and also the "Red Book of Hergest" (Oxford, Bodleian Library, Jesus College 111), which is dated to between 1382 and *c.* 1400 (Huws 2000, 8). The versions of *Peredur* found in these two manuscripts are very similar. A copy of the tale of *Peredur* is found in two further medieval manuscripts. The earliest known version is preserved in Aberystwyth, National Library of Wales, Peniarth 7 (hereafter Peniarth 7), dated *c.* 1300. Although there are some leaves missing, it can be seen that the version differs from the ones found in the Welsh Book of Rhydderch and the Red Book of Hergest. The story ends after Peredur lives with the Empress of Constantinople and the scribe of Peniarth 7 indicates that his version of the text ends here on f. 15v as a completed version: "Ac yvelly y tervyna kynnyd paredur ap Efrawc." (Luft, Thomas and Smith 2013, 35–36) [And thus ends the development of Peredur son of Efrawg. (Vitt 2010, 204)] This, of course, implies that the story was complete since it follows the same formulaic ending which is used in the *Four Branches of the Mabinogi*, "Ac uelly y teruyna y geing hon yma o'r Mabynnogyon" (Pwyll 23, 654) [And so ends this branch of the Mabinogion (Davies 2007, 21)]. This has led many scholars to believe that this may have been the original version, and that the additional section found in the two later manuscripts is a later augmentation.

A fragment of the text is also found in Aberystwyth, National Library of Wales, Peniarth 14 (hereafter Peniarth 14), dated to the first half of the fourteenth century. The end of Peredur's story is missing from this manuscript, as the story ends mid-sentence after Peredur's visit to see the first uncle. Therefore, it is impossible to know whether this version of the text agrees with the later manuscripts or whether it follows the short version found in Peniarth 7. Thus, we see that there are two versions of the tale of *Peredur* in the medieval Welsh manuscript tradition; we may add to this the fact that "the longer version of *Peredur* has become the definitive one." (Lloyd-Morgan 1981, 195)

The date of *Peredur* has been much debated.[2] Glenys Goetinck (1975; 1976; 1964) suggests that the tale dates from around 1135, while Stephen Knight (2000, 144) argues that the tale "need be much later than about 1150." Morfydd Owen (2000) argues for a date in the mid- to late-twelfth century. Brynley F. Roberts suggests that the romances date to *c.* 1200 (Roberts 1976, 225), while Rachel Bromwich agrees with Roberts "to locate the romances to about 1200." (Bromwich 1974, 155) Breeze (2003, 63) uses the reference to windmills as a guide to help date the tale of *Peredur* arguing that "*Peredur* could hardly have been written much before 1200." *Peredur* is now commonly attributed to *c.* 1200 during the reign of

---

2 For a good overview of the scholarly discussion regarding the date of the tale, *Peredur son of Efrawg*, see Breeze (2003, 60–61).

the Prince of Gwynedd, Llywelyn ab Iorwerth, or Llywelyn the Great (1173–1240), who was married to Joan, the daughter of King John. French was widely spoken in the court of Llywelyn the Great and as the Welsh and Anglo-Normans co-habited one can assume that the two cultures would influence each other and that literary borrowings would have been natural. There are more definite dates attributed to the tale of *Perceval*, with Chrétien's works widely held to have been composed in the second half of the twelfth century (Kelly 2006, 137), most likely around the 1170–1180s, and it is suspected that Chrétien's unfinished tale of *Perceval* or *Le Conte du Graal* dates to around 1181, and no later than 1191.

Peredur is the story of the upbringing of a young boy who wants to be a knight, and we learn about the education he receives from his uncles and his adventures on the road to achieving his aim. He is clueless about the code of conduct used in the court and the way he should behave when he meets ladies, but this is also a part of his training. The themes of education and training are central to the first part of the narrative (Roberts 1988, 37). During his training when he visits his uncle, there is a procession thought by some scholars to be the procession of the Grail, although the text does not mention the Grail at all. Peredur is knighted in Arthur's court and meets Angharad Law Eurawg, the maiden he loves the most. He then leaves Arthur's court and explores further adventures once he becomes a knight. This section has some characteristics of oral storytelling, such as the episodic nature of *Culhwch ac Olwen*, in which Culhwch completes the tasks in the quest for Olwen. In the case of *Peredur*, the adventures include fighting other knights, going hunting, meeting the Countess of Constantinople and overthrowing the knights sent to the Empress. Again, as in oral tradition, there are examples of triple repetition in the tale such as the Empress sending three messengers to Peredur, whom he rejects, three men visiting the Empress with a goblet and Peredur killing the three of them. After this episode, Peredur lives with the Empress for fourteen years, which is where this version, preserved in Peniarth 7, ends; as already noted, this may be the original form of the tale. However, there is, of course, a further section in the copies found in the White Book of Rhydderch and Red Book of Hergest. This section begins with the ugly maiden confronting Peredur in Arthur's court and then Peredur and Gwalchmai leaving Arthur's court together but going their separate ways. The tale then follows Gwalchmai's adventure for a short period before returning to Peredur who is seeking information about the Fortress of Wonders. The tale then echoes an episode from the story of *Culhwch ac Olwen* where Arthur and his men, including Peredur, are fighting the witches of Caerloyw. The tale ends by turning to the old King Arthur, who is depicted as a strong warrior, similar to how he is portrayed in the native Welsh prose of *Culhwch ac Olwen*, and a different portrayal from that in the three romances. Sioned Davies (2000, 88) convincingly argues that we cannot consider one author or one text for *Peredur*, as it reflects a continued tradition of copying, editing and re-writing for different audiences (cf. Hogenbirk, *supra*).

Many critics have written about the style and complex structure of *Peredur*.[3] For our purposes, it is simplest to discern four main sections: the first where Peredur is knighted in Arthur's court; the second section where he is with Angharad Law Eurawg; the third includes Peredur's adventures after becoming a knight until he meets the Empress; and the fourth runs from the appearance of the ugly maiden until the adventures of the Fortress of Wonders where the story ends. All four sections of this story are found in the White Book of Rhydderch and the Red Book of Hergest. Sections one, two and three are present in Peniarth 7. In the version found in Peniarth 14, the story comes to an end after Peredur's visit to his first uncle owing to the manuscript's mutilation.

In respect of the question of adaptation or translation of the three Welsh romances, there are various schools of thought:[4] one theory is that the stories are Celtic in origin, and were transmitted to France through the Breton *conteurs*, while others argue that this is highly unlikely. Others still have suggested that the only Celtic elements are the names and place-names, and that the tales reflect French society, while a further wide-spread argument is the common source theory, which states that the Welsh romances were created independently from the French romances, but that they were inspired by one common source which was probably French. Some "nationalistic" scholars, to employ Ceridwen Lloyd-Morgan's term (1986), argue that the Welsh romances are not indebted to Chrétien de Troyes at all, and are purely Welsh creations. The most recent scholarship in relation to this question suggests that the Welsh romances were adapted from the works of Chrétien de Troyes. Roberts (1992, 58) suggests that the transmission of both French and Welsh texts happened together and that Chrétien was the source for the Welsh romances, which were adapted for a Welsh audience. He explains:

> Significant differences between the Welsh and French texts make it unlikely that the Welsh stories are taken directly or without some adaptation from Chrétien, but a popular view has been that both versions derive independently from a common source, defined as French tales used by the poet.

3 According to Lloyd-Morgan (1981, 187–231), for instance, there are five main sections to the story. Glenys Goetinck (1975) has argued that there are four sections to the tale. Brynley F. Roberts (2000, 61) identifies three main parts to the story, with Arthur's court being the focal point each time.
4 Jones (1956–1957, 208–227); Foster (1959, 192–205); Roberts (1976, 203–243); Goetinck (1975); Lloyd-Morgan (1986, 78–91).

Roberts notes that the Welsh romances were adapted and written in the *cyfar-wydd*, or oral style,[5] much like the *Four Branches of the Mabinogi* and the tale of *Culhwch ac Olwen*. This can be seen as a way of engaging the audience, with new traditions in the story including the tournaments, the castles and chivalry. While this is different from the milieu of the native tales, the style and structure would have been very familiar to the Welsh audience.

Lloyd-Morgan (1991, 46) has considered the question of adaptation and/or translation extensively, cautioning that "too often it has been assumed that Wales was an island of primitive Celtic culture, where oral tradition reigned supreme." She stresses that the Welsh romances are adaptations of the French romances and that the Welsh redactors would tend to "follow the main narrative outline but to avoid close translation." (1991, 49) She bases her argument on the fact that the three romances must be adaptations rather than translations because, after the fourteenth century, no known native Welsh tales were composed. During this period, translations of many continental tales dominated Medieval Welsh liter-ary culture. Many French, English and Latin texts were directly translated into Welsh, though these were more strict translations and therefore much closer to the originals. Lloyd-Morgan (2000, 118) also highlights that there is no mention of the Grail in Welsh poetry from the earlier period or in the native triads, *Trioedd Ynys Prydain*. Through her consideration of the European context of *Peredur*, Lloyd-Morgan (2000, 126) is led to the conclusion that *Peredur* is indebted to more than one French romance, and that the author of the Welsh tale was also familiar with a number of other French romances from which he could borrow, and adapt, for the Welsh audience.

When comparing the three Welsh romances with their French counterparts there are clear similarities between the stories of *Geraint* and *Erec*, as well as between *Owain* and *Yvain*. However, *Peredur* and *Perceval* are perhaps the least similar of the three pairs. There are also clear differences between the style of *Peredur* and Chrétien's *Perceval*. The author of *Peredur* seems to have little inter-est in feelings, details and long descriptions, preferring instead to convey the background and describe incidents. Goetinck (1964, 61) further suggests that the author of *Peredur* has no interest in love or nature and that the characters in the story are mere "types". Chrétien, on the other hand, provides details about feel-ings and there is a clear emphasis on the hero's development throughout the tale, whereas Peredur's development is by no means as marked in the Welsh version. *Perceval* is, in other words, a much more complete and sophisticated version, while *Peredur* is much more reminiscent of an old saga (Goetinck 1964, 63). Fur-

---

5 The term *cyfarwydd* in Medieval Welsh means story-teller.

thermore, even when there are similarities between the two tales, the order of the episodes or details is usually different. For example, in the Welsh text, we learn first of Peredur's father and why his mother has nurtured him away from the life of the court, and then Peredur sees Arthur's knights and he tells his mother that he would like to become a knight, at which point she gives him her advice. In the French counterpart, by contrast, the order is different: Perceval sees the knights, we then learn of the father's death, and then the mother gives advice to her son, before he embarks on his quest to become King Arthur's knight. The emphasis in the Welsh text is on the innocence of a child, depicted through Peredur's character, which is quite different from Perceval's; the latter is perceived as stupid and a laughing stock.

The style of the two authors is also very different. *Peredur* is more concise in its rhetoric, which quickens the pace of the story, and the form is prose, as is more typical in Welsh and Irish storytelling, allowing for more emphasis on battles and attacks, thus bringing to mind the style of *Culhwch ac Olwen*.[6] In *Perceval*, Chrétien is more descriptive and, by using the verse form, is able to convey a very different mood and style. There are also a number of episodes in *Peredur* that are reminiscent of *Culhwch ac Olwen*. For example, the innocent depiction of Peredur's appearance seems to suggest a parody of the description of Culhwch as he rides his horse to King Arthur's court for the first time. Peredur looks very untidy on his horse (*Peredur* 9: 11–18;[7] Davies 2007, 66–67) as he leaves his mother, especially compared to the description of Culhwch, who looks immaculate as he seeks Arthur's aid at his court (*Culhwch* 3–4: 60–81;[8] Davies 2007, 180–181). They are both also unaware of the code of conduct required to gain access to the court of King Arthur: Culhwch learns of the convention of gaining access to the court by having a conversation with Arthur's gatekeeper, Glewlwyd Gafaelfawr, but rides in on his horse since he is unaware that he should leave his horse outside with the gatekeeper (*Culhwch* 6: 140–141; Davies 2007, 183). Peredur similarly rides in on his bony horse to the court of Arthur (*Peredur*, 12: 12–14; Davies 2007, 68).

A further example is provided by *Peredur* where it tells of Arthur fighting the witches of Caerloyw, a scene that is reminiscent of the episode in *Culhwch ac Olwen* where the witch's blood is needed to complete one of the tasks. Arthur's men are sent to kill the witch but are unsuccessful; therefore, Arthur steps in to kill her with his knife and he strikes her in half (*Culhwch* 41–42: 1205–1229; Davies 2007, 212–213). In the tale of *Peredur*, Arthur and his men are summoned to fight

---

6 It is worth noting that narrative is not used in verse form until the fourteenth century in Wales.
7 All references to *Peredur* are to Goetinck (1976).
8 All references to *Culhwch ac Olwen* are to Bromwich and Evans (1997).

the witches of Caerloyw. A witch kills one of Arthur's men in front of Peredur and he tells her to stop but she does not listen and instead kills another of Arthur's men. This prompts Peredur to strike the witch with his sword, before King Arthur and his men kill all of the witches (*Peredur* 70: 8–25; Davies 2007, 102). Perhaps pertinently, this episode actually does not occur in the French version, being possibly unique to the Welsh tradition, and this is not the only episode to fall into this category.

One example is provided by the episode with Angharad Law Eurawg, which is generally believed to have derived "from native Welsh tradition." (Lloyd-Morgan 2009, 133) Another is that of the Empress of Constantinople. The inverse is also true in some cases, such as the episodes that include Blanchefleur in the text of *Perceval*, which do not appear in the Welsh version. There is also no mention of the word "Grail" in the Welsh version, and there are only passing references to Christian institutions in *Peredur*, whereas in *Perceval* religion and religious institutions give structure to everyday life. Lloyd-Morgan believes that this "may perhaps reflect Welsh unease with spiritual elements in prose narratives still cast in a largely traditional mould." (Lloyd-Morgan 2009, 136) Furthermore, the episode of Gwalchmai in *Peredur* is very brief, and the author quickly turns its focus back to the adventures of Peredur. By contrast Gauvain's adventures in the text of *Perceval* are much longer: the knight leaves King Arthur's court at the same time as Perceval to seek adventures, and the French text follows Gauvain's adventures in great detail before returning for a very short period to those of Perceval.[9]

One custom that is removed almost completely from the Welsh adaptation is kissing. Although there are many examples of kissing observed in *Perceval*, there is only one example of a kiss included by the author of *Peredur*. This kiss happens between Peredur and the Maiden in the Pavilion, as Peredur kneels in front of the maiden and kisses her:

> Y vodrwy a gymerth Peredur, ac estwg ar pen y lin a rodi cusan y'r vorwyn, a chymryt y varch a chychwynu y ymdeith. (*Peredur* 11: 4–6)
> [Peredur took the ring. And he went down on his knee and kissed the maiden. And he took his horse and set off. (Davies 2007, 67)]

The fact that he has a ring in his hand reminds us of the proposition of marriage, but this is not a proposal, but rather a kiss of greeting from Peredur to the

---

9 Had Chrétien completed the text, it is suspected that he would have returned to the adventures of Perceval in greater detail, but this still does not detract from the large space given to the adventures of Gauvain.

maiden, which is a symbol of respect and gratitude. In this action, it is important to remember that Peredur follows his mother's advice as to how to behave in this situation:

> O gwely gwreic tec, gordercha hi kyn ny'th vynho. Gwell gwr a ffenedigach y'th wna no chynt. (*Peredur* 10: 1–3)
>
> [If you see a beautiful lady, make love to her even though she does not want you – it will make you a better and braver man than before. (Davies 2007, 66–67)]

The word "gorddercha" means the physical action of taking someone sexually (*Geiriadur Prifysgol Cymru* 1950, 631). But Peredur does not understand his mother's words in this instance as he just kisses the maiden, and afterwards confesses that he does not understand his own actions. This is the only example of a kiss in the eleven *Mabinogion* tales and the absence of the kiss in the prose tales suggests that this was not a part of Welsh literary culture.

When comparing this with the same episode in the French version, a great deal more detail is expressed.

> Li vaslex avoit les braz forz,
> si l'anbrace mout nicemant,
> car il nel sot fere autremant,
> mist la soz lui tote estandue,
> et cele s'est mout desfandue
> et deganchi quan qu'ele pot;
> mes desfansse mestier n'i ot,
> que li vaslez an un randon
> la beisa, volsist ele ou non,
> .XX. foiz, si com li contes dit,
> tant c'un anelan son doi vit,
> a une esmeraude mout clere (Chrétien de Troyes 1972, ll. 698–709)
>
> [But the boy had strong arms and embraced her – but gauchely, for that was the only way he knew. Then he laid her down full-length beneath him, and she struggled with all her might to get away; but she fought in vain, for whether she liked it or not the boy kissed her seven times in a row – so the story says – until he saw a ring on her finger crowned with a brilliant emerald. (Chrétien de Troyes 1982, 8–9)]

Here we see the positions of the characters: the maiden is held down underneath Perceval, and is put in a place of danger, as if he were going to rape her. We hear about her attempts to escape as she tries to fight him. It goes on to say that Perceval kisses her twenty times in a row. There is therefore a lot more drama in the French version, and the maiden's fear of Perceval is expressed in greater detail whereas in *Peredur*, the maiden greets him and makes him feel welcome. Also worth noting, in Old French – "baiser" means "to kiss", but its meaning has since evolved to mean "to take a person sexually", and one must wonder if any such connotation might have been intended. The mother's advice on maidens in the French version also differs:

> Se vos trovez ne pres ne loing
> dame qui d'aïe ait besoing,
> ne pucele desconselliee,
> la vostre aïe aparelliee
> lor soit, s'eles vos an requierent,
> que totes enors i afierent.
> Qui as dames enor ne porte,
> la soe enors doit estre morte.
> Dames et puceles servez,
> si seroiz par tot enorez;
> et se vos aucune an proiez,
> gardez que vos ne l'enuiez;
> ne fetes rien qui li despleise.
> De pucele a mout qui la beise;
> s'ele le beisier vos consant,
> le soreplus vos an desfant,
> se lessier le volez por moi.
> Et s'ele a enel an son doi,
> ou a sa ceinture aumosniere,
> se par amor ou par proiere
> le vos done, bon m'iert et bel
> que vos an portoiz son anel.
> De l'anel prandre vos doin gié,
> et de l'aumosniere, congié. (Chrétien de Troyes 1974, 21–22: 531–554)
> [If you encounter, near or far, a lady in need of help, or any girl in distress, be ready then to aid them if they request you to, for all honour lies in such deeds. When a man fails to honour ladies, his own honour must be dead. Serve ladies and girls, and you will be honoured everywhere. But if you should desire the love of any, take care that you don't annoy her by doing anything to displease her. And a maid who kisses gives much; so if she consents to kiss you, I forbid you to take more: for love of me, leave with the kiss. But if she has a ring on her finger or a purse at her waist, and for love or through your please she should give it to you, then in my eyes it would be fine and good that you should take her ring; yes, I give you leave to take the ring and purse. (Chrétien de Troyes 1982, 6–7)]

From the textual evidence here, I suggest that the kiss was a gesture later adopted from Middle English, since kissing as a phenomenon becomes more prominent in Welsh texts written later than the *Mabinogion*. Charlotte Ward (1992, 385) compares the Latin and the Welsh versions of the *Brut*, and says: "In Latin, greetings are always accompanied by kisses, but this public display of affection between men, appears to have been as alien to a medieval Welshman as it would be to a modern Welshman today." On this basis, it is likely that when the Welsh redactor was adapting the French tale for a Welsh audience, he did not consider this custom to be of importance.

From this all-too-brief comparison of elements from the two tales, the aims of both authors have shown themselves to be very different, and particularly that they are conscious of their task in targeting two very different audiences (cf. Taylor, *supra*). Furthermore, the evidence suggests that the text, *Peredur son of Efrawg*, is an adaptation of *Perceval*. A reflection of two different societies is found as we can see from the example of kissing in the Welsh adaptation, as well as from the new code of behaviour and the lack of understanding of the Grail. Elements derived from the oral tradition in the tale of *Peredur* resonate with the existing Welsh tradition, as it follows the formulaic and episodic structure found in the *Four Branches of the Mabinogi* and *Culhwch ac Olwen*. Additionally, the Welsh text is much shorter than is *Perceval*, with the author abbreviating many of the episodes when adapting the story for a Welsh audience. The tale has also been adapted to prose, the natural storytelling medium in Welsh, rather than maintaining the French verse. Indeed, the prose of *Peredur, Owain* and *Geraint* reflects a period of change in literary fashions, as no known Welsh prose has survived from the period, and no known tales of Welsh prose were composed after this period. In fact, during the late-thirteenth and fourteenth centuries, a new fashion of translating tales from the continent dominated the prose literature of the period. Lloyd-Morgan (2009, 140) explains that they were:

> [r]esponding to an increasing interest in fashionable French literature, [and] these texts provide a bridge not only between the old and the new, native and foreign, but also exemplify the gradual shift from orality to written culture, from public performance to private readings.

We must remember that the work of the medieval translator was rather different from that of the modern translator (Lloyd-Morgan 1985, 399; see also Taylor, *supra*). The task incorporated the freedom to translate directly, but also to discard anything thought to be irrelevant or not important to the Welsh audience, while traditions and customs peculiar to France would have been comprehensively adapted for the new Welsh audience (Lloyd-Morgan 1985, 404). Indeed, the Welsh and Anglo-Normans co-habited during the period when *Peredur son of Efrawg* was created, and during this time and even earlier, similar kinds of international influences can be traced in Welsh, even in the conservative medium of poetry (Haycock 1987).

The three Welsh romances depict a different life to that found in the *Four Branches of the Mabinogi* where the life of the tournaments, castles and knights as heroes reflects a new fashion and interest enjoyed by Welsh audiences. In the story of *Peredur son of Efrawg*, there are undoubtedly traces of such influences at work, as elsewhere in contemporary Welsh literature, and because of the complexity of old and new influences, we may never know with any certainty the full extent of the literary borrowings of the Welsh version from its French counterpart. Nevertheless, comparing the two reveals many of the fundamental and important differences between the expectations of audiences in France and Wales in this period.

References

Breeze, Andrew. "*Peredur son of Efrawg* and windmills." *Celtica* 24 (2003): 58–64.

Bromwich, Rachel. "Dwy Chwedl a Thair Rhamant." *Y Traddodiad Rhyddiaith yn yr Oesau Canol.* Ed. Geraint Bowen. Llandysul: Gwasg Gomer, 1974. 153–175.

Bromwich, Rachel, and D.S. Evans, eds. *Culhwch and Olwen: An Edition and Study of the Oldest Arthurian Tale.* Cardiff: University of Wales Press, 1997.

Chrétien de Troyes. *Perceval: The Story of the Grail.* Trans. Nigel Bryant. Cambridge: D.S. Brewer, 1982.

Chrétien de Troyes. *Les romans de Chrétien de Troyes, Le conte du Graal (Perceval), Tome I.* Ed. Félix Lecoy. Paris: Champion, 1972.

Davies, Sioned, trans. *The Mabinogion.* Oxford: Oxford University Press, 2007.

Davies, Sioned. "Cynnydd Peredur vab Efrawc." *Canhwyll Marchogyon: Cyd-destunoli Peredur.* Ed. Sioned Davies and Peter Wynn Thomas. Caerdydd: Gwasg Prifysgol Cymru, 2000. 65–90.

Davies, Sioned. "Written Text as Performance: The Implications for Middle Welsh Prose Narratives." *Literacy in Medieval Celtic Societies.* Ed. Huw Pryce. Cambridge: Cambridge University Press, 1988. 133–148.

Foster, Idris. "*Geraint, Owain* and *Peredur*." *Arthurian Literature in the Middle Ages.* Ed. R.S. Loomis. Oxford: Clarendon Press, 1959. 192–205.

Geiriadur Prifysgol Cymru: A Dictionary of the Welsh Language. Cardiff: University of Wales Press, 1950.

Goetinck, Glenys, ed. *Historia Peredur vab Efrawc.* Cardiff: University of Wales Press, 1976.

Goetinck, Glenys. *Peredur: A Study of Welsh Tradition in the Grail Legends.* Cardiff: University of Wales Press, 1975.

Goetinck, Glenys. "Peredur a Perceval." *Llên Cymru* 8 (1964): 58–64.

Haycock, Marged. "'Some Talk of Alexander and Some of Hercules': Three Early Medieval Poems from the Book of Taliesin." *Cambrian Medieval Celtic Studies* 13 (1987): 7–38.

Huws, Daniel. "Y Pedair Llawysgrif Ganoloesol." *Canhwyll Marchogyon: Cyd-destunoli Peredur.* Ed. Sioned Davies and Peter Wynn Thomas. Caerdydd: Gwasg Prifysgol Cymru, 2000. 1–9.

Jones, R.M. "Y Rhamantau Cymraeg a'u cysylltiadau Ffrangeg." *Llên Cymru* 4 (1956–1957): 208–227.

Kelly, Douglas. "Chrétien de Troyes." *The Arthur of the French.* Ed. Glyn S. Burgess and Karen Pratt. Cardiff: University of Wales Press, 2006. 135–185.

Knight, Stephen. "Resemblance and Menace: A Post-Colonial Reading of Peredur." *Canhwyll Marchogyon: Cyd-destunoli Peredur*. Ed. Sioned Davies and Peter Wynn Thomas. Caerdydd: Gwasg Prifysgol Cymru, 2000. 128–147.

Luft, Diana, Peter Wynn Thomas and D. Mark Smith, eds. "Peniarth 7." *Welsh Prose 1300–1425*. Cardiff: Cardiff University Press, 2013. Available at: <http://www.rhyddiaithganoloesol. caerdydd.ac.uk/en/ms-page.php?ms=Pen7&page=15v>.

Lloyd-Morgan, Ceridwen. "Migrating Narratives." *A Companion to Arthurian Literature*. Ed. Helen Fulton. Oxford: Wiley-Blackwell, 2009. 131–140.

Lloyd-Morgan, Ceridwen. "Y Cyd-destun Ewropeaidd." *Canhwyll Marchogyon: Cyd-destunoli Peredur*. Ed. Sioned Davies and Peter Wynn Thomas. Caerdydd: Gwasg Prifysgol Cymru, 2000. 113–127.

Lloyd-Morgan, Ceridwen. "French Text, Welsh Translators." *The Medieval Translator II*. Ed. Roger Ellis. London: Centre for Medieval Studies, Queen Mary and Westfield College, University of London, 1991. 45–63.

Lloyd-Morgan, Ceridwen. "Perceval in Wales: Late Medieval Welsh Grail Traditions." *The Changing Face of Arthurian Romance: Arthurian Studies XOI*. Ed. Alison Adams, Armel H. Diverres, Karen Stern and Kenneth Varty. Cambridge: Boydell Press, 1986. 78–91.

Lloyd-Morgan, Ceridwen. "Continuity and Change in the Transmission of Arthurian Material: Later Medieval Wales and the Continent." *Actes du 14e Congres International Arthurien, Rennes* (1984): 397–405.

Lloyd-Morgan, Ceridwen. "Narrative Structure in Peredur." *Zeitschrift für Celtische Philologie* 38 (1981): 187–231.

Owen, Morfydd E. "'Arbennic milwyr a blodeu marchogyon': cymdeithas *Peredur*." *Canhwyll Marchogyon: Cyd-Destunoli Peredur*. Ed. Sioned Davies and Peter Wynn Thomas. Cardiff: University of Wales Press, 2000. 92–112.

Roberts, Brynley F. "Y Cysyniad o Destun." *Canhwyll Marchogyon: Cyd-destunoli Peredur*. Ed. Sioned Davies and Peter Wynn Thomas. Caerdydd: Gwasg Prifysgol Cymru, 2000. 50–64.

Roberts, Brynley F. *Studies on Middle Welsh Literature*. New York: Edwin Mellen Press, 1992.

Roberts, Brynley F. "Dosbarthu'r Chwedlau Cymraeg Canol." *Ysgrifau Beirniadol* 15 (1988): 19–46.

Roberts, Brynley F. "Tales and Romances." *A Guide to Welsh Literature, vol. 1*. Ed. A.O.H. Jarman and Gwilym Rees Hughes. Swansea: Christopher Davies, 1976. 203–243.

Thomson, R.L., ed. *Pwyll Pendeuic Dyuet*. Mediaeval and Modern Welsh Series 1. Dublin: Dublin Institute for Advanced Studies, 1957.

Vitt, Anthony M. *Peredur vab Efrawc: Edited Texts and Translations of the MSS Peniarth 7 and 14 Versions*. MPhil dissertation: Aberystwyth University, 2010.

Ward, Charlotte. "Arthur in the Welsh Bruts." *Celtic Languages and Celtic Peoples: Proceedings of the Second North American Congress of Celtic Studies* (1992): 383–390.

Frank Brandsma
The *Roman van Walewein* and *Moriaen*: Travelling through Landscapes and Foreign Countries

In the Middle Dutch *Roman van Walewein*, the hero travels all the way to Endi (India).[1] This is further from home than any Arthurian knight has even ventured. Gaul, Ireland, Rome, Wales, those are the foreign, or not so foreign, regions visited by Arthur and his knights (Rouse and Rushton 2009). Walewein (aka Gauvain, Gawain), however, goes to a mysterious, foreign kingdom in a faraway land. In its presentation of the Arthurian setting, the *Roman van Walewein* displays an intriguing mixture of exotic otherworldliness and generic minimalism that makes it, on the one hand, representative of how space and geography are used in Arthurian romance, whereas, on the other hand, it comes up with an exceptionally foreign, yet also familiar other world. As we follow Walewein on his journey, we will encounter first the generic use of the setting, in respect of which we will also look at a second Middle Dutch romance (*Moriaen*), and then see how the text prepares its audience for Endi and its mysteries. Finally, we will come to Endi itself.

1 Carlioen and Dragon Mountain: the adventure begins

Made in Flanders around the middle of the thirteenth century, the *Roman van Walewein* is a Dutch original, to use a modern design term.[2] The story has no French source, even though the first author, Penninc, states in the prologue that he would have taken the story from the French, if he could have found it there (ll. 5–6). Walewein's quest, as created by Penninc and rounded off by a second

---

[1] Penninc and Vostaert (1957, 632). All further references to the *Roman van Walewein* are to Johnson and Claassens (2012); MNW (1998 s.v. Endi); REMLT (2016, s.v. India 1); but also Van Oostrom (2006, 262).

[2] For an overview of recent *Walewein* research, cf. Besamusca and Brandsma (2015).

Frank Brandsma (Utrecht University)

DOI 10.1515/9783110432466-027

author named Pieter Vostaert, is loosely based on an oral story (of the kind that would later be called a fairy tale) with a triple exchange structure, categorized by Aarne-Thompson under item number 550 and called "The Golden Bird" by the Grimm Brothers.[3] An enchanted prince turned into a speaking fox functions as the hero's helper in both the fairy tale and in the *Roman van Walewein*. Where the young prince in "The Golden Bird" exchanges the golden bird for a golden horse and the horse for the Princess of the Golden Castle, Walewein has to find a floating chessboard. To obtain that, he has to earn the sword with the two rings, which he will only receive in exchange for the exotic princess, Ysabele. Objects, setting and ending (to be discussed later) are all Arthurian in style in Penninc and Pieter Vostaert's text, which of course begins at Arthur's court, at Carlioen.

From Geoffrey's *Historia regum Britanniae* onwards, Caerleon in Wales has been one of the typical locations that Arthur as an itinerant king uses to hold court and feast with his knights and barons, waiting for an adventure to happen.[4] The narrator in the *Roman van Walewein* only states that King Arthur was in his hall in Carlioen (Johnson and Claassens 2012, l. 34); he does not mention the region or any specific landscape features. Like other locations in this text, and in Middle Dutch Arthurian romance in general, the court is a kind of set piece: no details about the castle, rooms or area are required to set the stage. It is Arthur's court, and that is apparently enough for the audience. When necessary, as we will see, spatial details are provided, but only on a need-to-know and just-in-time basis.

In Carlioen, an adventure presents itself immediately as an airborne chessboard comes in through the window and settles on the floor. It is beautifully made and ready to be played. Arthur's knights are, however, reluctant to do so. They are, somewhat fearfully, admiring the object, when it flies away again. Arthur then promises that whoever obtains the chess set for him will become his successor. Only when Arthur declares his intention to go after it himself does Walewein react. Reassured that the finder of the chessboard will indeed bear the crown, he takes on the quest.

At this point, the presentation of the setting becomes remarkable.[5] One would expect the chessboard to be gone, out of sight, while Walewein readies himself

---

3 Cf. Johnson and Claassens (2012, 8–9), with reference to Draak (1975), and for a more critical view, De Blécourt (2008); for the Golden Bird, see <http://www.verhalenbank.nl/items/show/51069>.

4 Lacy and Ashe (1997, 291 and frontispiece).

5 The analysis of this episode has benefited from discussions with Wim Gerritsen in the 1980s, on the basis of his as yet unpublished work on this scene. Cf. also Winkelman (1986), especially for the use of focalization (22–29) and Summerfield (1999, 119–120) for the use of "sight lines".

and his special horse, Gringolet, and takes leave of the king and queen, yet the strange object seems to be waiting to be followed. Sir Keye (Kay) has moved to the window and obviously still sees the chessboard hovering nearby, since he taunts Walewein, yelling:

> "Here Walewein, maerct ende verstaet:
> Haddi ghenomen enen draet
> Ende hadde den ant scaec ghestrect,
> So mochtijt nu hebben ghetrect
> Dat u niet ne ware ontvaren." (ll. 175–179)
> ["Sir Walewein, take note and listen: if you had taken a cord and had tied it to the chessboard, you might now be able to reel it in so that it would not have escaped you."]

Keye is asked to desist from this taunting, but he does have a point: the chessboard is still close by and seems easy to take. As Walewein rides off, the king and queen move from the hall to the battlements to see him go, whereas the other courtiers watch from the windows. Walewein sees the chessboard flying just in front of him:

> Ende hadt wel metter hant ghevaen,
> Maer hi liet dor der gore tale
> Die boven laghen in die zale:
> Hadsine sien daer achter vaen
> Endt hem danne ware ontgaen,
> Si mochter mede hare sceren maken. (ll. 218–223)
> [and he could have caught it in his hand, but he let it go on account of the gossip going on up in the hall: if they were to see him capture it and if it were then to escape him, they would make a mockery of him.]

It is as if Walewein's body and hands are in the field, close to the chessboard, while his ears and mind are still in the hall with the gazing and gossiping courtiers. The narrator gives us Walewein's thoughts, explaining why he does not grab the flying object. When Walewein rides into a valley, the narration returns to the court and king for a moment, and Arthur states that his eyes must now say goodbye to his knight (ll. 230–231).

Spatially, and with a strong focus on vision, the narration foregrounds the growing distance between quester and court. On the one hand, there are the king, queen and courtiers watching Walewein ride after the tantalizingly close chessboard; on the other hand, there is the hero, realizing he is still visible and deciding not to take the risk of making a fool of himself. There is a long line of sight from the castle's battlements to the empty fields. Only when he goes down into a valley is Walewein lost from the king's eyes and on his own. At this low point in the landscape, he is immediately confronted with a high mountain and the first test of his courage.

This set-up demonstrates beautifully Auerbach's assessment of the Arthurian setting (in Chrétien's *Yvain*):

> Die Welt der ritterlichen Bewährung ist eine Welt der Abenteuer; sie enthält nicht nur eine fast ununterbrochene Reihe von Abenteuern, sie enthält auch vor allem nichts anderes als das, was zum Abenteuer gehört; nichts was, was nicht Schauplatz oder Vorbereitung eines solchem wäre, wird in ihr angetroffen; es ist eine eigens für die Bewährung des Ritters geschaffene und präparierte Welt. (Auerbach 1988, 132)
> [The world of knightly proving is a world of adventure. It not only contains a practically uninterrupted series of adventures; more specifically, it contains nothing but the requisites of adventure. Nothing is found in it which is not either accessory or preparatory to an adventure. It is a world specifically created and designed to give the knight opportunity to prove himself. (Auerbach 1957, 119)]

The nameless mountain is only there for the adventure; it even opens in a mysterious way to let the chessboard and Walewein through. When it closes again, our hero is in the dark, unable to follow his target. Desperate, yet mindful of Keye's scorn should he return chessboard-less to court (ll. 280–282), Walewein prays and presses on. Just when he sees a light in the distance, he ends up in a dragon's nest with four young dragons, already standing on their feet and moving about. At this point, the narrator addresses the audience: "Wat radi Waleweine, den milden,/ Te doene, na dat es comen?" (ll. 322–323) [What would you suggest Walewein the Mild should do, when faced with this situation?] No answers from the implied listeners are recorded in the text, but Walewein takes his sword to the serpents. Although they fight him fiercely and inflict serious wounds, he manages to kill all four monsters. He finds a way out of the mountain and sees daylight, when the narrator mentions that this is the route the mother dragon uses to go to the nest.

Walewein quickly moves to the side of the entrance and pierces the dragon with his lance as she tries to enter and fry him with her flames. The lance breaks off in her body. As she fights her way in, the swipes of the dragon's tail enlarge the opening. Notwithstanding his dire position, this pleases Walewein:

> Deer Walewein stont ende louch
> Ende seide: "Dits wel mijn ghevoech,
> Tserpent heift mi die porte ondaen." (ll. 433–435)
> [Sir Walewein stood there and laughed, saying: "This suits me well, the dragon has opened the door for me!"]

The fight is far from over, however, and the dragon is winning: Walewein drops his sword, and the dragon manages to incapacitate him by grasping him with her enormous tail. She drags the exhausted hero into the mountain towards her nest. At this point, a remarkable and new situational detail is provided by the narrator: the dragon can no longer move through its usual passageway, because she is skewered by Walewein's lance. She gets stuck in what is now revealed to be a rather narrow tunnel. Walewein regroups somewhat, prays to the Lord to help him, finds his dagger and manages to stab the dragon through her navel into her heart, only to find himself stuck beneath her huge dead body in danger of being cooked in her hot blood. Finally, he is able to cut himself free. He escapes with fifteen wounds, his lance broken, his sword lost, horse missing, and no idea where the chessboard has gone. On his way out, he recovers his sword, and finds his horse standing near the exit, which turns out to be more suited to dragons than knights since it lies high above a river, with no way down.

As Thea Summerfield has shown, sending a copy of the *Walewein* translation to filmmakers like Steven Spielberg or Peter Jackson would not be out of the way, since the dragon episode is particularly reminiscent of an Indiana Jones-style movie, with lots of special effects, as used in *The Lord of the Rings* and *The Hobbit*.[6] Penninc, in other words, knows how to write a fast-moving action scene and uses the topical setting to great effect. As in the court scene, additional information is provided when necessary, like the narrowness of the passageway, which becomes evident only when the dragon gets stuck. The mountain and its inhabitants are made for the adventure, allowing the hero to be tested and to prove his prowess.

Even Walewein's horse is given the opportunity to prove itself. When Walewein and Gringolet find themselves on the high ledge above the river, the narrator again addresses the audience, foregrounding the horse: "Hoe sal hi neder comen up daerde/Met Gringolette sinen paerde?" (ll. 663–664) [How is Walewein to reach the valley with his horse Gringolet?][7] Walewein does not know what to do. He would rather die in a fight than jump to his death, yet staying on the ledge means starving. Gringolet then takes the decision out of his hands and makes the jump, with Walewein hanging on, wishing he had stayed in Carlioen. They survive the splash and Gringolet swims to the shore where they are able to rest and recover. There is also an additional detail: as horse and rider lie exhausted on the water's edge, Walewein first rubs his horse dry until it stands on its legs again, before he takes stock of his own situation (ll. 744–752). It is now a little after noon (l. 718), on the day after Walewein's departure.

---

6 Summerfield (1999); cf. also Van Oostrom (2006, 266) for a comparison of Walewein with James Bond.
7 For the special relationship between Walewein and Gringolet, see Hogenbirk (2000).

This brief summary of the first two episodes shows how situational the narration is, not so much with regard to elaborate topographical detail, but in respect of the manipulation of the setting to make it serve the adventure (cf. Fer-lampin-Acher, *supra*). Court, mountain and river only have those features that help shape the adventure; there is little or no superfluous information and the map seems empty apart from the adventurous, generic locations. After the river, Walewein's journey is uneventful until he arrives at the court of King Wonder, where he finds the chessboard. Although Penninc does not mention this expli-citly, Walewein has crossed the frontier between Arthur's kingdom and Wonder's realm. Before returning to our hero and another special river, we will consider the border of Arthur's realm in a related text, the *Roman van Moriaen*. This text demonstrates how, in texts with more than one protagonist, geographical fea-tures like the border may be used as meeting points and narrative devices.

2 The frontier – the "wegescede" in *Moriaen*

Like the *Roman van Walewein*, *Moriaen* is an indigenous romance. It was also created in the second half of the thirteenth century in Flanders, and Bart Besa-musca (1993, 23–39) has shown that there are strong intertextual links between the two romances (cf. also Van Oostrom 2006, 274–279). Of the original version, only small fragments remain, but we do have a complete, rewritten version in the *Lancelot Compilation* (The Hague, Koninklijke Bibliotheek 129 A 10; see Besa-musca 1993, 24, n. 28; Besamusca and Brandsma 2015, 7–9).[8]

Moriaen also begins at Arthur's court (Finet-Van der Schaaf 2009, l. 31 "in Bertangen" [in Britain]),[9] where the arrival of a wounded knight leads into a quest for Perchevael in which Lancelot and Walewein meet a Moor, the young knight Moriaen, who has come from faraway Moriane to find his father. He joins the quest, since his father Acglovael seems to be with Perchevael, who is his brother.

---

8 There is no modern English translation of *Moriaen*; the most recent edition gives the Middle Dutch text with a modern French translation (Finet-van der Schaaf 2009). There is a 1901, rather free and now archaic, translation by Jessie Weston, but this does not always do justice to the Middle Dutch text. The translations in what follows are my own. An important change in the compilation version is that Perchevael's role as Moriaen's father is transferred to his brother, Acglovael. The reason for this lies in the new context for the *Moriaen* in the compilation: Perche-vael dies a virgin in the next text in the *Compilation*, the *Queeste van den Grale* [the Quest of the Holy Grail], which precludes fatherhood in an earlier text in the series (cf. Oppenhuis de Jong 2000) and Hogenbirk (*supra*).

9 All references to *Moriaen* are to Finet-Van der Schaaf (2009).

The three knights then come to the border of Arthur's kingdom, where they find a four-way crossroads ("wegescede", l. 940) marked with a beautiful, inscribed cross. Walewein is well-educated and reads the inscription: the cross marks the frontier of Arthur's land, and whoever goes beyond it will soon find terrible adventures. Close by, the three companions find a hermitage and its inhabitant, who has seen two knights who looked like brothers pass by. They came down the road from Britain, and stopped at the cross to pray. Unfortunately, the hermit did not see which road they took, as he was himself praying in his hut. The three knights then decide to each take one of the three roads leading away from the cross, giving the story a larger geographical area to cover. Two of the three regions (the Land of Great Unreason, visited by Walewein who will be captured and almost executed; The Wild Land, inhabited by a monster, which Lancelot will slay) have little or no special spatial features. The third road, which Moriaen takes, however, leads to the sea. The cross and hermitage are to function as a meeting and information point in the rest of the story which, as usual in interlaced narratives, now diverges into three strands that will eventually converge again (cf. Brandsma 2010, 34–37, 92–111). Crosses, usually provided with a specific (hi)story, often play this role, especially in the Prose *Lancelot* and its translations.[10]

Moriaen travels to the seaside. Exceptionally, it is the real environment, rather than the generic topography that seems to have inspired the description of the landscape. He follows the hoof prints of two horses until he comes to the sea where one may take a boat to Ireland. The area is described: "Het was al heide ende sant:/ Hine vant daer anders geen lant;/ Daer nie wies gers no coren." (ll. 2389–2391) [There was only heather and sand, no arable land at all; no grass or corn grew there.] This is the somewhat desolate beach- and dune-scape that the *Moriaen* poet may well have been familiar with in Flanders, even though the closeness to Ireland suggests that it lies somewhere on the west side of England or Wales. Unable to find a ferryman (everyone thinks the Black Knight is the devil and flees), Moriaen returns to the cross, just in time to save Walewein who is to be executed right there. They are joined by Walewein's brother, Gariët, who then accompanies Moriaen in a second attempt to cross to Ireland. Using a modern

---

10 As a pseudo-chronicle, the Prose *Lancelot* has a precise chronological set-up, with a day-to-day narration of a knight's adventures within the interlaced narrative strands; geographically, things are less precise, but there are specific locations (e.g. a powerful opponent's dungeon, where a number of Arthur's knights end up) and meeting points, which help the audience to envisage the whereabouts of the different knights during a quest (cf. Ruberg 1963, 139). The role of the Black Cross in the great Lancelot quest in Part 3 (Préparation à la Queste/Agravain; Micha 1978–1983, vol. IV, LX, 3–LXI, 35; LXIV, 9) is quite similar to that of the border cross and hermitage in *Moriaen*. Cf. Brandsma (2010, xx, 92–111, 244 (diagram)).

hitchhiker's trick (Moriaen stays out of sight until Gariët has hired a ferryman), they come to Ireland and find Acglovael and Perchevael. Father and son are reunited, and it is decided that they will travel together to faraway Moriane and Moriaen's mother. They pick up Lancelot and Walewein at the crossroads, set free King Arthur, who has been kidnapped by the Irish King, and travel to Moriane.[11]

One would expect this mysterious land and its seductive princess to elicit elaborate descriptions, but the opposite is the case. The *Compilation* version wraps up the tale in less than one hundred lines: Moriaen leads the way to Moriane, where the knights display their prowess in such a way that Moriaen's mother is restored to her former position as the king's daughter. She is happily married to Acglovael, who stays in Moriane with wife and son, while the others return to Arthur's court in Karmeloet (l. 4689), where Galaat will soon arrive and the Grail quest is about to begin. It may have been different in the original Flemish *Moriaen*, but in the *Compilation* version there is nothing special or exotic about Moriane. Its inhabitants are black like Moriaen, but this detail has been divulged long before, when Moriaen first encountered Walewein and Lancelot (ll. 765–771), and is not even repeated in this final episode.

In comparison to the *Walewein* romance, to which we now return, *Moriaen* shows how an interlaced narrative uses the cross and hermitage on the border as a meeting and information point. Apart from the seaside details, the topography is as sparse, generic and adventure-driven as it was in the *Roman van Walewein*, even with regard to an intriguing and "other" land like Moriane. In Penninc's tale, this is about to change, as Endi comes into play and turns out to have paradise-like features.

3 Endi and the River of Purgatory

The generic scenery and geography in the *Roman van Walewein* (and *Moriaen*) gives way to a different kind of setting in the later sections of Penninc's romance and its conclusion by Pieter Vostaert. The shift into a more visionary, symbolic landscape does not coincide with the moment Vostaert takes over, at around l. 7780 of the 11,198 lines.[12] Well before that point, Penninc begins to provide more

---

11 Acglovael is seriously wounded when Moriaen finds him, and stays behind to recover. The knights return to Ireland by way of the cross to pick up Acglovael, before they set out for Moriane (ll. 4555–4599).

12 Cf. Van Dalen and Van Zundert (2007; 2008); Van Dalen (2007). See also, for a new perspective on the point where Vostaert takes over, Hugen and Warnar, forthcoming.

topographical details, especially in the description of Ravenstene Castle and in what might be called the "Rough Guide to Endi" given by King Amoraen.

Walewein has crossed the border and visited King Wonder, who owns the chess set but is willing to exchange it for the special sword with the two rings, which is in the possession of King Amoraen. So, Walewein's quest continues. He travels through forests and heaths, across mountains and through valleys (ll. 2848–2853), until he comes to the sea and sees a castle on a high rock. There seems to be no entrance and Walewein is puzzled until, like Moriaen, he discovers hoof prints in the sand (ll. 2898–2900). The road to the castle is submerged when the tide is in, and becomes passable at ebb. As in *Moriaen*, the scenery seems inspired by reality, and in this case is reminiscent of the monastery on the medieval Mont St Michel. Riding from the beach upwards through a tunnel, Walewein comes into the castle (ll. 2955–2957). It is called Ravenstene, and its ruler, King Amoraen, provides the famous knight, Walewein, with a warm welcome. The challenge of the sword with the two rings proves to be somewhat risky: if drawn by the wrong person, it will attack (ll. 3238–3373). Walewein turns out to be the sword's chosen wielder, and Amoraen is prepared to let him use the sword during his search for the third exchange element, the beautiful princess, Ysabele.

Amoraen has long been in love with this girl and knows a lot about her: he gives a long description (ll. 3410–3450) of her beauty, compares her, even though he has never met her, to other famous women, and explains that she will be hard to get, since her father King Assentijn keeps her in an impregnable castle in faraway Endi (l. 3457). The castle has twelve walls, separated by moats. Each wall has eighty towers and the gates in each of the twelve walls are guarded by eighty men. Within the walls, Ysabele has pleasant orchards and gardens in *locus amoenus* style, with all kinds of herbs, flowers and fruits, and even a golden tree, with golden birds making lovely music, powered by eight air bellows which are in turn operated by sixteen men (ll. 3503–3549). Under an olive tree, there is a fountain which finds its source in paradise (l. 3554): if a five-hundred-year-old man were to drink but a drop from its water, he would become as young and strong as when he was thirty (ll. 3586–3592).

The king's detailed description of Ysabele and the castle, tree and source in Endi runs to almost two hundred lines. This is in line with the attention to detail Penninc demonstrated when it came to objects like the chessboard and the sword, but this is the first time the setting is given the same attention. It prepares the audience for the enormous challenge Walewein will face in the final phase of his quest, even though not all of the details will prove relevant: the tree and source will only be mentioned once in the Endi episode. The whole description shows influence of the medieval imagery of the Otherworld, as Ad Putter (1999) has demonstrated. The twelve walls are a topical feature of the heavenly Jerusalem; the idea of coming to Paradise is also found in the Alexander romances; the tree and source come from the description of the land of Prester John (Putter 1999, 98).[13]

The thematic strand of the Otherworld, Paradise and the hereafter comes to prominence in the text from this point onwards. In a most remarkable episode *en route* to Endi (ll. 3676–4915), Walewein plays the role of lay confessor to an evil Red Knight he has defeated, and even wards off with sword and prayer the devils that come to take the knight's soul to hell (Jongen 2000; Zemel 2010, 3–4). He organizes the knight's burial and serves as acolyte at the requiem. The Red Knight's grateful ghost will have a role to play later on. To come to Endi, Walewein again travels through many forests and wastelands, suffering hardships which the narrator chooses not to recount (l. 4937), until he comes to the River of Purgatory. He sees a beautiful castle on the other side, yet is unable to cross: the only bridge consists of a sharp sword (ll. 4952–4975) and Walewein does not take up this intertextual challenge, which may have reminded the audience of the prose *Charrette* or Chrétien's *Lancelot* (Gerritsen, 1996).[14] Looking for an alternative route, Walewein sticks his lance into the water, whereupon it bursts into flames (l. 4988). Even prayer does not provide a solution here, since a little further down the river, the lance burns once more, before it even touches the water. Our hero is stuck. He retires to a nearby bower, where the fox, Roges, comes to his rescue. Since his own disenchantment relies on seeing Walewein and Ysabele together with King Wonder and his son, the fox-prince helps Walewein in many ways. Roges explains that the river cleanses souls. He shows Walewein how black soul birds dive into the water to wash away their sins and emerge as snow white birds flying off to heaven (ll. 5836–5855). The river comes straight out of hell and empties out into the "Lever zee" (l. 5955) [Liver Sea].[15] There is no way around it, but the fox knows a shortcut: he leads Walewein to a dark tunnel under the river. Finally, he has arrived in Endi.

King Assentijn's twelve-wall castle is the ultimate test for Walewein's prowess that Penninc's setting provides.[16] Even when the hero kills so many defenders that Walewein scholars interpret the whole scene as ironic, there are shortcuts,

---

13 For the mechanical tree and its musical birds, see Okken (1987).

14 Besamusca (1993, 61–66) discusses the work of Maartje Draak, Jef Janssens, Toos Verhage-Van den Berg and Johan Winkelman on this episode.

15 Zemel (2010, 18–21) analyses this episode, and Strijbosch (2000, 64–67) explores the Liver Sea in the Middle Dutch *Reis van Sint Brandaan* [The Voyage of Saint Brendan], a text about the hereafter that seems to resonate with much of Penninc's imagery of the river and Endi. Winkelman (2006) also discusses Purgatory, Paradise and the souls in this text.

16 Uyttersprot (2005) describes the narrative strategies employed in the Endi episode.

comparable to Roges' tunnel under the river.[17] Right at the first impregnable wall, Roges points Walewein to a small side gate (l. 6121), left open by servants, and thus he enters the castle. He then fights his way up to the fourth gate, where he manages to slip into the next circle with the fleeing defenders. After gate five, he finds a place to rest and sleeps until daybreak, eats a hearty breakfast and goes out to fight some more. When at gate number ten his super sword slips out of his hand (ll. 7260–7261), he is finally captured (l. 7327). The description of Walewein's individual achievements in Endi is "over the top": at one point, he is standing up to his ankles in blood (l. 6528), and afterwards dead defenders are taken away by the cart-full (twenty carts are needed in all; ll. 7662–7669) and he sustains no serious injuries, until bad luck leads to his capture.[18]

Now the lovely Ysabele comes into play. While Walewein is still in full fight, the tale switches to Ysabele, who asks her father for a "don contraignant" [an unconditional gift], without specifying what she will ask.[19] She has seen a handsome knight in a dream vision, and this is why she asks for the gift. At this point, it remains unclear what will happen with the gift. When Walewein has been taken, Ysabele watches him from inside the castle, as her father brings him in. Assentijn tells her that this must be the knight she dreamt about. She claims her gift now: she wishes to torment and punish the knight for a full night. Ysabele has, however, fallen madly in love with Walewein the moment she laid eyes on him (ll. 7386–7389). Her love grows when, in the dungeon, she overhears him lamenting his fate and declaring his love for the princess. When he is taken to her and sees her for the first time, he is also smitten (ll. 7761–7769), even though he fears she may torment him cruelly. She, however, is looking forward to making love to him, which will give her more joy than her beautiful orchard with the musical birds' tree and the fountain. In her private domain, she takes him to a lovely room, decorated with images from the stories of Troy and Alexander (ll. 7894–7906). It even has a secret hideaway, built by a craftsman killed for his efforts, in order to keep it secret (ll. 7912–7926). Like the "don contraignant", this is another example of how

---

17 See especially Uyttersprot (2004, 77–164) and Zemel (2010, 7–9).

18 Zemel (2005) compares Walewein's prowess in Endi to the feats of arms of knight in the *chansons de geste*, demonstrating that this genre influenced Penninc's narrative. The same goes for the love relationship and the presentation of Ysabele, which may have been inspired by the *chanson de geste*, *La Prise d'Orange* (cf. Zemel 2010).

19 Cf. Zemel (2008). Although the romance generally follows just one narrative strand, there are interlace sections with the alternation of two narrative strands, and this is one of those sections. Lines 7100–7210 describe the conversation of daughter and father and the granting of the "don".

Ysabele's actions are presented as premeditated.[20] Penninc prepares well for the crucial scenes in his narrative, and Pieter Vostaert uses this to his advantage.[21] We are now in the part of the text he wrote, without any directly notable or signposted transition (Hugen and Warnar, forthcoming).

The narrator refrains from describing in detail what Ysabele and Walewein do in the room: "Dan canic ju gheseggen niet wel" (l. 7946) [[This] I am not well able to tell you]. They are, however, observed by a spy, who reveals to the King what his daughter is up to. The lovers are besieged, and Ysabele urges Walewein to use the secret passageway. The courtly hero refuses to leave her (ll. 8111–8121) and fights bare-fisted until he is overcome and, like the princess, thrown into a dirty and cold dungeon. With his characters in these dire straits, Vostaert calls in a narrative option provided by Penninc: the ghost of the Red Knight, whose soul Walewein saved, appears and breaks Walewein's fetters. Ysabele is also freed, and they escape Endi by way of the tunnel under the river (ll. 8284–8451) to the bower where the fox is waiting with Gringolet. The narrator freely admits that he forgot to mention that Walewein even picked up his special sword on the way out (ll. 8429–8437).

After Endi, the story returns to more generic scenes (they are once again captured, and then escape; Ysabele is abducted and rescued) and scenery, even when Walewein and Ysabele take the faster option of a sailing voyage to Ravenstene (ll. 9496–9507). Once there, they discover that Amoraen has died and hopefully is now in Paradise (ll. 9527–9528), which saves Walewein from having to give up his lover. Finally, it takes just three hundred lines to wrap up the exchange narrative. They come to King Wonder and his son, which results in the undoing of Roges' enchantment. Walewein receives the chessboard in exchange for the wondrous sword, and returns with it and Ysabele to Arthur's court. The narrator leaves open whether he marries the princess, but there certainly is a happy end to the *Walewein*.

---

20 Ysabele's actions have been the subject of much debate among Walewein scholars; cf. especially Zemel (2008; 2010).

21 Cf. n. 13. A detailed analysis of the similarities and differences between the two authors with regard to the setting and topography is beyond the scope of this chapter. There certainly are characteristic differences in narrative technique, like the fact that Vostaert's narrator addresses his audience as "ju" [you] (e.g. ll. 7942, 7946, 8365, 8532, 9511, 9828, 10871, 10943, 10948, 11057, 11085, 11150, 11189, and even 11200 where the scribe of the Leiden manuscript (Leiden, UB, Ltk. 195) speaks), and rarely uses the more formal variants of "you": "ghi" (l. 8365), and "u" (l. 10833). For Vostaert's part, reference is made repeatedly to a source (e.g. ll. 9933, 10097, 10313, 10533, 10870, 11165) and, in contrast to the prologue, even to a French source (l. 11141).

4 Conclusion

In many ways, the Endi episode is strange. The association with India would lead one to expect exotic wonders, strange people with a foreign language and customs, perhaps even of the Muslim faith. Yet, Endi provides no such "otherness", nor does the story problematize or create any kind of difference from the generic Arthurian setting. Ysabele and Walewein fall in love without any hesitation, Ysabele resides in a precious *locus amoenus* and knows how to use the courtly "don contraignant", and there is nothing extraordinary about the fighting or weapons, even when Walewein's prowess is over the top. Endi does lie far away, but it is more Otherworld, and even Paradise-like, than exotic. The River of Purgatory and the story of saving the Red Knight's soul seem to relate to contemporary ideas of the hereafter and the world of the souls, and provide the tale with an unexpected spiritual layer, which disappears again as the narration returns to the triple exchange and quest scenario.[22]

When it comes to the presentation of the Arthurian world and its geography, both *Walewein* and *Moriaen* corroborate Auerbach's observation that these texts in general provide information about the setting on a what-is-needed-for-the-adventure basis, rather than describe topographical details as "couleur locale" [local colour] for their own sake, even when there are some minor, often sea- and beach-related, "realistic" descriptions that form minor exceptions to this rule. It is in the Endi episode that Penninc deviates quite drastically from this format, creating an intriguing yet puzzling Otherworld of soul birds, ghosts and burning water. Like the Sword Bridge, Walewein avoids the confrontation with this Otherworld, however, and Penninc provides him with a shortcut to the castle and the more "normal" world of defenders to fight, as well as a beautiful princess to fall in love with. Although the ghost is rather useful in Vostaert's part of the story, Vostaert does not otherwise take up Penninc's Otherworld elements; he brings the story to its conclusion in a generic way, with more fights to show off Walewein's heroic status and a rather *deus ex machina*-like solution to keep Walewein and Ysabele together and provide a happy end.

Acknowledgment: I would like to thank Bart Besamusca, Jelmar Hugen, John Verbeek and the editors of this volume for their comments on earlier versions of this chapter.

---

22 For the spiritual aspects, which are beyond the scope of this chapter see, for instance, Winkelman (2006).

References

Auerbach, Erich. *Mimesis. Dargestellte Wirklichkeit in der abendländischen Literatur*. Bern/
Stuttgart: Franke, 1988 [1946].
Auerbach, Erich. *Mimesis. The Representation of Reality in Western Literature*. Trans. Willard
Trask. Garden City, NY: Doubleday, 1957.
Besamusca, Bart. *Walewein, Moriaen en de Ridder metter mouwen: Intertekstualiteit in drie
Middelnederlandse romans*. Hilversum: Verloren, 2003.
Besamusca, Bart, and Frank Brandsma. "État présent: Arthurian Literature in Middle Dutch."
Journal of International Arthurian Studies 3 (2015): 1–31.
Brandsma, Frank. *The Interlace Structure of the Third Part of the Prose Lancelot*. Woodbridge:
D.S. Brewer, 2010.
De Blécourt, Willem. "'De gouden vogel', 'Het levenswater' en de Walewein. Over de
sprookjestheorie van Maartje Draak." *TNTL* 124 (2008): 259–277.
Draak, A. M. E. *Onderzoekingen over de roman van Walewein: (met een aanvullend hoofdstuk
over "Het Walewein onderzoek sinds 1936")*. Groningen et al.: Bouma's Boekhuis et al.,
1975.
Finet-van der Schaaf, Baukje. *Le Roman de Moriae*. Ed. and trans. Baukje Finet-van der Schaaf.
Grenoble: Ellug, 2009.
Gerritsen, W.P. "Walewein en de vurige rivier. *Roman van Walewein*, 4938–5093." *Tegendraads
genot: opstellen over de kwaliteit van middeleeuwse teksten*. Ed. Karel Porteman, Werner
Verbeke, Frank Willaert. Leuven: Peeters, 1996. 47–61.
Hogenbirk, Marjolein. "Walewein en Gringalet: trouwe kameraden." *Hoort wonder!: opstellen
voor W. P. Gerritsen bij zijn emeritaat*. Ed. Bart Besamusca, Frank Brandsma, Dieuwke van
der Poel. Hilversum: Verloren, 2000. 85–90.
Hugen, Jelmar, and Geert Warnar. "De *Roman van Walewein* als een onvoltooid verhaal met een
vervolg." *TNTL* 133 (2017): forthcoming.
Johnson, David, and Geert H.M. Claassens, ed. and trans. *Dutch romances I: Roman van
Walewein; II: Ferguut; III: Five interpolated romances from the Lancelot Compilation (Die
Wrake van Ragisel; Die riddere metter mouwen; Walewein ende Keye; Lanceloet en het hert
met de Witte Voet; Torec)*. Woodbridge: Boydell and Brewer, 2012.
Jongen, Ludo. "Walewein as Confessor: Crime and Penance in the *Roman van Walewein*." *King
Arthur in the Medieval Low Countries*. Ed. Geert H. M. Claassens and David F. Johnson.
Leuven: Leuven University Press, 2000. 45–58.
Lacy, Norris, and Geoffrey Ashe. *The Arthurian Handbook*. 2nd edn. New York/London: Garland,
1997.
Micha, Alexandre, ed. *Lancelot. Roman en prose du XIIIe siècle*. 9 vols. Geneva: Droz,
1978–1983.
MNW: *CD-rom Middelnederlands. Woordenboek en teksten*. Den Haag: SDU/Antwerpen:
Standaard uitgeverij, 1998.
Okken, Lambertus. *Das goldene Haus und die goldene Laube*. Amsterdamer Publikationen zur
Sprache und Literatur 72. Amsterdam: Rodopi, 1987.
Oppenhuis de Jong, Soetje. "Agloval and the compiler: the variant story of Acglovael in
the *Lancelot Compilation*." *King Arthur in the medieval Low Countries*. Ed. Geert H. M.
Claassens and David F. Johnson. Leuven: Leuven University Press, 2000, 113–124.

Penninc and Pieter Vostaert. *Roman van Walewein*. Ed. and trans. Johan H. Winkelman and
    Gerhard Wolf. Bibliothek mittelniederländischer Literatur V. Münster: Agenda, 2010.
Penninc and Pieter Vostaert. *De jeeste van Walewein en het schaakbord*. Ed. G.A. van Es. 2 vols.
    Zwolle: W.E.J. Tjeenk Willink, 1957.
Putter, Ad. "Walewein in the Otherworld and the Land of Prester John." *Originality and Tradition
    in the Middle Dutch Roman van Walewein*. Arthurian Literature XVII. Ed. Bart Besamusca
    and Erik Kooper. Cambridge: D.S. Brewer, 1999. 79–99.
REMLT: *Repertorium van Eigennamen in Middelnederlandse Literaire Teksten* <http://cf.hum.
    uva.nl/dsp/scriptamanent/remlt/remltindex.htm>.
Rouse, Robert, and Cory Rushton. "Arthurian Geography." *The Cambridge Companion to the
    Arthurian Legend*. Ed. Ad Putter and Elisabeth Archibald. Cambridge: Cambridge University
    Press, 2009. 218–234.
Ruberg, Uwe. *Raum und Zeit im Prosa-Lancelot*. Munich: Fink, 1963.
Strijbosch, Clara. *The Seafaring Saint. Sources and Analogues of the Twelfth-Century Voyage of
    Saint Brendan*. Trans. Thea Summerfield. Dublin: Four Courts Press, 2000.
Summerfield, Thea. "Reading a Motion Picture: Why Steven Spielberg Should Read the *Roman
    van Walewein*." *Originality and Tradition in the Middle Dutch Roman van Walewein*.
    Arthurian Literature XVII. Ed. Bart Besamusca, and Erik Kooper. Cambridge: D.S. Brewer,
    1999. 115–129.
Uyttersprot, Veerle. "Literair vuurwerk in Endi." *Maar er is meer. Avontuurlijk lezen in de Lage
    Landen. Studies voor Jozef D. Janssens*. Ed. Remco Sleiderink, Veerle Uyttersprot, Bart
    Besamusca. Leuven: Davidsfonds/Amsterdam: Amsterdam University Press, 2005. 13–26.
Uyttersprot, Veerle. *"Entie hoofsche Walewein, sijn gheselle was daer ne ghein". Ironie
    en het Walewein-beeld in de Roman van Walewein en in de Europese middeleeuwse
    Arturliteratuur*. Unpublished dissertation, University of Brussels, 2004.
Van Dalen, Karina. "Kwantificeren van stijl." *Tijdschrift voor Nederlandse taal- en letterkunde*
    123 (2007): 37–54.
Van Dalen, Karina, and Joris van Zundert. "The Quest for Uniqueness: Author and Copyist
    Distinction in Middle Dutch Arthurian Romances based on Computer-assisted Lexicon
    Analysis." *Yesterday's Words: Contemporary, Current and Future Lexicography*. Ed. Marijke
    Mooijaart and Marijke van der Wal. Cambridge: Cambridge Scholars Publishing, 2008.
    292–304.
Van Dalen, Karina, and Joris van Zundert. "Delta for Middle Dutch: Author and Copyist
    Distinction in *Walewein*." *Literary and Linguistic Computing* 22 (2007): 345–362.
Van Oostrom, Frits. *Stemmen op schrift. Geschiedenis van de Nederlandse literatuur vanaf het
    begin tot 1300*. Amsterdam: Bert Bakker, 2006.
Weston, Jessie. *Morien. A metrical Romance rendered into modern English prose from the
    mediaeval Dutch*. London: Nutt, 1901. <https://ebooks.adelaide.edu.au/w/weston/jessie_
    laidlay/morien/>.
Winkelman. Johan. "Walewein en God." *Nederlandse letterkunde* 11 (2006): 354–382.
Winkelman, Johan. "Arturs hof en Waleweins avontuur. Interpretatieve indicaties in de expositie
    van de Middelnederlandse Walewein." *Spiegel der Letteren* 28 (1986): 1–33.
Zemel, Roel. "Walewein en Ysabele in Endi." *Nederlandse letterkunde* 15 (2010): 1–28.
Zemel, Roel. "Op weg naar de vierde 'bede' in de Roman van Walewein." *Voortgang, jaarboek
    voor de neerlandistiek* 26 (2008): 75–92.
Zemel, Roel. "De Roman van Walewein en het heldenlied." *Maar er is meer. Avontuurlijk lezen in
    de Lage Landen. Studies voor Jozef D. Janssens*. Ed. Remco Sleiderink, Veerle Uyttersprot,

Bart Besamusca. Leuven: Davidsfonds/Amsterdam: Amsterdam University Press, 2005. 27–44.

Paloma Gracia
The Iberian Post-Vulgate Cycle: Cyclicity in Translation

Based on the above title, the reader might think that my contribution to this *Handbook* will be similar to that published in 2015 as "The *Post-Vulgate Cycle* in the Iberian Peninsula",[1] where I set out the Iberian witnesses related to this cycle and place the emphasis on the *Post-Vulgate* (hereafter *P-V*) as it was rewritten in the Iberian Peninsula, focusing on the perception and survival of its cyclical nature. However, the perspective and, therefore, the content of the present discussion will be diametrically different. The underlying reason for this is that my critical approach in the chapter included in *The Arthur of the Iberians* (2015), as well as in another study related to this subject (2011), was rather conservative, having been based on the conception of the *Post-Vulgate* as it was established by Fanni Bogdanow, who was also responsible for renaming the cycle, which had previously been known as the "Pseudo-Robert de Boron Cycle", the *Post-Vulgate Roman du Graal*. Following Bogdanow, scholarship has tended to understand the cycle as a recasting of the *Vulgate* that was inscribed by a single author and motivated by a single purpose. Contrastingly, this chapter will be based on a conception of the *P-V* that moves away from this notion.

Although Bogdanow continued to work on the *P-V* until relatively recently, and although some short fragments have been added to the manuscripts cited, she never changed the essence of the structure established in her *The Romance of the Grail* (1966, 11–13), which in her own words, is as follows:

> The Post-Vulgate *Roman du Graal* originally began with an account of the early history of the Grail – a version of the *Estoire del Saint Graal* similar to the Vulgate Version. This was followed, as in the latter, by the prose rendering of Robert de Boron's *Merlin* and by an account of Arthur's early wars against the rebel kings adapted from the Vulgate *Merlin* continuation. To the story of Arthur's wars is then added a new series of adventures not in the Vulgate

---

1 This study forms part of the work undertaken as part of the Research Project "The Arthurian cycle of *Post-Vulgate* under question: the nature of the model and the relationship between the Iberian derivatives reconsidered," FFI2016-78203-P, financed by the Ministry of Economy and Competitiveness of the Government of Spain and FEDER. I am sincerely grateful to Professor Celia Wallhead for assistance with the translation of this article into English. See Gracia (2015) for a fuller bibliography on the Iberian *P-V* and for a summary of the main problems.

Paloma Gracia (University of Granada)

DOI 10.1515/9783110432466-028

Merlin sequel and known formerly as the *Suite du Merlin* of the Huth MS. [...] In addition to the Huth MS., which is incomplete at the end, three other MSS. of the *Suite du Merlin* are now known, MS.B.N.fr. 112, Livre II, ff. 17b–58b, which contains a portion of the end of the romance, the single folio preserved in the State Archives of Siena, and the Cambridge MS. [...] No branch corresponding to the *Lancelot* proper of the Vulgate Cycle formed part of the *Roman du Graal*, but in order to supply a transition to the last sections of his work, the Post-Vulgate versions of the *Queste* and *Mort Artu*, our author adapted from the *Agravain* section of the Vulgate *Lancelot* and from the First Version of the prose *Tristan* a number of incidents which he combined with his own inventions [...] preserved in two manuscripts, B.N. fr. 112, *Livre* III, and B.N. fr. 12599. [...] The Post-Vulgate versions of the *Queste* and *Mort Artu* which conclude the *Roman du Graal* are based on the corresponding sections of the Vulgate Cycle, but have been remodelled. [...] No MS. contains the whole of the Post-Vulgate *Queste*, but fragments of it have been preserved in B.N. fr. 112, *Livre* IV and B.N. fr. 343. [...] Of the Post-Vulgate *Mort Artu* two small fragments have been preserved in French in B.N.Fr. 340.

According to Fanni Bogdanow, then, the *P-V* translated in the Iberian Peninsula consisted, like the French original, of an *Estoire del saint Graal*, a *Merlin* continued by a version of the *Suite du Merlin*, and a *Queste del saint Graal* and *Mort Artu*. Witnesses survive in both Portuguese and Spanish. In Portuguese, there are manuscripts of each of the three branches. Of the first part of the cycle, that is the *Libro de Josep Abaramatia* or *Estoria do Santo Graal*, there are two witnesses of the Portuguese translation. The older of the two consists of a single bifolium, retrieved from the binding of a notarial volume, preserved in Porto, Arquivo Distrital do Porto NO-CNSTS / 1 Liv. 12, cota 1 / 18 / 2 – CX 2, which has been dated to the end of the thirteenth century; the second witness is a complete version of the work preserved in a sixteenth-century manuscript in Lisbon (Torre do Tombo 643; hereafter Torre do Tombo 643). The section corresponding to the *Suite du Merlin* is called the *Libro de Merlin* and is preserved in Barcelona, Biblioteca de Catalunya 2434, made in the fourteenth century, while the final part is copied entirely in Vienna, ÖNB, 2594, made in the fifteenth century (cf. Moran, *supra*).

Of the Spanish version, we have only Salamanca, Biblioteca Universitaria de Salamanca, 1877 (hereafter Salamanca 1877; formerly Madrid, Biblioteca de Palacio Real, 2-G-5), compiled in 1469–1470 by Petrus Ortiz and containing sections of each of the parts of the cycle. There are important printed witnesses, too: the oldest is the *Baladro del Sabio Merlin con sus profecias* [shriek of the wise Merlin, with his prophecies], printed in Burgos by Juan of Burgos in 1498. The last two parts of the cycle were published together, but divided into two books, under the title *Demanda del Santo Grial con los maravillosos fechos de Lançarote y de Galaz su hijo* [quest for the Holy Grail, with the marvellous feats of Lançarote [Lancelot] and of Galaz [Galahad], his son]; of the 1515 Toledo edition of this version only the second book is preserved, that is, the *Demanda del Santo Grial*;

meanwhile, the Seville edition (1535) is the only one that contains a *Baladro* followed by a *Demanda*. The two editions of 1515 and 1535 seem to have derived independently from an edition published in Seville in 1500, but this is now lost (Gracia 2015).

In the passage cited above from *The Romance of the Grail*, Bogdanow was alluding to the three most extensive witnesses to the cycle: the Spanish *Baladro del Sabio Merlin*, which preserves the section corresponding to *Merlin*, and the Portuguese *Demanda do Santo Graal* and the Spanish *Demanda del Santo Grial*, both of which preserve fully the last part of the trilogy (the *Post-Vulgate Queste* and *Mort Artu*). In so doing, Bogdanow continued a critical tradition born at the same time as was the belief in the cycle, when Gaston Paris and Jacob Ulrich suggested the existence of a trilogy attributed to Robert de Boron in the introductory remarks to their edition of *Merlin: roman en prose*, published in 1886. Based on the so-called Huth manuscript (London, BL, Additional 38117), Paris and Ulrich advocated the existence of a trilogy formed by the prosifications of the *Joseph* and Robert de Boron's *Merlin*, followed by a version of the *Queste del saint Graal* and an abbreviated *Mort Artu*. Amongst the Iberian versions, Paris and Ulrich only knew the *Baladro del Sabio Merlin* in the incunable version of 1498, which they considered to be a translation of the Huth manuscript and to which they devoted several pages. A year later, in 1887, Gaston Paris composed a review of Reinhardstoettner's edition of the *Demanda do Santo Graal*, which had been published some months beforehand. In Reinhardstoettner's partial edition of the manuscript containing the Portuguese *Demanda*, Paris had found confirmation of some of the findings described in his and Ulrich's introduction to the Prose *Merlin*. Paris noted particularly the relationship between the Portuguese *Demanda* and the Huth *Merlin*, since the Portuguese version would thus have preserved the last part of the compilation to which it belongs: a *Queste del saint Graal* attributed to Robert de Boron. Many scholars of French literature then continued the work done by Paris and Ulrich, and their names are significant: H. Oskar Sommer in the first decade of the twentieth century; Eugène Vinaver during the forties; Cedric E. Pickford in the fifties and sixties and, soon after, Fanni Bogdanow, whose *The Romance of the Grail* was to be the most seminal study of the cycle.

Thus, the Portuguese *Demanda* and the 1498 *Baladro* have belonged to the reconstruction of the *P-V* since the beginning of the cycle's critical history. Not long after, in 1902, these witnesses were joined by the *Demanda del Santo Grial con los maravillosos fechos de Lançarote y de Galaz su hijo*, printed in 1535, and the Arthurian segments of the then codex 2-G-5 of the Biblioteca de Palacio (now Salamanca 1877), which had been made known by Otto Klob and published by Karl Pietsch under the title *Spanish Grail Fragments* in 1924 and 1925. Both witnesses, the 1535 *Demanda* and the Arthurian segments of Salamanca 1877, have been particularly important in the critical history of the trilogy because of their "cyclical" nature. Upon inspection, however, what arises is a sense that the existence of the so-called traces of the cyclical nature of the *P-V*, or at least the perception that late medieval Arthurian peninsular materials belonged to the same universe, is actually debatable.

1 The relationship between different languages and different sections

In a narrow sense, the relationship between the Portuguese and Spanish witnesses is limited to two factors: first, the link created between the Portuguese and Spanish *Demandas* by means of their both sharing a common ancestor; second, the first-person intervention of an authorial persona named Joam Vives/ Joannes Bivas that serves to connect the *Livro de Josep Abaramatia* (or *Estoria do Santo Graal*) with the Spanish *Demanda del Santo Grial*. The nature of the relationship is obviously very different in each of the two cases: the first associates versions of the same branch in different languages and is very complex. Indeed, many intricacies in respect of the obvious relationship of dependence between the Spanish and Portuguese *Demandas* have still not been entirely resolved by critics, although it is clear that both derive from a single (probably Portuguese) translation. The second link (the name by which the compiler, or perhaps the translator, refers to himself: Juan Vivas (Joam Vives/Joannes Bivas)) connects not only languages but also branches. This name appears twice in the *Libro de Josep Abaramatia*, and once in the Spanish *Demanda del Santo Grial*, and in a similar context in each case, although in the *Demanda del Santo Grial* the passage is clearly a later interpolation.

2 The trilogy: references to different sections and composite codices

Salamanca 1877 contains sections of all of the parts of the cycle: the *Libro de Josep Abarimatia*, *Libro de Merlin* and *Lançarote* (the name given by the copyist to the section corresponding to the *Mort Artu*). The *Josep* begins with the imprisonment of Joseph of Arimathea and ends with the narration of a series of events associated with King Evolat in Sarraz; this occupies ff. 252r–282r, and its content

corresponds to Sommer (1908–1916, I, 12–48). The *Libro de Merlin* is copied on
ff. 82v–296r, and corresponds to the narrative content of Paris and Ulrich (1886,
I, 1–33); *Lançarote* is the adaptation of a brief section of the *Mort Artu*. It occupies
ff. 298v–300v of the manuscript and corresponds to sections 630–654 of the Portuguese *Demanda*, and to chapters 394–417 of the Spanish *Demanda*; its abrupt
beginning and ending suggest that the segment is incomplete.

The fact that there are three segments and the third is an excerpt from the
Demanda has contributed to the idea that Petrus Ortiz would have extracted different sections from a codex of the entire trilogy. The *Demanda* is therefore the
third part of a whole. In support of this is the fact that, in the Spanish *Demanda
del Santo Grial*, Juan Vivas, in his authorial intervention, refers to his work as the
third part of a book:

> prometi de devisarla en tercera parte del libro, que devisa la *Demanda del Sancto Grial*, los
> cavalleros e las proezas que los cavalleros de la Mesa Redonda fizieron en aquella demanda
> [...] e como el Sancto Grial se fue de Inglaterra a la cibdad de Çarras (Ch. 52, f. 106)
> [I promised to narrate it in the third part of the book, which narrates the Quest of the Holy
> Grail, the knights and the exploits that the knights of the Round Table made in its quest [...]
> and how the Holy Grail left England and went to the city of Çarras.][2]

Additionally, this concurs with what is indicated by the inventory register of the
library of Queen Isabella I of Castile, which states that she possessed: "Otro libro
de pliego entero, de mano, en rromançe, que es la terçera parte de la *Demanda
del Santo Grial*, las cubiertas de cuero blanco." [Another book of folio size and
copied by hand in the Romance language, which is the third part of the *Quest of
the Holy Grail*, with white leather covers.] This reference seems to be specifying
that the copy concerned contained the third part or book of the *Demanda*, that is
to say, a *Demanda* properly designated as such, and perceived as a branch of a
cycle. Another register similarly suggests the possibility of a codex made up of a
Spanish *Estoire del saint Graal* and the *Demanda*: "Otro libro de pliego entero, de
mano, escripto en romançe, que se dize *Merlin*, con coberturas de papel de cuero
blancas, y habla de Joseph Avarimatin." (Ruiz García 2004) [Another book of folio
size copied by hand, written in Romance language, which is called *Merlin*, with
white leather covers, and speaks about Joseph Avarimatin.]

Something similar to Petrus Ortiz's proposed extraction of contents from a
source containing the entire trilogy could also have happened in the Portuguese
tradition, even though what is extant in Portuguese lacks witnesses that bring

---

2 The extracts of the *Demanda del Santo Grial* (Seville, 1535) have been taken from the copy preserved in Madrid, Biblioteca Nacional de España, R/3870.

together more than one branch. However, the notion that the individual branches, despite their appearing separately, together actually made up a cycle may have been widely understood. This is suggested, for example, by the title of Torre do Tombo 643: *Livro de Josep Abaramatia intetulado a primeira parte da Demanda do Santo Grial* [Book of Josep Abaramathia, designated/called the first part of the quest of the Holy Grail]. The specification here that this was the "first part" reveals quite overtly that the book should be understood as constituting just one branch of a cycle named, and/or completed by, the *Demanda do Santo Grial*.

3 The *Demanda del Santo Grial con los maravillosos fechos de Lançarote y de Galaz su hijo* (Seville, 1535)

The *Demanda del Santo Grial* was printed on at least three occasions although, as mentioned above, no copy of the supposed edition published in Seville in 1500 survives, while only the second book or *Demanda* is preserved in the edition printed in Toledo in 1515. The printed *Demanda* brings together, as its first and second books, a *Merlin* followed by its *Suite*, and a *Queste del saint Graal* and *Mort Artu*. Only the edition published in Seville in 1535 offers complete evidence of this. It contains a *Baladro*, derived from *Merlin*, followed by its *P-V Suite* and a *Demanda*, derived from the *P-V Queste-Mort Artu*, amongst which is inserted a sizeable collection of prophecies relating to events in Castilian politics under the title "Aqui comiençan las profecias del sabio Merlin, profeta dignissimo" [Here begin the prophecies of the wise Merlin, honourable prophet], of which the latest dates from 1467. We will also recall that is likely that the 1515 and 1535 editions derive, independently of each other, from the now-lost 1500 Seville edition.

While the biography of Merlin is given as an independent story in the 1498 *Baladro*, beginning with his birth and ending with his death, the life of the seer serves as a prelude to the adventure of the Grail in the 1535 edition. Both derive from a common ancestor to which they owe many of their principal characteristics, and with which they share the greater part of the work. Their respective versions are also very close textually; both include the same sections that are not encountered in the surviving French versions. These are the prophecies derived from the *Historia regum Britanniae*, and the episodes of Merlin's dream ("Ebron el Follon" and "Bandemagus"), as well as the profound revision of the ending that narrates the delivery of Merlin to the devils and his death as he utters that rending shriek or *baladro*. The second book of the printed editions of 1515 and

1535 (the *Demanda del Santo Grial*) also presents important innovations in relation to the *P-V Queste-Mort Artu*. The most important change is to the end of the
work, whereby the Spanish author substituted the *P-V* version with that of the
Vulgate, thus creating the so-called "Variant Version". The edition published in
Seville in 1535 is therefore the only truly "cyclical" witness of the *P-V*, in the sense
that it brings together more than one branch; its framework, though, cannot be
called typical.

In an article published in 2011, I maintained the thesis that the *Merlin* and the
Demanda branches were independent before 1500, the year of the publication of
the now-lost Seville edition, or 1515, the date of the Toledo edition:

> Un imprimeur, pouvant dater de la prétendue édition perdue de 1500, aurait antéposé à
> cette *Demanda* indépendante un *Baladro* également autonome, sous la formule du premier
> et du deuxième livre de la *Demanda del Sancto Grial* et donnant lieu ainsi à la configuration,
> conservée dans l'édition tolédane de 1515, bien que conservée uniquement dans la section
> *Demanda*, et uniquement préservée dans ses deux livres dans l'imprimé sévillane de 1535.
> (Gracia, 2011)
> [A printer, dating to the time of the alleged lost edition of 1500, would have preceded this
> independent *Demanda* with an equally independent *Baladro*, placing them under the
> header of the first and second books of the *Demanda del Sancto Grial*, thus giving rise to the
> configuration preserved in the edition published in Toledo in 1515, although preserved only
> in the *Demanda* section, and then only in its two books in the 1535 Seville edition.]

In that discussion, I put forward four arguments. First, the title of the 1498
Baladro del sabio Merlin con sus profecias (Gracia 2012) pre-dates (and is more
authentic than) that of "primero libro de la *Demanda del Santo Grial*" [first book
of the *Quest of the Holy Grail*], which is stated in the *incipit* of the 1535 *Baladro*
in the following form: "Aqui comiença el primero libro de la *Demanda del Santo
Grial* e primeramente se dira del nacimiento de Merlin." [Here begins the first
book of the *Quest of the Holy Grail*, and firstly it will explain the birth of Merlin.]
Second, in respect of the repetition of the story that explains the origin of the
Beste Glatissant [Questing Beast] in the Sevillian edition, I suggested it is prob-
able that this abbreviated narrative was incorporated into an already independent *Baladro*, like the one published in 1498, and that the repetition of stories in
the Sevillian edition is the consequence of having placed an independent *Merlin*
before a *Demanda* that already included the summary narrative. Third, in respect
of the strange addition of the prophecies that the Sevillian edition incorporates
after finishing its *Baladro* (following the statement that "Aqui se acaba el primero
libro de la *Demanda del Santo Grial*" [Here ends the first book of the *Quest of the
Holy Grail*]), I pointed out that the epigraph "Aqui comiençan las profecias del
sabio Merlin, profeta dignissimo" [Here begin the prophecies of the wise Merlin,
honourable prophet] serves as an introduction to a collection of prophecies about

the fifteenth-century politics of Castile that had been circulating independently. I suggested that it is, at the very least, surprising that the printer should jar the transition between the *Baladro* and the *Demanda* with this vast interpolation, and I thus raised the possibility that this addition had been made before, in an independent *Baladro*. Of course, in the eyes of the printer, the desire to offer everything about Merlin may well have taken precedence over the structure of the book and, therefore, the scenario in which the collection was added at a later date cannot be completely disregarded. Fourth, as regards the final tale in which Merlin gives himself to the devils and returns to hell, this is more likely to have occurred in an independent *Merlin* than in a version followed by a *Demanda*. The doomed destiny of the prophet, after all, opens a gap between the derivatives section of *Merlin* and the *Queste*, seriously damaging the overall coherence and understanding of the *Demanda*.

At the beginning of this study, however, I said that the critical perspective of this chapter would be different from my publications of 2011 and 2015, which are based on the conception of the *P-V* that was instigated by Paris and brought to culmination by Bogdanow. The rather different basis upon which I am operating here is one which suggests that certain parts of the *Vulgate* were indeed largely rewritten, perhaps most clearly the section of the *Suite du Merlin*, but that this adaptation was not necessarily made by a single author or at one single moment. This is a conception of the *P-V* that is less rigid and closer to the ideas expressed by Patrick Moran (2014, 656) in his chapter entitled "La question de l'existence du *Cycle Post-Vulgate*" where he states:[3]

> Que la *Suite*, la *Continuation* et la *Queste-Mort Artu post-Vulgate* partagent des affinités au niveau de leur *fabula* et de leur univers de fiction est indéniable [...] rien n'indique qu'elles aient été faites au même moment, qu'elles soient dues à la même personne ni même qu'elles aient jamais coexisté dans les mêmes manuscrits.
>
> [That the *Post-Vulgate Suite*, the *Continuation* and the *Queste-Mort Artu* share similarities in respect of their *fabula* and their fictional universe is undeniable [...] there is neither anything to suggest that they were composed at the same moment, nor that they are attributable to the same person, nor even that they ever existed in the same manuscripts.]

The design of the *P-V* that Paris initiated and Bogdanow finalized relies upon the idea that a manuscript of the cycle was brought to the Iberian Peninsula and translated there, which in turn implies a relationship between the Iberian wit-

---

3 Counter-arguments to the existence of the *P-V* cycle have rarely been formulated; see Szkilnik (2002) and Ménard (1993, 7–8; 1997, 9; 2007, 9–10). Gilles Roussineau also expressed doubts in the introduction to his edition of *La Suite du Roman de Merlin* (1996, 1, XXXVIII).

nesses that, I suggest, is doubtful. For example, at the same time as this conception of the trilogy connects the Iberian witnesses with one another, so it also isolates them, rather unnaturally, from their contemporary production in either French or Italian. Indeed, the study of medieval Iberian texts has tended to focus on their evolution by taking into account only the interventions of the Iberian authors and the adaptation of the original translation to their particular taste(s); in other words, the emphasis is on the influence of other Iberian literature. Critics have rarely, if ever, considered the possibility that certain features of late medieval Iberian Arthurian matter might be explained in the light of the contemporary foreign production such as, for example, the taste for the compilation of Arthurian matter into large codices, reflected in manuscripts such as Paris, BnF, fr. 112, copied for Jacques d'Armagnac by Micheau Gonnot in 1470 (Pickford 1960; Bogdanow 2005), the same year that Salamanca 1877 was produced. Nor has the possibility ever been considered that the 1498 edition might be related to the *Historia di Merlino* published by Lucas Dominici (printed in Venice in 1480). In short, the circumstances under which the editions of †1500, 1515 and 1535 were published were markedly different from those surrounding the production of the thirteenth-century manuscripts, both in Italy and in France, and even in the Iberian Peninsula. We must acknowledge, therefore, that these printed editions belong to a different universe than do their early manuscript forebears, one where copies of Arthurian texts are abundant, and where book planners have a wide spectrum of options for bringing together many and varied combinations.

The Spanish editions, I therefore argue, should be placed in the context of the codices copied for Jacques d'Armagnac, or that of the *Historia di Merlino* and even that of the *Merlin* of Antoine Vérard, published in 1498, the same year in which the *Baladro* of Burgos was published. We must additionally take into account the Venice and Paris *Merlins*, and into this context we should also place the Spanish manuscripts and printed books of the fifteenth and sixteenth centuries. For example, the *Historia di Merlino* combines the prose rendering of Robert de Boron's *Merlin* with some collections of prophecies derived from the *Prophéties de Merlin* attributed to Richard d'Irlande, which are interleaved in the biography of Merlin from his birth until his death (Visani 1994). In France, the most important printer of the moment, Antoine Vérard, was interested in the prose rendering of Robert de Boron's *Merlin* and published it directly alongside the *Prophéties* (cf. Taylor, *supra*). This is a compilation that collects various earlier materials, and adds to it new episodes such as the prose rendering of Robert de Boron's *Merlin*, the *Suite du Merlin* (*Vulgate*), the death of the prophet and the *Prophéties de Merlin*. In a similar vein, in the *Historia di Merlino* the prophecies are divided into two blocks, the second of which brings the sole surviving volume to a close, while in the *Merlin* by Vérard (Koble 2004) the prophecies contrastingly constitute a separate volume (the last, in fact). I contend that it is into this context that the 1498 edition, published by Juan of Burgos, should be placed. Juan's book includes the prose rendering of Robert de Boron's *Merlin*, followed by the *P-V Suite du Merlin* and the collection of prophecies derived from the *Historia regum Britanniae*, which are inserted after the enigma of the dragons is solved. It is not known, of course, whether the exemplar used by Juan of Burgos combined both biography and prophecies, or if he had read the *Historia di Merlino*, or, less likely, the *Merlin* of Vérard; the composition of this biography of Merlin, which brings together life and prophecies, is something that could just as easily have occurred independently in each of the three countries. However, with the exception of the prose rendering of Robert de Boron's *Merlin*, the source materials employed by Juan of Burgos are clearly different from those of his Venetian and Parisian colleagues. Indeed, it is quite possible that the *Prophéties de Merlin* had not yet been translated in the Iberian Peninsula, and that the dissemination of the *Suite du Merlin* (*Vulgate*) was scarce. Juan of Burgos therefore appears to narrate the biography of Merlin using only materials that had already been translated into Spanish (those associated with what we now know as the *P-V Cycle*), to which he adds a Spanish version of the prophecies of Merlin derived from the *Historia regum Britanniae*.

The important question as to when the prophecies might have been translated, or at least when they became associated with these materials, thus remains nebulous. It is possible that they were available in Seville in 1500, or in Toledo in 1515, since it was in the 1535 Seville edition of *Demanda del Santo Grial con los maravillosos fechos de Lançarote y de Galaz su hijo* that the publisher prefaced the *P-V Queste del saint Graal* with a *Merlin*, and followed it with the new collection of prophecies concerning Spanish politics of the fifteenth century. The 1535 Seville print therefore seems to be an example of a latterly-added *Merlin* to a *Queste*, or rather a *Queste* latterly prefaced by a *Merlin* (or, indeed, a *Demanda* latterly prefaced by a *Baladro*), than it is a witness that preserves the cyclic structure of a codex that had reached the Iberian Peninsula in the thirteenth century. Rather than constituting the physical preservation of a primitive cycle, the 1535 Seville edition is "un trompe-l'oeil, une illusion de cycle" [an optical illusion, an illusion of a cycle], to echo the words that Nathalie Koble (2004, 252) uses to define the *Merlin* of Antoine Vérard.[4]

In sum, certain characteristics of the Iberian texts contributed to the establishment in scholarly criticism of the tripartite structure of the *P-V*, especially the

---

4 On cyclicity in the late Arthurian romances, see Taylor (1994), Moran (2012) and Szkilnik (2004).

1535 *Demanda del Santo Grial* printed in Seville, but critics extrapolated that it harked back to a similarly-constructed primitive version, composed in the thirteenth century, and which is only reflected by the later printed versions. The printed editions of Burgos (1498) and Seville (†1500, 1515, 1535), I suggest, actually seem to be the product of a Europe-wide trend in Arthurian cyclical compilation, rather than a reflection of an earlier Iberian tradition in which the texts were necessarily compiled together. This is not to suggest, however, that the texts' inherent cyclicity was not understood at earlier stages. Indeed, two particular tendencies coexist in time and across texts: one is an interest in Merlin, whose life is covered from birth to death; the other is a fascination with the Grail, which needs an explanation prior to the arrival of the Grail at Arthur's court, as is set out in the Seville *Demanda*. One trend individualizes the narrative, as in the Burgos *Baladro*, while the other totalizes it, as is particularly the case in the 1535 Sevillian *Demanda del Santo Grial*. The perception that the Arthurian universe constitutes a whole is thus never lost, whether the texts are found together or apart, thanks to the repeated references to the various different sections in both the manuscripts and printed books.

References

Bogdanow, Fanni. "Micheau Gonnot's Arthuriad Preserved in Paris, Bibliothèque Nationale, fr. 112 and its Place in the Evolution of Arthurian Romance." *Arthurian Literature* 22 (2005): 20–48.

Bogdanow, Fanni. *The Romance of the Grail: A Study of the Structure and Genesis of a ThirteenthCentury Arthurian Prose Romance*. Manchester and New York: Manchester University Press and Barnes and Noble, 1966.

Gracia, Paloma. "The *Post-Vulgate Cycle* in the Iberian Peninsula." *The Arthur of the Iberians*. Ed. David Hook. Arthurian Literature of the Middle Ages 8. Cardiff: University of Wales Press, 2015. 271–288.

Gracia, Paloma. "Avatares ibéricos del ciclo artúrico de la *Post-Vulgate*: el título del *Baladro del sabio Merlín con sus profecías* (Burgos, 1498) y la colección profética derivada de la *Historia Regum Britanniae*." *Zeitschrift für romanische Philologie* 128 (2012): 507–521.

Gracia, Paloma. "Réflexions sur les remaniements du cycle *Post-Vulgate* dans la péninsule ibérique : la complexe perception cyclique d'une matière, qui peut être, à la fois, divisée en sections." *Temps et mémoire dans la littérature arthurienne*. Ed. Catalina Girbea, Andreea Popescu and Mihaela Voicu. Bucharest: University of Bucarest, 2011. 337–345.

Klob, Otto. "Beiträge zur Kenntnis der spanischen und portugiesischen GralLitteratur." *Zeitschrift für romanische Philologie* 26 (1902): 169–205.

Koble, Nathalie. "Le testament d'un compilateur: montages textuels et invention romanesque dans l'édition *princeps* des 'livres de Merlin' (Antoine Vérard, 1498)." *Du roman courtois*

au roman baroque. Actes du colloque des 2–5 juillet 2002. Ed. Emmanuel Bury and
Francine Mora, Paris: Belles Lettres, 2004. 251–264.

Ménard, Philippe. Preface to *Le Roman de Tristan en prose: version du manuscrit français 757
de la Bibliothèque nationale de France*. Ed. Christine Ferlampin-Acher. Paris: Champion,
2007. Vol. 5, 7–10.

Ménard, Philippe. Preface to *Le roman de Tristan en prose*. Ed. Laurence Harf-Lancner. Geneva:
Droz, 1997. Vol. 9, 9.

Ménard, Philippe. Preface to *Le roman de Tristan en prose*. Ed. Emmanuèle Baumgartner and
Michelle Szkilnik. Geneva: Droz, 1993. Vol. 6, 7–8.

Moran, Patrick. *Lectures cycliques. Le réseau inter-romanesque dans les cycles du Graal du XIIIe
siècle*. Paris: Champion, 2014.

Moran, Patrick. "Cycle ou roman-somme? Le *Cycle Vulgate* dans les manuscrits et les imprimés
du XVe siècle." *Le Moyen Âge par le Moyen Âge, même*. Ed. Laurent Brun et al. Paris:
Champion, 2012. 163–178.

Paris, Gaston. "Review of Karl von Reinhardstoettner, *Historia dos cavalleiros da Mesa Redonda
e da Demanda do Santo Graal*," *Romania* 16 (1887): 582–586.

Paris, Gaston, and Jacob Ulrich, eds. *Merlin: roman en prose du xiiie siècle publié avec la mise
en prose du poème de Robert de Boron d'après le manuscrit appartenant à M. Alfred H.
Huth*, Société des Anciens Textes Français. 2 vols. Paris: Firmin Didot, 1886.

Pickford, Cedric E. *L'Evolution du roman arthurien en prose vers la fin du Moyen Age, d'après le
manuscrit 112 du fonds français de la Bibliothèque nationale*. Paris: Nizet, 1960.

Pietsch, Karl. *Spanish Grail Fragments*. 2 vols. Chicago: The University of Chicago Press,
1924–1925.

Roussineau, Gilles, ed. *La Suite du Roman de Merlin. 2* vols. Geneva: Droz, 1996.

Ruiz García, Elisa. *Los libros de Isabel la Católica. Arqueología de un patrimonio escrito*.
Salamanca: Instituto de Historia del Libro y de la Lectura, 2004.

Szkilnik, Michelle. "Les sommes romanesques du Moyen Âge, cycles ou compilations?"
*Chemins tournants. Cycles et recueils en littérature des romans du Graal à la poésie
contemporaine*. Ed. Stéphane Michaud. Paris: Presses Sorbonne Nouvelle, 2004. 23–50.

Szkilnik, Michelle. "La cohérence en question: La *Suite-Merlin* et la constitution d'un cycle
romanesque." *Matéria de Bretanha em Portugal*. Ed. Leonor Curado Neves, Margarida
Madureira and Teresa Amado. Lisbon: Colibri, 2002. 9–27.

Sommer, H. Oskar, ed. *The Vulgate Version of the Arthurian Romances*. The Carnegie Institution
of Washington Publications 74. 8 vols. Washington, DC: The Carnegie Institution of
Washington, 1908–1916.

Taylor, Jane H.M. "Order from Accident: Cyclic Consciousness at the End of the Middle Ages."
*Cyclification. The Development of Narrative Cycles in the Chansons de Geste and the
Arthurian Romances*. Ed. Bart Besamusca et al. Amsterdam: Koninklijke Nederlandse
Akademie van Wetenschappen Verhandelingen, 1994. 59–73.

Visani, Oriana. "I testi italiani dell' *Historia di Merlino*." *Schede Umanistiche* 1 (1994): 17–62.

Michael Stolz
Wolfram von Eschenbach's *Parzival*: Searching for the Grail

Wolfram von Eschenbach's German Grail romance *Parzival*, written in the first and perhaps early second decade of the thirteenth century, comprises almost 25,000 verses in couplets. Following the structures of initials to be found in some of the oldest manuscripts, Karl Lachmann, the first modern editor of *Parzival*, divided the text into units of thirty verses, and – on a higher level – into sixteen books. A reference point for dating the poem can be found in the seventh book, with an allusion made to the vineyards of Erfurt being destroyed during a war between the Staufer Philip of Swabia and the Landgrave of Thuringia, Herman I, in 1203 (379:18–20; the consequences of crop shortfall may have lasted for up to a decade, hence this period of time could reasonably have separated the remark from the actual historical event: Mertens 2004, 243). In the rich manuscript tradition of the text, which contains over eighty witnesses dating from the thirteenth to the fifteenth century, four distinct redactions of Wolfram's *Parzival* can be discerned, all of which originate from the thirteenth century: *D, *m, *G, *T, of which *D and *m on the one hand, and *G and *T on the other, are more closely related (Stolz 2014, 457–459; variants of *D and *G are documented in the critical edition by Schirok (Wolfram von Eschenbach 2003) following Lachmann, while those of *D, *m and *G, *T are detailed in the electronic edition of the *Parzival*-Project, University of Bern).[1] Besides *Parzival*, Wolfram left a fragmentary side story of this novel, commonly referred to as *Titurel* and composed in stanzas, as well as another epic text belonging to the genre of *chanson de geste* called *Willehalm*, and some love poetry, especially dawn songs (*Tagelieder*).

---

1 For the complete list of manuscript sigla, see Stolz (2016b, 381).

Note: This article is indebted to the extensive research literature on Wolfram's Grail romance gathered in Nellmann (1994), Bumke (2004), Mertens (2003 and 2011/14). The primary texts are quoted after the editions of Chrétien's *Roman de Perceval* provided by Busby (Chrétien de Troyes 1993), and of Wolfram's *Parzival* provided by Lachmann/Schirok (Wolfram von Eschenbach 2003). Concerning the latter, I have consulted, and occasionally adapted with respect to the original Middle High German text and to the specific contexts in this article, the English translations by Hatto (1980) and Edwards (2004). I wish to thank Matthias Berger (Bern) and Christoph Pretzer (Cambridge) for revising this article linguistically.

Michael Stolz (University of Bern)

DOI 10.1515/9783110432466-029

1 Precursors: Chrétien's *Roman de Perceval ou le Conte du Graal* and others

Wolfram's main source for the *Parzival* is Chrétien de Troyes who, with his unfinished Old French *Roman de Perceval ou le Conte du Graal* (c. 1180–1190), introduced the motif of the Grail into Arthurian romance and therefore into European literature. Any primitive versions of the Grail story, which Chrétien may have known from oral Breton narrators, remain unknown. Concerning this matter, origins in Indo-European or Celtic contexts have been discussed, but these are hypothetical in many respects. Central components of the Grail story such as the unanswered question, the lance and the Grail itself may indeed have occurred in Celtic tales. But the written records in which these accounts are transmitted reveal the influence of later traditions represented by Chrétien's *Roman de Perceval*. Prototypes of the Grail topic can be traced in archaic Irish tales like the *Baile in scáil* and in the Cymric genre of *Mabinogion* [narratives of young heroes] with the story of *Peredur*, contained in manuscripts from the fourteenth century (see Morgans, *supra*). In both the Irish and the Cymric precursors, a precious vessel or dish is bound to the solemn transfer of sovereignty within a ruling family. Allowing for all the caveats inherent in any such reconstruction, the narrative pattern predating Chrétien might have looked as follows: an infant king grows up outside society and is put to initiatory tests. He encounters his uncle and is confronted with a symbolic task related to a vessel and a lance, both covered with blood. The task is associated with a question or riddle and – especially in the *Peredur*-tradition – with a wrong done to the family. The infant avenges this wrong and becomes king (Mertens 2003, 24; Mertens 2011/2014, 274–275).

2 The *Graal*

In Chrétien's *Roman de Perceval*, the magic vessel is called a *graal* (l. 3220), probably after the Latin word *gradale* for a big flat dish in which food is arranged in stages or "grades" (Mertens 2003, 35; Mertens 2011/2014, 266).[2] The word will reappear in Wolfram's *Parzival* as a proper name: "ein dinc, daz hiez der Grâl" (235:23, similarly 454:21) [a thing called the Grail] (see also Stolz 2010; Stolz

---

2 Other derivations from Latin *crater* [mixing vessel], or *cratis* [netting], as well as an occurrence of the expression *graalz* in Helinand of Froidmont's *Chronicon* are discussed by Bumke (2004, 235).

2016a, 270–274). But whereas Chrétien's *Graal* is a plate apparently large enough to be filled with fish (ll. 6420–6421), Wolfram's *Grâl* is a precious stone endowed with magic powers. As Chrétien states in the prologue, Count Philip of Flanders commissioned his *Conte du Graal* (l. 13). Philip died on the third crusade in 1191, which may have led Chrétien to abandon his work; Philip's father, on his return from the second crusade in 1150, had brought to Flanders a relic of some drops of Christ's blood assumed to have been collected by Joseph of Arimathea. This sort of relic adoration evident in the patron's family may also have influenced Chrétien's concept of the Grail (Mertens 2003, 26–27; Mertens 2011/2014, 264, 267–269). In this context, it is also worth mentioning a narrative variation outside Arthurian romance to demonstrate the diversity of the Grail topic around the year 1200.

3 Robert de Boron's *Estoire dou Graal*

In that time, Robert de Boron wrote his French *Estoire dou Graal* for Gautier de Montbéliard who, for his part, took the cross in 1199 (Mertens 2003, 83–103; Mertens 2011/2014, 276–278). Robert seems to have planned a cycle of three parts, of which it appears he was only able to finish the first one, called *Joseph d'Arimathie*. In this text, the Grail appears as a relic elevated over all other cult objects related to the Passion of Christ, such as the Veil of Veronica. It is the chalice used by Jesus Christ in the ceremony of the Last Supper and used in turn by Joseph of Arimathea to collect Christ's blood during his martyrdom. Due to its sacred context, the Grail is attributed grace-giving powers; it is conceived as the centre of a religious community with almost ecclesiastical status. Joseph, who was a member of the Jewish nobility, provides a model for Christian knighthood. Besides this, Robert furnishes the Grail with a sort of salvific history: after the dispersion of the Jews, Joseph of Arimathea leaves Palestine together with his sister and his brother-in-law, Bron (Hebron). Joseph inaugurates a table similar to that of the Last Supper (and evoking that of King Arthur) for celebrating a ceremony centred on the chalice and a meal of fish, the symbol of Christ; as the fish has been caught by Bron, the latter is called the "rich fisherman". The *Graal* is meant to be pleasant (*agreer*) to a community of the righteous who participate in the ceremony. An angel tells Joseph that after him, Bron will be the custodian of the Grail; Bron is to go to the West to attend the "third man", his grandson. In a later continuation of Robert's text (the so-called Didot-*Perceval*), this grandson is identified as Perceval. The genealogical concept of the subsequent custodies held by Joseph, Bron and the "third man" – somewhat similar to the three Ages of the Father, the Son and the Holy Spirit in Joachim of Fiore's contemporaneous doctrine – stakes a claim to historical truth. Accordingly, Robert calls his text an *estoire*, and not a *roman* as had his contemporary, Chrétien de Troyes, called his *Conte du Graal*.

Robert's *Joseph d'Arimathie* contains a Grail story that goes without the figure of Perceval (whose identification as the "third man" is part of a later version influenced by Chrétien). Whether Robert's text predates Chrétien's is not verified. However, both authors introduce the word "Graal" to refer to a magic vessel used in a cultish meal; and both describe a dynasty having a "rich fisherman" as its member (Bumke 2004, 235–236). In Chrétien's *Conte du Graal*, this fisherman is Perceval's cousin; in Wolfram's version he will be Parzival's uncle. However, in contrast to Robert of Boron, Chrétien and Wolfram both abstain from any explicit correlation of the Grail with the Passion of Christ.

4 Wolfram's Grail Story

In what follows, Wolfram's treatment of the Grail story will be discussed together with Chrétien's, but with a greater focus on Wolfram's perspective (based on Johnson 1999; Mertens 2003, 25–82; Bumke 2004, 54–124, 237–239; Mertens 2011/2014, 264–269, 279–283). Differences are emphasized, where relevant, while evidence of the manuscript tradition is included where it helps to understand the idiosyncrasy of the German poem. In light of Chrétien's unfinished text and Wolfram's narrative art, the German *Parzival* can arguably be called the most accomplished Arthurian Grail romance (cf. Kragl, *supra*). Wolfram not only completes his French source but also enriches it in many ways: he devises side stories as well as the profiles of numerous characters (who, in contrast to Chrétien's appellatives, bear individual names); he establishes a complex network of family relationships and enlarges Chrétien's Arthurian world with the realm of the Orient – which is also relevant, clearly, to the Grail. As an informant surpassing his deficient source, Wolfram introduces the enigmatic figure of Kyot, who, unlike Chrétien, has supposedly offered the authentic tale to the narrator (epilogue, 827:1–4). In all likelihood, this Kyot is a fictitious reference, used to cover Wolfram's own narrative inventions for information not provided by Chrétien. By means of this arrangement, narration itself proves to be one of the most prominent features of, and even a topic to be treated in, Wolfram's Grail romance (Bumke 2004, 215–232).

A peculiarity of Wolfram's narrative is the fact that the mysteries of the Grail are only gradually disclosed. This principle corresponds to the personality of the protagonist: Parzival is characterized as a foolish youngster who ignores the requests of his environment, making numerous mistakes and committing grave sins. His mother, Herzloyde, mourns the early death of her husband, Gahmuret (Parzival's father, whose adventures – without any model in Chrétien's *Conte du Graal* – are reported in books 1 and 2); she decides to educate her child far from the chivalrous world, in a solitary place, tellingly called Soltane by the German author (this is the start of book 3). But one day, young Parzival encounters a group of Arthurian knights and decides to search for King Arthur's court, leaving his dying mother behind. In Chrétien's *Conte du Graal*, Perceval sees his mother falling over, whereas in Wolfram's adaption Parzival does not turn back to watch her passing away. In a series of adventures, Parzival commits misconduct again, compromising innocent Jeschute (whom Wolfram presents as Erec's sister) in the eyes of her husband, Orilus, and killing his own relative, Ither, in order to deprive him of his vermilion armament when he first visits King Arthur's court. But after catching up on chivalrous education at the home of Gurnemanz, he also excels at chivalry, liberating Cundwiramurs, his future wife, from the besiegers who invade her territory (book 4). With these challenges braved, Parzival unwittingly enters the realm of the Grail for the first time (in book 5). The German narrator reports all these events while adopting Parzival's inadequate perspective and mixing it with his own observations and comments. This is also the case for the Grail ceremony the protagonist witnesses on his first visit at the Grail Castle, named Munsalvæsche. Only at a later stage, during his stay at the hermitage of his uncle, Trevrizent, (in book 9) will the mysteries of the Grail be revealed, when the hermit himself prominently adopts the role of narrator.

5 Genealogical structures

The genealogical structures in Wolfram's poem are of special interest, as Parzival combines the kinships of King Arthur on the patrilineal side and of the Grail on the matrilineal side (Bumke 2004, 169–176). As far as the siblings of his mother are concerned, Parzival has two aunts, Schoysiane and Repanse de schoye, the bearer of the Grail, as well as two uncles, the aforementioned Trevrizent and Anfortas, the Grail King, who is identical with the "rich fisherman" or "fisher king" (*Roi Pescheor*) in Chrétien's *Conte du Graal*. Wolfram thus enlarges the genealogical configurations of the Grail family from cousinship between Parzival and the Grail King to ancestry and succession, as, after Anfortas' regency, Parzival will become the Grail King himself. In the German poem, the maternal lineage is expanded by Anfortas' father, Frimutel, and by his grandfather, Titurel. When Parzival encounters the latter during his first visit to the Grail Castle, the narrator comments that the identity of this unnamed, "most handsome old man" (240:27) will be unveiled later; in order to illustrate this circuitous narrative, he employs the famous bowstring parable, which refers to a bowstring being stretched when the arrow is shot (241:1–30). At the end of the German poem, the next generation of the Grail family will also come into view: Parzival has two twin sons, Kardeiz and Loherangrin, of which only the latter is destined to become Grail King. Wolfram also mentions the marriage between Parzival's aunt Repanse de schoye and Parzival's half-brother Feirefiz, fathered by Gahmuret with the dark-skinned Oriental queen Belakane. Their son, Prester John, will assure the spread of Christendom in India, where the future kings adopt his name.

6 The Grail ceremony and its objects

The following description of the Grail ceremony concentrates on the objects Parzival is confronted with during his first visit to Munsalvæsche. Two types of things can be distinguished here: on the one hand are the objects Parzival comes into physical contact with; on the other are the objects he only looks at. Thus, cloak and sword as signs of sovereignty are contrasted with the lance and the Grail, the signs of the Grail mystery (for their function as signs, see Bumke 2001, 64–76). Other narrative features or items correlating with these objects will be discussed where relevant. Of special interest in this regard is the question that Parzival is expected to ask at the Grail Castle, the so-called redeeming question that could heal the suffering Grail King, Anfortas.

When Parzival arrives at Munsalvæsche, a chamberlain invests him with a cloak normally worn by Repanse de schoye, who is called the Grail Queen (228:8–16), whereas in Chrétien's *Conte du Graal* the cloak is conferred without such comment (ll. 3073–3074). In the French text, the Fisher King grants a precious sword to Perceval, a gift that Wolfram shifts to a moment after the Grail ceremony and the dinner with Anfortas and his court. In that context, as will be shown, the sword mutates from a sign of sovereignty to one of the Grail mystery.

A strange scene placed before the beginning of the Grail procession illustrates the fact that the protagonist is not yet mature enough to cope with the mysterious experience he is about to encounter. A "man deft in speech" (229:4), probably a jester, irritates Parzival, who, lacking the armour that has been taken off him, clenches his fist so furiously that blood shoots out of his nails and sprinkles his sleeves. Parzival, barely restrained from reacting violently by the attendant knights, proves to be unable to give an adequate verbal response to the jester. (229:4–22; see Weigand 1969 [1952]) This detail, not present in Chrétien, is equally suppressed in one of the main manuscripts of the German tradition: witness G (Munich, Staatsbibliothek, Cgm 19, mid-thirteenth century, missing 228:27–229:18). By carefully eliminating the scene, this codex, which constitutes the essential manuscript of version *G, suggests that the protagonist does not have any linguistic deficiencies.

Yet this linguistic inadequacy is also the cause of Parzival's failure while watching the Grail procession at Munsalvæsche. The unasked question is closely connected to the Grail ceremony, the sumptuousness of which Wolfram has significantly enlarged in respect to his French source. The German poet mentions numerous lights and candelabra, tables for hundreds of knights, golden dishes, and twenty-five beautiful maidens clothed in noble robes to serve in the procession.

7 The bloody lance and the silver knives

Before the start of the procession, a squire appears bearing a lance from whose blade blood is issuing, running down the shaft to his hand and stopping at the sleeve (231:17–22, the blood-splashed sleeve corresponds to Parzival's, mentioned in the previous scene). The presentation of the lance, carried along the four walls of the hall, evokes crying and grief. It might recall the Lance of Longinus, who thrust his spear into the flank of the crucified Christ to confirm his death, but neither Wolfram nor Chrétien hints overtly at this legend. This connection is only established in the *First Continuation* of Chrétien's *Perceval*, which was composed c. 1200. Here, the fact that the Lance of Longinus continues to bleed (which is not mentioned in the legend itself) becomes a tradition. At a later stage of the romance, a more rational explanation for the blood is given: during Parzival's stay at the hermitage, Trevrizent argues that the lance (presumably identical with the one in the Grail procession) is the poisoned weapon of a heathen who has wounded Anfortas in the testicles during a combat that he was fighting in the courtly service of a lady who was not destined by the Grail to be his lover (478:1–479:17). As a remedy, the lance has to be placed into Anfortas' wound, allowing the hot poison to draw the frost from his body (489:30–490:2; 490:11–17; Parzival also refers to the scene he has watched at the Grail Castle: 492:17–22).

The glass-coloured, ice-like frost is removed from the blade with two silver knives made by the wise smith, Trebuchet (490:18–22). These knives are a misconception that Wolfram formed from the "tailleoir d'argant" [silver plate] mentioned in Chrétien's description of the Grail procession (ll. 3231, 3287). Wolfram seems to have understood the *tailleoir* as a derivative of the French verb *taillier* [to cut], converted it (in plural form) into two sharp silver knives and set them as cutlery for the meal at Munsalvæsche ("zwei messer snîdende als ein grât", 234:18), before then altering them in Trevrizent's speech into instruments purifying the lance. It is likely that Wolfram changed the function of the knives, as well as the concept of the lance, during his long-term composition of the text: the mysteriously bleeding lance became a bloody lance to be cleaned by the silver knives.[3] The German expressions "bluotec sper" (255:11; 316:27) or "sper bluotec rôt" (490:2; 492:21) occurring in Wolfram's *Parzival* allow both interpretations, of a bleeding as well as of a bloody lance.

8 The Grail and the unasked question

While Chrétien includes the lance in the Grail procession, Wolfram introduces the latter only after the lance has been presented. The queen, Repanse de schoye, accompanied by the twenty-four maidens, conveys the Grail placed on a green-coloured cloth: "Upon a green achmardi she carried the perfection of Paradise, both root and branch; this was a thing called the Grail, earth's perfection's transcendence." (235:20–24; Stolz 2010, 189–191) During the meal, the Grail is placed on Anfortas' table, where Parzival sits down; in Chrétien's *Conte du Graal*, the Grail vessel passes the table during every course. Wolfram points to the fact that the Grail, similar to a magic table, offers all sorts of food and drink (238:8–239:7). Puzzled by the mysterious occurrence and remembering Gurnemanz, who has advised him not to ask too many questions, Parzival refrains from enquiring, "how it stands with this household?" (239:8–17) The wording of the unasked question might well be a reflex from Chrétien, where Perceval abstains from asking, "whom does the Grail serve?" (ll. 3292–3293) Later, in the French text, Perceval's female cousin informs him that the questions of why the lance was bleeding and where the Grail procession was heading would have healed the Fisher King and restored his sovereignty (ll. 3552–3570, 3583–3590). This is different in Wolfram's romance, where Parzival is expected to ask Anfortas: "hêrre, wie stêt iwer nôt?" (484:27) ["Lord, what is the nature of your distress?"], as Trevrizent later teaches his nephew during the stay at the hermitage.

Parzival's stop at his uncle's enclave – a cave situated in a rock face – on Good Friday initiates the extensive revelation of the Grail's mysteries, given first

---

3 Both paragraphs in book 5 and 9 are commented on in Nellmann (1994, 575–579, 694–695; 1996).

by the narrator, and then by the hermit himself (book 9). At the start, the syncretistic history of the Grail, grounded in a blend of the three monotheistic religions, is explained. The heathen astronomer Flegetanis, son of a Jewish mother and a Muslim father, has read the name of the Grail in the stars (453:23–454:23). His visions result in a statement: "er jach, ez hiez ein dinc der grâl" (454:21) [he said that a thing was called the Grail]. This phrase resumes almost verbatim the verse occurring in the procession scene: "daz was ein dinc, daz hiez der grâl" (235:23) [this was a thing called the Grail]. Both times, the fact that "the thing" is called by the name "Grail" is emphasized. The second occurrence, following the first mention on the narrative axis, but preceding it on the historical one, combines Flegetanis' vision with a verbal utterance in which the Grail might be named for the very first time. It seems telling that a significant difference between the versions *D, *m and *G, *T (otherwise rare in book 9) arises at this point, as *G, *T have the variant "er jach, ez wære ein dinc der grâl" [he said that [there] *was* a thing [called?] the Grail] (see Stolz 2016a, 272–274). Obviously, the verb alternatives *wære* [[there] was] and *hiez* [was called] – the latter of which is also to be found in the verb sequence of verse 235:23 – highlight either the real or the linguistic existence of the Grail. The variant *wære*, as *G, *T have it, represses the linguistic aspect, and might be correlated to the missing jester scene (as it occurs in manuscript G), which announces Parzival's deficient linguistic behaviour at Munsalvæsche.

9 The Grail history

One important detail of Flegetanis' testimony is the fact that "a troop left the Grail on earth and rose high above the stars" before Christian people ("baptised fruit") had to take care of it (454:24–30). It is debatable whether this may allude to the "neutral angels" who stayed impartial after Lucifer's fall, referred to later in the text (471:15–29; 798:11–22). The "prime version of the Grail history" ("dirre âventiure gestifte", 453:14), transmitted as a written record of Flegetanis' account (455:1), is found by Kyot, the narrator's above-mentioned authority, in Toledo, the intercultural centre of erudition and translation in medieval Spain. There he decodes the history of the Grail, composed in "heathen" (Arabian or Hebrew?) letters, supported in his understanding by the fact that he is a Christian (453:11–22). Furthermore, Kyot has studied chronicles in Britain, France and Ireland – the original territories of the historical Grail legend – to look for the history of the Grail family, and discovered it in "Anschouwe" (455:2–12) [Anjou].

At this point, Trevrizent, engaging in a dialogue with Parzival, resumes the narration (456:5–502:30). In the course of this conversation, the "hidden tidings of the Grail" (452:30) are disclosed: Parzival learns that the Grail is a stone with the dubious name "lapsit exillis" (469:7; "lapsit exillis" in *D and in *G, "lapis exilis" in *m, "jaspis ex illix" in *T; for the Grail name in context with the neutral angels, see Ranke 1946, Engl. transl. 2000; for the variants of the Grail name see Nellman 2000). Its rejuvenating and life-saving powers prevent human beings from dying during the week following their having seen it (469:14–27); this is also the reason why the heavily wounded Grail King, Anfortas, lives on (480:25–29). Every Good Friday, which is also the day of Parzival's arrival at Trevrizent's hermitage, the power of the Grail, including the charms of the magic table, is renewed with a host brought by a dove from heaven (470:1–20). The Grail stone is similar to a magic bowl with appearing and vanishing inscriptions that indicate the names of boys and virgins destined for the service of the Grail (470:21–471:14). This community of guardians resembles a sacred order, and the boys, after having become knights, are called "templeise" (468:28), recalling the order of the Templars (which had been founded in 1120). Before these knights and maidens assumed guardianship of the stone under the rule of the Grail family, the "neutral angels" already alluded to by the narrator fulfilled this task (471:15–29). Thus, the legend of the Grail is projected back to the beginning of history.

Similar to the lance, the Grail evokes religious ideas without being limited to a merely Christian dimension. The "neutral angels" might have their origin in Jewish traditions. Its form of a stone and the green colour of the achmardi it is covered with could, from an Islamic perspective, also be connected with the Kaaba and the colour of the prophet Mohamed (Mertens 2003, 72). The date of Parzival's arrival at the hermitage is the Christian Good Friday, and Trevrizent uses a psalter to help Parzival regain the temporal orientation he has lost (460:25–27). Nevertheless, Wolfram reduces the apparently ecclesiastical components (chapel, priest, formal confession and Eucharist) that Chrétien uses for the scenery, and the hermit Trevrizent declares himself a layman (462:11). All of these details, including the fact that women participate in the pseudo-liturgical Grail ceremony in Munsalvæsche, point to a religious mentality of the kind practised by lay people in the twelfth century (Mertens 2003, 73; Bumke 2004, 94, 131–132). In this lay perspective, Parzival, after having omitted the redeeming question at Munsalvæsche, is brought back to religious life. Trevrizent declares that, besides the unasked question, Parzival's greatest sins are the deaths caused to his mother and to his relative, Ither (499:20–22; 501:3–5). However, when the hermit absolves his nephew from his sins, this act has no canonical character (501:17–18; 502:25–26).

10 The Grail Sword

The Grail Sword that Parzival receives at Munsalvæsche is also mentioned in the context of sins (501:1). Unlike in Chrétien, where Perceval is endowed with the Sword before he watches the Grail ceremony (ll. 3130–3184), Wolfram's Parzival receives the Sword after the procession has ended. This deferment goes hand-in-hand with a shift of the Sword's function, which mutates from a sign of sovereignty to one of the Grail mystery. In Wolfram's romance, the Sword, once used by Anfortas in combat, is closely linked to the redeeming question. The narrator explicitly refers to it as a hint by which Parzival "was admonished to ask the question" (240:6) and he complains: "Alas that he did not ask then!" (240:3) The correlation of the sword and the unasked question is repeatedly emphasized in the poem (254:15–30; 316:21–23); and it also returns in Trevrizent's statements about Parzival's sins: "Your uncle gave you a sword, too, by which you have been granted sin, since your eloquent mouth unfortunately voiced no question there." (501:1–4) Apart from this, the Grail Sword, forged by Trebuchet like the silver knives (253:29), turns out to be an almost blind motif, ostensibly adopted from Chrétien (and from some interpolations in certain *Perceval*-manuscripts), appearing at intervals with some inconsistency throughout Wolfram's poem (Stolz 2016a). Its role as a guiding theme and sign used to urge Parzival – as well as the audience of the text – to ask for the secrets of the Grail and its narrative environs is supported by the fact that, soon after mentioning the Sword (fifteen days in the story, but only some lines later in the narrative: 501:11), Trevrizent discloses that the "handsome old man" is Titurel (501:19–502:3), just as was announced in the bowstring parable (241:1–30).

11 Searching for the Grail

Repeated references to the lance, the silver knives and the Grail Sword occur when Parzival meets his cousin, Sigune, shortly after the visit at the Grail Castle (book 5) and when his failure is proclaimed publicly by the hideous Grail messenger, Cundrie, in the presence of King Arthur and his court (book 6). In both cases, Parzival – and the audience – are partly informed about the secrets of the Grail before Trevrizent gives his more comprehensive explanations (book 9). Cundrie accuses Parzival of having committed a sin (316:23); her execration provokes Parzival to resign any joy before having seen the Grail: "That is the goal to which my thoughts chase me." (329:25–28) With this sentence, Parzival starts his intentional search for the Grail, whose realm he has entered inadvertently before. This is also the classical moment of crisis that occurs in the conventional scheme of Arthurian romance, for example in Chrétien's *Erec* and *Yvain*, both adapted in German by Hartmann von Aue. According to this scheme, the protagonist, after having failed in a first course of adventures, starts a second one to repair his fault, namely the neglect of the ruler's and the husband's duties in *Erec* and *Yvain*, respectively. In the Grail novel, this second course is altered, as it is split up and distributed between two protagonists: Perceval/Parzival searches for the Grail, whereas Gauvain/Gawan, the Arthurian model knight, proves himself in secular adventures of chivalry and courtly love. In the subsequent parts of the German poem (books 7–8, 10–14), the narration concentrates on Gawan, while Parzival stays in the background. Among other things, Gawan is charged with searching for the Grail by Vergulaht, who, defeated by Parzival, has himself been obligated to search for the Grail. However, Gawan's particular achievement will be the liberation of four hundred maidens and four queens, the latter being his own and King Arthur's relatives, detained by the magician Clingschor at Schastel marveile, the secular counterpart of Munsalvæsche.

Regarding Parzival's search for the Grail, it is striking that he rejects any divine guidance. After Cundrie's execration, Parzival asks, "Alas, what is god?" (332:1), which recalls a question he had addressed to his mother in Soltane, "Alas, mother, what is god?" (119:17), and which leads to his conclusion: "Now, I'll refuse Him service." (332:7) Willingly, Parzival accepts God's enmity at this moment, an acceptance abandoned only during his stay at Trevrizent's hermitage. There, Parzival admits that his "highest anxiety concerns the Grail, thereafter the one concerning (his) own wife." (467:26–27)

12 The redeeming question

The miraculous conclusion of the Grail story, which is of course not contained in Chrétien's unfinished romance, offers Parzival a second chance at Munsalvæsche. After a perilous combat with his half-brother, Feirefiz, during which the kinship of both is revealed only at the very last moment (book 15), the threads of the narrative are tied together. With the marriage of Repanse de schoye and Feirefiz, and their offspring, Prester John, future king of India, the Grail and the Grail family will unite Orient and Occident (book 16). Before this ending is achieved, though, Parzival and Feirefiz, guided by the messenger, Cundrie, return to Munsalvæsche. There, Parzival asks for the place where the Grail is kept: "Tell me where the Grail here lies." (795:21) The demand introduced by the imperative phrase "saget mir" ["tell me"], occurring in versions *D, *m, is altered into "nu zeiget mir" ["do show me"] in versions *G, *T. Favouring the visual aspect of display, *G, *T again tend towards a suppression of verbal communication in this verse. Turning to the Grail and kneeling down, Parzival now pronounces the redeeming question, asking: "œheim, waz wirret dier?" (795:29) ["Uncle, what troubles you?"] This wording is somewhat different from the sentence Trevrizent suggested at the hermitage: "hêrre, wie stêt iwer nôt?" (484:27) ["Lord, what is the nature of your distress?"]. The title of "Lord" yields to the kinship term "uncle", and the polite plural form "iwer" to the more intimate pronoun "dier", which, rhyming with "stier" in the following verse (the bull as part of the Silvester legend quoted there), even evokes Wolfram's Franconian dialect (the standard form being "dir"; see Gärtner 2004, 3032). The question having been asked, Anfortas recovers immediately and Parzival is declared the new Grail King.

13 Trevrizent's "retraction"

Subsequently, Parzival joins his wife, Cundwiramurs, and his twin sons, Kardeiz and Loherangrin, whom he meets for the very first time after having left their mother five years previously. Before that, however, he encounters Trevrizent again, who admits "ich louc durch ableitens list/ vome grâl, wiez umb in stüende." (798:6–7) ["I have lied about the Grail and its circumstances in order to distract from it."] The whole episode (798:1–30) is highly problematic, as Trevrizent seems to retract a number of former statements, including the one concerning the "neutral angels", the first guardians of the Grail, who are now evoked as God's adversaries, condemned forever (798:11–22). In this context, Trevrizent declares: "it has ever been uncustomary that anyone, at any time, might gain the Grail by fighting." (798:24–26) The deliberate search or even battle for the Grail seems to be forbidden to anyone. It is unclear to which utterance Trevrizent actually refers when he confesses his lie: is it to the doctrine of the "neutral angels" or to the second chance Parzival has been given to ask the redeeming question, with the latter seeming impracticable according to Trevrizent's earlier explanation (484:1–2)? (Nellmann 1994, 776; Groos 1995, 220–241) Trevrizent's unsettling "retraction" is also reflected in the manuscript transmission, as some witnesses eliminate the entire passage, whereas others try to ascribe the statement to different characters, like Feirefiz, such as the manuscripts of version *m (Stolz 2004, 39–41).

14 The inconsistencies of the Grail: visual appearance, verbalization and ambiguity

Trevrizent's announcement is also characteristic of the general "inconsistencies" and even of the "messiness" that the Grail topic entails when verbalized (Groos 1995, 241). Viewed in this light, Trevrizent, as an intra-diegetic figure, represents the difficulties the narrator runs into when trying to come to grips with the Grail matter. The lie told "durch ableitens list" (798:6) [to distract from it] might even be correlated with the narrative act itself and its deferred revelations of the Grail secrets: "ableiten" [to distract] is morphologically and semantically close to "umbe leiten" (241:16) [to redirect, or to lead astray], one of the key terms used in the bowstring parable (Herberichs 2012, 64–65). The story of the Grail turns out to be a series of delegated speech acts and references ranging from the narrator to Trevrizent, to Kyot, to the chronicles and to Flegetanis, who is said to have read the name of the Grail in the stars (Mertens 2011/2014, 281). In fact, the visual appearances of the Grail and its surroundings are central in the poem, as becomes obvious with the splendour of the Grail procession so unintelligible to Parzival during his first visit to Munsalvæsche. When the ceremony is repeated after Parzival has asked the redeeming question, the Grail remains invisible to Feirefiz, who has to wait for his burlesque baptism, which is almost exclusively motivated by his love for Repanse de schoye, before seeing the Grail. But besides the visual aspect, the verbalization of the Grail and its story is obviously fundamental from the moment it is first named by Flegetanis. On a meta-diegetic level, speaking about the Grail also refers to the audience, which has to decode the various perspectives and frequently ambiguous messages concerning the Grail following Parzival's imperfect perception of it, as reported by the narrator. In this respect, the search for the Grail and its imponderables pertains to the listeners and readers of Wolfram's Grail story, who have kept up their interest in the topic to the present day.

The diversity of different viewpoints is also manifest in the manuscript transmission, of which some examples have been given above. The continuing fascination the story held in medieval times is documented by the *Rappoltsteiner Parzifal*, a text in which Wolfram's *Parzival* was combined with German translations of the Old French Continuations of Chrétien's unfinished *Conte du Graal* (Mertens 2011/14, 297–300; Chen 2015; see also Taylor, *supra*). In this extensive conglomeration of over 60,000 lines, discrepancies are almost unavoidable. For instance, Parzival is shown healing Anfortas twice, once in vengeance (the old motif from the Celtic tradition, resumed in the French *Continuation* by Manessier), and once by asking the redeeming question (following Wolfram). When Parzival returns to Munsalvæsche for this purpose, Wolfram's text is supplemented by segments relating that King Arthur and his court escort the future Grail King. This new arrangement combining the realm of the Grail with an Arthurian entourage proves to be an "Arthurizing of the Grail." (Mertens 1998, 288–300) Thus, the Grail topic is given back to the poetic genre of Arthurian romance from which it emerged, where it was first formed by its literary founder, Chrétien de Troyes.

References

Achnitz, Wolfgang. *Deutschsprachige Artusdichtung des Mittelalters. Eine Einführung.* Berlin and Boston: De Gruyter, 2012.

Bumke, Joachim. *Wolfram von Eschenbach.* 8th edn. Sammlung Metzler 36. Stuttgart and Weimar: J.B. Metzler, 2004.

Bumke, Joachim. *Die Blutstropfen im Schnee. Über Wahrnehmung und Erkenntnis im* Parzival *Wolframs von Eschenbach.* Hermaea 94. Tübingen: Niemeyer, 2001.

Burns, E. Jane. "Quest and Questioning in the Conte du graal." *Romance Philology* 41 (1988): 251–266.

Chen, Yen-Chun. *Ritter, Minne und der Gral: Komplementarität und Kohärenzprobleme im "Rappoltsteiner Parzifal".* Studien zur historischen Poetik 18. Heidelberg: Universitätsverlag Winter, 2015.

Chrétien de Troyes. *Le Roman de Perceval ou Le Conte du Graal.* Ed. Keith Busby. Tübingen: Niemeyer, 1993.

Gärtner, Kurt. "Grundlinien einer literarischen Sprachgeschichte des deutschen Mittelalters." *Sprachgeschichte. Ein Handbuch zur Geschichte der deutschen Sprache und ihrer Erforschung.* 2nd edn. Ed. Werner Besch, Anne Betten, Oskar Reichmann and Stefan Sonderegger. Handbücher zur Sprach- und Kommunikationswissenschaft 2.4. 4 vols. Berlin and New York: De Gruyter, 2004. IV, 3018–3042.

Groos, Arthur. *Romancing the Grail. Genre, Science, and Quest in Wolfram's* Parzival. Ithaca, NY and London: Cornell University Press, 1995.

Groos, Arthur, and Norris J. Lacy, eds. *Perceval/Parzival. A Casebook.* New York and London: Routledge, 2002.

Haferland, Harald. "Die Geheimnisse des Grals. Wolframs *Parzival* als Lesemysterium?" *Zeitschrift für deutsche Philologie* 113 (1994): 23–51.

Hartmann, Heiko. *Einführung in das Werk Wolframs von Eschenbach.* Einführungen Germanistik. Darmstadt: Wissenschaftliche Buchgesellschaft, 2015.

Herberichs, Cornelia. "Erzählen von den Engeln in Wolframs *Parzival.* Eine poetologische Lektüre von Trevrizents Lüge." *Beiträge zur Geschichte der deutschen Sprache und Literatur* 134 (2012): 39–72.

Johnson, Sidney. "Doing his own Thing: Wolfram's Grail". *A Companion to Wolfram's* Parzival. Ed. Will Hasty. Studies in German Literature, Linguistics, and Culture. Rochester, NY and Woodbridge: Camden House, 1999. 77–95.

Loomis, Roger Sherman. *The Grail: From Celtic Myth to Christian Symbol.* Cardiff: University of Wales Press; New York: Columbia University Press, 1963.

Mertens, Volker. "*Parzival* II. Der Stoff: Vorgaben und Fortschreibungen." *Wolfram von Eschenbach: Ein Handbuch*. Ed. Joachim Heinzle. 2 vols. Berlin and Boston: De Gruyter, 2011; students' edition 2014. 264–307.

Mertens, Volker. "Geschichte und Geschichten um den Gral." *Kulturen des Manuskriptzeitalters*. Ed. Arthur Groos and Hans Jochen Schiewer. Transatlantische Studien zu Mittelalter und Früher Neuzeit 1. Göttingen: V&R unipress, 2004. 237–258.

Mertens, Volker. *Der Gral. Mythos und Literatur*. Universal-Bibliothek 18261. Stuttgart: Reclam, 2003.

Mertens, Volker. *Der deutsche Artusroman*. Universal-Bibliothek 17609. Stuttgart: Reclam, 1998.

Nellmann, Eberhard. "*Lapsit exillis? Jaspis exillix?* Die Lesarten der Handschriften." *Zeitschrift für deutsche Philologie* 119 (2000): 416–420.

Nellmann, Eberhard. "Produktive Missverständnisse. Wolfram als Übersetzer Chrétiens." *Wolfram-Studien XIV: Übersetzen im Mittelalter. Cambridger Kolloquium 1994*. Ed. Joachim Heinzle, L. Peter Johnson and Gisela Vollmann-Profe. Berlin: Erich Schmidt, 1996. 134–148.

Nellmann, Eberhard. "Stellenkommentar." Wolfram von Eschenbach. *Parzival*. Ed. Karl Lachmann. Trans. Dieter Kühn. Rev. Eberhard Nellmann. Bibliothek des Mittelalters 8,1/2; Bibliothek deutscher Klassiker 110. 2 vols. Frankfurt am Main: Deutscher Klassiker Verlag, 1994. II, 443–790.

Parzival-Project, University of Bern: <www.parzival.unibe.ch>.

Pérennec, René. "Percevalromane." *Höfischer Roman in Vers und Prosa*. Ed. René Pérennec and Elisabeth Schmid. Germania Litteraria Mediaevalis Francigena 5. Berlin and New York: De Gruyter, 2010. 169–220.

Ranke, Friedrich. "Zur Symbolik des Grals bei Wolfram von Eschenbach." *Trivium* 4 (1946): 20–30; English translation: "The Symbolism of the Grail in Wolfram von Eschenbach." Trans. Adelheid Thieme. *The Grail: A Casebook*. Ed. Dhira B. Mahoney. New York and London: Garland, 2000. 367–377.

Schirok, Bernd. " *Parzival* III.1. Die Handschriften und die Entwicklung des Textes." *Wolfram von Eschenbach: Ein Handbuch*. Ed. Joachim Heinzle. 2 vols. Berlin and Boston: De Gruyter, 2011; students' edition 2014. 308–334.

Stolz, Michael. "Dingwiederholungen in Wolframs *Parzival*." *Dingkulturen: Verhandlungen des Materiellen in Literatur und Kunst der Vormoderne*. Ed. Anna Mühlherr, Heike Sahm, Monika Schausten and Bruno Quast. Berlin and Boston: de Gruyter, 2016a. 267–293.

Stolz, Michael. "Von den Fassungen zur Eintextedition. Eine neue Leseausgabe von Wolframs Parzival." *Überlieferungsgeschichte transdisziplinär. Neue Perspektiven auf ein germanistisches Forschungsparadigma*. Ed. Dorothea Klein, Horst Brunner and Freimut Löser. Wissensliteratur im Mittelalter 52. Wiesbaden: Dr. Ludwig Reichert, 2016b. 353–388.

Stolz, Michael. "Chrétiens *Roman de Perceval ou le Conte du Graal* und Wolframs *Parzival*: Ihre Überlieferung und textkritische Erschließung." *Wolfram-Studien XXIII: Wolframs Parzival-Roman im europäischen Kontext. Tübinger Kolloquium 2012*. Ed. Klaus Ridder, Susanne Köbele and Eckart Conrad Lutz. Berlin: Erich Schmidt, 2014. 431–478.

Stolz, Michael. "A Thing Called the Grail. Oriental 'Spolia' in Wolfram's *Parzival* and its Manuscript Tradition." *The Power of Things and the Flow of Cultural Transformations. Art and Culture between Europe and Asia*. Ed. Lieselotte E. Saurma-Jeltsch and Anja Eisenbeiß. Berlin and Munich: Deutscher Kunstverlag, 2010. 188–216.

Stolz, Michael. "*Ine kan decheinen buochstap*: Bedingungen vorneuzeitlichen Schreibens am Beispiel der Überlieferung von Wolframs *Parzival*." "*Mir ekelt vor diesem tintenklecksenden Säkulum*": *Schreibszenen im Zeitalter der Manuskripte*. Ed. Martin Stingelin, Davide Giuriato and Sandro Zanetti. Zur Genealogie des Schreibens 1. Munich: Wilhelm Fink, 2004. 22–53.

Weigand, Hermann J. "A Jester at the Grail Castle in Wolfram's *Parzival*." *PMLA* 67 (1952): 485–510; reprinted in *Wolfram's* Parzival: *Five Essays with an Introduction*. Ed. Ursula Hoffmann. Ithaca, NY and London: Cornell University Press, 1969. 75–119.

Wolfram von Eschenbach. Parzival *with* Titurel *and the Love-Lyrics*. Trans. Cyril Edwards. Arthurian Studies 56. Woodbridge and Rochester, NY: D.S. Brewer, 2004.

Wolfram von Eschenbach. *Parzival*. Studienausgabe. Ed. Karl Lachmann and Bernd Schirok. Trans. Peter Knecht. 2nd edn. Berlin and New York: De Gruyter, 2003.

Wolfram von Eschenbach. *Parzival*. Trans. Arthur T. Hatto. London: Penguin, 1980.

Laura Chuhan Campbell
Chrétien de Troyes' *Erec et Enide*: Women in Arthurian Romance

Chrétien's story of Erec and Enide is an Arthurian love story with a difference. Focusing on the relationship of a married couple, as opposed to the more conventional adulterous courtly love, it considers the relative obligations of husbands and wives in relation to both each other and the society in which they live. The story begins when Erec, son of King Lac, pursues a foreign knight, who has offended Guinevere, to a town in which a "sparrowhawk festival" is being held. The rules of this custom dictate that the knight with the most beautiful lover should ask her to remove a sparrowhawk from its perch; if another knight believes his lady to be more beautiful and, therefore, more deserving of the sparrowhawk, he may issue a challenge. Erec wishes to participate as an excuse to engage the foreign knight – the current reigning champion – in a fight, but he cannot do it without the help of a lady. He asks the host, an impoverished vavasour, if he would permit his beautiful daughter to enter the competition in order to give Erec a pretext to challenge the foreign knight. This request is accompanied by a marriage proposal, which is willingly accepted. All goes according to plan and the daughter, whose name is Enide, becomes Erec's wife. After their wedding, however, Erec's wish to spend all of his time in bed with Enide attracts criticism from his peers. Enide is troubled by these accusations, and her discomfort leads her to tell Erec about the gossip she has heard; offended, Erec insists she accompany him on an adventure in the forest. He forbids her from speaking to him in any circumstance, but when she is the first to see a group of knights ready to attack ahead of them, she breaches his command in order to warn him. Despite his retributions, she continues to warn him of danger on successive occasions. Due to Erec's prowess and Enide's verbal dexterity, the couple succeeds in evading attack from knights, thieves, a count who wishes to abduct Enide and another who attempts to marry her while Erec is unconscious and presumed dead. Finally, it is revealed that Erec had been testing Enide's love the whole time, and that she has confirmed her devotion to him by acting out of concern for his life instead of blindly following his commands. After having completed a final adventure called the *Joie de la cort* [Joy of the Court], Erec and Enide return to Arthur's court to find out that Erec's father has died, and that they are to be crowned king and queen.

Laura Chuhan Campbell (Durham University)

DOI 10.1515/9783110432466-030

The romance raises questions about the status of women as wives and lovers, as well as interrogating the roles they should play within male chivalric practices. Much of the adventure is told from Enide's perspective, giving the audience an insight into her thoughts and emotions. Reto Bezzola (1968, 86) has argued that *Erec et Enide* can be understood not just in the conventional sense of the development and education of the knight, but also in terms of Enide's training to become a proper courtly lady. The adventure, in other words, allows her to find her place in the aristocratic and chivalric world that she has suddenly entered by marriage. Many of the issues this story raises are staple sources of contention for both medieval misogyny and modern feminism: ownership of women's bodies, the status of their voice, the gendered oppositions between activity and passivity, the public and the private. In Arthurian literature, these issues are conventionally solidified into the "typical" female characters of the queen, the courtly wife, the fairy mistress and the nameless *amies* [female friend or, often, girlfriend] who act as a chivalric accessory or object of dispute between men. Enide's physical journey from her home to Arthur's court, through their forest adventure to her ultimate coronation, will see her repeatedly pushed into occupying one or more of these roles, often against her will. Her reactions to being silenced, commodified and objectified within different chivalric interactions reveals an inherent tension in the way in which female subjectivity is encoded in the masculine world of medieval romance.

1 Two customs and an engagement: the pros and cons of female passivity

Women in Arthurian literature operate both within the masculine system of chivalry, and outside of it. In order to play a part in this man's world, they are generally expected to be passive and submissive. Nowhere is this more evident than in the two customs that open the text: the white stag hunt (during which, Guinevere is insulted by the unknown knight whom Erec then pursues) and the sparrowhawk contest. The role of women in both of these customs is to act as a decorative accessory to male chivalric prowess. As in the sparrowhawk contest, the custom of the white stag hunt collocates a physical contest between men with a beauty contest between women: whoever succeeds in killing the stag during the hunt may kiss the most beautiful lady at court. In both cases, the value of male action is bolstered by the attractiveness of his partner; the difference, however, is that while male bodies are judged according to their active capacities as hunters or warriors, female bodies are – quite predictably – measured as passive receptacles of male desire. This dichotomy is reinforced by the connection between the animals at the centre of both customs, the stag and sparrowhawk, and the ladies whose superiority in beauty is designated by obtaining them. Hunting deer and hunting with sparrowhawks were pursuits reserved for the aristocracy (Bord and Mugg 2004, 149; Linder 2009, 4 and 13), therefore both the beautiful ladies and the status-symbol animals act as accessories that indicate the winner's nobility and physical skill.

The betrothal of Erec and Enide, which takes place at the same time that Erec asks to enlist her in the sparrowhawk contest, mirrors the sexual politics of the custom: Enide, like the sparrowhawk, becomes an object to be obtained, a prize for the knight whose prowess can match her beauty. As critics have observed, the engagement plays out as a transaction between two men, Enide's father and Erec; though Enide is delighted ("joianz et liee", l. 685),[1] her involvement is purely passive (McCracken 1993, 108–110; Simpson 2007, 237; Stahuljak et al. 2011, 118). After Erec asks her father for a "un don" (l. 631) [a gift], Enide is quite literally handed over to him:

> Lors l'a pris par mi le poing:
> «Tenez, fet il, je la vos doing.»
> Erec lieemant la recut (ll. 677–679)
> [Then he took her by the hand. "Here," said he, "I give her to you." (45)][2]

This transaction exemplifies Simon Gaunt's argument that the exchange of women in romance has the function of cementing male homosocial relationships (1995, 73–74).

Just as the ladies in the competition are commodities intended to increase the renown of their lovers, the exchange of Enide between her father and Erec is mutually beneficial to the standing of both. Erec acquires a wife who perfectly complements his own personal qualities: "Mout estoient igal et per/ De courteisie et de biauté" (ll. 1492–1493) [They were very well and evenly matched in courtliness, in beauty, and in great nobility (56)], as well as one allowing him to participate in, and win, the sparrowhawk contest: "Or a quanque il li estut" (l. 680) [Now he had everything he needed (45)]. Meanwhile, the father is delivered from his life of poverty and given new titles and lands. The couple's clear sexual interest in each other will be signalled after their marriage, but the narra-

---

1 All references are to the edition of *Erec et Enide* in Chrétien de Troyes (1994).
2 All translations are from Kibler (1991) (the translation of *Erec et Enide* is by Carleton W. Carroll), except where an alternative manuscript is cited.

tion of the engagement itself focuses purely on Enide's value as a status symbol for the benefit of her male guardians. The betrothal and contest, then, are linked through Enide's passivity and objectification. Her participation in both is even characterized linguistically by a grammatical passivity; in the first example, the passive voice is used and, in the second, she is the object of the sentence, while Erec is the subject:

> Mes mout estoit joianz et liee
> Qu'*ele li estoit* otroiee (ll. 685–686; my emphasis)
> [she was very joyful and happy that *she had been granted* to him (45; my emphasis)]

> Sa pucele *fet* avant trere (l. 826; my emphasis)
> [[he] had his damsel come forward (47)]

She may be central to the narrative here, but just like the sparrowhawk, she is merely an indicator of prestige for whomever deems themselves worthy of possessing her.

The customs and engagement, then, establish an initially harmonious partnering between Erec and Enide, based on the logic that a woman's beauty augments and complements the beauty and bravery of her lover. Tom Artin (1974, 70–72) has highlighted the fact that Enide is compared to a mirror (ll. 437–442), an ambivalent symbol with multiple potential significances. In this initial episode, she appears to mirror Erec in the straightforward sense; her own beauty reflects Erec's beauty, prowess and courtliness. Indeed, as Guinevere notes, only a man with Erec's qualities could "conquer" a woman such as Enide: "Qui par ses armes puet conquerre/ Si bele dame en autre terre" (ll. 1730 –1732) [who can win such a beautiful lady by deeds of arms in another land (59)]. Enide is declared the unanimous winner of the white stag custom, despite Gauvain's fears, at the beginning of the text, that selecting the lover of one knight over all the others may provoke conflict. Gauvain had foreseen potential disagreements as to the identity of the most beautiful lady, but everyone in fact agrees that Enide is worthy of the title: "Beisier la poez quitemant,/ Tuit l'otroions comunemant." (ll. 1792–1793) [You may freely kiss her; we all concede it with one voice (59)]. This unanimity not only elevates Enide above other ladies, but also reflects and projects Erec's superiority – as she is his fiancée, it is his victory as much as hers.

Nevertheless, all is not as perfect as it seems. After their wedding, Erec falls into his period of *recreantise* [languor or laziness]: instead of participating in tournaments and attending to his duties as a prince, he spends half the day in bed with his new wife. Whereas the engagement scene appeared to be an emotionless transaction, Erec and Enide's passion for each other now comes into play. Yet, just as in the engagement scene, the narration of Erec's *recreantise* still casts Erec as the active subject and Enide as the passive object:

> Mes tant *l'ama* Erec d'amors,
> Que d'armes mes ne li chaloit,
> Ne a tornoiement n'aloit.
> N'avoit mes soing de tornoier:
> A sa fame *volt* dosnoier,
> Si an *fist* s'amie et sa drue.
> En li *a mis* antendue,
> En acoler et an besier. (ll. 2446–2453; my emphasis)
> [But Erec was so in love with her that he cared no more for arms, nor did he go to tournaments. He no longer cared for tourneying; he wanted to enjoy his wife's company, and he made her his lady and his mistress. He turned all his attention to embracing and kissing her. (67)]

Although Enide will blame herself for this: "Dons l'ai ge honi tot por voir" (l. 2517) ["Now I have truly shamed him" (68)], she has apparently taken no active part in seducing Erec or convincing him to spend all his time with her – in fact, she is more aware than Erec of his error in this. Yet her passivity, which made her seem like an ideal wife at the beginning of the text, has begun to cause problems. Just as Erec made her an accessory to his chivalric status in the first section, he has now made her into his sexual object, and each time, she has let herself be defined by him (cf. Griffiths, *infra*). As E. Jane Burns (1993, 176) argues, men continually attempt to define the place of women within the narrative; their versions of how female characters fit into the stories that they create "so often elide the speaking, knowing female subject." Enide has passively allowed Erec, her father and the court to dictate who she is and what role she plays, with both positive and negative results. Her comparison to a mirror initially suggested that she was a reflection of Erec's beauty and nobility, but the figure of the mirror in the Middle Ages was also used to represent a window onto an unattainable ideal: the sum of spiritual virtues, or the perfect courtly lady (see Goldin 1967, 5–6). Enide's beauty and apparent wifely perfection is perhaps too good to be true; she becomes, for Erec, an incorporeal ideal that can be moulded into his chivalric accessory, his compliant wife or his sex object, as he sees fit. Treating women as passive objects to be exchanged and redefined at will can sometimes be convenient in Arthurian romance, but omitting female subjectivity and choice can also lead to conflict, just as allowing men to define the most beautiful lady in the white stag custom has the potential to introduce discord among the knights. Perhaps the conflict was avoided this time not just because of Enide's clearly superior beauty, but because the winner was selected not by Arthur, but by Guinevere – a woman who, due to her social position, carries a level of authority that compensates, to some extent, for her objectification.

2 Disobedient devotion: Enide's refusal to stay silent

Erec has so far treated Enide like a passive object, and eventually this is to his own detriment; however, his treatment of her during their journey into the forest does not initially suggest any improvement on that matter. He gives her two commands: first, to ride ahead of him, and second, to refrain from speaking to him in any circumstance. By riding behind Enide, Erec is in essence using her as bait. He knows that other knights they encounter will be tempted to fight him for the right to abduct her. This is a standard motif in Arthurian literature, justified by a custom that is first outlined in Chrétien's *Le Chevalier de la charrette* (ll. 1308–1322; see also Hinton, *infra*): if a knight meets an unaccompanied lady while on his adventures, then he is honour-bound to protect her. If, however, he encounters a woman who is accompanied by another knight, he may challenge the knight for the right to take the woman, if he can beat him in combat. This scenario once again casts the lady both as a status symbol and passive commodity; in the words of Roberta Krueger (1996, 7):

> the custom thus assures not the protection of the maiden's autonomy, but her value as a possession or prize for those knights between whom she is the object of dispute. Within the chivalric honor system, the woman becomes an object of exchange.

This role that Erec now outlines for Enide is thus no different than the one she was forced to play in the sparrowhawk contest, or the betrothal, except that the injunction for her to remain silent further reinforces the fact of her objectification. The knights who approach them in the first instance certainly see her in this regard, although they are robbers who intend simply to take Enide and her possessions without respecting the custom. Her value as a possession is even more evident, when, after Erec has defeated the knights and taken their horses, a second group of robber knights conspires to abduct Enide and the horses that she is leading. As they divide the spoils in advance, the lady and the palfreys are regarded as equally fair game, drawing further analogies between Enide and the domestic animals captured by her husband:

> Ce dist li uns que il avroit

La dame ou il toz an moerroit,
Et li autres dist que suens iert
Le destriers veirs, que plus n'an quiert
De trestot le gaaing avoir.
Li tierz dist qu'il avroit le noir.
"Et je le blanc", ce dist li quarz. (ll. 2956–2963)
[One said he would have the lady or die in the attempt, and another said the dappled charger would be his – that was all he wanted of the booty. The third said he would have the black. "And I the white!" said the fourth. (73)]

She has already been defined as an object to obtain, exchange and manipulate, but now Erec's injunction not to speak further reduces her to the status of a dumb animal.

But passive as she may have been at the start of the text, Enide is not in fact a dumb animal. She has the capacity to speak and assert herself; her speech to Erec in bed and her interior monologues in the forest show her to be a thinking, feeling subject, despite the patriarchal acts of definition that attempt to deprive her of that subjectivity. Her reasonable decision that it would be better for her to warn Erec of the knights' attack and incur retribution than to see him killed (ll. 2978–2995) attributes to her not only subjectivity, but rationality. Zrinka Stahuljak et al. (2011, 123) have warned against an overly modern interpretation of Enide's visible thought processes as a positive marker of individuality; as they argue, individuality in Chrétien's works is a sign of alienation, a lone voice that should, but does not, fit into the collective identity to which the character belongs. The introduction of Enide's voice coincides with the moments in which allowing herself to be treated as a passive object becomes no longer tenable. Erec may have benefited from treating Enide as an accessory during the betrothal and the sparrowhawk contest, but his character begins to suffer when he allows her to become the source of his *recreantise*, and, as Enide understands it, he is putting himself in danger by not allowing her to warn him of oncoming attacks. If the man who defines what female role Enide should play should lose his life or reputation because of that choice, then where does that leave her? Silence is no longer an option in either case, because by accepting to be a silent object of Erec's possession, she is utterly dependent on him. She therefore speaks to warn Erec of the rumours about him, just as she violates his order to stay silent to tell him about the attacking knights in the forest. Paradoxically, she must disobey his command in order to retain the right to remain his compliant wife; she believes it is his prerogative to abandon her (ll. 3754–3755) or even kill her if she breaks her silence: "Il m'ocirra. Asez, m'ocie!" (l. 2993) ["He'll kill me. All right, let him!" (73)]. Her only choice is to rebel against the passivity that has left her in a contradictory position, and she does so primarily by using her voice.

Joan Tasker Grimbert (1989, 64–70) has observed that the value of Enide's speech is complicated by a gendered relationship between actions and words. Erec demonstrates that gossip about his *recreantise* is untrue by undertaking an adventure and becoming active; he proves those words wrong through his deeds. As a woman in medieval society, Enide does not have recourse to physical action in the same way that Erec does. Instead, her words *are* her deeds. She proves her devotion to Erec through her speech acts. The relationship between Enide's actions and her words is encapsulated in the way that the narration brings her physical body to bear on the use of her voice. This is initially articulated as a struggle between her body and her voice; as she develops and becomes increasingly self-reliant, her voice and her body seem to function in harmony. At the beginning of the journey, when she breaks her silence to warn Erec of oncoming attackers, she speaks, so that he may act on their behalf. At one point, this is described in terms of a battle between her voice and her body. The narration underlines the relationship between the two by focusing on the mechanical processes involved in the physical act of speech:

> A li meïsmes s'an consoille;
> Sovant del dire s'aparoille
> Si que la leingue se remuet,
> Mes la voiz pas issir n'an puet,
> Car del peor estraint les danz,
> S'anclost la parole dedanz.
> Et si se justise et destraint:
> La boche clot, les danz estraint
> Que la parole hors n'an aille.
> A li a prise grant bataille. (ll. 3737–3746)
> [She deliberated within herself; often she prepared to speak so that her tongue moved but her voice could not escape, for out of fear she clenched her teeth and withheld the words inside. Thus she controlled and restrained herself; she closed her mouth and clenched her teeth, so that the words would not get out; she battled with herself. (83)]

Erec's command over her persona is so pervasive that in order to disobey him, she must wrestle with it for control of her own body. Her body wishes to remain passive, while her voice wants to be active.

Her next speech act is not only more proactive, but shows Enide to be more in command of the relationship between her speech and her body. When the couple takes up lodging in the domain of a count named Galoain, she responds to the sexual advances of the Count by telling him that she will willingly marry him if he ambushes Erec the following morning. As the narrative voice assures us, this is merely a ruse, thought up by Enide on the spot when the Count threatens to have Erec killed immediately if she does not agree to become his lover. She saves them both by telling Erec of her plans, allowing them to escape the ambush by leaving early in the morning. Whereas previously, her speech led Erec to act on their behalf, now it is her speech act itself that saves them both. Yet, once again, her words are underscored with physicality, this time through the images she creates in her discourse. In her initial rejection of the Count's advances, she imagines a negation or dissolution of her body by insisting that she would rather have never been born, or would rather be burned alive than betray Erec (ll. 3346–3349). Then later, when she pretends to seduce him, she again invokes her body in a sexual context: "Je vos voldroie ja santir/An un lit, certes, nu a nu" (ll. 3408–3409) ["Indeed, I should already like to feel you naked beside me in a bed." (79)]. In doing this, Enide not only actively delivers her husband from death and herself from rape, but she increasingly breaks out of the passive role that she can no longer reasonably occupy. Having previously allowed men to cast her as an incorporeal ideal that fits into a standard mould – as a sex object, an accessory, a pawn in masculine relationships – she now subverts the Count's attempts to define her as such, and uses this against him. The Count willingly believes that Enide's outraged response to his advances was simply because she was testing his devotion, his image of her informed by his "fervid misogynistic portrait of the proud woman." (Simpson 2007, 314) He is also ready to accept her assertion that she *wants* to be abducted and taken away from her husband, imagining a passive complicity on the part of the woman when she represents an object of dispute between two knights; this standard scenario of chivalric literature becomes, when told by Enide, "a dream, a trick, a mirage." (Burns 1993, 178) So far in the romance, men have imagined her body according to an intangible and malleable ideal; it is now Enide herself who manipulates the projection of her own body as an ideal by prompting the Count to imagine her naked.

In this way, her speech not only plays a progressively more active part in their adventures, but also provides a way for her to define herself as a loyal wife to Erec, rather than to passively allow herself to be defined by others – including Erec himself, who has thus far been treating her as if she had somehow betrayed him. In her manipulation of the Count, she parodies the roles that she has been cast in, in order to prove that loyalty. In the following adventure, however, she aggressively affirms her status as Erec's wife by choosing death over life. When Erec faints and she believes him to be dead, Enide decides to kill herself, only to be saved by God, who "la fet tarder un peu" (l. 4672) [caused her to delay a little (94)] before a treacherous count named Oringle arrives to abduct her. Her wish to join Erec in death, macabre as it may be, is a radical act of self-definition; she will be nothing if not Erec's wife and future queen. She vociferously protests her abduction by, and re-marriage to, Oringle, both with her voice and with her body, physically resisting as much as is possible:

Si li ont a force donee
Car ele mout le refusa (ll. 4769–4770)
[[they] gave her by force to the count, though she vigorously refused him. (95)]

Si l'ont sor un faudestuel
Feite aseoir, outre son vueil (ll. 4785–4786)
[They made her sit upon a faldstool against her will. (95)]

She refuses to eat and drink, frequently faints and withstands a physical beating without changing her mind. This mirrors both the abnegation of her body and consciousness in her planned suicide, as well as her prior claim that she would rather be burned alive than leave Erec. Enide's rejection of Oringle's attempt to appropriate her as an object and an accessory is a further affirmation of her right to choose her fate; as Stahuljak et al. (2011, 128) note, her vocal protest against her marriage to Oringle contrasts with the silence of her initial consent to marry Erec. Since Erec is believed to be dead, she asserts her voice and bodily autonomy without relying on him to perform on behalf of her voice – he, of course, wakes up and rescues her, but she does not know that he is alive at the time.

Enide, then, becomes increasingly astute and active in her use of her voice – which, for a woman, holds the value of both action and speech. She has been previously cast as an object to be exchanged, or a blank canvas for the projection of idealized models of femininity, upon which male characters projected their fantasies of commodifying women's bodies for their social and personal gain. The increasing intrusion of her physicality into those speech acts constitutes a progressive rejection of the way in which her body has been instrumentalized by others. By the final adventure, she has asserted her own ideal self as a real body, not an intangible fantasy. Of course, she is a woman in Arthurian romance, a genre which was born out of the work of misogynistic clerics – she cannot escape being idealized and instrumentalized (Gaunt 1993, 85). Yet by affirming her choice of Erec as husband, and his queen as her role, she exercises a conscious and autonomous choice.

3 Women vs. chivalry: the spectre of the fairy mistress

Enide's journey, from passive accessory to accidental temptress, and to queen-in-the-making, has produced a more active female subject, whose presence is no longer at odds with Erec's participation in chivalric activity. As we have already observed, Enide did not appear to seduce Erec deliberately into abandoning his knightly duties – if anything, he is responsible for his own *recreantise*. The journey has also been an educational process for him, as he has learned to articulate his relationship with Enide by fighting on her behalf, rather than expressing it in purely sexual terms (Gallien 1975, 20). Despite this, however, the narrative establishes a series of analogies that seem to compare Enide – as she was at the beginning of the text – to malignant female characters that conventionally challenge and undermine chivalry. In these comparisons, she is cast as both a fairy and a Dido-figure, characters who are not only sexually independent, but who deliberately keep their lovers away from their manly obligations. Even if Enide's sexual passivity at the beginning is not held up as an ideal in comparison – given that it still leads to Erec's *recreantise* – the analogies manifest a persistent anxiety about the role of women in the world of chivalry, and the power of sexuality to disrupt masculine activities.

The final adventure of the story, called the *Joie de la cort* [Joy of the Court], introduces a couple that appears to be a mirror image of Erec and Enide during Erec's period of *recreantise*. These similarities evoke an additional connection between Enide and the figure of the fairy in Arthurian literature. To complete the *Joie de la cort* adventure, Erec must enter a magically-enclosed garden, and defeat the knight who resides there. We are later told that the knight's name is Mabonagrain, and that he is trapped in the garden due to a promise he has made to his lover. Evoking the motif of the *don contraignant* [rash promise], Mabonagrain's lover asked him to grant her a gift, which he vowed to do without knowing what it was. As it turned out, she wished him to stay with her in the magic garden until he was defeated by another knight. The scenario brings to light the same problems of activity and passivity in love, as well as the interface between the public and the private, that plagued the initial stages of Erec and Enide's marriage (Lacy 1980, 79–80; Simpson 2007, 428). Their passionate private relationship damaged his reputation by confining him to a feminized private sphere, just as Mabonagrain is unable to participate in normal chivalric activity when confined to the garden. He becomes inactive, as Erec was at the beginning, waiting for challengers to come to him, rather than proactively participating in tournaments. The fact that Enide is revealed to be the lover's cousin, and that Mabonagrain spent some time growing up in Erec's father's court, further reinforces the connection between the two couples.

Scholars have pointed out that Mabonagrain's lover corresponds to the character of the fairy mistress, another standard figure in Arthurian literature (Fourquet 1955–1956, 300; Larrington 2006, 52–54; Meneghetti 1976, 376). The *Joie de la cort* story reflects a narrative trope most famously associated with the enchantress Morgan, but not exclusively connected with her; it can be found, in various iterations, in, for example, Marie de France's *Lanval*, the *Lai de Guingamor* and the Prose *Tristan* (in the abduction of Tristan's father, Meliadus). A mortal man is lured into the Otherworld by a beautiful fairy, who takes him away from the court and keeps him as her lover (see Harf-Lancner 1984, 199–214). The similarities between the upside-down world of the fairy's domain and both the *Joie de la cort* situation and Erec and Enide's marital bliss are obvious. The garden parallels the Otherworld in its inversion of the gender balance of the courtly world; here, women are in charge, and their words are a source of power to rival men's actions (Burns 1993, 184–185; Larrington 2006, 50). As Larrington (*supra*) observes, the happiness a knight can achieve from his *amie* alone (which is figured through these imaginary feminized spaces) challenges the nature of chivalry itself, which is active and public by definition.

Through the fairy analogy, then, Enide's presence as a sexual distraction for Erec posits her as a disruptive force in the proper workings of chivalry. This is reinforced by the symbolic associations of two objects that are presented to Enide at the beginning and the end of her journey, both of which offer metaphorical readings of her personal development during the narrative. One derives from the Celtic imagery of the *matière de Bretagne* [Matter of Britain], the other from the classical world, thus underscoring Chrétien's *conjointure* of different cultural narratives (see Murray 2008). The first object is the chasuble that Guinevere presents Enide with at her wedding. The needlework on the chasuble, we are told, is the work of Morgan, and was made as a present for her lover. It was obtained by Guinevere "par engin mout grant" (l. 2383) [by great ingenuity (my translation)] from the Emperor Gassa. The fact that the chasuble has been passed from Morgan (a fairy) to the Guinevere (a queen) recalls Enide's development during the course of the text. Stahuljak et al. (2011, 113–129) have argued that Enide's learning process during the journey teaches her how to use her voice with the proper authority of a queen; she learns to understand the value of speech and silence at the right times, as well as how to use her voice to advise her husband and speak with authority, just as Guinevere does (see also McCracken 1993, 116). Whereas the fairy archetype and Mabonagrain's lover use their voices to undermine chivalry, Enide's various trials have taught her how to use her voice to ensure its proper function. She correctly understands that she must intervene to stop Erec's fight with Guivret when she knows her husband is too weak to survive it (ll. 5027–5046), yet she also knows that it is right to avoid verbally expressing her reservations when Erec decides to attempt the *Joie de la cort* (ll. 5825–5828). Just as the chasuble is passed between the fairy and the queen, Enide has developed from the former conception of femininity to the latter – from one that inadvertently subverted chivalry to one that accepts her proper place to act within it. Even the queen, however, is said to have employed trickery in order to obtain the chasuble, just as Enide tricks Count Galoain in order to save herself and Erec; the

comparison, although ultimately positive for Enide, reveals an implicit suggestion that even the most respected women are capable of deception (see Simpson
2007, 460).

This same schema is reflected in the saddle Enide receives near the end of her
journey as a gift from Guivret. Carvings on the saddle depict the story of Aeneas,
and in particular, his abandonment of his passionate affair with Dido in favour
of a more measured and politically-expedient marriage to Lavinia. Joseph Wittig
(1970) has suggested that the Aeneas reference should be read as another analogy
of Erec and Enide's relationship, who have abandoned their unproductive love
in favour of a more reasonable love that does not constrain Erec's public duties
(see also Burgess 1984, 79–80). The way in which the story carved on the saddle
is told re-engages the interaction between sexual passivity and activity. Dido is
described as an active subject, who "received [Aeneas] into her bed" ("Dido an
son lit le reçut" (ll. 5338–5339)); Lavinia, on the other hand, is passively "conquered" by Aeneas, and listed alongside the lands he has also acquired:

> Comant Eneas puis conquist
> Laurente et tote Lombardie
> Et Lavine, qui fu s'amie. (ll. 5336–5338)[3]
> [How Aeneas then conquered Laurentum, all of Lombardy, and Lavinia, who was his lover.
> (my translation)]

Enide's development from a fairy-figure to a queen is therefore recast here as a
development from a Dido to a Lavinia, signifying the same opposition between a
woman who challenges male chivalry to one who knows her place within it. The
comparison does not map exactly onto Enide herself (see Wittig 1970, 241); where
her passivity was viewed as negative, her ability to use her initiative actively is
regarded as more compatible with her role as Erec's wife. Nor did she actively
seduce Erec in the manner suggested by the analogy with Dido. Nevertheless, the
comparison signifies a broader apprehension in relation to the place of women in
chivalric society, and one that goes beyond Enide herself as an individual.

---

3 This reference to Lavinia has been omitted from the Guiot copy of the manuscript (Paris, BnF,
fr. 794), which is used for a number of editions. I have quoted, in this case, from Fritz's edition of
Paris, BnF, fr. 1376. See Simpson (2007, 391–392).

4 Conclusion

Enide's story demonstrates the contradictions that emerge from the status of women in Arthurian romance, which is dominated by a chivalric ideology that excludes female subjectivity, while being simultaneously under threat from it. Chivalry's system of homosocial relations demands that women are passive objects to be exchanged and fought over, and it is the response of female characters to that objectification that adds layers of intrigue and conflict. Enide is all too happy to internalize that objectification until she realizes that it places her in an impossible position; she is forced to exert her autonomous choice in order to save her marriage, her husband and herself. As a woman, however, she can never quite escape the spectre of female sexuality and desire, which have the potential to interfere with masculine activities. The figure of the fairy mistress looms large over the early stages of Erec and Enide's marriage, casting a shadow that Enide must work hard to escape. Women in Arthurian romance may occupy a set of standard roles such as the lady to be fought over, the beloved queen, the helpful maid or the dangerously autonomous fairy, but these roles offer more of a starting point for female figures than a fixed persona. Enide must find her place in the chivalric world by at times embodying, at times subverting these roles; they offer a paradigm of behaviours that are both a help and a hindrance to her in different situations.

References

Artin, Tom. *The Allegory of Adventure: Reading Chrétien's* Erec and Yvain. Lewisburg, PA: Bucknell University Press, 1974.

Bezzola, Reto R. *Le sens de l'aventure et de l'amour*. Paris: La Jeune Parque, 1968.

Blanchard, Joël, and Michel Quereuil, eds. *Le roman de Tristan en prose (version du manuscrit fr. 757 de la Bibliothèque nationale de Paris)*. Volume I. Paris: Champion, 1997.

Bord, Lucien-Jean, and Jean-Pierre Mugg. *La chasse au Moyen Âge: Occident latin, VIe-XVe siècle*. Paris: Gerfault, 2008.

Burgess, Glyn S. *Chrétien de Troyes: Erec et Enide*. London: Grant & Cutler, 1984.

Burgess, Glyn S., and Leslie C. Brook, eds. *Cambridge French Arthurian Literature. Volume IV: Eleven Old French Narrative Lays*. Cambridge and Rochester, NY: D.S. Brewer, 2007.

Burns, E. Jane. *Bodytalk: When Women Speak in Old French Literature*. Philadelphia, PA: University of Pennsylvania Press, 1993.

Chrétien de Troyes. *Œuvres complètes*. Ed. Daniel Poirion, Anne Berthelot, Peter F. Dembowski, Sylvie Lefèvre et al. Paris: Gallimard, 1994.

Fourquet, Jean. "Le rapport entre l'œuvre et la source chez Chrétien de Troyes et le problème des sources bretonnes." *Romance Philology* 9 (1955): 298–312.

Gallien, Simone. *La conception sentimentale de Chrétien de Troyes*. Paris: Nizet, 1975.

Gaunt, Simon. *Gender and Genre in Medieval French Literature*. Cambridge: Cambridge University Press, 1995.

Goldin, Frederick. *The Mirror of Narcissus in the Courtly Love Lyric*. Ithaca, NY: Cornell University Press, 1967.

Grimbert, Joan Tasker. "Misrepresentation and Misconception in Chrétien de Troyes: Nonverbal and Verbal Semiotics in Erec et Enide and Perceval." *Sign, Sentence, Discourse: Language in Medieval Thought and Literature*. Ed. Julian N. Wasserman and Lois Roney. Syracuse, NY: Syracuse University Press, 1989. 50–79.

Harf-Lancner, Laurence. *Les fées au moyen âge Age: Morgane et Mélusine, la naissance des fées*. Paris: Champion, 1984.

Kibler, William W., ed. and trans. *Chrétien de Troyes: Arthurian Romances*. London: Penguin, 1991.

Koble, Nathalie, and Mireille Séguy, eds. *Lais bretons (XIIe-XIIIe siècles): Marie de France et ses contemporains*. Paris: Champion, 2011.

Krueger, Roberta L. "Love, Honour, and the Exchange of Women in *Yvain*: Some Remarks on the Female Reader." *Arthurian Women: A Casebook*. Ed. Thelma S. Fenster. New York: Routledge, 2000. 3–18.

Lacy, Norris J. *The Craft of Chrétien de Troyes: An Essay on Narrative Art*. Leiden: Brill, 1980.

Larrington, Carolyne. *King Arthur's Enchantresses: Morgan and her Sisters in Arthurian Tradition*. London: I.B. Tauris, 2006.

Linder, Olivier. "Un monde d'oiseaux de proie: Quelques exemples de figuration animalière du discours sur nature et norreture." *Déduits d'oiseaux au Moyen Âge*. Ed. Chantal Connochie-Bourgne. Aix-en-Provence: Presses Universitaires de Provence, 2009. 179–192.

McCracken, Peggy. "Silence and the Courtly Wife: Chrétien de Troyes's *Erec et Enide*." *The Arthurian Yearbook* 3 (1993): 105–124.

Meneghetti, Maria Luisa. "'Joie de la cort': intégration individuelle et métaphore sociale dans *Erec et Enide*." *Cahiers de civilisation médiévale* 19 (1976): 371–379.

Murray, Sarah-Jane. *From Plato to Lancelot: A Preface to Chrétien de Troyes*. Syracuse, NY: Syracuse University Press, 2008.

Simpson, James R. *Troubling Arthurian Histories: Court Culture, Performance and Scandal in Chrétien de Troyes's* Erec. Oxford: Peter Lang, 2007.

Stahuljak, Zrinka, Virginie Greene, Sarah Kay, Sharon Kinoshita and Peggy McCracken, eds. *Thinking Through Chrétien de Troyes*. Cambridge: D.S. Brewer, 2011.

Wittig, Joseph S. "The Aneas-Dido Allusion in Chrétien's *Erec et Enide*." *Comparative Literature* 22 (1970): 237–253.

Gareth Griffith

Merlin: Christian Ethics and the Question of Shame

From the beginning, the Arthur of medieval literature was a Christian man in a Christian culture. His legendary origins may have been in pre-Christian Europe, but from the texts of Geoffrey of Monmouth and Chrétien de Troyes onwards, even though he is presented as a figure from long ago, or as semi-mythic, he also lives in a religious milieu that would be broadly familiar to contemporary audiences in the predominantly Christian Europe of the twelfth (and later of the thirteenth, fourteenth and fifteenth) century. Alongside the dwarves and giants, the magic and the mysterious, sit priests and bishops, holy hermits and knights attending mass before they go on their quests. In this context, the knightly virtues and ideals that Arthur and his court embodied were thus presented as in some sense Christian, too – the ideal Arthurian knight was also one form of ideal Christian.

Yet this inevitably created tensions between courtly and Christian ideals. Some Christian virtues (such as pious devotion to God, humility and selflessness) were readily absorbed into the chivalric ideal. Others needed negotiation. Self-sacrifice, for example, could be made a knightly ideal, but if this morphed into passivity it could seem merely to be unheroic weakness. It was not impossible for Arthurian literature to explore a passively suffering hero, as *Sir Gawain and the Green Knight* makes clear, but even in that narrative the idea of active combat still had to be present in the narrative, even if it was skirted over (such as in Gawain's encounters with wild men and animals on the way to Castle Hautdesert), displaced onto other characters besides the hero (the hunts of deer, boar and fox) or recoded (the wars of words in the bedroom).

Nevertheless, from the viewpoint of Christian theology, virtue is essentially Christ-likeness, and so in theological terms an Arthurian knight (or Arthur himself) is only virtuous to the extent that he is like Christ. This resemblance was not so impossible as it might appear to a modern reader; there was a lively tradition in medieval piety that presented the crucified Christ as a triumphant knight, most famously in *Piers Plowman*:

> This Jesus of his gentries wol juste in Piers armes,
> In his helm and in his haubergeon (Langland 1995, B-Text, Passus XVIII, ll. 22–23)

Gareth Griffith (University of Bristol)

DOI 10.1515/9783110432466-031

From the other side of the question, romance texts found inventive ways to close the gap between idealized medieval knighthood and Christ-like models of behaviour. This seems to be the reason behind Malory's invention of the episode of the healing of Sir Urry, as it allows his hero, Launcelot, to work a miracle, and thus conform to a model of Christian hagiographic virtue. Even so, the very effort needed to bring these worlds together emphasizes the gap between them; the scene from *Piers Plowman* is only possible because it is in an allegorical dream, with all the possibilities for symbolism that such a shifting, unreal setting provides. Malory feels compelled to invent the miracle of Sir Urry precisely because Launcelot has come back from the Grail Quest knowing that he is morally compromised by his affair with Guenevere. Nor are these isolated instances; the figures of Arthurian romance are frequently caught in the tension between courtly and Christian ideals.

One of these ideals, which became increasingly prominent in the medieval Arthurian tradition in the later Middle Ages, was the importance attached to a knight's honour and "worship", that is to say his fame, reputation and public standing in the wider community of knighthood. This is the primary homosocial value in the predominantly male world of the Arthurian court, the chief currency that knights seek to accrue and maintain in their relationships with each other, and the measure of their worth and power. Nevertheless, the very value placed upon honour helped to ensure that various narrative pressures (such as the desire to instruct an audience, or to create tension, or to make a character more admirable) sooner or later require stories about honour to embrace the presence of something to act as its opposite, whether as a weakness to set off the picture of heroic strength, or as a threat of vice that the core virtue of knighthood can overcome. Megan Leitch (2015, 13) has argued persuasively for treason as fulfilling this role in romances of the fifteenth-century, but in the wider Arthurian tradition the unavoidable opposite of honour is shame. These two needs – to make heroes in some way Christ-like, and to negotiate the issue of honour and shame – are at the heart of Arthurian literature's dialogue with medieval Christianity. The rest of this essay will examine their effect in an often-neglected text, the work of "a lost Arthurian" (Dalrymple 2000, 155) which brings both to the fore.

1 A poet without "honour"

The fifteenth-century Middle English poem *Merlin* is a translation of the Old French Vulgate *Estoire de Merlin* made by the London *civis et pelliparius* [citizen and skinner], Henry Lovelich, for a fellow skinner, Henry Barton, in about 1425

(Ackerman 1952a, 476). The poem was edited by Ernst A. Koch in the nineteenth century, but modern interest in the poem properly dates from 1952, when Robert W. Ackerman published two scholarly pieces on it. The first was a concerted attempt to rescue the poem from obscurity and put its poet on the scholarly agenda; the second was only a short note making a minor but revealing point. Other scholars had expressed doubt as to whether the poet's surname was "Lovelich" or "Lonelich"; Ackerman knew for certain it was Lovelich. He knew this because the poet makes it clear in a "crude and unsyntactical" (Ackerman 1952b, 532) Latin pun:

> yow preyeth, lordynges, to hauen mynde of this
> Gallina Ciligo Amo Similis (ll. 21595–21596)[1]

As he notes, the second line here can be translated "hen rye love like" (Ackerman 1952b, 532). In fact, Koch had already noted this in the margin of his edition. In other words, while few scholars had written on the text, it seems that even fewer had actually read it properly.

This detail is indicative of the curious paradox of this text, which is simultaneously marginal and central to the medieval Arthurian tradition. It is regularly mentioned by name in modern essays that survey Arthurian romance, or the literature of the fifteenth century, but nearly always in passing: it has rarely received sustained scholarly attention. On the one hand, it is arguably an obscure work, the product of an amateur poet whose industry outpaced his skill (its 27,852 lines are in a rather rough-and-ready four-beat metre), a text that seems not to have circulated very widely in its own period (it survives in a single manuscript), and which has been largely overlooked by modern scholarship – "ignored even by those dedicated to the analysis of dullness", as Michelle R. Warren (2008, 113) neatly puts it. Yet it is also the fullest medieval account in English of the story of Merlin, from the French Vulgate, which itself derives from the *Merlin* romance linked to Robert de Boron. This of course was one of the most important and influential contributions to the Arthurian story in the Middle Ages, and thus in making a new version of this material, Lovelich was solidly within a long and popular narrative and textual tradition.[2] It is also an important example of how the Arthurian stories could be adapted for new audiences (see Taylor, *supra*): as in recent years

---

1 All quotations from the *Merlin* are taken from Koch's edition (Lovelich 1903; 1913; 1932), lightly modernized. I use the forms of names found in Lovelich's text to refer to characters in his poem, but more familiar forms to speak about characters in the wider Arthurian tradition.

2 For details of many of these romances, see other contributions to this volume, in particular Byrne (*supra*) and Moran (*supra*); see also Bryant (2001, esp. 1–3).

Lovelich has finally received proper critical attention, a recurrent theme in the scholarship has been the fact that he is a London guildsman writing for other London guildsmen, rather than a royal or noble court.[3] Barton, the skinner at whose "instaunce" Lovelich undertook the *Merlin* and his earlier, almost equally lengthy translation, *History of the Holy Grail*, was Sheriff of London 1405–1406 and twice Lord Mayor of the same city (1416–1417 and 1428–1429; Dalrymple 2000, 156). Lovelich's immediate audience is thus a civic, mercantile one, and the knightly court of the text is now reflected in the similarly homosocial and close-knit world of a London guild. Lovelich's text is therefore uniquely revealing in the ways in which it interacts with the Arthurian tradition in a new milieu, in its preoccupation not only with London but more pervasively with the nature of leadership (in a king or a counsellor) and in the private and public relations of people who sleep together (showing kings and queens to be subject to the same uncertainties and difficulties in communication as anyone else further down the social scale). In particular, it is a poem with powerful things to say about the ideals of Christ-like heroism and honour/shame.

2 Arthurian (anti-)Christ

An Arthurian story centred on Merlin, rather than on Arthur himself or on one or more of his knights, offers some obvious advantages in the depiction of Christ-like virtue. There is no need to recount details of him in battle (the behaviour that "worship" requires of a knight, even a king-knight), and he is acknowledged as a figure with more than normal power, whether prophetic, scientific or magical. Yet this is not the whole story, since battle (and Merlin's involvement in it) does occupy huge swathes of Lovelich's poem. Moreover, the figure of Merlin as he was available to the fifteenth century brings with him dangers as well. Ever since Robert de Boron's *Merlin*, written in the closing years of the twelfth century, the story of Merlin had opened with a council of demons seeking to find a riposte to the incarnation of Christ. This council always concludes with the decision to create a prophet who will mislead people into following him and his demonic masters, and this prophet will be Merlin. The story thus consciously echoes and perverts the narratives of the birth of Christ and its theological significances. Different versions of the story suggest different ways in which God subsequently intervenes to frustrate this plan (at least partially), but these origins always mean

---

3 See, for example, Dalrymple (2000), Warren (2008) and Radulescu (2013, esp. Ch. 3).

that some threat of evil hangs over the character of Merlin.[4] He can be said to mirror Christ, but in two senses: he repeats the Christ-story, but he also reverses it (at least partially). His origins and identity are shaped by notions of supernatural incarnation and dual nature, which link him to Christology, but in Merlin's case the result is not a hypostatic union but a hybrid, a man part human and part demon. It is up to any text to choose how far to exploit this tension, and how far to seek to efface it.

In Lovelich's case, the tension is repeatedly brought to the fore. For one thing, the language used to describe Merlin is very mixed. To some he is simply "the devel" (l. 3202), but several characters (and the narrator) call him a "devyn" (as at ll. 3246, 3306, 3392). Of course, the word recurs partly because it is a potential rhyme for the tricky "Merlyne", but it is also found mid-line, so this cannot be the only reason. In context, the primary sense of this word must be taken as "One who predicts future events by astrology or augury, or by the interpretation of dreams, signs, or oracles; astrologer, augur, prophet, soothsayer, sorcerer" (MED, s.v. "divin(e)", 2.(a)), but the related sense "Divine nature, divineness" (3.(a)) is made present, too. The rhyme of "Merlyn" and "devyn" is therefore more than the product of pragmatic utility; it significantly and repeatedly links two words which both contain within themselves elements that are orthodox and potentially heretical.

It is true that scholars have rarely paid attention to this kind of verbal detail in Lovelich's *Merlin*, rarely viewing his translation as being the product of much poetic flair, or motivated by any particular purpose or emphasis.[5] On the contrary, they have focused on his closeness to the French original: Raluca Radulescu (2013, 90) notes his "faithful approach to his source [...] [h]is competence in Old French [...] the accuracy of his translation and close attention to detail" and summarizes other scholars who have found his poems "insufficiently original". Yet the work of Dalrymple (2000) and others has begun to shine a light on the sheer mass of the poem, and shows that there is much to be said for Lovelich's careful choice of vocabulary. Moreover, the *Merlin* does show some evidence of having had more than one source, which suggests that the work of translation was not merely mechanical reproduction, but involved the (at least partly) conscious selection and combination of materials.[6] This in turn ought to prompt his readers

---

4 For more on this, see Griffith (2012, 102–104).

5 Catherine Batt (1994, 272–273), for example, is ambivalent about any discernible intent in Lovelich's avoidance of the use of a direct translation of the French phrase *cors a cors*.

6 Holland (1973, 91) shows that in at least one case Lovelich knows of alternative proper names for a character, drawn from more than one source.

to be open to the idea that Lovelich is doing more than churning out lines by the hundred; he is shaping a narrative in line with particular interests (whether consciously or unconsciously held). The character of Merlin, central to the poem throughout its length, is naturally one of these interests, and Lovelich's conception of it can be discerned through attentive reading.

For example, there are numerous occasions where, in context, a word or phrase subtly emphasizes the Christ-likeness of Merlin, especially (and notably) in recalling details unique to the gospel of Luke. This is especially marked in the infancy narrative of Merlin; the later bulk of the poem focuses heavily on battle, a context in which Christ-likeness is hard to portray, but these first few thousand lines are concerned with Merlin's conception, birth and family, and here the parallels are much easier to see. As a starting point, we might take the morning after Merlin's conception, where the narrative contains numerous phrases that glance at the biblical account of the annunciation: when Merlin's mother realizes what has happened, "thanne cam it in hire mynde anon/ that the enemy hire hadde ouergon." (ll. 629–630) Here, "ouergon" recalls the angel's words to Mary: "Spiritus Sanctus *superveniet* in te et virtus Altissimi *obumbrabit* tibi" (Luke 1.35, my emphasis) [The Holy Ghost *shall come upon* thee and the power of the Most High shall *overshadow* thee].[7] Merlin's mother continues the parallel, declaring "me is befalle a destyne/ that neuere fyl to womman but to me." (ll. 657–658) This is akin to the angel's greeting "benedicta tu in mulieribus" (Luke 1.28) [blessed art thou among women], but whereas the angelic words speak of unique favour, Merlin's mother is the object of treatment equally unique, but entirely negative in its import. Her confessor adds "Ful of the devel thou art, ful pleyn" (l. 700), which inevitably brings to mind the Vulgate's "ave gratia plena" (Luke 1.28) [Hail, full of grace] even as it inverts it. In each of these cases, the double-mirroring of Christ is present in Merlin: repetition involves reversal.

After this cluster, echoes of the gospel narratives are more widely spaced, but still continue. The women who ask what Merlin is to be called (l. 988) are reminiscent of those in Luke 1.62 who ask what name is to be given to John the Baptist; these same women predict "for hym schalt thou suffren ful gret peyn", a prediction surely modelled on that of Simeon, who tells Mary (speaking of the effect that Christ will have on various people) "et tuam ipsius animam pertransiet gladius" (Luke 2.35) [And thy own soul a sword shall pierce]. Sometimes there is no direct parallel, but evidence that the language and symbolism of the Bible were things that Lovelich wanted to associate with his central figures, such as

---

7 All biblical quotations taken from the Vulgate, with English translation from the Douay-Rheims version.

when we are told (l. 1105) that Merlin's mother is kept in a tower awaiting trial for precisely forty days; is this her "wilderness experience", preparing her for the life and teaching of her son to begin (cf. Luke 4.1-13)? In the trial itself, the judges take particular care to ascertain from experienced women that a child cannot be conceived without "mannes compeny", a phrase used three times in seven lines (ll. 1206–1212); the emphasis on the idea of a virgin birth is unmistakeable, even if that is not what has happened in this case.

In some instances, the double-mirroring serves strongly to highlight the ways in which Merlin is *not* like Christ. Early in his adult life, Merlin is out riding and encounters a funeral:

> it happede vpon a day,
> As thorwgh a town thanne lay here way,
> A chyld toward beryeng was there ibore,
> and moche ful sore wepyng was therefore. (ll. 2433–2436)

This chance encounter with the funeral procession of a child recalls an incident from the life of Christ recorded only by Luke in chapter 7 of his gospel. There Jesus stops the cortège of a widow's only son (his age is not specified, but his identity as a son suggests youth), in order to raise the corpse to life again, "misericordia motus super ea" (Luke 7) [being moved with mercy towards her]. Merlin's response to the similar situation is very different: he laughs. He then proceeds to expose the fact that the child is the illegitimate son of the very priest conducting the burial. Sensational and doubtless entertaining as this revelation is, it nonetheless could not be said to be motivated by *misericordia* [mercy]; at best it springs from *iusticia* [justice], and at worst sheer mischief, since Merlin's public declaration brings shame on the priest and on the boy's mother. Thus in *Merlin* the central character remains poised between demonic inspiration and Christ-like vocation. In a number of respects, especially in the early part of the poem, it is the latter which Lovelich chooses to draw out and emphasize. Nevertheless, the question of shame continues to follow him – the possibility of personal shame about his own origins, but also shame as something he repeatedly brings on others around him.

3 The nature(s) of shame

Although shame (*infamia*) was a key concept in moral theory throughout the Middle Ages, its very ubiquity meant that it was not often subjected to analysis or definition. The most important discussion of it for medieval thinking was in fact pre-medieval, coming from Aristotle's *Ethics* (Book 4, ch. 9).[8] Here, Aristotle said that shame was a feeling rather than a state of character; that it was a form of fear (fear of dishonour); that it was not a virtue in itself, but that no-one incapable of feeling shame could be considered virtuous; and that it was nonetheless more becoming to the young, who are expected to "live by feeling and therefore commit many errors" (Ross 1999, 71) than to the old, who should not be doing anything of which they need feel ashamed. These observations are strikingly predictive of Arthurian literature. The fear of dishonour is key to knightly conduct in many Arthurian texts; for a knight to be good he must know what shame is, know that he could feel it, fear to do so, and arrange his conduct accordingly.

Beyond the schoolroom, it was the writers of stories (like Lovelich) who explored shame most fully, giving examples and showing how it might be experienced in practice. Once again, Arthurian literature is at the forefront of this exploration, this time showing that shame is not only distinguished according to the age of the person feeling it. Firstly, the experience of shame is distinguished by social class. Thus Radulescu (2013, 106) notes that in his *History of the Holy Grail*, Lovelich "places emphasis on honour as an aristocratic virtue." Since, like honour, shame is in essence a public phenomenon, it can only exist where there are others present to observe. But only people of the right class or with a particular office to fulfil can claim the right to look and thus to judge someone worthy of honour or shame. It may be acceptable to behave in a particular way in front of those of lower social standing, but this same behaviour becomes dishonourable once those of one's own (noble) class are present to see it. Lancelot may, *in extremis*, ride in a cart when only the carter is present (see Hinton, *supra*), but shame occurs when other, more nobly born observers can see him.

Even more notably, shame is also a gendered phenomenon. The kinds of shame that men are likely to encounter in the Arthurian world relate to a failure of prowess in battle, or in keeping one's word (*Sir Gawain and the Green Knight* is the obvious example of the latter, but depends also on a fear of the former, too). For women, shame is far more likely to result from transgressing sexual norms, in particular through sex outside of marriage. In medieval tellings of the story of Lancelot and Guinevere, both face possible shame for having committed treason against their lord, but the sexual sin is usually tied more closely to Guinevere than to Lancelot. This gendered dichotomy of shame is very strongly present in Lovelich's *Merlin*, but with greater variety than might be expected. Not all male shame comes from battle, for example. When Ban and Bors present themselves at

---

8 This is the authority quoted, for example, by Thomas Aquinas in his *Summa Theologiae*, I, XCV, 3, in the discussion of whether Adam would be capable of shame.

the court of king Leodegan, but refuse to say who they are, he accepts them, but asks them to declare their identities: he suspects they are men of higher rank than he is, and if that is the case, "hit myhte ben gret schame to me/ of yow servise to taken, certeinle." (ll. 13743–13744) Shame here is public and concerned with rank, but peaceable.

In a martial context, Lovelich exploits the relationship between two subtly different senses of the word "schame". One of these, in essence, means "defeat", and it is in this sense that Merlin warns the barons who are unconvinced of Arthur's legitimacy, and prepare for war, "that fowlyche scholen ye ben schamed alle." (l. 8134) In the event, they are quickly put on the run in battle, but reflect "a schame hyt were to hem echon,/ and he so lyhtly schold from hem gon." (ll. 8343–8344) Here "schame" is closer to the modern sense of the word, and it is brought on by military failure. Yet this kind of shame can also be brought on by the prospect of an inglorious victory. In the wars of Arthur's succession, his small army attacks a vastly superior force led by eleven kings, "and whanne the xi kynges on a rewe/ behelden hemself so manye and the tother so fewe/ thanne sore aschamed were they echon." (ll. 10695–10697) They do not at this point think they will lose, but to win with the odds so heavily in their favour is unchivalric, dishonourable and shaming.

Male shame can be simply due to a personal rebuff in battle, such as being unhorsed. When five of the kings making war on Arthur are beaten and unhorsed, "aschamed they weren and of here lyves lothe." (l. 11018) In an earlier battle, Lwcawns is unhorsed, but other knights come to his rescue:

> anon sire lwcawns, that worthy knyght,
> vppon that hors fulsone he was,
> and sory man and angry in that plas,
> that his schamefulnesse wolde avenge. (ll. 10974–10977)

Even here, though, in two apparently similar instances of male shame, a distinction is made which helps to establish the difference between the good and bad sides. Arthur's enemies respond to shame by a self-destructive emotion; in contrast, Lwcawns responds with action and a determination to destroy others in revenge. This, it would seem, is the approved way of dealing with male military shame.

In this way, shame can be actively invoked as a motivator to virtuous action, and it is no surprise to find Merlin creating shame to this end. When Arthur hesitates to fight the Giant of Toraise, Merlin calls him a coward:

> And whanne kyng Artheur herde Merlyne speken so,
> and that coward he clypede hym thanne,
> Ful sore aschamed was that worthy manne. (ll. 15018–15020)

The result is, of course, that Arthur fights and overcomes the giant; as with Lwcawns, male shame is productive of heroic action. However, this is only the case for good characters with a substantial role to play in the narrative. For bad people, shame is a punishment: Merlin, in explaining the significance of the dragons found in the attempt to build a tower, reveals in front of the council that Costantyn was falsely killed: "and whanne Fortager herde this/ Ful sore he was aschamed, iwys." (ll. 2933–2934) This shame goes nowhere. Similarly, marginal characters are not given the chance to make shame productive: the families of the hired murderers who had made Fortager king, and whom he then had executed, come and complain to him: "Mochel schame has thou vs don." (l. 1864) Fortager will eventually be deposed, but not directly because of their shame.

In contrast, female shame in the poem is predominantly sexual, and produces only acts of defence, since women were denied personal access to the means of making amends through heroic action which constituted the male remedy for shame. It is also, surprisingly, often experienced in private. Whilst women are subjected to public scrutiny and condemnation as part of a shaming process in the poem, they use the language of shame in private or in interior thoughts – indeed, when the subject of shame moves into the public arena, it can also be re-gendered, and become male shame (cf. Larrington, *supra*).

There are two extended examinations of female shame in the poem, each relating to the complex and potentially scandalous conception of a main character. In the lead-up to Merlin's birth, the demon responsible sets himself to destroy the family of the woman who will become Merlin's mother. He incites a young man to sleep with one of the sisters in the family,

> and whanne be hire he hadde don folye
> the devel anon it schewede openlye,
> and disclawndred it al the contre,
> the more schame to hem that it scholde be. (ll. 235–238)

These few lines are full of the language of dishonour ("folye", "disclawndred", "schame") which is intensified by repeated language of exposure ("schewede openlye", "al the contre"). This is shame as a weapon; Merlin's exposure of the dead child's parentage, discussed above, shows him to take after his father in this troubling respect.

Once Merlin is conceived, and later born, public exposure and the threat of shame is the major theme of the poem, until Merlin is able to vindicate his mother. This theme is present from the moment that she awakes after the demon has raped her:

> sche besowhte God with humble chere
> that in this world neuere schamed sche were. (ll. 633–634)

Her first thought on waking is to pray that she will not be public shamed. Whether this prayer is answered is something of a textual crux; certainly, in the end Merlin is able to show that she is an innocent victim, but not until after she has suffered much at the court of popular opinion, and in a real court, too. Shame is therefore not just a final verdict; it is a process, too, and one that can be undeservedly applied.

It is perhaps surprising that the language of shame is most intensively used in the poem in relation to Arthur's conception. Indeed, the tale of Arthur's origins and birth can be retold simply from examining the word "schame" in the poem. It is present from the beginning in Uther's attempts to make Ygwern sleep with him; when first aware of the king's desires for her, she responds:

> how longe hath the kyng a tretour be,
> that my lord so worschepith to-forn me
> and me wolde don so fowl a schame,
> and thereto bryngen me into endeles blame? (ll. 4815–4818)

This is a skilful deployment of the language of honour and shame, drawing attention to the complex honouring-relationships in play. In courtly theory, the king ought to be the most honourable and most honoured person, yet courtly behaviour requires him also to honour his nobles and (for other reasons) their wives. Ygwern is required to honour the king as king, but also her husband, since he is her "lord". Yet by seeking to seduce Ygwern, the king has become a "tretour" to his retainer, the Duke (which hints at the paradox of a king being a "tretour" to the state, essentially to himself), and thus a hypocrite since he gives the husband "worschep" in public in order to give the wife "schame" in private. Lovelich's poetic skill is quite equal to suggesting so much in so short a span, and he ends emphatically by rhyming "schame" with "blame", making it clear where his focus lies. As yet, this shame is private, but it will soon move into the public sphere.

The king is not put off by her response, and sends Ygwern a cup to drink from; when she sees the gift and hears the king's request, which her husband unsuspectingly makes into a command to her, she sees through it:

ful red sche wax, and aschamed sche ferde,
and dorste not refusen hire lordis byddyng (ll. 4889–4890)

The tension in honouring-relationships that Ygwern's earlier words suggested
has now come into effect: honour breeds shame. Yet the unsuspecting Duke soon
finds out the reason for the king's attention to his wife, and leaves the court in
protest:

The dewk aftyr his cownseille thanne sente anon,
and tolde hem the cause ful pleynly,
the cause of his comeng so hastely,
and what schame the kyng gan hym purchase,
that cawsed hym to voyden out of that plase.
and whanne they herden his pleyneng,
they yoven the dewk good comfortyng,
and seiden: "he that schame to his lige wyle purchase,
on hym may be-happen the same grace!" (ll. 5022–5030)

Two things have now happened: the shame has become public, and it has become
male. Ygwern is not mentioned at all in this passage; instead, the subject of the
Duke's speech is "what schame the kyng gan *hym* purchase" (my emphasis). It is
a shame given by a man to a man, and it is the council of men who wish it back
on the king. From this point onwards, it will be men who speak publicly of the
shame relating to the affair, and Ygwern and the king who continue to speak of
it in private.

It will also henceforth be Merlin who takes control of the concept of shame.
It will be Merlin who finally declares to the barons that Uther is Arthur's father,
referring as he does so to Ygwern's "schamfulnesse" (l. 7998). Long before that,
it is Merlin who removes the initial shame by arranging for Uther to sleep with
Ygwern and subsequently marry her, and he who tells the king not to ask who the
child's father is, to avoid causing her shame:

"For yif thow axe that lady mylde
be whom that sche goth so with childe,
sche schal not konnen the answere
ho that is the fadyr, in non manere,
so that gret schame to hire schal be [...]" (ll. 5785–5789)

Two things are notable about the shame in view here. Firstly, it is never suggested that Uther should confess to his wife that he is the father of the child she
presumes to be illegitimate: there is no possibility of removing female shame at
the expense of creating male shame. Secondly, the "schame" that Merlin seeks

to avoid is, once again, private – the distress Ygwern will feel at not being able to answer her husband, presumably in private conversation. Both aspects (the unwillingness of men to remove female shame at their own cost, and the internalized nature of female shame) highlight how women suffer more from shame in the poem than men do.

This imbalance is openly acknowledged by Merlin, when he asks the king to give him Arthur to bring up himself. He wants to do this partly because it was his plot that was responsible for the conception, but also for a second reason:

> "and ek also the modyr aschamed scholde be
> hyt forto norschen, ful sekerle;
> for wommen ne haven non wyt therto
> here owene cownseille to helen so. [...]" (ll. 5751–5754)

Women, says Merlin, remain ashamed because they cannot keep their own secrets. This is not only misogynistic, but demonstrably untrue in the poem. It is the men (Merlin chief among them) who have persistently chosen to make private matters public, and so bring shame on others; it is the female characters who speak of shame in private, sometimes only to themselves.

4 Of *Merlin*, Christ and shame

Christ-likeness simultaneously invoked and refuted in the life of its hero; a complex examination of shame as a deeply gendered phenomenon, manifesting itself in a plurality of forms of public justice and private torment; read carefully, Lovelich's poem is eloquent in its dissection of some of the key themes and preoccupations of the Arthur myth in the later Middle Ages. The sheer size of the text has prevented it from receiving as much careful reading as it deserves, a situation not helped by its tendency to prolixity, and the view (until recently) that fifteenth-century poetry was not worth troubling much about. Nevertheless, as I hope to have shown here, it is a key part of the late medieval discourse of Arthur, especially in an English context. In its huge scope, and in its moments of individual brilliance, it shines a spotlight on fault lines in the values of the Arthurian world, which threatened to pull that world apart even as they provided the energy that made it so compelling to write about and to encounter as an audience. Lovelich experiments boldly with what a Christ-like hero would look like in Arthur's world; if Merlin is finally unable to live up to that model, this is not surprising, not just because of the height at which that bar is set, but also because of ambiguities about the character that Lovelich inherited from his sources, and which he in fact highlights to dramatic effect. This is nowhere truer than in Merlin's manipulation of the categories of shame, which he seeks to control as he does other aspects of Arthur's court. Lovelich's poem incorporates this into a wider examination of the concept of shame, showing its class-based and highly gendered nature, but also its flexibility and utility as a lens for understanding what makes people in Arthur's world truly tick.

References

Ackerman, Robert W. "Henry Lovelich's *Merlin*." *PMLA* 67 (1952a): 473–484.

Ackerman, Robert W. "Henry Lovelich's Name." *Modern Language Notes* 67 (1952b): 531–533.

Aristotle. *Ethics*. Trans. W.D. Ross. Kitchener, ONT: Batoche Books, 1999.

Batt, Catherine. "'Hand for Hand' and 'Body for Body': Aspects of Malory's Vocabulary of Identity and Integrity with Regard to Gareth and Lancelot." *Modern Philology* 91 (1994): 269–287.

Boffey, Julia, and A.S.G. Edwards, eds. *A Companion to Fifteenth-Century English Poetry*. Woodbridge: D.S. Brewer, 2013.

Bryant, Nigel, trans. *Merlin and the Grail: The Trilogy of Arthurian Romances Attributed to Robert de Boron*. Woodbridge: Boydell and Brewer, 2001.

Dalrymple, Roger. "'Evele knowen ye Merlyne, in certeyn': Henry Lovelich's *Merlin*." *Medieval Insular Romance: Translation and Innovation*. Ed. Judith Weiss, Jennifer Fellows and Morgan Dickson. Woodbridge: D.S. Brewer, 2000. 155–167.

Griffith, Gareth. "Merlin." *Heroes and Anti-Heroes in Medieval Romance*. Ed. Neil Cartlidge. Woodbridge: D.S. Brewer, 2012.

Holland, William E. "Formulaic Diction and the Descent of a Middle English Romance." *Speculum* 48 (1973): 89–109.

Langland, William. *The Vision of Piers Plowman*. Ed. A.V.C. Schmidt. London: J.M. Dent, 1995.

Lawrence-Mathers, Anne. *The True History of Merlin the Magician*. New Haven, CT: Yale University Press, 2012.

Leitch, Megan. *Romancing Treason: The Literature of the Wars of the Roses*. Oxford: Oxford University Press, 2015.

Lovelich, Henry. *Merlin: A Middle-English Metrical Version of a French Romance by Henry Lovelich, Skinner and Citizen of London*. Ed. Ernst A. Koch. 3 vols. London: Early English Text Society, 1904, 1913, 1932.

Radulescu, Raluca L. *Romance and its Contexts in Fifteenth-Century England: Politics, Piety and Penitence*. Woodbridge: D.S. Brewer, 2013.

Scott, Kathleen L. "Past Ownership: Evidence of Book Ownership by English Merchants in the Later Middle Ages." *Makers and Users of Medieval Books: Essays in Honour of A.S.G. Edwards*. Ed. Carol M. Meale and Derek Pearsall. Woodbridge: D.S. Brewer, 2014. 150–177.

Warren, Michelle R. "Lydgate, Lovelich and London Letters." *Lydgate Matters: Poetry and Material Culture in the Fifteenth Century*. Ed. Lisa H. Cooper and Andrea Denny-Brown. New York: Palgrave Macmillan, 2008. 113–138.

Weiss, Judith, Jennifer Fellows and Morgan Dickson, eds. *Medieval Insular Romance: Translation and Innovation*. Woodbridge: D.S. Brewer, 2001.

Siân Echard

De ortu Walwanii and Historia Meriadoci: Technologies in/of Romance

There is relatively little scholarship on the two Latin romances dealt with in this chapter, and a good bit of what does exist has been focused on two related issues, the dating and authorship of the works. While I have argued in the past, following Mildred Leake Day, for a date in the latter part of the twelfth century (Echard 1998; see also Day 1984b; 1988; 2013), what is of particular importance in this chapter, is *how*, exactly, arguments for dating and authorship proceed. The range of suggested dates runs from the twelfth through to the early-fourteenth centuries, with arguments based on romance motifs and analogues (Bruce 1898–1900; Brugger 1923; Nicholson 2000; Berthet et al. 2007),[1] philosophical concepts (Galyon 1978),[2] and the capital R that appears in a manuscript rubric to the *Historia Meriadoci* (Day 1984b; 1988; Larkin 2004, though these point to different authors from different centuries).[3] The most persistent thread in arguments over dating, however, focuses on objects and technologies in the *De ortu Walwanii*: on the surcoat that gives Gawain his sobriquet as the "Knight of the Surcoat"; on the nasal pieces of helmets; on the carefully-described ships; and on the Greek fire that features in a major naval battle. The *Historia Meriadoci*, generally agreed to

---

1 J. Douglas Bruce edited the romances in 1898 and 1900, with an edition of both, along with a new introduction, appearing in 1913. His interest in romance analogues for many of the episodes led him to argue for a thirteenth-century date, and so to dismiss the possible authorship of Robert of Torigni (see n. 3 below). The recent French translation of the romances also argues that the romance elements suggest a thirteenth-century date (Berthet et al. 2007, 19–20). Helen Nicholson also argues for a thirteenth-century date, based on similarities of some sections of the text to the *Itinerarium peregrinorum et gesta regis Ricardi*, an account of the Third Crusade.
2 Aubrey Galyon (1978) detects in the *De ortu* the thirteenth-century philosophical preoccupation with the theory of illumination.
3 In her editions of the two romances (1984a and 1988), Mildred Leake Day argues for the authorship of Robert of Torigni, abbot of Mont St Michel from 1154 to 1186. The romances were attributed to Robert by John Bale (see Morriss 1908), and Day develops support for the idea in part by arguing for a twelfth-century date, on the basis of such features as details of armour and ship construction. Peter Larkin (2004), however, suggests that the indicative "R" is commonly used by Ranulf Higden, the fourteenth-century author of the *Polychronicon*; like Day, he then uses contextual, historical material to support his arguments; in this case, in favour of a fourteenth- rather than a twelfth-century author.

Siân Echard (University of British Columbia)

DOI 10.1515/9783110432466-032

be by the same hand, is dated by association with the first text (and so with its significant objects), and also by concerns it reveals about such legal issues as trial by combat and forest law.[4] The *Historia Meriadoci* blends a fascination for everyday technologies, such as the means used to cook food during the forest exile with which the text opens, with one for fantastical settings, such as the mysterious castle in which Meriadoc and his companions have a series of strange adventures. I suggest that scholarly interest in using the objects and technologies of these texts to date them has led us to overlook the obvious, and that is the significance of objects in these romances in the first place. The laser-like scrutiny in these texts of clothing, buildings, settings and technologies moves objects to the centre of the stage. In his now classic essay, Bill Brown (2001, 4) suggests that "We begin to confront the thingness of objects when they stop working for us." (cf. Johnston, *supra*) The objects in these Latin Arthurian romances, on the other hand, become things because they reveal so clearly how they do work for us; or rather, what their role in the technology of romance itself actually is.

The *De Ortu Walwanii*, which survives in only one, early fourteenth-century, manuscript (London, BL, Cotton Faustina B VI), is a prose account of the early adventures of Gawain, set in the fifth century. Gawain, the illegitimate son of King Arthur's sister Anna and Loth, son of the King of Norway, is sent away as a baby, and raised in ignorance of his lineage by a poor man named Viamandus. Viamandus had come across Gawain in the ship of the merchants to whom Anna had entrusted the infant and a considerable treasure, and had seized both child and treasure in the merchants' absence. The treasure underwrites Viamandus' move to Rome with Gawain, when the latter is a child of seven. Before dying when Gawain is twelve, Viamandus reveals the truth of Gawain's origin to the Pope, and both agree the young man should be kept in the dark for the time being. He is raised by the Emperor as a Roman knight, and comes to be known as the "Knight of the Surcoat". He sets off to the Holy Land, in order to engage in single combat on behalf of the Christians besieged in Jerusalem. Among the adventures encountered on the way is a furious naval battle with a pagan fleet armed with Greek fire. After successfully defeating the pagan champion outside Jerusalem, Gawain journeys to King Arthur's court, carrying (unbeknownst to him) the tokens of his parentage. Here he helps the Arthurians defeat the enemy army besieging the Castle

---

4 As was the case with the romance elements in the *De ortu*, there is disagreement as to how the legal preoccupations might lead us to date the text, with Day and others arguing for a twelfth-century date to coincide with Henry II's expansion of forest law, and Porter (1992) arguing that the judicial duel is presented in terms derived from Magna Carta, so that the text must be of the thirteenth century.

of Maidens, and Arthur reveals to him his true identity as "Gawain, nephew of Arthur". There is a good deal more to the rather complex plot of this romance, but this brief summary draws attention to the two elements I wish to focus on here, the surcoat and the description of Greek fire. The surcoat shows how the trappings of martial chivalry come to stand for both the individual knight and the system in which he is embedded. The encounter with Greek fire places that metonymy in a world whose coordinates are both fantastical and recognizably contemporary. The hybrid technology, an amalgam of marvellous and mundane ingredients, then invites a scrutiny of the technology of the narrative itself.

The surcoat is presented in the text as a new and distinctive fashion (hence its role in arguments over the dating of the romance). When Gawain is fifteen, he is knighted by the Emperor, and triumphs in the martial games held to celebrate a group of new knights. He dresses for these games in "a purple tunic, [...] placing it over his armour. He called it a surcoat for armour." [5] The style is so novel ("for before this, it was no one's practice to wear a tunic of this sort while in armour") that the other young knights immediately ask Gawain about it. He replies that its purpose is for decoration (*ad hornatum*), and is promptly hailed as "[n]ew knight with the surcoat for his armour." [6] In this way, the "Knight of the Surcoat" is born, and Gawain retains the name until he claims his real name, and the family relationships that go along with it, at the very end of the text.

While the sobriquet dwells on the garment alone, it matters as well that the surcoat is *purpureus*. While the term can indeed be translated by the word "scarlet", as used by Day in her edition and translation of the text, the primary meaning is purple, the imperial colour. Gawain puts on his surcoat in Rome, as a protegé of the Emperor and, though he does not know it at the time, as a scion of a royal house. His mother had delivered the infant to the merchants who were to take him away and raise him, with a variety of markers of his status, including an embroidered, richly bejeweled *pallium*, a signet ring worn by the king on feast days, and a document (*cartam*) with the royal seal, laying out the infant's parentage. Their ship was also laden with a wealth of gold, silver, and rich clothing (*preciosarumque vestium innumerabilem copiam*).[7] It is this wealth that Viaman-

---

5 "[...] tunicam sibi paraverat purpuream, [...]; tunicam armature nuncupavit." (Day 1984a, 18) All translations into English are my own.

6 "Dumque a militibus quereretur cur eam super arma induisset, neque enim antea huiusmodi tunica armis septus aliquis usus fuerat, respondit se tunicam armature ad hornatum adhibuisse. Ad quod responsum ei ab omni acclamatur exercitu; 'Novus miles cum tunica armature, novus miles cum tunica armature.'" (Day 1984a, 18)

7 "[...] negociatores suscipiunt, cum quo genitrix eis auri et argenti preciosarumque vestium innumerabilem copiam contulit. Tradidit quoque ingentis precii pallium, insertis gemmis auro

dus uses to fund his successful self-presentation at Rome as a nobleman. In medieval British Latin usage, a *pallium* can be a royal cloak, an archbishop's cloak, or an altarcloth, and the word occurs in collocation with *purpureus* in more than one text. The signet ring and the *carta* witness the growing importance, in the Angevin empire, of a documentary culture built on charters whose seals testified to their veracity and the impermeability of their textual contents (and, by extension, their contents – laws, land-claims, pedigrees, and so on). Gawain's surcoat, then, is only the latest in a series of aristocratic objects that have followed him for his whole life. So charged with meaning are these objects that we tend to read them as metonymic of Gawain himself, just as the eager young knights do in the name they choose for him. The focus on objects in the text suggests the object-oriented metonymy is the stuff of romance itself. To put the matter colloquially, you can tell a knight by his stuff.

The romance has a traditional Fair Unknown plot, and the young Gawain proves himself by triumphing in a series of encounters, relying on his martial abilities alone. As often happens in such narratives, Gawain's outsider status allows a questioning of the practices and persons of the dominant culture, as for example when he unhorses his own uncle, King Arthur, after the king has pridefully chosen to ignore the warnings of his queen; or when he succeeds in the battle at which the Arthurians have failed, taunting them for their weakness. But the point of a typical Fair Unknown story is not (usually) that a man can succeed in a chivalric society through skill, regardless of his background; instead, it is that the martial class has inborn abilities that reveal themselves, no matter the circumstances. There is, in short, a kind of chivalric charisma around figures like Gawain. His instinctive choice of the purple surcoat – to set himself apart, to distinguish himself visually, as he is also (though he does not know it) distinguished by blood – is a choice framed by the other significant objects that travel with him, unseen by him but closely regarded by both internal and external audiences. The surcoat is a purple exclamation mark, revealing the aristocratic privilege of martial life. It is an object that draws our gaze in a particular context, and so becomes the thing that reveals the social machinery underlying the narrative motif.

The *De ortu*'s long, peculiar digression on Greek fire, in the narration of the naval battle between Gawain's fleet and a pagan one, concretizes another part

---

undique intextum, necnon et anulum lapide smaragdino insignitum, quem a rege custodiendum acceperat quo ipse dum taxat festivis diebus uti solebat. Cartam eciam regis sigillo signatam addidit, cuius textus eum certis insinuabat indiciis ex regis Norwegie nepote sororeque Arturi progenitum Waluuaniumque a genitrice nominatum." (Day 1984a, 4)

of this machinery, and that is the technology of war. The weapon is introduced only after a preliminary naval encounter, during which the battle-readiness of the opposing fleets is minutely described. The centurion who commands the ship on which Gawain is travelling sits in a tower (*turre*) that has been set up in the stern of the ship (*in puppe erexerat*) (Day 1984a, 60). There are weathervanes and banners fixed to the mastheads to indicate the direction of the wind. Five ships have rams (*rostratas*), and the text details the iron-covered projections, with hooks and armour "in the manner of the crested beak of a cock,"[8] along with towers allowing javelins and stones to be hurled from above. When the battle is joined, the text runs through a range of weapons, including axes, swords, javelins, catapults – "every kind of weapon"[9] – all directed at the Knight of the Surcoat's armoured ship. The machinery of war literally encircles the signifier of chivalric knighthood. It is at this moment that the opposing fleet hurls Greek fire, and the text stops to describe how the fearsome weapon is made.

The recipe for Greek fire includes poisonous toads force-fed for three months with dove meat and honey and then nursed by a lactating animal; water snakes that have been fed on human bodies, a three-headed flame-spewing poisonous asp; the gall bladder and testicles of a shape-shifting wolf; a marvellous stone called a *ligurius*; the head, heart and liver of an ancient crow; the blood of a red-haired man; and the blood of a dragon. Many of the ingredients prompt descriptive digressions, as we learn, for example, how dangerous the asp's venom is, or how the shape-shifting wolf was created, or how to prepare the red-headed man to be bled, or how to catch a dragon. The process for making Greek fire from these ingredients (as well as from the more mundane sulphur, pitch, resin, olive oil, tartar and petroleum) is described in great detail, with particular attention to the vessel and bellows used, along with the complex arrangement of tubes, valves and windows that serve to control the temperature and collect the liquid. The manuscript has a doodle next to this particular passage of a figure putting his finger to his mouth in a sort of "hmm" gesture – at least one reader found this description either intriguing, confusing, or both.

It is something of an anticlimax when, after several pages of description of this sort, we return to the battle. While the weapon does envelope the centurion's ship in flames, Gawain saves the day by leaping onto the enemy ship, defeating the enemy single-handed, and in a single sentence. Our attention, in other words, has been wholly on the many strange ingredients that make up Greek fire, but the fire itself gets second billing. The narrative observes that the naval battle con-

---

8 "[...] ad modum galli cristatis rostris munita." (Day 1984a, 62–64)
9 "[...] omni telorum [...] genere." (Day 1984a, 66)

cludes "not without the greatest danger,"[10] but both the brevity of the narration once Greek fire is actually introduced and the odd negative construction here, seem to acknowledge that our interest is elsewhere.

The Greek fire digression mixes marvellous with real ingredients, and describes a recognizable process of creating a chemical reaction, in a liquid that is both fantastical, in the world of the romance, and real, in the world of the text (as the inclusion of the more likely ingredients also underlines). It has been suggested that the point of the Greek fire episode is to stress, by means of the use of an actual weapon that was both novel and feared when the text was written, that "the world of the story is no longer quite the world of Arthur and his knights. It is already, even in the twelfth century, the modern world, where warfare is impersonal and death holds no glory." (Day 1984a, xxvii) The contrast developed between the description and the weapon's use, however, suggests something else is going on. The ingredients that become the focus of our attention are the fantastical ones; the process that concretizes the weapon in front of us is both "real" and imaginary. Greek fire becomes a kind of liminal object, one that holds in tension the worlds of romance and contemporary martial activity. Brown used the image of the dirty window to explain how we begin to notice the thingness of objects (once the window is dirty, we cannot look through it, but must look at it; Brown 2001, 4; see also Johnston *supra*). I would suggest that the incongruent fit between the ingredients of Greek fire (with the narrative expectations those engender), and the almost mundane and cursory reality of its (nevertheless potentially deadly) use, makes of the weapon a kind of two-way mirror. From one side, we see the fantastical technology of romance; from the other, the contemporary reality of combat. And that two-way view crystallizes for us that romance is itself a thing. It would be easy to suggest that the incongruities in the Greek fire digression are meant to cause us to see the thing-ness, and so to break the machine that is romance. I wonder, however, if the point is not, instead, to make us first notice that romance *is* a machine, and then to wonder what, exactly, it is doing.

Like the *De ortu*, the *Historia Meriadoci* is also found in London, BL, Cotton Faustina B VI (where it is the first text; it is immediately followed by the *De ortu*). It is also found in Oxford, Bodleian Library, Rawlinson B 149, a somewhat later manuscript whose contents also include the story of Apollonius of Tyre, and a Latin Alexander romance. The story abounds in folklore and romance motifs, though like the *De ortu* it also has elements that critics have recognized as reflecting contemporary concerns, in this case regarding judicial duels, forest law and

---

10 "[...] non sine maximo discrimine [...]" (Day 1984a, 80).

attitudes towards mercenaries. The romance trappings are, however, far more pronounced in this text than in the other, and many readers have attempted to categorize and classify these features. Like the *De ortu*, the *Historia Meriadoci* has elements of a Fair Unknown story, since like Gawain, Meriadoc is estranged from his rightful heritage and makes his way, through much of the story, by virtue of his skill at arms. Other folkloric and hero-tale episodes that various critics have detected in the plot include the "*Enfances* of the Hero" (in a variant called the "endangered childhood"); the "Combat at the Ford"; the "Faery Mistress"; the "Perilous Castle"; the "Abduction", with parallels drawn in particular to the stories of Havelock the Dane (Day 1988, xxiii–xxxvi). There are also historical texts that have been suggested as influences; in short, the romance is a mixture of a sometimes bewildering range of features, as the brief synopsis below makes clear.

Meriadoc is the son of Caradoc, King of Cambria. When Caradoc is killed by men employed by his brother Griffin, his wife dies of grief, and their two children, Meriadoc and Orwen, are rescued from execution and spirited away by Ivor, the royal huntsman, and raised in the forest by Ivor and his wife, Morwen. Five years later, Meriadoc is seized by Kay and borne off to Arthur's court, while Orwen is taken away by Urien of Scotland. Eventually Morwen is reunited with Orwen in Scotland; Ivor is reunited with Meriadoc at Arthur's court and then they too head to Scotland, bringing the siblings and their caretakers back together. Meriadoc enlists the king's aid against Griffin, who is eventually defeated. Rather than take up the throne of Cambria, however, Meriadoc remains a knight, and after defeating several challengers in Arthur's court, rides off with his new companions in search of adventure. On his way to rescue the daughter of the Emperor of the Alemanni, he and his men come across two strange castles in a strange forest, and are temporarily separated by a series of bewildering experiences. At last, they escape and are reunited, and Meriadoc rescues the emperor's daughter. The Emperor betrays him and tries to have him killed, but Meriadoc escapes, joins forces with the Gauls against the Emperor, is victorious, and marries the princess and founds a royal dynasty.

The author begins by calling his narrative a *historia* (Day 1988, 2), and the first episode, in which evil counsellors turn Griffin against his brother, echoes the concerns of contemporary court satire about false counsellors. The forest childhood of Meriadoc and his sister, on the other hand, at first blush suggests the similar beginnings for romance figures such as Perceval. There is at the outset, then, an uneasy mixture of generic signals. I want to concentrate on one moment in this first movement of the narrative, and that is the digression about forest food. Romance can be notoriously unspecific about the matters of everyday life. Sir Gawain's miserable journey in search of the Green Knight's castle in *Sir*

Gawain and the Green Knight is remarkable precisely because we are rarely asked to imagine what it would be like to ride through fierce winter weather in armour, and to sleep outside with no shelter. The *Historia Meriadoci*, however, not only tells us that the children and their guardians gather fruit, nuts and herbs, but also pauses to explain how it is possible to cook food without pots. They build a pyre of logs and light it from the top; use the heat from the burnt wood to heat rocks; dig two pits connected by a channel that can be blocked and unblocked; fill one pit with water and the other with meat wrapped in leaves; tip the hot material from the fire into the water to boil it; release that water into the food pit.

While this passage is not as long as the one detailing the heating of Greek fire in the *De ortu*, both suggest a fascination with what could be seen as everyday technological magic – how things can be heated, distilled, cooled, and so on, whether to produce weapons or food. Like the Greek fire passage, this is also a liminal point in the text, a place where an objectified technology reveals an uneasy joining of romance and "real" worlds. The narrative touches several times on forest life and forest law; for example, Meriadoc's judicial duels at Arthur's court are focused on the claims of various knights to tracts of forest land. The childhood forest exile is a romance motif to be sure, but here, in the cooking description, it rubs up against a technology said to originate from the all-too-real phenomenon of forest outlaws. The digression begins by referring to "men exiled as a result of crimes against estate or homeland, far removed from the normal routines of life, hiding in the depths of the forest and woods."[11] Henry II was famous, or infamous, for the claims he made on the forests, both expanding his rights and vigorously pursuing any perceived infringement of those rights.[12] If this is a later twelfth-century text, the state of the forests would mean much in a learned (that is, Latinate) audience's mind; in later centuries, the question of forest jurisdiction continues to be a lively one. The outlaws whose know-how is borrowed in this passage are presented as both criminals and exiles. Their cooking method is literally a life-saver for the outlaws and for our romance exiles. The seeping of one forest world into the other, by means of a closely-observed technology, blurs the lines between the worlds and, perhaps, raises the question of what kind of cultural work the romance is meant to do.

The forest entered by Meriadoc and his men on their way to rescue the Emperor's daughter is, we are told, "so vast and savage, that no one had ever been able

---

11 "[...] homines prediis vel patria scelere exigente expulsi, publica ab conversacione remocius semoti, saltus slivarumque latebras [...]" (Day 1988, 40)
12 For more on this, see Young (1979).

to measure its length nor its width."[13] This forest is said to be home to every kind of fear and hallucination-inducing phantom. Inside the forest, day and night do not behave as the knights expect, further adding to the sense of disorientation. It is in this state that Meriadoc encounters "remarkable buildings, of the most marvellous and excellent workmanship, with carved and painted columns and high ceilings, built of marble and porphyry, with an inlaid floor, all encircled by a high wall and a deep moat."[14] He passes through a courtyard and into a great hall, where, at the top of a set of porphyry stairs, a beautiful lady reclines on a couch. All around are all manner of ornaments, decorations and noblemen playing at various games; when Meriadoc is invited to dine with the lady, the description of the feast emphasizes the "splendidus apparatus" (Day 1988, 122) [splendid accessories] of the feast. It has been suggested that the lady, who chides Meriadoc for not recognizing her, is Fortuna, and certainly this part of the text involves a number of startling reversals of fortune, before the hero finally triumphs.

Particularly important for our purposes, however, is the close attention paid to the fabric and contents of the marvellous castle. Scenes like this are not unusual in romance – a lavish feast, surrounded by evidence of opulent, aristocratic wealth, is a common element. The detail here gains added significance in part because of the text's persistent interest in perception and interpretation (Echard 1998), and also because this is not the only fantastical building Meriadoc and his men encounter. When a bizarre encounter with the lady's seneschal causes Meriadoc and his men to flee, they find themselves on horseback in a rushing river. Back in the forest, an intense storm drives many of the men to shelter in a second castle, despite the warnings of one of their number who knows its negative properties (no one, he says, may return from it without shame). Again the interior is described, as we read about a hall, an upper room with walls covered in hangings and with carpets all over the floor. There is a warm fire, and stables filled with straw. Despite the appearance of aristocratic comfort, however, a strange terror grips the men, so that when Meriadoc finally enters, he has to urge them to set aside their fear and set the table. He runs through various rooms in the castle, pillages the kitchen (throwing an irate guardian down the kitchen-well) and finally leaves the castle in pursuit of another of its angry inhabitants.

---

13 "Erat [...] vasta nimis et horrida, quam cuius esset latitudinis vel longitudinis nullus unquam rimari potuit." (Day 1988, 114)

14 "[...] ingencia edificial [...], miri et preclari operis columpnis celatis et depictis, celsis laquearibus, ex lapide marmoreo et porphiritico tabulatis parietum constructis et constratis, omnia circumcirca alta fossa valloque prerupto cingente." (Day 1988, 116)

The two castles are built environments whose narrative purpose seems to be to draw the eyes of both the characters and the reader, and then to bewilder both audiences, first through the dizzying display of the richness of aristocratic life, and then through the apparently random peculiarities characteristic of romance locales. The level of detail makes each seem solid, before each vanishes into the narrative mist. In both cases, a specific route through the castle is described, and the parts are enumerated – the courtyard, hall, stairs and high table (*curia, aula, gradus, celsior mensa*; Day 1988, 118–122) of the first building; and the gates, hall, upper tower hall, stables, chambers, kitchen and well (*aditus, aula, turris superior, stabula, thalamum, coquina, puteus*; Day 1988. 132–142) of the second. Against this familiar solidity, the strange events play out, and when their strangeness drives our protagonist twice back into the bewildering forest of romance, we are encouraged to see them afresh, not as natural aristocratic environments, but as parts of the romance machine, as stages where narrative is made and advanced. And it matters that, as in the Greek fire digression, these fantastic environments also contain the ordinary and everyday (such as the kitchen well or the stables). Once again, the laying bare of the operations of the text encourages us first to notice how it is working, and then perhaps to interrogate the chivalric martial culture in which it is embedded.

Throughout this essay, I have followed convention and described these Latin texts as romances. Despite the importance of Geoffrey of Monmouth in establishing the story of King Arthur, Latin is not, of course, the normal language of romance, whose very name declares its vernacularity. Certainly, both the *De ortu Walwanii* and the *Historia Meriadoci* abound in recognizable romance motifs and structures. But the treatment of objects and technologies suggests something of a sideways glance. These texts repeatedly offer us what is familiar, and then defamiliarize it. If these are twelfth-century romances, then perhaps we are seeing the pieces of the new genre-machine being explored and assembled, even in an experimental fashion. If they date to a period when that machine has become ubiquitous, then perhaps those same pieces, particularly their exaggerations, suggest a kind of fantastical contraption intended to highlight, play with or even mock the cogs and wheels we have become accustomed not to seeing. Whatever the case, the objects in these romances repeatedly dirty our windows, or turn them into (funhouse) mirrors, and in so doing, they confront us, to quote the *De ortu*, with "the thing as it is."[15]

---

15 "[...] rem ut erat." (Day 1984a, 62)

References

Archibald, Elizabeth. "Variations on Romance Themes in the *Historia Meriadoci*." *Journal of the International Arthurian Society* 2 (2014): 3–19.

Archibald, Elizabeth. "Arthurian Latin Romance." *The Arthur of Medieval Latin Literature: The Development and Dissemination of the Arthurian Legend in Medieval Latin*. Ed. Siân Echard. Cardiff: University of Wales Press, 2011. 132–145.

Berthet, Jean-Charles, Martine Furno, Claudine Marc, and Philippe Walter, trans. *Arthur, Gauvain et Mériadoc. Récits arthuriens latins du XIIIe siècle*. Grenoble: ELLUG, 2007.

Brown, Bill. "Thing Theory." *Critical Inquiry* 28 (2001): 1–22.

Bruce, J. Douglas, ed. Historia Meriadoci *and* De Ortu Waluuanii: *Two Arthurian Romances of the XIIIth Century in Latin Prose*. Baltimore, MD: Johns Hopkins, 1913.

Bruce, J. Douglas, ed. *Vita Meriadoci: An Arthurian Romance now first edited from the Cottonian MS. Faustina B.VI of the British Museum*. Baltimore, MD: MLA, 1900.

Bruce, J. Douglas, ed. *De Ortu Waluuanii: An Arthurian Romance now first edited from the Cottonian MS. Faustina B.VI of the British Museum*. Baltimore, MD: MLA, 1898.

Brugger, Ernst. "Zu *Historia Meriadoci* und *De Ortu Walwanii*." *Zeitscrhift für französische Sprache und Literatur* 5/6 (1923): 247–280.

Cross, Roseanna. "'Heterochronia' in *Thomas of Erceldoune*, *Guingamor*, 'The Tale of King Herla', and *The Story of Meriadoc, King of Cambria*." *Neophilologus* 92 (2008): 163–175.

Day, Mildred Leake. "Dating *De ortu Waluuanii* from Twelfth-Century Ship Design." *Arthuriana* 23 (2013), 98–110.

Day, Mildred Leake, ed. *The Story of Meriadoc, King of Cambria*. New York: Garland, 1988.

Day, Mildred Leake, ed. *The Rise of Gawain, Nephew of Arthur*. New York: Garland, 1984a.

Day, Mildred Leake. "Scarlet Surcoat and Gilded Armor: Literary Tradition and Costume in *De Ortu Waluuanii* and *Sir Gawain and the Green Knight*." *Arthurian Interpretations* 15 (1984b): 53–58.

Day, Mildred Leake. "*Historia Meriadoci* and *Arthur and Gorlagon*: Two Arthurian Tales in a Unique Fifteenth-Century Collection of Latin Romances (Rawlinson B.149)." *Fifteenth-Century Studies* 17 (1980): 67–71.

Echard, Siân. *Arthurian Narrative in the Latin Tradition*. Cambridge: Cambridge University Press, 1998.

Galyon, Aubrey. "*De Ortu Walwanii* and the Theory of Illumination." *Neophilologus* 62 (1978): 335–341.

Larkin, Peter. "Constructing a Hybrid National Hero: Gawain and *De ortu Waluuanii*." *Other Nations: The Hybridization of Medieval Insular Mythology and Identity*. Ed. Wendy Marie Hoofnagle and Wolfram R. Keller. Heidelberg: Universitätsverlag Winter, 2011. 145–164.

Larkin, Peter. "A Suggested Author for *De ortu Waluuanii* and *Historia Meriadoci*: Ranulph Higden." *Journal of English and Germanic Philology* 103 (2004): 215–231.

Morriss, Margaret Shove. "The Authorship of the *De Ortu Waluuanii* and the *Historia Meriadoci*." *PMLA* 23 (1908): 599–645.

Nicholson, Helen. "Following the Path of the Lionheart: The *De Ortu Walwanii* and the *Itinerarium Peregrinorum et Gesta Regis Ricardi*." *Medium Ævum* 69 (2000): 21–33.

Porter, David W. "The *Historia Meriadoci* and Magna Carta." *Neophilologus* 76 (1992): 136–146.

Young, Charles R. *The Royal Forests of Medieval England*. Philadelphia, PA: University of Pennsylvania Press, 1979.

Charmaine Lee
Jaufre: Genre Boundaries and Ambiguity

Jaufre is an Occitan Arthurian romance. This simple statement conceals a whole series of problems starting from the fact that, apart from the much shorter, Celtic-themed romance, *Blandin de Cornoalha*, *Jaufre* is the only Arthurian romance in Occitan to have come down to us. Indeed, it is one of the few examples of narrative in Occitan to have survived at all and most of it tends to be derived from the troubadour lyric, presenting in narrative form concerns more generally expressed in this tradition. So, to go back to my opening statement, the term "Occitan" is not usually associated with either "romance" or "Arthurian" and the three terms together inevitably point to a hybrid.

This is underscored by the fact that even the author seems to be unsure as to which genre his text belongs. While medieval authors are often frustratingly imprecise in the terminology they use to define genre, and it is the modern reader who has felt the need to impose fixed categories on a literary corpus that seems to have followed different criteria (Busby 2008), the terminology used by the anonymous author to refer to his work does give us food for thought. He begins by saying it is a "conte" (l. 1) [a tale], but a few lines later he describes it as "novas" (ll. 16, 21).[1] *Novas* is the term now employed to refer to shorter narrative texts presenting courtly conceits, such as those by Raimon Vidal, but as Huchet (1992) and Limacher-Riebold (1997) have pointed out, it is also used by the author of the romance of *Flamenca*. Literally meaning "news", like the Italian *novella*, *novas* seems to imply oral discourse, but it is also a specifically Occitan term and its use here tends to stress the Occitan nature of the text. Later on in the prologue, however, the author refers to his text as a "canchon" (ll. 85–90) [song], which has been interpreted as an allusion to the *chansons de geste* (Huchet 1992, 277; Spetia 2012, 191–195), elements of which are present in *Jaufre* (Espadaler 2002). However, I believe that here it alludes to the *canso*, the troubadour song, since the author also claims to have heard its *razon*, that is the tale of the events leading to its composition, and this concerns King Arthur. By introducing Arthur and his court in a context that recalls the performance of a *canso*, the author seems to be saying that he is combining this *matière* with that pertaining to lyric poetry. This would fit the view that Occitan narrative texts produce a "fictionalization of the

---

1 References to *Jaufre* are from the edition by Lee (2006a).

Charmaine Lee (University of Salerno)

DOI 10.1515/9783110432466-033

lyric tradition" (Huchet 1992, 278; Di Luca 2014, 14), although Huchet (1992, 297) believes that *Jaufre* has failed to bring this about because the Arthurian subject matter resists being combined with the lyric tradition and remains foreign to it. On the contrary, I would say that it is a success, as seems implicit in the fact that finally, at the very end of the tale, it is called a "roman" (l. 10967) [romance]: the merger of the Arthurian subject with the *novas* and *canso* has led to the creation of a new, specifically Occitan *roman*, as I hope to show in the rest of this chapter on this highly entertaining, but often ambiguous romance.

Jaufre has come down to us in two complete manuscripts and six fragments which fall into two families, an Occitan branch formed by manuscript *A* and fragments *e, f, g, h*, and a northern Italian branch consisting of manuscript *B* and two fragments, *c* and *d*, which are actually passages copied in troubadour anthologies.[2] The scribe responsible for *B* has been identified as one Iohannes Iacobi, perhaps from Bologna (Brunetti 2004), who is known to have copied the *Chanson d'Aspremont* and the romance of *Florimont*; this, along with the number of manuscripts, albeit fragmentary, points to a greater success of the romance compared to others whose circulation is limited to the area straddling the Pyrenees. *Jaufre* was also reworked in prose in the fifteenth century in French and Castilian, the latter being part of what must have been a wider Iberian reception that ranges from the frescoes illustrating the story in the Aljafería Palace in Zaragoza, commissioned by Peter IV of Aragon, to a version in Tagalog, a native language of the Philippines.

The story conforms to those Arthurian romances that focus on the adventures of a single knight in his quest to obtain a fief and a lady. In close to 11,000 lines it tells of a young man, Jaufre, who goes to Arthur's court and asks to be knighted in order to go off and seek the villainous Taulat de Rogimon, who a little earlier had burst into the court, killed a knight before the queen's very eyes and threatened to return the same day (Pentecost) every year to repeat the affront. The search for Taulat is the main narrative thread of the first half of the romance, which, after a series of encounters with some quite monstrous and diabolical knights, ends with Taulat's defeat and capture. The second part tells of the conquest of a wife, Brunissen, met during the quest for Taulat, and a fief, the castle of Monbrun,

---

2 The *sigla* used here are the standard ones employed by Brunel (1943), except for *g* and *h*, which were discovered later. *A* = Paris, BnF, fr. 2164; *B* = Paris, BnF, fr. 12571; *c* = Rome, Biblioteca Apostolica Vaticana, Vat. lat. 3206 (*chansonnier L*); *d* = New York, Pierpont Morgan Library, M. 819 (*chansonnier N*); *e* = Nîmes, Archives départementales du Gard, F (001) 083, pièce 3, notaire de Vallerauge; *f* = Nîmes, Archives départementales du Gard, F (001) 083, pièce 4, notaire de Bagnols-sur-Cèze; *g* = Rodez, Archives départementales de l'Aveyron, 50 J, fonds Balsa de Firmi; *h* = Barcelona, Institut Municipal d'Història, B-109.

which is Brunissen's dowry. The romance thus has the typical bipartite structure of Arthurian romances, with a first part devoted mainly to chivalric valour and the second to proving oneself as a lover (Köhler 1988 [1956]; Southworth 1973).

Behind this apparently simple structure lies a greater complexity involving the overall meaning of the text, its themes and motifs, and some more external details such as who wrote the romance, who commissioned it and when. These questions have yet to find a definite answer, yet they are fundamental for a correct interpretation, which depends on being able to place the text in the appropriate historical context. The author seems to delight in being deliberately ambiguous by suggesting at the very end of the romance that the authors are actually two and, more importantly, by dedicating his work to a king of Aragon without ever naming him. As a result modern criticism of *Jaufre* has invariably tended to revolve around these problems. Attempts have been made to identify the king of Aragon on the basis of the two sections of text that praise him (ll. 58–84, 2626–2640), trying to make the description fit one or other of the different candidates: Alfonso II (1162– 1196), Peter II (1196–1213) and James I (1213–1276), the first or the last being the main contenders.[3] Alternatively, some scholars have endeavoured to refer the apparently precise temporal references, particularly in the first part of the romance, to a year in which Whitsunday fell on 12th June, as it seems to in *Jaufre* (Pinkernell 1972b). Neither method of investigation is entirely satisfactory; the passages in praise of the king do not differ greatly from similar eulogies found, for example, in many *planhs* [laments], including the series of parodical *planhs* pronounced for Jaufre himself when he is thought to be dead and therefore cannot help identify the king (Ferrero 1962, 133; Lee 2000). The same may be said of the chronological indications, which are in fact ambiguous, even differing from one manuscript to another (Limentani 1977, 79–92; Kay 1979). So once more the author plays games with his audience by seeming to be precise when in fact he is just giving a general measure of time, which might be a week or a month, according to the scribe rather than the author.

More recently Espadaler (1997; 1999–2000; 2011) has argued for a later date, not only on the basis of the allusions to dates, but also because some of the expressions that praise the king of Aragon are identical to those directed at James

---

3 The earlier date is favoured by Lejeune (1948; 1953), Pirot (1972, 498–506, 517), Eckhardt (1984, 89–92) and Alibert (2015), while the later date is preferred by Brunel (1943, I, xxxviii), Jeanroy (1941), Remy (1959), Limentani (1977), Gaunt and Harvey (2006). Lewent (1945–1946) suggests two versions, a view followed by De Riquer (1955), Gómez Redondo (1996, 15), Girbea (2008) and, to a certain extent, Lazzerini (2010), who prefers 1242 and 1272. A date of composition at the end of James's reign is proposed by Espadaler (1997; 1999–2000; 2011) and Asperti (1999, 355–356).

I by the Catalan troubadour Cerveri de Girona in his moral treatise *Maldit-Bendit*, composed in 1271. Since he assumes that it is the author of *Jaufre* who is quoting Cerveri and not the other way around, Espadaler concludes that the romance must be later than 1271, perhaps written in 1272, a year in which Whitsun fits the date implied by the text. However, the objection still stands that we have no way of knowing whether the author of *Jaufre* quoted Cerveri, or vice versa, not to mention that these expressions are not entirely unique. Nevertheless the basis of the investigation is sound, and there can be no real doubt that the king to whom the romance is dedicated is James I, though not necessarily at such a late date.

Still this path of research is fruitful in that it considers the romance's intertextual relationships, which are in fact numerous. Indeed, if we accept Bakhtin's theory that the novel is a polyphonic genre, then *Jaufre* stands as a precursor, in the same way as *Tirant lo Blanc* or *Don Quixote*. As said before, the author of *Jaufre* seems to be attempting to create a specifically Occitan Arthurian romance, a kind of romance that will distance itself from the French genre. To bring this about he has moved in several directions: using material derived from Chrétien's works as well as later Arthurian romances; introducing Arthurian motifs excluded from Chrétien's canon; weaving the main tenets of courtly lyric poetry into his story.

As for many later Arthurian romances, the main point of reference for *Jaufre* is Chrétien de Troyes (Schmolke-Hasselmann 1998), which makes it safe to say that the elusive king of Aragon cannot be Alfonso II, who was on the throne while Chrétien was still composing his works. *Jaufre* moreover bears many similarities to *Perceval*, Chrétien's final romance (Pontecorvo 1938; Limentani 1977, 78–101; Gaunt and Harvey 2006), which is often rewritten parodically (Fleischman 1981; Jewers 2000, 54–82), such as when Jaufre, exhausted after several adventures, discovers Brunissen's garden and falls asleep there, only to be awoken by three different knights who try to capture him, while he believes it is always the same one. The scene recalls Perceval's trance on seeing the drops of blood in the snow, which remind him of his sweetheart Blanchefleur and he also takes three different knights for one. Or similarly, Perceval fails to ask the question about the Grail, while Jaufre constantly asks why the people at Brunissen's castle cry out in anguish at regular intervals, only to be threatened with death each time (Huchet 1994). References to *Perceval* sometimes take the form of literal quotations, even with the use of the same rhyme words, such as when Kay makes his first appearance at court (*Jaufre*, ll. 123–112; *Perceval*, ll. 2791–2793).[4] The episode continues with the well-known motif of Arthur's refusal to eat before some adventure takes place, which first appears in *Perceval*, and is repeated almost verbatim in *Jaufre*

---

4 All references to the romances of Chrétien are to Poirion's edition: Chrétien de Troyes (1994).

(ll. 141–152; *Perceval*, ll. 2818–2824) with additional commentary along the lines of "you have seen it many times", implying the author's awareness of how topical the motif had become.

Jaufre also shares many features with *Yvain* (Hunt 1988; Spetia 2012). Both texts begin at a plenary court on Whitsunday; the episode in which Jaufre causes a tempest by breaking the head of a statue is reminiscent of the storm at the fountain in *Yvain*. The *bovier* that Jaufre meets on his travels hints, though in a rather comic fashion, at the wild herdsman (*Bouvier*) in *Yvain* (cf. Lodén, *supra*). Jaufre's horse acts out a *planh* for his master when he believes him to be dead, just as the lion does for Yvain. Meanwhile, the character of Harpin de la Montagne in *Yvain* has several traits in common with both the giant leper and Fellon d'Albarua in *Jaufre*. Indeed the tendency to split episodes from *Yvain* and place them at different points in his tale is one of the ways in which the author of *Jaufre* reuses Chrétien's text, to the point that Spetia (2012, 137) asks whether he might have had a written copy before him. As a matter of fact, all of Chrétien's romances appear between the lines in a recurrent game of quotations, a kind of "spot the romance". The list of knights at Arthur's court in the opening scene (ll. 96–110) more or less corresponds to that in *Erec et Enide* (ll. 1667–1690): it includes Gawain, Lancelot, Tristan, Yvain, Erec, Kay, Perceval, Calogrenant, Cligès, Kaherdin, Caradoc, Briebras. A further twist of irony is that at l. 1697 in *Erec*, the list names "Gilflez, li filz Do, et Taulas", the very protagonists of *Jaufre*, that is Jaufre, Girflez (the fils Dovon) and Taulat de Rogimon; thus Chrétien's romances provide the plot outline and characters for the Occitan author.

Chrétien's second romance, *Cligès*, has mainly supplied material for the love interest; in particular the monologues pronounced by Jaufre and Brunissen during the night of their first and second meetings at Monbrun follow those of Cligès' parents, Alixandre and Soredamor, as they realize they have fallen in love while on the ship taking them from England to Brittany. Like Soredamor (ll. 984–1009), Brunissen (ll. 7543–7576), wonders whether it would be acceptable for her, as a woman, to make the first move. Here, too, as Spetia remarked in respect of *Yvain*, a single episode has been divided and placed in two different parts of the romance, the author again pointing to his source by including Cligès and Fenice among the famous couples evoked here by Brunissen (ll. 7626–7628).

Finally, the entire story is set in motion by an event, the insult to the queen and subsequent *queste* [quest], which brings to mind the *Chevalier de la charrette* (*Lancelot*), in which the protagonist also acts as a liberator and defender of the weak, a role frequently taken on by Jaufre. Moreover, *Jaufre* ends much like *Lancelot*. The view that there might be two authors is based on the fact that at the very end of the romance (ll. 10967–10968, present only in *B*) the author begs for a prayer to be said for he who began the romance, presumably leaving it unfinished, and he who ended it; indeed if one began, or wrote a version, around 1170, while the other reworked it around 1225–1230, this would solve the problem of the identity of the king of Aragon.[5] A closer examination suggests that the author is most likely casting a sly glance at his model, where we discover that Godefrei de Leigni brought the tale to an end following Chrétien's instructions (ll. 7102–7107). We are also told that Chrétien stopped writing when Lancelot was "anmurez" [imprisoned] in a tower by Meleagant (l. 7109), which constitutes a possible ending for the romance, a "prison of love" from which Lancelot cannot escape, just as Chrétien cannot get out of his tale of adultery. In *Jaufre*, too, the protagonist is *anmurez*, but in the lepers' house, where the author threatens to leave him because he is disgusted at the decline of courtly values. It is only for love of the king of Aragon, whose court keeps such customs alive, that he will free Jaufre and carry on with his tale (ll. 2623–2649). So the romance continues, no longer inspired by the relative of Arthur and Gawain alluded to at the beginning (ll. 85–93), but by the king of Aragon himself, thus replacing Arthur's court with that of Aragon.

Moreover, an examination of the style (Stimming 1888) and structure (Southworth 1973) points to a single author since the language and stylistic features are the same throughout, while the different episodes are arranged symmetrically in the two parts, with characters who appear in the first part, such as the lepers' rather bizarre mother, returning in the second. In addition, the main body of the romance is framed by two parallel adventures involving Arthur being carried off by a beast, which turns out to be a knight and enchanter from his court. These two episodes have been interpreted in different ways (Huchet 1989; Lecco 2003, 3–14; Gouiran 2005): they increase the symmetry governing the text and are connected by the theme of clothes, with the knights of the Round Table undressing in the first episode to soften Arthur's fall in case the horned beast to which he has become attached drops him off the cliff. Then, they don the wrong clothes, while at the end Arthur celebrates the safe outcome by ordering new clothes to be made for his knights. It may well be, as Fraser (1995) has argued, that the author is somehow celebrating the southern bourgeoisie involved in the textile industry, but I would also agree with Huchet (1989, 99; 1994, 173) that this represents the manner in which the author has "undressed", or dismantled Arthurian romance

---

5 The theory of two authors was first formulated by Raynouard (1817, II, 286) and (1883, 178), then by Pontecorvo (1938), Jauss (1953–1954), De Riquer (1955), Pinkernell (1972b), Gómez Redondo (1996, 15); Stimming (1888), Lewent (1945–1946), Jeanroy (1941), Brunel (1943, I), Remy (1959), Eckhardt (1982–1983), Huchet (1989), Arthur (1992, xiv–xvi), Lee (2003a) believe in a single author.

only to dress it anew in Occitan garb. No ends are left loose in this tale that begins at Carduel and ends at Monbrun, starting with praise of king Arthur and ending with that of Jaufre, again passing the baton from one court to another and stressing Jaufre's feats, despite the fact that he is only a *novel cavalier*, just like the king of Aragon. An implicit link is thus created between Jaufre and the king.

This unnamed king, moreover, cannot be Alfonso II, because *Jaufre* also alludes to the tradition derived from Chrétien. A number of parallels exist with the romance of *Yder* (Espadaler 2002), as well as the *Continuation-Gauvain* or *First Continuation* of *Perceval*: in ll. 6653–6655, for instance, Jaufre mocks Kay recalling the time he was struck by a roast peacock; significantly this occurs in a part of the *First Continuation* (Limentani 1977, 84; Lorenzo Gradín 1997, 203) where Girflez, the fils Dovon (*Gilflez, li filz Do*), has gone missing. More recently Alibert (2015) has argued for a much closer intertextual relationship between these two texts, especially the part known as the "Livre de Caradoc", which also features the motif of Arthur's refusal to eat before having an adventure, as well as a knight-enchanter, Eliavrés, similar to the character in *Jaufre*, who, we should remember, is never actually identified as Merlin, however much we might be tempted to make that connection. Alibert uses his conclusions to argue for a common, more archaic source for both the *First Continuation* and *Jaufre* in an attempt to push back the date of the romance, which he believes must be around 1176. *Jaufre* does indeed contain some archaic features, beginning with the fact that the protagonist's description upon his first appearance (face blushed by the sun, golden to reddish hair, clothes apparently of shot silk, and a wreath of flowers in his hair) likens him to a sun god, and in fact he seems to gain strength during the daylight and weaken at night. Moreover, Taulat's killing of the knight at court and his threat to repeat the deed every year clearly points to the cycle of nature, much in the same way as *Sir Gawain and the Green Knight*, a romance to which *Jaufre* can also be likened (Alibert 2015, 47). But these features do not necessarily point to an earlier date: *Sir Gawain* dates from the late-fourteenth century.

Jaufre also bears some resemblance to another thirteenth-century romance, the *Biaus descouneüs* (Limentani 1977: 100; Lecco 2003: 34–40; Lee 2006b).[6] Indeed the author almost points to this source by including Lo Bels Desconegutz among the knights present at Arthur's court (l. 108), while the name does not feature in the comparable list in *Erec et Enide*. The protagonists of both

---

6 There seems to be some significance in the fact that Claude Platin, who published a prose reworking of *Jaufre* in 1530, combined the two romances. Moreover several motifs listed in Guerreau-Jalabert (1992) only appear in *Jaufre* and the *Biaus descouneüs*, and in very few other romances.

romances have to choose between a human princess and a fairy lover, though in *Jaufre* the danger posed by the "fada de Gibel" [fairy of Gibel] for Brunissen is virtual. Brunissen's castle is shaken by cries of woe that recall the sinister noises at Blonde Esmerée's castle in the *Biaus descouneüs*. More to the point, however, both romances are "open" in that their *dénouement* depends on someone beside the author. In the *Biaus descouneüs* it is the author's lady, to whom the work is dedicated, who could change the ending were she to accept the author's courtship, while in *Jaufre* it is the king of Aragon, as we have seen, who is responsible for the tale's being continued and concluded. The *Biaus descouneüs* has been compared to a *chanson*, the romance serving as a request to the lady (Guthrie 1984), whereas *Jaufre* could be likened to a *sirventes* [service song] in praise of the king of Aragon, the implicit subject of the text.

All this serves to alter the perspective of the Arthurian world informing Chrétien's romances, which is no longer able to fulfil its traditional role as guarantor of civilized society as people come to rely more and more on Jaufre to act this part. This becomes clear when the *fada de Gibel* goes to Arthur's court to ask for help against Fellon d'Albarua, only to discover that there are no knights left there to carry out her request; only Jaufre will be able to defeat Fellon and restore order to her underwater kingdom. Thus, while using Chrétien and the tradition derived from his works, the author of *Jaufre* distances himself from him, first by frequently offering parodical and/or comical readings of his romances, which frustrate the audience's expectations and lead the text in a new direction, and then by turning to motifs that have not found a place in Chrétien's canon, in particular ones that seem to have circulated on the Mediterranean "periphery" of Arthurian legend, appearing one way or another in Italy, Catalonia and southern France. Four episodes in *Jaufre* involve this material: the *fada de Gibel*, the sculpted head causing a tempest enabling Jaufre to escape from the lepers' house, the *fada*'s enemy Fellon d'Albarua, and Arthur riding the horned beast in the first episode (Lee 2007).

The *fada*, who could have become a rival in love for Brunissen, is most probably to be identified with Morgan and connected to the legends of Arthur's survival in a cave under Mount Etna (*Mongibello*), which seem to have developed under the Normans in Sicily and been registered for the first time by Gervase of Tilbury in the *Otia imperialia* (Graf 2002, 321–338; Pioletti 1989; Ueltschi 2005). Reference to this legend is made in vernacular texts hailing from Italy, France and Catalonia from the twelfth to the fourteenth centuries. The oldest of these, the epic poem *La Bataille Loquifer*, a text belonging to the *Guillaume d'Orange Cycle* that mixes epic material with the Matter of Britain, contains two more such motifs. Here the protagonist, Rainouart, kills his father Desramé, cuts off his head and throws it into the sea causing a tempest, just as Jaufre does with the sculpted head he breaks in order to escape from the lepers' enchanted house. Though this particular motif probably originated in the eastern Mediterranean (Ménard 1987; Varvaro 1998a, 1998b), it is found once again in the *Otia imperialia* in a chapter entitled "De insulis Mediterranei maris" [the Mediterranean islands], along with the tale of Arthur in Mount Etna.

In the *Bataille Loquifer*, Rainouart also fights the monster Chapalu who, once defeated, turns into a handsome knight. This beast is none other than Cath Palug, the monstrous cat mentioned in the Welsh Black Book of Carmarthen (Aberystwyth, National Library of Wales, Peniarth 1), who defeats Arthur in some Arthurian tales, as is recalled by a number of troubadours (Pirot 1972, 448). The description of Chapalu is akin to that of Fellon d'Albarua, the *fada*'s enemy, whose "mouth larger than a leopard's, stretching from ear to ear" is somewhat feline;[7] Fellon, too, ceases to be seen as monstrous once he is defeated. The *Bataille Loquifer* has Sicilian connections and a dangerous looking cat seems to threaten and defeat Arthur on the mosaic floor in Otranto Cathedral in southern Italy, again a product of the Norman dukes in that area. Here, as well as being confronted by the cat, Arthur is riding a horned beast, similar to a goat. Perhaps connected to tales of Arthur leading a wild hunt, one of which features in the above-mentioned chapter of the *Otia imperialia*, this image also brings to mind the first adventure in *Jaufre* where Arthur becomes attached to the horns of a beast and is carried around dangling rather inelegantly from them. It is not clear what kind of beast this is, though the illuminator pictures it as a bull in *A*. What is important, however, is that once more the author of *Jaufre* has had recourse to motifs deriving from legends that must have circulated perhaps orally around the Mediterranean. Gervase of Tilbury, who recorded several of these, was employed for a time at the court of William II of Sicily where he no doubt came into contact with these "other" pre-Galfridian Arthurian legends (Bresc 1987).

These different episodes, then, may be associated with an Occitan and Mediterranean tradition in opposition to the more mainstream Arthurian legend and help to set the romance apart from this latter. But *Jaufre* is specifically an Occitan romance and, like most narrative texts from this area, it offers, woven into the plot, a fictionalization of the courtly lyric tradition. The text contains many passages that recall different lyric genres as well as the ideas expressed by some major troubadours. A first such genre is the *planh*, or lament, a number of which are pronounced by different characters, including Jaufre's horse, when he is thought to have drowned in the fountain where the *fada* has pushed him in order to obtain his help in fighting Fellon. Elsewhere the genre is featured in

---

7 Translation from Arthur (1992, 155–156).

the *salut*, a lyric epistle in which a lover addresses his lady, and which appears in the two episodes when Jaufre and Brunissen lie awake thinking about how they will declare their love for each other (ll. 7405–7441; 7611–7642). When they finally find the courage, the conversation is reminiscent of a further troubadour genre, the *tenso*, with Brunissen pretending she does not know that Jaufre loves her (ll. 7757–7825). This kind of poetry in dialogue form between a lover and his lady features frequently in the body of texts attributed to the *trobairitz*, the female troubadours, and indeed many of Brunissen's reflections on love conform to the *trobairitz* pattern (De Riquer 1995): she believes a woman should not give her love to a *ric ome* (ll. 3806–3808) [nobleman], a man more noble than herself, like Azalais de Porcairagues. She compares her love for Jaufre to that of famous literary couples, a feature both of the *salut* and the poetry of the Contessa de Dia, who, like Brunissen, also wishes to embrace her lover in bed (ll. 7346–7348).

Jaufre, on the other hand, thinks and talks like a troubadour: he is attracted to Brunissen at first by the sight of her beauty (ll. 7405–7411); he feels completely within her power (ll. 7412–7417) and cannot defend himself against her (ll. 3638–3650). He is too shy to declare his love (ll. 7397–7400) but to deserve her love he must follow specific norms of behaviour (ll. 7306–7321). Though much of this falls into the more general typology of courtly concepts, it does seem to echo a particular group of poets and poems present, together with the passages of *Jaufre*, in troubadour songbooks *L* and *N*, as well as in Raimon Vidal's *novas*, *En aquel temps*, a text also copied into these manuscripts (Lee 2003b). These are poets who insist on the need to keep courtly values alive at a time when it seemed they were being neglected, which, as we have seen, is also a concern of the author of *Jaufre*, who was going to stop writing for this very reason, were it not for the king of Aragon. It would appear that the Italian compilers of troubadour songbooks *L* and *N* read the romance as a plea for courtly behaviour and, indeed, taken as a whole it is the tale of a young, landless knight, who gains a rich and powerful lady and her fiefs, thanks to his bravery and prowess, thus reaffirming the basic courtly tenets at the level of both plot and story (Fuksas 2011; Lee 2013).

These same issues also inform the poetry of a slightly later troubadour, who has more than one aspect in common with *Jaufre*, Guilhem de Montanhagol. Guilhem was active from 1233 to 1257 (Ricketts 1964, 17); he was doubtless a witness to the Treaty of Paris in 1229, which marked the end of the Albigensian crusade, and, during the years in which he composed his poetry, he would have observed the decline of southern society, with its main counties falling to Louis XI's brothers. His most successful song, *Nulhs hom no val ni deu esser prezatz* (*BdT* 225, 10), at least judging by the eighteen manuscripts that contain it, reads almost like a manifesto. Like *Jaufre* it develops the theme of *laudatio temporis acti* [lamenting the decline of past times], while at the same time insisting on the importance of *mezura* [dignity/self-restraint] and the need to safeguard honour, especially a lady's, since ladies in this increasingly uncourtly world hesitate to give their love for fear of being dishonoured (Lee 2005). This sentiment is echoed by Brunissen, who is afraid to fall in love; she is rich and powerful, but definitely single (ll. 3076–3078) and apparently intent on staying so (ll. 6929–6931). Brunissen, for all intents and purposes, is sterile, just as her land has been rendered sterile by Taulat's torture of her lord, Melian, who thus appears as an echo of the Fisher King in the Grail legend (Lecco 2003, 14; Alibert 2011). However, as Kaltenbach (1998, 92–93) has argued, this *terre gaste* [waste land] may be seen as the Midi tortured by the Albigensian crusade and its aftermath, which is also the cause of the decline of courtesy, as exemplified by Taulat's behaviour which lacks *mezura* [measure]: his killing of the knight at Arthur's court is explicitly described as *desmesura* (ll. 6101–6104) [unmeasured]. Thus, he is to be condemned both in the context of Arthurian romance, as well as in that of courtly ideology (Szabics 2010, 489–490). Once Jaufre has rid society of this evil, Brunissen is able to concede her love. The many points of contact between the ideas inspiring both Guilhem de Montanhagol and *Jaufre* lead once more to the conclusion that the king of Aragon praised in the romance is the same as that invoked by Guilhem in his poetry: *lo reys Jacmes* [King James], who was still pursuing his interests in the south of France around 1230–1240, before Provence and Toulouse passed to the Capetians.

In conclusion, *Jaufre* contains references to most of the Arthurian tradition from Chrétien to his immediate followers, but also to pre-Galfridian motifs, which may well have reached the south of France via the Plantagenets (Schmolke-Hasselmann 1998, 249–250; Girbea 2008, 13). The English presence in south-west France lasted until 1453 and included several monarchs who exploited the legend for their own ends: Henry II, Edward I and Edward III. At the same time the story is interwoven with courtly ideology as developed in troubadour lyric poetry, thus proving that the *roman* is indeed a hybrid, formed of *cansos*, *razos* and *novas* as implied in the prologue. As the story progresses, it becomes clear that Jaufre stands for the king of Aragon, a fact that is underscored by the expression, *noveltz cavaliers* [new knight], applied to the king in the prologue and later to Jaufre. Our hero replaces Arthur, for he leaves the court after his wedding, to set up his own court at Monbrun, having proven throughout that he is better than Arthur at fulfilling the latter's duties. Though the idea that *Jaufre* is anti-French has been denied by some (Girbea 2008, 17), I would say that it must at least be described as pro-Aragon as, within the context of events at the time, the king of Aragon was pitted against the French. The conflict between Charles of Anjou and James I fits the later date when the Aragonese were probably preparing their involvement in Sicily, which would have taken place after the Sicilian Vespers in 1282. Alternatively, it is also possible that the events reflected here refer rather to the period in which Charles was being installed as count of Provence, and his brother, Alfonso, as count of Toulouse in the mid-1240s. If the Albigensian crusade may be seen as having caused the different *terres gastes* present in the romance, fertility, prosperity and peace are restored by James/Jaufre, whose name, moreover, recalls the legendary first count of Barcelona to gain independence from the Franks, *Guifré el Pilós* [Wilfred the Hairy] (Lejeune 1948, 271; Spetia 2012, 197). That all this was to remain wishful thinking, while the Midi was taken over by the French and James gave up his rights in France with the treaty of Corbeil in 1258 and turned his attention towards the wider Mediterranean, is another story.

References

Alibert, Laurent. "Enrasigament meravilhós e re-escritura critica: lo rei trucat dins *Jaufré*." *Nouvelles recherches en domaine occitan: approches interdisciplinaires. Colloque de l'Association internationale d'études occitanes (Albi, 11–12 juin, 2009)*. Ed. Wendy Pfeffer and Jean Thomas. Turnhout: Brepols, 2015. 41–51.

Alibert, Laurent. "La *terre gaste* dans le *Roman de Jaufre*: au-delà de l'influence de Chrétien." *Revue des langues romanes* 115 (2011): 163–181.

Arthur, Ross G., trans. Jaufre: *An Occitan Arthurian Romance*. New York and London: Garland, 1992.

Asperti, Stefano. "La letteratura catalana medievale". *L'area iberica*. Ed. Valeria Bertolucci, Carlos Alvar and Stefano Asperti. Rome-Bari: Laterza, 1999. 325–408.

Bresc, Henri. "Excalibur en Sicile." *Medievalia* 7 (1987): 7–21.

Brunel, Clovis. *Jaufre. Roman arthurien du XIIIe siècle en vers provençaux*. 2 vols. Paris: Société des anciens textes français, 1943.

Brunetti, Giuseppina. "Un capitolo dell'espansione del francese in Italia: manoscritti e testi a Bologna fra Duecento e Trecento." *Bologna nel Medioevo. Atti del Convegno (Bologna, 28–29 October 2002). Quaderni di filologia romanza* 17 (2004): 125–164.

Busby, Keith. "Narrative Genres." *The Cambridge Companion to Medieval French Literature*. Ed. Simon Gaunt and Sarah Kay. Cambridge: Cambridge University Press, 2008. 139–152.

Cerverí de Girona. "*Maldit-Bendit*." *Obras completas del trovador Cerverí de Girona*. Ed. Martín de Riquer. Barcelona: Instituto español de Estudios Mediterráneos, 1947. 323–341.

Chrétien de Troyes. *Oeuvres complètes*. Ed. Daniel Poirion. Bibliothèque de la Pléiade. Paris: Gallimard, 1994.

De Riquer, Isabel. "Géneros trovadorescos en el *Jaufré*." *La narrativa in Provenza e Catalogna nel XIII e XIV secolo*. Ed. Fabrizio Beggiato. Pisa: Edizioni ETS, 1995. 11–26.

De Riquer, Martín. "Los problemas del *Roman provenzal de Jaufre*." *Recueil de Travaux offerts à M. Clovis Brunel*. 2 vols. Paris: Société de l'Ecole des Chartes, 1955. II, 435–461.

Di Luca, Paolo. "Il *Roman du Conte de Toulouse*. Un frammento di *chanson de geste* occitana?" *Quaderni di filologia e lingue romanze* 29 (2014): 7–36.

Eckhardt, Caroline D. "An Aragonese King, a Norman Count, an Arabic Enemy: The Curious Historical Context of *Jaufré*." *Courtly Romances: A Collection of Essays*. Ed. Guy R. Mermier. Detroit, MI: Fifteenth Century Symposium, 1984. 89–107.

Eckhardt, Caroline D. "Two Notes on the Authorship of *Jaufre*: Sir Kay gets the bird: the King of Aragon reigns." *Romance Notes* 23 (1982–1983): 191–196.

Espadaler, Anton M. "'La cort del plus onrat rei': Jacques Ier d'Aragon et le Roman de *Jaufré*." *Revue des langues romanes* 115 (2011): 183–198.

Espadaler, Anton M. "Sobre la densitat cultural del *Jaufre*." *Literatura i cultura a la Corona d'Aragó, s. XIII–XV*. Ed. Lola Badía, Miriam Cabré and Sadurní Martí. Barcelona: Publicacions de l'Abadia de Montserrat/Curial, 2002. 335–353.

Espadaler, Anton M. "El final de *Jaufre* i, novament, Cerverí de Girona." *Boletín de la Real Academia de Buenas Letras de Barcelona* 47 (1999–2000): 321–334.

Espadaler, Anton M. "El Rei d'Aragó i la data del *Jaufre*." *Cultura neolatina* 57 (1997): 199–207.

Ferrero, Giuseppe Guido. "Appunti sul *Jaufré*." *Cultura neolatina* 22 (1962): 123–140.

Fleischman, Suzanne. "*Jaufre* or Chivalry Askew: Social Overtones of Parody in Arthurian Romance." *Viator* 12 (1981): 101–129.

Fraser, Veronica. "Humour and Satire in the Romance of *Jaufre*." *Forum for Modern Language Studies* 31 (1995): 223–233.

Fuksas, Anatole Pierre. "Formato testuale e articolazione argomentativa delle versioni del *Jaufre* conservate nei canzonieri trobadorici L e N." *Studi mediolatini e volgari* 57 (2011): 131–142.

Gaunt, Simon, and Ruth Harvey. "The Arthurian Tradition in Occitan Literature." *The Arthur of the French: The Arthurian Legend in Medieval French and Occitan Literature*. Ed. Glyn S. Burgess and Karen Pratt. Cardiff: University of Wales Press, 2006. 528–545.

Girbea, Catalina. "De Girflet à Jaufré: destin et devenir d'un personnage arthurien." *Revue des langues romanes* 112 (2008): 7–32.

Gómez Redondo, Fernando, trans. *Jaufre*. Madrid: Gredos, 1996.

Gouiran, Gérard. "Le roi et le chevalier-enchanteur: les mésaventures du roi Arthur dans le *Roman de Jaufré*." *Materiali arturiani nelle letterature di Provenza, Spagna, Italia*. Ed. Margherita Lecco. Alessandria: Edizioni dell'Orso, 2005. 17–40.

Graf, Arturo. *Miti, leggende e superstizioni del medio evo*. Ed. Clara Allasia and Walter Meliga. Milan: Bruno Mondadori, 2002 [1925].

Guerreau-Jalabert, Anita. *Index des motifs narratifs dans les romans arthuriens français en vers (XIIe–XIIIe siècles)*. Geneva: Droz, 1992.

Guthrie, Jeri S. "The Je(u) in *Le Bel Inconnu*. Autoreferentiality and Pseudo-Autobiography." *Romanic Review* 75 (1984): 147–161.

Huchet, Jean-Charles. "*Jaufre* et le graal." *Vox romanica* 53 (1994): 156–174.

Huchet, Jean-Charles. "*Jaufre* et *Flamenca*. *Novas* ou Romans?" *Revue des langues romanes* 96 (1992): 275–300.

Huchet, Jean-Charles. "Le roman à nu: *Jaufre*." *Littérature* 74 (1989): 91–99.

Hunt, Tony. "Text and pré-texte. *Jaufré* and *Yvain*." *The Legacy of Chrétien de Troyes*. Ed. Norris J. Lacy, Douglas Kelly and Keith Busby. 2 vols. Amsterdam: Rodopi, 1988. II, 125–141.

Jauss, Hans Robert. "Die Defigurierung des Wunderbaren und der Sinn der Aventüre im *Jaufre*." *Romanistisches Jahrbuch* 6 (1953–1954): 60–75.

Jeanroy, Alfred. "Le roman de *Jaufre*." *Annales du Midi* 53 (1941): 363–390.

Jeanroy, Alfred. "Le soulèvement de 1242 dans la poésie des troubadours." *Annales du Midi* 16 (1904): 311–329.

Jewers, Caroline. *Chivalric Fiction and the History of the Novel*. Gainsville, FL: University Press of Florida, 2000.

Kaltenbach, Nikki L. *Le Roman de Jaufre. A Jungian Analysis*. New York et al.: Peter Lang, 1998.

Kay, Sarah. "The Contrasting Use of Time in the Romances of *Jaufre* and *Flamenca*." *Medioevo romanzo* 6 (1979): 37–62.

Köhler, Erich. "Forma e struttura del romanzo arturiano." *Il romanzo*. Ed. Maria Luisa Meneghetti. Bologna: il Mulino, 1988. 147–169.

Lazzerini, Lucia. "La lezione di Chrétien e la militanza politica in *Flamenca* e nel *Jaufre*." *Silva portentosa. Enigmi, intertestualità sommerse, significati occulti nella letteratura romanza dalle origini al Cinquecento*. Modena: Mucchi, 2010. 445–199.

Lecco, Margherita, ed. *Materiali arturiani nelle letterature di Provenza, Spagna, Italia*. Alessandria: Edizioni dell'Orso, 2005.

Lecco, Margherita. *Saggi sul romanzo del XIII secolo*. Alessandria: Edizioni dell'Orso, 2003.

Lee, Charmaine. "*Versi d'amore e prose di romanzi*: The Reception of Occitan Narrative Genres in Italy." *Tenso* 28 (2013): 18–32.

Lee, Charmaine. "Re Artù dall'Italia alla Spagna." *Mediterranoesis. Voci dal Medioevo e dal Rinascimento mediterraneo*. Ed. Roberta Morosini and Cristina Perissinotto. Rome: Salerno, 2007. 43–60.

Lee, Charmaine, ed. *Jaufre*. Rome: Carocci, 2006a.

Lee, Charmaine. "*Jaufre* e il *Conte du Graal* trent'anni dopo." *Medioevo romanzo* 30 (2006b): 38–52.

Lee, Charmaine. "Guilhem de Montanhagol and the Romance of *Jaufre*." *Etudes de langue et de littérature médiévales offertes à Peter T. Ricketts à l'occasion de son 70ème anniversaire*. Ed. Dominique Billy and Anne Buckley. Turnhout: Brepols, 2005. 405–417.

Lee, Charmaine. "L'auteur de *Jaufre* et celui du *Chevalier à la charrette*." *Scène, évolution, sort de la langue et la littérature d'oc. Actes du VII Congrès international de l'AIEO (Reggio Calabria-Messina juillet 2002)*. Ed. Rossana Castano, Saverio Guida and Fortunata Latella. 2 vols. Roma: Viella, 2003a. I, 479–491.

Lee, Charmaine. "I frammenti del *Jaufre* nei canzonieri lirici." In *Actas del XXIII Congreso Internacional de Lingüística y Filología Románica (Salamanca, 24–30 septiembre 2001)*. Ed. Fernando Sánchez Miret. 5 vols. Tübingen: Niemeyer, 2003b. IV, 135–147.

Lee, Charmaine. "L'elogio del re d'Aragona in *Jaufre*." *Actas del VIII Congreso Internacional del Asociación Hispánica de Literatura Medieval (Santander, septiembre 1999)*. Santander: AHLM-Gobierno de Cantábria, 2000. 1051–1060.

Lejeune, Rita. "Le roman de *Jaufré*, source de Chrétien de Troyes?" *Revue belge de philologie et d'histoire* 31 (1953): 717–747.

Lejeune, Rita. "La date du roman de *Jaufré*. A propos d'une édition récente." *Le Moyen Age* 54 (1948): 257–299.

Lewent, Kurt. "The Troubadours and the Romance of *Jaufre*." *Modern Philology* 43 (1945–1946): 153–169.

Limacher-Riebold, Ute. *Entre "novas" et "romans". Pour l'interprétation de "Flamenca"*. Alessandria: Edizioni dell'Orso, 1997.

Limentani, Alberto. *L'eccezione narrativa. La Provenza medievale e l'arte del racconto*. Turin: Einaudi, 1977.

Lorenzo Gradín, Pilar. "*Jaufre* o el orden ambiguo." *De l'aventure épique à l'aventure romanesque. Mélanges offerts à André de Mandach par ses amis, collègues et élèves*. Ed. Jacques Chocheyras. Frankfurt and New York: Peter Lang, 1997. 201–219.

Ménard, Philippe. "La tête maléfique dans la littérature médiévale. Etude d'une croyance magique." *Rewards and Punishments in the Arthurian Romances and Lyric Poetry of Medieval France: Essays Presented to Kenneth Varty*. Cambridge: D.S. Brewer, 1987. 89–99.

Pinkernell, Gert. "Realismus (v. 1–6234) und Märchenhaftigkeit (v. 6235–10956) in der Zeitstruktur des provenzalischen *Jaufre*-Romans (Ein Beitrag zur Stützung der Zwei-Verfasser-Theorie)." *Germanisch-romanische Monatsschrift* 53 (1972a): 357–376.

Pinkernell, Gert. "Zur Datierung des provenzalischen *Jaufre*-Roman." *Zeitschrift für romanische Philologie* 88 (1972b): 105–110.

Pioletti, Antonio. "Artù, Avallon, l'Etna." *Quaderni medievali* 28 (1989): 6–35.

Pirot, François. *Recherches sur les connaissances littéraires des troubadours occitans et catalans des XIIe et XIIIe siècles*. Barcelona: Real Academia de Buenas Letras, 1972.

Platin, Claude. *L'hystoire de Giglan filz de Messire Gauvain qui fut roy de Galles et de Geoffrey de Maience son compagnon*. Lyon: Claude Nourry, 1530.

Pontecorvo, Aurelia. "Una fonte del *Jaufre*." *Archivum Romanicum* 22 (1938): 399–401.

Raynouard, François. *Choix des poésies originales des troubadours*. 6 vols. Paris: Firmin Didot, 1816–1821.

Remy, Paul. "*Jaufré*." *Arthurian Literature in the Middle Ages*. Ed. Roger Sherman Loomis. Oxford: Oxford University Press, 1959. 400–405.

Ricketts, Peter T. "*Castitatz* chez Guilhem de Montanhagol." *Revue des langues romanes* 77 (1966): 147–149.

Ricketts, Peter T., ed. *Les poésies de Guilhem de Montanhagol. Troubadour provençal du XIIIe siècle*. Toronto: Pontifical Institute of Mediaeval Studies, 1964.

Schmolke-Hasselmann, Beate. *The Evolution of Arthurian Romance. The Verse Tradition from Chrétien to Froissart*. Cambridge: Cambridge University Press, 1998 [1980].

Southworth, Marie-José. *Etude comparée de quatre romans médiévaux. Jaufre, Fergus, Durmart, Blancadrin*. Paris: Nizet, 1973.

Spetia, Lucilla. *"Li conte de Bretaigne sont si vain et plaisant". Studi sull' Yvain e sul Jaufre*. Soveria Mannelli: Rubbettino, 2012.

Stimming, Albert. "Über den Verfasser des *Roman de Jaufre*." *Zeitschrift für romanische Philologie* 12 (1888): 323–347.

Szabics, Imre. "Interférences de motifs dans le *Roman de Jaufre* et les romans arthuriens de Chrétien de Troyes." *Revue des Langues romanes* 114 (2010): 489–503.

Ueltschi, Karine. "Sibylle, Arthur et Sainte Agathe: les monts italiens comme carrefour des autres mondes." *Materiali arturiani nelle letterature di Provenza, Spagna, Italia*. Ed. Margherita Lecco. Alessandria: Edizioni dell'Orso, 2005. 141–62.

Varvaro, Alberto. "Ancora sul *gouffre de Satilie* da Walter Map ai Templari." *Zeitschrift für romanische Philologie* 114 (1998a): 651–656.

Varvaro, Alberto. "A proposito delle credenze magiche nella letteratura medievale." *Miscellanea Medievalia. Mélanges offerts à Philippe Ménard*. Ed. J. Claude Faucon, A. Labbé and D. Quéruel. 2 vols. Paris: Champion, 1998b. II, 1445–1452.

Index

This index provides references to names of people/characters, place names, important objects, manuscript shelfmarks and titles of primary texts. The names of editors of primary texts and scholars are included only where their works are included as core subject in a discussion (rather than as supporting criticism). In the interests of navigational ease, text titles commencing with an article are indexed by the first proper word, with the article transposed to the end of the entry. The same is true of honorifics/personal titles (e.g. "Sir"), except where that title is the first word of a primary text's title. Character names with different spellings across different languages are usually maintained and given as separate entries so as to aid navigation to a particular text or set of texts (e.g. Gawain/Gauvain/Walewain/Gwalchmei, and so on), but cross-references are occasionally given when the editors deemed this to be helpful.

CPSIA information can be obtained
at www.ICGtesting.com
Printed in the USA
BVHW070754070121
597230BV00004B/321